Greenhill Books

The Greenhill
Military Small Arms
Data Book

The Greenhill
Military Small Arms
Data Book

Ian V. Hogg

Greenhill Books, London
Stackpole Books, Pennsylvania

The Greenhill Military Small Arms Data Book
First published in 1999 by
Greenhill Books, Lionel Leventhal Limited,
Park House, 1 Russell Gardens, London NW11 9NN
and

Stackpole Books,
5067 Ritter Road, Mechanicsburg, PA 17055, USA

British Library Cataloguing in Publication Data
Hogg, Ian V. (Ian Vernon), 1926–
The Greenhill military small arms data book
1. Firearms – Handbooks, manuals, etc.
2. Firearms – History – Handbooks, manuals, etc.
I. Title 623.4'4

ISBN 1-85367-360-9

Library of Congress Cataloging-in-Publication Data
Hogg, Ian V., 1926–
The Greenhill military small arms data book / by Ian V. Hogg.
p.   cm.
Includes bibliographical references and index.
ISBN 1-85367-360-9
1. Firearms. I. Title. UD380.H5G4 1999
683.4—dc21   98-46534
CIP

Edited and designed by Donald Sommerville
Printed and bound in Great Britain by The Bath Press, Bath

Contents

List of Illustrations

Photographs have been selected to illustrate examples of the various features which are mentioned in the descriptive sections of the data entries so that there can be no doubt as to what is meant by, for example, 'open-frame' or 'perforated jacket'. Two of the weapons shown did not find military use and accordingly do not have entries in the body of the book.

Preface

The aim of this book is simply to provide, in one place, all the basic information relating to military weapons of the metallic cartridge era; a brief description, the cartridge used, the dimensions, weight, magazine capacity, rate of fire and muzzle velocity. Space considerations have led to a fairly ruthless selection, and the listing is confined to weapons actually used by military or police forces, or produced for sale or offer to such forces. This includes a number of weapons which were produced for military use but not adopted, but which were of sufficient importance in the overall development of military weapons to appear in books and museums and are thus likely to produce a demand for information. Regrettably there are still a few weapons for which reliable information has not yet made an appearance in time for publication, and in one or two places 'not known' or 'not available' will be found instead of some piece of data.

In the normal course of events acquiring such data is often difficult. It demands a substantial library of reference books, and even that may not produce the one elusive figure that is needed. Moreover, comparisons of several reference sources frequently produce as many differences of opinion over a single dimension. Every dimension in this book has come either from an authoritative source – for example a maker's manual or a government handbook – or has been physically checked on an actual weapon. Nevertheless, it would be well to warn the reader at the outset that the dimensions given here may occasionally be slightly at variance with a set of measurements made on another example of any particular weapon. It is not uncommon to pick up two weapons, nominally identical but made in different years or in different factories, and find small differences in length or weight. Rifles, for example, frequently differ in weight because of the density of the wood used in the furniture. Revolvers made in the late 19th century often differ in barrel length by a millimetre or two, simply because of the hand-fitting and fettling that always went on during final assembly.

Weapons have been listed mainly by their common names – Mauser, Webley, Luger, Vickers and so on – and weapons of the same name supplied to different countries are listed under these headings in order of country. Where no commonly used name exists – where the title is simply M1905 or MG 42 – then the weapon is listed under the country of origin or main country of employment. In this respect no distinction is made between Tsarist Russia, the USSR, and post-Communist Russia – all are included under the heading 'Russia' where appropriate. To assist in finding the various weapons a comprehensive index, with cross references, is provided.

Since firearms are of little use when divorced from their ammunition, particular care has been taken to identify the actual cartridge used (as opposed to merely noting the calibre). A list of dimensions of all the cartridges used by the listed weapons is also provided.

For those uncertain of technicalities a glossary has been included, which expands on some of the expressions used in the brief descriptions. Each weapon entry includes an abbreviated version of the name of its manufacturer(s). Fuller versions of these names are separately listed. Manufacturers' names like these can sometimes be of assistance in dating a weapon, since the style or title of a company frequently changed and the markings on their weapons changed with it. Finally there is a 'Who's Who' section giving fuller details concerning notable inventors, designers and manufacturers, both individuals and organisations.

The data in the main weapons' chapters is arranged in standard form. First, a heading with the common name of the weapon or maker and country of origin. Following this is, where applicable, the country of use and the short title of the manufacturer. Then comes a brief description followed by the dimensions and performance figures. *Length* means the overall length of the weapon from one extremity to the other. In the case of sniping and other rifles with adjustable butts the length given is the mid-point of the available adjustment. *Weight* is the weight of the unloaded weapon fitted with an empty magazine where applicable, unless otherwise stated. Water-cooled machine guns are weighed without the water. *Barrel length* is the length from the closed bolt face to the muzzle, excluding flash hiders or other muzzle attachments, unless otherwise noted. *Rifling* specifies the number of rifling grooves and the direction of twist, as seen from the breech. The twist is constant unless otherwise stated. *Muzzle velocity* is the figure claimed by the maker or military authority. In cases where similar lengths of barrel firing the same cartridge produce different figures, this may be due to the tolerance between bullet and rifling, or to national preferences for propellant. *Cyclic rate* is the rate of fire assuming an uninterrupted supply of ammunition in a new gun and is generally a median of high and low values quoted by the maker. This, again, can depend upon many variables including propellant, belt weight, bore clearances and lubrication.

Finally I would like to acknowledge my indebtedness to the Ministry of Defence Pattern Room, and Mr Herbert Woodend, its Curator, for permitting me to examine weapons and consult its unrivalled technical library in my search for some of the more elusive figures, and to Mr John Walter for ransacking his files to find obscure pieces of information for me – and for reminding me of things I might otherwise have overlooked.

GLOSSARY

ACCELERATOR

Mechanical device found in recoil-operated automatic weapons. Interposed between the barrel and the bolt, by means of leverage it imparts a greater speed to the bolt than would be achieved by the movement of the barrel alone. The most common application is in the .50 Browning machine gun.

ACP

Automatic Colt Pistol. A descriptive abbreviation added behind the calibre notation of .25 (6.35mm), .32 (7.65mm) and .45 (11.43mm) automatic pistol cartridges originally developed for use in Colt designs of pistol in those calibres, in order to distinguish these cartridges from others of similar calibre but different characteristics and dimensions.

ADVANCED PRIMER IGNITION

A system of operation commonly found in submachine guns, in which the cartridge primer is struck and fired while the breech bolt is still moving forward and loading the cartridge into the weapon's chamber. The explosion force must therefore arrest the moving mass of the bolt before it can make it recoil, so introducing a short delay which is sufficient to allow the bullet to leave the gun barrel, and the chamber pressure to drop, before the breech is opened. The adoption of this system also allows a reduction to be made in the weight of the bolt and the distance of its recoil stroke, permitting the design of a more compact weapon. Analogous to 'Differential recoil' (*qv*).

ANNULAR GROOVED CHAMBER

The chamber of a firearm in which an annular groove or grooves have been formed so that one or more indented rings run around the chamber. On firing, the metal of the cartridge case expands into this annular groove and thus the case is retained in place in the chamber and is not forced out by gas pressure. It is used in blowback weapons as a method of delaying the opening of the breech; the amount of expansion of the case is below the elastic limit for the metal, and thus, once the gas pressure drops (after the bullet has left the muzzle) the case metal contracts to, or close to, its original dimension and the case can then be extracted by the momentum of the breech block.

ANVIL

A metal 'pimple' which lies in front of the primer cap of a small arms cartridge so that when the firing pin or hammer strikes the cap, the pyrotechnic composition inside is crushed between the tip of the firing pin or hammer and the anvil, so generating the flash which ignites the propellant. The anvil may be formed in the body of the cartridge case, or it may be a separate component which is fitted into the cap during manufacture. *See* 'Berdan primer' and 'Boxer primer'.

ASSAULT RIFLE

A light and compact selective-fire automatic rifle firing a cartridge of such power that it can deliver effective fire to a range of about 500 metres, but at the same time will permit the weapon to be fired in the automatic mode from the shoulder.

AUTOMATIC PISTOL

Strictly, an automatic weapon is one which will fire once the trigger is pressed and will continue firing so long as the trigger remains pressed and there is ammunition. Less strictly the term is applied to any form of self-loading pistol.

AUTOMATIC REVOLVER

(1) A revolver in which the energy of discharge is used to re-cock the hammer and align a fresh chamber behind the barrel.
(2) The term 'Automatic' was also frequently applied to American revolvers in the 1890–1910 period to indicate automatic extraction and ejection of the spent cases when the barrel was hinged down.

BALL

Term used to describe an inert bullet for small arms, having kinetic energy only. The term is derived from antiquity, when bullets from smooth-bore muskets were actual balls of lead.

BARREL

That component of a firearm through which the projectile is launched and which gives direction to it.

BARREL EXTENSION

A frame attached to the barrel of a weapon which carries the bolt and which usually carries a means of locking the bolt to the extension so as to hold the bolt closed during firing.

BELTED

Type of cartridge which has a raised belt around the body, ahead of the extraction groove. Invented and patented by J.G. Accles, a Birmingham ammunition maker, as an alternative method of positively locating the cartridge case inside the gun chamber, it also has the added bonus of strengthening the case against very high internal pressures.

BELT FED

An automatic weapon in which the ammunition feed system takes the form of a flexible belt in which the cartridges are carried.

BERDAN PRIMER

A type of primer cap used with small arm ammunition, named for Colonel Hiram Berdan, US Ordnance Department, who invented it in the 1860s. The principal feature is that the anvil forms part of the cartridge case, there being a number of flash holes alongside the anvil to permit the passage of flame from the cap to the propelling powder. The Berdan primer is used in almost all military ammunition. *Cf* 'Boxer primer'.

BLOWBACK

A weapon in which the breech is kept closed by the inertia of the breech-block and pressure of the recoil spring, so that, on firing, the chamber pressure 'blows the bolt back' once it overcomes this inertia. Hence, such a breech is not positively locked.

BLOW-FORWARD

Analogous to blow-back but working in the opposite direction; on firing the barrel of the weapon is blown forward by the chamber pressure, allowing the empty case to be withdrawn by a fixed extractor, and a spring returns the barrel to chamber the next cartridge.

BOLT

A device which closes the breech of a weapon; usually infers a separate component moving within the body of the weapon.

BOLT ACTION

Breech closure of a small arm by means of a hand-operated bolt moving in prolongation of the weapon's axis. May be a 'turnbolt' in which the bolt is pushed forward and then turned down to lock by means of a handle; or a 'straight pull bolt' in which the manual action is a simple reciprocating movement and the bolt is turned and locked by cam or wedge action.

BOTTLE-NECKED

A cartridge case in which the mouth is sharply reduced in diameter to hold the bullet or projectile. It allows the case to hold the desired amount of propellant without being excessively long.

BOXER PRIMER

Primer cap for small arm cartridges invented by Colonel Edward Boxer, Superintendent of the Royal Laboratory at Woolwich Arsenal in the 1860s. It is distinguished from the Berdan primer (*qv*) by having the anvil as a separate component which is fitted into the cap before insertion into the cartridge case. There is a single central flash hole in the case, leading from the cap chamber to the interior of the case and the propellant charge. The Boxer primer is preferred for sporting ammunition since it is easy to push out the fired cap from a used case, using a thin rod through the central flash hole, so allowing the case to be reloaded. Military ammunition is now never reloaded, so that the Berdan primer is preferred as being an easier manufacturing and assembly proposition.

BOX MAGAZINE

A method of ammunition supply in the form of a metallic or plastic box, either detachable from the weapon or integral with it, below, above, or to one side of the weapon. The cartridges are held inside the box and propelled to the mouth of the magazine by a spring, from where they are fed into the weapon's chamber.

BROWNING LINK

Method of locking a pistol breech devised by John Browning. The barrel carries a link, pinned loosely beneath the breech. The other end of the link is pinned loosely to the pistol frame. When ready to fire, the barrel is held forward and lugs on its upper surface engage with recesses inside the pistol slide. On firing, slide and barrel recoil together, but the link forces the rear of the barrel to move in an arc, so that the lugs are withdrawn from their recesses. Once completely clear, the slide is free to recoil, while the barrel is held by the link. The time taken for the barrel to become disconnected from the slide is sufficient to permit the bullet to leave the muzzle and the chamber pressure to fall to a safe level.

BROWNING CAM

An improvement on the swinging link system, in which a piece of metal beneath the breech is formed into a cam path which rides upon a pin in the pistol frame. This forces the rear of the barrel down, disconnecting it from the slide and then holding it while the slide continues to recoil.

BROWNING-PETTER CAM

Similar to the Browning cam but instead of an open-jawed piece of metal, the cam is a curved slot in a solid piece beneath the chamber.

CALIBRE

The internal diameter of a gun barrel; strictly, the diameter of a cylinder which will just fit inside the bore; more usually, the diameter between two opposite lands.

CARBINE

A short rifle, usually to the same basic design as the standard infantry rifle, but intended for use by cavalry, who required a shoulder arm of a conveniently short length for carriage in the saddle, or by engineers, artillery and similar troops whose primary equipment is not the shoulder arm but who require one for self-defence.

CARTRIDGE

Strictly speaking, 'cartridge' means the propelling charge for a firearm, but in the context of small arms it is always taken to mean the complete round – bullet, propelling charge, cartridge case and primer cap.

CARTRIDGE BRASS

A mixture of 70 percent copper and 30 percent zinc, from which cartridge cases are traditionally made.

CASELESS CARTRIDGE

A small arm cartridge which dispenses with the conventional metallic or plastic case and has the propellant formed into a solid mass attached to the bullet. It may or may not incorporate the means of ignition.

CENTRE FIRE

A cartridge which carries its percussion cap centrally in the base; and, by extension, a weapon using centre-fire ammunition.

CHAMBER

The enlarged and shaped area of the interior of the gun barrel at the breech, into which the cartridge fits.

CHAMBER LOADED INDICATOR

A pin or other device which gives visual and tactile indication of the presence of a cartridge in the chamber.

CHANGE LEVER

A lever or switch on a firearm which allows the firer to choose between modes of fire, *eg* single shots or automatic fire. Also called a 'Selector lever'.

CHARGER

Method of loading a magazine firearm in which a number of cartridges are held in a metal frame. The action is opened, the frame positioned at the entrance to the magazine, and the cartridges then pressed down by the thumb so as to be stripped from the frame and loaded into the magazine. The empty charger is then discarded.

CLIP

Method of loading a magazine firearm in which a number of cartridges are held in a metal frame. The action is opened and the entire frame, with cartridges, is placed in the magazine. When the action is closed a spring-loaded arm forces up the cartridges inside the clip, so that as the action is worked a fresh cartridge is presented. As the last cartridge is loaded the clip is ejected from the weapon. It is important to realise that without the clip, the weapon cannot be loaded or operated except as a single-loader, and the magazine cannot be 'topped up' with loose cartridges.

CLOSED BOLT

A weapon in which the bolt is closed, though not necessarily locked, when the firing impulse is applied.

COMPENSATOR

A device on the muzzle of a firearm which diverts some of the emerging gas and forces it upwards, so developing a downward thrust to counteract the rise of the weapon muzzle during firing.

COOK-OFF

Colloquial expression for the premature ignition of the propelling charge of a small arm cartridge caused by induced heat from the gun chamber walls after prolonged firing.

CRANE

A hinged arm, attached to the revolver frame, which carries the cylinder arbor and the cylinder, allowing the cylinder to be swung out of the frame sideways for loading.

CYCLE OF OPERATION

The complete routine of operations required in an automatic weapon, covering firing, breech unlocking, extracting, ejecting, cocking, feeding, chambering and breech locking. Not all functions may be present, some may overlap, and the order of their occurrence may change.

CYCLIC

Rate of fire of an automatic weapon assuming an unlimited and continuous supply of ammunition, *ie* the rate of fire not taking into account the need to change magazines or insert fresh belts.

CYLINDER

That part of a revolver which contains the ammunition; it revolves and presents a loaded chamber behind the barrel for each operation of the trigger.

CYLINDER RELEASE

A mechanism to permit the rapid removal of a revolver cylinder from the frame to allow replacement with a pre-loaded cylinder or to facilitate rapid reloading, notably in the days before collective ejection systems became common. Generally took the form of a catch retaining the arbor pin, so that releasing the catch allowed the pin to be withdrawn and thus free the cylinder.

CYLINDER STOP

A part of the lockwork which rises from the frame of a revolver and, engaging in a recess in the cylinder, locates the cylinder so that one chamber is aligned with the barrel ready to fire. After the trigger has been operated to fire the pistol, the stop is withdrawn, so freeing the cylinder and allowing it to be revolved to the next chamber.

DE-COCKING LEVER

Lever which safely lowers the hammer of a cocked automatic pistol, allowing it to be carried safely; it can also be used, in some designs, to re-cock the weapon when required. Operation of this lever usually moves the firing pin from the hammer path or places a block between the hammer and the pin prior to releasing the hammer.

DELAYED BLOWBACK

A blowback (*qv*) weapon in which an additional restraint or brake is placed on the bolt or other breech closure so as to delay or slow down the opening, but without actually locking the breech. Also known as 'Retarded blowback'.

DIFFERENTIAL RECOIL

The principle of firing a weapon during the run-out period, that is while the barrel and breech are still running forward after the recoil of the previous shot. By firing an instant before the parts reach the end of their stroke, the recoil force has firstly to arrest the momentum of the moving parts and then drive them back in recoil. This arresting action absorbs a proportion of the recoil force and thus there is less force left to be transmitted to the body of the gun, and therefore to the mounting. First developed for artillery weapons by Colonel Deport of the French Army in 1907, it has also been applied to a few machine-gun designs, notably the Czech/British Besa guns. The system of operation known as 'Advanced primer ignition' (*qv*) might be considered a form of differential recoil.

DISCONNECTOR

Part of the trigger mechanism of a semi-automatic weapon which disconnects the trigger from the remainder of the firing train after each shot; the firer must therefore release the trigger and take a fresh pressure to fire the next shot. This prevents the weapon firing continuously for a single pressure of the trigger. The change mechanism in a selective fire weapon, which permits either single shots or automatic fire, is usually operated by moving the disconnector in or out of engagement.

DISINTEGRATING LINK BELT

A belt of ammunition for an automatic weapon in which the individual metal links are held together by the actual rounds of ammunition. Thus, when the round has been pulled out of the belt to be loaded into the gun the link falls free.

DOUBLE ACTION

A firing mechanism employing a hammer, in which the hammer can be raised and cocked by the thumb and then released by the trigger, or it can be raised, cocked, and released by a longer pull of the trigger.

DOUBLE PULL

A type of trigger used with some selective fire weapons in which pulling the trigger causes a single shot to be fired; pulling the trigger further, against the pressure of an additional spring, provides automatic fire.

DOUBLE TRIGGER

A type of firing mechanism used with some selective fire weapons in which there are two triggers, one providing single shots and the other automatic fire. In some cases the triggers may be combined into a single unit, pivoted in the centre; pulling back on the top section provides single shots and on the bottom section produces automatic fire. Another method is to have two triggers but press only the front one; the first pressure produces single shots, but further pressure causes the front trigger to bear against the rear trigger and thus commence automatic firing. The rear trigger is never actually touched by the finger.

DRUM MAGAZINE

A circular magazine into which the rounds are loaded axially or radially and propelled towards the feed lips by a spring or by a mechanism driven by the gun. The spring system is more usual, being employed on the Thompson, Lahti and other submachine guns; the mechanical system is uncommon, and was used on the Lewis machine gun.

EJECTOR

Device for throwing empty cartridge cases out of a firearm; in the case of a revolver, usually a star-shaped plate in the centre of the cylinder which is forced out by some mechanism and, catching beneath the rims of the cases, pushes them out of the chambers. It thus extracts and ejects in one movement. In the case of an automatic weapon, usually a fixed metal piece which intercepts the empty case as it is withdrawn from the breech by the extractor and knocks it clear of the weapon. There are, however, many variations on this theme.

EXTRACTOR

Device used actually to pull the cartridge case from the chamber of a weapon; as noted above, in revolvers this is usually done by one mechanism which also ejects the case clear of the weapon. In other weapons it is almost always a claw attached to the bolt or breech unit which engages with the cartridge case and pulls it from the chamber during recoil, presenting it to the ejector. It is possible to have an automatic weapon without an extractor or ejector, relying upon residual gas pressure to blow the case out as the breech is opened, though this can pose a problem when trying to unload an unfired round.

FEEDWAY

That part of a weapon where a cartridge, taken from the feed system, is positioned ready to be loaded into the chamber.

FERMETURE NUT

A system of locking the breech of a light machine gun, used in some Hotchkiss and Benet-Mercie designs from about 1909 to the 1930s. It consists of a collar with interrupted lugs which surrounds the weapon's chamber. Operated by a gas piston, it is given a part-revolution which disengages the interrupted lugs from similar lugs on the breech block, which is then free to be withdrawn by further movement of the gas piston. When the breech block returns and reloads the chamber, the fermeture nut is rotated back and the lugs secure the block to the barrel.

FLASH ELIMINATOR

A device fitted to the muzzle of a small arm to cool the emergent propellant gases so that they do not inflame on contact with the air.

FLASH HIDER

A conical muzzle attachment to a gun designed to conceal the weapon's flash from the firer, since it can dazzle him in poor light conditions. May also serve as a flash eliminator, though a hider is usually less efficient than a properly designed eliminator.

FLIP REARSIGHT

A rear sight for a small arm consisting of two notches or apertures mounted at right-angles to each other and pivoted, so that either can be rotated into position, providing two alternative range settings.

FLUTED CHAMBER

A gun chamber in which a number of grooves, parallel with the axis of the barrel, are cut. These grooves extend into the bore of the gun but do not reach the mouth of the chamber. On firing, some of the propellant gas leaks down these grooves and thus 'floats' the case on a layer of high-pressure gas, compensating for the pressure inside the case. These are used with high-pressure weapons in which the breech tends to begin opening whilst the internal pressure is high. If the chamber wall were plain, the internal pressure would cause the body of the cartridge case to stick firmly against the chamber, and any rearward movement of the bolt would probably tear the base off the cartridge. By floating the case, there is less resistance to movement, and the bolt can begin opening without risk of damage.

In the case of the SIG Stgw57 automatic rifle, the grooves perform a different function. Some of the grooves are longer and extend to the rear edge of the chamber where they align with two holes in the face of the closed bolt. On firing, propellant gas flows down the grooves and through the holes into the bolt, where the gas pressure pushes on the bolt body and assists in withdrawing the locking rollers, thus releasing the bolt so that it can open. *And see* 'Annular Grooved Chamber'.

FOLDING TRIGGER

A trigger which is hinged so as to fold forwards beneath the frame of the pistol, so allowing it to be carried easily in a pocket without the trigger catching.

FURNITURE

Those parts of a small arm which are solely for facilitating its handling, such as the stock, pistol grip, butt and fore-end, sling swivels, bipod, muzzle cap and similar items.

GAS SEAL REVOLVER

A type of revolver in which the cylinder and barrel are mechanically forced together before firing, so that no gap exists between the barrel and the chamber mouth, preventing any leak of gas and thus any waste of the power of the cartridge. Invariably requires a special cartridge.

GATE LOADING

Method of loading a solid-frame revolver. A hinged 'gate' is formed in the recoil shield; this can be opened to allow the chamber in front of it to be loaded. The cylinder is then moved round until the next cylinder is aligned and that one is loaded. After firing the gate is opened and the empty cartridge extracted. Gates may be cross-connected to the hammer to ensure that the gun cannot be accidentally fired during loading.

GPMG

General Purpose Machine Gun. A machine gun capable of being employed either as a bipod-mounted squad automatic weapon or as a tripod-mounted sustained-fire weapon.

GRIP SAFETY

A safety device forming part of the grip of a pistol and connected in some manner to the firing mechanism. Unless this grip is held tightly and forced inwards, the firing mechanism is interrupted and the weapon cannot fire. It prevents accidental firing of the weapon due to dropping it or mishandling, but, contrary to common myth, is not intended to prevent suicide.

HANGFIRE

An ignition failure in a propelling charge, resulting in a delay between applying the firing impulse and having the charge explode. Invariably due to some defect in the ammunition.

HEADSPACE

The permitted clearance between the base of the loaded cartridge and the face of the bolt or breech-block when the bolt or breech-block is closed and, where applicable, locked. Too little headspace and the bolt will not close, or it may close but not lock; or, if the bolt closes, the firing pin may pierce the primer cap prematurely. Too much headspace and the firing pin may not strike the cap with sufficient force to fire it, and the cartridge, if it does fire may set back out of the chamber, so permitting gas to leak around the case or the case to expand and jam tightly in the chamber, giving difficult extraction. Gauges are provided for armourers to measure headspace, and various methods are adopted to permit it to be adjusted.

HINGED FRAME

A weapon in which the barrel, and in the case of revolvers, the cylinder, form a separate unit which is attached to the rest of the weapon by a hinge bolt, so that by releasing a catch the barrel can be tipped down to expose the rear end or the chambers of a revolver. Generally taken to mean a barrel which tips down; those which tip in any other direction are so identified in their description. The term generally applies to revolvers, though hinged-frame automatic pistols are not uncommon.

HIT PROBABILITY

The chance, expressed as a percentage, of a round fired by any weapon hitting the target. Hit probability, usually contracted to Ph, is the product of the effect of a number of factors including: the accuracy of the weapon; the accuracy of the sighting or fire control system; the accuracy of the ammunition; the skill of the firer. Thus, if the accuracy of the weapon is assessed as 95% and the accuracy of the firer at 50%, then the overall Ph will be .95 x .50 = .475. And if the accuracy of all four factors is 95%, then the Ph of the system will be .08; in other words only 8 shots out of every hundred can be expected to hit the target. A few minutes with a calculator will show that to have a 90 percent chance of hitting, you require all four elements to be of the order of 98% or better. Since the flight of the bullet is governed by the standard laws of probability, it follows that there is not, nor ever will be, a weapon with a Ph of 100.

HOLD-OPEN DEVICE

A catch or stop in the mechanism of a self-loading weapon which prevents the breech closing after the last round in the magazine has been fired. Serves as an indication that the weapon requires reloading and also holds the loading system open, ready for replenishment.

INERTIA FIRING PIN

A firing pin for an automatic pistol which is shorter than the tunnel in which it rests. Thus, when the hammer is lowered and presses on the pin, the front end does not protrude through the bush in the breech face and does not touch the cartridge cap. Only the violent blow of a properly released hammer will overcome the natural inertia of the pin and drive it forward far enough to pass through the breech face and strike the cap with sufficient force to fire the cartridge. The pin invariably has a small spring around its front end, pushing back against a collar, so that as the hammer rebounds after firing, the pin withdraws behind the breech face and cannot therefore strike the cap of the next cartridge as the breech closes.

INTERRUPTOR

A device in a self-loading weapon which disconnects the trigger from the sear after a shot has been fired, requiring the firer to release the trigger and take a fresh pressure in order to fire the next round. This prevents automatic action which would otherwise result if the trigger remained pressed and the sear disengaged. Also called the 'Disconnector'.

KNOX-FORM

That part of the barrel of a small arm (principally a rifle) which is formed externally with flat surfaces so that a spanner can be used to screw the barrel into the receiver, and so proportioned that by matching one flat with an index mark on the receiver, the gun sight is vertical. A corruption from 'Nock's Form', after Nock, the English gunsmith who invented the idea.

LANDS

The raised portions of a gun barrel between the grooves of the rifling.

LEVER ACTION

Method of opening the breech of a rifle by the use of a lever lying below the butt and usually forming an extension of the trigger guard. The most common examples are the various rifles by Winchester, Savage and Marlin. Rarely seen on military weapons due to the difficulty of using a lever action when lying prone.

LMG

Light Machine Gun; a generally-used abbreviation to describe the infantry squad automatic weapon. Normally a machine gun which is capable of being carried and operated by one man.

LOCK TIME

The elapsed time between pressing the trigger and the explosion of the cartridge. Important in target shooting where the shortest possible lock time is desirable so as to reduce the chance of any shift of aim. This generally requires a fairly sensitive trigger mechanism, but is also dependent upon the general system of firing mechanism adopted.

LONG RECOIL

A system of operation of automatic weapons which relies upon the barrel and locked breech recoiling together for a distance at least as long as a complete unfired cartridge. At the end of this stroke the bolt is unlocked and held, while the barrel is allowed to run back to its forward position. During this movement the cartridge case is extracted and ejected and a fresh round placed in the feedway. The bolt is then released, runs forward to chamber a round, locks, and the weapon is ready to fire. Not common in any type of firearm, least of all in pistols, but several notable designs of the past have employed it.

MACHINE CARBINE

Term adopted by the British Army in the 1939–40 period to describe submachine guns. It showed a fundamental misunderstanding of the term 'carbine', and was generally ignored. It remained the official terminology for the Sten gun ('Carbine, Machine, Sten, 9mm') but was abandoned when the Sterling was introduced in 1957 (as the 'Gun, Submachine, 9mm, L2A1').

MACHINE GUN

Automatic weapon intended to provide fire support for infantry or to arm aircraft or armoured vehicles, or provide air defence. May be classed as 'light' – to be operated by one or two men and easily carried, usually magazine fed; or 'medium' – rifle-calibre, belt-fed, tripod-mounted and capable of sustained fire; or 'heavy' – more than rifle calibre, sustained fire, belt-fed, tripod-mounted; or 'general-purpose' – capable of being used in either the light or medium role.

MACHINE PISTOL

A loose term, which can sometimes be found applied to submachine guns; strictly, it means a pistol which has its firing mechanism adapted so that it can fire in the full-automatic mode if required.

MACHINE RIFLE

An obsolescent term used to describe a heavy-barrelled automatic rifle capable of being used as a light machine gun. It differs from the 'true' light machine gun in not having an interchangeable barrel and by being based directly upon an existing automatic rifle design.

MAGAZINE

A feed system for a firearm in which cartridges are kept in an integral or attachable container. May be a 'Box Magazine', rectangular in shape and holding ammunition in a column or columns; or a 'Drum magazine', circular in shape and holding the ammunition radially, feeding it by rotation or spring power to the feedway of the weapon. A 'Saddle Drum magazine' consists of two drums connected by a unit which contains the feed exit, so that the whole sits across the top of the weapon with one drum on each side. Magazines may be of metal or plastic; the disposable magazine has yet to find military approval.

MAGAZINE HOUSING

That part of the receiver of the weapon into which a removable magazine fits so as to present the cartridges to the feedway.

MAGAZINE SAFETY

Safety device incorporated in some automatic pistols whereby the weapon will not fire if the magazine is removed. Intended as a precaution so that, when dismantling, any round inadvertently left in the chamber will not be fired. Not generally liked by military authorities since there is always the danger that the firer may be surprised while changing magazines and be unable to use the one round he has loaded.

MISFIRE

Total failure of a propelling charge to ignite. Often due to a defect in the ammunition, but it can also be caused by mechanical defects in the weapon, particularly faults in the protrusion of the striker or firing pin, a weak or broken firing pin spring, or excessive cartridge-head clearance.

MMG

Medium Machine Gun. Obsolescent term referring to rifle-calibre machine guns used in the sustained-fire support role. Generally water-cooled, *eg* the Vickers, Maxim and Browning M1917 patterns.

MUZZLE BRAKE

A muzzle attachment similar to a compensator but intended to turn the emerging gases and drive them rearwards so as to pull on the muzzle and thus reduce the recoil. Not common on small arms, though they will be found on heavy calibre (12.7mm etc) sniping rifles and anti-tank rifles in order to reduce the felt recoil, and on some military rifles capable of automatic fire in order to reduce the recoil and make them more controllable. On the whole, though, muzzle brakes are disliked because they generally direct the blast at the soldier's companions.

NON-EJECTING

A class of revolver in which there is no provision for ejecting the spent cartridges, and the only way to re-load is to remove the cylinder, punch out the cases with a suitable implement, re-load the cylinder and replace it. Also used to describe shotguns from which the empty case must be removed by hand, having been loosened and partially extracted by the ejector.

OPEN BOLT

A weapon is said to fire 'from an open bolt' when the bolt is held back from the empty chamber in the cocked condition and, when the trigger is pressed, the bolt runs forward propelled by a spring to load a round into the chamber and fire it. On releasing the trigger the bolt is again held back. This system, used with automatic weapons, allows air to circulate through the barrel between bursts of fire for cooling purposes, and it is usually simpler to design and manufacture than a weapon which 'fires from a closed bolt'. Its principal drawback is the shift of balance experienced by the firer as the bolt runs forward for the first shot, which usually disturbs the aim. For this reason some selective fire weapons are designed so that in automatic fire they operate from an open bolt, but for single-shot, deliberate, fire they fire from a closed bolt.

OPEN-TOPPED SLIDE

A form of automatic pistol slide in which the forward section of the upper surface is removed; in some cases a small section at the front end may be left, to carry the front sight and generally stiffen the construction, thus giving the effect of a very large ejection opening: *eg* various Beretta models. In other cases the two sides are joined at the front below the barrel: *eg* the Mannlicher M1900/05 model.

OPEN-FRAME REVOLVER

A revolver in which the barrel unit is secured to the frame only in front of the trigger area, and there is no link between the top of the barrel and the standing breech; thus the top of the cylinder is entirely exposed. The most common examples are the percussion Colt revolvers.

PARABELLUM

Based upon the Latin phrase *Si vis pacem, para bellum* ('If you wish for peace, prepare for war') and coined by DWM and registered as a Trade Mark and as their telegraphic address, 'Parabellum Berlin', in 1900. The word then attached itself to two products of the company, the Parabellum (Luger) pistol and the Parabellum machine gun, and, by extension, to the 7.65mm and 9mm pistol cartridges developed specifically for use with the Parabellum pistol.

For those readers who are unfamiliar with the expression, a 'telegraphic address' was used in the days of cheap and quick communication by telegrams – messages written on a form, handed to a Post Office, and from there sent by voice or telegraph, across a telephone line, to the addressee's town, where the message was again written out on a form and then delivered by messenger to the addressee. These telegrams were charged by the word. And thus, writing 'Deutsche Waffen und Munitionsfabrik, Eichborndamm 127, Berlin-Borsigwalde' cost money. Large firms therefore registered 'Telegraphic Addresses' of one or two words and these were used instead of the company's name and address. In this case, 'Parabellum, Berlin' directed the message to the correct address at less expense.

PRAWL

That part of the butt frame of a revolver which curves back over the web of the thumb and thus prevents the grip riding down in the hand when firing.

REBATED RIMLESS

A form of small arm and cannon cartridge case in which the extraction rim is smaller in diameter than the base of the case. Adopted in blowback weapons where it is desirable that the entire case be inside the chamber before being fired, or in weapons of unusual calibre so that the extracting rim conforms to a standard bolt face dimension.

REBOUNDING HAMMER

A pistol or rifle hammer which, having fallen and fired the cap, then 'rebounds' by spring or cam action so as to lift slightly and thus withdraw the firing pin from proximity with the cap. This prevents inadvertent discharge by dropping the weapon or when closing the breech or cylinder.

RECEIVER

The action body of a small arm; the casing covering the breech and breech mechanism; the housing for the bolt or breech block.

RECOIL

The rearward movement of a gun or other firearm due to reaction to the ejection of the projectile from the muzzle.

RECOIL INTENSIFIER

A device attached to the muzzle of a recoil-operated machine gun which impedes the muzzle blast and thus amplifies the rearward thrust on the barrel, so giving greater impulse to the automatic mechanism.

RECOIL OPERATION

A term descriptive of automatic and self-loading weapons which depend upon the recoil of the weapon to actuate the automatic or self-loading mechanism. In general, the barrel is permitted to recoil so as to deliver impetus to the mechanism; the recoil may be long (*qv*) or short, the latter being more common. Familiar weapons using recoil operation are the various Browning machine guns and the Colt automatic pistol.

RECOIL SHIELD

The round plate, usually forming part of the standing breech, which conceals the rear of a revolver cylinder. It prevents the recoil shock shaking the cartridges loose in their chambers, which, in the absence of the shield, would tend to jam the rotation of the cylinder.

RECOIL SPRING

The spring in an automatic weapon which returns the bolt or slide after firing; sometimes, and perhaps more accurately, called the 'return spring'.

REGULATOR

A valve on a gas-operated automatic weapon through which a proportion of the propellant gas is diverted to the actuating mechanism. It is provided with an adjustment, usually a number of different-sized ports, so that more or less gas can be admitted to the system so as to give extra power to overcome stiffness from lack of lubrication, heat expansion, dirt or other causes. In some weapons the regulator may permit the gas to be entirely shut off so as to allow the weapon to be used for launching grenades; in such cases the automatic action is not required and all the gas can be applied to the grenade.

RETARDED BLOWBACK

A blowback (*qv*) automatic weapon in which the rearward movement of the bolt or breech-block is mechanically impeded so as to slow down its initial movement and thus permit the chamber pressure to drop to safe limits before the breech begins to open. Often used to permit the firing of a more powerful cartridge than would be advisable in a simple blowback mechanism but without adding the complication and expense of a locked breech. Also called 'delayed blowback'.

REVOLVER

(1) A pistol in which a rotating cylinder is positioned behind the barrel and presents loaded chambers in succession to be fired.

(2) A machine gun or cannon in which a revolving mechanism strips the ammunition from the feed belt and presents it to the barrel for firing, *eg* the Degtyarev DShK and various aircraft cannons.

(3) A machine gun or cannon using a group of barrels which revolve and which fire at a specific point in their revolution, using the remainder of the cycle for feed and extraction; *eg*, the Gatling gun.

RF

See Rimfire

RIBBED BARREL

Commonly found on revolvers, where the barrel is forged with a stiffening rib above it, into which the foresight blade is formed or fixed. The object is to give the barrel rigidity without adding as much weight as would be required if it were forged as a thicker cylinder.

RIFLE

A shoulder-fired long arm with rifled barrel; the primary weapon of the infantryman.

RIFLING

Method by which an elongated projectile is given stabilising spin when discharged from a firearm. In the most usual system the barrel of the weapon is incised with helical grooves so that under the pressure of the propelling gas the surface of the bullet engraves into these grooves and the bullet is thus forced to revolve as it moves forward. Other systems have been, and sometimes still are, used: *eg* the barrel can be formed internally as a polygon and then twisted.

RIMFIRE

A cartridge in which the priming composition is distributed around the hollow rim and therefore the pistol must direct its firing pin on to the rim and squash it between pin and chamber face. The system was very popular in the early days of cartridge weapons, since it was easier to make than the early centre-fire designs, but because the case metal has to be soft in order to be squashed by the firing pin, it cannot withstand much internal pressure and the system is now used only in .22 calibre pistols and low-powered 9mm shotguns.

RIMLESS

Cartridge case which has an extraction groove in the base, the rim thus exposed being the same diameter as the head of the case. Such a design makes feeding from a magazine more reliable, there being no exposed rims to jam. However, the location of the cartridge in the chamber is controlled by the shoulder (in the case of a bottle-necked round) or by the forward edge of the case (in the case of a straight-sided round) and this can gradually creep forward under the effects of wear and erosion. Weapons using rimless cases are therefore often provided with some means of adjusting the headspace.

RIMMED

Cartridge case with an upstanding rim at the base, which butts against the chamber face to position the cartridge. Nowadays usually confined to revolvers and manually-operated rifles but used in some target automatic pistols.

ROD EJECTION

System of ejection used with gate-loaded (*qv*) revolvers in which a rod, carried below the barrel or on a swinging arm, can be forced back to drive the empty case out of the chamber and through the loading gate.

ROLLING BLOCK

Method of breech closure in which the breech block is pivoted below the chamber and swings back and down to open. There are several variations on this theme, differing largely in the method of locking the block and transmitting the firing impulse. Perhaps the best known is the Remington system in which the closed block is supported and locked by the hammer as it falls.

ROTATING BARREL

Method of locking the breech of a semi-automatic pistol. Breech block and barrel are locked together by an interrupted lug system; they recoil together but a lug on the barrel is drawn through a helical groove on the gun's frame, so causing the barrel to rotate until the breech lugs are unlocked. The barrel then stops moving while the breech-block continues rearward to complete the cycle of operation. On closing the breech after re-loading, the forward movement rotates the barrel into the locked position.

SEAR

A lever or catch connected to the trigger, which holds the hammer or firing pin back until trigger pressure moves it to release the hammer or pin.

SELECTIVE FIRE

Term used to describe small arms which are capable of firing single shots semi-automatically or of firing full automatic, the choice being governed by some form of switch or controller.

SELF-COCKING

A firing mechanism in which the action of cocking and releasing the hammer or firing pin is performed by pulling back the trigger. Sometimes called 'double action only', which is a contradiction in terms.

SELF-LOADING

The proper term for any weapon which, by the agency of recoil or other firing-induced force, extracts and ejects the empty case and reloads and recocks, leaving the weapon ready to fire when the trigger is next pressed. The common 'automatic' pistol is properly called a self-loading pistol.

SEMI-RIMMED

Cartridge case which has an extraction groove like a rimless case, but in which the rim so exposed is slightly larger than the head of the case. This means that the rim can position the case correctly in the chamber but is not sufficiently large to interfere with feeding from the magazine. Invented by John Browning and first used with the 7.65mm ACP cartridge.

SET TRIGGER

Trigger mechanism used with target weapons in which a lever or button 'sets' the trigger by taking up all the slack in the system, and thereafter a very slight pressure on the trigger is sufficient to fire the weapon.

SHEATHED TRIGGER

Form of trigger, usually found on early revolvers, in which a sheath formed in the frame conceals the trigger except when the hammer has been cocked; at this point the trigger moves forward and is sufficiently exposed to be pressed to fire the weapon. Also called a 'stud trigger'. Occasionally found on some early automatic pistols.

SILENCER

Device attached to the muzzle of a weapon, or incorporated into its construction, whereby the gases emerging from the barrel are trapped, circulated until their temperature and pressure have dropped, and then released to the atmosphere. This prevents the usual noise of the muzzle blast. More generally called 'sound moderators' today, since the result is rarely completely silent and because, unless sub-sonic ammunition is used, the bullet noise is still considerable.

SINGLE ACTION

A pistol which must be manually cocked before every shot by drawing back the hammer or striker. An automatic pistol is said to be single action when it must be manually cocked by drawing back the slide or hammer before firing the first shot; subsequent shots perform the single-action cocking automatically.

SLIDE STOP

A catch in the frame of an automatic pistol which can be used to lock the slide to the rear for cleaning or dismantling or, automatically moved by the magazine platform, locks the slide open to indicate that the last shot in the magazine has been fired. Can be manually released or, in some designs, is automatically released by inserting a full magazine.

SOLID FRAME

A type of revolver in which the frame is forged in one piece, with an aperture into which the cylinder fits. The cylinder may be capable of being swung out on a crane (*qv*) or, in older or cheap designs, may have to be gate-loaded or entirely removed to re-load.

STANAG

NATO-speak for 'Standardisation Agreement'. A typical such agreement is STANAG 2324 which lays down the dimensions and tolerances for an optical or electro-optical sight mount for small arms.

STANDING BREECH

A fixed part of the pistol frame which abuts against the base of the cartridge in the firing position and carries the firing pin or the firing pin bush. Principally found in revolvers and single-shot pistols, but some odd forms of automatic pistol also have standing breeches.

STIRRUP LATCH

A method of securing the top strap of a hinged frame revolver to the standing breech. It consists of a metal frame with flat top and curved sides, hinged to the standing breech, and with a thumb-operated arm. The whole thing resembles a stirrup upside-down, and when the arm is pressed, the top section is hinged back, releasing the end of the top strap. Common on Webley revolvers.

STRIKER

A firing pin of generous proportions which is driven by a spring, and thus has sufficient momentum to fire the cartridge cap.

SUBMACHINE GUN

An automatic or selective fire weapon, compact, and firing pistol ammunition. This has been the definition of a submachine gun for most of its existence, but in the mid-1980s a new variety of weapon, firing assault rifle ammunition but of submachine gun dimensions, began to appear under this name. In addition, the Soviets and their neighbours in central Europe have invariably called the AK family of assault rifles 'submachine guns'.

SUB-SONIC

Below the speed of sound (1118ft/340m per second at sea level). Term applied to ammunition which in its normal form is super-sonic but is specially loaded to reduce the velocity to the sub-sonic level for use with silenced firearms. A supersonic bullet creates a noise as it passes through the air – the 'sonic bang' – and this negates the effect of a silenced weapon to a great extent. Sub-sonic ammunition used with a silenced weapon reduces the noise level to the point where it is impossible to determine where the bullet came from.

TIP-UP REVOLVER

A hinged-frame revolver in which the hinge between the barrel unit and the frame is between the top strap and the standing breech, so that when opened, the barrel rises.

TOGGLE LOCK

A method of locking the bolt or breech-block of an automatic weapon by using a two-lever linkage. One end is attached to the barrel extension, the other to the bolt, and in the middle is a hinge. With the bolt closed, the two levers lie flat, and any thrust is resisted. As the weapon recoils, some mechanism is used to raise the central hinge, and once this occurs the strut-like resistance fails and the two levers can fold up, allowing the bolt to move backwards and open the breech. First used on the Maxim machine gun, most famously used on the Parabellum pistol, and found on a variety of Swiss automatic weapons designed by Colonel Furrer, Superintendent of the Thun arsenal 1925–45, who had a predilection for this mechanism. It is rarely seen otherwise, since it demands fine machining and very consistent ammunition performance.

The toggle may also be used as a delaying mechanism for a delayed blowback weapon, either by positioning the hinge points above the line of recoil so that the recoil force tends to open the toggle, though at a considerable mechanical disadvantage (the Pedersen rifle) or by having the toggle folded in the closed position and making the recoil force unfold it (the Schwarzlose machine gun).

TWO-PART BOLT

A mechanism to provide delayed blowback action of an automatic weapon. It consists of a bolt in two parts, the front light and the rear heavy, together with some delaying element between the two, *eg* a lever or rollers engaging in a recess in the receiver. On firing, blowback action of the cartridge case forces the light forward section backwards; the lever or rollers must then be disengaged from their lodgement by this pressure before the rearward movement can be imparted to the heavy section of the bolt which, by reason of its inertia, adds a further delay before it begins to move back, taking the forward section and the locking device with it. The first application of this principle appears in a 1912 patent by Kiraly, and it was used by him in a variety of weapons in the 1930–40 period, notably the Hungarian Danuvia submachine guns, the SIG-Neuhausen submachine gun and the Kiraly-Ende KE-7 light machine gun. It has since been used in improved form in the Heckler & Koch and CETME rifles and submachine guns, in the French FA-MAS rifle and AAT-52 machine gun, and in the SIG Stgw57 rifle.

WINDAGE

(1) The difference in diameter between the calibre of a gun and the external diameter of the projectile.

(2) Lateral adjustment of a weapon's sight in order to compensate for a cross-wind blowing across the trajectory. (Principally an American usage).

ZEROING

The act of adjusting the sights of the weapon to the axis of the gun barrel, so that when fired the bullet strikes at the point of aim. When the adjustment has been performed, the weapon is said to be 'zeroed'. Correctly done, it will take into account not only the various idiosyncrasies of the individual weapon but the eyesight defects of the firer.

LIST OF MANUFACTURERS

This section is organised alphabetically according to the abbreviated versions of names used for the various manufacturing companies in the gun-by-gun chapters that follow. Fuller names of the companies are listed here, in many cases along with some details of their operations. More comprehensive information on the most prominent organisations and individuals can also be found in the *Inventors, Designers & Manufacturers* chapter (*see* pages 246–74).

AAI
AAI Corporation, Baltimore, Md., USA.

Accles
Accles Arms & Ammunition Mfg Co, Perry Barr, Birmingham, England.

Set up by James G Accles in 1894 and took over the assets of Grenfell & Accles and of the Gatling Arms & Ammunition Co. In Liquidation 1899.

Accuracy Int
Accuracy International, Portsmouth, England.

Adams (UK)
Adams Patent Small Arms Co, London, England. 1864–81.
Adams Patent Small Arms Mfg Co, W. Watts Locke & Co Proprietors. 1881–94.

Adams (US)
Adams Revolving Arms Co, New York NY, USA.

Set up by the English Adams brothers *ca* 1862 to sell revolvers during the Civil War. Manufacture was by the Massachusetts Arms Co.

Adasa
Armamentos de Aviación SA, Madrid, Spain.

Company set up to procure weapons for the Spanish Air Force. It later dabbled in manufacture but appears to have gone out of business by the early 1960s.

A&E
Armos y Equipos SRL, Córdoba, Argentina.

AI Corp
American International Corp., Salt Lake City, Utah, USA.

Amberg
Königliche Bayerische Gewehrfabrik, Amberg, Bavaria, Germany.

Anschütz
J.G. Anschütz GmbH, Ulm-a-d-Donau, Germany.

Ares
Ares Inc., Port Clinton, Ohio, USA.

Armaguerra
Armaguerra srl, Cremona, Italy.

ArmaLite
ArmaLite Div of Fairchild Engine & Airplane Co, Costa Mesa, Calif., USA. 1954–83.

Armalite Inc
ArmaLite Incorporated, Geneseo, Ill., USA. 1995– .

Arms Research
Arms Research Associates, Stone Park, Ill., USA.

Armstrong
Sir William Armstrong & Co, Elswick Works, Newcastle-upon-Tyne, England. 1847–97.

The company then took over Joseph Whitworth & Co to become Armstrong-Whitworth, then joined Vickers to become Vickers-Armstrong, and eventually vanished into Vickers

Arsenal
Arsenal, Kazanlak, Bulgaria.

Ascaso
Francisco Ascaso, Tarrasa, Cataluña, Spain.

Small factory which made copies of the government-issue Astra 400 for the Republicans in the Spanish Civil War.

Aserma
Aserma Manufacturing, New Germany, South Africa.

Astra-Unceta
Astra-Unceta y Cia SA, Guernica, Vizcaya, Spain.

Began in 1907 as Pedro Unceta y Juan Esperanza, Eibar; moved to Guernica in 1913 and became Esperanza y Unceta, adopted 'Astra' as their principal trade-name in 1914, became Unceta y Cia in 1926, Astra-Unceta in 1955 and Astra Gernika SA in 1994.

Auto-Ordnance
Auto-Ordnance, West Hurley, NY, USA.

This company was set up in New York in mid-1916 and went on to develop the Thompson submachine gun. It was never commercially successful and after its principal financial backer died in 1928 Thompson lost control of the firm. It changed hands several times until in 1951 it was sold to Numrich Arms Corporation who thereafter operated it as a subsidiary

Barrett
Barrett Firearms Mfg Co, Murfreesboro, Tenn., USA.

Bayonne
Manufacture d'Armes de Bayonne, Bayonne, France. 1921–88.

Beardmore
Beardmore Engineering Co., Glasgow, Scotland.

Beaumont
Frans Beaumont, Maastricht, The Netherlands.

Patentee and manufacturer of Dutch service revolvers and rifles, 1873–1905.

Becker
Becker & Hollander, Suhl, Germany. *Ca* 1885–1945.

Beistegui
Beistegui Hermanos, Eibar, Spain. 1915–36.

Benelli
Benelli Armi SpA, Urbino, Italy. *Ca* 1850– .

Beretta
Pietro Beretta SpA, Gardone Val Trompia, Italy. 1680– .

Bergmann
Th. Bergmann Waffenfabrik, Suhl, Germany. 1885–1918.
Bergmann's Industriewerke, Gaggenau, Germany. 1918–45.

Bern
Eidgenossische Waffenfabrik Bern, Bern, Switzerland.

Government arsenal since 1875. Name changed in 1993 to W+F Bern (*qv*).

Bernardelli
Vincenzo Bernardelli SpA, Gardone Val Trompia, Italy. 1865– .

BHS
BHS (Pvt) Ltd, Bulawayo, Rhodesia. 1976–80.

Bilbao
Bilbao SA Industria y Comércio, São Paulo, Brazil.

Blake
J.H. Blake, New York, NY, USA. *Ca* 1890–1910.

Bofors
Bofors Carl Gustav AB, Eskilstuna, Sweden.

Originally an ironworks, became a gunmaker in 1883, specialising in artillery. Moved into the small arms field in 1993 by taking over FFV.

Bonehill
C.G. Bonehill, Birmingham, England. 1872– .

Braendlin
Braendlin & Sommerville, Birmingham, England. 1867–71.
Braendlin Armoury, Birmingham. 1871–88.
Braendlin Armoury Co, Birmingham. 1888–1915.

Breda
Società Italiana Costruzioni Meccaniche Ernesto Breda, Brescia, Italy.

Brescia
Real Fabbrica d'Armi, Brescia, Italy.

Bridge
Bridge Tool & Die Manufacturing Co., Philadelphia, Pa., USA.

Brixia
Metallurgica Bresciana Tempini, Brescia, Italy. 1908–15.

Brünn
Waffenwerke Brünn, Brno, Czechoslovakia.

The Brno factory of Ceska Zbrojovka under the German occupation, 1938–45.

BSA
Birmingham Small Arms Co Ltd., Birmingham, England. 1861–73.
Birmingham Small Arms & Metal Co Ltd. 1873–97.
Birmingham Small Arms Co Ltd. 1901–19.
BSA Guns Ltd. 1919–84.
BSA Guns (1984) Ltd. 1984–92.

Burnside
Burnside Rifle Co, Providence, RI, USA. 1859–67.

Operated by Charles Jackson, who had taken Burnside's patents in settlement of debts.

Bushman
Bushman Ltd, Frogmore, St Albans, England.

Cadillac Gage
Cadillac Gage Corp, Warren, Mich., USA.

Carl Gustav
Carl Gustav Staatsgevärsfaktori, Eskilstuna, Sweden.

Became FFV in the 1970s.

Carmichael
W.T. Carmichael Ltd., Melbourne, Australia.

Castelli
Armi Castelli, Brescia, Italy.

Cataluña
Industrias de Guerra do Cataluña, Barcelona, Spain.

CETME
Centro de Estudios Tecnicos de Materiales Especiales, Madrid, Spain.

CEV
Companhia de Explosivos Valparaiba, Rio de Janiero, Brazil.

Christiana
Hovedarsenalet, Christiana, Norway.

Chuo Kogyu
Chuo Kogyu Kaisha Ltd, Niikura, Tokyo, Japan.
Absorbed Nambu Rifle Mfg Co in 1936.

CIS
Chartered Industries of Singapore, Singapore.

Colt
Colt's Patent Firearms Manufacturing Co, Hartford, Conn, USA. 1847–1947.
Colt's Manufacturing Co. 1947–55.
Colt's Patent Firearms Manufacturing Co. 1955–64.
Firearms Division of Colt Industries. 1964–89.
Colt Manufacturing Corp. 1990– .

Cordier
Cordier & Cie, Bellefontein, Switzerland.

COW
Coventry Ordnance Works, Coventry, England. *Ca* 1904–25.

Cranston
Cranston Arms Co, Providence, Rhode Island, USA.

A 'paper company' formed by Universal Windings Co of Providence to manufacture the Johnson automatic rifle in 1941–42 since at that time the Johnson Automatics Co had no manufacturing capability. The factory was located in Cranston, a suburb of Providence.

Cugir
Cugir Arsenal, Cugir, Romania.

CZ Brno
Ceskoslovenska Zbrojovka, Brno, Czechoslovakia. 1919–46. *See also* Brünn.
Zbrojovka Brno, Brno. 1946– .

CZ Prague
Ceska Zbrojovka a.s., Prague and Strakonice, Czechoslovakia. 1921– .

Daewoo
Daewoo Precision Industries, Pusan, South Korea.

Dai-Nippon
Dai-Nippon Heiki Kogyo, Notobe, Japan.
Sub-contractors to Nagoya Arsenal. *Ca* 1940–42.

Danuvia
Danuvia, Budapest, Hungary.

Danzig
Königliche Gewehrfabrik Danzig, West Prussia.

Darne
R. & P. Darne et Cie (later Darne SA), St Étienne, France. 1881–1979.
Much of their manufacture was actually contracted-out to Astra-Unceta of Spain.

Demro
Demro Products Inc., Manchester, Conn., USA.

Diecasters
Diecasters Ltd, Melbourne, Australia.

Diemaco
Diemaco, Kitchener, Ontario, Canada.

Dresse-Laloux
Dress-Laloux & Cie, Liège, Belgium.

Dreyse
F. Dreyse, Sommerda, Germany, 1841–1901, after which the name was purchased by Rheinmetall (*qv*).

Ductile Steel
Ductile Steel Co., Short Heath, Staffs., England. 1940–42.

DWM
Deutsche Waffen und Munitionsfabrik, Berlin, Germany. 1897–1945.

Eagle Arms
Eagle Arms Division of ArmaLite Inc., Geneseo, Ill., USA.

EBO
Hellenic Arms Industry SA (abbreviated as EBO from the Greek version of the name), Athens, Greece.

Echeverria
Star-Bonifacio Echeverria y Cia, Eibar, Spain

Enfield
Royal Small Arms Factory, Enfield Lock, England. 1854–1988.
After which the operation was purchased by British Aerospace/Royal Ordnance and transferred to the Royal Ordnance Factory, Nottingham, England.

Erfurt
Königliche Preussische Gewehrfabrik, Erfurt, Germany.
Established 1815 near Dusseldorf, moved to Erfurt 1862, dismantled under the orders of the Allied Disarmament Commission in 1919–20.

Erma
Erma-Werke, B. Giepel GmbH, Erfurt, Germany. 1919–45.
Erma-Werke GmbH, München-Dachau, Germany. 1949–

Euskalduna
Euskalduna y Cia, Placencia, Spain.

Evans

Evans Rifle Mfg Co, Mechanics Falls, Mass., USA. *Ca*. 1871–79, when bankrupt.

FAMAE

Fábrica de Material de Ejército, Santiago, Chile.

Previously known as Fábrica de Material de Guerra.

FBP

Fábrica de Braco de Prata, Lisbon, Portugal.

FEG

See Fegyvergar *below*.

Fegyvergyar

Fegyver es Gepgyar Reszvenytarsasag, Budapest, Hungary. From *ca* 1880–1945.

Then became Femaru es Szersazamgepgyar NV, until *ca* 1985, then the FEG Arms & Gas Appliances Factory.

Feinmechanik

Feinmechanische Werke GmbH, Erfurt, Germany

FFV

Forsvarets Fabriksverk, Eskilstuna, Sweden.

Formed by an amalgamation of Carl Gustav and Husqvarna in the 1970s. Became part of Bofors Ordnance in 1993.

FIAT

Fabbrica Italiana Automobili Torino, Turin, Italy.

FMAP

Fábrica Militar de Armas Portátiles 'Domingo Matheu', Rosario, Argentina.

FN

Fabrique Nationale des Armes de Guerre SA, Herstal, Liège, Belgium. 1889–1990.
FN Nouvelle Herstal SA, Liège. 1990–97.
FN Herstal SA. 1997– .

FNA

Fábrica Nacional de Armas, Mexico City, Mexico.

FNAB

Fabbrica Nazionale d'Armi, Brescia, Italy.

FNMI

FN Manufacturing Inc, Columbia, SC, USA.

American factory of FN Herstal.

Franchi

Luigi Franchi SpA, Fornaci, Brescia, Italy.

Francotte

August Francotte & Cie, Liège, Belgium.

Gabilondo

Founded at Eibar, Spain, in 1904 as Gabilondos y Urresti; one of the Gabilondo brothers left in 1909 and it then became Gabilondo y Urresti until 1920 when the firm moved to Elgoeibar and became Gabilondo y Cia. In 1936 it changed its name to Llama-Gabilondo y Cia, and in 1940 moved to Vitoria (*see* Llama).

Galand

C.F. Galand, Liège, Belgium. *Ca* 1855–1914.

Garate

Garate, Anitua y Cia, Eibar, Spain. *Ca* 1880–1936.

Gasser

Leopold Gasser, Vienna and St Polten, Austria. 1880–1914.

Gatling

Gatling Arms & Ammunition Co, Birmingham, England.

Formed in 1888 to market the Gatling machine gun in Europe and manufactured the Dimancea revolver until liquidated in 1890.

GEC

General Electric (USA), Burlington, Vt., USA.

Later became General Electric Aerospace, and in the early 1990s was taken over by Lockheed Martin.

Gevelot

Marin Batard-Gevelot (d.1846) set up Gevelot & Cie in 1820 to make percussion caps. Issy factory built by 1826.
Gevelot & Gaupillat 1883–85.
Société Française des Munitions (1885 to date)

The GG trademark was used after SFM took over and the name was revived in recent years.

GG

Golden Gun Company, Turku, Finland

GIAT

Groupement Industriel des Armamentes Terrestres, Saint-Cloud, France. 1950–90.

GIAT Industries, Saint-Cloud. 1990– .

Gibbs

Gibbs Rifle Co. Inc., Martinsburg, West Virginia, USA. 1992– .

This company, a subsidiary of Navy Arms Co, acquired the rights to the Parker-Hale rifle designs and manufactures them under the Parker-Hale name.

Glisenti

Società Siderurgica Glisenti, Turin, Italy.

Glock

Glock GmbH, Deutsch-Wagram, Austria.

Began making pistols in 1982, but had been a manufacturer of knives and edged tools for several years prior.

Greene

Greene Rifle Works, Worcester, Mass., USA. *Ca* 1860–66.

Grünig

Grünig & Elmiger, Malters, Switzerland.

Guide Lamp

Guide Lamp Division of General Motors, Detroit, Mich., USA.

Gustloff

Gustloff-Werke, Weimar, Germany.

Haenel
C.G. Haenel Gewehr & Fahrradfabrik, Suhl, Germany. 1840–1945, after which it became one of the founders of VEB, the East German state-controlled gunmakers' co-operative.

Haerens R
Haerens Rüstkammer, Copenhagen, Denmark.

Haerens T
Haerens Tøjhus, Copenhagen, Denmark.

Haerens V
Haerens Vaabenarsenal, Copenhagen, Denmark.

Hafdasa
Hispano-Argentino Fábrica de Automóviles SA, Buenos Aires, Argentina.

Halcon
Halcon SA, Buenos Aires, Argentina.

Hanyang
Hanyang Arsenal, Hanyang (now Wuhan), Hupeh Province, China.

Harrington
Harrington & Richardson, Worcester, Mass., USA.

Harris
Harris Gun Works, Phoenix, Ariz., USA.

Heckler & Koch
Heckler & Koch GmbH, Oberndorf/Neckar, Germany. 1949– .

Purchased by British Aerospace in 1992.

Hefah
Hefah & Co, Wednesfield, Staffs., England. 1941–43.

Helenius
Gunsmith Helenius, Salo, Finland.

Hembrug
Koninklijk Geweerfabrik, Hembrug, The Netherlands.

Henry
Alexander Henry & Co, Edinburgh, Scotland. *Fl* 1855–69
Alexander Henry, London, England. 1869– .
Henry Rifled Barrel Co, London. 1875–76.
Henry Rifled Barrel, Engineering & Small Arms Co. Ltd., London. 1876–1900.
Henry Military Rifle Co., London. 1875–78.

High Standard
High Standard Inc, Hartford, Conn., USA. 1926–85.

Originally barrel-makers, they bought the remains of the Hartford Arms Co in 1932 and used Hartford's pistol design as a basis for their own developments.

Hispano
Hispano-Suiza SA, Geneva, Switzerland.

Hopkins
Hopkins & Allen, Norwich, Conn., USA. 1868–1917.

Hotchkiss
Société de la Fabrication des Armes à Feu Portative Hotchkiss et Cie, Saint-Denis, Paris, France.

Howa
Howa Industries, Aichi, Japan.

Hughes
Hughes Helicopters & Ordnance Systems, Culver City, Calif., USA.

Later taken over by McDonnell Douglas.

Husqvarna
Husqvarna Vapenfabrik AB, Huskvarna, Sweden.

Ibarzabal
Teodoro Ibarzabal, Eibar, Spain.

IBM
International Business Machines Corp., Poughkeepsie, NY, USA.

IBRAP
Indústria Brasileira do Mecanica de Precisão Lds., Belo Horizonte, Brazil.

IMBEL
Indústria de Materiais Bélico do Brasil, São Paulo, Brazil.

IMI
Israel Military Industries, Ramat Ha Sharon, Israel. 1950–93, 1996– .

The company became Ta'as Israel Industries in 1993–96, but then reverted to the original name.

Imperia
Imperia SA, Nessonvaux, Liège, Belgium

INA
Indústria Nacional de Armas SA, São Paulo, Brazil

Inagaki
Inagaki Gun Factory, Tokyo, Japan. 1924–45.

INDEP
Indústria Nacional de Defesa do Exército Português, Lisbon, Portugal.

Inglis
John Inglis & Co, Toronto, Canada.

Ingram
The Ingram submachine gun has been through several hands including POC and SWD Inc (*qv*), see the *Inventors, Designers and Manufacturers* chapter for a more complete explanation.

Inland
Inland Division of General Motors, Dayton, Ohio, USA.

Interdynamic
Interdynamic of America, Miami, Fla., USA.

International Harvester
International Harvester Corp., Chicago, Ill., USA.

IOG
International Ordnance Group, San Antonio, Texas, USA.

IPME
Institute of Precise Mechanical Engineering, Klimovsk, Russia.

Irwin
Irwin-Pedersen Arms Co, Grand Rapids, Mich., USA.

Ishapore
Ishapore Rifle Factory, Ishapore, India.

Ithaca
W.H. Baker & Co, Ithaca, NY, USA. 1883–89.
Ithaca Gun Co, Ithaca. 1889–1988.
Ithaca Gun Co, Kingferry, NY, USA. 1988– .

ITM
Industrial Technology & Machines AG, Solothurn, Switzerland. 1984–89.

Then absorbed into Sphinx Engineering and its products sold under the Sphinx name thereafter.

Izhevsk
Izhevsk Rifle Factory, Izhevsk, Russia.

Made rifles and machine guns from the time of the Tsar through the Communist era. Privatised in the early 1990s and now operates as Izhmash (*below*).

Izmash
Ishevsk Machinery Factory, Izhevsk, Russia.

Formerly the Izhevsk Rifle Factory. This organisation also controls a number of subsidiary joint-stock companies which appear to have been set up by the various design bureau leaders – *eg* the Kalashnikov Joint Stock Company (Izhmash).

Jinsen
Jinsen Arsenal, Jinsen (now Inchon), Korea.

Built by Japanese; 1923–45.

Johnson
Johnson Automatics Mfg Co, Cranston, Rhode Island, USA. 1936–44.

Joslyn
Joslyn Arms Co., Stonington, Conn., USA. 1855–66.

Junker & Ruh
Junker & Ruh AG, Karlsruhe, Germany.

Kayaba
Kayaba Kogyo, Tokyo, Japan.

Sub-contractors to Nagoya Arsenal, *ca* 1940–42.

KBP
Instrument Design Bureau (KBP), Tula, Russia.

Klin
Klin-Zlatoust Engineering Works, Zlatoustovsk, Russia.

Knight
Knight's Armament Co, Vero Beach, Fla., USA.

Knorr
Knorr-Bremse AG, Lichtenberg, Berlin, Germany.

København
Gevaerfabriken København, Copenhagen, Denmark.

Koishikawa
Koishikawa Arsenal, Tokyo, Japan.

Kokura
Kokura Arsenal, Kokura, Japan. 1927–45.

Kongsberg
Kongsberg Vapenfabrik, Kongsberg, Norway.

Kovrov
Kovrov Machine Gun Factory, Kovrov, Russia.

Kragujevac
Originally called Kragushevats, in Serbia, it was the site of the Serbian national arsenal from the 1870s. It was rebuilt and equipped with modern machinery by Fabrique National of Belgium in the early 1900s. Became known as Voini Techniki Zavod (Army Technical Factory) in the 1920s. More or less destroyed 1939–45, it was reconstituted as Crvena Zastava (Factory of the Red Flag), and in 1990 changed its name to Zastava Arms.

Krieghoff
Heinrich Krieghoff Waffenfabrik, Suhl, Germany. Pre-1945.
H. Krieghoff GmbH, Ulm/Donau, Germany. Post-1945.

KSN
K.S.N. Industries Ltd., Kfar Saba, Israel.

Kwantung
Kwantung Arsenal, Kwantung (now Yipinglang), Yunnan Province, China.

La Coruña
Fábrica Nacional de Armas, La Coruña, Spain.

Part of the Santa Barbara organisation.

La France
La France Specialties, San Diego, Calif., USA.

Lamson
E.G. Lamson & Co, Windsor, Vt. USA. *Fl* 1865–66.

Landes
Maschinenfabrik Landes, Munich, Germany.

LAR
L.A.R. Manufacturing Co., West Jordan, Utah, USA.

Lee Arms
Lee Arms Co, Wilkes Barre, Penn, USA. *Ca* 1865–85.

Lefaucheaux
Eugene Lefaucheaux, Paris France.

Liège
Fabrique d'Armes de l'État, Liège, Belgium.

Liègeoise
Precision Liègeoise SA, Herstal, Belgium.

Lines
Lines Brothers, London, England.

Lithgow
Small Arms Factory, Lithgow, NSW, Australia.

LIW
LIW Division of Denel Pty, Pretoria, South Africa.
Formerly Lyttleton Engineering Works.

Llama
Llama-Gabilondo y Cia SA, Vitoria, Spain. 1936– .
For earlier history *see* Gabilondo.

Lockheed
Lockheed Martin Armament Systems, Burlington, Vt., USA.

Loewe
Ludwig Loewe & Co, Berlin, Germany.
Amalgamated with a cartridge company in 1896 to become DWM (*qv*).

Long Branch
Long Branch Small Arms Factory, Long Branch, Ontario, Canada.

LSA
London Small Arms Co., London, England. 1866–1925.

Lübeck
Berlin-Lübecker Maschinenfabrik, Lübeck, Germany.

Lucznik
Zaklady Metalowe Lucznik, Radom, Poland.

Lysaght
Lysaght Pty, Newcastle, NSW, Australia.

Lyttleton
Lyttleton Engineering Co, Pretoria, South Africa.

Maadi
Maadi Military & Civil Industries Co, Cairo, Egypt.
Originally known as State Rifle Factory No.54 and located in Port Said.

MAB
Manufacture d'Armes de Bayonne, Bayonne, France. 1921–88.
A private company manufacturing automatic pistols.

MAC
Military Armaments Corp, Atlanta, Georgia, USA.
Made the Ingram submachine gun, *ca* 1976–82.

MAC Chatellerault
Manufacture d'Armes Chatellerault, Chatellerault, France.
State arms factory, particularly noted for machine guns.

McDonnell
McDonnell Douglas Helicopter Systems, Mesa, Arizona, USA.

McMillan
McMillan Gun Works Inc, Phoenix, Arizona, USA.

Madsen
Dansk Industri Syndikat AS 'Madsen', Copenhagen, Denmark.
Now known as DISA Systems, and no longer in the firearms business.

MAN
Maschinenfabrik Augsburg-Nürnberg, Augsburg, Germany.

Manroy
Manroy Engineering, Beckley, East Sussex, England.

Manufrance
Manufacture Française d'Armes et Cycles de Saint Étienne, St Étienne, France.
Later (post-1945) adopted the name Manufrance SA.

Manurhin
Manufacture de Machines du Haut-Rhin, Mulhouse-Bourtzwiler, France.
Began firearms manufacture in the early 1950s. Later changed its name to 'Manurhin' and later to 'Manurhin Defense' until taken over by GIAT in 1990. It still retains its own identity within the GIAT organisation and markets arms under the Manurhin name. Also a major producer of ammunition-making machinery.

MAP
Manufacture d'Armes de Paris, Saint-Denis, France.
State arms factory; rifles. World War I period.

Marlin
John M. Marlin, New Haven, Conn., USA. 1870–1915.
Marlin-Rockwell Corp., New Haven. 1915–23.
Marlin Firearms Co, New Haven. 1923–69.
Marlin Firearms Co., North Haven, Conn., USA. 1969– .

MAS
Manufacture d'Armes de St Étienne, St Étienne, France.
State arms factory; rifles, submachine guns, pistols.

MAT
Manufacture d'Armes de Tulle, Tulle, France.

Mauser
Gebruder Mauser, Oberndorf/Neckar, Germany. 1872–74.
Gebruder Mauser & Co. 1874–84.
Waffenfabrik Mauser. 1884–1922.
Mauserwerke AG. 1922–45.
Mauserwerke Oberndorf AG. 1950– .

Maxim
Maxim Gun Co., Ltd, Hatton Garden, London.

Mechem
Mechem, Silverton, South Africa.

Mendoza
Productos Mendoza SA, Mexico City, Mexico.

Menz
Waffenfabrik August Menz, Suhl, Germany. 1914–37.

Meriden
Meriden Manufacturing Co., Meriden, Conn., USA.
Ca 1863–67.

Mexicanas
Fábrica de Armas Mexicanas, Mexico City, Mexico.

MKEK
Makina ve Kimya Endustrisi Kurumu, Ankara, Turkey.

Mukden
Mukden Arsenal, Manchuria. *Ca* 1922; taken over by
Japan 1931–45.

NA&ACo
National Arms & Ammunition Co, Birmingham,
England.

Founded 1872 by Westley Richards & Maj Gen Dixon.
Made Mauser rifles and 11mm ammunition for Germany,
Snider and Martini-Henry rifles for UK, Martini and
Westley Richards rifles commercially, but failed to prosper.
Holford Mills factory sold to Gatling in 1888 and the
Sparkbrook factory in Montgomery St taken over by the
government when the company collapsed in 1896.

Nagant
Emile Nagant, Liège, Belgium. ?–1910.
Fabrique d'Armes Leon Nagant, Liège. ?–1910.
Fabrique d'Armes et Automobiles Nagant Frères, Liège.
1910–14.

Nagoya
Nagoya Arsenal, Nagoya, Japan. 1923–45.

Nambu
Nambu Rifle Manufacturing Co., Kokubunji, Tokyo,
Japan. 1927–36.

Nanking
Nanking Arsenal, Nanking (now Nanjing), China.

Set up by Japan *ca* 1943–45.

National Postal
National Postal Meter Co., Rochester, NY, USA.

Neuhausen
Name under which products of the Schweizer Industrie
Gesellschaft (SIG) of Neuhausen-am-Rheinfalls,
Switzerland, were sold in the 1930s.

Norinco
China North Industries Corporation, Beijing, China.

Sales organisation for the Chinese national munitions
factories.

North American
North American Arms Co, Quebec, Canada. 1917–20.

Set up for wartime production of various weapons, notable
for producing a small number of Colt .45 auto
pistols on contract. The end of the war caused cancellation
of the contract after about 100 pistols had been made.

NRF1
National Rifle Factory No.1, Birmingham, England.
1915–18.

Oberspree
Waffenwerke Oberspree, Kornbusch & Co, Berlin,
Germany.

Omori
Omori Factory, Division of Minebea Co, Tokyo, Japan.

Orbea
Orbea Hermanos, Eibar, Spain.

Ost-Schweiz
Ost-Schweizerische Buchsenmacherei, St Gallen,
Switzerland.

Oviedo
Fábrica Nacional de Armas, Oviedo, Spain.

Now part of the Santa Barbara organisation.

OVP
Officina Villar Perosa, Villar Perosa, Turin, Italy.

Parker-Hale
Parker-Hale Ltd, Birmingham, England. 1900–92.

In 1992 the rights and patents to Parker-Hale rifles were
sold to the Gibbs Rifle Co (*qv*) who then began making
rifles under the Parker-Hale name.

Parinco
Parinco SA, Madrid, Spain.

Persia
State Rifle Factory, Mosalsalsasi, Persia (Iran).

Peruana
Industria Peruana, Fábrica de Armes de Los Andes, Peru.

Manufactured the Ingram Model 6 under licence in the
1950s.

Petit Syndicat
Short-lived amalgamation of four Liège gunmakers –
Ancion & Cie, Dress-Laloux, Francotte and Pirlot – in the
1870s to manufacture the Comblain rifle.

Pfenninger
Rudolf Pfenninger, Stäfa, Switzerland.

PGM
PGM Precision sarl, La Chambre, France.

Pieper
Henri & Nicolas Pieper, Herstal, Belgium. 1866–1905.

Then became Ancien Établissments Pieper until about
1955.

Pirlot
Pirlot Frères, Liège, Belgium.

Placencia
Fábrica Nacional de Armas, Placencia, Spain.
Now part of the Santa Barbara organisation.

POC
Police Ordnance Co., Los Angeles, Calif., USA. 1949–53.

POF
Pakistan Ordnance Factory, Wah Cantonment, Pakistan.

Povaske Strojarne
CZ Brno factory at Povaske Strojarne, Czech Republic.

Pratt & Whitney
Pratt & Whitney Mfg Co, Hartford, Conn., USA.

Precise Engineering
Institute of Precise Mechanical Engineering, Izhevsk, Russia.

Providence
Providence Tool Co, Providence, Rhode Island, USA.

PSM
Pabrik Sendjata dan Mesiu, Bandung, Indonesia.

PT
Pindad PT Pindad, Kiaracondong, Bandung, Indonesia.

Puteaux
Atelier d'Armes de Puteaux, Paris, France.

Quality
Quality Hardware & Machine Co., Chicago, Ill., USA.

Radom
Fabrika Brony w Radomu, Radom, Poland.

Ramo
Ramo Manufacturing Inc., Nashville, Tenn., USA.

Rangoon
Burmese Army Workshops, Rangoon, Burma.

Remington
Eli Remington & Son, Ilion, NY, USA. 1816–86.
Remington Arms Co, Bridgeport, Conn., USA. 1886–1912.
Remington Arms-UMC, Bridgeport. 1912–35.
Remington Arms Co, Bridgeport. 1935– .

Repousmetal
SA Repousmetal, Brussels, Belgium.

Rexim
Rexim SA, Geneva, Switzerland.

RH-ALAN
RH-ALAN Ltd., Zagreb, Croatia.

Rheinmetall
Rheinische Metallwaren und Maschinenfabrik, Sommerda, Germany.

Richardson
Richardson & Overman, Philadelphia, Pa., USA. *Ca* 1860–65.

Robar
Robar Companies Inc., Phoenix, Arizona, USA.

Rochester
Rochester Defense Corporation, Rochester, NY, USA.

Rock Island
Rock Island Arsenal, Rock Island, Ill., USA.

Rock-Ola
Rock-Ola Corporation, Chicago, Ill., USA.

ROF (F)
Royal Ordnance Factory, Fazakerley, Liverpool, England.

ROF (M)
Royal Ordnance Factory, Maltby, Yorkshire, England.

Rome
Officina Costruzioni d'Artiglieria, Rome, Italy.

Romtehnica
Romtehnica, Bucharest, Romania.

Ronge
J.B. Ronge Fils, Liège, Belgium.

Ross
Ross Rifle Co, Quebec, Canada. 1903–17.

RPB
R.P.B. Industries, Atlanta, Georgia, USA.

Ruger
Sturm, Ruger & Co Inc, Southport, Conn., USA. 1949– .

Rychner
Rychner & Keller, Aarau, Swizterland

SACM
Société Alsacienne des Constructions Mécaniques, Cholet, France. 1930–40.

Saco
Saco Division, Maremont Corporation, Saco, Maine, USA.
Later became Saco Defense Inc.

Saginaw
Saginaw Steering Division of General Motors, Saginaw and Grand Rapids, Mich., USA.

St Chamond
Compagnie des Forges et Aciers de la Marine, St Chamond, France.

St Étienne
Manufacture Nationale des Armes de Saint Étienne, St Étienne, France.

Sako
Oy Sako AB, Riihimaki, Finland.

San Cristóbal
Armeria de San Cristóbal, Benemérita de San Cristóbal, Dominican Republic. National Arsenal, established in the 1950s with assistance from Beretta of Italy.

Santa Barbara
Empresa Nacional de Industrias Militares 'Santa Barbara', La Coruña and Madrid, Spain.

Spanish government arsenal which also makes sporting rifle actions and barrels.

Sauer & Sohn
J.P. Sauer & Sohn GmbH, Suhl, Germany. 1751–1945.
J.P. Sauer & Sohn GmbH, Eckernforde, Germany. 1948– .

Sauerbrey
Valentin Sauerbrey, Basle, Switzerland.

Savage
Savage Arms Corp., Utica, NY, and Chicopee Falls, Mass., USA. 1894– .

Schilling
V. Chr. Schilling, Suhl, Germany. 1816–1934.

Schutz & Larsen
Schutz & Larsen, Otterup, Denmark.

Schwarzlose
Andreas W. Schwarzlose GmbH, Berlin, Germany. 1893–1919.

Sedgley
R.F. Sedgley Inc, Philadelphia, Pa., USA.

Sestroretsk
Imperial Arsenal, Sestroretsk, Russia; after 1917 became Sestroretsk Rifle Factory.

SIA
Società Anonima Italiana G. Ansaldo, Armstrong & Co.

SIG
Schweizerische Industrie Gesellschaft, Neuhausen am Rheinfalls, Switzerland. 1853– .

SIMA-CIFAR
SIMA-CIFAR, Base Naval, Callao, Peru.

Peruvian Navy arsenal and weapon development agency.

Simson
Waffenfabrik Simson & Co, Suhl, Germany. *Ca* 1860–1932.

Became Berliner-Suhler Waffen und Fahrzeugwerke AG in 1932 and was then seized in *ca* 1936 to become part of the Gustloff-Werke combine.

SITES
SITES SpA, Turin, Italy.

Skoda
Waffenwerke Skoda, Pilsen, Bohemia (Czech Republic).

Smith-Corona
L.C. Smith & Corona Typewriter Co, Pittsburg, Pa., USA.

Smith & Wesson
Smith & Wesson, Springfield, Mass., USA. 1852– .

Socimi
Società Costruzioni Industriale di Milano, Milan, Italy.

SOFAM
Société de Fabrication des Armaments et Moteurs, Paris, France.

Sola
Société Luxembourgoise des Armes SA, Ettelbruck, Luxembourg.

Soleil
Louis Soleil, Liège, Belgium.

Sollux
Sollux AG, Vienna, Austria.

Solothurn
Solothurn AG, Solothurn, Switzerland. Originally a small engineering firm, taken over by Rheinmetall in the early 1920s and used as their design and development agency so as to evade the Versailles Treaty. Weapons developed were then manufactured by Steyr (*qv*) and marketed by Steyr-Solothurn AG.

Spandau
Königliche Gewehrfabrik Spandau, Berlin, Germany.

Spangenberg
Spangenberg & Sauer, Suhl, Germany. *Fl* 1870–90.

Sparkbrook
Royal Small Arms Factory, Sparkbrook, Birmingham, England.

Spencer
Spencer Repeating Rifle Co., Boston, Mass., USA. 1860–69.

Springfield
Springfield Armory, Springfield, Mass., USA. 1782–1975. US Government arsenal.

SSA
Standard Small Arms Co., Birmingham, England. 1915–18.

Standard
Standard Products Co., Port Clinton, Ohio, USA.

Star
Star-Bonifacio Echeverria SA, Eibar, Spain.

Steiger
W. von Steiger & Cie, Thun, Switzerland.

Steiner
Walter Steiner Eisenkonstructionen, Suhl, Germany.

Sterling
Sterling Armaments Co., Dagenham, England.

Steyr
Josef Werndl, Steyr, Austria. 1864–69.
Österreichische Waffenfabrik Gesellschaft GmbH, Steyr. 1869–1919.
Steyr-Werke AG. 1919–34.
Steyr-Daimler-Puch, Steyr. 1934–90.
Steyr-Mannnlicher GmbH, Steyr. 1990– .

A subsidiary company, Steyr-Solothurn AG, existed 1934–45 as a marketing organisation for military weapons made by Steyr, Rheinmetall and Solothurn AG.

Suhl
Productionsgenossenschaft, Suhl, Germany. *Fl* 1880s.

Sumitomo
Sumitomo Heavy Industries, Tokyo, Japan.

SWD Inc
S.W.D. Inc., Atlanta, Georgia, USA. *See* Ingram.

Ta'as
Ta'as Israel Industries, Ramat Hasharon, Israel. 1993–96.

See also IMI for the company's history before and after these dates.

Tallinn
State Arsenal, Tallinn, Estonia.

Tampeeren
Tampeeren Asepaja Oy, Tampere, Finland.

Tarrasa
Industrias de Guerra de Cataluña, Tarrasa.

Spanish Republican factory established during the Civil War, 1936–39.

Technika
Technika, Budapest, Hungary.

Terni
Fabbrica Nazionale d'Armi, Terni, Italy.

TGE
Tokyo Gas & Electric Co, Tokyo, Japan.

Tikkakoski
Oy Tikkakoski AB, Tikkakoski, Finland.

Torino
Reale Fabbrica d'Armi de Torino, Turin, Italy.

Torre
Reale Fabbrica d'Armi de Torre Annunziata, Torre Annunziata, Italy.

Tientsin
Tientsin Arsenal, Tientsin (Tianjin), China.
Set up by Japan, *ca* 1943–45.

Tøjhus
København Tøjhus, Copenhagen, Denmark.

Tokyo Juki
Tokyo Juki Company, Tokyo, Japan.

Sub-contractors to Nagoya Arsenal, 1940–45.

Toyo Juki
Toyo Juki Company, Hiroshima, Japan.

Sub-contractors to Nagoya Arsenal, 1940–45.

Trocaola
Trocaola, Aranzabal y Cia, Eibar, Spain. *Ca* 1903–36.

TRW
Thompson-Ramo-Woolridge Inc., Cleveland, Ohio, USA.

Tula
Imperial Arsenal, Tula, Russia.

Uhersky Brod
CZ Brno factory at Uhersky Brod, Czech Republic.

Underwood
Underwood-Elliott-Fisher Co., Hartford, Conn., USA.

Uralsk
Enterprise Metallist, Uralsk, Kazakhstan.

USMG
United States Machine Gun Co, Meriden Conn., USA.

Valmet
1. Valtions Metallathedas, Helsinki, Finland. Finnish rifle arsenal; made Mosin-Nagant rifles and Lahti pistols.

2. Valtrions Kivaaritedhas, Jyvaskyla, Finland. Finnish state engineering factory set up in 1917 and made pistols, SMGs and rifles.

3. These amalgamated to form: Valmet AB, Jyvaskyla, Finland. Taken over by Sako in 1992.

Våpensmia
Våpensmia AS, Dokka, Norway.

Vektor
Vektor Division of Denel Pty, Pretoria, South Africa.

Vickers
Albert Vickers Ltd, Crayford, Kent, England.
Vickers, Son & Maxim Ltd, Crayford.
Vickers Ltd, Crayford. 1919–39.
Vickers-Armstrong Ltd, Crayford & Newcastle-upon-Tyne.

Viking
Viking Systems Inc., Arlington, Virginia, USA.

Voere
Voere Tiroler Jadg- und Sportwaffenfabrik, Kufstein, Austria.

Vorwerke
Vorwerke & Cie, Barmen, Germany. 1914–18.

Voini Techniki Zavod
See Kragujevac.

Vsetín
Zbrojovka Vsetín, Vsetín, Czech Republic.

W+F Bern

Waffenfabrik Bern, Berne, Switzerland.

National arsenal, formerly known as Eidgenossische Waffenfabrik Bern (*see* Bern).

Walther

Carl Walther Waffenfabrik, Zella Mehlis, Germany.
 1886–1945.

Then re-organised in Ulm-a-d-Donau in 1950 and now known as Carl Walther Waffenfabrik, Ulm/Donau, Germany.

Warnant

L. & J. Warnant Frères, Hognee, Belgium. *Ca* 1850–1914.

Warner

James Warner, Springfield, Mass., USA. *Ca* 1864–66.

Warsaw

National Rifle Factory, Warsaw, Poland. 1922–39.

Weaver Arms

Weaver Arms Ltd, Escondido, Calif., USA.

Webley

Originated as Philip Webley in 1845; became P. Webley & Son (1859–97); The Webley & Scott Revolver & Arms Company (1897–1906) and finally Webley & Scott Ltd (1906–) all of Birmingham, England.

Western States

Western States Arms Co., Midvale, Utah, USA.

Principally a distributor and dealer but was peripherally involved with the American 180 submachine gun in the mid-1960s. Appears to have gone out of business by 1975

Westinghouse

New England Westinghouse Co., Springfield, Mass., USA.

Westley Richards

Westley Richards, Birmingham England. 1840–59.
Westley Richards & Co., Birmingham. 1859–73.
Westley Richards & Co Ltd, Birmingham. 1873– .

Whitehead

Whitehead Moto-Fides, Livorno, Italy.

Whitney

Whitney Arms Co, Whitneyville, Conn., USA.
 Ca 1840–88, when bought out by Winchester.

Winchester

New Haven Arms Co., New Haven, Conn., USA.
 1857–60
Winchester Repeating Arms Co., New Haven.
 1860–1932.

In 1932 the company was bought by the Western Cartridge Co., owned by a man called Olin. The gunmaking business continued under the Winchester Repeating Arms name, while the ammunition-making component became the Winchester-Western Division of the Olin Mathieson Chemical Company. This arrangement continued until the late 1970s when Olin decided to concentrate on the ammunition side, and sold the gunmaking business, which then became the U.S. Repeating Arms Company, New Haven, Conn. The ammunition part became Olin-Winchester, East Alton, Illinois, USA.

Witten

Eisenwerke Witten, Witten-a-d-Ruhr, Germany.

WSI

Weapons Systems Inc., Malden, Mass., USA.

Zastava Arms

Post-1990 name for Kragujevac arsenal and its successors; *see* Kragujevac.

Zbrojovka Brno

Ceskoslovenska Zbrojovka, Brno, Czech Republic. 1919– .

Zürich

Zürich Zeughaus, Zurich, Switzerland.

PISTOLS

The weapons in this section are, for the most part, listed under their maker's name or under the names commonly associated with them; unfortunately this system cannot be easily applied to the profusion of European military revolvers of the later years of the 19th century, and these are listed under their country of adoption. Many of these revolvers were contract-made to a design drawn up by a military commission, or bought from some foreign source which is now untraceable, or produced by a military arsenal factory using a collection of features which could be ascribed to various designers. To classify, for example, all French revolvers as 'Chamelot-Delvigne' or all Swiss as 'Schmidt-Galand' is therefore arguable at best, and in order to avoid long discussions of the pros and cons of obscure design features and their weight in deciding the parentage of particular designs, the national route has been taken.

It could probably be argued that every pistol ever made has been taken into battle at some time or another, officially or unofficially, but in order to keep a sense of proportion, this section confines itself to those weapons actually authorised for military service or made with military adoption in view. Even with this proviso, there are still a few surprises.

ADAMS Britain
Adams (UK)

Dean & Adams Revolver Pistol, Converted, Mark 1
1868. Conversion of Beaumont-Adams muzzle-loading percussion revolvers of 1856 to breech-loading cartridge pattern. Solid-frame, hexagonal barrel, double-action revolver with smooth cylinder. Gate-loaded, rod-ejection. Prominent squared prawl on butt.

Cartridge: .450 Adams
Length: 11.62in (295mm)
Weight: 2lb 6oz (1080g)
Barrel: 5.63in (143mm), 4 grooves, rh
Magazine: 6-round cylinder
Muzzle velocity: 650 ft/sec (198 m/sec)

Pistol, Adams, Centre-Fire, BL, Mark 2
1872. Generally similar to Mark 1 but of new construction. Note the 'BL' in the designation indicating the adoption of breech-loading.

Cartridge: .450 Adams
Length: 11.18in (284mm)
Weight: 2lb 6oz (1080g)
Barrel: 6.0in (152mm), 4 grooves, rh
Magazine: 6-round cylinder
Muzzle velocity: 650 ft/sec (198 m/sec)

Pistol, Adams, Centre-Fire, Mark 3
1872. As for Mark 2 but with an improved ejector rod system mounted on a swivel at the front of the frame.

Cartridge: .450 Adams
Length: 10.83in (275mm)
Weight: 2lb 5oz (1060g)

Barrel: 6.0in (152mm), 4 grooves, rh
Magazine: 6-round cylinder
Muzzle velocity: 650 ft/sec (198 m/sec)

Pistol, Adams, Centre-Fire, Mark 4
1872. Conversion of original Mark 1 pistols by substituting a fresh design of trigger mechanism to overcome faulty cylinder operation.

ASCASO Spain
Ascaso

1936–39. The Ascaso was a direct copy of the Astra 400 pistol manufactured by a Republican workshop operating under the name of a well-known political firebrand assassinated shortly after the beginning of the Spanish Civil War. The finish was not up to Astra standards, but it worked well enough and several hundred appear to have been made.

Cartridge: 9 × 23mm Largo
Length: 9.25in (235mm)
Weight: 1lb 15oz (878g)
Barrel: 5.90in (150mm), 4 grooves, rh
Magazine: 8-round box.
Muzzle velocity: 1181 ft/sec (360 m/sec)

ASERMA South Africa
Aserma

ADP Mark II.
1994. Synthetic frame with moulded-in rails; steel slide. Semi-automatic; retarded blowback by venting gas into a cylinder in the frame, where it resists a piston attached to the slide; self-cocking trigger mechanism; manual safety.

Cartridge: 9 × 19mm Parabellum
Length: 6.30in (160mm)
Weight: 1lb 4oz (567g)
Barrel: 3.58in (96.5mm), 4 grooves, rh
Magazine: 10- or 15-round box
Muzzle velocity: 1115 ft/sec (340 m/sec)

ASTRA Spain
Astra-Unceta
Model 300

1923–47. A smaller version of the Model 400 (*below*). Adopted in 9mm Short calibre by the Spanish prison service and the Spanish Navy. Some 23,000 bought by the German Army in France in 1943–44.

Cartridge: 9 × 17mm Short
Length: 6.30in (160mm)
Weight: 1lb 6oz (635g)
Barrel: 3.9in (99mm), 6 grooves, rh
Magazine: 7-round box
Muzzle velocity: 890 ft/sec (271 m/sec)

Model 400

1921–46. Virtually Astra's re-design of the Campo-Giro Model 1913-16. It retained the 'water-pistol' shape of the Campo-Giro but improved the manufacture and minor details. Blowback, concentric recoil spring around the barrel, internal hammer-fired, grip safety, manual safety, magazine safety. Standard Spanish Army pistol 1921–46.

Cartridge: 9 × 23mm Largo
Length: 9.25in (235mm)
Weight: 1lb 15oz (878g)
Barrel: 5.91in (150mm), 6 grooves, rh
Magazine: 8-round box
Muzzle velocity: 1181 ft/sec (360 m/sec)

Model 600

1943–46. Smaller version of the Model 400 in 9mm Parabellum calibre, made for the German government in 1943–44 and thereafter sold commercially.

Cartridge: 9 × 19mm Parabellum
Length: 8.07in (205mm)
Weight: 2lb 0oz (908g)
Barrel: 5.24in (133mm), 6 grooves, rh
Magazine: 8-round box
Muzzle velocity: 1181 ft/sec (360 m/sec)

Model 900

1927–55. Outwardly a copy of the Mauser c/96 Military Model, though the internals differ somewhat in detail. A sliding cover on the left side of the frame allows access to the breech lock and trigger mechanism. Charger-loaded magazine in front of trigger, 'broom-handle' butt, ring hammer.

Cartridge: 7.63 × 25mm Mauser
Length: 12.48in (317mm)
Weight: 3lb 1oz (1390g)
Barrel: 5.51in (140mm), 6 grooves, rh
Magazine: 10-round box
Muzzle velocity: 1329 ft/sec (405 m/sec)

Model 901

1928. A version of the Model 900 with a fire selector switch on the right side of the frame, permitting automatic fire. Fixed magazine in front of trigger, Wooden holster-stock. Sold to China in the 1930s.

Cartridge: 7.63 × 25mm Mauser
Length: 11.42in (290mm)
Weight: 2lb 12oz (1247g)
Barrel: 5.51in (140mm), 6 grooves, rh
Magazine: 10-round box
Muzzle velocity: 1329 ft/sec (405 m/sec)
Cyclic rate: 900 rds/min.

Model 902

1929. This is the 901 with a longer barrel and a fixed 20-shot magazine in front of the trigger. Also sold to China in the 1930s.

Cartridge: 7.63 × 25mm Mauser
Length: 12.48in (330mm)
Weight: 3lb 6oz (1519g)
Barrel: 7.08in (180mm), 6 grooves, rh
Magazine: 20-round box
Muzzle velocity: 1575 ft/sec (480 m/sec)
Cyclic rate: 900 rds/min

Model 903 & Model 903E

1932. A further variant, introducing a detachable magazine. Some to China, most to the German Army in France, 1940–41. Model 903 was the original, Model 903E the principal production model, which differed in minor details of the magazine platform and magazine release.

Cartridge: 7.63 × 25mm Mauser
Length: 12.13in (308mm)
Weight: 2lb 13oz (1275g)
Barrel: 6.30in (160mm), 6 grooves, rh
Magazine: 10- or 20-round box
Muzzle velocity: 1509 ft/sec (460 m/sec)
Cyclic rate: 900 rds/min

Model 904

A development design, this was more or less a Model 903 with a rate-reducing device set into the butt in order to bring the rate of fire down to a controllable figure. Very few were made, the results of the development being applied to the Model F (*below*).

Cartridge: 7.63 × 25mm Mauser
Length: 12.13in (308mm)
Weight: 2lb 13oz (1275g)
Barrel: 6.30in (160mm), 6 grooves, rh
Magazine: 10- or 20-round box
Muzzle velocity: 1509 ft/sec (460 m/sec)
Cyclic rate: 350 rds/min

Model F

1933-35. The final version of the Model 900 series. It was chambered for the 9mm Largo cartridge and fitted with the rate retarder developed in the Model 904. Fire selector switch on right side of frame. Supplied to the Guardia Civil, but production was interrupted by the Civil War and never resumed.

Cartridge: 9 × 23mm Largo
Length: 13.0in (330mm)

Weight: 3lb 6oz (1528g)
Barrel: 7.09in (180mm), 6 grooves, rh
Magazine: 10- or 20-round box
Muzzle velocity: 1350 ft/sec (411 m/sec)
Cyclic rate: 350 rds/min

Falcon

1956 This is the sole surviving model derived from the Campo-Giro design and is sold widely as a police pistol. It it a blowback, hammer-fired weapon with the familiar round slide of the Astra 400 series and is found in 7.65mm and 9mm Short calibres.

Cartridge: 7.65 × 17SR Browning
Length: 6.46in (164mm)
Weight: 1lb 8oz (668g)
Barrel: 3.88in (98.5mm), 6 grooves, rh
Magazine: 8-round box (7-round in 9mm)
Muzzle velocity: 870 ft/sec (265 m/sec)

Model A-80

Completely new design, which appears to have looked at the SIG pistols for inspiration. Recoil-operated, double-action with a de-cocking lever under the left grip. Automatic firing pin safety, loaded chamber indicator. Also in other calibres.

Cartridge: 9 × 19mm Parabellum
Length: 7.09in (180mm)
Weight: 2lb 3oz (985g)
Barrel: 3.80in (96.5mm), 6 grooves, rh
Magazine: 15-round box
Muzzle velocity: 1148 ft/sec (350 m/sec)

Model A-90

1985. Improved A-80. Improved double-action mechanism, adjustable sights, automatic firing pin safety, manual safety. Larger magazine capacity.

Cartridge: 9 × 19mm Parabellum
Length: 7.09in (180mm)
Weight: 2lb 3oz (985g)
Barrel: 3.80in (96.5mm), 6 grooves, rh
Magazine: 17-round box
Muzzle velocity: 1148 ft/sec (350 m/sec)

Model A-100

Similar to the A-90 but without manual safety, reliance being placed on the firing pin safety and de-cocking lever. Available in .40 S&W, 9mm Parabellum or .45ACP

Specifications: as for A-90

Police revolver

Solid-frame, side-opening cylinder, shrouded ejector rod, double-action, square butt. Fixed sights. Specifically for police and military use.

Cartridge: .357 Magnum
Length: 8.35in (212mm)
Weight: 2lb 5oz (1040g)
Barrel: 3.03in (77mm), 6 grooves, rh
Magazine: 6-round cylinder
Muzzle velocity: 1394 ft/sec (425 m/sec)

BALLESTER-MOLINA Argentina
Hafdasa

Broadly based on the Colt M1911 and of similar appearance and operation.

Cartridge: .45 ACP
Length: 9.00in (228mm)
Weight: 2lb 8oz (1.14kg)
Barrel: 5.0in (127mm), 6 grooves, rh
Magazine: 7-round box
Muzzle velocity: 860 ft/sec (262 m/sec)

BARRACUDA Belgium
FN

Revolver made in the 1975–90 period. A conventional five-round double-action weapon with side-opening cylinder. In .357 Magnum or .38 Special chambering. It was also available chambered for the 9mm Parabellum cartridge and therefore required the use of a special clip to hold the rimless cartridges and permit them to be extracted.

Cartridge: 9 × 19mm Parabellum
Length: 8.03in (204mm)
Weight: 2lb 5oz (1.05kg)
Barrel: 3.0in (76.2mm), 6 grooves, rh
Magazine: 5-round cylinder
Muzzle velocity: 1115 ft/sec (340 m/sec)

BEHOLLA Germany
Becker

German semi-automatic pistol made by Becker & Hollander of Suhl 1915–18. A simple pocket blowback, it was adopted as an emergency pistol by the German Army. It was also manufactured under the names Leonhardt, Menta and Stenda.

Cartridge: 7.65mm Browning
Length: 5.50in (140mm)
Weight: 1lb 6oz (628g)
Barrel: 2.88in (73mm), 6 grooves, rh
Magazine: 7-round box
Muzzle velocity: 860 ft/sec (262 m/sec)

BELGIUM
See also Barracuda, Browning & FN Herstal
Troopers' M1871 revolver
Pirlot

Chamelot-Delvigne pattern solid-frame, gate-loaded, rod-ejection, double-action. Octagonal barrel with round reinforce at rear, smooth cylinder.

Cartridge: 11 × 17.5mm French Ordnance
Length: 11.62in (295mm)
Weight: 2lb 6oz (1077g)
Barrel: 4.41in (112mm), 4 grooves, rh
Magazine: 6-round cylinder
Muzzle velocity: 722 ft/sec (220 m/sec)

Officers' M1878 revolver
Nagant
Solid frame, gate-loaded, rod-ejection, double-action. Octagonal barrel with round reinforce, fluted cylinder.

Cartridge: 9 × 23R Belgian Nagant
Length: 10.63in (270mm)
Weight: 2lb 1oz (940g)
Barrel: 5.51in (140mm), 4 grooves, rh
Magazine: 6-round cylinder
Muzzle velocity: 650 ft/sec (198 m/sec)

NCOs' M1883 revolver
Nagant
Generally similar to the M1878 design but with a short reinforce to the barrel, smooth cylinder and single-action

Cartridge: 9 × 23R Belgian Nagant
Length: 10.86in (276mm)
Weight: 2lb 2oz (950g)
Barrel: 5.51in (140mm), 4 grooves, rh
Magazine: 6-round cylinder
Muzzle velocity: 650 ft/sec (198 m/sec)

BERETTA Italy
Beretta
Model 1915
Blowback automatic pistol with internal hammer. Slide has an ejection port and is also cut away for most of the barrel, leaving only sufficient at the front end to support the foresight. Normally found in 9mm Short calibre but numbers were made in 7.65mm Browning and a very small number were chambered for the 9mm Glisenti cartridge.

Cartridge: 9 × 17mm Short
Length: 5.90in (150mm)
Weight: 1lb 4oz (570g)
Barrel: 3.30in (84mm), 6 grooves, rh
Magazine: 8-round box
Muzzle velocity: 875 ft/sec (266 m/sec)

Model 1922
Sometimes listed as the **Model 1915/19**. This was an improved Model 1915, the principal visible change being the adoption of the open-topped slide which has virtually been a Beretta trademark ever since. Improved trigger pull due to redesigned lockwork.

Cartridge: 9 × 17mm Short
Length: 5.75in (146mm)
Weight: 1lb 7oz (670g)
Barrel: 3.50in (87mm), 4 grooves, rh
Magazine: 7-round box
Muzzle velocity: 875 ft/sec (266 m/sec)

Model 1923
Similar to the M1922 but chambered for the 9mm Glisenti cartridge and with an external hammer. Also fitted with a buffer to cushion the slide recoil. About 3000 made; almost all went to either the Italian or Argentine police forces.

Cartridge: 9 × 19mm Glisenti
Length: 7.0in (177mm)
Weight: 1lb 12oz (800g)
Barrel: 3.50in (87mm), 4 grooves, rh

Magazine: 7-round box
Muzzle velocity: 1000 ft/sec (305 m/sec)

Model 1931
A further improvement on the M1922, this has the open-topped slide and external hammer, with wooden grips inset with a medallion carrying the Italian Navy badge.

Cartridge: 7.65 × 17SR Browning
Length: 5.98in (152mm)
Weight: 1lb 9oz (700g)
Barrel: 3.46in (88mm), 4 grooves, rh
Magazine: 8-round box
Muzzle velocity: 985 ft/sec (300 m/sec)

Model 1934
The perfected Beretta design based on the 1915 original. The frame was shaped so as to fit the hand more comfortably and the whole weapon built to withstand rigorous service. No significant change in the general shape or operation from the previous model.

Cartridge: 9 × 17mm Short
Length: 5.90in (150mm)
Weight: 1lb 8oz (660g)
Barrel: 3.40in (86.5mm), 6 grooves, rh
Magazine: 7-round box
Muzzle velocity: 804 ft/sec (245 m/sec)

Model 1935
This was the Model 1934 in 7.65mm calibre and with a lighter slide, for use by the Italian Navy and Air Force.

Cartridge: 7.65 × 17SR Browning
Length: 5.83in (148mm)
Weight: 1lb 10oz (730g)
Barrel: 3.35in (85mm), 6 grooves, rh
Magazine: 8-round box
Muzzle velocity: 985 ft/sec (300 m/sec)

Model 1951
1976. Beretta's first locked-breech pistol, using a wedge lock similar to that of the Walther P38. The open-topped slide was retained. Hammer-fired, single-action.

Cartridge: 9 × 19mm Parabellum
Length: 8.0in (203mm)
Weight: 1lb 15oz (890g)
Barrel: 4.50in (114mm), 6 grooves, rh
Magazine: 8-round box
Muzzle velocity: 1300 ft/sec (396 m/sec)

Model 1951R
A special variant of the Model 1951 for the Carabinieri and other Special Forces, this was a 1951 with longer barrel, a selective fire switch permitting automatic fire, an extended magazine and a wooden handgrip at the front of the slide.

Cartridge: 9 × 19mm Parabellum
Length: 8.35in (212mm)
Weight: 2lb 15oz (1350g)
Barrel: 4.92in (125mm), 6 grooves, rh
Magazine: 10-round box
Muzzle velocity: 1312 ft/sec (400 m/sec)
Cyclic rate: 750 rds/min

Model 81

1976. Principally for commercial sale but widely used as a police weapon. A blowback pistol, it used the same open-topped slide as the 1934 but in a more modern and streamlined contour and with double-action trigger.

Cartridge: 7.65 × 17SR Browning
Length: 6.77in (172mm)
Weight: 1lb 8oz (670g)
Barrel: 3.82in (97mm), 6 grooves, rh
Magazine: 12-round box
Muzzle velocity: 984 ft/sec (300 m/sec)

Model 84

1976. As for the Model 81 but in 9mm Short calibre.

Cartridge: 9 × 17mm Short
Length: 6.77in (172mm)
Weight: 1lb 7oz (660g)
Barrel: 3.82in (97mm), 6 grooves, rh
Magazine: 13-round box
Muzzle velocity: 918 ft/sec (280 m/sec)

Other variants

The Models 81 and 84 fathered a wide range of variants – **81BB, 82BB, 84BB, 85BB**, and so on – with chamber-loaded indicators, automatic firing pin safety, smaller capacity magazines and .22LR versions, all of which were for the commercial market and which, apart from the various options, all had the same characteristics as the Model 81.

Model 86

1985. An unusual variant of the Model 84 pattern, this had the barrel formed with a lug beneath the muzzle which was hinged to the frame. The slide did not have the usual front sight bridge but remained open at the front end. A catch on the frame released the barrel and a spring lifted the breech end up for cleaning or loading.

Cartridge: 9 × 17mm Short
Length: 7.28in (185mm)
Weight: 1lb 7oz (660g)
Barrel: 4.37in (111mm), 6 grooves, rh
Magazine: 8-round box
Muzzle velocity: 1017 ft/sec (310 m/sec)

Model 92

1976. This was really an updated M1951, using the same form of breech lock but with double-action trigger and a more modern shape. Frame-mounted safety catch, loaded chamber indicator. Magazine release in heel of butt. Like the Model 81/84, the Model 92 spawned an incredible number of variants, which will be dealt with somewhat summarily.

Cartridge: 9 × 19mm Parabellum
Length: 8.54in (217mm)
Weight: 2lb 1oz (950g)
Barrel: 4.92in (125mm), 6 grooves, rh
Magazine: 15-round box
Muzzle velocity: 1280 ft/sec (390 m/sec)

Model 92D

Self-cocking (or 'double-action only') version of the Model 92F in which the hammer always follows the slide on reloading, so as to come to rest in the double-action position. No hammer spur. No safety devices, and no levers or controls on the slide.

Model 92DS

Self-cocking, as for the Model 92D, but with a safety catch on the slide.

Model 92F

As for the Model 92SB but with the trigger-guard shaped for a two-handed grip, a wedge-like magazine bottom which gives an improved grip, and a lanyard ring at the heel of the butt. Barrel is chromed and the pistol is finished externally in Bruniton, a Teflon-like protective coating.

Model 92F Compact

Shorter version of the Model 92F; dimensions as for the 92SB Compact (*below*).

Model 92FC Compact Type M

As for the 92F Compact but with a thinner butt and an eight-round single-column magazine.

Model 92 FS

As for the 92SB but with the trigger guard formed for the two-handed grip, extended magazine base, magazine release in the butt behind the trigger-guard, new butt plates, chromed barrel, Bruniton finish and a new lanyard ring, all of which were required to bring the 92 into accordance with the US Army's specification. It was selected as the US Army **M9** pistol.

Specifications: as for the Model 92S, *below*

Model 92FS Compact

Shortened version of the 92FS with the same features.

Specifications: as for the SB-C, *below*

Model 92 FS Compact Type M

The FS Compact with a reduced magazine capacity, so as to provide a more slender grip.

Specifications: as for the SB-C, except
Weight: 1lb 11oz (875g)
Magazine: 8-round box

Model 92FS Inox

A model 92 FS in stainless steel finish.

Model 92G

Variant of the 92FS but fitted with a de-cocking lever only and no form of applied safety. Adopted by the French Gendarmerie Nationale (hence 'G'); for further details *see* France, PA-MAS G-1.

Model 92S

As for the Model 92 but with safety catch/de-cocking lever on the slide.

Weight: 2lb 2oz (980g)

Model 92SB

As Model 92 but with ambidextrous safety lever on the slide, magazine release moved to beneath the trigger guard and can be fitted on right or left side, automatic firing pin safety. Butt straps grooved front and rear.

Model 92SB Compact (or SB-C)
Shortened version of the Model 92.

Cartridge: 9 × 19mm Parabellum
Length: 7.76in (197mm)
Weight: 2lb 0oz (910g)
Barrel: 4.29in (109mm), 6 grooves, rh
Magazine: 13-round box
Muzzle velocity: 1280 ft/sec (390 m/sec)

Model 92SB Compact Type M
As for the SB-C but with an 8-round magazine which had a small spur at the front bottom for use as a finger rest.

Model 93R
The updated equivalent of the 1951R, a selective fire pistol with a down-folding handgrip at the front of the frame, a folding metal butt-stock which clips to the bottom of the butt grip, and an extended barrel with muzzle compensator. The fire selector permits single shots, 3-round bursts or full automatic fire.

Cartridge: 9 × 19mm Parabellum
Length: 9.45in (240mm)
Weight: 2lb 8oz (1120g)
Barrel: 6.14in (156mm), 6 grooves, rh
Magazine: 15- or 20-round box
Muzzle velocity: 1230 ft/sec (375 m/sec)
Cyclic rate: 1100 rds/min

Model 96 Series
All variants in the Model 96 series are to the same specification as the similarly-identified model in the 92 series but chambered for the .40 Smith & Wesson cartridge.

Model 98 Series
There are two entirely distinct series under this name. The first series existed *ca* 1980–90 and was made up of variants of the Model 92 chambered for the 7.65mm Parabellum cartridge. The name was revived *ca* 1993 and now refers to variants of the Model 92 chambered for the 9 x 21mm IMI cartridge.

Models 92, 96 or 98 Stock, Combat and Brigadier
These pistols are variants of the basic numbered model specifically designed for competitive shooting and are variously modified, decorated and adorned with sights, weights, compensators and so forth.

Model 99
Ca 1980–90. This appears to have been an escapee from the Model 96 first series, being a Model 92SB Compact Type M chambered for the 7.65mm Parabellum cartridge.

Centurion Series
The Centurion pistols have the frame and magazine capacity of the stock Model 92 or 96 FS models but with the reduced length barrel and slide of the Compact versions. Special D, G and DS Centurions are the same but with the various special features of the D, G and DS variants.

BERGMANN Germany
Bergmann

Bergmann-Bayard
Designed by Theodor Bergmann, made by the Ancien Établissments Pieper of Liège, who added the word 'Bayard' since it was their trademark. Locked breech, charger-loaded detachable box magazine in front of trigger, hammer-fired. A variant model was manufactured in Denmark as the **Model 1910**. It can be recognised from the markings and the over-sized grip plates.

See Denmark

Cartridge: 9 × 23mm Largo
Length: 10.00in (254mm)
Weight: 2lb 4oz (1020g)
Barrel: 4.0in (101mm), 6 grooves, lh
Magazine: 6- or 10-round box
Muzzle velocity: 1300 ft/sec (395 m/sec)

BERNARDELLI Italy
Bernardelli

P-018-9
Ca 1980. Recoil-operated, double-action automatic pistol using a locking block breech. Hammer-fired, somewhat square in outline. A 7.65mm version was made for police and commercial sale.

Cartridge: 9 × 19mm Parabellum
Length: 8.38in (213mm)
Weight: 2lb 7oz (1105g)
Barrel: 4.80in (122mm), 6 grooves, rh
Magazine: 14-round box
Muzzle velocity: 1148 ft/sec (350 m/sec)

BROWNING Belgium
FN

Model 1900
Blowback, internal hammer, rounded slide top with fluted forward section separating barrel shroud from spring case. Prominent side-plates.

Cartridge: 7.65 × 17SR Browning
Length: 6.75in (170mm)
Weight: 1lb 6oz (640g)
Barrel: 4.00in (101mm), 6 grooves, rh
Magazine: 7-round box
Muzzle velocity: 950 ft/sec (290 m/sec)

Model 1903
The pistol which laid down the now-conventional form of frame and all-enveloping slide. Blowback, internal hammer-fired, grip safety. Can be found with tangent sights and with the butt slotted for a shoulder-stock. Simple construction led to wide copying of this design in Spain and elsewhere, though rarely in the same calibre.

Cartridge: 9 × 20SR Browning Long
Length: 8.00in (203mm)
Weight: 2lb 0oz (910g)
Barrel: 5.0in (127mm), 4 grooves, lh
Magazine: 7-round box
Muzzle velocity: 1050 ft/sec (329 m/sec)

Model 1910

Rounded slide due to placing recoil spring around barrel. Blowback, striker-fired, grip safety. Found in 7.65mm or 9mm Short calibres.

Cartridge: 7.65 × 17SR Browning
Length: 6.00in (152mm)
Weight: 1lb 5oz (600g)
Barrel: 3.50in (89mm), 6 grooves, rh
Magazine: 7-round box
Muzzle velocity: 925 ft/sec (282 m/sec)

Model 1910/22

The Model 1910 with a longer barrel and the slide lengthened by a bayonet-fitting tubular extension. Butt extended for larger magazine. Blowback, striker-fired, grip safety. Found in 7.65mm or 9mm Short calibres.

Cartridge: 9 × 17mm Short
Length: 7.00in (178mm)
Weight: 1lb 9oz (708g)
Barrel: 4.50in (114mm), 4 grooves, lh
Magazine: 9-round box
Muzzle velocity: 875 ft/sec (266 m/sec)

Model 1935 High-Power

Locked breech, using the Browning cam method of unlocking slide from barrel. Thick grip to accommodate large magazine. Hammer-fired. May be found with tangent sights or with the butt slotted for a shoulder stock. Made in Canada 1942–45 for British and Chinese Nationalist forces and correspondingly marked.

Cartridge: 9 × 19mm Parabellum
Length: 7.75in (197mm)
Weight: 2lb 3oz (1000g)
Barrel: 4.72in (120mm), 4 grooves, rh
Magazine: 13-round box
Muzzle velocity: 1148 ft/sec (350 m/sec)

High-Power Mark 2

1980. The Model 35 with ambidextrous safety catch, anatomical grips, wider sights and a phosphated finish.

Specifications: similar to the Model 1935.

High-Power Mark 3

1989. Re-design of the High-Power with new dimensions of the frame and slide to improve strength, and manufacture by new computer-controlled machinery. Sights dovetailed into the slide to permit changing; enlarged ejection port; new grips.

Cartridge: 9 × 19mm Parabellum
Length: 7.87in (200mm)
Weight: 2lb 1oz (930g)
Barrel: 4.65in (118mm), 6 grooves, rh
Magazine: 13-round box
Muzzle velocity: 1148 ft/sec (350 m/sec)

High-Power Mark 3S

The same as the Mark 3 but with an automatic firing pin safety system. Intended for police use.

Specifications: as for the Mark 3

BDA 9

1990. Browning Double Action. A redesign of the High-Power to compete with modern double-action automatic pistols. Operation is the same Browning cam system but with a double-action trigger, de-cocking lever, and trigger guard shaped for a two-handed grip.

Cartridge: 9 × 19mm Parabellum
Length: 7.87in (200mm)
Weight: 2lb 0oz (915g)
Barrel: 4.66in (118.5mm), 6 grooves, rh
Magazine: 14-round box
Muzzle velocity: 1148 ft/sec (350 m/sec)

BDAO

1992. Browning Double Action Only. A variant of the BDA 9 with a self-cocking trigger mechanism. After each shot the hammer drops to rest clear of the firing pin and is cocked and dropped by the trigger. Automatic firing pin safety. No cocking spur on the hammer.

Cartridge: 9 × 19mm Parabellum
Length: 7.87in (200mm)
Weight: 1lb 15oz (870g)
Barrel: 4.66in (118.5mm), 6 grooves, rh
Magazine: 14-round box
Muzzle velocity: 1148 ft/sec (350 m/sec)

BDA 380

1982–90. Actually the Beretta Model 81 with a solid-topped slide, FN grips and markings. Originally known as the **FN 140DA**. Blowback, hammer-fired, double-action, with hammer de-cocking when the safety catch on the slide is applied. Found in 7.65mm or 9mm Short calibres.

Cartridge: 9 × 17mm Short
Length: 6.81in (173mm)
Weight: 1lb 7oz (640g)
Barrel: 3.82in (97mm), 6 grooves, rh
Magazine: 12-round box
Muzzle velocity: 984 ft/sec (300 m/sec)

CAMPO-GIRO Spain
Astra-Unceta

Model 1904

Development model. Cylindrical slide, locked breech, recoil-operated by laterally moving slide controlled by cam track in frame. Hammer-fired.

Cartridge: 7.65 × 17SR Browning
Length: 6.81in (173mm)
Weight: 1lb 4oz (560g)
Barrel: 4.55in (115.5mm), 6 grooves, rh
Magazine: 8-round box
Muzzle velocity: 984 ft/sec (300 m/sec)

Model 1913

Cylindrical slide with top ejection port and prominent finger-grips alongside it. Magazine release beneath the trigger guard. Blowback, hammer-fired, manual safety. About 1000 made for Spanish Army.

Cartridge: 9 × 23mm Bergmann-Bayard
Length: 9.33in (237mm)
Weight: 2lb 3oz (995g)
Barrel: 6.46in (164mm), 6 grooves, rh
Magazine: 8-round box
Muzzle velocity: 1115 ft/sec (340 m/sec)

Model 1913-16

1916. Modified version of the M1913. Safety catch improved, magazine release moved to the heel of the butt, two grip screws instead of one. 13,000 manufactured for Spanish Army 1916–19.

Cartridge: 9 × 23mm Bergmann-Bayard
Length: 9.56in (243mm)
Weight: 2lb 4oz (1029g)
Barrel: 6.60in (168mm), 6 grooves, rh
Magazine: 8-round box
Muzzle velocity: 1115 ft/sec (340 m/sec)

CHINA
State factories
Type 54

A direct copy of the Soviet Tokarev TT-33 pistol, distinguishable by the Chinese markings and the narrow finger grip grooving on the slide.

Cartridge: 7.62 × 25mm Soviet Pistol
Length: 7.68in (195mm)
Weight: 1lb 15oz (890g)
Barrel: 4.53in (115mm), 4 grooves, rh
Magazine: 8-round box
Muzzle velocity: 1378 ft/sec (420 m/sec)

Type 59

Direct copy of the Soviet Makarov PM pistol, distinguishable only by the Chinese markings.

Cartridge: 9 × 18mm Makarov
Length: 6.38in (162mm)
Weight: 1lb 10oz (730g)
Barrel: 3.78in (96.5mm), 4 grooves, rh
Magazine: 8-round box
Muzzle velocity: 1030 ft/sec (314 m/sec)

Type 64

Blowback automatic pistol with integral silencer. The breech may be manually locked to obviate mechanical noise on firing. Bulbous silencer/jacket with smaller tubular extension beneath. Fires a distinctive Chinese rimless version of the 7.65mm Browning cartridge.

Cartridge: 7.65 × 17mm rimless
Length: 8.74in (222mm)
Weight: 4lb 0oz (1810g)
Barrel: 3.75in (95mm), 4 grooves, rh
Magazine: 9-round box
Muzzle velocity: 673 ft/sec (205 m/sec)

Type 67

Improved version of the Type 64; the difference is in the silencer, which is now a simple cylindrical jacket around the barrel.

Cartridge: 7.65 × 17mm rimless
Length: 8.90in (226mm)
Weight: 2lb 5oz (1050g)
Barrel: 3.50in (89mm), 4 grooves, rh
Magazine: 9-round box
Muzzle velocity: 787 ft/sec (240 m/sec)

Type 77

A blowback automatic pistol with 'one-hand' cocking; instead of holding it in one hand and gripping the slide with the other, the front of the trigger guard is pulled back with the fore-finger and this cocks the slide. Used by the military and police officers in China.

Cartridge: 7.65 × 17mm rimless
Length: 5.83in (148mm)
Weight: 1lb 2oz (500g)
Barrel: 3.43in (87mm), 4 grooves, rh
Magazine: 7-round box
Muzzle velocity: 1043 ft/sec (318 m/sec)

Type 80

Selective fire machine pistol based upon the layout of the Mauser c/96 with a detachable magazine in front of the trigger-guard. The magazine is canted forward, doubtless to improve the feed. Flatter and more 'modern' butt than the Mauser, and a clip-on extending butt-stock can be fitted to the butt.

Cartridge: 7.62 × 25mm Soviet Pistol
Length: 11.81in (300mm)
Weight: 2lb 7oz (1100g)
Barrel: 7.28in (185mm), 4 grooves, rh
Magazine: 10- or 20-round box
Muzzle velocity: 1542 ft/sec (470 m/sec)

COLT USA
Colt
Model 1873 revolver

1873. Also known as the 'Frontier' and 'Peacemaker'. Solid frame, single-action, gate-loading, rod-ejection. Characteristic Colt outline which can scarcely be mistaken for anything else.

Cartridge: .45 Colt
Length: 13.0in (330mm)
Weight: 2lb 8oz (1134g)
Barrel: 7.50in (190mm), 6 grooves, lh
Magazine: 6-round cylinder
Muzzle velocity: 886 ft/sec (270 m/sec)

New Navy M1889 revolver

1889–1908. Solid frame, double-action, side-opening with hand ejection. Cylinder rotation anti-clockwise. Hard rubber butt grips. A .38 revolver on a .41 frame.

Cartridge: .38 Long Colt
Length: 11.0in (279mm)
Weight: 2lb 2oz (964g)
Barrel: 6.0in (152mm), 6 grooves, lh
Magazine: 6-round cylinder
Muzzle velocity: 787 ft/sec (240 m/sec)

New Army M1892 revolver

As for the New Navy 1889 but with walnut grips and a separate cylinder bolt.

New Army M1894 revolver

The same as the 1892 but with a positive trigger lock to prevent the trigger moving unless the cylinder was properly aligned with the barrel.

New Marine M1905 revolver

The same as the New Army but with chequered butt grips and a rounded butt. Incorporated the trigger lock and had a 5-grooved barrel.

Army Special M1908 revolver

Generally similar to the New Army model but more robust and with clockwise cylinder rotation.

Cartridge: .38 Special
Length: 11.25in (285mm)
Weight: 2lb 4oz (1020g)
Barrel: 6.0in (152mm), 6 grooves, lh
Magazine: 6-round cylinder
Muzzle velocity: 865 ft/sec (263 m/sec)

New Service M1909 revolver

Double-action, solid-frame, swing-out cylinder, with clockwise rotation.

Cartridge: .45 Colt
Length: 10.75in (273mm)
Weight: 2lb 8oz (1134g)
Barrel: 5.50in (140mm), 6 grooves, lh
Magazine: 6-round cylinder
Muzzle velocity: 853 ft/sec (260 m/sec)

M1917 revolver

The M1909 modified to accept the .45 ACP cartridge, loaded with two half-moon clips.

Cartridge: .45 ACP
Length: 10.75in (273mm)
Weight: 2lb 8oz (1134g)
Barrel: 5.50in (140mm), 6 grooves, lh
Magazine: 6-round cylinder
Muzzle velocity: 860 ft/sec (262 m/sec)

M1911 pistol

Recoil-operated using the Browning swinging link lock, single-action, hammer-fired. Straight butt backstrap, short hammer spur, grip safety.

Cartridge: .45 ACP
Length: 8.50in (216mm)
Weight: 2lb 8oz (1134g)
Barrel: 5.0in (127mm), 6 grooves, lh
Magazine: 7-round box
Muzzle velocity: 860 ft/sec (262 m/sec)

M1911A1 pistol

As for M1911 but with longer hammer spur, hump-backed rear grip strap, chamfered trigger and frame behind trigger.

Specifications: the same.

M15 General Officers' pistol

1972. M1911A1 cut down and rebuilt by Rock Island Arsenal. As for the M1911A1 but smaller. Brass plate in left grip with the owner's name engraved.

Cartridge: .45 ACP
Length: 7.90in (200mm)
Weight: 2lb 4oz (1030g)
Barrel: 4.17in (106mm), 6 grooves, lh
Magazine: 7-round box
Muzzle velocity: 800 ft/sec (245 m/sec)

CZ Czechoslovakia

vz 1922
CZ Brno

Or 'Nickl-Pistole', having been designed by Josef Nickl of Mauser. Locked breech, using a rotating barrel, round-topped slide with oblique finger grips. Rectangular butt with wooden grips, barrel flush with slide front.

Cartridge: 9 × 17mm Short
Length: 6.0in (152mm)
Weight: 1lb 6oz (620g)
Barrel: 3.54in (90mm), 6 grooves, rh
Magazine: 8-round box
Muzzle velocity: 984 ft/sec (300 m/sec)

vz/1924
CZ Prague

The 1922 modified as a result of manufacture being handed to a different company, who made changes to suit their own methods. Locking system and general appearance remained the same, but a magazine safety was added, the trigger was changed, and the butt slightly flared out at the bottom. Barrel protrudes from slide front. Originally with wood grips, later with hard rubber.

Cartridge: 9 × 17mm Short
Length: 6.0in (152mm)
Weight: 1lb 8oz (700g)
Barrel: 3.55in (91mm), 6 grooves, rh
Magazine: 8-round box
Muzzle velocity: 984 ft/sec (300 m/sec)

vz/1927
CZ Prague

A re-design of the vz/1924 to do away with the rotating barrel and turn it into a blowback pistol, and change the calibre. Identifiable by finger grips on the slide being vertical not oblique. Adopted by the German Army after 1938 as the **Pistole Mod 27(t)** and will be found so marked.

Cartridge: 7.65 × 17SR Browning
Length: 6.25in (159mm)
Weight: 1lb 9oz (710g)
Barrel: 3.82in (97mm), 6 grooves, rh
Magazine: 8-round box
Muzzle velocity: 920 ft/sec (280 m/sec)

vz/1938
CZ Prague

Blowback, striker-fired, self-cocking pistol. Large and clumsy for its calibre, the slide is hinged to the front of the frame and can be released and hinged up to withdraw the barrel for cleaning.

Cartridge: 9 × 17mm Short
Length: 7.7in (196mm)
Weight: 2lb 0oz (912g)
Barrel: 4.72in (120mm), 6 grooves, rh
Magazine: 8-round box
Muzzle velocity: 1017 ft/sec (310 m/sec)

vz/1950
CZ Prague

Blowback, hammer-fired, double-action pistol apparently inspired by the Walther PP, though with some small changes. The trigger-guard is solid, and there is a stripping catch in the frame; the chamber loaded indicator protrudes to the side instead of the rear, and the safety catch is on the frame rather than the slide. Refused by the Army because of its calibre, it was issued to the Czech police.

Cartridge: 7.65 × 17SR Browning
Length: 6.6in (167mm)
Weight: 1lb 7oz (660g)
Barrel: 3.75in (94mm), 6 grooves, rh
Magazine: 8-round box
Muzzle velocity: 920 ft/sec (280 m/sec)

vz/1952
CZ Prague

Recoil-operated, locked breech using a two-part roller-locked breech block, hammer-fired automatic pistol. Strong, elegant, unnecessarily complicated.

Cartridge: 7.62 × 25mm Soviet Pistol
Length: 8.23in (209mm)
Weight: 2lb 2oz (960g)
Barrel: 4.72in (120mm), 4 grooves, rh
Magazine: 8-round box
Muzzle velocity: 1300 ft/sec (396 m/sec)

CZ1975
CZ Brno

This was introduced commercially but soon found favour with military and police forces. Conventional recoil-operated automatic pistol using the Browning-Petter cam lock. Hammer-fired, double-action, frame-mounted safety catch.

Cartridge: 9 × 19mm Parabellum
Length: 8.0in (203mm)
Weight: 2lb 3oz (980g)
Barrel: 4.72in (120mm), 6 grooves, rh
Magazine: 15-round box
Muzzle velocity: 1300 ft/sec (396 m/sec)

1975 Full-auto
CZ Brno

Variant of the CZ1975 with selective full-automatic fire ability. Exposed muzzle formed as a compensator, and a clip on the front end of the frame into which a loaded magazine fits to act as a front grip.

Cartridge: 9 × 19mm Parabellum
Length: 8.0in (206mm)
Weight: 2lb 4oz (1020g)
Barrel: 4.72in (120mm), 6 grooves, rh
Magazine: 15- or 25-round box
Muzzle velocity: 1300 ft/sec (396 m/sec)
Cyclic rate: 1000 rds/min

vz/82
CZ Prague

Blowback, double-action, hammer-fired. Ambidextrous safety catch and magazine release, automatic firing pin safety. Trigger guard acts as dismantling catch and is linked so that it cannot be opened if the magazine is in, and the magazine cannot be inserted until it is closed.

Cartridge: 9 × 18mm Makarov
Length: 6.77in (172mm)
Weight: 1lb 12oz (800g)
Barrel: 3.78in (96mm), 6 grooves, rh
Magazine: 12-round box
Muzzle velocity: 1017 ft/sec (310 m/sec)

DAEWOO South Korea
Daewoo

DP51

1990. Delayed blowback automatic pistol, hammer-fired. Automatic firing pin safety, aluminium alloy frame, ambidextrous safety catch.

Cartridge: 9 × 19mm Parabellum
Length: 7.48in (190mm)
Weight: 1lb 12oz (800g)
Barrel: 4.13in (105mm), 6 grooves, rh
Magazine: 10- or 13-round box
Muzzle velocity: 1152 ft/sec (351 m/sec)

DH40

The same pistol as the DP51 but firing the .40 Smith & Wesson cartridge.

Cartridge: .40 Smith & Wesson
Length: 7.48in (190mm)
Weight: 2lb 3oz (980g)
Barrel: 4.21in (107mm), 6 grooves, rh
Magazine: 10- or 12-round box
Muzzle velocity: 984 ft/sec (300 m/sec)

DENMARK

Revolver M1871/81
Unknown

Conversion from an 1871 Lefaucheaux-Francotte pinfire revolver. Open frame, gate-loaded, rod-ejection, octagonal barrel, smooth cylinder, rounded butt.

Cartridge: 12 × 15R French Thick Rim
Length: 10.12in (257mm)
Weight: 2lb 2oz (970g)
Barrel: 5.03in (128mm), 7 grooves, rh
Magazine: 6-round cylinder
Muzzle velocity: 787 ft/sec (240 m/sec)

Officers' M1880 revolver
Warnant

Solid frame, gate-loaded, rod-ejection, double-action. Round barrel with half-length octagonal reinforce at the rear, fluted cylinder with reinforce at the rear.

Cartridge: 9 × 17R Danish
Length: 9.09in (231mm)
Weight: 1lb 12oz (780g)
Barrel: 4.41in (112mm), 7 grooves, rh
Magazine: 6-round cylinder
Muzzle velocity: 656 ft/sec (200 m/sec)

Troopers' M1882 revolver
Warnant

Solid frame, gate-loaded, rod-ejection, double-action. Round barrel with octagonal reinforce. Fluted cylinder.

Cartridge: 9 × 17R Danish
Length: 10.23in (260mm)
Weight: 2lb 0oz (920g)
Barrel: 5.51in (140mm), 7 grooves, rh
Magazine: 6-round cylinder
Muzzle velocity: 690 ft/sec (210 m/sec)

Officers' M1880/85 revolver
Warnant
Generally similar to the Troopers' model but shorter and lighter

Cartridge: 9 × 17R Danish
Length: 9.06in (230mm)
Weight: 1lb 11oz (775g)
Barrel: 4.33in (110mm), 7 grooves, rh
Magazine: 6-round cylinder
Muzzle velocity: 656 ft/sec (200 m/sec)

M1891
Ronge
Hinged frame, double-action, self-ejecting. Half round, half octagonal barrel.

Cartridge: 9 × 17R Danish
Length: 10.23in (260mm)
Weight: 1lb 15oz (900g)
Barrel: 5.39in (137mm), 6 grooves, rh
Magazine: 6-round cylinder
Muzzle velocity: 656 ft/sec (200 m/sec)

M1910 Automatic Pistol
Haerens T & Pieper
This is the Bergmann-Bayard as supplied to the Spanish Army in 1905, adopted by the Danes in 1911. Originally made by Pieper in Belgium, this arrangement was terminated by World War 1 and manufacture began in Denmark in 1922. The Danish product differed from the original design by using larger wood or Bakelite grips, and by having the lock cover-plate retained by a screw instead of a spring. They were marked 'M1910/21' with Danish inscriptions; earlier weapons refurbished to the same standard by the change of grips were also marked 'M1910/21' but retained their original Belgian inscriptions.

Cartridge: 9 × 23mm Bergmann-Bayard
Length: 10.0in (254mm)
Weight: 2lb 4oz (1020g)
Barrel: 4.0in (101mm), 6 grooves, rh
Magazine: 6- or 10-round box
Muzzle velocity: 1300 ft/sec (395 m/sec)

DIMANCEA Britain
Gatling
1888–90. Invented by Captain Dimancea of the Romanian Army, this was an unusual self-cocking revolver. It had a high-sided frame concealing a star-wheel firing pin mechanism, and a spur on this frame released the barrel and cylinder to pivot sideways for loading and extraction. Whether or not these revolvers were supplied to the Romanian Army remains a matter of conjecture.

Cartridge: .450 Short CF
Length: 11.22in (285mm)
Weight: 2lb 0oz (920g)

Barrel: 5.51in (140mm), 6 grooves, rh
Magazine: 6-round cylinder
Muzzle velocity: 750 ft/sec (228 m/sec)

DREYSE Germany
Rheinmetall
7.65mm
Ca 1907. Originally for commercial sale, adopted for military use by German Army in 1917. Blowback, striker-fired, unusual construction with stepped slide and breech-block.

Cartridge: 7.65 × 17SR Browning
Length: 6.30in (160mm)
Weight: 1lb 9oz (710g)
Barrel: 3.66in (93mm), 4 grooves, rh
Magazine: 7-round box
Muzzle velocity: 985 ft/sec (300 m/sec)

9mm
Ca 1912. Never officially adopted but known to have been used by German troops. Blowback, striker-fired, very strong return spring leading to an unusual method of construction to permit cocking the slide without compressing the return spring. Limited production.

Cartridge: 9 × 19mm Parabellum
Length: 8.12in (206mm)
Weight: 2lb 5oz (1050g)
Barrel: 5.0in (126mm), 6 grooves, rh
Magazine: 8-round box
Muzzle velocity: 1181 ft/sec (360 m/sec)

ENFIELD Britain
Enfield
Pistol, Revolver, Breech-Loading, Enfield, Mark 1
1880. Six-shot, hinged-frame, double-action revolver. Recognisable by the reverse-curved frame in front of the cylinder, which, when the barrel is hinged down, acts as a lever to pull the cylinder forward, leaving a fixed extractor to pull the cartridges from the chambers. Front portion of the chambers rifled; interior parts nickel-plated. British pistols browned, Indian service pistols nickel-plated externally. Wedge-shaped foresight.

Cartridge: .455 Enfield Mk 2
Length: 11.45in (291mm)
Weight: 2lb 8oz (1148g)
Barrel: 5.87in (149mm), 6 grooves, rh
Magazine: 6-round cylinder
Muzzle velocity: 673 ft/sec (205 m/sec)

Pistol, Revolver, Breech-Loading, Enfield, Mark 2
1882. Improved model of the Mark 1. Nickel-plating removed from interior parts, cylinders taper-bored smooth, rounded foresight, smooth butt grips.

Cartridge: .455 Enfield Mk 2 or .476 Mk 3
Length: 11.45in (291mm)
Weight: 2lb 9oz (1150g)
Barrel: 5.87in (149mm), 6 grooves, rh
Magazine: 6-round cylinder
Muzzle velocity: 688 ft/sec (210 m/sec)

Pistol, Revolver, No 2, Mark I

1932. Copy of a Webley design, and similar in appearance to earlier Webley Mark 6, though smaller. Hinged-frame, double-action revolver.

Cartridge: .38 British
Length: 10.24in (260mm)
Weight: 1lb 11oz (780g)
Barrel: 5.0in (127mm), 6 grooves, rh
Magazine: 6-round cylinder
Muzzle velocity: 673 ft/sec (590 m/sec)

Pistol, Revolver, No 2, Mark I*

1938. As for No 2, Mark 1 but with the hammer spur removed and the mainspring lightened to give a better double-action-only pull. Originally special to Royal Tank Regiment but became general issue and most Mark 1 pistols were converted to Mark 1* in course of maintenance and repair.

Specifications: as for Mark 1

Pistol, Revolver, No 2, Mark I**

1942. Mark 1* revolvers manufactured without the hammer stop as a wartime concession to speed manufacture. Found to be unsafe, and from 1945 all were recalled, fitted with hammer stops and reverted to Mark 1 status.

FABRIQUE NATIONALE Belgium
FN
See also **Barracuda & Browning**

FN Five-SeveN

1995. Developed to act as a companion to the FN P-90 Personal Defence Weapon (*see* Submachine Guns, FN) and fires the same cartridge. Steel slide, composite frame. Delayed blowback using cams to hold the slide while barrel recoils 3mm to unlock the cams. Loaded chamber indicator, striker-fired. Pulling trigger compresses firing pin spring, then releases pin.

Cartridge: 5.7 × 28mm P90
Length: 8.19in (208mm)
Weight: 1lb 6oz (618g)
Barrel: 4.82in (122.5mm), 6 grooves, rh
Magazine: 20-round box
Muzzle velocity: 2133 ft/sec (650 m/sec)

FAMAE Chile
FAMAE

.38 Special

Conventional solid-frame, double-action, side-opening revolver. Used by Chilean military and police forces.

Cartridge: .38 Special
Length: 7.13in (181mm)
Weight: 1lb 9oz (696g)
Barrel: 2.50in (63.4mm), 6 grooves, rh
Magazine: 6-round cylinder
Muzzle velocity: ca 935 ft/sec (285 m/sec)

FRANCE
See also **Galand, Le Français, MAB & Manurhin**

Navy M1870 Modifie N
Lefaucheaux

Solid frame, gate-loading, rod-ejection, double-action. Round barrel, smooth cylinder, wood grips with slight prawl. Trigger guard continued down the front of the butt as a finger rest.

Cartridge: 11 × 17.5R French Ordnance
Length: 9.41in (239mm)
Weight: 2lb 5oz (1050g)
Barrel: 4.76in (121mm), 4 grooves, rh
Magazine: 6-round cylinder
Muzzle velocity: 820 ft/sec (250 m/sec)

M1873
MAS

Double-action, solid-frame, gate-loading, rod-ejection revolver. Part-round, part-hexagonal barrel, smooth cylinder with rear reinforce, wood butt grips.

Cartridge: 11 × 17.5R French Ordnance
Length: 9.45in (240mm)
Weight: 2lb 8oz (1145g)
Barrel: 4.53in (115mm), 4 grooves, rh
Magazine: 6-round cylinder
Muzzle velocity: 804 ft/sec (245 m/sec)

M1874
MAS

Officers' model. Fluted cylinder, longer than that of the M1873; chemically browned. More precise manufacture and better finish than M1873.

Cartridge: 11 × 17.5R French Ordnance
Length: 9.41in (239mm)
Weight: 1lb 15oz (900g)
Barrel: 4.45in (113mm), 4 grooves, rh
Magazine: 6-round cylinder
Muzzle velocity: 804 ft/sec (245 m/sec)

Mle. 1892 (Modèle d'Ordonnance)
MAS

Solid frame, double-action, right side opening cylinder. Barrel may be round or hexagonal with a round reinforce.

Cartridge: 8 × 27R Lebel revolver
Length: 9.33in (237mm)
Weight: 1lb 14oz (840g)
Barrel: 4.61in (117mm), 6 grooves, rh
Magazine: 6-round cylinder
Muzzle velocity: 720 ft/sec (219 m/sec)

M1935A
SACM

Single-action, recoil-operated automatic pistol using the Browning link method of locking, hammer-fired. Curved butt, generally excellent finish.

Cartridge: 7.65 × 19.8mm Longue
Length: 7.72in (196mm)
Weight: 1lb 10oz (750g)
Barrel: 4.72in (120mm), 4 grooves, rh
Magazine: 8-round box
Muzzle velocity: 1100 ft/sec (335 m/sec)

M1935S
MAC Chatellerault

1938. Simplified version of the M1935A for hurried production on the eve of war. Single instead of multiple lugs locking slide and barrel together, trigger mechanism simplified, low-quality finish, more angular shape.

Cartridge: 7.65 × 19.8mm Longue
Length: 7.40in (188mm)
Weight: 1lb 11oz (770g)
Barrel: 4.21in (107mm), 4 grooves, rh
Magazine: 8-round box
Muzzle velocity: 1082 ft/sec (330 m/sec)

M1950
MAC Chatellerault

This is more or less the M1935S re-designed around the 9mm Parabellum cartridge. Slightly more elegant, considerably better finish, plastic wrap-around butt grip.

Cartridge: 9 × 19mm Parabellum
Length: 7.64in (194mm)
Weight: 2lb 2oz (975g)
Barrel: 4.37in (111mm), 4 grooves, rh
Magazine: 9-round box
Muzzle velocity: 1100 ft/sec (335 m/sec)

PA-MAS G-1
MAS

1992. This is the Beretta Model 92G double-action automatic pistol manufactured under license by the Manufacture d'Armes de St Étienne. The Model G (for Gendarmerie) is the same as the Model FS except that it has no safety device other than the de-cocking lever. When the lever is released, after lowering the hammer, it flies back to the 'ready' position and the pistol can be fired by pulling through on the trigger.

Cartridge: 9 × 19mm Parabellum
Length: 8.54in (217mm)
Weight: 2lb 2oz (960g)
Barrel: 4.92in (125mm), 6 grooves, rh
Magazine: 15-round box
Muzzle velocity: 1138 ft/sec (347 m/sec)

FROMMER Austria-Hungary
Fegyvergyar

Stop

Also called the Model 1912, this is a complicated long-recoil pistol using a double recoil spring inside a tunnel on the top of the receiver. Bolt and barrel recoil within the receiver, and the bolt rotates to lock and unlock. Hammer-fired, grip safety. Adopted in 7.65mm by the Honved, the Hungarian reserve element of the Austro-Hungarian Army, It was also produced in 9mm Short calibre, but this model was never officially adopted in military service.

Cartridge: 7.65 × 17SR Browning
Length: 6.5in (165mm)
Weight: 1lb 4oz (567g)
Barrel: 3.93in (99mm), 4 grooves, rh
Magazine: 7-round box
Muzzle velocity: 986 ft/sec (300 m/sec)

Model 29

The Model 1929 replaced the 'Stop' as the official issue (though the latter remained in use until 1945). The 29 is a simple blowback weapon, very robust, and easily recognised by a raised, ribbed, grip which is pinned to the rear of the slide. Hammer-fired, grip safety. The 7.65mm calibre was also dropped, 9mm Short becoming the new standard.

Cartridge: 9 × 17mm Short
Length: 6.77in (172mm)
Weight: 1lb 12.5oz (751g)
Barrel: 3.93in (100mm), 4 grooves, rh
Magazine: 7-round box
Muzzle velocity: 886 ft/sec (270 m/sec)

Model 37M

This replaced the 29 as the official 9mm Hungarian sidearm in 1938; manufacture continued under German occupation, the weapons being in 7.65mm calibre and marked 'P Mod 37' and the manufacturer's code 'jhv'. In original Hungarian form it is a conventional blowback, hammer-fired and with a grip safety. As modified by German request, the 7.65mm models after mid-1941 were fitted with a manual safety catch at the left rear of the frame.

Cartridge: 9 × 17mm Short
Length: 6.80in (173mm)
Weight: 1lb 10oz (737g)
Barrel: 3.93in (100mm), 4 grooves, rh
Magazine: 7-round box
Muzzle velocity: 886 ft/sec (270 m/sec)

Cartridge: 7.65 × 17SR Browning
Length: 7.20in (183mm)
Weight: 1lb 11oz (765g)
Barrel: 4.33in (110mm), 4 grooves, rh
Magazine: 7-round box
Muzzle velocity: 985 ft/sec (300 m/sec)

GALAND France
Galand

M1870

Open-frame revolver with an operating arm hinged just below the muzzle and extending back and down to form the trigger guard. When pressed down, this forces the barrel and cylinder forward to extract the cartridge. Double-action, wood or chequered composition butt with prawl. Adopted in Russia as the **Ordnance Revolver M1870**. Commercial models in calibres from 7mm to 12mm.

Cartridge: 12 × 15R French Thick Rim
Length: 9.25in (235mm)
Weight: 2lb 3oz (990g)
Barrel: 4.92in (125mm), 12 grooves, rh
Magazine: 6-round cylinder
Muzzle velocity: *ca* 656 ft/sec (200 m/sec)

GARATE, ANITUA Spain
Garate

Pistol Old Pattern No 1 Mark 1

Spanish hinged-frame revolver, a copy of the Harrington & Richardson top-break models of *ca* 1890. Manufactured in

.455 calibre, it was adopted by the British Army as an emergency revolver in November 1915, and declared obsolete in 1921, remaining weapons being sold off through the gun trade. Double-action, hinged frame, simultaneous ejection.

Cartridge: .455 Webley Mk 6
Length: 11.02in (280mm)
Weight: 23.4oz (663g)
Barrel: 5.12in (130mm), 5 grooves, rh
Magazine: 6-round cylinder
Muzzle velocity: 656 ft/sec (200 m/sec)

GASSER Austria-Hungary
Gasser

See also **Gasser-Kropatschek & Rast & Gasser**

Gasser Austrian M1870
This is an open-frame revolver, the barrel secured to the frame by a bolt. Gate-loading, plain cylinder with rear end reinforced, hand ejector rod, double-action. Round barrel with hexagonal rear end, Note that these revolvers were also sold commercially with different barrel lengths.

Cartridge: 11.3 × 35R Austrian Gasser
Length: 12.6in (320mm)
Weight: 3lb 0.3oz (1369g)
Barrel: 6.85in (174mm), 6 grooves, rh
Magazine: 6-shot cylinder
Muzzle velocity: 690 ft/sec (210 m/sec)

M1874
This differed in having a steel action body instead of iron.

Cartridge: 11.3 × 35R Austrian Gasser
Length: 14.76in (375mm)
Weight: 3lb 5oz (1520g)
Barrel: 9.25in (235mm), 6 grooves, rh
Magazine: 6-round cylinder
Muzzle velocity: 755 ft/sec (230 m/sec)

Navy M1874
This had the barrel locked by a spring wedge, but was otherwise similar to the army model.

Montenegrin Gasser
These revolvers are generally based on the M1870 Army; early models were open-frame gate-loaded, later models solid-frame gate-loaded, still later hinged frame with ejector plate. They come in a wide variety of sizes and calibres, usually large, and vary between being well-finished with gold inlay work and rough iron finish. Examples are:

Open frame
Cartridge: 11.5 × 36R Gasser
Length: 10.24in (260mm)
Weight: 3lb 3oz (1000g)
Barrel: 5.04in (128mm), 6 grooves, rh
Magazine: 6-shot cylinder
Muzzle velocity: 731 ft/sec (223 m/sec)

Solid frame
Cartridge: 11.5 × 36R Gasser
Length: 14.70in (373mm)
Weight: 3lb 4oz (1474g)
Barrel: 9.13in (232mm), 6 grooves, rh
Magazine: 6-shot cylinder
Muzzle velocity: 804 ft/sec (245 m/sec)

Hinged frame
Cartridge: 11.5 × 36R Gasser
Length: 14.80in (376mm)
Weight: 3lb 3oz (1450g)
Barrel: 9.05in (230mm), 6 grooves, rh
Magazine: 6-shot cylinder
Muzzle velocity: 804 ft/sec (245 m/sec)

GASSER-KROPATSCHEK Austria-Hungary
Gasser

Austrian Infantry Officers' M1873
Scaled-down version of the Gasser 1870/74, with a hexagonal barrel with no reinforce at the rear end. Plain cylinder with no reinforce. Double-action, gate-loaded. Austrian infantry officer issue.

Cartridge: 9 × 26R Gasser-Kropatschek
Length: 9.05in (230mm)
Weight: 1lb 11oz (770g)
Barrel: 4.72in (120mm), 6 grooves, rh
Magazine: 6-round cylinder
Muzzle velocity: 722 ft/sec (220 m/sec)

GERMANY
See also **Beholla, Bergmann, Dreyse, Heckler & Koch, Luger, Mauser, Sauer, Schwarzlose, SIG-Sauer, Walther & Werder**

Reichsrevolver M1879
Dreyse, Erfurt, Haenel, Sauer & Sohn, Schilling & Spangenberg
Or 'Troopers' Model'. Designed by a Committee and produced by various firms on contract, this agriculturally simple weapon was officially in service until 1909 and many survived to appear in 1945. Single-action, solid-frame, gate-loading, non-ejecting revolver. Safety catch on the left side of the frame. Usually carry regimental markings on the backstrap of the butt.

Cartridge: 10.6 × 24.5R German Ordnance
Length: 12.20in (310mm)
Weight: 2lb 4oz (1030g)
Barrel: 7.20in (183mm), 6 grooves, rh
Magazine: 6-round cylinder
Muzzle velocity: 673 ft/sec (205 m/sec)

Reichsrevolver M1883
As M1879
Or 'Officers' Model'. The same simple design as the M1879 but with a shorter barrel and a more rounded butt.

Cartridge: 10.6 × 24.5R German Ordnance
Length: 10.25in (260mm)
Weight: 2lb 0oz (920g)
Barrel: 4.96in (126mm), 6 grooves, rh
Magazine: 6-round cylinder
Muzzle velocity: 640 ft/sec (195 m/sec)

Pistole M
State factories
Issued to the East German forces, the Pistole M was a locally manufactured copy of the Soviet Makarov, and showed a few differences. There was no loaded chamber indicator; it used a leaf spring for the hammer instead of a

coil spring; and there were some small differences in the trigger mechanism.

Cartridge: 9 × 18mm Makarov
Length: 6.30in (160mm)
Weight: 1lb 9oz (710g)
Barrel: 3.58in (91mm), 4 grooves, rh
Magazine: 8-round box
Muzzle velocity: 1033 ft/sec (315 m/sec)

GLISENTI Italy
Glisenti

Model 1910

Recoil-operated automatic pistol using 'prop-up' locking. Slab-sided receiver, well-raked butt, slender barrel. Prominent stripping catch at front of receiver below barrel. Striker-fired.

Cartridge: 9 × 19mm Glisenti
Length: 8.22in (207mm)
Weight: 1lb 13oz (820g)
Barrel: 3.91in (100mm), 6 grooves, rh
Magazine: 7-round box
Muzzle velocity: 1050 ft/sec (320 m/sec)

GLOCK Austria
Glock

Model 17

1983. Original model. Military/police automatic pistol, using a large proportion of synthetic material in its construction. Self-cocking trigger mechanism with automatic safeties. Browning cam breech lock, double-action, striker-fired.

Cartridge: 9 × 19mm Parabellum
Length: 7.32in (186mm)
Weight: 1lb 6oz (625g)
Barrel: 4.50in (114mm), 6 grooves, rh
Magazine: 17-round box
Muzzle velocity: 1263 ft/sec (385 m/sec)

Model 17L

As for Model 17 but with longer barrel and slide.

Cartridge: 9 × 19mm Parabellum
Length: 8.86in (225mm)
Weight: 1lb 8oz (670g)
Barrel: 6.02in (153mm), 6 grooves, rh
Magazine: 17- or 19-round box
Muzzle velocity: 1263 ft/sec (385 m/sec)

Model 18C

Full automatic version of the Model 17; parts not interchangeable with any other model to prevent illegal conversions. Muzzle compensator concealed by slide. Extra-length 33-round magazine available.

Cartridge: 9 × 19mm Parabellum
Length: 7.32in (186mm)
Weight: 1lb 5oz (587g)
Barrel: 4.50in (114mm), 6 grooves, rh
Magazine: 17- or 33-round box
Muzzle velocity: 1115 ft/sec (340 m/sec)
Cyclic rate: 1200 rds/min

Model 19

Compact version of the Model 17.

Cartridge: 9 × 19mm Parabellum
Length: 6.85in (174mm)
Weight: 1lb 5oz (595g)
Barrel: 4.01in (102mm), 6 grooves, rh
Magazine: 16- or 17-round box
Muzzle velocity: 1148 ft/sec (350 m/sec)

Model 20

As for Model 17 but chambered for the 10mm Auto cartridge.

Cartridge: 10mm Auto
Length: 7.59in (193mm)
Weight: 1lb 12oz (785g)
Barrel: 4.60in (117mm), 6 grooves, rh
Magazine: 15-round box
Muzzle velocity: 1115 ft/sec (340 m/sec)

Model 21

As for Model 17 but chambered for the .45 ACP cartridge

Cartridge: .45 ACP
Length: 7.60in (193mm)
Weight: 1lb 10oz (745g)
Barrel: 4.60in (117mm), 6 grooves, rh
Magazine: 15-round box
Muzzle velocity: 820 ft/sec (250 m/sec)

Model 22

As for Model 17 but chambered for the .40 S&W cartridge.

Cartridge: .40 Smith & Wesson
Length: 7.32in (186mm)
Weight: 1lb 7oz (650g)
Barrel: 4.66in (118mm), 6 grooves, rh
Magazine: 13-round box
Muzzle velocity: 984 ft/sec (300 m/sec)

Model 23

As for Model 19 but chambered for .40 S&W cartridge.

Cartridge: .40 Smith & Wesson
Length: 6.85in (174mm)
Weight: 1lb 5oz (600g)
Barrel: 4.01in (102mm), 6 grooves, rh
Magazine: 13-round box
Muzzle velocity: 968 ft/sec (295 m/sec)

Model 24

As for Model 17L but chambered for the .40 S&W cartridge and with a solid barrel (ie no muzzle compensator).

Cartridge: .40 Smith & Wesson
Length: 8.86in (225mm)
Weight: 1lb 10oz (750g)
Barrel: 6.02in (153mm), 6 grooves, rh
Magazine: 15-round box
Muzzle velocity: 1017 ft/sec (310 m/sec)

Model 24C

As for Model 24 but with a muzzle compensator cut into the barrel.

Specifications: the same, except
Muzzle velocity: 1000 ft/sec (305 m/sec)

Model 25

To the same general design as the Model 17 but chambered for the 9mm Short/.380 Auto cartridge.

Cartridge: 9 × 17mm Short
Length: 6.85in (174mm)
Weight: 1lb 4oz (570g)
Barrel: 4.01in (102mm), 6 grooves, rh
Magazine: 15-round box
Muzzle velocity: 885 ft/sec (270 m/sec)

Model 26 Sub-Compact

Uses the standard Glock features but is smaller in all dimensions than any other model.

Cartridge: 9 × 19mm Parabellum
Length: 6.30in (160mm)
Weight: 1lb 3.75oz (560g)
Barrel: 3.46in (88mm), 6 grooves, rh
Magazine: 10-round box
Muzzle velocity: 1115 ft/sec (340 m/sec)

Model 27 Sub-Compact

Similar to Model 26 but chambered for the .40 S&W cartridge.

Cartridge: .40 Smith & Wesson
Length: 6.30in (160mm)
Weight: 1lb 3.75oz (560g)
Barrel: 3.46in (88mm), 6 grooves, rh
Magazine: 9-round box
Muzzle velocity: 935 ft/sec (285 m/sec)

HECKLER & KOCH Germany
Heckler & Koch

VP70

Blowback, self-cocking, striker-fired semi-automatic with burst-fire option when the shoulder stock is attached. Considerable use of synthetic materials in manufacture.

Cartridge: 9 × 19mm Parabellum
Length: 8.03in (204mm)
Weight: 1lb 13oz (820g)
Barrel: 4.57in (116mm), 4 grooves polygonal, rh
Magazine: 18-round box
Muzzle velocity: 1181 ft/sec (360 m/sec)

P7M8

Delayed blowback, self-cocking, striker-fired automatic pistol. Delay by propellant gas entering a cylinder and resisting the movement of a piston connected to the slide. Unique grip safety device in front edge of grip prevents trigger cocking the weapon unless the grip is squeezed.

Cartridge: 9 × 19mm Parabellum
Length: 6.73in (171mm)
Weight: 1lb 12oz (800g)
Barrel: 4.13in (105mm), 4 grooves polygonal, rh
Magazine: 8-round box
Muzzle velocity: 1148 ft/sec (350 m/sec)

P7M13

Similar to the P7M8 but with a larger-capacity magazine and small dimensional differences.

Cartridge: 9 × 19mm Parabellum
Length: 6.88in (175mm)

Weight: 1lb 13oz (820g)
Barrel: 4.13in (105mm), 4 grooves polygonal, rh
Magazine: 13-round box
Muzzle velocity: 1148 ft/sec (350 m/sec)

P7M10

Similar to the P7M8 but chambered for the .40 Smith & Wesson cartridge and with a magazine capacity of 10 rounds. Limited numbers produced.

P7K3

Similar in appearance to the P7M8 but without the delay system, functioning as a pure blowback weapon. Similar squeeze-cocking system

Cartridge: 9 × 17mm Short
Length: 6.30in (160mm)
Weight: 1lb 10oz (750g)
Barrel: 3.68in (96.5mm), 4 grooves polygonal, rh
Magazine: 8-round box
Muzzle velocity: 902 ft/sec (275 m/sec)

P9S

Delayed-blowback, double-action automatic pistol. Delay by roller-locked two-part breech-block as in other H&K weapons. Internal hammer with a pin protruding from the slide to indicate cocked condition. Small numbers were also made in 7.65mm Parabellum and .45ACP calibres.

Cartridge: 9 × 19mm Parabellum
Length: 7.56in (192mm)
Weight: 1lb 15oz (880g)
Barrel: 4.01in (102mm), 4 grooves polygonal, rh
Magazine: 9-round box
Muzzle velocity: 1148 ft/sec (350 m/sec)

USP

1993. Universal Self-loading Pistol. Modern, squared-off style of locked-breech double-action pistol using the Browning cam lock. Built around the .40 S&W cartridge, but then adapted to .45ACP and 9mm Parabellum. Recoil buffering device.

Cartridge: .40 Smith & Wesson
Length: 7.64in (194mm)
Weight: 1lb 11oz (780g)
Barrel: 4.25in (108mm), 4 grooves polygonal, rh
Magazine: 13-round box
Muzzle velocity: 935 ft/sec (285 m/sec)

Cartridge: .45ACP
Length: 7.87in (200mm)
Weight: 1lb 14oz (840g)
Barrel: 4.41in (112mm), 4 grooves polygonal, rh
Magazine: 10-round box
Muzzle velocity: 885 ft/sec (270 m/sec)

Cartridge: 9 × 19mm Parabellum
Dimensions: as for .40 S&W
Weight: 1lb 10oz (750g)
Magazine: 15 rounds,
Muzzle velocity: 1150 ft/sec (350 m/sec)

Mark 23 Mod 0

Special variant of the USP (*above*) developed to meet a US Special Forces demand. Generally as for the USP but with longer slide and barrel prepared for silencer.

Cartridge: .45ACP
Length: 9.65in (245mm)
Weight: 2lb 10oz (1210g)
Barrel: 5.87in (149mm), 4 grooves polygonal, rh
Magazine: 12-round box
Muzzle velocity: 885 ft/sec (270 m/sec)

P11-ZUB

Ca 1988. Underwater pistol for Special Forces. Fires dart projectiles from a factory-loaded 5-round cylinder which is loaded into the five-barrelled weapon and electrically fired.

Cartridge: 7.62 × 36mm Special
Length: 7.87in (200mm)
Width: 2.36in (60mm)
Sight base: 5.75in (146mm)
Weight: 2lb 5oz (1.20kg)
Barrel length: (7.08in) 180mm

IMBEL Brazil
IMBEL

M973

This is a slightly re-designed version of the Colt M1911A1 pistol in 9mm calibre. The re-design is largely a re-shaping of the barrel contour and barrel bush to improve accuracy. The other mechanical features are entirely to the Colt pattern. In the 1980s production of the same pistol in .45 ACP calibre was instituted.

Cartridge: 9 × 19mm Parabellum
Length: 8.38in (213mm)
Weight: 2lb 4oz (1010g)
Barrel: 5.04in (128mm), 6 grooves, rh
Magazine: 8-round box
Muzzle velocity: 1148 ft/sec (350 m/sec)

9mm MD1

This has the same appearance as the M973, *ie* a copy of the Colt M1911A1, but is smaller and is a pure blowback weapon.

Cartridge: 9 × 17mm Short
Length: 7.56in (192mm)
Weight: 2lb 1oz (943g)
Barrel: 4.09in (104mm), 6 grooves, rh
Magazine: 7-round box
Muzzle velocity: 886 ft/sec (270 m/sec)

9mm MD2

This is generally similar to the 9mm MD1 but is built from frame components of the M973 and hence has a deeper butt and a larger-capacity magazine.

Specifications: as for the MD1, except
Weight: 2lb 4oz (1016g)
Magazine: 10-round box

.38 Super MD1

This is to the same design and uses many of the same parts as the 9mm M973 pistol, but is chambered for the .38 Super cartridge. The barrel is to the standard Colt-designed straight pattern.

Cartridge: .38 Super Auto
Length: 8.62in (219mm)

Weight: 2lb 6oz (1078g)
Barrel: 5.08in (129mm), 6 grooves, rh
Magazine: 9-round box
Muzzle velocity: 1280 ft/sec (390 m/sec)

.38 Super MD2

As for the .38 Super MD1 above but the barrel is shaped at the muzzle and the barrel bush is modified to improve accuracy.

Cartridge: .38 Super Auto
Length: 8.62in (219mm)
Weight: 2lb 6oz (1078g)
Barrel: 5.04in (128mm), 6 grooves, rh
Magazine: 9-round box
Muzzle velocity: 1280 ft/sec (390 m/sec)

ITALY
See also Beretta, Bernardelli & Glisenti

Troopers' Revolver M1872
Brescia, Castelli, Glisenti

Solid-frame, double-action, gate-loaded, rod-ejecting revolver. Hexagonal barrel, wood grips, lanyard ring. Fluted cylinder retained by spring wedge.

Cartridge: 10.4 × 20R Italian Ordnance
Length: 11.42in (290mm)
Weight: 2lb 7oz (1110g)
Barrel: 6.30in (160mm), 6 grooves, rh
Magazine: 6-round cylinder
Muzzle velocity: 837 ft/sec (255 m/sec)

M1886
Glisenti, Brescia and others.

Solid-frame, single-action, folding trigger, gate-loaded. Hexagonal barrel, fluted cylinder, safety catch on left rear of butt.

Specifications: not known

M1889
Castelli, Glisenti, Brescia and others

Solid-frame, double-action, gate-loaded, rod-ejecting revolver. Loading gate linked with hammer on the Abadie system to prevent inadvertent firing. Two models; one with round barrel and trigger guard for officers and NCOs, the other with hexagonal barrel, no trigger guard and a folding trigger for the rank and file. The latter model appears not the have been made after 1914.

Cartridge: 10.4 × 20R Italian Ordnance
Length: 9.25in (235mm)
Weight: 2lb 2oz (950g)
Barrel: 4.53in (115mm), 6 grooves, rh
Magazine: 6-round cylinder
Muzzle velocity: 836 ft/sec (255 m/sec)

ITHACA USA
Ithaca

Name found on Colt M1911A1 pistols manufactured by the Ithaca Gun Company of Ithaca, New York, between 1943 and 1945, a total of 441,557 being made.

JAPAN

26th Year revolver
Koishikawa
1893. Hinged frame self-cocking revolver; general design of the frame follows Nagant style, barrel lock is based on Smith & Wesson practice of the period, and the lock mechanism is similar to European designs. Identifiable by the large frame hinge bolt and the peculiar spur-less hammer.

Cartridge: 9 × 22R Japanese Revolver
Length: 8.50in (216mm)
Weight: 1lb 15oz (880g)
Barrel: 4.72in (120mm), 6 grooves, lh
Magazine: 6-round cylinder
Muzzle velocity: 640 ft/sec (195 m/sec)

Nambu Type A, 4th Year
Koishikawa & TGE
1915. Recoil-operated, striker-fired automatic pistol; using a 'prop-up' wedge lock. Well-raked but thin butt with wooden grips, prominent cocking-piece at rear of receiver, tapered barrel. Ejection port on top of receiver. Grip safety on front of grip. Single recoil spring on left side of frame.

Cartridge: 8 × 21mm Nambu
Length: 8.98in (228mm)
Weight: 1lb 15oz (880g)
Barrel: 4.72in (120mm), 6 grooves, rh
Magazine: 8-round box
Muzzle velocity: 1100 ft/sec (335 m/sec)

Nambu Type B (Baby)
Koishikawa & TGE
1909. Smaller version of the Type A, for officers.

Cartridge: 7 × 20mm Nambu
Length: 6.73in (171mm)
Weight: 1lb 5oz (590g)
Barrel: 3.27in (83mm), 6 grooves, rh
Magazine: 7-round box
Muzzle velocity: 1000 ft/sec (305 m/sec)

Nambu 14th Year
Koishikawa, Kokura, Nagoya & Nambu
1925. Improved version of the 4th Year Type A. Minor internal manufacturing changes, safety catch added at forward left side of frame and grip safety removed, dual recoil springs fitted. In *ca* 1937 a variant was produced with a much larger trigger-guard for use with gloved hands.

Cartridge: 8 × 21mm Nambu
Length: 8.94in (227mm)
Weight: 2lb 0oz (900g)
Barrel: 4.76in (121mm), 6 grooves, rh
Magazine: 8-round box
Muzzle velocity: 1100 ft/sec (335 m/sec)

Type 94 pistol
Chuo Kogyo & Nambu
1934. Recoil operated, locked breech using a vertical block, striker-fired automatic pistol of idiosyncratic appearance. Wedge-shaped butt, slab-sided receiver, tubular barrel, grooved cocking piece forming the rear top of the receiver.

Cartridge: 8 × 21mm Nambu
Length: 7.09in (180mm)

Weight: 1lb 12oz (790g)
Barrel: 3.15in (80mm), 6 grooves, rh
Magazine: 6-round box
Muzzle velocity: 1000 ft/sec (305 m/sec)

New Nambu
Omori
1961. Conventional solid-frame, double-action revolver with side-opening cylinder, based on Smith & Wesson practice. Used by Police and Maritime Safety Guards.

Cartridge: .38 Special
Length: 7.76in (197mm)
Weight: 1lb 8oz (680g)
Barrel: 3.03in (77mm), 6 grooves, rh
Magazine: 5-round cylinder
Muzzle velocity: 722 ft/sec (220 m/sec)

Inagaki
Inagaki
1941. Submitted to the Japanese Army but refused, and was adopted in some quantity by the Japanese Navy. A conventional fixed-barrel blowback automatic pistol, the only odd features being a leaf spring acting as the return spring and another acting as the internal hammer.

Cartridge: 7.65 × 17SR Browning
Length: 6.50in (165mm)
Weight: 1lb 7oz (650g)
Barrel: 4.53in (115mm), 4 grooves, rh
Magazine: 8-round box
Muzzle velocity: 985 ft/sec (300 m/sec)

Hamada (1)
Japan Gun
1941–44. Produced in response to a Japanese Army demand, this was little more than a copy of the Browning Model 1910 in 7.65mm Browning calibre but with a more rectangular slide and a full-length frame.

Hamada (2)
Japan Gun
In 1942 the Japanese Army requested a pistol chambering the standard 8mm Nambu cartridge, and the Japan Gun Co redesigned their Hamada pistol accordingly. This, however, was not 'politically correct'; an Army pistol had to be designed by the Army, so a commission was hastily assembled, made some cosmetic changes, and the Hamada (2) resulted. The result was a conventional slide-and-frame fixed-barrel blowback pistol of which about 500 appear to have been completed.

Cartridge: 8 × 21mm Nambu
Length: 6.97in (177mm)
Weight: 1lb 10oz (750g)
Barrel: 3.74in (96mm), 6 grooves, rh
Magazine: 6-round box
Muzzle velocity: 1050 ft/sec (320 m/sec)

JERICHO Israel
IMI

Model 941R
1991. Recoil-operated, using Browning cam breech-locking, hammer-fired automatic pistol in either 9mm Parabellum, .40 S&W or .41 Action Express calibres.

Prominent prawl on the butt grip, front end of slide sloped back. Slide-mounted safety catch also acts a de-cocking lever.

Cartridge: 9 × 19mm Parabellum
Length: 8.15in (207mm)
Weight: 2lb 7oz (1100g)
Barrel: 4.41in (112mm), 6 grooves, rh
Magazine: 16-round box
Muzzle velocity: 1247 ft/sec (380 m/sec)

Model 941F
The same as the Model 941R but with the safety catch mounted on the frame and automatic firing pin safety.

Specifications: as for Model 941R

Model 941FS
Short version of the Model 941F. Features the same, dimensions differ.

Cartridge: 9 × 19mm Parabellum
Length: 7.24in (184mm)
Weight: 2lb 0oz (990g)
Barrel: 3.54in (90mm), 6 grooves, rh
Magazine: 16-round box
Muzzle velocity: 1083 ft/sec (330 m/sec)

Model 941FB
Similar to the 941FS but with a shorter butt and reduced magazine capacity.

Specifications: as for 941FS, except
Weight: 2lb 1oz (945g)
Magazine: 13-round box

KSN Israel
KSN

Golan
1994. This began life as the Zastava Arms CZ99 pistol, made in Yugoslavia. Due to the political situation there, production barely got under way. The rights were acquired by KSN Industries of Israel and the pistol is now known as the Golan. The design appears to have been copied from the SIG-Sauer 220 series, showing similar contours and controls. Recoil-operated, cam-locked breech, hammer-fired. Alloy frame, steel slide.

Cartridge: 9 × 19mm Parabellum
Length: 6.69in (170mm)
Weight: 1lb 13oz (835g)
Barrel: 3.86in (98mm), 6 grooves, rh
Magazine: 15-round box
Muzzle velocity: 1214 ft/sec (370 m/sec)

Kareen Mark 2
1994 This is a copy of the Browning High-Power with a light alloy frame and ambidextrous safety catch. Cosmetic changes to the slide grips etc.

Cartridge: 9 × 19mm Parabellum
Length: 7.80in (198mm)
Weight: 2lb 2oz (960g)
Barrel: 4.64in (118mm), 6 grooves, rh
Magazine: 13- or 15-round box
Muzzle velocity: 1246 ft/sec (380 m/sec)

Kareen Mark 2 Compact
A shortened version of the Kareen Mark 2.

Cartridge: 9 × 19mm Parabellum
Length: 6.02in (153mm)
Weight: 2lb 0oz (920g)
Barrel: 3.86in (98mm), 6 grooves, rh
Magazine: 13-round box
Muzzle velocity: 1214 ft/sec (370 m/sec)

LAHTI Finland
Valmet & Husqvarna

M35 (Finland)
Valmet
1935. In outline, the shape of the butt and tapering barrel resemble the Luger (Parabellum) but with a flat-topped receiver having an internal bolt locked by a vertically-moving yoke. Recoil-operated, striker-fired.

Cartridge: 9 × 19mm Parabellum
Length: 9.21in (234mm)
Weight: 2lb 12oz (1442g)
Barrel: 4.72in (120mm), 6 grooves, rh
Magazine: 8-round box
Muzzle velocity: 1148 ft/sec (350 m/sec)

M40 (Sweden)
Husqvarna
A version of the Finnish M35 manufactured in Sweden. The dimensions differ, and this version has a hexagonal reinforce where the barrel meets the receiver, the trigger guard is more oval, and the foresight is taller and with a vertical rear face.

Cartridge: 9 × 19mm Parabellum
Length: 9.57in (243mm)
Weight: 2lb 13oz (1265g)
Barrel: 4.72in (120mm), 4 grooves, rh
Magazine: 7-round box
Muzzle velocity: 1148 ft/sec (350 m/sec)

LE FRANÇAIS France
Manufrance

Military Model
Introduced in 1928 in the hopes of a military contract; the French Army purchased a few but the remainder were sold commercially and to police forces until 1939. A blowback pistol with the barrel hinged to drop down far enough for cleaning the chamber. A magazine safety releases the barrel when the magazine is withdrawn. Ejection by chamber pressure.

Cartridge: 9 × 20SR Browning Long
Length: 8.0in (203mm)
Weight: 2lb 6oz (1090g)
Barrel: 5.50in (140mm), 6 grooves, rh
Magazine: 8-round box
Muzzle velocity: 1000 ft/sec (305 m/sec)

LEONHARDT
See Beholla

LIBERATOR USA
Guide Lamp
M1942

A single-shot pistol assembled from steel stampings and intended to be air-dropped to resistance forces in enemy-occupied territory. Smooth-bored, it had a manually-operated breech block and manually-cocked striker. The butt held five .45 ACP cartridges. The round was loaded, fired, and then the breech was opened and the empty case poked out with a pencil or stick prior to reloading.

Cartridge: .45 ACP
Length: 5.55in (141mm)
Weight: 1lb 0oz (454g)
Barrel: 3.97in (101mm), smoothbore
Magazine: none
Muzzle velocity: 820 ft/sec (250 m/sec)

LLAMA Spain
Llama
Model 11

Also known as the **Llama Especial**. 1934–56. Recoil-operated, hammer-fired, locked breech using the Browning link system. Rather slender butt, more square to the receiver than usual on Colt copies, and with the toe kicked forward to make a finger rest.

Cartridge: 9 × 19mm Parabellum
Length: 8.46in (215mm)
Weight: 2lb 6oz (1075g)
Barrel: 5.0in (127mm), 6 grooves, rh
Magazine: 8-round box
Muzzle velocity: 1181 ft/sec (360 m/sec)

Model IX-C

Recoil-operated automatic pistol based on the Colt M1911 and using the same locking system. Hammer-fired, manual safety. Principal change from the Colt is the large magazine capacity.

Cartridge: .45 ACP
Length: 8.50in (216mm)
Weight: 2lb 4oz (1020g)
Barrel: 5.0in (127mm), 6 grooves, rh
Magazine: 13-round box
Muzzle velocity: 836 ft/sec (255 m/sec)

M-82

Modern design of double-action automatic pistol, hammer-fired, using a wedge lock similar to the Walther P38. Slide-mounted safety catch.

Cartridge: 9 × 19mm Parabellum
Length: 8.23in (209mm)
Weight: 2lb 7oz (1105g)
Barrel: 4.49in (114mm), 6 grooves, rh
Magazine: 15-round box
Muzzle velocity: 1300 ft/sec (396 m/sec)

LUGER Germany
DWM, Erfurt, Mauser & Simson

All Luger (Parabellum) pistols are to the same basic design: recoil-operated, locked by means of a toggle, striker-fired. All have a safety catch, some have a grip safety in addition.

The pistols listed below are the definitive year models. The various Luger pistols adopted in other countries are all copies of one of these models, identifiable solely by their national markings and minor variations to suit national preferences.

German Navy M1904

Also known as the Pistole MM '04. Long barrel, two-position flip rear sight, grip safety on guns made before 1915–18, butt-stock lug at heel of butt, no rebound lock on toggle.

Cartridge: 9 × 19mm Parabellum
Length: 10.51in (267mm)
Weight: 2lb 3oz (1010g)
Barrel: 5.90in (150mm), 6 grooves, rh
Magazine: 8-round box
Muzzle velocity: 1132 ft/sec (345 m/sec)

German Army M1908

Also known as the Pistole '08. Standard barrel, manual safety catch, no rebound lock on toggle, no grip safety, coil mainspring, fixed rear sight. Stock lug on butt after 1913.

Cartridge: 9 × 19mm Parabellum
Length: 8.50in (216mm)
Weight: 1lb 15oz (885g)
Barrel: 3.94in (100mm), 6 grooves, rh
Magazine: 8-round box
Muzzle velocity: 1100 ft/sec (335 m/sec)

Artillery '08

Also known as the Long '08. Long barrel, ramp sight on rear of barrel, stock lug, no grip safety, no rebound lock.

Cartridge: 9 × 19mm Parabellum
Length: 12.48in (317mm)
Weight: 2lb 7oz (1105g)
Barrel: 7.87in (200mm), 6 grooves, rh
Magazine: 8-round box
Muzzle velocity: 1230 ft/sec (375 m/sec)

SWITZERLAND
M1900
W+F Bern

Slender barrel, grip safety, rebound lock in right toggle grip, leaf mainspring.

Cartridge: 7.65 × 21.5mm Parabellum
Length: 9.33in (237mm)
Weight: 1lb 15oz (890g)
Barrel: 4.72in (120mm), 4 grooves, rh
Magazine: 8-round box
Muzzle velocity: 1148 ft/sec (350 m/sec)

M1906
W+F Bern

Generally as for the M1900 but without the rebound lock and with a coil mainspring.

Cartridge: 7.65 × 21.5mm Parabellum
Length: 9.21in (234mm)
Weight: 1lb 15oz (890g)
Barrel: 4.65in (118mm), 4 grooves, rh
Magazine: 8-round box
Muzzle velocity: 1148 ft/sec (350 m/sec)

M 1906/29
W+F Bern

Slender barrel, long grip safety, plain toggle grips, U-notch fixed rear sight, front end of receiver is round.

Cartridge: 7.65 × 21.5mm Parabellum
Length: 9.45in (240mm)
Weight: 2lb 1oz (935g)
Barrel: 4.72in (120mm), 4 grooves, rh
Magazine: 8-round box
Muzzle velocity: 1200 ft/sec (365 m/sec)

MAB France
MAB

PA-15

Ca 1960. Delayed blowback using rotating barrel, hammer-fired automatic pistol. Large capacity magazine.

Cartridge: 9 × 19mm Parabellum
Length: 8.0in (203mm)
Weight: 2lb 6oz (1090g)
Barrel: 4.49in (114mm), 6 grooves, rh
Magazine: 15-round box
Muzzle velocity: 1148 ft/sec (350 m/sec)

MAKAROV Russia
State Factories

PM

1950. Based on the Walther PP, a blowback pistol with double-action trigger, hammer-fired. Safety catch on slide acts as a de-cocking lever.

Cartridge: 9 × 18mm Makarov
Length: 6.30in (160mm)
Weight: 1lb 7oz (663g)
Barrel: 3.58in (91mm), 4 grooves, rh
Magazine: 8-round box
Muzzle velocity: 1033 ft/sec (315 m/sec)

MANNLICHER Austria
Steyr

Models 1901 & 1905

Unique design with sloping butt, thin frame and exposed barrel, open-top slide. Delayed blowback by spring and cam action, hammer-fired, integral charger-loaded magazine in butt. **M1901** had rear sight mounted on the barrel above the chamber, **M1905** on the rear of the breech-block, otherwise identical.

Cartridge: 7.63 × 21mm Mannlicher M1901
Length: 9.65in (245mm)
Weight: 2lb 0oz (910g)
Barrel: 6.10in (155mm), 4 grooves, rh
Magazine: 8-round integral box
Muzzle velocity: 1023 ft/sec (312 m/sec)

M1903

To the Mauser pattern, curved butt and frame, bolt moving in barrel extension, exposed barrel, box magazine in front of trigger. Locked breech, block propped by lugs, hammer-fired. Occasionally found with butt-stock attachment.

Cartridge: 7.65 × 25mm Mannlicher M1903
Length: 11.02in (280mm)
Weight: 2lb 4oz (1020g)
Barrel: 4.52in (115mm), 6 grooves, rh
Magazine: 6-round box
Muzzle velocity: 1181 ft/sec (360 m/sec)

MANURHIN France
Manurhin

Revolver MR73

1973. A conventional double-action, solid-frame, side-opening six-shot revolver. Found in various barrel lengths and styles, though the most usual service model has a 4-inch barrel and is fitted with fixed sights. A replacement cylinder for 9mm Parabellum cartridges is available for conversion.

Cartridge: .357 Magnum
Length: 9.17in (233mm)
Weight: 2lb 1oz (950g)
Barrel: 4.0in (101.6mm), 6 grooves, rh
Magazine: 6-round cylinder
Muzzle velocity: 1312 ft/sec (400 m/sec)

MAUSER Germany
Mauser

c/96

The classic 'Broom-handle' design. Long, slender barrel, rounded butt with wood grips, charger-loaded box magazine in front of trigger. Recoil-operated, block locking, hammer-fired.

Cartridge: 7.63 × 25mm Mauser
Length: 11.02in (280mm)
Weight: 2lb 8oz (1130g)
Barrel: 4.72in (120mm), 4 grooves, rh
Magazine: 10-round box
Muzzle velocity: 1444 ft/sec (440 m/sec)

c/96/M1916

The c/96 re-barrelled and modified to fire the 9mm Parabellum cartridge, a wartime expedient for the German Army. Weapons so modified have a large figure 9 carved into the grips and coloured red. 9mm c/96 pistols with a black 9 in the butt, or with no marks at all, were commercially produced after the war from spare parts.

Cartridge: 9 × 19mm Parabellum
Length: 11.65 (296mm)
Weight: 2lb 8oz (1120g)
Barrel: 5.55in (141mm), 4 grooves, rh
Magazine: 10-round box
Muzzle velocity: 1181 ft/sec (360 m/sec)

M1912 Military

Improved c/96. No major dimensional changes but the barrel was rifled with six grooves instead of four, and an improved safety catch fitted.

M1930 Military

Further improvement on the c/96 pattern, by lengthening the barrel and fitting a new three-position safety catch.

Cartridge: 7.63 × 25mm Mauser
Length: 11.57in (294mm)
Weight: 2lb 10oz (1188g)
Barrel: 5.55in (141mm), 6 grooves, rh
Magazine: 10-round box
Muzzle velocity: 1453 ft/sec (443 m/sec)

Model 711

A revision of the Model 1930 to provide it with a removable magazine in order to compete with Spanish copies in the Far East market.

M712 'Schnellfeuerpistole' (Nickl)

1930. Selective fire machine pistol based on the Model 711. Removable magazine, selector switch on the left side of the frame in the form of a two-position lever. Automatic control designed by Josef Nickl.

Cartridge: 7.63 × 25mm Mauser
Length: 11.25in (285mm)
Weight: 2lb 11oz (1210g)
Barrel: 5.27in (134mm), 6 grooves, rh
Magazine: 10- or 20-round box
Muzzle velocity: 1476 ft/sec (450 m/sec)

M712 'Schnellfeuerpistole' (Westinger)

1931. This was the same pistol as above but with a more reliable automatic selector system designed by Karl Westinger. Identified by the diamond-shaped selector switch on the left side of the frame. Dimensions remained the same. With the wooden butt-stock fitted, these pistols were 25.25in (641mm) long and weighed 4lb 13oz (2.0kg) with stock fitted and a loaded 10-round magazine in place.

M1914

Blowback, striker-fired pistol for police and self-defence, but frequently adopted as a military pistol. Open-topped slide with the front end bridged underneath the barrel. Knurled catch at front end of slide locks the barrel in place. Warp-round carved wood or hard rubber grip. Safety catch locks on safe and is released by push-button. Magazine safety.

Cartridge: 7.65 × 17SR Browning
Length: 6.0in (152mm)
Weight: 1lb 5oz (600g)
Barrel: 3.45in (87mm), 6 grooves, rh
Magazine: 8-round box
Muzzle velocity: 984 ft/sec (300 m/sec)

M1934

Improved version of the M1914; some very minor changes in manufacture, *eg* the barrel retaining catch is no longer machined and knurled.

Specifications: the same.

HsC

1937. Modern double-action blowback pistol designed to compete with the Walther PP. Very streamlined shape, web of steel between frame and trigger-guard, only the hammer spur shows at the rear, safety catch on slide does not drop hammer.

Cartridge: 7.65 × 17SR Browning
Length: 6.0in (152mm)
Weight: 1lb 5oz (600g)
Barrel: 3.38in (86mm), 6 grooves, rh
Magazine: 8-round box
Muzzle velocity: 984 ft/sec (300 m/sec)

M80SA

1988–95. This was the Hungarian FEG P9, a commercial copy of the Browning High-Power, delivered to Mauser 'in the white' and then finished by Mauser to a high standard and marked with the Mauser name. It is, in fact, a copy of the Browning High-Power.

Cartridge: 9 × 19mm Parabellum
Length: 8.0in (203mm)
Weight: 2lb 0oz (900g)
Barrel: 4.64in (118mm), 6 grooves, rh
Magazine: 14-round box
Muzzle velocity: 1181 ft/sec (360 m/sec)

M90DA

1988-95. The FEG P9R finished by Mauser in the same way as the M80SA *above*; the difference being that this is a double-action version of the Browning High-Power.

Specifications: as for the M80SA, except
Weight: 2lb 2oz (1000g)

M90 Compact

Short version of the M90DA *above*.

Cartridge: 9 × 19mm Parabellum
Length: 7.40in (188mm)
Weight: 2lb 1oz (950g)
Barrel: 4.13in (105mm), 6 grooves, rh
Magazine: 13-round box
Muzzle velocity: 1148 ft/sec (350 m/sec)

MENTA
See Beholla

NAMBU
See Japan

NETHERLANDS
Beaumont

M1873 Army 'Old Model'

Solid frame, double-action, gate-loaded. Rounded butt with wood grips and rounded prawl. Octagonal barrel, plain cylinder.

Cartridge: 9.4 × 20R Dutch
Length: 11.14in (283mm)
Weight: 2lb 13oz (1285g)
Barrel: 6.34in (161mm), 8 grooves, rh
Magazine: 6-round cylinder
Muzzle velocity: 590 ft/sec (180 m/sec)

KNIL M1891

Solid frame, double-action, gate-loaded, rod-ejection. Octagonal barrel with round reinforce, fluted cylinder. For use by Colonial Army.

Cartridge: 9.4 x 20R Dutch
Length: 8.74in (222mm)
Weight: 1lb 13oz (825g)
Barrel: 4.45in (113mm), 4 grooves, rh
Magazine: 6-round cylinder
Muzzle velocity: 557 ft/sec (170 m.sec)

NORTH KOREA
State arsenals

Type 64

Ca 1950. A close copy of the Browning M1900 blowback pistol. May be found with a shortened slide and with the muzzle threaded for a silencer.

Cartridge: 7.65 x 17SR Browning
Length: 6.73in (171mm)
Weight: 1lb 6oz (624g)
Barrel: 4.01in (102mm), 6 grooves, rh
Magazine: 7-round box
Muzzle velocity: 951 ft/sec (290 m/sec)

Type 68

A much-modified copy of the Tokarev TT-33. Shorter and more bulky; finger grip grooves on the slide slope forward; barrel formed with Browning lug instead of link, slide stop stronger, firing pin retained by a plate instead of a cross-pin, magazine release at heel of butt.

Cartridge: 7.62 x 25mm Soviet Pistol
Length: 7.28in (185mm)
Weight: 1lb 12oz (795g)
Barrel: 4.25in (108mm), 4 grooves, rh
Magazine: 8-round cylinder
Muzzle velocity: 1296 ft/sec (395 m/sec)

NORWAY
Nagant

Ordnance Revolver M1883

Nagant pattern. Solid frame, double-action, gate-loading, rod-ejection. Hexagonal barrel, fluted cylinder, wood grips.

Cartridge: 9 x 23R Belgian Nagant
Length: 10.51in (267mm)
Weight: 2lb 1oz (940g)
Barrel: 5.51in (140mm), 4 grooves, rh
Magazine: 6-round cylinder
Muzzle velocity: 689 ft/sec (210 m/sec)

Ordnance Revolver M1887

Nagant design; generally similar to the M1883 but firing a smaller cartridge.

Cartridge: 7.5 x 22R Norwegian Nagant
Length: 9.21in (234mm)
Weight: 1lb 12oz (795g)
Barrel: 4.45in (113mm), 4 grooves, rh
Magazine: 6-round cylinder
Muzzle velocity: 738 ft/sec (225 m/sec)

OBREGON (Mexico)
Mexicanas

1934–38. A semi-automatic pistol with Colt-like appearance but having the front of the slide more rounded, due to the rotating barrel breech locking system. Encouraged by the Mexican government, about 1000 pistols were made but were never adopted by the Army and were disposed of commercially.

Cartridge: .45 ACP
Length: 8.50in (216mm)
Weight: 2lb 8oz (1130g)
Barrel: 5.0in (127mm), 6 grooves, lh
Magazine: 7-round box
Muzzle velocity: 860 ft/sec (262 m/sec)

POLAND
Radom

Radom

Manufactured by Fabrika Brony w Radomu, the Polish national arsenal, 1935–39. A semi-automatic pistol of Polish design but leaning heavily on the Colt/Browning system. Original Polish pistols are marked with the Polish eagle on the slide. Manufacture continued 1939–44 under German occupation, and such weapons are marked 'Pistole 35(p)'. Recoil operated, Browning cam, hammer-fired, de-cocking lever.

Cartridge: 9 x 19mm Parabellum
Length: 8.31in (211mm)
Weight: 2lb 5oz (1.05kg)
Barrel: 4.53in (115mm), 6 grooves, rh
Magazine: 8-round box
Muzzle velocity: 1150 ft/sec (350 m/sec)

P-64

Polish version of the Soviet Makarov, a double-action blowback, hammer-fired, safety catch/de-cocking lever on slide.

Cartridge: 9 x 18mm Makarov
Length: 6.10in (155mm)
Weight: 1lb 6oz (636g)
Barrel: 3.30in (84mm), 4 grooves, rh
Magazine: 6-round box
Muzzle velocity: 1030 ft/sec (314 m/sec)

P-83

Cheaper and simpler version of the P-64; made from pressings and welds, rather than machined raw metal.

Cartridge: 9 x 18mm Makarov
Length: 6.49in (165mm)
Weight: 1lb 9oz (730g)
Barrel: 3.54in (90mm), 4 grooves, rh
Magazine: 8-round box
Muzzle velocity: 1043 ft/sec (318 m/sec)

P-93

A further improvement on the P-64 and P-83, mainly by a change in contours to suit the two-handed grip and moving the de-cocking lever to the top of the left side grip.

Cartridge: 9 x 18mm Makarov
Length: 7.0in (178mm)
Weight: 1lb 10oz (750g)

Barrel: 3.93in (100mm), 4 grooves, rh
Magazine: 8-round box
Muzzle velocity: 1050 ft/sec (320 m/sec)

PORTUGAL

Ordnance Revolver M1878 (System Abadie)
Soleil

Officers' Model. Double-action, solid-frame, gate-loaded, rod-ejection. Octagonal barrel, fluted chamber, wood grips. Ejector rod in slotted housing. Abadie system of linking loading gate to hammer to prevent inadvertently firing while loading.

Cartridge: 9.1 × 17.5R Portuguese Abadie
Length: 8.58in (218mm)
Weight: 1lb 11oz (752g)
Barrel: 4.45in (113mm), 4 grooves, lh
Magazine: 6-round cylinder
Muzzle velocity: 558 ft/sec (170 m/sec)

Ordnance Revolver M1886 (System Abadie)
Soleil

Troopers' Model. Double-action, solid-frame, gate-loaded, rod-ejection. Octagonal barrel, fluted chamber, wood or rubber grips. Ejector rod in slotted housing of different design to the 1878. Abadie loading gate.

Cartridge: 9.35 × 17.5R Portuguese Abadie
Length: 9.84in (250mm)
Weight: 1lb 14oz (835g)
Barrel: 5.59in (142mm), 4 grooves, lh
Magazine: 6-round cylinder
Muzzle velocity: 531 ft/sec (162 m/sec)

Savage
Savage

This commercially-made American semi-automatic pistol was adopted by the Portuguese Army and some paramilitary forces in World War One when the supply of their regulation Parabellum pistols was halted. It is a delayed blowback weapon, using barrel rotation to unlock the breech, delay being achieved by the inertia of the barrel and the counter-rotation impulse given by the bullet passing through the rifling.

M/908
Savage

1915. This is the Savage commercial M1907 pattern, distinguishable by the widely-spaced finger grips on the slide, the serrated 'hammer' tip showing at the rear of the slide, sheet-metal grip plates and the bulged-forward toe of the butt.

Cartridge: 7.65 × 17SR Browning
Length: 6.57in (167mm)
Weight: 1lb 4oz (567g)
Barrel: 3.78in (96mm), 6 grooves, rh
Magazine: 10-round box
Muzzle velocity: 984 ft/sec (300 m/sec)

M/915
Savage

This is the Savage commercial Model 1915 and is generally similar to the 1908 but without the exposed 'hammer' tip and with the addition of a grip safety.

Cartridge: 7.65 × 17SR Browning
Length: 7.0in (178mm)
Weight: 1lb 8oz (680g)
Barrel: 3.78in (96mm), 6 grooves, rh
Magazine: 10-round box
Muzzle velocity: 984 ft/sec (300 m/sec)

RAST & GASSER Austria
Gasser

Model 1870

Open frame, single-action, round barrel, gate loading, rod-ejection. Round barrel, plain cylinder.

Cartridge: 11.3 × 35R Austrian Gasser
Length: 14.76in (375mm)
Weight: 3lb 4oz (1474g)
Barrel: 9.25in (235mm), 4 grooves, rh
Magazine: 5-round cylinder
Muzzle velocity: 787 ft/sec (240 m/sec)

Model 1870/74

A smaller version of the M1870. Round barrel, fluted cylinder.

Cartridge: 11.3 × 35R Austrian Gasser
Length: 12.79in (325mm)
Weight: 2lb 2oz (963g)
Barrel: 7.28in (185mm), 4 grooves, rh
Magazine: 5-round cylinder
Muzzle velocity: 770 ft/sec (235 m/sec)

Model 1898

Solid frame, gate-loaded, double-action revolver, Smooth cylinder, butt at right-angle to the frame, Frame-mounted firing pin. Loading gate connected to hammer to prevent firing whilst loading. Austrian infantry issue.

Cartridge: 8 × 27R Rast & Gasser
Length: 8.86in (225mm)
Weight: 2lb 2oz (955g)
Barrel: 4.57in (116mm), 4 grooves, rh
Magazine: 8-round cylinder
Muzzle velocity: 787 ft/sec (240 m/sec)

REMINGTON USA
Remington

Model 1875 Army

1875–90. Solid frame, single-action, gate-loading, rod-ejection revolver. Identifiable by the triangular web between ejector rod casing and front of frame.

Cartridge: .44 Remington
Length: 12.0in (305mm)
Weight: 2lb 12oz (1245g)
Barrel: 7.5in (191mm), 5 grooves, lh, increasing twist
Magazine: 6-round cylinder
Muzzle velocity: 660 ft/sec (206 m/sec)

ROYAL Spain
Beistegui

M1927

Machine pistol based on the Mauser c/96 pattern, the first of this type. Selector switch on left side of frame for automatic or semi-automatic fire. Various barrel lengths, and can be found with fixed 10-round magazine or removable 20-round type. Small recess in frame above trigger on both sides. Sold with a wooden holster-stock which clips to the butt.

Cartridge: 7.63 × 25mm Mauser
Length: 11.61in (295mm)
Weight: 2lb 14oz (1297g)
Barrel: 5.5in (140mm), 6 grooves, rh
Magazine: 10-round fixed or 20-round removable box
Muzzle velocity: 1410 ft/sec (430 m/sec)
Cyclic rate: 850 rds/min

MM31-1

1931. Improved model of the M1927. Differs in having a larger recess in the frame, above the trigger, and by the selector lever being moved forward on the frame and slightly above the trigger. Fixed magazine only. 140mm or 180mm barrel.

Cartridge: 7.63 × 25mm Mauser
Length: 13.0in (330mm)
Weight: 3lb 3oz (1451g)
Barrel: 7.09in (180mm), 6 grooves, rh
Magazine: 10-round fixed box
Muzzle velocity: 1624 ft/sec (495 m/sec)
Cyclic rate: 850 rds/min

MM31-2

1931. Variant of the MM31-1 with 20-round fixed barrel, increasing the weight to 3lb 9oz (1633g).

MM31-3

1932. Further variant of the MM31 using removable 10-, 20-, or 30-round magazines. Identified by a square recessed panel above the grips. Magazines are unique to this gun.

MM31-4

1933. Final version of the MM31; no square recessed panel above grips, removable magazines are interchangeable with Mauser types.

Cartridge: 7.63 × 25mm Mauser
Length: 11.42in (290mm)
Weight: 3lb 0oz (1361g)
Barrel: 5.51in (140mm), 6 grooves, rh
Magazine: 10- or 20-round removable box
Muzzle velocity: 1483 ft/sec (452 m/sec)
Cyclic rate: 850 rds/min

MM34

1935. New model still based on the Mauser pistol but with the addition of a rate reducer and a finned barrel to assist in cooling. Rate regulating lever in a recess in the top of the left butt grip. Very limited production due to the seizure of the factory by Republican forces and its later destruction.

Cartridge: 7.63 × 25mm Mauser
Length: 12.91in (328mm)
Weight: 3lb 7oz (1580g)

Barrel: 7.0in (178mm), 6 grooves, rh
Magazine: 10- or 20-round removable box
Muzzle velocity: 1624 ft/sec (495 m/sec)
Cyclic rate: variable between *ca* 650 & 850 rds/min

RUBY Spain
Gabilondo and sub-contractors

Model 1915

Blowback, internal hammer-fired, semi-automatic pistol of cheap construction, copied from the Browning M1903 design. Manufactured by several companies in Eibar, Spain, to meet French and Italian Army demands in 1915–18, and formed the foundation of innumerable cheap commercial pistols in the 1920–35 period.

Cartridge: 7.65 × 17SR Browning
Length: 6.06in (154mm)
Weight: 1lb 12oz (785g)
Barrel: 3.46in (88mm), 6 grooves, lh
Magazine: 9-round box
Muzzle velocity: 984 ft/sec (300 m/sec)

RUSSIA
State factories
See also **Galand, Makarov, Stechkin & Tokarev**

Revolver, Nagant, M1895

Gas-seal revolver. Solid frame, double-action, gate-loading, rod-ejection. Cylinder moves forward to enclose the rear end of the barrel when the trigger is pressed. Abnormally long firing pin.

Cartridge: 7.62 × 38R Nagant
Length: 9.25in (235mm)
Weight: 1lb 12oz (810g)
Barrel: 4.48in (114mm), 4 grooves, rh
Magazine: 7-round cylinder
Muzzle velocity: 950 ft/sec (290 m/sec)

PSM

1975. Blowback, double-action automatic pistol. Generally a reduced Makarov, designed with particular attention to a slim contour. Safety catch behind the slide, drops the hammer when moved to the safe position.

Cartridge: 5.45 × 18mm Soviet
Length: 6.30in (160mm)
Weight: 1lb 3oz (460g)
Barrel: 3.35in (85mm), 6 grooves, rh
Magazine: 8-round box
Muzzle velocity: 961 ft/sec (293 m/sec)

PSS

Ca 1990. Silent pistol, firing a special 'piston' cartridge which retains the explosion inside the case when fired. Otherwise a simple blowback weapon, double-action with an internal hammer; frame-mounted safety catch de-cocks hammer.

Cartridge: 7.62 × 42mm SP-4
Length: 6.57in (165mm)
Weight: 1lb 4oz (700g)
Barrel: not known, probably no more than 30mm
Magazine: 6-round box
Muzzle velocity: 656 ft/sec (200 m/sec)

SPP-1

Ca 1985. Underwater pistol. Four-barrelled, loaded by a clip carrying four dart projectiles. Self-cocking trigger then fires each dart in succession.

Cartridge: 4.5mm SPS dart
Length: 6.30in (244mm)
Weight: 1lb 3oz (950g)
Barrel: estimated 3.35in (54mm), smoothbore
Muzzle velocity: 820 ft/sec (250 m/sec) in air

SAUER Germany
Sauer & Sohn

Model 1914

Blowback, striker-fired, automatic pistol. Cylindrical slide, return spring around the fixed barrel, separate breech-block held in rear of slide by screwed cap.

Cartridge: 7.65 × 17SR Browning
Length: 5.70in (145mm)
Weight: 1lb 4oz (570g)
Barrel: 2.95in (75mm), 6 grooves, rh
Magazine: 7-round box
Muzzle velocity: 918 ft/sec (280 m/sec)

Model 30

1930. Also called the 'Behordenmodell' ('Authorities' Model'). Generally the same as the Model 1914 but with a more rounded butt contour. Widely used as a police pistol.

Cartridge: 7.65 × 17SR Browning
Length: 5.75in (146mm)
Weight: 1lb 6oz (620g)
Barrel: 3.03in (77mm), 6 grooves, rh
Magazine: 7-round box
Muzzle velocity: 918 ft/sec (280 m/sec)

Model 38H

1938. The same basic blowback weapon as the previous models but with a more modern and streamlined appearance, slide and breech-block in one piece, internal hammer, double-action, de-cocking lever on left side of grip

Cartridge: 7.65 × 17SR Browning
Length: 6.73in (171mm)
Weight: 1lb 9oz (720g)
Barrel: 3.27in (83mm), 4 or 6 grooves, rh
Magazine: 8-round box
Muzzle velocity: 984 ft/sec (300 m/sec)

SAVAGE
See Portugal

SCHWARZLOSE Germany
Schwarzlose

M1898 Standard

Recoil-operated, breech locking by rotating bolt, striker-fired automatic pistol. Well-raked butt, slender tubular receiver, tapering barrel. Prominent rear sight above chamber and slide stop and safety levers on the left side of the frame. Striker protrudes from rear of receiver and acts as cocking handle

Cartridge: 7.63 × 25mm Mauser
Length: 10.75in (273mm)
Weight: 2lb 1oz (940g)
Barrel: 6.42in (163mm), 4 grooves, rh
Magazine: 7-round box
Muzzle velocity: 1477 ft/sec (450 m/sec)

SIG Switzerland
SIG

P210-1

1948. Recoil-operated, breech locking by Browning-Petter can, single-action, hammer-fired automatic pistol. Slide runs on outside frame rails; hammer and mainspring unit removable. Polished finish and wood grips.

Cartridge: 9 × 19mm Parabellum
Length: 8.46in (215mm)
Weight: 1lb 15oz (900g)
Barrel: 4.72in (120mm), 6 grooves, rh
Magazine: 8-round box
Muzzle velocity: 1100 ft/sec (335 m/sec)

P210-2

As above, but sand-blasted finish and plastic grip plates.

P210-4

Special production model for West German Border Police.

P210-5

Target version with 150mm barrel

P210-6

Target version with 120mm barrel.

SIG-SAUER Switzerland/Germany
SIG & Sauer & Sohn

P220

Recoil-operated, double-action, hammer-fired automatic pistol. Breech locking by Browning cam, the squared-off area of the chamber locking into the ejection opening in the slide. De-cocking lever on top of left grip.

Cartridge: 9 × 19mm Parabellum
Length: 7.80in (198mm)
Weight: 1lb 10oz (750g)
Barrel: 4.41in (112mm), 6 grooves, rh
Magazine: 9-round box
Muzzle velocity: 1132 ft/sec (345 m/sec)

P225

Similar design to the P220 but smaller.

Cartridge: 9 × 19mm Parabellum
Length: 7.09in (180mm)
Weight: 1lb 10oz (740g)
Barrel: 3.86in (98mm), 6 grooves, rh
Magazine: 8-round box
Muzzle velocity: 1115 ft/sec (340 m/sec)

P226

1980. Designed to compete in the US Army trials. Similar to the P220 but larger magazine, ambidextrous magazine catch behind trigger.

Cartridge: 9 × 19mm Parabellum
Length: 7.72in (196mm)
Weight: 1lb 15oz (875g)
Barrel: 4.41in (112mm), 6 grooves, rh
Magazine: 15- or 20-round box
Muzzle velocity: 1132 ft/sec (345 m/sec)

P228

1988. Compact version of the P226.

Cartridge: 9 × 19mm Parabellum
Length: 7.09in (180mm)
Weight: 1lb 13oz (825g)
Barrel: 3.86in (98mm), 6 grooves, rh
Magazine: 13-round box
Muzzle velocity: 1115 ft/sec (340 m/sec)

P229

1991. Generally as for the P228 but chambered for the .40 Smith & Wesson cartridge. Later available in 9mm Parabellum and .357 SIG.

Cartridge: .40 Smith & Wesson
Length: 7.80in (180mm)
Weight: 1lb 15oz (865g)
Barrel: 4.41in (98mm), 6 grooves, rh
Magazine: 12-round box
Muzzle velocity: 968 ft/sec (295 m/sec)

P239

Similar to earlier models but with a slightly deeper frame and a more pronounced taper of the frame front. Originally designed in .357 SIG calibre, later extended to .40 S&W and 9mm Parabellum.

Cartridge: .357 SIG
Length: 6.77in (172mm)
Weight: 1lb 13oz (830g)
Barrel: 3.62in (92mm), 6 grooves, rh
Magazine: 7-round box
Muzzle velocity: 1345 ft/sec (410 m/sec)

SMITH & WESSON USA

Smith & Wesson

M1869 Army revolver

Also known as **No 3 First Model**, Single-action. Hinged-frame, automatic extraction, ribbed barrel, sharply curved square butt, fluted cylinder. Prominent hinge bolt. Army issue examples have 'U.S.' on top of barrel and serial numbers between 125 and 2199.

Cartridge: .44 S&W American
Length: 13.38in (340mm)
Weight: 2lb 9oz (1160g)
Barrel: 8.0in (203mm), 5 grooves, rh
Magazine: 6-round cylinder
Muzzle velocity: 650 ft/sec (198 m/sec)

M1870 Russian

Similar to the M1869 but with improved rifling and firing a much-improved cartridge. Distinguished by the rounded butt with slight prawl, and a finger-rest under the trigger guard.

Cartridge: .44 S&W Russian
Length: 12.0in (305mm)

Weight: 2lb 8oz (1135g)
Barrel: 6.50in (165mm), 5 grooves, rh
Magazine: 6-round cylinder
Muzzle velocity: 771 ft/sec (235 m/sec)

M1874 Schofield

Similar to the M1869 but with an improved barrel latch attached to the frame instead of the top strap, a round recoil plate in the frame, and a shorter ejector housing under the barrel.

Cartridge: .45 Smith & Wesson
Length: 12.40in (315mm)
Weight: 2lb 8oz (1140g)
Barrel: 7.0in (178mm), 5 grooves, rh
Magazine: 6-round cylinder
Muzzle velocity: 771 ft/sec (235 m/sec)

M1875 Schofield

Improved model; no recoil shield, barrel latch has oval centre section seen from above, knurled trigger of slightly changed shape. No change in dimensions

Mark 2 Hand Ejector, First Model

Also known as **New Century** or **Triple Lock**. 1908. In 1915 a quantity were supplied to the British Army in .455 calibre. Solid-frame, double-action, side-opening revolver. Cylinder and crane use three locks to secure in position, and the ejector rod is shrouded.

Cartridge: .455 Webley Mk 2
Length: 11.73in (298mm)
Weight: 2lb 6oz (1075g)
Barrel: 6.50in (165mm), 5 grooves, rh
Magazine: 6-round cylinder
Muzzle velocity: 656 ft/sec (200 m/sec)

M1917

This was the Mark 2 Hand Ejector, Second Model, modified to fire a .45 ACP cartridge by using two semi-circular clips to provide something for the ejector to work against. Similar to the First Model but the triple lock was abandoned, as was the barrel shroud for the ejector rod. It was also supplied in .455 calibre to the British Army in 1916.

Cartridge: .45 ACP
Length: 10.78in (274mm)
Weight: 2lb 4oz (1020g)
Barrel: 5.50in (140mm), 6 grooves, rh
Magazine: 6-round cylinder
Muzzle velocity: 860 ft/sec (262 m/sec)

Military & Police

1905. A solid-frame, side-opening, double-action revolver of conventional form. Data is for a 6-inch barrel version, but the model was available in various barrel lengths and finishes.

Cartridge: .38 Special
Length: 11.10in (282mm)
Weight: 1lb 15oz (880g)
Barrel: 6.0in (152mm), 5 grooves, rh
Magazine: 6 -round cylinder
Muzzle velocity: 870 ft/sec (265 m/sec)

Victory Model

1942–45. This was a wartime 'no-frills' version of the standard Military and Police model, produced for government use. It was issued in 4-inch and 2-inch barrel versions, most of the latter being taken by the US Department of Justice, while the larger weapons went to the US Army, Navy and Defense Supplies Corporation.

Cartridge: .38 Smith & Wesson
Length: 8.46in (215mm)
Weight: 1lb 14oz (860g)
Barrel: 4.0in (101mm), 5 grooves, rh
Magazine: 6-round cylinder
Muzzle velocity: 745 ft/sec (227 m/sec)

.38-200 (or K-200)

1940–45. A special version of the standard Military and Police revolver, with the chambers dimensioned to suit the British .380 Mark 2 cartridge. The grips indicate its age; from 1940 to January 1942 they were chequered walnut with inlet S&W monograms; after that they were smooth wood without monograms. From 1940 to January 1942 the gun was made in 4-, 5- and 6-inch barrel lengths and had a polished blue finish. After that date it was produced only in 5-inch barrel form and with a sandblasted blue finish. A total of 568,204 were supplied to British and Empire forces and they remained in use until the middle 1950s.

Cartridge: .38 Smith & Wesson
Length: 10.20in (260mm)
Weight: 2lb 0oz (907g)
Barrel: 5.0in (127mm), 5 grooves, rh
Magazine: 6-round cylinder
Muzzle velocity: 600 ft/sec (183 m/sec)

STAR Spain
Echeverria

Super B

Spanish Army pistol 1946–82. Resembles the Colt M1911A1 but uses the Browning cam system of locking and has no grip safety. Dismantling latch on right side of frame.

Cartridge: 9 × 19mm Parabellum
Length: 8.74in (222mm)
Weight: 2lb 4oz (1020g)
Barrel: 5.12in (130mm), 4 grooves, rh
Magazine: 8-round box
Muzzle velocity: 1312 ft/sec (400 m/sec)

Model 28DA

Tested by Spanish Army *ca* 1982 but not adopted. Short recoil, Browning cam locking, slide runs inside the frame. Hammer-fired, double-action, ambidextrous safety catch, loaded chamber indicator.

Cartridge: 9 × 19mm Parabellum
Length: 8.07in (205mm)
Weight: 2lb 8oz (1140g)
Barrel: 4.33in (110mm), 4 grooves, rh
Magazine: 15-round box
Muzzle velocity: 1246 ft/sec (380 m/sec)

Model 28P DA

Compact version of the 28DA with the same features.

Cartridge: 9 × 19mm Parabellum
Length: 7.60in (193mm)
Weight: 2lb 6oz (1100g)
Barrel: 3.86in (98mm), 6 grooves, rh
Magazine: 15-round box
Muzzle velocity: 1214 ft/sec (370 m/sec)

Model 28PK DA

As for the 28P DA but with a light alloy frame instead of forged steel.

Specifications: as for 28P DA, except
Weight: 1lb 14oz (860g)

Model 30M

Adopted by Spanish Army in 1989. An improved version of the 28DA.

Cartridge: 9 × 19mm Parabellum
Length: 8.07in (205mm)
Weight: 2lb 8oz (1140g)
Barrel: 4.69in (119mm), 6 grooves, rh
Magazine: 15-round box
Muzzle velocity: 1246 ft/sec (380 m/sec)

Model 30PK

Similar to the 30M but smaller and with a light alloy frame.

Cartridge: 9 × 19mm Parabellum
Length: 7.60in (193mm)
Weight: 1lb 14oz (860g)
Barrel: 3.86in (98mm), 6 grooves, rh
Magazine: 15-round box
Muzzle velocity: 1214 ft/sec (370 m/sec)

STENDA
See Beholla

STECHKIN Russia
State factories

9mm Stechkin

Blowback automatic, double-action, hammer-fired, based on Walther PP design. Service pistol of Soviet Army *ca* 1955–75. Selective fire capability. Wooden holster-stock.

Cartridge: 9 × 18mm Makarov
Length: 8.86in (225mm)
Weight: 2lb 4oz (1020g)
Barrel: 5.50in (140mm), 4 grooves, rh
Magazine: 20-round box
Muzzle velocity: 1115 ft/sec (340 m/sec)
Cyclic rate: 750 rds/min

STEYR Austria
Steyr

8mm Roth-Steyr M1907

Service pistol of the Hungarian cavalry element of the Austro-Hungarian Army 1908–18. Marked 'Steyr' and 'W-n' above the butt. No commercial model made. Unique shape, with a cylindrical barrel casing, slab-sided receiver, round, knurled, cocking piece at rear. Breech locked by rotating barrel, striker part-cocked by recoil, part by trigger pull. Charger-loaded integral box magazine in butt.

Cartridge: 8 × 19mm Roth-Steyr
Length: 9.17in (233mm)
Weight: 2lb 4oz (1020g)
Barrel: 5.16in (131mm), 4 grooves, rh
Magazine: 10-round box
Muzzle velocity: 1050 ft/sec (320 m/sec)

9mm Steyr M1911

Service pistol of the Austrian element of the Austro-Hungarian Army, 1912–18 and of the Austrian Army thereafter. Numbers converted to 9mm Parabellum calibre after 1938 and marked P'08 on the slide. Recoil-operated self-loader, rotating barrel lock, hammer-fired, integral magazine in butt. Also supplied to Chile and Romania prior to 1914.

Cartridge: 9 × 23mm Steyr
Length: 8.46in (215mm)
Weight: 2lb 2oz (964g)
Barrel: 5.04in (128mm), 4 grooves, rh
Magazine: 8-round box
Muzzle velocity: 1185 ft/sec (361 m/sec)

GB

1980–90. Delayed blowback automatic pistol, delay by gas pressure in annular space between barrel and slide. Double-action, hammer-fired.

Cartridge: 9 × 19mm Parabellum
Length: 8.54in (217mm)
Weight: 1lb 4oz (845g)
Barrel: 5.35in (136mm), 4 grooves polygonal, rh
Magazine: 18-round box
Muzzle velocity: 1247 ft/sec (380 m/sec)

SPP (Special Purpose Pistol)

1988. Similar to the Steyr TMP submachine gun but without the forward grip and firing semi-automatic only. Synthetic receiver and frame, recoil-operated, breech locked by rotating barrel. Magazine housing in pistol grip, small fore-end grip with spur to keep fingers away from the muzzle.

Cartridge: 9 × 19mm Parabellum
Length: 12.68in (322mm)
Weight: 2lb 13oz (1300g)
Barrel: 5.12in (130mm), 6 grooves, rh
Magazine: 15- or 30-round box
Muzzle velocity: ca 1214 ft/sec (370 m/sec)

SUPER AZUL Spain
Beistegui

Super Azul

This was actually a version of the Royal MM31 selective-fire machine pistol marketed under another name. Copy of the Mauser 712 design with magazines made interchangeable with the Mauser.

Cartridge: 7.63 × 25mm Mauser
Length: 11.42in (290mm)
Weight: 3lb 2oz (1400g)
Barrel: 5.51in (140mm), 6 grooves, rh
Magazine: 10-, 20- or 30-round box
Muzzle velocity: 1476 ft/sec (450 m/sec)

SWEDEN
See also Lahti

Troopers' M1871
Francotte & Husqvarna

Lefaucheaux-Francotte. First issues made by Francotte of Liège. Later (1878) by Husqvarna. Single-action, gate-loaded. Swept-back butt, round barrel, plain cylinder.

Cartridge: 11 × 17.5R French Ordnance
Length: 12.20in (310mm)
Weight: 2lb 9oz (1175g)
Barrel: 5.90in (150mm), 4 grooves, rh
Magazine: 6-round cylinder
Muzzle velocity: 804 ft/sec (245 m/sec)

M1884
Husqvarna

Generally resembles the French M1873 design: with solid-frame, double-action, gate-loading, and rod-ejection. Round barrel with half-length octagonal reinforce, plain cylinder.

Cartridge: 11 × 17.5R French Ordnance
Length: 9.45in (240mm)
Weight: 2lb 5oz (1040g)
Barrel: 4.53in (115mm), 4 grooves, rh
Magazine: 6-round cylinder
Muzzle velocity: 787 ft/sec (240 m/sec)

Officers' M1887
Nagant

Solid-frame, double-action revolver. Hexagonal barrel, fluted cylinder. Gate loading, rod-ejection.

Cartridge: 7.5 × 22R Norwegian Nagant
Length: 9.25in (235mm)
Weight: 1lb 11oz (770g)
Barrel: 4.53in (115mm), 6 grooves, rh
Magazine: 6-round cylinder
Muzzle velocity: 738 ft/sec (225 m/sec)

Ordnance Model 1893
Husqvarna

Nagant design. Double-action, solid-frame, gate-loaded, rod-ejection. Hexagonal barrel, fluted cylinder, wood grips.

Cartridge: 7.5 × 22R Norwegian Nagant
Length: 9.25in (235mm)
Weight: 1lb 12oz (790g)
Barrel: 4.49in (114mm), 6 grooves, rh
Magazine: 7-round cylinder
Muzzle velocity: 738 ft/sec (225 m/sec)

SWITZERLAND
See *also* Luger, SIG & SIG-Sauer
M1872 10.4mm CF or RF
Pirlot

Generally called the Chamelot, Delvigne & Schmidt from the three designers who had the principal influence on it, this pistol was made by Pirlot of Liège, 1873–79. Solid frame, double-action revolver. Gate-loaded, rod-ejection. Hexagonal barrel, fluted cylinder.

Cartridge: .10.4 × 20R Swiss Ordnance
Length: 10.83in (275mm)
Weight: 1lb 8oz (680g)
Barrel: 5.90in (150mm), 4 grooves, rh
Magazine: 6-round cylinder
Muzzle velocity: 610 ft/sec (185 m/sec)

Troopers' M1878 10.4mm CF
Chamelot, Delvigne & Schmidt. Similar to the M1872 but the ejector rod is not held in a slotted shroud.

Cartridge: 10.4 × 20R Swiss Ordnance
Length: 9.25in (235mm)
Weight: 1lb 10oz (737g)
Barrel: 4.57in (116mm), 4 grooves, rh
Magazine: 6-round cylinder
Muzzle velocity: 610 ft/sec (185 m/sec)

Ordnance Revolver M1882
Solid frame, double-action, gate-loaded, rod-ejection. Hexagonal barrel, fluted cylinder, composition grips.

Cartridge: 7.5 × 23R Swiss Revolver
Length: 8.98in (228mm)
Weight: 1lb 13oz (810g)
Barrel: 4.53in (115mm), 6 grooves, rh
Magazine: 6-round cylinder
Muzzle velocity: 725 ft/sec (221 m/sec)

Ordnance Revolver M1929
Solid frame, double-action, gate-loaded, rod-ejection. Round barrel, fluted cylinder. Butt rather more rounded than the M1882, foresight larger. Bakelite grips.

Cartridge: 7.5 × 23R Swiss Revolver
Length: 8.98in (228mm)
Weight: 1lb 11oz (770g)
Barrel: 4.53in (115mm), 6 grooves, rh
Magazine: 6-round cylinder
Muzzle velocity: 725 ft/sec (221 m/sec)

TOKAREV Russia
State factories
TT-30
1930. Recoil-operated, single-action, hammer-fired automatic pistol. Breech locking by Browning link, with lugs machined on upper surface of barrel. Hammer and mainspring in a detachable sub-assembly.

Cartridge: 7.62 × 25mm Soviet Pistol
Length: 7.68in (195mm)
Weight: 1lb 13oz (822g)
Barrel: 4.50in (114mm), 4 grooves, rh
Magazine: 8-round box
Muzzle velocity: 1427 ft/sec (435 m/sec)

TT-33
1933. Improved version, simplified to speed up manufacture. Barrel lugs are now collars running all round the barrel. Slight changes in the contour of the frame and in the lockwork sub-assembly.

Cartridge: 7.62 × 25mm Soviet Pistol
Length: 7.72in (196mm)
Weight: 1lb 14oz (850g)
Barrel: 4.57in (116mm), 4 grooves, rh
Magazine: 8-round box
Muzzle velocity: 1378 ft/sec (420 m/sec)

TOKAGYPT Egypt
Fegyvergar
A licensed copy of the Tokarev TT-33 pistol, manufactured by Fegyvergar of Hungary but made in 9mm Parabellum calibre for the Egyptian Army in the 1950s.

Cartridge: 9 × 19mm Parabellum
Length: 7.64in (194mm)
Weight: 2lb 1oz (910g)
Barrel: 4.49in (114mm), 6 grooves, rh
Magazine: 7-round box
Muzzle velocity: 1148 ft/sec (350 m/sec)

TROCAOLA ARANZABAL Spain
Trocaola
Pistol, Old Pattern, No 2 Mark I
A hinged-frame, double-action revolver, a scaled-up imitation of a Smith & Wesson hinged-frame model of *ca* 1890, which was adopted by the British Army as an emergency weapon in 1915 and declared obsolete in 1921.

Cartridge: .455 Webley Mk 6
Length: 11.02in (280mm)
Weight: 1lb 8oz (680g)
Barrel: 5.12in (130mm), 5 grooves, rh
Magazine: 6-round cylinder
Muzzle velocity: 656 ft/sec (200 m/sec)

UZI Israel
IMI
Uzi Pistol
A shortened and converted form of the Uzi sub-machine gun with some changes in the components so as to prevent conversion back to automatic fire capability. Blowback operation, cocking handle on top of receiver, magazine in pistol grip, trigger guard shaped for two-handed grip.

Cartridge: 9 × 19mm Parabellum
Length: 9.45in (240mm)
Weight: 3lb 10oz (1650g)
Barrel: 4.53in (115mm), 4 grooves, rh
Magazine: 20-round box
Muzzle velocity: 1148 ft/sec (350 m/sec)

VEKTOR South Africa
LIW

SP-1

1993. Recoil-operated, double-action, hammer-fired automatic pistol, using a wedge locking system. Steel slide, aluminium alloy frame. Ambidextrous safety catch.

Cartridge: 9 × 19mm Parabellum
Length: 8.26in (210mm)
Weight: 2lb 3oz (995g)
Barrel: 4.65in (118mm), 4 grooves polygonal, rh
Magazine: 15-round box
Muzzle velocity: 1181 ft/sec (360 m/sec)

Z-88

1988. In spite of some minor modifications to suit manufacturing methods and fitting a reversible magazine catch, this is essentially the Beretta 92 made in South Africa. Recoil-operated, double-action, hammer-fired automatic pistol, using a wedge lock. Open-topped slide.

Cartridge: 9 × 19mm Parabellum
Length: 8.54in (217mm)
Weight: 2lb 3oz (995g)
Barrel: 4.92in (125mm), 6 grooves, rh
Magazine: 15-round box
Muzzle velocity: 1148 ft/sec (350 m/sec)

WALTHER Germany
Walther

Model 4

Ca 1912. Blowback, internal hammer, automatic pistol. Developed for use as a police and military pistol by extending the barrel of the existing Model 3 and adding an extension to the slide by means of a bayonet catch, in the same manner as the later Browning 1910/22. In military service 1914–18.

Cartridge: 7.65 × 17SR Browning
Length: 6.00in (152mm)
Weight: 1lb 3oz (550g)
Barrel: 3.35in (85mm), 6 grooves, rh
Magazine: 6-round box
Muzzle velocity: 984 ft/sec (300 m/sec)

Model 6

1915. An enlarged Model 4 to fire the 9mm Parabellum cartridge. It remained a blowback design, with a very strong return spring and a heavy slide. Unpopular, production was discontinued in 1917.

Cartridge: 9 × 19mm Parabellum
Length: 8.25in (210mm)
Weight: 2lb 2oz (960g)
Barrel: 4.75in (121mm), 4 grooves, rh
Magazine: 8-round box
Muzzle velocity: 1148 ft/sec (350 m/sec)

PP

1929. Blowback, double-action, hammer-fired automatic pistol. Safety catch on slide acts as de-cocking lever. Can be found in .22LR, 6.35mm, 7.65mm or 9mm Short calibres, the two smaller being uncommon.

Cartridge: 9 × 17mm Short
Length: 6.38in (162mm)
Weight: 1lb 9oz (710g)
Barrel: 3.35in (85mm), 6 grooves, rh
Magazine: 8-round box
Muzzle velocity: 950 ft/sec (289 m/sec)

PPK

1929. A smaller version of the PP, differing in the frame construction and using a wrap-around butt grip instead of separate plates. Usually with a finger-rest on the magazine.

Cartridge: 7.65 × 17SR Browning
Length: 5.83in (148mm)
Weight: 1lb 5oz (590g)
Barrel: 3.15in (80mm), 6 grooves, rh
Magazine: 7-round box
Muzzle velocity: 984 ft/sec (300 m/sec)

P38

1938. Recoil-operated, double-action, hammer-fired automatic pistol. Wedge locking, safety lever on slide drops hammer when applied and lifts firing pin out of alignment.

Cartridge: 9 × 19mm Parabellum
Length: 8.38in (213mm)
Weight: 2lb 2oz (960g)
Barrel: 5.0in (127mm), 6 grooves, rh
Magazine: 8-round box
Muzzle velocity: 1148 ft/sec (350 m/sec)

P1

1956. Postwar revival of the P38 for West Germany. Minor changes due to different manufacturing machinery.

Cartridge: 9 × 19mm Parabellum
Length: 8.56in (218mm)
Weight: 1lb 11oz (772g)
Barrel: 4.88in (124mm), 6 grooves, rh
Magazine: 8-round box
Muzzle velocity: 1148 ft/sec (350 m/sec)

P1A1

1988. Compact version of the P1. Same mechanism, but short barrel and all-enveloping slide. Automatic firing pin safety, de-cocking lever at top of left grip. Intended as the replacement for the P1 in German Army service but approval was withheld due to lack of funding and the project was dropped.

Cartridge: 9 × 19mm Parabellum
Length: 7.05in (179mm)
Weight: 1lb 12oz (808g)
Barrel: 3.54in (90mm), 6 grooves, rh
Magazine: 8-round box
Muzzle velocity: 1148 ft/sec (350 m/sec)

P5

1989. This appears to be the P1A1 completed by Walther as a private venture and offered for military use.

Cartridge: 9 × 19mm Parabellum
Length: 7.09in (180mm)
Weight: 2lb 3oz (795g)
Barrel: 3.54in (90mm), 6 grooves, rh
Magazine: 15-round box
Muzzle velocity: 1148 ft/sec (350 m/sec)

P5 Compact

Even more compact version. Same full-slide outline as the P5 but smaller.

Cartridge: 9 x 19mm Parabellum
Length: 6.61in (168mm)
Weight: 1lb 11oz (780g)
Barrel: 3.11in (79mm), 6 grooves, rh
Magazine: 8-round box
Muzzle velocity: 1148 ft/sec (350 m/sec)

P88

1988. Entirely new design using Browning cam locked breech. Full length slide with ejection port on top acting as the locking recess for the barrel. Double-action, with ambidextrous safety catch on frame acting as de-cocking lever. Stripping catch on frame above trigger.

Cartridge: 9 x 19mm Parabellum
Length: 7.36in (187mm)
Weight: 1lb 15oz (900g)
Barrel: 4.02in (102mm), 6 grooves, rh
Magazine: 15-round box
Muzzle velocity: 1181 ft/sec (360 m/sec)

P-88 Compact

1992. Replacement for the P88, different frame contour, safety catch/de-cocking lever moved to rear of the slide.

Cartridge: 9 x 19mm Parabellum
Length: 7.13in (181mm)
Weight: 1lb 13oz (822g)
Barrel: 3.81in (97mm), 6 grooves, rh
Magazine: 14- or 16-round box
Muzzle velocity: 1148 ft/sec (350 m/sec)

P99

1996. Recoil-operated, locked breech using Browning cam, internal hammer-fired automatic pistol. Synthetic frame, steel slide. Front of frame formed into rails for mounting laser or aiming spot. Automatic firing pin safety, de-cocking lever.

Cartridge: 9 x 19mm Parabellum
Length: 7.09in (180mm)
Weight: 1lb 5oz (600g)
Barrel: 4.02in (102mm), 6 grooves, rh
Magazine: 10- or 16-round box
Muzzle velocity: *ca* 1181 ft/sec (360 m/sec)

WEBLEY Britain
Webley

Pistol, Webley, Mark 1

1887. Hinged frame, self-extracting, double-action revolver. Birds-head butt with lanyard ring, stirrup lock in front of hammer to hold frame locked. Black Vulcanite grips.

Cartridge: .442 Revolver
Length: 10.25in (260mm)
Weight: 2lb 3oz (992g)
Barrel: 4.0in (102mm), 7 grooves, rh
Magazine: 6-round cylinder
Muzzle velocity: 698 ft/sec (213 m/sec)

Pistol, Webley, Mark 1*

1894. Mark 1 revolvers with the recoil shield (behind the cylinder) fitted into a dove-tailed slot in the standing breech so as to be more easily replaceable.

Specifications: as for Mark 1

Pistol, Webley, Mark 1**

1915. Conversion on repair of Mark 1 and 1* revolvers by fitting them with the Mark 4 barrel and Mark 5 cylinder.

Pistol, Webley, 6-inch Barrel, Mark 1*

1915. Conversion on repair of Marks 1 and 1* revolvers by fitting them with the 6-inch barrel of the Mark 5 or 6 revolver and the Mark 5 cylinder.

Pistol, Webley, Mark 2

1894. Differences from Mark 1 include the recoil shield, new hammer with larger spur, change in the butt shape.

Cartridge: .445 Webley Mk 1
Length: 9.25in (235mm)
Weight: 2lb 3oz (995g)
Barrel: 4.0in (102mm), 7 grooves, rh
Magazine: 6-round cylinder
Muzzle velocity: 705 ft/sec (215 m/sec)

Pistol, Webley, Mark 2*

1915. A quantity of Mark 2 pistols were repaired and fitted with Mark 4 hammers and were given this nomenclature.

Pistol, Webley, Mark 2**

1915. Conversion on repair of Mark 2 pistols by fitting a Mark 4 barrel and Mark 5 cylinder.

Pistol, Webley, 6-inch Barrel, Mark 2**

1915. Conversion on repair by fitting the 6-inch Mark 5 or 6 barrel and the Mark 5 cylinder.

Pistol, Webley, Mark 3

1897. Differs from previous models by having the cylinder axis pin forming part of the barrel forging and the addition of an automatic cam to operate the self-extracting mechanism. In 1905 numbers were fitted with 6-inch barrels for sale to officers.

Cartridge: .445 Webley Mk 1
Length: 9.49in (241mm)
Weight: 2lb 5oz (1050g)
Barrel: 4.0in (102mm), 7 grooves, rh
Magazine: 6-round cylinder
Muzzle velocity: 705 ft/sec (215 m/sec)

Pistol, Webley, Mark 4

1899. Differed from Mark 3 in using a different quality steel in the manufacture, improved trigger stop and cylinder slots, and the ratchet teeth of the extractor mechanism were case-hardened. The hammer was made lighter. As with the Mark 3, some were fitted with 6-inch barrels after 1905, for sale to officers.

Cartridge: .445 Webley Mk 1
Length: 9.25in (235mm)
Weight: 2lb 4oz (1020g)
Barrel: 4.0in (102mm), 7 grooves, rh
Magazine: 6-round cylinder
Muzzle velocity: 705 ft/sec (215 m/sec)

Pistol, Webley, Mark 5

1913. Differed from Mark 4 in having a larger-diameter cylinder radiussed on the rear edge, and the frame suitably modified to clear it.

Cartridge: .445 Webley Mk 2
Length: 9.25in (235mm)
Weight: 2lb 3oz (1005g)
Barrel: 4.0in (102mm), 7 grooves, rh
Magazine: 6-round cylinder
Muzzle velocity: 590 ft/sec (180 m/sec)

Pistol, Webley, w/6in Barrel, Mark 5

1915. Differs from Mark 5 in having a longer barrel with removable foresight blade and fixing screw

Pistol, Webley, Mark 6

1915. Differs from Mark 5 in having a longer barrel, square butt, removable foresight, 'and a number of internal components changed in minor respects, making them special to this pistol.'

Cartridge: .455 Webley Mk 6
Length: 11.25in (286mm)
Weight: 2lb 7oz (1090g)
Barrel: 6.0in (152mm), 7 grooves, rh
Magazine: 6-round cylinder
Muzzle velocity: 650 ft/sec (198 m/sec)

Pistol, Revolver, Webley, .38 Mark IV

Trade pattern, adopted 1942. Similar to the Enfield Pistol, Revolver, No 2 but had no sideplate, and therefore the trigger was fitted through a slot in the underside of the frame. The trigger guard was detachable and secured by two screws. The cylinder stop formed part of the trigger.

Cartridge: .380 British
Length: 10.50in (266mm)
Weight: 1lb 11oz (760g)
Barrel: 5.0in (127mm), 7 grooves, rh
Magazine: 6-round cylinder
Muzzle velocity: 600 ft/sec (183 m/sec)

WEBLEY-FOSBERY Britain
Webley

Model 1914.

Although not an officially-adopted weapon, many were used in the 1914–18 war. Automatic revolver, recoil-operated by the barrel/cylinder unit sliding across the frame to cock the hammer and revolve the cylinder by means of a pin in the frame running in zig-zag grooves in the cylinder. Based upon the contemporary Webley revolver and with a distinct family likeness.

Cartridge: .455 Webley Mk 2
Length: 10.51in (267mm)
Weight: 2lb 6oz (1075g)
Barrel: 6.0in (152mm), 7 grooves, rh
Magazine: 6-round cylinder
Muzzle velocity: 650 ft/sec (198 m/sec)

WEBLEY & SCOTT Britain
Webley

Name applied to automatic pistols manufactured by Webley & Scott, thus distinguishing them from the revolvers made by the same company which were simply called 'Webley'.

Pistol, Self-loading, Webley & Scott, .455in Mark 1

1913. Re-titled 'Pistol, &c, No 1 Mark 1' in 1915. Recoil-operated, hammer-fired automatic pistol. Characteristic square receiver, exposed barrel, butt almost at right-angles. Grip safety.

Cartridge: .455 Webley & Scott
Length: 8.50in (216mm)
Weight: 2lb 8oz (1134g)
Barrel: 5.0in (127mm), 6 grooves, rh
Magazine: 7-round box
Muzzle velocity: 738 ft/sec (225 m/sec)

Pistol, Self-loading, Webley & Scott, .455 No 2 Mark 1

1915. Differed from the No 1 Mark 1 in having a safety catch and no grip safety, minor improvements to bolt and hammer, and with the bottom of the butt formed to take a detachable butt-stock.

Specifications: as for No 1 Mk 1

Model 1909

Designed for commercial sale, adopted by the South African police in 1920. Similar to the Mark 1 model but the slide has a rounded top, and the wood grips are shaped to run forward close to the trigger guard. Manual safety.

Cartridge: 9 × 20SR Browning Long
Length: 8.0in (203mm)
Weight: 2lb 2oz (964g)
Barrel: 5.50in (140mm), 6 grooves, rh
Magazine: 8-round box
Muzzle velocity: 1115 ft/sec (340 m/sec)

Roumanian Model

1923. Similar to the M1909 but chambered for the 9mm Steyr cartridge. Grip safety.

Cartridge: 9 × 23mm Steyr
Length: 8.40in (213mm)
Weight: 2lb 4oz (1020g)
Barrel: 5.0in (127mm), 6 grooves, rh
Magazine: 8-round box
Muzzle velocity: 1184 ft/sec (361 m/sec)

WERDER (Germany)
Amberg

Werder Mod 1869 (Bavarian Lightning)

Single shot, dropping block operated by thumb lever above breech. Deep slab-sided receiver, round barrel with hexagonal reinforce. Wood butt grips.

Cartridge: 11.5 × 35R Werder
Length: 14.84in (377mm)
Weight: 3lb 10oz (1645g)
Barrel: 8.86in (225mm), 4 grooves, rh
Magazine: none
Muzzle velocity: ca 656 ft/sec (200 m/sec)

YOVANOVITCH Yugoslavia
Kragujevac

Model 1931
A blowback semi-automatic pistol designed by Yovanovitch and made by Voini Techniki Zavod, Kragujevac. Resembles the Browning 1910, but the slide is tapered and the bolt is a separate item, retained by a screwed cap at the rear end. There are serrated grips at the rear of the slide for cocking and loading. It has been said that this pistol was also made in 6.35mm and 7.65mm Browning calibres, but no specimen has ever been seen.

Cartridge: 9 × 17mm Short
Length: 7.25in (184mm)
Weight: 1lb 6oz (624g)
Barrel: 4.06in (103mm), 6 grooves, rh
Magazine: 8-round box
Muzzle velocity: 885 ft/sec (270 m/sec)

ZASTAVA Yugoslavia
General name for arms produced by the Yugoslavian national factory at Kragujevac. Originally built in the 1920s, it was known as Voini Techniki Zavod (Army Technical Factory) but after 1945 changed its name to Zavodi Crvena Zastava (roughly equivalent to 'National Arsenals') until 1990 when it was privatised and became 'Zastava Arms'. Its current name and condition is unknown.

Model M57
Recoil-operated, single-action, hammer-fired automatic pistol using a Browning cam lock. It is the Yugoslav-made version of the Soviet Tokarev TT-33 pistol.

Cartridge: 7.62 × 25mm Soviet Pistol
Length: 7.87in (200mm)
Weight: 1lb 15oz (900g)
Barrel: 4.57in (116mm), 4 grooves, rh
Magazine: 9-round box
Muzzle velocity: 1476 ft/sec (450 m/sec)

Models M70 & M70A
This is simply the M57 design done into 9mm Parabellum calibre and differs only in having 6-groove rifling and a muzzle velocity of 1082 ft/sec (330 m/sec.). The **M70A** is a variant which differs in having a slide-mounted safety catch which locks the firing pin.

Model M 70
Confusingly, this is a reduced-size version of the 9mm Parabellum M70, with the mechanism simplified to a blowback mode and chambered for the 7.65mm cartridge. It uses an external hammer and has a magazine safety.

Cartridge: 7.65 × 17SR Browning
Length: 6.50in (165mm)
Weight: 1lb 10oz (740g)
Barrel: 3.70in (94mm), 6 grooves, rh
Magazine: 8-round box
Muzzle velocity: 984 ft/sec (300 m/sec)

Model M70(k)
The same as the small Model 70 but chambered for the 9mm Short cartridge.

Specifications: as for the 7.65mm M70, except
Weight: 1lb 9oz
Muzzle velocity: 853 ft/sec (260 m/sec)

Model M88, M88A
A modernized version of the original M57/M70 design, with a completely different butt shape and a less angular outline, but the basic Browning link mechanism remains the same.

Cartridge: 9 × 19mm Parabellum
Length: 6.89in (175mm)
Weight: 1lb 11oz (780g)
Barrel: 3.78in (96mm), 6 grooves, rh
Magazine: 8-round box
Muzzle velocity: 1066 ft/sec (325 m/sec)

CZ-99
1992. This was announced in 1992, and appeared to be a close copy of the SIG P220. Few were made before political events overtook Zastava Arms, and the design was bought by an Israeli company.

See KSN, Golan

Model 1983 revolver
A conventional solid-frame, double-action, side-opening revolver broadly based on Smith & Wesson practice. Very deep frame below the hammer, ventilated rib on the barrel and a full-length shroud for the ejector rod under the barrel. Various barrel lengths available.

Cartridge: .357 Magnum
Length: 7.40in (188mm)
Weight: 1lb 15oz (900g)
Barrel: 4.01in (102mm), 6 grooves, rh
Magazine: 6-round cylinder
Muzzle velocity: 1148 ft/sec (350 m/sec)

COMPARATIVE TABLES

Weapons are arranged in ascending order of calibre, with automatic pistols covered first, then revolvers and single shot weapons. Overall lengths and barrel lengths are given in inches, weights in ounces and muzzle velocity in feet per second.

AUTOMATIC PISTOLS

Pistol	Date	Calibre	Length	Barrel	Weight	Magazine	Velocity
Russia: PSM	1975	5.45 × 18	6.30	3.35	19	8	961
FN Five-SeveN	1995	5.7 × 28	8.19	4.82	22	20	2133
Nambu Type B (Baby)	1909	7 × 20	6.73	3.27	21	7	1000
China: Type 54		7.62 × 25	7.68	4.53	31	8	1378
China: Type 80		7.62 × 25	11.81	7.28	39	10/20	1542
CZ vz/52	1952	7.62 × 25	8.23	4.72	34	8	1300
North Korea: Type 68	1953	7.62 × 25	7.28	4.25	28	8	1296
Tokarev TT-30	1930	7.62 × 25	7.68	4.50	29	8	1427
Tokarev TT-33	1933	7.62 × 25	7.72	4.57	30	8	1378
Zastava M57	1957	7.62 × 25	7.87	4.57	31	9	1476
Mannlicher 1901 & 1905	1901 & 05	7.63 × 21	9.65	6.10	32	8	1023
Astra Model 900	1927	7.63 × 25	12.48	5.51	49	10	1329
Astra Model 901	1928	7.63 × 25	11.42	5.51	44	10	1329
Astra Model 902	1929	7.63 × 25	12.48	7.08	54	20	1575
Astra Model 903	1932	7.63 × 25	12.13	6.30	45	10/20	1509
Astra Model 904	1933	7.63 × 25	12.13	6.30	45	10/20	1509
Mauser c/96	1896	7.63 × 25	11.02	4.72	40	10	1444
Mauser M/30	1930	7.63 × 25	11.57	5.55	42	10	1453
Mauser M712 Schnellfeuer	1931	7.63 × 25	11.25	5.27	43	10/20	1476
Royal M27	1927	7.63 × 25	11.61	5.50	46	10/20	1410
Royal MM31-1	1931	7.63 × 25	13.00	7.09	51	10	1624
Royal MM31-4	1933	7.63 × 25	11.42	5.51	48	10/20	1483
Royal MM34	1935	7.63 × 25	12.91	7.00	55	10/20	1624
Schwarzlose Standard	1898	7.63 × 25	10.75	6.42	33	7	1477
Super Azul	1933	7.63 × 25	11.42	5.51	50	10/20/30	1476
Astra Falcon	1956	7.65 × 17	6.46	3.88	24	8	870
Beholla	1915	7.65 × 17	5.50	2.88	22	7	860
Beretta 1931	1931	7.65 × 17	5.98	3.46	25	8	985
Beretta 1935	1935	7.65 × 17	5.83	3.35	26	8	985
Beretta 81	1976	7.65 × 17	6.77	3.82	24	12	984
Browning 1900	1900	7.65 × 17	6.75	4.00	22	7	950
Browning 1910	1910	7.65 × 17	6.00	3.50	21	7	925
Campo-Giro	1904	7.65 × 17	6.81	4.55	20	8	984
China Type 64		7.65 × 17	8.74	3.75	64	9	673
China Type 67		7.65 × 17	8.90	3.50	37	9	787
China Type 77		7.65 × 17	5.83	3.43	18	7	1043

Pistol	Date	Calibre	Length	Barrel	Weight	Magazine	Velocity
CZ vz/27	1927	7.65×17	6.25	3.82	25	8	920
CZ vz/50	1950	7.65×17	6.60	3.75	23	8	920
Dreyse	1907	7.65×17	6.30	3.66	25	7	985
Frommer Stop	1912	7.65×17	6.50	3.93	20	7	986
Frommer 37M	1940	7.65×17	7.20	4.33	27	7	985
Inagaki	1941	7.65×17	6.50	4.53	23	8	985
Mauser M1914	1914	7.65×17	6.00	3.45	21	8	984
Mauser HsC	1937	7.65×17	6.00	3.38	21	8	984
North Korea: Type 64	1950	7.65×17	6.73	4.01	22	7	951
Ruby	1915	7.65×17	6.06	3.46	28	9	984
Savage	1907	7.65×17	6.57	3.78	20	10	984
Savage	1915	7.65×17	7.00	3.78	24	10	984
Sauer M14	1914	7.65×17	5.70	2.95	20	7	918
Sauer M30	1930	7.65×17	5.75	3.03	22	7	918
Sauer 38H	1938	7.65×17	6.73	3.27	25	8	984
Walther Model 4	1912	7.65×17	6.00	3.35	19	6	984
Walther PPK	1929	7.65×17	5.83	3.15	21	7	984
Zastava M70		7.65×17	6.50	3.70	26	8	984
France: M1935A	1935	7.65×19.5	7.72	4.72	26	8	1100
France: M1935S	1938	7.65×19.5	7.40	4.21	27	8	1082
Luger: Swiss M1900	1900	7.65×19.5	9.33	4.72	31	8	1148
Luger: Swiss M1906	1906	7.65×19.5	9.21	4.65	31	8	1148
Luger: Swiss M06/29	1929	7.65×19.5	9.45	4.72	33	8	1200
Mannlicher M1903	1903	7.65×25	11.02	4.52	36	6	1020
Roth-Steyr M'07	1907	8×19	9.17	5.16	36	10	1050
Hamada 2	1942	8×21	6.97	3.74	26	6	1050
Nambu 4th Year	1915	8×21	8.98	4.72	31	8	1100
Nambu 14th Year	1925	8×21	8.94	4.76	32	8	1100
Type 94	1934	8×21	7.09	3.15	28	6	1000
Astra Model 300	1923	9×17	6.30	3.90	22	7	890
Beretta 1915	1915	9×17	5.90	3.30	20	8	875
Beretta 1922	1922	9×17	5.75	3.50	23	7	875
Beretta 1934	1934	9×17	5.90	3.40	24	7	804
Beretta 84	1976	9×17	6.77	3.82	23	13	918
Beretta 86	1985	9×17	7.28	4.37	23	8	1017
Browning 1910/22	1922	9×17	7.00	4.50	25	9	875
Browning BDA 380	1982	9×17	6.81	3.82	23	12	984
CZ vz/22	1922	9×17	6.00	3.54	22	8	984
CZ vz/24	1924	9×17	6.00	3.55	24	8	984
CZ vz/38	1938	9×17	7.70	4.72	32	8	1017
Frommer M29	1929	9×17	6.77	3.93	27	7	886
Frommer M37	1937	9×17	6.80	3.93	26	7	886
Glock 25	1995	9×17	6.85	4.01	20	15	885
Heckler & Koch P7K3		9×17	6.30	3.68	26	8	902
IMBEL 9mm MD1		9×17	7.56	4.09	33	7	886
IMBEL 9mm MD2		9×17	7.56	4.09	36	10	886
Walther PP	1929	9×17	6.38	3.35	25	8	950
Yovanovitch	1931	9×17	7.25	4.06	22	8	885
China: Type 59		9×18	6.38	3.78	26	8	1030
CZ vz/82	1982	9×18	6.77	3.78	28	12	1017

Pistol	Date	Calibre	Length	Barrel	Weight	Magazine	Velocity
Makarov PM	1950	9 × 18	6.30	3.58	23	8	1033
Poland: P-64	1964	9 × 18	6.10	3.30	22	6	1030
Poland: P-83	1983	9 × 18	6.49	3.54	25	8	1043
Poland: P-93	1993	9 × 18	7.0	3.93	26	8	1050
Stechkin	1955	9 × 18	8.86	5.50	36	20	1115
Aserma ADP Mk 2	1994	9 × 19	6.30	3.58	20	10/15	1115
Astra Model 600	1943	9 × 19	8.07	5.24	32	8	1181
Astra A-80	1980	9 × 19	7.09	3.80	35	15	1148
Astra A-90	1985	9 × 19	7.09	3.80	35	17	1148
Astra A-100	1990	9 × 19	7.09	3.80	35	17	1148
Beretta 1923	1923	9 × 19	7.0	3.50	28	7	1000
Beretta 1951	1951	9 × 19	8.00	4.50	31	8	1300
Beretta 1951R	1953	9 × 19	8.35	4.92	47	10	1312
Beretta 92	1976	9 × 19	8.54	4.92	33	15	1280
Beretta 92SB Compact	1978	9 × 19	7.76	4.29	32	13	1280
Beretta 93R	1978	9 × 19	9.45	6.14	40	15/20	1230
Bernardelli P-018	1980	9 × 19	8.38	4.80	39	14	1148
Browning 1935 High-Power	1935	9 × 19	7.75	4.72	35	13	1148
Browning High-Power Mk 3	1989	9 × 19	7.87	4.65	33	13	1148
Browning BDA 9	1990	9 × 19	7.87	4.66	32	14	1148
Browning BDAO	1992	9 × 19	7.87	4.66	31	14	1148
CZ 1975	1975	9 × 19	8.00	4.72	35	15	1300
Daewoo DP51	1990	9 × 19	7.48	4.13	28	10/13	1152
Dreyse	1912	9 × 19	8.12	5.00	37	8	1181
France: M1950	1950	9 × 19	7.64	4.37	34	9	1100
France: PA-MAS G-1	1992	9 × 19	8.54	4.92	34	15	1138
Glisenti M1910	1910	9 × 19	8.22	3.91	29	7	1050
Glock 17	1983	9 × 19	7.32	4.50	22	17	1263
Glock 17L	1985	9 × 19	8.86	6.02	24	17/19	1263
Glock 18C	1986	9 × 19	7.32	4.50	21	17/33	1115
Glock 19	1988	9 × 19	6.85	4.01	21	16/17	1148
Glock 26	1994	9 × 19	6.30	3.46	10	10	1115
Heckler & Koch VP70	1978	9 × 19	8.03	4.57	29	18	1181
Heckler & Koch P7M8	1979	9 × 19	6.73	4.13	28	8	1148
Heckler & Koch P7M13	1981	9 × 19	6.88	4.13	29	13	1148
Heckler & Koch P9S	1972	9 × 19	7.56	4.01	31	9	1148
Heckler & Koch USP	1993	9 × 19	7.64	4.25	26	15	1150
IMBEL M973	1973	9 × 19	8.38	5.04	36	8	1148
Jericho 941R	1991	9 × 19	8.15	4.41	39	16	1247
Jericho 941FS	1993	9 × 19	7.24	3.54	32	16	1083
KSN Golan	1994	9 × 19	6.69	3.86	29	15	1214
KSN Kareen Mk 2	1994	9 × 19	7.80	4.64	34	13/15	1246
KSN Kareen Mk 2 Compact	1995	9 × 19	6.02	3.86	32	13	1214
Lahti M35 (Finland)	1935	9 × 19	9.21	4.72	44	8	1148
Lahti M40 (Sweden)	1940	9 × 19	9.57	4.72	45	7	1275
Llama Model 11	1934	9 × 19	8.46	5.00	38	8	1181
Llama M-82	1983	9 × 19	8.25	4.49	39	15	1300
Luger Navy '04	1904	9 × 19	10.51	5.90	35	8	1132
Luger Army '08	1908	9 × 19	8.50	3.94	31	8	1100
Luger Long '08	1914	9 × 19	12.48	7.87	39	8	1230

Pistol	Date	Calibre	Length	Barrel	Weight	Magazine	Velocity
MAB PA-15	1960	9×19	8.00	4.49	38	15	1148
Mauser c/96/M16	1916	9×19	11.65	5.55	40	10	1181
Mauser M80	1988	9×19	8.00	4.64	32	14	1181
Mauser M90 Compact	1990	9×19	7.40	4.13	33	13	1148
Radom	1935	9×19	8.31	4.53	37	9	1150
SIG P-210	1948	9×19	8.46	4.72	31	8	1100
SIG-Sauer P-220		9×19	7.80	4.41	26	9	1132
SIG-Sauer P-225		9×19	7.09	3.86	26	8	1115
SIG-Sauer P-226	1980	9×19	7.72	4.41	31	15/20	1132
SIG-Sauer P-228	1988	9×19	7.09	3.86	29	13	1115
Star Super B	1946	9×19	8.74	5.12	36	8	1312
Star 28DA	1980	9×19	8.07	4.33	40	15	1246
Star 28P DA		9×19	7.60	3.86	38	15	1214
Star 28PK DA		9×19	7.60	3.86	30	15	1214
Star 30M	1988	9×19	8.07	4.69	40	15	1246
Star 30PK	1989	9×19	7.60	3.86	30	15	1214
Steyr GB	1980	9×19	8.54	5.35	30	18	1247
Steyr SPP	1988	9×19	12.68	5.12	45	15/30	1214
Tokagypt		9×19	7.64	4.49	33	7	1148
Uzi		9×19	9.45	4.53	58	20	1148
Vektor SP-1	1993	9×19	8.26	4.65	35	15	1181
Vektor Z-88	1988	9×19	8.54	4.92	35	15	1148
Walther Model 6	1915	9×19	8.25	4.75	34	8	1148
Walther P38	1938	9×19	8.38	5.00	34	8	1148
Walther P1	1956	9×19	8.56	4.88	27	8	1148
Walther P1A1	1988	9×19	7.05	3.54	28	8	1148
Walther P5	1989	9×19	7.09	3.54	35	15	1148
Walther P5 Compact		9×19	6.61	3.11	27	8	1148
Walther P88	1988	9×19	7.36	4.02	31	15	1181
Walther P88 Compact	1992	9×19	7.13	3.81	29	14/16	1148
Walther P99	1996	9×19	7.09	4.02	21	10/16	1181
Zastava M80		9×19	6.89	3.78	27	8	1066
Browning 1903	1903	9×20	8.00	5.00	32	7	1050
Le Français Military	1928	9×20	8.00	5.50	38	8	1000
Webley & Scott SA Police	1909	9×20	8.0	5.50	34	8	1115
Ascaso	1936	9×23	9.25	5.90	31	8	1181
Astra Model 400	1921	9×23	9.25	5.91	31	8	1181
Astra Model F	1933	9×23	13.00	7.09	54	10/20	1350
Bergmann-Bayard	1910	9×23	10.00	4.00	36	6/10	1300
Campo-Giro M1913	1913	9×23	9.33	6.46	35	8	1115
Campo-Giro M1913-16	1916	9×23	9.56	6.60	36	8	1115
Denmark: M1910	1921	9×23	10.00	4.00	36	6/10	1300
Steyr M1911	1911	9×23S	8.46	5.04	34	8	1185
Webley & Scott Roumanian	1923	9×23S	8.40	5.00	36	8	1184
SIG-Sauer P-239		.357 SIG	6.77	3.62	29	7	1345
IMBEL .38 Super MD1		.38 Sup	8.62	5.08	38	9	1280
IMBEL .38 Super MD2		.38 Sup	8.62	5.04	38	9	1280
Glock 20		10	7.59	4.60	28	15	1115
Daewoo DH40	1992	.40	7.48	4.21	35	10/12	1152
Glock 22		.40	7.32	4.66	23	13	984

Pistol	Date	Calibre	Length	Barrel	Weight	Magazine	Velocity
Glock 23		.40	6.85	4.01	21	13	968
Glock 24		.40	8.86	6.02	26	15	1017
Heckler & Koch USP	1993	.40	7.64	4.25	27	13	935
SIG-Sauer P-229	1991	.40	7.80	4.41	31	12	968
Ballester-Molina	1938	.45	9.00	5.00	40	7	860
Colt M1911/1911A1	1911	.45	8.50	5.00	40	7	860
Colt M15 General Officers'	1972	.45	7.90	4.17	36	7	800
Glock 21		.45	7.60	4.60	26	15	820
Heckler & Koch USP	1993	.45	7.87	4.41	30	10	885
Heckler & Koch Mk 23 Mod 0	1993	.45	9.65	5.87	42	12	885
Llama IX-C		.45	8.50	5.00	36	13	836
Obregon	1934	.45	8.50	5.00	40	7	860
Webley & Scott Mk 1	1913	.455	8.50	5.00	40	7	738

REVOLVERS & SINGLE SHOT PISTOLS

Pistol	Date	Calibre	Length	Barrel	Weight	Chambers	Velocity
Norway: Nagant	1887	7.5×22	9.21	4.45	28	6	738
Sweden: Nagant	1887	7.5×22	9.25	4.53	27	6	738
Sweden: Ordnance	1893	7.5×22	9.25	4.49	28	6	738
Switzerland: Ordnance	1882	7.5×23	8.98	4.53	29	6	725
Switzerland: Ordnance	1929	7.5×23	8.98	4.53	27	6	725
Russia: Nagant, Gas seal	1895	7.62×38	9.25	4.48	28	7	950
Austria: Rast & Gasser	1898	8×27	8.86	4.57	34	8	787
France: Mod d'Ordonnance	1892	8×27	9.33	4.61	30	6	720
Astra Police	1970	.357	8.35	3.03	37	6	1394
Manurhin MR73	1973	.357	9.17	4.0	33	6	1312
Zastava	1983	.357	7.40	4.01	31	6	1148
Colt Army Special	1908	.38	11.25	6.0	36	6	865
Colt New Navy	1889	.38	11.0	6.0	34	6	787
Enfield Pistol Rev No 2	1932	.38	10.24	5.0	27	6	673
FAMAE	1978	.38	7.13	2.5	25	6	935
Japan: New Nambu	1961	.38	7.76	3.03	24	5	722
S&W Military & Police	1905	.38	11.10	6.00	31	6	870
S&W Victory	1942	.38	8.46	4.00	30	6	745
S&W 38-200	1940	.38	10.20	5.00	32	6	600
Webley Mark 4	1942	.38	10.50	5.00	27	6	600
Denmark: Officers'	1880	9×17	9.09	4.41	28	6	656
Denmark: Officers'	1885	9×17	9.06	4.33	27	6	656
Denmark: Ronge	1891	9×17	10.23	5.39	31	6	656
Denmark: Troopers'	1882	9×17	10.23	5.51	32	6	690
FN Barracuda	1975	9×19	8.03	3.00	37	5	1115
Japan: 26th Year	1893	9×22	8.50	4.72	31	6	640
Norway: Nagant	1883	9×23	10.51	5.51	33	6	689
Belgian: Officers'	1878	9×23	10.63	5.51	33	6	650
Belgian: NCOs'	1883	9×23	10.86	5.51	34	6	650
Gasser-Kropatschek	1872	9×26	9.05	4.72	27	6	722
Portugal: Abadie	1878	9.1×17.5	8.58	4.45	27	6	558

Pistol	Date	Calibre	Length	Barrel	Weight	Chambers	Velocity
Portugal: Abadie	1886	9.35 × 17.5	9.84	5.59	30	6	531
Netherlands: Old Army	1873	9.4 × 20	11.14	6.34	45	6	590
Netherlands: KNIL	1897	9.4 × 20	8.74	4.45	29	6	557
Italy: Troopers'	1872	10.4 × 20	11.42	6.30	39	6	837
Italy: Bodeo	1889	10.4 × 20	9.25	4.53	34	6	836
Switzerland: M1872	1872	10.4 × 20	10.83	5.90	24	6	610
Switzerland: Troopers'	1878	10.4 × 20	9.25	4.57	26	6	610
Reichsrevolver: Troopers'	1879	10.6 × 24	12.20	7.20	36	6	673
Reichsrevolver: Officers'	1883	10.6 × 24	10.25	4.96	32	6	640
Belgium: Troopers'	1871	11 × 17.5	11.62	4.41	38	6	722
France: Navy, Mod. N	1870	11 × 17.5	9.41	4.76	37	6	820
France: MAS	1873	11 × 17.5	9.45	4.53	40	6	804
France: MAS, Officers'	1874	11 × 17.5	9.41	4.45	31	6	804
Sweden: Troopers'	1871	11 × 17.5	12.20	5.90	41	6	804
Sweden: Husqvarna	1884	11 × 17.5	9.45	4.53	37	6	787
Austria: Gasser	1870	11.3 × 35	12.6	6.85	48	6	690
Austria: Gasser	1874	11.3 × 35	14.76	9.25	53	6	755
Austria: Rast & Gasser	1870	11.3 × 35	14.76	9.25	51	5	787
Austria: Rast & Gasser	1874	11.3 × 35	12.79	7.28	34	5	770
Werder	1869	11.5 × 35	14.80	8.86	58	SS	656
Gasser, Montengrin Open Frame	1875	11.5 × 36	10.24	5.04	35	6	731
Gasser, Montengrin Solid frame	1875	11.5 × 36	14.70	9.13	52	6	804
Gasser, Montenegrin Hinge frame	1875	11.5 × 36	14.8	9.05	51	6	804
Smith & Wesson Army	1869	.44	13.38	8.0	41	6	650
Smith & Wesson Russian	1870	.44	12.0	6.50	40	6	771
Remington 1875 Army	1875	.44	12.0	7.50	44	6	660
Webley Mark I	1887	.442	10.25	4.00	35	6	698
Colt M1917	1917	.45	10.75	5.50	40	6	860
Colt New Service	1909	.45	10.75	5.50	40	6	853
Colt M1873	1873	.45	13.0	7.50	40	6	886
Liberator	**1942**	.45	5.55	3.97	16	SS	820
Smith & Wesson Schofield	1874	.45	12.40	7.0	40	6	771
Smith & Wesson M1917	1917	.45	10.78	5.50	36	6	860
Adams Conv'td Mk I	1868	450	11.62	5.63	38	6	650
Adams BL, Mk 2	1872	.450	11.18	6.0	38	6	650
Adams CF, Mk 3	1872	450	10.83	6.0	37	6	650
Dimancea	1888	.450	11.22	5.51	32	6	750
Enfield: BL, Mk I	1880	.455	11.45	5.87	40	6	673
Enfield: BL, Mk 2	1882	.455	11.45	5.87	41	6	688
Garate: Pistol O.P.	1915	.455	11.02	5.12	23	6	656
Smith & Wesson Triple Lock	1915	.455	11.73	6.50	38	6	656
Trocaola Pistol O.P	1915	.455	11.02	5.12	24	6	656
Webley Mark 2	1894	.455	9.25	4.00	35	6	705
Webley Mark 3	1897	.455	9.49	4.00	37	6	705
Webley Mark 4	1899	.455	9.25	4.00	36	6	705
Webley Mark 5	1913	.455	9.25	4.00	35	6	590
Webley Mark 6	1915	.455	11.25	6.00	39	6	650
Webley-Fosbery	1914	.455	10.51	6.00	38	6	650
Denmark: M1871/81	1881	12 × 15	10.12	5.03	34	6	787
France: Galand	1870	12 × 15	9.25	4.92	35	6	656

SUBMACHINE GUNS

All weapons in this section are blowback, selective fire, firing from an open bolt, unless otherwise described.

ADASA Spain
Adasa
1953. Designed by Vorgrimmler, made by Armamentos de Aviación SA of Madrid in small number for Spanish Air Force. One-piece pressed steel receiver and tapered perforated barrel jacket, metal stock folding beneath receiver, pistol grip. More or less based on the Soviet PPS-42 internally. Said to be capable of firing 9mm Parabellum or 9 x 23mm Largo without adjustment.

Cartridge: 9mm Parabellum or Largo
Length, butt extended: 32.0in (813mm)
Length, butt folded: 24in (610mm)
Weight: 7lb 0oz (3.17kg)
Barrel: 9.85in (250mm), 6 grooves, rh
Magazine: 30-round box
Muzzle velocity, 9mm Parabellum: 1200 ft/sec (365 m/sec)
Cyclic rate: 600 rds/min

AGRAM Croatia
RH-ALAN
1997– . Pressed steel and welded construction; tubular receiver which also forms a short slotted barrel jacket. Muzzle protrudes, threaded for silencer. No butt; pistol grip and trigger, magazine housing and a plastic forward handgrip resembling a thumb-hole rifle stock. Cocking handle on left side, ejection on right. Two models: the **Agram 2000** has two-range flip rear sight, **Agram 2002** has tangent leaf rear sight.

Cartridge: 9mm Parabellum
Length: 13.8in (350mm)
Weight: 4lb 3oz (1.9kg)
Barrel: 6.0in (152mm), 6 grooves, rh
Magazine: 20- or 32-round box
Muzzle velocity: ca1200 ft/sec (365 m/sec)
Cyclic rate: not known

AKABA Egypt
Maadi
Ca 1970. Simplified copy of the Carl Gustav. Uses the Carl Gustav receiver and mechanism, but with a plain barrel and no jacket, a shorter pistol grip, and a sliding wire folding stock. The rear sight is close to the rear end of the receiver, not ahead of the bolt slot as in the Carl Gustav.

Cartridge: 9mm Parabellum
Length, butt extended: 29.0in (737mm)
Length, butt folded: 19.0in (482mm)
Weight: not known
Barrel: 5.9in (150mm), 6 grooves, rh
Magazine: 36-round box
Muzzle velocity: ca 1250 ft/sec (380 m/sec)
Cyclic rate: 700 rds/min

ALFA GP-1 Brazil
IBRAP
Ca 1978–82. Tubular receiver over rectangular frame, two pistol grips, forward holding spare magazine, rear acting as magazine housing, and folding tubular butt. Prototypes and pre-production models for test, but no production.

Cartridge: 9mm Parabellum
Length, butt extended: 24.5in (620mm)
Length, butt folded: 16.5in (420mm)
Weight: 7lb 1oz (3.20kg)
Barrel: 9.0in (230mm), micro-grooved, rh
Magazine: 30-round box
Muzzle velocity: ca 1350 ft/sec (410 m/sec)
Cyclic rate: 550 rds/min

AMERICAN 180 USA
AI Corp, Voere & Western States
Designed 1958–60 by Casull and Eskelson in the USA, made as the **Casull Model 290 Carbine** by Western States Arms, Midvale, Utah 1965–66. Rights sold in 1969 to American International Corp, who licensed manufacture to Voere of Austria. It has re-appeared periodically from 1960

to 1990 but without achieving any major adoption. Blowback, drum feed, using .22 rimfire ammunition. Faintly reminiscent of the Thompson but with a Lewis-type drum and wooden furniture.

Cartridge: .22 Long Rifle RF
Length: 35.25in (895mm)
Weight: 5lb 12oz (2.60kg)
Barrel: 16.5in (419mm), 6 grooves, rh
Magazine: 177- or 290-round drum
Muzzle velocity: 1350/1650 ft/sec (410/503 m/sec)
Cyclic rate: 1200/1600 rds/min, depending on ammunition

ANDREWS Britain
BSA

1943. Designed by an Australian and manufactured in proto-type form by BSA, this was a Sten-type blowback weapon, but had the bolt supported by two rods which ran above and below the barrel and were retained at their front end by nuts. The pistol grip was simply a hollow steel tube and the butt was formed by the spare magazine. It was apparently considered awkward to hold, the receiver being rather fat, but on trials it performed better than the Sten Mark 4. Further trials eliminated the Andrews and various other contenders in favour of the Patchett (*qv*).

Cartridge: 9mm Parabellum
Weight: 6lb 3oz (2.80kg)
Length: 26.50in (673mm)
Barrel: 6.80in (172mm), 4 grooves, rh
Magazine: 30-round box
Muzzle velocity: 1180 ft/sec (360 m/sec)
Cyclic rate: 660 rds/min

ARAC Spain
SOFAM

Ca 1950–55, for converting M1898 Mauser rifles to selec-tive fire submachine guns. The barrel, stock and trigger assembly of the rifle were used, plus a new receiver and magazine housing, and a bolt based on that of the Erma MP40. Only made in small quantity.

Cartridge: 9mm Parabellum
Length: 34.75in (882mm)
Weight: 7lb 0oz (3.17kg)
Barrel: 11.85in (300mm), 6 grooves, rh
Magazine: 32-round box
Muzzle velocity: 1300 ft/sec (396 m/sec)
Cyclic rate: 600 rds/min

ARES USA
Ares

Compact weapon which folded into itself for carriage or concealment. Introduced in the mid-1980s, offered until early 1990s, no response and project abandoned. It was then copied by the Russians as the PP-90 (*qv*).

Cartridge: 9mm Parabellum
Length, folded: 10.3in (262mm)
Length, unfolded: 19.8in (503mm)
Weight, with full 20-round magazine: 5lb 4oz (2.38kg)
Barrel: 7.25in (184mm)
Magazine: 20- or 32-round box

Muzzle velocity: *ca* 1250 ft/sec (380 m/sec)
Cyclic rate: 650 rds/min

ARGENTINA
See also Hafdasa, Halcon & MEMS
FMK-3
FMAP

Ca 1986. Tubular receiver on rectangular frame, short exposed barrel, sliding wire butt, pistol grip/magazine housing.

Cartridge: 9mm Parabellum
Length, butt extended: 27.2in (690mm)
Length, butt closed: 20.5in (520mm)
Weight: 7lb 15oz (3.6kg)
Barrel: 11.4in (290mm), 6 grooves, rh
Magazine: 25- or 40-round box
Muzzle velocity: 1312 ft/sec (400 m/sec)
Cyclic rate: 600 rds/min

PA 3 DM
FMAP

Pistola Ametralladora 3, Domingo Matheu. Early nomen-clature for what eventually became known as the **FMK-3 Mod 2.**

PAM-1
FMAP

1952. Pistola Ametralladora M-1. A copy of the US M3A1 differing slightly in dimensions and in being produced only in 9mm Parabellum calibre. The **PAM-2**, introduced in 1960, was the same weapon but with the addition of a grip safety behind the magazine housing.

Cartridge: 9mm Parabellum
Length, butt extended: 28.54in (725mm)
Length, butt retracted: 21.06in (535mm)
Weight: 6lb 9oz (2.99kg)
Barrel: 7.87in (200mm), 6 grooves, rh
Magazine: 40-round box
Muzzle velocity: 1200 ft/sec (365 m/sec)
Cyclic rate: 450 rds/min

ARMAGUERRA Italy
Armaguerra

O.G.44

Ca 1944–48. Wood stock, sheet metal receiver. Bolt has an upper forward extension running in a tubular casing above the barrel. Less than 20 prototypes made.

Cartridge: 9mm Parabellum
Length: 31.0in (787mm)
Weight: 7lb 0oz (3.17kg)
Barrel: 11.5in (292mm), 6 grooves, rh
Magazine: 20- or 40-round box
Muzzle velocity: *ca* 1280 ft/sec (390 m/sec)
Cyclic rate: 500 rds/min

ARMS RESEARCH USA
Arms Research

KF-AMP

1985–88. The exact connection is not known, but the mechanical drawings of this weapon are identical with those of the Interdynamic MP-9 weapon, and it seems probable that the Interdynamic firm sold the design to Arms Research Associates. There are some minor changes in the final product; this weapon does not have a perforated barrel jacket, but has a longer amount of barrel exposed in front of the receiver; it has no front grip, the magazine in its housing serving for this purpose; and the skeleton butt of thin tubing folds round to lie along the left side of the receiver. Limited production.

Cartridge: 9 × 19mm Parabellum
Length, stock extended: 20.55in (603mm)
Length, stock folded: 12.48in (273mm)
Weight: 3lb 15oz (1.13kg)
Barrel: 5.0in (76.2mm), 6 grooves, rh
Magazine: 20-, 36-, 60- or 108-round box
Muzzle velocity: 1181 ft/sec (360 m/sec)
Cyclic rate: 800 rds/min

ARSENAL SHIPKA Bulgaria
Arsenal

1996. Tubular receiver, rectangular synthetic frame and pistol grip, folding wire butt. Magazine in front of trigger guard. Designed for export and available in 9mm Makarov or Parabellum chambering.

Cartridge: 9 × 18mm Makarov
Length, butt extended: 24.6in (625mm)
Length, butt folded: 13.3in (338mm)
Weight: 4lb 14oz (2.22kg)
Barrel: 5.9in (150mm), 4 grooves, rh
Magazine: 32-round box
Muzzle velocity: 1050 ft/sec (320 m/sec)
Cyclic rate: 700 rds/min

Cartridge: 9mm Parabellum
Length, butt extended: 28in (710mm)
Length, butt folded: 16.14in (410mm)
Weight: 5lb 5oz (2.41kg)
Barrel: 7.8in (200mm), 6 grooves, rh*
Magazine: 25-round box
Muzzle velocity: 1250 ft/sec (380 m/sec)
Cyclic rate: 700 rds/min

* A version with a 150mm barrel also available in this calibre

ATLANTIC Spain

Sales name for the Star TN-35 when offered for test in the USA in 1942.
See Star TN-35

AUSTEN Australia
Diecasters & Carmichael

'Australian Sten'. An amalgam of the Sten design with the bolt, telescoping mainspring housing and folding butt of the Erma MP40. Some 20,000 were made in Australia 1943–45.

Mark I

This had the barrel, barrel retaining collar and trigger mechanism frame of the Sten, with a forward grip and folding butt.

Cartridge: 9mm Parabellum
Length, butt extended: 33.25in (845mm)
Length, butt folded: 21.75in (552mm)
Weight: 8lb 12oz (3.97kg)
Barrel: 7.80in (198mm), 6 grooves, rh
Magazine: 28-round box
Muzzle velocity: 1200 ft/sec (366 m/sec)
Cyclic rate: 500 rds/min

Mark II

This was produced only in limited numbers in 1944–45 and differed principally in having a two-piece cast aluminium receiver and frame.

Cartridge: 9mm Parabellum
Specifications: as for Mk I, except
Weight: 8lb 8oz (3.85kg)

AUSTRALIA
See also **Austen & Owen**

F-1
Lithgow

1962. Locally developed design owing some features to the Owen and some to the Sterling. Cylindrical receiver with straight-line wood butt and perforated barrel jacket. Pistol grip, top-mounted curved magazine. Raised offset sights.

Cartridge: 9mm Parabellum
Length: 28.15in (715mm)
Weight: 7lb 3oz (3.26kg)
Barrel: 8.0in (203mm), 6 grooves, rh
Magazine: 34-round box
Muzzle velocity: 1250 ft/sec (381 m/sec)
Cyclic rate: 600 rds/min

BAKSAN Russia
IPME

1995. One-hand personal defence weapon, resembling an over-sized automatic pistol. Recoil-operated, locked breech, muzzle brake, folding single-strut butt, selective fire. Under development 1995– .

Cartridge: 9mm Parabellum or Makarov
Length, butt extended: 25.6in (650mm)
Length, butt folded: 18.9in (480mm)
Weight: 3lb 15oz (1.8kg)
Barrel: n/a
Magazine: 20-round box in pistol grip
Muzzle velocity, 9mm Para: *ca* 1250 ft/sec (380 m/sec)
Cyclic rate: 900 rds/min

BERETTA Italy
Beretta

Model 1918
Derived by fitting the barrel, receiver and mechanism of the Villar Perosa machine gun into a wooden stock, with new trigger mechanism, and adding a folding bayonet. Automatic fire only. Result looks like a rifle until the top-mounted magazine is fitted. Built 1918, designed by Marengoni. In service to 1945.

Cartridge: 9mm Parabellum
Length: 33.5in (851mm)
Weight: 7lb 3oz (3.26kg)
Barrel: 21.5in (318mm), 6 grooves, rh
Magazine: 25-round box
Muzzle velocity: *ca* 1250 ft/sec (380 m/sec).
Cyclic rate: 900 rds/min

Model 1938A
Wood stock, tubular receiver, slotted barrel jacket, bayonet. Produced 1938–48. Numerous minor variations in models supplied to different countries.

Cartridge: 9mm Parabellum
Length: 37.25in (946mm)
Weight: 9lb 4oz (4.19kg)
Barrel: 12.4in (315mm), 6 grooves, rh
Magazine: 10-, 20- or 40-round box
Muzzle velocity: 1378 ft/sec (420 m/sec)
Cyclic rate: 600 rds/min

Model 38/42
Wood furniture, tubular receiver, fluted barrel with two-slot compensator, two triggers. Designed by Marengoni in 1942, production 1943– *ca* 1950.

Cartridge: 9mm Parabellum
Length: 31.5in (800mm)
Weight: 7lb 3oz (3.26kg)
Barrel: 8.4in (214mm), 6 grooves, rh
Magazine: 20- or 40-round box
Muzzle velocity: *ca* 1250 ft/sec (380 m/sec)
Cyclic rate: 550 rds/min

Model 38/44
Simplified version of 38/42 with simpler bolt and mainspring. In production late 1945– *ca* 1953.

Specifications: as for 38/42

Model 38/49
Similar to 38/44 but with additional cross-bolt safety catch in the fore-end. Numerous minor variations for customer option. Sold widely 1949–62.

Specifications: as for 38/42

Model 1
Tubular receiver, fluted barrel with two-slot compensator and hooded foresight, alloy frame, wood grips and fore-end, folding butt of Erma MP40 type. Designed 1941 by Marengoni for Italian airborne troops, limited production.

Cartridge: 9mm Parabellum
Length, butt extended: 28in (711mm)
Length, butt folded: 20in (508mm)
Weight: 8.0lb (3.62kg)
Barrel: 7.8in (200mm), 6 grooves, rh
Magazine: 20- or 40-round box
Muzzle velocity: *ca* 1250 ft/sec (380 m/sec)
Cyclic rate: 550 rds/min

Model 3
All-metal design by Marengoni. Tubular receiver, pistol grip with grip safety, smooth barrel with two-slot compensator, sliding wire butt. May be found with folding bayonet. Production 1956– .

Cartridge: 9mm Parabellum
Length, butt extended: 28in (710mm)
Length, butt folded: 20in (508mm)
Weight: 7lb 10oz (3.47kg)
Barrel: 7.8in (200mm), 6 grooves, rh
Magazine: 20- or 40-round box
Muzzle velocity: *ca* 1250 ft/sec (380 m/sec)
Cyclic rate: 550 rds/min

Model 5
Similar to 38/49 but with a form of grip safety let into the finger-grooves in the fore-end. Production 1957–59.

Specifications: as for 38/42

Models 6 to 11
These were prototypes for the eventual Model 12 and came in a variety of shapes and sizes; they are unlikely to be encountered. All designed by Salza in 1952–57.

Model 12
All-metal except for wooden butt; also with side-folding metal butt. Tubular receiver, short exposed barrel, two pistol grips, magazine in front of trigger-guard, prominent front and rear caps on receiver. Production 1959– *ca* 1980 in Italy, but continues in Brazil and Indonesia under licence.

Cartridge: 9mm Parabellum
Length, fixed butt: 26in (660mm)
Length, metal butt extended: 25.4in (645mm)
Length, butt folded: 16.43in (417mm)
Weight: 6lb 9oz (3.0kg)
Weight, metal butt: 6lb 10oz (3.0kg)
Weight, wood butt: 7lb 8oz (3.40kg)
Barrel: 7.9in (200mm), 6 grooves, rh
Magazine: 20-, 32- or 40-round box
Muzzle velocity: *ca* 1250 ft/sec (380 m/sec)
Cyclic rate: 550 rds/min

Model 12S
Improved model 12 introduced *ca* 1983. New thumb-operated fire selector/safety catch and improved butt catch operation.

Cartridge: 9mm Parabellum
Length, wood butt: 26.0in (660mm)
Length, metal butt extended: 26.0in (660mm)
Length, metal butt folded: 16.45in (418mm)
Weight: 7lb 1oz (3.02kg)
Barrel: 7.8in (200mm), 6 grooves, rh
Magazine: 20-, 32- or 40-round box
Muzzle velocity: *ca* 1250 ft/sec (380 m/sec)
Cyclic rate: 550 rds/min

BERGMANN Germany
Bergmann, Junker & Ruh, Pieper & Walther

MP18
Bergmann

1916. The grandfather of all submachine guns and the weapon which more or less dictated design for the next 25 years. Recognisable by the perforated barrel jacket, wood stock and side-feeding snail magazine entering obliquely if original, or side-feeding box magazine feeding at right-angles if modified in 1920–23 for police use. No single-shot capability, full automatic fire only. Designed by Louis Schmeisser.

Cartridge: 9mm Parabellum
Length: 32.10in (815mm)
Weight: 9lb 3oz (4.17kg)
Barrel: 7.8in (200mm), 6 grooves, rh
Magazine: 32-round 'snail'; or 20- or 32-round box
Muzzle velocity: *ca* 1250 ft/sec (380 m/sec)
Cyclic rate: 400 rds/min

MP28
Bergmann & Pieper

Improved version of the MP18 with selective fire, new rear sight, improved firing pin and return spring. Made from 1929 onward, and under licence in Belgium.

Cartridge: 9mm Parabellum
Length: 32in (813mm)
Weight: 8lb 13oz (4.0kg)
Barrel: 7.8in (200mm), 6 grooves, rh
Magazine: 20-, 32- or 50-round box
Muzzle velocity: *ca* 1250 ft/sec (380 m/sec)
Cyclic rate: 500 rds/min

MP34
Walther

Similar in general outline to the MP28 but with slotted barrel jacket, a cocking handle like a rifle bolt at the rear of the receiver, and a magazine feeding from the right-hand side. Manufacture was contracted-out to Walther and about 2000 made.

Cartridge: 9mm Parabellum
Length: 33in (838mm)
Weight: 8lb 15oz (4.06kg)
Barrel: 7.8in (200mm), 6 grooves, rh
Magazine: 24- or 32-round box
Muzzle velocity: *ca* 1250 ft/sec (380 m/sec)
Cyclic rate: 650 rds/min

MP35/I
Junker & Ruh

Slightly modified form of the MP34; modifications to bolt and sear, buffer spring omitted, bolt safety fitted at rear of receiver. Manufacture contracted-out to Junker & Ruh on orders of the Waffen-SS, and about 40,000 made.

Specifications: as for MP34

BERNARDELLI Italy
Bernardelli

VB

Developed in 1947 for the postwar market. Resembles the Beretta 38/44 with wooden butt and tubular receiver but smooth barrel and five-slot compensator on muzzle. About 500 were made but it was not competitive with other designs and manufacture ceased in 1949.

Cartridge: 9mm Parabellum
Length: 32.7in (830mm)
Weight: 7lb 7oz (3.37kg)
Barrel: 11.8in (300mm), 6 grooves, rh
Magazine: 20- or 40-round box
Muzzle velocity: 1350 ft/sec (410 m/sec)
Cyclic rate: 600 rds/min

BISON Russia
Izmash

Ca 1990. Developed by V. Kalashnikov and bears some similarities to his father's famous rifle, *eg* the safety lever. Rectangular receiver and perforated fore-end covering barrel. Side-folding tubular butt. Helical magazine beneath barrel. Prototypes only, awaiting further development.

Cartridge: 9 mm Makarov
Length, butt extended: 26.0in (660mm)
Length, butt folded: 16.73in (425mm)
Weight: 4lb 10oz (2.10kg)
Barrel: n/a
Magazine: 64-round helical feed
Muzzle velocity: *ca* 1115 ft/sec (340 m/sec)
Cyclic rate: 700 rds/min

BLYSKAWICZA Poland

1943. Based upon the Sten Mark II, manufactured in Resistance workshops in Warsaw in 1943–44. It used a similar bolt/spring/receiver, but had the magazine housing fixed and feeding from below. The trigger section was set back and below the receiver and carried a folding metal butt which moved up and forward over the top of the receiver. The safety catch was inside the trigger guard and locked the trigger, and there was also a grip safety. About 700 guns were manufactured in seven workshops around Warsaw and all were used in the Warsaw Rising of 1944. Eight are known to survive.

Specifications: none available

BRONDBY M1933 Denmark
Maker not known

1933. Developed in Denmark in the early 1930s and submitted to the British Army for test in 1938. It was favourably reported on but nothing came of it. The weapon resembles a carbine, was gas operated with the gas cylinder above the barrel, fired from an open bolt but locked the breech before firing. It formed one member of a series of similar weapons, rifle, light machine gun and this 'machine carbine'.

Cartridge: 7.63mm Mauser
Length: 34.25in (870mm)
Weight: 5lb 2oz (2.32kg)
Barrel: 16.73in (425mm), 4 grooves, rh
Magazine: 15-round box
Muzzle velocity: *ca* 1650 ft/sec (500 m/sec)
Cyclic rate: 800 rds/min

BSA Britain
BSA
Developed in 1945 and submitted to the British Army but turned down in favour of the Patchett/Sterling. Had a prominent plastic fore-end which acted as cocking device; curved magazine on left, tubular receiver, pistol grip and folding two-strut butt.

Cartridge: 9mm Parabellum
Length, butt extended: 27.5in (698mm)
Weight: 5lb 10oz (2.54kg)
Barrel: 8.0in (203mm), 6 grooves, rh
Magazine: 32-round curved box
Muzzle velocity: *ca* 1300 ft/sec (396 m/sec)
Cyclic rate: 530 rds/min

BSA-KIRALY Britain
BSA
Designed by Kiraly of Hungary, engineered by BSA in England, submitted for trial May 1939. Wood rifle-type stock, long barrel with thin slotted jacket, tubular receiver, Used a two-part bolt for delayed blowback operation. Complex trigger mechanism to regulate rate of fire. Not adopted.

Cartridge: 9 x 25mm Mauser Export
Length: 38.75in 984mm)
Weight: 8lb 8oz (3.85kg)
Barrel: 16.125in (409mm), 6 grooves, rh
Magazine: 40 rounds
Muzzle velocity: 1480 ft/sec (450 m/sec)
Cyclic rate: 730 rds/min

BURMA
BA-52
Rangoon
Burmese manufacture, *ca* 1949–53, based upon the Italian TZ-45. Barrel jacket, tubular receiver, sliding wire stock, grip safety on magazine housing.

Cartridge: 9mm Parabellum
Length, butt extended: 32.00in (813mm)
Length, butt folded: 22in (559mm)
Weight: 6lb 12oz (3.06kg)
Barrel: 10.0in (254mm), 6 grooves, rh
Magazine: 40-round box
Muzzle velocity: 1377 ft/sec (420 m/sec)
Cyclic rate: 500 rds/min

BUSHMAN Britain
Bushman
One-hand 'Personal Defence Weapon' using an electronic rate regulating system. Offered in Britain in the 1980s without success, design then sold to the USA.

Cartridge: 9mm Parabellum
Length: 10.86in (276mm)
Weight: 6lb 7oz (2.92kg)
Barrel: 3.24in (82.5mm), 6 grooves, rh
Magazine: 20-, 28- or 32-round box
Muzzle velocity: *ca* 1155 ft/sec (352 m/sec)
Cyclic rate: 450 rds/min

BXP South Africa
Mechem
Ca 1984. Rectangular receiver, short barrel with perforated jacket, single-strut folding butt, may be fitted with collimating sight. Accessories include silencer, grenade launcher. Used by South African Army and Police.

Cartridge: 9mm Parabellum
Length, butt extended: 23.9in (607mm)
Length, butt folded: 15.24in (387mm)
Weight: 5lb 12oz (2.73kg)
Barrel: 8.18in (208mm), 6 grooves, rh
Magazine: 22- or 32-round box
Muzzle velocity: *ca* 1250 ft/sec (380 m/sec)
Cyclic rate: 800 rds/min

CANADA
C1
Long Branch
Based upon the Sterling, differing in having a 30-round magazine with conventional follower instead of rollers, and using the FN-FAL bayonet. Introduced 1958 and will probably be entirely replaced by the C8 carbine (*see* Rifles, Diemaco) by 2000.

Cartridge: 9mm Parabellum
Length, butt extended: 27in (686mm)
Length, butt folded: 19.4in (493mm)
Weight: 6lb 8oz (2.95kg)
Barrel: 7.79in (198mm), 6 grooves, rh
Magazine: 30-round curved box
Muzzle velocity: *ca* 1200 ft/sec (365 m/sec)
Cyclic rate: 550 rds/min

CARL GUSTAV Sweden
Carl Gustav

m/45 Series
Designed in 1944–45, produced until *ca* 1960; also made under licence in Egypt and Indonesia. Tubular receiver, tubular perforated barrel jacket, prominent foresight wings, squared-off pistol grip, tubular butt folding to the right side. Early models (**m/45**) used the 50-round Suomi magazine; later models (**m/45A**) had an add-on magazine housing to take a 36-round magazine, but which could be removed to permit use of the Suomi. From *ca* 1952 the magazine housing was a permanent fitting, the Suomi magazine was dropped, and the weapon became the **m/45B**.

Cartridge: 9mm Parabellum:
Length, butt extended: 31.8in (808mm)
Length, butt folded: 21.7in (552mm)
Weight: 7lb 14oz (3.59kg)
Barrel: 8.38in (213mm), 6 grooves, rh
Magazine: 36-round box
Muzzle velocity: 1345 ft/sec (410 m/sec)
Cyclic rate: 600 rds/min

CETME C-2 Spain
Santa Barbara
Developed by CETME in the later 1970s, not adopted by the Spanish Army, but remains available. Similar appear-

ance to the Sterling with perforated barrel jacket, tubular receiver and left side mounted straight magazine. Butt folds beneath weapon and forms a forward handgrip. An unusual feature is the dimensioning of the chamber so that this weapon can fire 9 x 19mm Parabellum or 9 x 23mm Largo ammunition interchangeably.

Cartridge: 9mm Parabellum or 9 x 23mm Largo
Length, butt extended: 28.35in (720mm)
Length, butt folded: 19.7in (500mm)
Weight: 6lb 5oz(2.87kg)
Barrel: 8.35in (212mm), 4 grooves, rh
Magazine: 32-round box
Muzzle velocity, Parabellum: 1066 ft/sec (325 m/sec)
Muzzle velocity, Largo: 1115 ft/sec (340 m/sec)
Cyclic rate: 600 rds/min

CEV Brazil
CEV

M9-M1
Developed *ca* 1982 onward but seems to be in a permanent state of final development. Tubular receiver and top-vented barrel jacket, plastic fore-end, folding stock, grip safety.

Cartridge: 9mm Parabellum
Length: n/a
Weight: 6lb 10oz (3.0kg)
Barrel: 9.0in (227mm), 6 grooves, rh
Magazine: 30-round box
Muzzle velocity: 1312 ft/sec (400 m/sec)
Cyclic rate: 600 rds/min

CHINA
State factories

Type 36
Copy of the US M3A1 (*qv*). Dimensions the same as the American original, but examples distinguishable by poorer quality and Chinese markings.

Type 43
Adopted during the Korean War this is simply a Chinese-made copy of the Russian PPS-43 design, to which reference should be made for dimensions etc.

Type 50
As with the Type 43, the Type 50 was adopted during the Korean War in the form of the Russian PPSh-41, after which copies were made in China from 1951 onward. Although a copy, there are some slight differences in construction, *eg* lighter wood furniture and a rubber bolt buffer.

Cartridge: 7.62mm Soviet Pistol
Length: 33.75in (867mm)
Weight: 8lb 0oz (3.63kg)
Barrel: 10.75in (273mm), 4 grooves, rh
Magazine: 35-round curved box
Muzzle velocity: 1400 ft/sec (426 m/sec)
Cyclic rate: 900 rds/min

Type 64 Silenced
This weapon used the bolt mechanism of the Type 43 (*above*) in a new receiver, and allied it to an integral silencer system. A fire selector was added. The silencer is the usual multi-baffle Maxim type. Rectangular receiver with curved top, curved magazine below, long tubular silencer/barrel assembly, pistol grip, folding butt.

Cartridge: 7.62mm Soviet Pistol
Length, butt extended: 33.2in (843mm)
Length, butt folded: 25in (635mm)
Weight: 7lb 8oz (3.5kg)
Barrel: 9.6in (244mm), 4 grooves, rh
Magazine: 30-round curved
Muzzle velocity: 980 ft/sec (298 m/sec)
Cyclic rate: 1000 rds/min

Type 79
Introduced in the early 1980s, this uses a gas tappet driving an operating rod to propel a bolt carrier and rotating bolt. This results in a very light weapon capable of selective fire. Rectangular receiver with Kalashnikov-type safety, pistol grip, long exposed barrel with short gas attachment in front of receiver, folding butt.

Cartridge: 7.62mm Soviet Pistol
Length, butt extended: 29.13in (740mm)
Length, butt folded: 18.5in (470mm)
Weight: 4lb 3oz (1.9kg)
Barrel: n/a
Magazine: 20-round box
Muzzle velocity: 1640 ft/sec (500 m/sec)
Cyclic rate: 650 rds/min

Type 85
Broadly resembles the Type 79 but is a much simpler blow-back design with a tubular receiver and folding butt.

Cartridge: 7.62mm Soviet Pistol
Length, butt extended: 24.72in (628mm)
Length, butt folded: 17.48in (444mm)
Weight: 4lb 3oz (1.9kg)
Barrel: n/a
Magazine: 30-round curved box
Muzzle velocity: 1640 ft/sec (500 m/sec)
Cyclic rate: 780 rds/min

Type 85 Silenced
This replaced the Type 64 Silenced (*above*) and is simply the same sort of weapon but using the receiver and bolt assembly of the Type 85 gun. There are some small detail differences in the silencer and the weapon is regulated to fire a sub-sonic cartridge, though it will still fire normal ammunition.

Cartridge: 7.62mm Soviet Pistol sub-sonic
Length, butt extended: 34.2in (869mm)
Length, butt folded: 16in (631mm)
Weight: 5lb 8oz (2.5kg)
Barrel: 9.80in (249mm), 4 grooves, rh
Magazine: 30-round curved box
Muzzle velocity: *ca* 985 ft/sec (300 m/sec)
Cyclic rate: 800 rds/min

COBRA USA
Ingram

Name applied to a variation of the Ingram M10 and M11 guns in which the receiver was of stamped metal, the bolt of stamped metal filled with lead, and similar cost- and labour-saving measures were employed. Development was done *ca* 1977 by Ingram but nothing went into production.

Specifications: as for the standard Ingram weapons, *which see*

COBRAY USA
SWD Inc

The Ingram M11 gun was manufactured under this name during the late-1970s/mid-1980s in two models: the **M11** in 9mm Short/.380 Auto calibre, and the **M11/9** in 9mm Parabellum. It is believed that very few were made.

COLT USA
Colt

Model 635

This Colt gun introduced in the early 1990s is simply a short M16 carbine in 9mm calibre with a blowback bolt system and a telescoping butt.

Cartridge: 9mm Parabellum
Length, butt extended: 28.75in (730mm)
Length, butt retracted: 25.6in (650mm)
Weight: 5lb 12oz (2.59kg)
Barrel: 10.50in (267mm), 6 grooves, rh
Magazine: 20- or 32-round box
Muzzle velocity: *ca* 1300 ft/sec (396 m/sec)
Cyclic rate: *ca* 900 rds/min

COOK USA
Maker not known

Ca 1950–60. Made entirely from steel tubes apart from the rectangular magazine housing which was also the pistol grip. The tubular receiver also formed the buttstock, and there was a forward handgrip. Prototypes only.

Cartridge: 9mm Parabellum or .45 ACP
Length: 23.28in (591mm)
Weight: 7lb 0oz (3.17kg)
Barrel: 9.5in (241mm), 6 grooves, rh
(US M3 for .45, Sten for 9mm)
Magazine: 30- or 32-round box
Muzzle velocity, .45: 920 ft/sec (280 m/sec)
Muzzle velocity, 9mm: 1200 ft/sec (380 m/sec)
Cyclic rate: 550 rds/min

CZ Czechoslovakia
CZ Brno

CZ 1938

Wood stock with short fore-end, long barrel with odd double magazine housing. Production began in 1938 and was curtailed by the German occupation and never resumed.

Cartridge: 9mm 17mm Short (.380 Auto)
Length: 31in (787mm)
Weight: 8lb 0oz (3.63kg)
Barrel: 8.5in (216mm), 6 grooves, rh
Magazine: 24-round box or 94-round drum

Muzzle velocity: 950 ft/sec (290 m/sec)
Cyclic rate: 600 rds/min

CZ 47

Produced 1947–48, sold in small numbers to South America. Similar to the CZ 1938 but with a more conventional magazine housing, the drum option having been abandoned.

Cartridge: 9mm Parabellum
Length: 30.85in (784mm)
Weight: 6lb 6oz (2.90kg)
Barrel: 7.80in (200mm), 6 grooves, rh
Magazine: 40-round box
Muzzle velocity: *ca* 1250 ft/sec (380 m/sec)
Cyclic rate: 560 rds/min

CZ 247 & CZ 347

The **CZ 247** was similar to the CZ 47 but with a bayonet lug. The **CZ 347** was an experimental design of the CZ 47 chambered for the 7.62mm Soviet Pistol cartridge.

CZ 23

Ca 1948. Tubular receiver and barrel housing, short exposed barrel, pistol grip forms magazine housing, separate fore-end. Notable for introducing the 'overhung' or 'telescoping' bolt which partly encloses the barrel when closed. Issued to Czech Army and later sold to Syria, Cuba and other countries.

Cartridge: 9mm Parabellum
Length: 27 in (685mm)
Weight: 6lb 13oz (3.08kg)
Barrel: 11.2in (284mm), 6 grooves, rh
Magazine: 24- or 40-round box
Muzzle velocity: 1250 ft/sec (380 m/sec)
Cyclic rate: 600 rds/min

CZ 24

As for the CZ 23, but chambered for the 7.62mm Soviet Pistol cartridge to conform with Warsaw Pact standardisation. In fact the Czechs developed their own cartridge of somewhat higher velocity than the Soviet original, which required some changes internally such as a heavier bolt.

Cartridge: 7.62mm Soviet Pistol
Length: 26.6in (676mm)
Weight: 7lb 4oz (3.28kg)
Barrel: 11.2in (284mm), 4 grooves, rh
Magazine: 32-round box
Muzzle velocity: *ca* 1800 ft/sec (548 m/sec)
Cyclic rate: 600 rds/min

CZ 25

Same weapon as the CZ 23 but with a folding metal buttstock.

Specifications: as for CZ 23, except
Length, butt folded: 17.5in (445mm)

CZ 26

Similar to the CZ 25 but for the 7.62mm Soviet Pistol cartridge, with similar changes to the CZ 24.

Cartridge: 7.62mm Soviet Pistol
Length, butt extended: 27in (686mm)
Length, butt folded: 17.5in (445mm)

Weight: 7lb 4oz (3.28kg)
Barrel: 11.20in (285mm), 4 grooves, rh
Magazine: 32-round box
Muzzle velocity: *ca* 1800 ft/sec (548 m/sec)
Cyclic rate: 600 rds/min

ZK 383

1933. A relic of the period when the submachine gun was still looking for a tactical role. Heavy, with wooden butt and fore-end, perforated barrel jacket, bipod, quick-change barrel, an insert in the bolt which could be removed to obtain a faster rate of fire, and a tangent sight graduated to 800 metres range. Used by Bulgaria 1938–63, by Germany 1938–45, and some South American countries.

Cartridge: 9mm Parabellum
Length: 35.43in (900mm)
Weight: 9lb 9oz (4.33kg)
Barrel: 12.79in (325mm), 6 grooves, rh
Magazine: 30-round box
Cyclic rate: 1250 ft/sec (381 m/sec)
Cyclic rate: 500 or 700 rds/min

ZK 383H

1946. Simplified version of the ZK 383 for possible adoption by Czech Army. Wood butt; ribbed wooden fore-end in front of trigger-guard, slotted barrel jacket. Magazine and housing fold forward to lie beneath the barrel. Dimensions probably similar to those of the ZK 383. Prototypes only.

ZK 383P

1939. Variant of the ZK 383 for police use. No bipod, and a simple two-range flip aperture sight. Dimensions as for ZK-383 but somewhat lighter.

DAEWOO South Korea
Daewoo

KIA

Ca 1988. A mini-assault rifle, this design is based on the Daewoo K2 rifle and is gas operated with a rotating bolt. It is simply a short-barrelled rifle with a single-strut folding stock and in addition to semi- and full-automatic fire offers three-round bursts.

Cartridge: 5.56 × 45mm
Length, butt extended: 33in (838mm)
Length, butt folded: 25.7in (653mm)
Weight: 6lb 5oz (2.87kg)
Barrel: 10.35in (263mm), 6 grooves, rh
Magazine: 20- or 30-round box
Muzzle velocity: 2690 ft/sec (820 m/sec)
Cyclic rate: *ca* 800 rds/min

DANUVIA Hungary
Danuvia

Model 39M

1938–39, first issued 1941. Full-stocked rifle style, bayonet lug, tubular receiver. Box magazine beneath folds forward into recess in stock fore-end. Delayed blowback using two-part bolt. A variant Model 39A had a side-folding butt, but few were made. Total production about 8000.

Cartridge: 9 × 25mm Mauser Export
Length: 41.25in (1047mm)
Weight: 8lb 3oz (3.72kg)
Barrel: 19.65in (500mm), 6 grooves, rh
Magazine: 40-round box
Muzzle velocity: 1525 ft/sec (465 m/sec)
Cyclic rate: 750 rds/min

Model 43M

Ca 1942, produced 1943–45. Essentially the 39M with shorter barrel, folding stock, pistol grip, and new magazine housing which cants the magazine to improve the feed angle.

Cartridge: 9 × 25mm Mauser Export
Length, butt extended: 37.5in 952mm)
Length, butt folded: 29.5in (750mm)
Weight: 8lb 0oz (3.63kg)
Barrel: 16.7in (424mm), 6 grooves, rh
Magazine: 40-round box
Muzzle velocity: 1450 ft/sec (442 m/sec)
Cyclic rate: 750 rds/min

DAUGS M44 Finland
Tikkakoski

A modification by W. Daugs of the Tikkakoski Arsenal, of the Russian PPS-43. Change of calibre and adapted to use Suomi magazines. Remained Finnish Army standard until the 1960s. Full automatic fire only.

Cartridge: 9mm Parabellum
Length, butt extended: 32.7in (830mm)
Length, butt folded: 24.45in (621mm)
Weight: 6lb 3oz (2.81kg)
Barrel: 9.84in (250mm), 4 or 6 grooves, rh
Magazine: 36- or 50-round box, or 71-round drum
Muzzle velocity: *ca* 1300 ft/sec (396 m/sec)
Cyclic rate: 650 rds/min

DEMRO USA
Demro

TAC-1

1974. Designed by Gerald Fox, this was originally called the Fox Carbine, but ran into legal problems since there was already a 'Fox' shotgun. About 100 weapons, mostly in semi-automatic form, were made by the Tri-C Corporation until its factory burned down in 1976. Fox then sold the patents to the Demro Corporation who produced it as the TAC-1, though the magazine housing still had the name 'Fox Carbine' cast into it. Slab-sided receiver, exposed barrel with muzzle compensator, wooden fore-end, magazine housing in front of trigger guard. Unusual in having a three-figure combination lock let into the receiver above the trigger as a very positive form of safety device. Removable wooden stock.

Cartridge: .45 ACP or 9 × 19mm Parabellum
Length, without stock: 19.37in (492mm)
Length, with stock fitted: 29.0in (717mm)
Weight: 7lb 12oz (3.51kg)
Barrel: 10.5in (266mm), 6 grooves, rh
Magazine: 30-round box (.45); 32- or 50-round box (9mm)
Muzzle velocity, .45: 935 ft/sec (295 m/sec)

Muzzle velocity, 9mm: 1250 ft/sec (380 m/sec)
Cyclic rate: 700 rds/min

DUX 53 Spain
Oviedo

A variant of the Daugs M44 which was developed by Daugs and others in Spain. One thousand were issued to the German Border Police in 1954 but no other major orders. Full automatic fire only.

Cartridge: 9mm Parabellum
Length, butt extended: 32.5in (826mm)
Length, butt folded: 24.25in (615mm)
Weight: 7lb 11oz (3.49kg)
Barrel: 9.84in (250mm), 6 grooves, rh
Magazine: 50-round Suomi box
Muzzle velocity: *ca* 1300 ft/sec (396 m/sec)
Cyclic rate: 500 rds/min

DUX 59 Germany
Anschütz

Developed by Anschütz, 1956–59, as an improved model of the DUX 53. Apart from a new curved magazine and moving the safety catch to above the left grip, changes were largely cosmetic. Perforated jacket now tubular instead of square. Few were made before the agreement between Daugs and Anschütz collapsed.

Cartridge: 9mm Parabellum
Length, butt extended: 31.2in (792mm)
Length, butt folded: 22.83in (580mm)
Weight: 6lb 10oz (3.0kg)
Barrel: 9.84in (250mm), 6 grooves, rh
Magazine: 32- or 40-round curved box
Muzzle velocity: 1300 ft/sec (396 m/sec)
Cyclic rate: 550 rds/min

EL SALVADOR
HB-1
Maker unknown

1958–60; prototypes only. Resembles the Beretta 38/44 with wood stock, perforated jacket and cross-bolt safety in the stock. Bayonet lug.

Cartridge: 9mm Parabellum
Length: 34.0in (850mm)
Weight: 8lb 4oz (3.74kg)
Barrel: 10in (254mm), 6 grooves, rh
Magazine: 30-round box
Muzzle velocity: 1300 ft/sec (396 m/sec)
Cyclic rate: 740 rds/min

ERMA Germany
Erma
MPE

1931. Wooden half-stock with unique hand-grip all in one piece. Cylindrical receiver, slotted barrel jacket, magazine feeds from the left side. First Erma design to use the Vollmer one-piece bolt and telescoping mainspring casing. The weapon was copied in Spain during World War II and chambered for the 9mm Largo cartridge.

Cartridge: 9mm Parabellum
Length: 35.04in (890mm)
Weight: 9lb 3oz (4.15kg)
Barrel: 9.84in (250mm), 6 grooves, rh
Magazine: 20- or 30-round box
Muzzle velocity: 1250 ft/sec (381 m/sec)
Cyclic rate: 500 rds/min

MP38

1936. A milestone weapon: the first to use a practical folding butt, the first to be made entirely of metal and plastics. Cylindrical machined steel receiver with longitudinal fluting to lighten it. Hexagonal barrel-retaining nut, hook-like wedge under the barrel for holding the barrel in a vehicle firing-port. Hooded front sight, plastic frame and pistol grip, tubular butt folds underneath the receiver. Magazine housing with large hole in it. Automatic fire only.

Cartridge: 9mm Parabellum
Length, butt extended: 32.75in (832mm)
Length, butt folded: 24.80in (630mm)
Weight: 9lb 0oz (4.14kg)
Barrel: 9.72in (247mm), 6 grooves, rh
Magazine: 32-round box
Muzzle velocity: 1250 ft/sec (381 m/sec)
Cyclic rate: 500 rds/min

MP40

1940. The MP38 re-engineered to make it easier and cheaper to produce. Can be distinguished from the MP38 by the smooth receiver and the solid magazine housing with strengthening flutes pressed in. Automatic fire only.

Cartridge: 9mm Parabellum
Length, butt extended: 32.80in (833mm)
Length, butt folded: 24.80in (630mm)
Weight: 8lb 14oz(4.03kg)
Barrel: 9.84in (250mm), 6 grooves, rh
Magazine: 32-round box
Muzzle velocity: 1250 ft/sec (381 m/sec)
Cyclic rate: 500 rds/min

EMP 44

1943. Made entirely of steel tubing, drawn and welded. Double magazine housing; slotted jacket; prominently raised sights. Prototypes only.

Cartridge: 9mm Parabellum
Length: 28.34in (720mm)
Weight: 8.0 lb (3.63kg)
Barrel: 9.84in (250mm), 6 grooves, rh
Magazine: 32-round MP38 box
Muzzle velocity: 1300 ft/sec (396 m/sec)
Cyclic rate: 500 rds/min

EMP 56

A 1956 design by Louis Camillis, a Frenchman. Some work was done by Erma, now in Dachau, but the financial backer withdrew and it became the **Mauser Model 57**, *which see.*

EMP 58

1958. Virtually a postwar improvement on the MP40, using the same Vollmer-designed telescoping spring casing and bolt. Butt folds over the top of the receiver. Exposed barrel.

Cartridge: 9mm Parabellum
Length, butt extended: 27.56in (700mm)
Length, butt folded: 18.11in (460mm)
Weight: 6lb 10oz (3.0kg)
Barrel: 6.49in (165mm), 6 grooves, rh
Magazine: 32-round MP38 box
Muzzle velocity: 1250 ft/sec (380 m/sec)
Cyclic rate: 700 rds/min

EMP 59

Germany; improved MP 58, limited production 1959 for German Army trials. Simplified construction, receiver and slotted jacket one piece, telescoping two-strut butt.

Cartridge: 9mm Parabellum
Length, butt extended: 28.75in (730mm)
Length, butt folded: 19.3in (490mm)
Weight: 7lb 1oz (3.20kg)
Barrel: 8.27in (210mm), 6 grooves, rh
Magazine: 30-round box
Muzzle velocity: 1250 ft/sec (380 m/sec)
Cyclic rate: 620 rds/min

EMP 60

Germany; even simpler development of the MP 58/59, for German Army trials 1960. Flat-sided stamped receiver/jacket, side-folding steel butt, angular appearance.

Cartridge: 9mm Parabellum
Length, butt extended: 31.1in (790mm)
Length, butt folded: 20.48in (520mm)
Weight: 7lb 5oz (3.30kg)
Barrel: 9.45in (240mm), 6 grooves, rh
Magazine: 36-round Carl Gustav box
Muzzle velocity: 1300 ft/sec (396 m/sec)
Cyclic rate: 500 rds/min

ERO Croatia
RH-ALAN

Ca 1994. A copy of the Israeli Uzi though slightly heavier at 7.87lb (3.57kg). The other dimensions and performance are the same as the Uzi (*qv*).
See also Mini ERO

FINLAND
See also Daugs, Jati-Matic, Pelo & Suomi

GG-95
GG

1997– . Name applied to the Jati-Matic submachine gun manufactured by the Golden Gun company of Turku, Finland.
See Jati-Matic

FN HERSTAL Belgium
FN

FN

Ca 1953–5. Wood butt, rifle-type trigger, tubular receiver, long barrel in perforated jacket with four-slot compensator. Limited production.

Cartridge: 9mm Parabellum
Length: 34.45in (875mm)

Weight: 8lb 3oz (3.72kg)
Barrel: 9.8in (250mm), 6 grooves, rh
Magazine: 40-round Beretta box
Muzzle velocity: 1310 ft/sec (400 m/sec)
Cyclic rate: 600 rds/min

FN P-90

'Personal Defence Weapon'. 1990– . Synthetic casing, built-in collimating sight, transparent magazine lies on top of receiver with rounds at 90° to barrel axis, feeds through a turntable; ejection downward through the grip. Fires from a closed bolt.

Cartridge: 5.7 x 28mm
Length: 19.68in (500mm)
Weight: 5lb 9oz (2.54kg)
Barrel: 10.35in (263mm), 8 grooves, rh
Magazine: 50-round box
Muzzle velocity: 2345 ft/sec (715 m/sec)
Cyclic rate: 900 rds/min

FNAB Italy
FNAB

1943. Machined receiver, perforated barrel jacket, muzzle compensator, pistol grip, single-strut folding buttstock on right side. About 7000 made. Selective fire, delayed blowback by two-part bolt, fires from closed bolt.

Cartridge: 9mm Parabellum
Length, butt extended: 31.1in (790mm)
Length, butt closed: 20.7in (526mm)
Weight: 7lb 1oz (3.20kg)
Barrel: 7.8in (200mm), 6 grooves, rh
Magazine: 20- or 40-round box
Muzzle velocity: 1250 ft/sec (380 m/sec)
Cyclic rate: 400 rds/min

FRANCHI Italy
Franchi

LF-57

1953. Rectangular receiver/jacket with barrel set low; perforations in jacket, short exposed muzzle. Pistol grip, side-folding butt. Used by Italian Navy in 1960–70 period.

Cartridge: 9mm Parabellum
Length, butt extended: 26.7in (680mm)
Length, butt closed: 16.5in (420mm)
Weight: 7lb 2oz (3.22kg)
Barrel: 8.1in (205mm), 6 grooves, rh
Magazine: 20- or 40-round box
Muzzle velocity:1260 ft/sec (384 m/sec)
Cyclic rate: 500 rds/min

FURRER Switzerland
Bern

MP41/44

Developed by Furrer at Bern Arsenal 1936–42; recoil-operated, used a form of toggle lock similar to that of the Luger pistol but laid on its side. Slotted barrel jacket, forward handgrip, pistol grip and wood butt. Notable swelling of the receiver on the left side to accommodate the action of the toggle. Highly expensive and difficult to make. Only 4800 made in three years.

Cartridge: 9mm Parabellum
Length: 30.5in (775mm)
Weight: 11lb 6oz (5.15kg)
Barrel: 9.8in (250mm), 6 grooves, rh
Magazine: 40-round box
Muzzle velocity: 1312 ft/sec (400 m/sec)
Cyclic rate: 900 rds/min

GERÄT POTSDAM Germany
Mauser

By Mauser, Oberndorf, 1944. An exact copy of the British Sten Mark II, even down to the inspector's and proof marks. It is virtually impossible to distinguish between this and a genuine Sten without very critical examination. 25,000 were made for use by the 'Werewolves' but most were issued to the German Army and used in NW Europe.

Specifications: exactly as for the Mark II Sten

GERMANY
See also **Bergmann, Dux, Erma, Gerät Potsdam, Haenel, Heckler & Koch, Mauser & Walther**

MP 3008
Mauser, Steiner, other unidentified

1944. German copy of the Sten gun, differing in using a fixed magazine housing with vertical feed, a wooden butt and a longer barrel. Several different makers and many minor variations between them.

Cartridge: 9mm Parabellum
Length: 31.50in (800mm)
Weight: 6lb 8oz (2.95kg)
Barrel: 7.72in (196mm), 6 or 8 grooves, rh
Magazine: 32-round box
Muzzle velocity: 1250 ft/sec (381 m/sec)
Cyclic rate: 500 rds/min

GEVARM France
Gevelot

D-3 and D-4

Ca 1955-60; by Gevelot branch of Société Française des Munitions. Tubular receiver, sweeping wooden butt, small frame and pistol grip, perforated and corrugated short jacket on long barrel.

Cartridge: 9mm Parabellum
Length: 31.2in (800mm)
Weight: 8lb 1oz (3.65kg)
Barrel: 12.6in (320mm), 6 grooves, rh
Magazine: 32-round box
Muzzle velocity: 1310 ft/sec (400 m/sec)
Cyclic rate: 600 rds/min

GREECE

EBO EMP5
EBO

Locally manufactured licensed copy of the Heckler & Koch MP5.

Specifications: as for the MP5

HAENEL Germany
Haenel

Haenel MP41

1941. A major variation of the MP40 (*see* Erma), in effect the receiver, barrel and magazine housing of the MP40 mounted into a wooden half-stock based on the Bergmann MP28 and with a Bergmann-type fire selector added to permit single shot firing. Developed by Hugo Schmeisser, manager of the Haenel works and the only variation of the MP38 or 40 which can properly be called 'Schmeisser'.

Cartridge: 9mm Parabellum
Length: 34.05in (865mm)
Weight: 8lb 2oz (3.70kg)
Barrel: 9.84in (250mm), 6 grooves, rh
Magazine: 32-round box
Muzzle velocity: 1250 ft/sec (381 m/sec)
Cyclic rate: 500 rds/min

HAFDASA C-4 Argentina
Hafdasa

Ca 1949. Marriage of the Sten receiver, barrel and magazine, with the folding stock and pistol grip of the MP40. Small quantity produced.

Cartridge: 9mm Parabellum
Length, butt extended: 31.2in (792mm)
Length, butt closed: 21in (533mm)
Weight: 7lb 0oz (3.17kg)
Barrel: 7.75in (197mm), 6 grooves, rh
Magazine: 30-round box
Muzzle velocity: 1200 ft/sec (365 m/sec)
Cyclic rate: 600 rds/min

HALCON Argentina
Halcon

M/943

Tubular receiver, long finned barrel with over-sized compensator, wood butt and pistol grip in one piece, prominent rear overhang of receiver. Used by Argentine Army and Police in mid-1940s.

Cartridge: .45 ACP (police), or 9mm Parabellum (army).
Length: 33.4in (850mm)
Weight: 10lb 7oz (4.63kg)
Barrel: 11.5in (292mm), 6 grooves, rh
Magazine: 17- or 30-round box
Muzzle velocity, .45ACP: 950 ft/sec 290 m/sec)
Cyclic rate: 700 rds/min

M/946

Improved M/943 by shortening barrel, smaller compensator, folding butt based on MP40, separate pistol grip. Used by Argentine Army and small numbers exported.

Cartridge: .45 ACP
Length: 31.1in (790mm)
Weight: 8lb 14oz (4.05kg)
Barrel: 6in (152mm), 6 grooves, rh
Magazine: 17- or 30-round box
Muzzle velocity: 920 ft/sec 280 m/sec)
Cyclic rate: 700 rds/min

ML-57

Ca 1957. M/946 of simplified all-metal construction, using separate firing pin and hammer. Side-folding stock. Single trigger and change lever.

Cartridge: 9mm Parabellum
Length, butt extended: 30.7in (780mm)
Length, butt folded: 21in (535mm)
Weight: 6lb 15oz (3.15kg)
Barrel: 8.86in (225mm), 6 grooves, rh
Magazine: 40-round box
Muzzle velocity: 120 ft/sec (365 m/sec)
Cyclic rate: 520 rds/min

ML-60

A later model, this had two triggers instead of a change lever, rear trigger giving automatic fire. Neither model went into production.

ML-63

1963. Cylindrical receiver with end cap, side cocking handle, tapered smooth barrel with muzzle brake. Front grip acts as magazine housing, well-raked pistol grip with two triggers giving auto or single shot fire. Usually with sliding wire butt, though wooden butt models have been noted.

Cartridge: 9mm Parabellum
Length, butt extended: 23.62in (690mm)
Length, butt closed: 19.68in (500mm)
Weight: 8lb 1oz (3.65kg)
Barrel: 6.69in (170mm), 6 grooves, rh
Magazine: 42-round box
Muzzle velocity: 1148 ft/sec (350 m/sec)
Cyclic rate: 600 rds/min

HECKLER & KOCH Germany
Heckler & Koch

HKMP5

Ca 1964. Pressed steel receiver/barrel jacket; plastic butt fitting over the end of the receiver (**MP5A2**) or metal sliding butt (**MP5A3**). Safety/fire selector switch above grip on left side. Cocking handle left side, in barrel jacket. Delayed blowback, delay by roller-locked breech; selective fire, later models also with three-round burst option, or two-round burst option from early 1990s. Fires from closed bolt.

MP5A2

Cartridge: 9mm Parabellum
Length: 26.7in (680mm)
Weight: 5lb 10oz (2.55kg)
Barrel: 8.86in (225mm), 6 grooves, rh
Magazine: 15- or 30-round curved box
Muzzle velocity: 1312 ft/sec (400 m/sec)
Cyclic rate: 800 rds/min

MP5A3

Cartridge: 9mm Parabellum
Length, butt extended: 26in (660mm)
Length, butt closed: 19.3in (490mm)
Weight: 5lb 10oz (2.55kg)
Barrel: 8.86in (225mm), 6 grooves, rh
Magazine: 15- or 30-round curved box
Muzzle velocity: 1312 ft/sec (400 m/sec)
Cyclic rate: 800 rds/min

MP5SD

Silenced version of the basic MP5; has fatter barrel jacket and extended silencer casing. Six variants as follows:

MP5SD1

Has receiver end cap and no butt-stock.

Cartridge: 9mm Parabellum
Length: 21.65in (550mm)
Weight: 6lb 3oz (2.8kg)
Barrel: 5.75in (146mm), 6 grooves, rh
Magazine: 15- or 30-round curved box
Muzzle velocity: 935 ft/sec (285 m/sec)
Cyclic rate: 800 rds/min

MP5SD2

Fixed butt-stock.

Length: 30.7in (780mm)
Weight: 6lb 13oz (3.1kg)

MP5SD3

Folding butt.

Length, butt extended: 30.7in (780mm)
Length, butt folded: 24in (610mm)
Weight: 7lb 8oz (3.4kg)

MP5SD4

As for MP5SD1, but with added three-round burst control.

MP5SD5

As for MP5SD2, but with added three-round burst control.

MP5SD6

As for MP5SD3, but with added three-round burst control.

MP5K

Compact version of the MP5 for police and counter-terrorism forces. Forward hand grip, no butt-stock. Four variant models as follows:

MP5K

Basic model, with iron sights, or telescope mount.

Cartridge: 9mm Parabellum
Length: 12.8in (325mm)
Weight: 4lb 6oz (2.0kg)
Barrel: 4.52in (115mm), 6 grooves, rh
Magazine: 15- or 30-round curved box
Muzzle velocity: 1230 ft/sec (375 m/sec)
Cyclic rate: 900 rds/min

MP5KA1

Smooth upper surface to avoid catching in clothing. Small sights.

MP5KA4

As for MP5K, but with three-round burst control.

MP5KA5

As for MP5KA1, but with three-round burst control.

MP5K-PDW

Developed by H&K USA for special forces etc. As for the MP5K but with a side-folding butt and three lugs on the barrel for attachment of a silencer or grenade launcher. The butt may be removed and replaced by a cap on the receiver. Optional two- or three-round burst facility.

Cartridge: 9mm Parabellum
Length, butt extended, suppressor fitted: 31.5in (800mm)
Length, butt closed: 14.48in (368mm)
Weight: 6lb 2oz (2.79kg)
Barrel: 5.5in (140mm), 6 grooves, rh
Magazine: 15- or 30-round curved box
Muzzle velocity: 1230 ft/sec (375 m/sec)
Cyclic rate: 900 rds/min

MP5/10

A 'product-improved' MP5 developed for the US law enforcement market. As for the MP5A2 or A3, but chambered for the 10mm Auto cartridge and with a carbon-fibre reinforced straight box magazine, and dual-magazine clamp allowing two magazines to be attached and rapidly switched into the firing position. Various sight and firing options, including two- or three-round bursts, may be fitted.

Cartridge: 10mm Auto
Length, fixed butt: 26.8in (680mm)
Length, butt extended: 26.0in (660mm)
Length, butt closed: 19.3in (490mm)
Weight, fixed butt: 5lb 14oz (2.67kg)
Weight, folding stock: 6lb 4oz (2.85kg)
Barrel: 8.86in (225mm), 6 grooves, rh
Magazine: 30-round straight box
Muzzle velocity: 1450 ft/sec (442 m/sec)
Cyclic rate: 800 rds/min

MP5/40

As for the MP5/10, but chambered for the .40 Smith & Wesson cartridge. Muzzle velocity *ca* 1150 ft/sec (350 m/sec), depending upon ammunition.

HK53

Although chambered for a rifle cartridge this weapon is widely used as a submachine gun by security forces. It generally resembles the MP5 but with a prominent exposed barrel and flash hider and a much deeper magazine. The weapon is available only with a metal two-strut sliding butt.

Cartridge: 5.56 × 45mm
Length, butt extended: 29.7in (755mm)
Length, butt closed: 22.1in (563mm)
Weight: 6lb 12oz (3.05kg)
Barrel: 8.3in (211mm), 6 grooves, rh
Magazine: 25-round curved box
Muzzle velocity: 2460 ft/sec (750 m/sec)
Cyclic rate: 700 rds/min

MP2000

1988. An unusual weapon for H&K, this was a pure blow-back design, hammer-fired from a closed bolt, and with a switchable gas vent on the chamber which could be opened when a suppressor was fitted, so as to drop the velocity to subsonic levels. Slab-sided receiver with fore-grip, tubular stock sliding in groove in the receiver, normal H&K pistol grip and selector switch, curved magazine. If fitted with suppressor, would have forward bolt lock for silent firing. Made in small numbers for evaluation in 1988–90 but never put into production.

Cartridge: 9 × 19mm Parabellum
Length, stock extended: 22.24in (565mm)

Length, stock folded: 15.24in (387mm)
Weight: 6lb 2oz (2.78kg)
Barrel: n/a
Magazine: 30-round box
Muzzle velocity: *ca* 1245 ft/sec (380 m/sec)
Cyclic rate: 880 rds/min

HISPANO-SUIZA Switzerland
Hispano

MP 43/44

1943. Actually the Finnish Suomi manufactured in Switzerland under licence when production of the Furrer MP41 lagged behind schedule. Differed from the Finnish model in having fitments for the Swiss bayonet and using a box magazine instead of the Suomi drum.

Cartridge: 9mm Parabellum
Length: 34.00in (863mm)
Weight: 10lb 8oz (4.79kg)
Barrel: 12.50in (318mm), 6 grooves, rh
Magazine: 50-round box
Muzzle velocity: 1300 ft/sec (396 m/sec)
Cyclic rate: 800 rds/min

HOTCHKISS France
Hotchkiss

Universal

1949. Complicated design in order to be compact; magazine folds, butt and pistol grip fold, barrel telescopes back into the receiver. Result was expensive and difficult to make, weapon was used in Indo-China and by Venezuela but no other sales. Ceased manufacture in the late 1950s.

Cartridge: 9mm Parabellum
Length, butt extended: 30.6in (775mm)
Length, butt closed: 21.2in (538mm)
Length, butt closed and barrel telescoped: 17.1in (435mm)
Weight: 7lb 8oz (3.4kg)
Barrel: 10.8in (270mm), 6 grooves, rh
Magazine: 32-round box
Muzzle velocity: 1312 ft/sec (400 m/sec)
Cyclic rate: 650 rds/min

HOVEA m/49 Denmark
København

1949. Similar to the Carl Gustav, developed by Husqvarna in competition for the Swedish Army. Denmark bought the rights and built it as the Hovea. Tubular receiver/barrel jacket, side-folding butt, two-prong magazine housing to take Suomi magazines.

Cartridge: 9mm Parabellum
Length, butt extended: 31.8in (808mm)
Length, butt closed: 21.6in (548mm)
Weight: 7lb 6oz (3.35kg)
Barrel: 8.46in (215mm), 4 or 6 grooves, rh
Magazine: 36-round box
Muzzle velocity: 1250 ft/sec (380 m/sec)
Cyclic rate: 600 rds/min

HUNGARY
See also Danuvia

KGP-9
Fegyvergyar

Ca 1990– . Rectangular receiver of steel plate and castings, side-folding butt, pistol grip, short exposed barrel retained by knurled nut. Barrel can be removed and replaced by longer (250mm) barrel if required. Large plastic fore-end. Curved cocking handle on top of receiver, offset to one side.

Cartridge: 9mm Parabellum
Length, butt extended: 24.2in (615mm)
Length, butt folded: 13.97in (355mm)
Weight: 6lb 1oz (2.75kg)
Barrel: 7.48in (190mm), 6 grooves, rh
Magazine: 25-round box
Muzzle velocity: 1280 ft/sec (390 m/sec)
Cyclic rate: 900 rds/min

M48
State factories
1948. An identical copy of the Russian PPSh-41.

HYDE USA
Marlin

Model 35

1935–40. Generally resembles the Thompson, with forward grip, finned barrel and Cutts Compensator, but with a tubular receiver and a rear cocking knob which oscillated during firing.

Cartridge: .45 ACP
Length: 35in (890mm)
Weight: 9lb 8oz (4.31kg)
Barrel: 11.25in (286mm), 7 grooves, rh
Magazine: 20-round box
Muzzle velocity: 920 ft/sec (280 m/sec)
Cyclic rate: 725 rds/min

HYDE-INLAND USA
Marlin

M2

1942. Designed by Hyde, developed by Inland Division of General Motors, made by Marlin Firearms Co. Full-stocked with exposed barrel and pistol grip. Approved as Substitute Standard as US Army M2 in April 1942. Production difficult, ceased after about 500 had been made and M3 had entered service.

Cartridge: .45 ACP
Length: 32.1in (825mm)
Weight: 9lb 4oz (4.19kg)
Barrel: 12.1in (307mm), 4 grooves, rh
Magazine: 20- or 30-round Thompson box
Muzzle velocity: 960 ft/sec (293 m/sec)
Cyclic rate: 500 rds/min

IMBEL Brazil
Imbel

MD-2

Ca 1980. Developed from an earlier attempt, the MD-1, this was an interesting concept: to adapt as many parts as possible of the FN-FAL rifle (already in manufacture in Brazil) and make a submachine gun out of them. Stock, receiver and pistol grip have a definite family relationship with the FAL rifle; there is a short fore-end with a thick jacketed barrel protruding. Large protecting wings around foresight.

Cartridge: 9mm Parabellum
Length: 30.31in (770mm)
Weight: 7lb 15oz (3.60kg)
Barrel: 8.70in (221mm), 4 grooves, rh
Magazine: 15- or 30-round box
Muzzle velocity: 1312 ft/sec (400 m/sec)
Cyclic rate: 700 rds/min

IMPERIA Belgium
Imperia

MI-53

1954. This was nothing more than the Mark 2 Sten with a re-designed frame and trigger mechanism housing, together with a pistol grip, and a sliding wire stock. Barrel, bolt, magazine housing and magazine, and receiver were all refurbished Sten parts. Produced for submission to the Belgian Army but was beaten to the post by the Vigneron; it appears to have been sold commercially for a short time in the mid-1950s.

Cartridge: 9mm Parabellum
Length, butt extended: 31.50in (800mm)
Length, butt closed: 20.10in (510mm)
Weight: 6lb 15oz (3.15kg)
Barrel: 8.0in (203mm), 4 grooves, rh
Magazine: 32-round curved box
Muzzle velocity: 1200 ft/sec (365 m/sec)
Cyclic rate: 600 rds/min

INA Brazil
INA

M/950

1950. A copy of the Madsen m/46 made under licence by the Indústria Nacional de Armas SA. Prominently marked with the Brazilian crest and 'EXÉRCITO BRASILEIRO'. A minor variant is the **m/953** which has a larger magazine housing with a wire clip around it and the cocking handle moved from the top of the receiver to the right-hand side. Full-automatic fire only.

Cartridge: .45 ACP
Length, butt extended: 31.25in (794mm)
Length, butt closed: 21.5in (546mm)
Weight: 7lb 8oz (3.4kg)
Barrel: 8.38in (213mm), 4 grooves, rh
Magazine: 30-round box
Muzzle velocity: 920 ft/sec (280 m/sec)
Cyclic rate: 650 rds/min

INDEP Portugal
INDEP

LUSA A1

1986. Receiver in a double-cylinder form with an overhung bolt moving in the upper portion and the barrel attached to the lower. Sliding wire butt, pistol grip. Two versions, one with fixed barrel with perforated jacket, the other with plain removable barrel.

Cartridge: 9mm Parabellum
Length, butt extended: 23.6in (600mm)
Length, butt closed: 17.5in (445mm)
Weight: 5lb 8oz (2.5kg)
Barrel: 6.3in (160mm), 6 grooves, rh
Magazine: 30-round box
Muzzle velocity: 1280 ft/sec (390 m/sec)
Cyclic rate: 900 rds/min

LUSA A2

1994. Improved A1; more substantial metal sliding butt, detachable barrel only, which can be replaced by integral barrel/silencer. Three-round burst facility added.

Cartridge: 9mm Parabellum
Length, butt extended: 23.0in (585mm)
Length, butt closed: 18.0in (458mm)
Weight: 6lb 3oz (2.85kg)
Barrel: 6.3in (160mm), 6 grooves, rh
Magazine: 30-round box
Muzzle velocity: 1280 ft/sec (390 m/sec)
Cyclic rate: 900 rds/min

INDONESIA

PM Model 7
PSM

1957. A locally-designed weapon. Cylindrical steel receiver, perforated barrel jacket, muzzle compensator, pistol grip, sliding wire stock. Large magazine housing acting as fore grip. Hinged cover on the ejection port locks the bolt in place when closed. Automatic fire only.

Cartridge: 9mm Parabellum
Length, butt extended: 33.07in (840mm)
Length, butt retracted: 21.26in (540mm)
Weight: 7lb 4oz (3.29kg)
Barrel: 10.78in (274mm), 6 grooves, rh
Magazine: 33-round box
Muzzle velocity: 1250 ft/sec (381 m/sec)
Cyclic rate: 600 rds/min

INGRAM USA

Model 6
POC

1949–52. Cylindrical receiver, wooden butt and pistol grip, and separate wooden fore-end in front of magazine housing and supporting the barrel. Some had a wooden hand-grip similar to the Thompson M1928 beneath the barrel instead of the fore-end. Available in 9mm Parabellum, .38 Super and .45 calibres.

Cartridge: .45 ACP
Length: 30.0in (762mm)
Weight: 7lb 4oz (3.29kg)

Barrel: 9.0in (228mm), 6 grooves, rh
Magazine: 30-round box
Muzzle velocity: 920 ft/sec (280 m/sec)
Cyclic rate: 600 rds/min

M10
Ingram

1964– *ca* 1985. Compact rectangular receiver with short exposed barrel, sliding wire butt, magazine in pistol grip. Barrel threaded for silencer. Possibly 16,000 Ingrams of all types were made and distributed in small parcels over several countries. Manufacture by several companies at various times, most of which went into liquidation.

Cartridge: 9mm Parabellum
Length, butt extended: 22in (559mm)
Length, butt closed: 11.73in (298mm)
Weight: 6lb 0oz (2.72kg)
Barrel: 5.75in (146mm), 6 grooves, rh
Magazine: 32-round box
Muzzle velocity: 1200 ft/sec (380 m/sec)
Cyclic rate: 1050 rds/min

The M10 is also available in .45 ACP calibre.

Dimensions: same
Magazine: 30-round box
Muzzle velocity: 920 ft/sec (280 m/sec)
Cyclic rate: 1145 rds/min

M11
RPB

Ca 1970–85. As for the M10 but slightly smaller, being chambered for the 9mm Short (.380 Auto) cartridge. A compact and handy weapon, but few seem to have been sold.

Cartridge: 9 × 17mm Short
Length, butt extended: 18.1in (460mm)
Length, butt closed: 9.76in (248mm)
Weight: 3lb 8oz (1.59kg)
Barrel: 5.08in (129mm), 6 grooves, rh
Magazine: 16- or 32-round box
Muzzle velocity: 961 ft/sec (293 m/sec)
Cyclic rate: 1200 rds/min

INTERDYNAMIC USA
Interdynamic

MP-9

1985–88. Very compact weapon derived from a semi-automatic 'tactical pistol'. Cylindrical receiver and perforated barrel jacket; forward hand grip beneath jacket; pistol grip at rear of receiver, magazine in front of trigger guard. Stub of muzzle exposed. Sliding wire butt like US M3.

Cartridge: 9 × 19mm Parabellum
Length, stock extended: 20.55in (522mm)
Length, stock folded: 12.48in (317mm)
Weight: 3lb 15oz (1.80kg)
Barrel: 5.0in (127mm), 6 grooves, rh
Magazine: 36-round box
Muzzle velocity: 1245 ft/sec (380 m/sec)
Cyclic rate: 900 rds/min

IOG USA
MP2
RPB
1980. Tubular receiver, foregrip beneath sight, large compensator, pistol grip/magazine housing. No butt. Trigger and grip safety control fire selection; press grip safety then trigger for automatic, press trigger then grip safety for single shots. 100 guns made 1980 but no known production thereafter and company probably folded by 1985.

Cartridge: 9mm Parabellum
Length: 13.25in (337mm)
Weight: 4lb 0oz (1.81kg)
Barrel: n/a
Magazine: 18- or 32-round box
Muzzle velocity: 1085 ft/sec (330 m/sec)
Cyclic rate: 750 rds/min

IRAN
Persia
Model 22
1943. The Model 22 is simply a better-finished copy of the Soviet PPSh-41, made with Soviet licence and assistance from 1943 to some time in the 1950s. Prior to 1945 the weapon was in 7.62mm calibre; some time in the late 1940s the design was re-worked to 9mm Parabellum and weapons later issued to the Iranian Army were 9mm calibre.

Cartridge: 7.62 × 25mm Soviet Pistol or 9mm Parabellum
Length: 33.19in (843mm)
Weight: 8lb 4oz (3.75kg)
Barrel: 10.55in (268mm), 4 grooves, rh
Magazine: 35-round box
Muzzle velocity, 7.62mm: 1500 ft/sec (457 m/sec)
Cyclic rate: 900 rds/min

ITALY
See also Armaguerra, Beretta, Bernardelli, FNAB, Franchi, Lercker, OVP, Revelli, Socimi, Spectre & Villar Perosa

TZ-45
Maker unknown
1945. Cylindrical receiver, pistol grip, sliding wire stock of unusual length. Forward magazine housing with grip safety. Flimsy barrel jacket, slotted muzzle compensator. About 6000 made.

Cartridge: 9mm Parabellum
Length, butt extended: 33.46in (850mm)
Length, butt retracted: 21.46in (545mm)
Weight: 7lb 3oz (3.26kg)
Barrel: 9.05in (230mm), 6 grooves, rh
Magazine: 20- or 40-round box
Muzzle velocity: 1198 ft/sec (365 m/sec)
Cyclic rate: 550 rds/min

JAPAN
Type 100/40
Kokura & Nagoya
1940–43. Wooden half-stock, tubular receiver, perforated barrel jacket with large bayonet bar beneath, muzzle compensator. About 10,000 made in Kokura Arsenal, plus about 6,000 of a folding-stock variant at Nagoya Arsenal. Reported as unreliable because of weak ammunition.

Cartridge: 8 × 21mm Nambu
Length, fixed butt: 36in (914mm)
Length, butt extended: 34in (864mm)
Length, butt closed: 22.25in (565mm)
Weight: 7lb 8oz (3.40kg)
Barrel: 9.0in (228mm), 6 grooves, rh
Magazine: 30-round box
Muzzle velocity: 1100 ft/sec (335 m/sec)
Cyclic rate: 450 rds/min

Type 100/44
Nagoya
1944–45. Similar to wooden butt 100/40 model but simplified manufacture, no bayonet bar, longer and thinner compensator, faster firing. About 8000 made at Nagoya Arsenal.

Cartridge: 8 × 21mm Nambu
Length: 36in (914mm)
Weight: 8lb 8oz (3.86kg)
Barrel: 9.20in (234mm), 6 grooves, rh
Magazine: 30-round box
Muzzle velocity: 1100 ft/sec (335 m/sec)
Cyclic rate: 800 rds/min

JATI-MATIC Finland
Tampereen
Ca 1985. Bolt recoils up an inclined plane to slow its action and improve stability. Pressed steel receiver appears to be at an angle to the barrel; pistol grip with magazine housing in front. No butt, forward hand grip folds under receiver. Design licensed to China in the 1980s but not followed up and has reverted to a Finnish coy. (*see* Finland, GG-95).

Cartridge: 9mm Parabellum
Length: 14.76in (375mm)
Weight: 4lb 5oz (1.95kg)
Barrel: 8.0in (203mm), 6 grooves, rh
Magazine: 20- or 40-round box
Muzzle velocity: 1181 ft/sec (360 m/sec)
Cyclic rate: 650 rds/min

KALASHNIKOV
See Rifles

KEDR Russia
Klin
Developed in early 1970s to replace the Stechkin machine pistol. Rectangular pressed steel receiver, exposed barrel, pistol grip, butt folds over the receiver. Various accessories – silencer, flash suppressor, laser spot – developed.

Cartridge: 9 × 18mm Makarov
Length, butt extended: 21.25in (540mm)
Length, butt folded: 11.8in (300mm)
Weight: 3lb 1oz (1.40kg)
Barrel: 4.7in (120mm) 4 grooves, rh
Magazine: 20- or 30-round box
Muzzle velocity: ca 1117 ft/sec (310 m/sec)
Cyclic rate: 850 rds/min

KIPARIS Kazakhstan
Uralsk

1997– . Pressed steel rectangular receiver with composite pistol grip and steel butt folding over receiver. Exposed barrel with knurled retaining nut, threaded for silencer.

Cartridge: 9 × 18mm Makarov
Length, butt extended: 23.2in (590mm)
Length, butt folded: 12.52in (318mm)
Weight: 3lb 7oz (1.57kg)
Barrel: n/a
Magazine: 20- or 30-round box
Muzzle velocity: 1100 ft/sec (335 m/sec)
Cyclic rate: 900 rds/min

KLIN Russia
Klin

The KLIN is a KEDR (*described above*) optimised to fire the hotted-up 9mm 57-N Makarov cartridge, presumably by fitting a stiffer return spring and/or buffer. It appears that a small number were made in 1994 to prove the concept, but no production has taken place since then.

Cartridge: 9mm 57-N-181SM
Length, butt extended: 21.25in (540mm)
Length, butt folded: 12.07in (305mm)
Weight: 3lb 1oz (1.41kg)
Barrel: 4.7in (120mm), 4 grooves, rh
Magazine: 20- or 30-round box
Muzzle velocity: *ca* 1410 ft/sec (430 m/sec)
Cyclic rate: *ca* 1100 rds/min

KOVROV Russia
Kovrov

AEK 919

1997– . Rectangular steel receiver in polymer frame with pistol grip. Sliding butt. Exposed barrel retained by knurled nut. Magazine in pistol grip.

Cartridge: 9 × 18mm Makarov
Length, butt extended: 19.5in (495mm)
Length, butt folded: 12.8in (325mm)
Weight: 3lb 10oz (1.65kg)
Barrel: 8.85in (225mm), 4 grooves, rh
Magazine: 20- or 30-round box
Muzzle velocity: 1115 ft/sec (330 m/sec)
Cyclic rate: n/a

LABORA Spain
Cataluña

1938. Wood butt, pistol grip, machined steel tubular receiver, barrel with broad cooling rings, prominent front sight, sling swivel beneath muzzle. Receiver closed by large knurled cap. Believed not more than 5,000 were ever made.

Cartridge: 9 × 23mm Largo
Length: 31.75in (806mm)
Weight: 9lb 6oz (4.26kg)
Barrel: 10.25in (260mm), 4 grooves, rh
Magazine: 36-round box
Muzzle velocity: 1312 ft/sec (400 m/sec)
Cyclic rate: 750 rds/min

LA CORUÑA Spain
La Coruña

Ca 1960. Name under which the Rexim Favor Mark 4 submachine gun was offered for sale by the La Coruña Arsenal of Spain.
See Rexim Favor

LA FRANCE USA
La France

M16K

1996. Based on the M16 rifle and of similar appearance but with a cylindrical fore-end/handguard to the muzzle, with a pronged flash-hider. Magazine housing altered to take a thin straight magazine. Fixed butt, carrying handle with rear sight, high-set front sight.

Cartridge: .45 ACP
Length: 26.61in (676mm)
Weight: 8lb 8oz (3.86kg)
Barrel: 7.24in (184mm), 6 grooves, rh
Magazine: 30-round box
Muzzle velocity: 853 ft/sec (260 m/sec)
Cyclic rate: 625 rds/min

LANCHESTER Britain
Sterling

1941. Copy of the Bergmann MP28 but with stock based on the Lee-Enfield rifle stock, bayonet attachments for Lee-Enfield sword bayonet, changed method of opening the receiver, and highly-polished brass magazine housing. Use confined to Royal Navy. A **Mark 1★** variant removed the fire selector and permitted only automatic fire, and most Mark 1 guns were converted to this form during their life. It remained in naval service until the early 1960s.

Cartridge: 9mm Parabellum
Length: 33.5in (851mm)
Weight: 9lb 10oz (4.37kg)
Barrel: 7.90in (200mm), 6 grooves, rh
Magazine: 50-round box
Muzzle velocity: 1200 ft/sec (365 m/sec)
Cyclic rate: 600 rds/min

LERCKER Italy
Maker unknown

Ca 1950. One-hand machine pistol. Resembles an ordinary blowback pistol with tubular receiver and barrel secured by knurled nut. Selector switch on left side. Cocking knob at rear, fires from open bolt. About 100 made.

Cartridge: 6.35 × 16mm Auto Pistol
Length: 7.25in (184mm)
Weight: 2lb 1oz (0.95kg)
Barrel: 4.0in (102mm), 6 grooves, rh
Magazine: 20-round box
Muzzle velocity: 820 ft/sec (250 m/sec)
Cyclic rate: 1000 rds/min

MADSEN Denmark
Madsen

m/45

1945. Wooden half-stock with handgrip notch in the underside of the fore-end, or wooden fore-end with folding metal butt. Rectangular receiver, the rear portion being a movable slide with breech-block. This is pulled back to cock the weapon, which thus fires from an open bolt. Like the Polish PM 63, this is really an overgrown full-automatic pistol.

Cartridge: 9mm Parabellum
Length, fixed butt, or folding butt extended: 31.50in (800mm)
Length, butt retracted: 21.65in (550mm)
Weight: 7lb 0oz (3.15kg)
Barrel: 12.40in (315mm), 4 grooves, rh
Magazine: 50-round box
Muzzle velocity: 1312 ft/sec (400 m/sec)
Cyclic rate: 850 rds/min

m/46

1946. A completely new design, the receiver being in two pressed-steel halves hinged together at the rear end and secured by the barrel nut screwed on over both halves. This allows the weapon to be completely dismantled when necessary for cleaning or repair. Rectangular receiver, conical barrel nut, pistol grip with tubular skeleton stock hinged to it, cocking slide on top of receiver, grip safety behind the magazine housing.

Cartridge: 9mm Parabellum
Length, butt extended: 31.50in (800mm)
Length, butt retracted: 21.50in (546mm)
Weight: 7lb 0oz (3.17kg)
Barrel: 7.75in (196mm), 4 grooves, rh
Magazine: 32-round box
Muzzle velocity: 1250 ft/sec (381 m/sec)
Cyclic rate: 500 rds/min

m/50

1950. A minor improvement on the m/46, this had a cocking knob instead of the slide, so that it was no longer necessary to unscrew the cocking slide before dismantling the weapon. There were also some slight dimensional changes.

Cartridge: 9mm Parabellum
Length, butt extended: 30.75in (780mm)
Length, butt retracted: 20.86in (530mm)
Weight: 7lb 0oz (3.17kg)
Barrel: 7.83in (200mm), 6 grooves, rh
Magazine: 32-round box
Muzzle velocity: 1250 ft/sec (381 m/sec)
Cyclic rate: 550 rds/min

m/53

1953. A further advance in the design, this introduced a new curved magazine and the barrel locking nut actually screws on to the barrel and clasps the front of the two-part receiver instead of screwing directly on to the receiver as before.

Cartridge: 9mm Parabellum
Length, butt extended: 31.50in (800mm)
Length, butt retracted: 20.86in (530mm)
Weight: 7lb 0oz (3.17kg)
Barrel: 7.8in (197mm), 6 grooves, rh
Magazine: 32-round box
Muzzle velocity: 1250 ft/sec (381 m/sec)
Cyclic rate: 550 rds/min

MAS France
MAS

STA-1924

1924. Broadly based on the Bergmann MP18. Wooden half-stock with curved vertical magazine at front end. Cylindrical receiver, no barrel jacket, but bipod attached close to muzzle. About 1000 issued, principally in North Africa, but then abandoned on financial grounds. Blowback, full automatic fire only.

Cartridge: 9mm Parabellum
Length: 32.83in (834mm)
Weight: 7lb 11oz (3.50kg)
Barrel: 8.86in (225mm), 4 grooves, rh
Magazine: 32-round box
Muzzle velocity: 1200 ft/sec (365 m/sec)
Cyclic rate: 600 rds/min

MAS 38

1938. Rectangular receiver, fixed wooden butt, long exposed barrel, pistol grip, box magazine. Barrel is at an angle with the receiver to avoid high sight line. Bolt can be locked by pressing trigger forward. May be found rebarrelled for 7.62mm Soviet cartridge after capture by Vietcong.

Cartridge: 7.65mm Longue
Length: 28.90in (734mm)
Weight: 6lb 5oz (2.87kg)
Barrel: 8.82in (224mm), 4 grooves, rh
Magazine: 32-round box
Muzzle velocity: 1151 ft/sec (351 m/sec)
Cyclic rate: 600 rds/min

MAT France
MAT

MAT 49

1949. Stamped steel frame and receiver, pistol grip with grip safety locking bolt and trigger. Magazine folds forward beneath barrel. Wire telescoping stock.

Cartridge: 9mm Parabellum
Length, butt extended: 28.35in (720mm)
Length, butt retracted: 18.11in (460mm)
Weight: 7lb 11oz (3.50kg)
Barrel: 8.97in (228mm), 4 grooves, rh
Magazine: 20- or 32-round box
Muzzle velocity: 1283 ft/sec (390 m/sec)
Cyclic rate: 600 rds/min

MAUSER Germany
Mauser

Model 57
1957. Originally developed by Erma, then transferred to Mauser. Cylindrical receiver with end caps, pistol grip magazine housing, folding forward handgrip and folding tubular two-strut butt. Limited production.

Cartridge: 9mm Parabellum
Length, butt extended: 24.0in (610mm)
Length, butt retracted: 16.93in (430mm)
Weight: 6lb 15oz (3.15kg)
Barrel: 10.24in (260mm), 6 grooves, rh
Magazine: 32-round box
Muzzle velocity: 1197 ft/sec (365 m/sec)
Cyclic rate: 800 rds/min

MEMS Argentina
A&E

Model 67
Cylindrical receiver, long slender barrel with compensator. Pistol grip. Magazine housing acts as forward grip. Two-strut tubular butt folds down and under the receiver.

Cartridge: 9mm Parabellum
Length, butt extended: 31.50in (800mm)
Length, butt retracted: 25.19in (640mm)
Weight: 7lb 5oz (3.30kg)
Barrel: 7.08in (180mm), 12 grooves, rh
Magazine: 40-round box
Muzzle velocity: 1197 ft/sec (365 m/sec)
Cyclic rate: 850 rds/min

MENDOZA Mexico
Mendoza

HM-3
1975. Cylindrical receiver on rectangular frame, short exposed barrel. Pistol grip acts as magazine housing and also incorporates a grip safety. Single strut butt folds to the left side and the butt-plate doubles as a forward handgrip when folded.

Cartridge: 9mm Parabellum
Length, butt extended: 25.00in (635mm)
Length, butt retracted: 15.55in (395mm)
Weight: 5lb 15oz (2.69kg)
Barrel: 10.04in (255mm), 6 grooves, rh
Magazine: 32-round box
Muzzle velocity: 1300 ft/sec (396 m/sec)
Cyclic rate: 600 rds/min

MINI-ERO Croatia
RH-ALAN

1996. Appears to be a copy of the Mini-Uzi, but with a telescoping wire butt. Same rectangular receiver, central pistol grip/magazine housing, grip safety.

Cartridge: 9mm Parabellum
Length, butt extended: 21.46in (545mm)
Length, butt retracted: 12.60in (320mm)
Weight: 4lb 14oz (2.20kg)
Barrel: 5.90in (150mm), 4 grooves, rh

Magazine: 20- or 30-round box
Muzzle velocity: 1155 ft/sec (352 m/sec)
Cyclic rate: 1100 rds/min

NORTH KOREA
State factories

Type 49
1949–55. A near-identical copy of the Russian PPSh-41, the only difference being in the rear sight, which in this weapon is an aperture rather than a notch.

Specifications and performance: as for the PPSh-41

NORTH VIETNAM
State factories

K-50M
This was a Vietnamese variation of the Chinese Type 50, which itself was a copy of the Russian PPS-43. The changes made include removing the folding butt and replacing it with a sliding wire butt; cutting away most of the perforated barrel jacket and tapering the remains; reshaping the lower receiver and curtailing the upper; and removing the muzzle compensator.

Cartridge: 7.62 × 25mm Soviet Pistol
Length, butt extended: 29.76in (756mm)
Length, butt retracted: 22.48in (571mm)
Weight: 7lb 8oz (3.40kg)
Barrel: 10.60in (269mm), 4 grooves, rh
Magazine: 35-round box
Muzzle velocity: 1600 ft/sec (488 m/sec)
Cyclic rate: 700 rds/min

ORITA Romania
Cugir

M1941
1941–44. Wooden butt and half-stock, cylindrical receiver, long tapering barrel. Mostly made from machined components. Magazine housing at tip of fore-end, long thin magazine. Prominent tangent sight to 500 metres in front of chamber.

Cartridge: 9mm Parabellum
Length: 35.20in (894mm)
Weight: 7lb 10oz (3.46kg)
Barrel: 11.69in (297mm), 6 grooves, rh
Magazine: 25-round straight or 32-round curved box
Muzzle velocity: 1250 ft/sec (381 m/sec)
Cyclic rate: 600 rds/min

OVP Italy
OVP

Ca 1920. In effect, one barrel of the Villar Perosa twin machine gun (listed *below* as a Submachine Gun) removed and fitted with a rifle-type butt and a double trigger assembly. Split sleeve acts as a cocking handle, small barrel jacket added as a forward hand grip.

Cartridge: 9 × 19mm Glisenti
Length: 35.50in (901mm)
Weight: 8lb 1oz (3.67kg)
Barrel: 11.0in (279mm), 6 grooves, rh

Magazine: 25-round box
Muzzle velocity: 1250 ft/sec (381 m/sec)
Cyclic rate: 900 rds/min

OWEN Australia
Lysaght

Mark 1

1941. Cylindrical receiver, overhead magazine, quick-remove barrel to permit stripping, pistol grip forward handgrip, wood or metal skeleton butt, muzzle compensator. Early models had cooling fins on barrel. Almost always painted in camouflage colours.

Cartridge: 9mm Parabellum
Length: 32.0in (813mm)
Weight: 9lb 5oz (4.21kg)
Barrel: 9.75in (247mm), 7 grooves, rh
Magazine: 33-round box
Muzzle velocity: 1378 ft/sec (420 m/sec)
Cyclic rate: 700 rds/min

Mark 2

1943. Modified version of the Mark 1 with different method of attaching butt and with a bayonet lug above the muzzle compensator to receive a special tubular-haft bayonet. Prototypes only.

Specifications: as for Mark 1, except
Weight: 7lb 10oz (3.47kg)

PARINCO Spain
Parinco

CI-3R

1958. Cylindrical receiver, short perforated barrel jacket, long tapering barrel with muzzle compensator. Pistol grip and trigger mechanism cover are of plastic and hinge down at the rear end to permit stripping. Sliding wire butt and vertical box magazine. Small quantity adopted by Spanish Army, may also have been sold to South America in 9mm Parabellum calibre.

Cartridge: 9 × 23mm Largo
Length, butt extended: 31.50in (800mm)
Length, butt retracted: 24.40in (620mm)
Weight: 6lb 0oz (2.72kg)
Barrel: 10.0in (254mm), 6 grooves, rh
Magazine: 32-round box
Muzzle velocity: 1200 ft/sec (365 m/sec)
Cyclic rate: 600 rds/min

PATCHETT Britain
Sterling

Mark 1

1944. Cylindrical receiver, pistol grip at point of balance, side-feeding magazine, perforated barrel jacket, collapsible butt folds down and forward under receiver. About 110 made, used D-Day and Arnhem by 6th Airborne Division.

Cartridge: 9mm Parabellum
Length, butt extended: 28.0in (711mm)
Length, butt retracted: 18.0in (457mm)

Weight: 6lb 3oz (2.81kg)
Barrel: 8.25in (210mm), 6 grooves, rh
Magazine: 32-round Sten box
Muzzle velocity: 1200 ft/sec (365 m/sec)
Cyclic rate: 600 rds/min

PELO Finland
Sako

1956. Cylindrical receiver with end cap; short barrel retained by knurled nut. Alloy pistol grip, detachable wooden butt. Unusual magazine; right side opens downwards and compresses the magazine spring as it does so; a pre-packed clip of ammunition is then dropped in and the magazine cover closed, so releasing the spring to press upwards on the cartridges. Limited production.

Cartridge: 9mm Parabellum
Length, with butt: 20.27in (515mm)
Length, without butt: 15.35in (390mm)
Weight, without butt: 4lb 10oz (2.10kg)
Barrel: 8.86in (225mm), 6 grooves, rh
Magazine: 30-round box
Muzzle velocity: 1200 ft/sec (365 m/sec)
Cyclic rate: 600 rds/min

POLAND
See also **Blyskawicza**

PM 63
Radom

1964. Resembles an oversized pistol with a folding butt. The rear portion of the receiver top is the slide and breech-block which reciprocates during firing and contains a rate retarder. The folded butt can be used as a front firing grip. Pistol grip acts as magazine housing. Prominent spoon-type muzzle compensator.

Cartridge: 9 × 18mm Makarov
Length, butt extended: 22.95in (583mm)
Length, butt retracted: 13.11in (333mm)
Weight: 3lb 15oz (1.80kg)
Barrel: 6.0in (152mm), 6 grooves, rh
Magazine: 15- or 25-round box
Muzzle velocity: 1060 ft/sec (323 m/sec)
Cyclic rate: 600 rds/min

PM 84
Lucznik

1983. Rectangular receiver with conventional reciprocating bolt inside, two cocking handles, wire butt folds underneath receiver, pistol grip acts as magazine housing. Short exposed muzzle with barrel retaining nut.

Cartridge: 9 × 18mm Makarov
Length, butt extended: 22.64in (575mm)
Length, butt retracted: 14.76in (375mm)
Weight: 4lb 9oz (2.07kg)
Barrel: 7.28in (185mm), 6 grooves, rh
Magazine: 15- or 25-round box
Muzzle velocity: 1083 ft/sec (330 m/sec)
Cyclic rate: 600 rds/min

PM 84P
Lucznik

1985. As for the PM 84 above but chambered for the 9mm Parabellum cartridge for export sale.

Cartridge: 9mm Parabellum
Length, butt extended: 22.64in (575mm)
Length, butt retracted: 14.76in (375mm)
Weight: 4lb 12oz (2.17kg)
Barrel: 7.28in (185mm), 6 grooves, rh
Magazine: 15- or 25-round box
Muzzle velocity: 1181 ft/sec (360 m/sec)
Cyclic rate: 640 rds/min

PM 98
Lucznik

1998. Improved version of the PM 84P. New sliding wire stock, fore-end grip with space for laser or aiming spot projector. Slightly larger and more robust.

Cartridge: 9mm Parabellum
Length, butt extended: 23.82in (605mm)
Length, butt retracted: 15.94in (405mm)
Weight: 5lb 1oz (2.30kg)
Barrel: 7.28in (185mm), 6 grooves, rh
Magazine: 15- or 25-round box
Muzzle velocity: 1181 ft/sec (360 m/sec)
Cyclic rate: 640 rds/min

POC Peru
Peruana

Model 6

1951. This is the Ingram Model 6 manufactured in Peru under a licence granted by POC. The dimensions are different.

Cartridge: .45 ACP
Length: 30.25in (768mm)
Weight: 7lb 0oz (3.17kg)
Barrel: 9.0in (229mm), 6 grooves, rh
Magazine: 30-round box
Muzzle velocity: 950 ft/sec (290 m/sec)
Cyclic rate: 650 rds/min

PORT SAID Egypt
Maadi

Ca 1960, A licence-produced version of the Carl Gustav m/45 which has remained in production ever since. Although visually similar it has some minor differences in dimensions, due to different manufacturing practices.

Cartridge: 9mm Parabellum
Length, butt extended: 31.81in (808mm)
Length, butt retracted: 21.65in (550mm)
Weight: 8lb 1oz (3.65kg)
Barrel: 8.38in (213mm), 6 grooves, rh
Magazine: 36-round box
Muzzle velocity: 1312 ft/sec (400 m/sec)
Cyclic rate: 600 rds/min

PORTUGAL
See also INDEP
M/948
FBP

Stamped body, trigger unit and sliding wire butt of the US M3A1 allied to a bolt and spring casing based on the MP40, plus a locally designed barrel with bayonet lug.

Cartridge: 9mm Parabellum
Length, butt extended: 32in (813mm)
Length, butt closed: 25.0in (625mm)
Weight: 8lb 3oz (3.77kg)
Barrel: 9.8in (250mm), 6 grooves, rh
Magazine: 32-round box
Muzzle velocity: 1260 ft/sec (384 m/sec)
Cyclic rate: 500 rds/min

M/976
FBP

Improved M/948 by dispensing with the telescoping spring case, adding a grip safety and three-way safety catch/selector switch. and putting a perforated jacket around the barrel. In service into the later 1980s.

Cartridge: 9mm Parabellum
Length, butt extended: 31.5in (800mm)
Length, butt closed: 25.8in (655mm)
Weight: 6lb 14oz (3.12kg)
Barrel: 9.8in (250mm), 6 grooves, rh
Magazine: 32- or 36-round box
Muzzle velocity: 1260 ft/sec (384 m/sec)
Cyclic rate: 650 rds/min

PPD, PPS, PPSh
For PPD, PPS, PPSh *designs see* **Russia**

RAN Belgium
Repousmetal

1953. Cylindrical receiver, sliding wire stock, barrel with muzzle compensator. May have folding bayonet. Plastic pistol grip; magazine housing acts as fore-grip. Grip safety.

Cartridge: 9mm Parabellum
Length, butt extended: 31.25in (794mm)
Length, butt retracted: 23.0in (584mm)
Weight: 6lb 8oz (2.95kg)
Barrel: 11.81in (300mm), 6 grooves, rh
Magazine: 32-round box
Muzzle velocity: 1395 ft/sec (425 m/sec)
Cyclic rate: 630 rds/min

RATMIL Romania
Romtehnica

1995. Wedge-shaped rectangular receiver with rounded top, short slotted barrel jacket, pistol grip at rear of receiver, box magazine ahead of trigger, single-strut wire folding stock. Single shots and three-round bursts only.

Cartridge: 9mm Parabellum
Length, butt extended: 25.60in (650mm)
Length, butt retracted: 16.73in (425mm)
Weight: 5lb 15oz (2.70kg)
Barrel: n/a

Magazine: 30-round box
Muzzle velocity: 1214 ft/sec (370 m/sec)
Cyclic rate: 650 rds/min

REISING USA
Harrington

Model 50
1941. Wooden-stocked almost to the muzzle, cylindrical receiver, partly-finned barrel, large muzzle compensator. Magazine housing beneath receiver. Fore-end slotted underneath for the cocking handle. Delayed blowback, using a rising bolt to obtain delay.

Cartridge: .45 ACP
Length: 35.75in (908mm)
Weight: 6lb 12oz (3.06kg)
Barrel: 11.0in (279mm), 6 grooves, rh
Magazine: 12- or 20-round box
Muzzle velocity: 920 ft/sec (280 m/sec)
Cyclic rate: 550 rds/min

Model 55
1943. Mechanism of the Model 50 in a new wooden stock which terminated in a pistol grip and then had a flimsy wire folding skeleton butt. No muzzle compensator.

Cartridge: .45 ACP
Length, butt extended: 31.25in (794mm)
Length, butt retracted: 22.25in (565mm)
Weight: 6lb 4oz (2.83kg)
Barrel: 10.50in (266mm), 6 grooves, rh
Magazine: 12- or 20-round box
Muzzle velocity: 920 ft/sec (280 m/sec)
Cyclic rate: 550 rds/min

REVELLI Italy
Name sometimes applied to the Villar Perosa submachine gun (see OVP and Villar Perosa), particularly those which were manufactured by the Canadian General Electric Co. in 1917–18, A.B. Revelli being the designer.

REXIM Switzerland
Rexim

Favor
Ca 1952. Cylindrical receiver with knurled end cap. Slotted barrel jacket with bayonet socket beneath the muzzle. Skeleton metal folding butt, pistol grip. Various barrel lengths and butt types were made as demonstration samples. Guns made in Spain; Swiss firm failed in 1957. Spanish guns were sold off as La Coruña, mostly to Turkey.

Cartridge: 9mm Parabellum
Length, butt extended: 34.35in (873mm)
Length, butt retracted: 24.35in (617mm)
Weight: 10lb 5oz (4.67kg)
Barrel: 13.35in (340mm), 6 grooves, rh
Magazine: 32-round box
Muzzle velocity: 1400 ft/sec (427 m/sec)
Cyclic rate: 600 rds/min

RHODESIA
See also Rhogun
R-76
Maker unknown
1976. Rectangular receiver, pistol grip, sliding wire butt. Sloping magazine housing acts as a front grip and accepts Browning High-Power pistol magazines. Plain barrel held by knurled nut. Limited production. Other barrel lengths.

Cartridge: 9mm Parabellum
Length, butt extended: 30.0in (762mm)
Length, butt retracted: 22.0in (558mm)
Weight: 6lb 11oz (3.03kg)
Barrel: 10.0in (254mm), 6 grooves, rh
Magazine: 13-, 20- or 30-round box
Muzzle velocity: 1300 ft/sec (396 m/sec)
Cyclic rate: 500 rds/min

RHOGUN Rhodesia
BHS
1978. Cylindrical receiver on rectangular frame. Pistol grip acts as magazine housing. Sliding wire butt, folding front grip. Grip safety which lifts magazine into feedway. Limited production.

Cartridge: 9mm Parabellum
Length, butt extended: 26.0in (660mm)
Length, butt retracted: 18.0in (457mm)
Weight: 8lb 13oz (4.0kg)
Barrel: 10.0in (254mm), 4 grooves, rh
Magazine: 25-round box
Muzzle velocity: 1250 ft/sec (381 m/sec)
Cyclic rate: 660 rds/min

RUGER USA
Ruger
MP-9
1994. Designed by Uzi Gal ca 1985, modified by Ruger. Rectangular receiver, the upper part being steel, the lower synthetic material. Short exposed barrel retained by knurled nut. Pistol grip acts as magazine housing, front edge of trigger-guard as fore-grip, and there is a skeleton frame extending from the bottom of the pistol grip to the rear of the receiver. A folding butt telescopes and folds down to lie against this frame. Fires from a closed bolt.

Cartridge: 9mm Parabellum
Length, butt extended: 21.89in (556mm)
Length, butt retracted: 14.80in (376mm)
Weight: 6lb 10oz (3.0kg)
Barrel: 6.81in (173mm), 6 grooves, rh
Magazine: 32-round box
Muzzle velocity: 1148 ft/sec (350 m/sec)
Cyclic rate: 600 rds/min

RUSSIA
State factories, unless noted otherwise
See also **Baksan, Bison, KEDR, KLIN & Kovrov**

Note also that the Kalashnikov family of weapons is covered in the Rifles chapter

A-91
IPME

1995. More properly a short assault rifle, since it can be chambered for 5.45mm, 5.56mm, 7.62 x 39mm or the special 9 x 39mm cartridge. Gas operated, locked breech, selective fire. Plastic fore-end with prominent gas tube to barrel; spoon-type muzzle compensator; folding butt; unusually deep (front-to-rear) magazine; pistol grip; vertical cocking handle on left side.

Cartridge: various (*see above*)
Length, butt extended: 23.78in (604mm)
Length, butt folded: 15.15in (385mm)
Weight: 3lb 13oz (1.75kg)
Barrel: 7.97in (200mm)
Magazine: 20-round box
Muzzle velocity: 1870–2230 ft/sec (570–680 m/sec), depending on ammunition
Cyclic rate: 700–900 rds/min, depending on ammunition

9A-91
IPME

The 9A-91 is similar to the above, but chambered for the special 9 x 39mm low-velocity cartridge and provided with a silencer.

PPD-34/38

Pistol Pulyemet Degtyarev. 1938. Generally based on the Bergmann MP28, but with selective fire and with an aperture under the fore-end for a special drum magazine. Wooden half-stock, perforated barrel jacket, receiver end cap, prominent tangent sight.

Cartridge: 7.62 x 25mm Soviet Pistol
Length: 30.70in (780mm)
Weight: 8lb 4oz (3.73kg)
Barrel: 10.62in (270mm), 4 grooves, rh
Magazine: 25-round box or 71-round drum
Muzzle velocity: 1590 ft/sec (485 m/sec)
Cyclic rate: 800 rds/min

PPD-40

1940. Improved version of the PPD-34/38 which gave up the box/drum magazine set up and adopted an entirely new drum based on the Finnish Suomi, resulting in a gap in the fore-end for the magazine to slot in side-ways.

Cartridge: 7.62 x 25mm Soviet Pistol
Length: 30.60in (777mm)
Weight: 8lb 2oz (3.70kg)
Barrel: 10.63in (270mm), 4 grooves, rh
Magazine: 71-round drum
Muzzle velocity: 1590 ft/sec (485 m/sec)
Cyclic rate: 800 rds/min

PPS-42

Pistol Pulyemet Sudaev. 1942. Among the cheapest and simplest designs ever made, the PPS is entirely of stamped sheet steel, except for the bolt, has two wood grips and a scrap of leather as a bolt buffer. Rectangular receiver merges into perforated barrel jacket which has the end turned over to form a muzzle brake and barrel support. Forward section of the jacket is a separate item, riveted to the rear section. Two-strut metal butt-stock folds up and over to lie across the ejection port. Magazine housing for unique curved box magazine.

Cartridge: 7.62 x 25mm Soviet Pistol
Length, butt extended: 35.04in (890mm)
Length, butt retracted: 25.0in (635mm)
Weight: 6lb 9oz (2.99kg)
Barrel: 10.83in (275mm), 4 grooves, rh
Magazine: 35-round box
Muzzle velocity: 1590 ft/sec (485 m/sec)
Cyclic rate: 700 rds/min

PPS-43

1943. Improved model of the PPS-42. Shorter butt which, when folded, lies behind the ejection port. Receiver and entire jacket stamped out of one piece of metal, larger fore-sight protecting wings, safety catch squared-off instead of rounded.

Cartridge: 7.62 x 25mm Soviet Pistol
Length, butt extended: 32.28in (820mm)
Length, butt retracted: 24.60in (625mm)
Weight: 7lb 8oz (3.39kg)
Barrel: 10.0in (254mm), 4 grooves, rh
Magazine: 35-round box
Muzzle velocity: 1590 ft/sec (485 m/sec)
Cyclic rate: 700 rds/min

PPSh-41

Pistol Pulyemet Shpagin. 1941. Similar to the PPD models but cheaper and quicker to make. Slotted barrel jacket with rudimentary compensator, prominent hinge-bolt on fore-end to allow barrel to tip for stripping, drum magazine slightly tilted forward. Selective fire, with selector switch inside trigger guard, though late 1944–45 manufacture often omitted this feature.

Cartridge: 7.62 x 25mm Soviet Pistol
Length: 33.0in (838mm)
Weight: 8lb 0oz (3.64kg)
Barrel: 10.50in (266mm), 4 grooves, rh
Magazine: 35-round box or 71-round drum
Muzzle velocity: 1590 ft/sec (485 m/sec)
Cyclic rate: 900 rds/min

PP-90
Uralsk

1995. This appears to have been copied from the Ares folding submachine gun. Rectangular receiver and stock, one folding around the other, the two containing the magazine when folded and forming a rectangular metal box some 11 x 3.5 inches (270 x 90mm). It has been offered on the export market for some time but it is not known whether there have been any takers. Automatic fire only.

Cartridge: 9mm Parabellum
Length, unfolded: 19.29in (490mm)
Weight: 4lb 1oz (1.83kg)
Barrel (estimated): 5.12in (130mm)
Magazine: 30-round box

Muzzle velocity: 1050 ft/sec (320 m/sec)
Cyclic rate: 650 rds/min

SACO USA
Saco

Model 683

Ca 1985. Conventional blowback weapon designed with an eye to simplicity and cheapness of manufacture. Most parts of stamped steel. Cylindrical receiver, into which the butt telescopes; cylindrical slotted barrel jacket, conical flash hider. Large carrying handle with tubular sight unit. Rectangular frame with pistol grip.

Cartridge: 9mm Parabellum
Length, butt extended: 27.52in (699mm)
Length, butt retracted: 20.47in (520mm)
Weight: 7lb 5oz (3.31kg)
Barrel: 8.0in (203mm), 6 grooves, rh
Magazine: 25-round box
Muzzle velocity: 1300 ft/sec (396 m/sec)
Cyclic rate: 650 rds/min

SAF Chile
FAMAE

1990. Based largely upon the SIG 540 assault rifle which is manufactured in Chile under licence, and uses several components. Modifications have been made to the SIG firing mechanism to incorporate a three-round burst option. Fixed or folding butt versions. Can be fitted with silencer. Fires from a closed bolt.

Cartridge: 9mm Parabellum
Length, butt fixed or extended: 25.28in (640mm)
Length, butt retracted: 16.14in (410mm)
Weight, fixed butt: 5lb 15oz (2.70kg)
Weight, folding butt: 6lb 6oz (2.90kg)
Barrel: 7.87in (200mm), 6 grooves, rh
Magazine: 20- or 30-round box
Muzzle velocity: 1280 ft/sec (390 m/sec)
Cyclic rate: 1200 rds/min

Mini-SAF
FAMAE

1991. Same basic mechanism as the SAF, same receiver, very short barrel, forward handgrip, no butt-stock. Made for concealed carrying.

Cartridge: 9mm Parabellum
Length: 12.20in (310mm)
Weight: 5lb 1oz (2.30kg)
Barrel: 4.53in (115mm), 6 grooves, rh
Magazine: 20- or 30-round box
Muzzle velocity: 1214 ft/sec (370 m/sec)
Cyclic rate: 1200 rds/min

SEDGLEY USA
Sedgley

1940. Commercially produced and sold, though in very small numbers. Wooden half-stock, cylindrical receiver, slotted barrel jacket, straight box magazine in front of fore-end.

Cartridge: 9mm Parabellum
Length: 35.0in (889mm)
Weight: 7lb 8oz (3.40kg)
Barrel: 11.0in (279mm), 6 grooves, rh
Magazine: 20-round box
Muzzle velocity: 1312 ft/sec (400 m/sec)
Cyclic rate: 450 rds/min

SIG Switzerland
SIG

M1920

Licensed copy of the Bergmann MP18. Wood half-stock with finger grooves, cylindrical receiver, perforated barrel jacket. Magazine feeds from the left side. Sold to Finland in 7.65mm Parabellum, marked 'SA'; to China and Japan in 7.63mm Mauser. Japanese models have bayonet fittings. Full-automatic fire only.

Cartridge: 7.65 × 21.5mm Parabellum
Length: 33.07in (840mm)
Weight: 11lb 2oz (5.04kg)
Barrel: 8.27in (210mm), 4 grooves, rh
Magazine: 50-round box
Muzzle velocity: 1200 ft/sec (365 m/sec)
Cyclic rate: 600 rds/min

M1930

Revised model of the M1920 with a front hand-grip, magazine feeding from the right and slotted to show ammunition state.

Specifications: as for the M1920

MKMO

1933. Full-stocked, short exposed muzzle. Delayed blowback using Kiraly two-piece bolt. Magazine folds forward and up into a slot in the fore-end. Oblique finger-grips in fore-end. Various calibres. Bayonet fitting. Automatic only.

Cartridge: 9 × 25mm Mauser
Length: 40.35in (1025mm)
Weight: 9lb 4oz (4.19kg)
Barrel: 19.68in (500mm), 6 grooves, rh
Magazine: 40-round box
Muzzle velocity: 1600 ft/sec (487 m/sec)
Cyclic rate: 900 rds/min

MKMS

1935. Simplified version of the MKMO, using a solid bolt and straight blowback operation. Limited numbers only.

Specifications: as for MKMO

MKPO

1935. Short version of the MKMO intended for police use. No bayonet fitting, smaller magazine, very short exposed muzzle. Various calibres.

Cartridge: 9mm Parabellum
Length: 32.38in (820mm)
Weight: 8lb 6oz (3.80kg)
Barrel: 11.81in (300mm), 6 grooves, rh
Magazine: 30-round box
Muzzle velocity: 1312 ft/sec (400 m/sec)
Cyclic rate: 900 rds/min

MKPS

1937. Straight blowback version of the MKMO, using a one-piece bolt.

Specifications: as for MKPO

MP41

1940. Made for Swiss Army trials, at which the Furrer design (*qv*) was selected. Prototype and trials quantity production only. Used the straight blowback, one-piece bolt system from the MKMS. Wood butt, pistol grip and fore-end; finned barrel, Cylindrical receiver with right side cocking handle. Hinged magazine housing in front of the trigger; magazine folds up and forward to lie in a slot in the fore-end. Full automatic fire only.

Cartridge: 9mm Parabellum
Length: 31.50in (800mm)
Weight: 9lb 10oz (4.38kg)
Barrel: 12.05in (306mm), 6 grooves, rh
Magazine: 40-round box
Muzzle velocity: 1312 ft/sec (400 m/sec)
Cyclic rate: 850 rds/min

MP44

1943. An improved version of the MP41. Wood butt now extends to a part-stock enclosing the frame as far as the magazine housing. Stamped steel perforated fore-end, hollow to receive the fold-forward magazine. Selective fire by two-stage trigger. May also be found with a muzzle compensator.

Cartridge: 9mm Parabellum
Length: 32.38in (830mm)
Weight: 8lb 11oz (3.951kg)
Barrel: 11.81in (300mm), 6 grooves, rh
Magazine: 40-round box
Muzzle velocity: 1378 ft/sec (420 m/sec)
Cyclic rate: 800 rds/min

MP46

Variant model of the MP44, differing simply in having finger-grooves pressed into the metal fore-end and a fixed firing pin in the bolt.

Specifications: same

MP48

1948. Entirely new design. Wood pistol grip and short stock supports tubular receiver; exposed barrel, magazine folds up and forward to lie beneath barrel. Sliding steel rod butt; early production slides in grooves cut in outer surface of stock; later production slides into grooves on inner surface. Adopted by Chilean Army.

Cartridge: 9mm Parabellum
Length, butt extended: 28.15in (715mm)
Length, butt retracted: 24.0in (610mm)
Weight: 8lb 2oz (3.70kg)
Barrel: 7.87in (200mm), 6 grooves, rh
Magazine: 40-round box
Muzzle velocity: 1200 ft/sec (365 m/sec)
Cyclic rate: 700 rds/min

MP310

1958. Further improvement on the MP48 pattern. Cylindrical receiver with end cap, plastic covered frame, magazine housing and magazine fold forward and provide safety. Sliding wire butt. Two-stage trigger pull gives semi- or full-automatic fire.

Cartridge: 9mm Parabellum
Length, butt extended: 28.94in (735mm)
Length, butt retracted: 24.01in (610mm)
Weight: 7lb 9oz (3.42kg)
Barrel: 7.87in (200mm), 6 grooves, rh
Magazine: 40-round box
Muzzle velocity: 1200 ft/sec (365 m/sec)
Cyclic rate: 900 rds/min

SIMA-CIFAR Peru
SIMA-CIFAR

MGP 79A

1979. Cylindrical receiver over rectangular frame, side-folding butt. May have bare barrel retained by nut or by a perforated jacket which can also act as a forward grip. There is also a forward grip incorporated in the magazine housing, as well as a pistol grip. An unusual feature is the provision of separate safety and selector switches positioned so that they can be used by both hands when on the grips.

Cartridge: 9mm Parabellum
Length, butt extended: 31.85in (809mm)
Length, butt retracted: 21.42in (544mm)
Weight: 6lb 13oz (3.09kg)
Barrel: 9.33in (237mm), 12 grooves, rh
Magazine: 20- or 32-round box
Muzzle velocity: 1345 ft/sec (410 m/sec)
Cyclic rate: 700 rds/min

MGP 84

1982, when known as the **MGP-15**. Re-designed and re-introduced as the MGP 84 in 1985. Cylindrical receiver on rectangular frame, receiver concealing barrel. Central pistol grip acts as magazine housing. Single-strut folding butt. Accepts Uzi magazine.

Cartridge: 9mm Parabellum
Length, butt extended: 19.29in (490mm)
Length, butt retracted: 10.67in (271mm)
Weight: 5lb 1oz (2.31kg)
Barrel: 6.0in (152mm), 12 grooves, rh
Magazine: 20- or 32-round box
Muzzle velocity: 1122 ft/sec (342 m/sec)
Cyclic rate: 650 rds/min

MGP 87

1987. Generally similar to the MGP 79A, but with a shorter barrel and shorter folding butt and the cocking handle is turned up and made more prominent.

Cartridge: 9mm Parabellum
Length, butt extended: 30.16in (766mm)
Length, butt retracted: 19.69in (500mm)
Weight: 6lb 6oz (2.90kg)
Barrel: 7.64in (194mm), 12 grooves, rh
Magazine: 20- or 32-round box
Muzzle velocity: 1187 ft/sec (362 m/sec)
Cyclic rate: 700 rds/min

MGP 14 pistol carbine

1994. This is the MGP 84 modified to fire in the semi-automatic mode only.

Specifications: the same, except
Weight: 5lb 6oz (2.45kg)

MGP 14 assault pistol

1994. This is the MGP 14 without the folding butt and with an additional front hand grip.

Specifications: the same

SKORPION Czechoslovakia
CZ Brno

vz/61

1960. Could fairly be called a machine pistol, since it could be used in one hand and fired the 7.65mm Browning pistol cartridge. Rectangular receiver, wooden pistol grip, short curved magazine, short barrel, wire stock folds up and over the top of the receiver. Inertia-operated rate regulator in pistol grip. A licensed copy was made by Zastava Arms (*see* Yugoslavia, M84) in the early 1990s.

Cartridge: 7.65 × 17SR Browning
Length, butt extended: 28.95in (522mm)
Length, butt retracted: 24.0in (270mm)
Weight: 2lb 14oz (1.31kg)
Barrel: 4.53in (115mm), 6 grooves, rh
Magazine: 10- or 20-round box
Muzzle velocity: 968 ft/sec (295 m/sec)
Cyclic rate: 700 rds/min

vz/63, 64, 68

These were variants of the vz/61; the **vz/63** fired the 9mm Short (.380 Auto) cartridge, the **vz/64** the 9mm Makarov, and the **vz/68** the 9mm Parabellum. This is according to the advertising brochures; nobody to my knowledge has ever seen one of these variations and no reliable dimensions have ever been published.

SMITH & WESSON USA
Smith & Wesson

Light Rifle

1939. In spite of the name, a submachine gun by most definitions. Cylindrical receiver, plain jacketed barrel, unusually deep (front-to-back) magazine which incorporates a chute for empty cases. Revolver-style pistol grip. Intended as a police weapon, it was offered to Britain 1940; some were bought by the Royal Navy and fitted with a single-strut folding butt attached to the bottom of the grip in 1942. Semi-automatic only, though full-auto prototypes were made and tested.

Cartridge: 9mm Parabellum
Length: 30.50in (845mm)
Weight: 8lb 10oz (3.92kg)
Barrel: 9.75in (247mm), 6 grooves, rh
Magazine: 20-round box
Muzzle velocity: 1240 ft/sec (378 m/sec)

Type 76

1967. Based on the Carl Gustav m/45 (*qv*), though somewhat different in appearance. Cylindrical receiver, barrel

secured by knurled nut, pistol grip with tubular skeleton folding butt. Ambidextrous safety/selector fitted. Limited numbers produced.

Cartridge: 9mm Parabellum
Length, butt extended: 28.95in (735mm)
Length, butt retracted: 20.25in (514mm)
Weight: 7lb 4oz (3.29kg)
Barrel: 8.0in (203mm), 6 grooves, rh
Magazine: 36-round box
Muzzle velocity: 1250 ft/sec (381 m/sec)
Cyclic rate: 720 rds/min

SOCIMI Italy
Socimi

Type 821

Ca 1985. Rectangular pressed steel receiver, pistol grip, short barrel with knurled retaining nut. Single-strut butt pivots below the end of the receiver, swings right and forward. Pistol grip acts as magazine housing.

Cartridge: 9mm Parabellum
Length, butt extended: 23.62in (600mm)
Length, butt retracted: 15.75in (400mm)
Weight: 5lb 6oz (2.45kg)
Barrel: 7.87in (200mm), 6 grooves, rh
Magazine: 32-round box
Muzzle velocity: 1247 ft/sec (380 m/sec)
Cyclic rate: 600 rds/min

SOLA Luxembourg
Sola

Super

1954. Cylindrical receiver with end cap, long barrel with compensator, short perforated jacket at front of receiver. Frame runs full receiver length, pistol grip, sliding wire stock.

Cartridge: 9mm Parabellum
Length, butt extended: 35.0in (890mm)
Length, butt retracted: 24.0in (610mm)
Weight: 6lb 6oz (2.90kg)
Barrel: 12.0in (305mm), 6 grooves, rh
Magazine: 32-round box
Muzzle velocity: 1400 ft/sec (425 m/sec)
Cyclic rate: 550 rds/min

Light

1957. Simplified model of the Super. Pistol grip attached directly to receiver, no frame. No perforated jacket. No compensator on muzzle. Met with no success and company left the firearms business.

Cartridge: 9mm Parabellum
Length, butt extended: 31.0in (790mm)
Length, butt retracted: 22.50in (570mm)
Weight: 6lb 0oz (2.72kg)
Barrel: 7.87in (200mm), 6 grooves, rh
Magazine: 32-round box
Muzzle velocity: 1250 ft/sec (365 m/sec)
Cyclic rate: 550 rds/min

SPECTRE Italy
SITES

M-4
Ca 1985. Rectangular receiver and slotted barrel jacket; butt folds over the top of the receiver. Pistol grip. Magazine is unusually thick four-column design. Fires from a closed bolt using unique double-action trigger and hammer system. Forced ventilation of barrel. No mechanical safety devices. 'Sinusoidal' rifling claimed to reduce friction and increase velocity.

Cartridge: 9mm Parabellum
Length, butt extended: 22.83in (580mm)
Length, butt retracted: 13.78in (350mm)
Weight: 6lb 6oz (2.90kg)
Barrel: 5.12in (130mm), 4 grooves, rh
Magazine: 30- or 50-round box
Muzzle velocity: 1312 ft/sec (400 m/sec)
Cyclic rate: 850 rds/min

STAR Spain
Star

SI-35
1935. Wooden butt and half-stocked to magazine housing. Cylindrical receiver with prominent tangent rear sight. Long, slender barrel with slotted jacket, Cam-delayed blowback action, two selectable rates of automatic fire.

Cartridge: 9 × 23mm Largo
Length: 35.45in (900mm)
Weight: 8lb 4oz (3.74kg)
Barrel: 10.60in (270mm), 6 grooves, rh
Magazine: 10-, 30- or 40-round box
Muzzle velocity: 1350 ft/sec (412 m/sec)
Cyclic rate: 300 or 700 rds/min

RU-35
A version of the SI-35 which had only one rate of automatic fire, *viz* 300 rds/min.

TN-35
A variant of the SI-25 which had only one rate of automatic fire, *viz* 700 rds/min. A prototype of this weapon in .38 Super Auto calibre was demonstrated in the USA in 1940 as the Atlantic, but was turned down.

Z-45
1944. Based on the German MP40 but has the cocking handle on the right side, a perforated barrel jacket, and a barrel which can be removed by simply unscrewing it. Muzzle compensator. Locking catch on cocking handle which locks the bolt in the forward position. Two-stage trigger; pull for single shots, pull further for automatic.

Cartridge: 9 × 23mm Largo
Length, butt extended: 33.0in (838mm)
Length, butt retracted: 22.80in (579mm)
Weight: 8lb 8oz (3.86kg)
Barrel: 7.80in (198mm), 6 grooves, rh
Magazine: 30-round box
Muzzle velocity: 1250 ft/sec (381 m/sec)
Cyclic rate: 450 rds/min

Z-62
1960. Cylindrical receiver, perforated barrel jacket, folding single-strut butt. Well-raked pistol grip central with magazine housing in front. Exposed muzzle, prominent sight protectors. Also found in 9mm Largo calibre.

Cartridge: 9mm Parabellum
Length, butt extended: 27.60in (701mm)
Length, butt retracted: 18.90in (480mm)
Weight: 6lb 5oz (2.87kg)
Barrel: 7.91in (201mm), 6 grooves, rh
Magazine: 20-, 30- or 40-round box
Muzzle velocity: 1200 ft/sec (380 m/sec)
Cyclic rate: 550 rds/min

Z-70/B
1971. Generally similar to the Z-62, being an improved version with a new trigger mechanism. Quick distinguishing mark is the trigger, which is solid on the Z-62 but a thin and separate item on the Z-70/B. Also found in 9mm Largo calibre.

Cartridge: 9mm Parabellum
Length, butt extended: 27.60in (701mm)
Length, butt retracted: 18.90in (480mm)
Weight: 6lb 5oz (2.87kg)
Barrel: 7.91in (201mm), 6 grooves, rh
Magazine: 20-, 30- or 40-round box
Muzzle velocity: 1247 ft/sec (380 m/sec)
Cyclic rate: 550 rds/min

Z-84
1984. Rectangular receiver with short muzzle protruding from barrel nut. Central pistol grip acting as magazine housing. Ejection port on top of receiver. Folding two-strut butt. Prominent sight protectors.

Cartridge: 9mm Parabellum
Length, butt extended: 24.21in (615mm)
Length, butt retracted: 16.14in (410mm)
Weight: 6lb 10oz (3.0kg)
Barrel: 8.46in (215mm), 6 grooves, rh
Magazine: 25- or 30-round box
Muzzle velocity: 1312 ft/sec (400 m/sec)
Cyclic rate: 600 rds/min

STEN Britain
Mark I
ROF (F) & BSA
1940. Cylindrical receiver with end-cap; smooth barrel jacket same diameter as the receiver, spoon-type muzzle compensator/flash hider. Short wooden fore-end, folding wooden fore-grip, fixed magazine housing, feeding from the left. Skeleton metal stock, may have short wood filler at front end.

Cartridge: 9mm Parabellum
Length: 35.25in (895mm)
Weight: 7lb 3oz (3.30kg)
Barrel: 7.75in (196mm), 6 grooves, rh
Magazine: 32-round box
Muzzle velocity: 1250 ft/sec (381 m/sec)
Cyclic rate: 550 rds/min

Mark 1*
ROF (F) & BSA
1941. Simplified model of the Mark 1. Did away with the wooden fore-end and handgrip, replaced by sheet-metal cover over trigger mechanism. Did away with flash hider/compensator.

Cartridge: 9mm Parabellum
Length: 31.25in (794mm)
Weight: 7lb 0oz (3.18kg)
Barrel: 7.80in (198mm), 6 grooves, rh
Magazine: 32-round box
Muzzle velocity: 1250 ft/sec (381 m/sec)
Cyclic rate: 550 rds/min

Mark 2
ROF (F) & BSA
1942. Shorter and handier model. Same receiver and trigger unit, single-strut butt-stock, removable barrel retained by perforated sleeve which acted as a forward hand grip, rotatable magazine housing with spring plunger lock. Magazine feeds from the left. Most common model of the Sten, some 3.5 million made.

Cartridge: 9mm Parabellum
Length: 30.0in (762mm)
Weight: 6lb 8oz (2.99kg)
Barrel: 7.75in (196mm), 2 or 6 grooves, rh
Magazine: 32-round box
Muzzle velocity: 1250 ft/sec (381 m/sec)
Cyclic rate: 550 rds/min

Mark 2S
Enfield
1942. Silenced version of the Mark 2. Same receiver but long cylindrical silencer/barrel with canvas foregrip laced around it.

Cartridge: 9mm Parabellum
Length: 35.75in (908mm)
Weight: 7lb 12oz (3.56kg)
Barrel: 3.50in (87mm), 6 grooves, rh
Magazine: 32-round box
Muzzle velocity: 1000 ft/sec (305 m/sec)
Cyclic rate: 450 rds/min

Mark 3
Lines & Long Branch
1942. Development of the Marks 1 and 2 in constructional methods. Same mechanism, trigger housing and skeleton butt, but the entire receiver and barrel jacket are one piece of welded tubing and the barrel is not removable. The magazine housing is fixed, welded to the receiver. Sighting/stiffening rib along the top of the receiver and jacket. No flash hider.

Cartridge: 9mm Parabellum
Length: 30.0in (762mm)
Weight: 7lb 0oz (3.22kg)
Barrel: 7.75in (196mm), 6 grooves, rh
Magazine: 32-round box
Muzzle velocity: 1250 ft/sec (381 m/sec)
Cyclic rate: 550 rds/min

Mark 4
Enfield
1943. Prototypes only, intended for use by airborne troops. **Mark 4A** had pistol grip midway along receiver, folding steel strip stock; **Mark 4B** had pistol grip at end of receiver, folding steel strip stock. Short perforated sleeve like Mark 2 but with conical flash hider. Insufficient improvement to warrant production.

Cartridge: 9mm Parabellum
Length, butt extended: 27.50in (698mm)
Length, butt folded: 17.50in (443mm)
Weight: 7lb 8oz (3.45kg)
Barrel: 3.75in (95mm) with flash hider, 6 grooves, rh
Magazine: 32-round box
Muzzle velocity: 1250 ft/sec (381 m/sec)
Cyclic rate: 570 rds/min

Mark 5
ROF (F) & BSA
1944. Generally as for the Mark 2 but better quality of manufacture and finish. Used wooden butt-stock and pistol grip, and the muzzle was formed with lugs for the Lee-Enfield rifle bayonet. Early models had a forward hand-grip but this was soon abandoned.

Cartridge: 9mm Parabellum
Length: 30.0in (762mm)
Weight: 8lb 9oz (3.90kg)
Barrel: 7.75in (196mm), 6 grooves, rh
Magazine: 32-round box
Muzzle velocity: 1250 ft/sec (381 m/sec)
Cyclic rate: 600 rds/min

Mark 6
Enfield
1944. Silenced version of the Mark 5. Same butt, pistol grip and receiver, but long barrel/silencer assembly.

Cartridge: 9mm Parabellum
Length: 33.75in (857mm)
Weight: 9lb 8oz (4.31kg)
Barrel: 3.75in (95mm), 6 grooves, rh
Magazine: 32-round box
Muzzle velocity: 1000 ft/sec (305 m/sec)
Cyclic rate: 475 rds/min

STERLING Britain
Sterling

L2A1
1953. Developed from the Patchett and similar in appearance. Cylindrical receiver, perforated barrel jacket, well-raked pistol grip at centre of balance, curved magazine feeding from left. Collapsible stock folding underneath the receiver.

Cartridge: 9mm Parabellum
Length, butt extended: 27.17in (690mm)
Length, butt retracted: 19.0in (483mm)
Weight: 6lb 0oz (2.72kg)
Barrel: 7.80in (198mm), 6 grooves, rh
Magazine: 34-round box
Muzzle velocity: 1280 ft/sec (390 m/sec)
Cyclic rate: 550 rds/min

L2A2

1955. Differed from L2A1 in several small details of manufacturing convenience; strengthened butt, larger sight aperture, fixed firing pin etc.

Specifications: as for L2A1

L2A3

1956. With further modifications: chamber to NATO dimensions, front sight adjustable by Allen key, removable trigger-guard, etc.

Specifications: as for L2A1

L34A1

1966. Silenced version of the L2A3. Standard receiver, pistol grip, butt and magazine, then long cylindrical barrel/silencer assembly with short wooden fore-end beneath.

Cartridge: 9mm Parabellum
Length, butt extended: 34.02in (864mm)
Length, butt retracted: 25.98in (660mm)
Weight: 7lb 15oz (3.60kg)
Barrel: 7.80in (198mm), 6 grooves, rh
Magazine: 34-round box
Muzzle velocity: 1017 ft/sec (310 m/sec)
Cyclic rate: 550 rds/min

Police Carbine.

1960. This was the standard military L2A1, but with the mechanism altered so as to allow semi-automatic fire only.

Specifications: as for L2A1

STEYR Austria
Steyr

MPi 69

1969–93. Rectangular receiver, central pistol grip acting as magazine housing, short barrel with knurled retaining nut. Sliding wire stock. Sling attached to cocking handle so as to provide a fast means of cocking.

Cartridge: 9mm Parabellum
Length, butt extended: 26.38in (670mm)
Length, butt retracted: 18.31in (465mm)
Weight: 6lb 14oz (3.13kg)
Barrel: 10.24in (260mm), 6 grooves, rh
Magazine: 25- or 32-round box
Muzzle velocity: 1250 ft/sec (381 m/sec)
Cyclic rate: 550 rds/min

MPi 81

1980. The same weapon as the MPi 69 but with a conventional cocking handle and the sling attachments on the side of the receiver.

Specifications: the same, except
Cyclic rate: 700 rds/min.

AUG-9

1986. This is actually a variant of the Steyr AUG rifle in which the normal barrel and locking bolt system is replaced by a 9mm barrel and a blowback bolt system, and the magazine housing is fitted with an adapter which allows the insertion of a 9mm magazine. The plastic casing, carrying handle with optical sight, full hand-guard pistol grip and folding forward grip of the rifle are retained.

Cartridge: 9mm Parabellum
Length: 26.18in (665mm)
Weight: 7lb 5oz (3.30kg)
Barrel: 16.54in (420mm), 6 grooves, rh
Magazine: 25 or 32-round box
Muzzle velocity: 1312 ft/sec (400 m/sec)
Cyclic rate: 700 rds/min

TMP

1990. Tactical Machine Pistol. Locked-breech weapon using rotating barrel. Frame and receiver are of synthetic material and incorporate a guide rail for the bolt. Pistol grip acting as magazine housing, forward grip. Barrel threaded for silencer. No butt-stock. The basic weapon is also produced in semi-automatic form, with no front grip, as the Special Purpose Pistol (*see* Pistols, Steyr SPP)

Cartridge: 9mm Parabellum
Length: 11.10in (282mm)
Weight: 2lb 14oz (1.30kg)
Barrel: 5.12in (130mm), 6 grooves, rh
Magazine: 15- or 30-round box
Muzzle velocity: 1180 ft/sec (360 m/sec)
Cyclic rate: 900 rds/min

STEYR-SOLOTHURN Switzerland/Austria
Steyr

1930. Also called the Solothurn **S1-100** and **MP34(ö)**. Wooden butt with half-stock, perforated barrel jacket, side-mounted magazine, prominent cocking knob on right. Exceptionally well made, machined from solid steel and highly finished. Unusual magazine loading slot in the magazine housing allows filling magazine from clips. Made in various calibres.

Cartridge: 9mm Parabellum
Length: 33.50in (850mm)
Weight: 8lb 8oz (3.87kg)
Barrel: 7.75in (196mm), 6 grooves, rh
Magazine: 32-round box
Muzzle velocity: 1250 ft/sec (381 m/sec)
Cyclic rate: 500 rds/min

SUOMI Finland
Tikkakoski

M26

1926. Wooden half-stock, cylindrical receiver, slotted barrel jacket. Unique 'hump-backed' butt-stock, and equally unique very curved magazine which bends up under the barrel jacket. Cocking device is a knob beneath the rear receiver cap. Lever at right front of fore-end unlocks barrel, allowing it to be rotated and withdrawn from the receiver.

Cartridge: 7.65 x 21.5mm Parabellum
Length: 36.02in (915mm)
Weight: 9lb 11oz (4.39kg)
Barrel: 13.58in (345mm), 6 grooves, rh
Magazine: 36-round box
Muzzle velocity: 1250 ft/sec (381 m/sec)
Cyclic rate: 750 rds/min

M31

1931. Wooden half-stock of conventional appearance, cylindrical receiver, long slotted barrel jacket, may have muzzle compensator. Fore-end slotted to accept a drum or box magazine. Barrel locking lever on right front of fore-end. Finnish Army weapons were modified in *ca* 1954 to take the 36-round Carl Gustav magazine.

Cartridge: 9mm Parabellum
Length: 36.02in (870mm)
Weight: 9lb 11oz (4.60kg)
Barrel: 13.58in (315mm), 6 grooves, rh
Magazine: 20- or 50-round box; or 40- or 71-round drum
Muzzle velocity: 1312 ft/sec (400 m/sec)
Cyclic rate: 900 rds/min

M37-39
Husqvarna

1939. Manufactured under licence in Sweden, this was simply a short model of the M31. Cylindrical receiver with end cap, slotted barrel jacket, wooden butt extending to the magazine housing, large trigger-guard, small hooked cocking handle. Numbers were also sold to Norway, Denmark, Indonesia and Egypt in the late 1940s.

Cartridge: 9mm Parabellum
Length: 30.31in (770mm)
Weight: 8lb 9oz (3.90kg)
Barrel: 8.38in (213mm), 6 grooves, rh
Magazine: 50-round box
Muzzle velocity: 1200 ft/sec (365 m/sec)
Cyclic rate: 900 rds/min

MP44/46

1946. Modification of the Daugs M44 (*qv*) to use the 36-round Carl Gustav magazine instead of the 71-round Suomi drum. Also made to a better standard of finish.

Cartridge: 9mm Parabellum
Length: 32.50in (828mm)
Weight: 6lb 3oz (2.84kg)
Barrel: 9.80in (248mm), 4 grooves, rh
Magazine: 36-round box
Muzzle velocity: 1310 ft/sec (402 m/sec)
Cyclic rate: 650 rds/min

TALLINN Estonia
Tallinn

Model 1923

A near-copy of the Bergmann MP18. Wood stock and fore-end, cylindrical receiver, finned barrel inside slotted jacket. Sling swivels on the jacket and butt. Left side feeding magazine.

Cartridge: 9mm Parabellum
Length: 31.89in (810mm)
Weight: 9lb 8oz (4.31kg)
Barrel: 8.27in (210mm), 6 grooves, rh
Magazine: 40-round box
Muzzle velocity: 1200 ft/sec (365 m/sec)
Cyclic rate: 600 rds/min

THOMPSON USA
M1928A1
Auto-Ordnance & Savage

1928. Probably the best-known submachine gun in the world, thanks to Hollywood. Rectangular receiver, finned barrel, muzzle compensator, removable wooden butt, large rear sight, well-raked pistol grip. Drum or box magazines. Delayed blowback using Blish system of slipping inclined faces.

Cartridge: .45 ACP
Length, with butt: 33.75in (857mm)
Length, without butt: 25.0in (635mm)
Weight: 10lb 12oz (4.87kg)
Barrel: 10.50in (268mm), 6 grooves, rh
Magazine: 20-round box or 50-round drum
Muzzle velocity: 920 ft/sec (280 m/sec)
Cyclic rate: 700 rds/min

M1
Auto-Ordnance & Savage

1942. Simplified version of the M1928A1; delayed blowback mechanism removed and simple blowback with a heavier bolt substituted. Forward hand grip replaced by wooden fore-end with finger grooves. Box magazine only. Butt no longer removable.

Cartridge: .45 ACP
Length: 32.0in (813mm)
Weight: 10lb 7oz (4.74kg)
Barrel: 10.50in (198mm), 6 grooves, rh
Magazine: 20- or 30-round box
Muzzle velocity: 920 ft/sec (280 m/sec)
Cyclic rate: 700 rds/min

M1A1
Auto-Ordnance & Savage

1942. As for the M1 but with a fixed firing pin forming part of the bolt instead of a separate firing pin and hammer.

Specifications: the same

UNITED DEFENSE USA
Marlin

UD M42

1941. Wooden stock, cylindrical receiver, part-finned barrel, box magazine, pistol grip and forward pistol grip – very 'Thompson' in outline. Produced as a private venture, purchased by US Government and distributed to various allied forces and to OSS. Prototypes were also made in .45 calibre but no production.

Cartridge: 9mm Parabellum
Length: 32.25in (820mm)
Weight: 9lb 1oz (4.17kg)
Barrel: 11.0in (279mm), 6 grooves, rh
Magazine: 20-round box
Muzzle velocity: 1312 ft/sec (400 m/sec)
Cyclic rate: 700 rds/min

URU Brazil
Bilbao

Model 2

1977. Rectangular frame, cylindrical receiver and perforated barrel jacket, short exposed muzzle. Largely made of stampings and drawn tubing. Pistol grip; forward magazine housing acts as a handgrip. Detachable butt may be of wood or a single-strut tubular steel type.

Cartridge: 9mm Parabellum
Length, butt fitted: 26.42in (671mm)
Length, butt removed: 17.05in (433mm)
Weight: 6lb 9oz (3.0kg)
Barrel: 6.89in (175mm), 6 grooves, rh
Magazine: 30-round box
Muzzle velocity: 1276 ft/sec (389 m/sec)
Cyclic rate: 750 rds/min

USA

See also **AI Corp, American, Ares, Arms Research, Cobra, Cobray, Colt, Cook, Demro, Hyde, Hyde-Inland, Ingram, Interdynamic, IOG, La France, Reising, RPB, Ruger, SACO, Sedgley, Smith & Wesson, SWD Inc, Thompson, United Defense, Viking, Weaver Arms & WSI**

M1, M1928A1 & M1A1

See Thompson

M2

See Hyde

M3

Guide Lamp

1942. The 'Grease Gun' – the American equivalent of the Sten. Cylindrical receiver, short barrel retained by knurled nut, metal pistol grip, sliding wire butt. Hinged ejection port cover locks bolt in forward position. Retracting handle on right side cocks bolt. Calibre could be changed to 9mm Parabellum by changing bolt and barrel and inserting adapter to take Sten magazines, but it rarely was.

Cartridge: .45ACP
Length, butt extended: 30.00in (762mm)
Length, butt retracted: 22.75in (577mm)
Weight: 8lb 15oz (4.05kg)
Barrel: 8.0in (203mm), 4 grooves, rh
Magazine: 30-round box
Muzzle velocity: 920 ft/sec (280 m/sec)
Cyclic rate: 450 rds/min

M3A1

Guide Lamp & Ithaca

1944. Improved M3. Retracting handle mechanism removed; bolt had a hole on the side into which a finger was inserted to cock the bolt. Longer hinged cover would lock bolt either forward or cocked when closed.

Cartridge: .45 ACP
Length, butt extended: 29.75in (756mm)
Length, butt retracted: 22.75in (577mm)
Weight: 8lb 3oz (3.71kg)
Barrel: 8.0in (203mm), 4 grooves, rh
Magazine: 30-round box

Muzzle velocity: 920 ft/sec (280 m/sec)
Cyclic rate: 450 rds/min

UZI Israel
IMI & FN

Uzi

Ca 1954. Distinctive pressed steel receiver with large wing protectors for fore and rear sights, cocking knob on top. Short plastic fore-end, pistol grip acting as magazine housing, wooden butt or collapsible steel butt.

Cartridge: 9mm Parabellum
Length, fixed butt or butt extended: 25.60in (650mm)
Length, butt retracted: 18.50in (470mm)
Weight: 8lb 4oz (3.75kg)
Barrel: 10.23in (260mm), 4 grooves, rh
Magazine: 25- or 32-round box
Muzzle velocity: 1312 ft/sec (400 m/sec)
Cyclic rate: 600 rds/min

Mini-Uzi

1981. A smaller version of the Uzi, with a side-folding single-strut metal butt and a special short magazine, though standard Uzi magazines can also be used.

Cartridge: 9mm Parabellum
Length, butt extended: 23.62in (600mm)
Length, butt retracted: 14.17in (360mm)
Weight: 5lb 15oz (2.70kg)
Barrel: 7.75in (197mm), 4 grooves, rh
Magazine: 20-, 25- or 32-round box
Muzzle velocity: 1155 ft/sec (352 m/sec)
Cyclic rate: 950 rds/min

Micro-Uzi

1982. The smallest version of the Uzi. Similar to the Mini-Uzi, with the same type of side-folding stock which serves as a forward hand grip when folded. The bolt has a tungsten insert to provide weight and keep the rate of fire to a controllable figure.

Cartridge: 9mm Parabellum
Length, butt extended: 18.11in (460mm)
Length, butt retracted: 9.84in (250mm)
Weight: 4lb 5oz (1.95kg)
Barrel: 4.61in (117mm), 4 grooves, rh
Magazine: 20-round box
Muzzle velocity: 1082 ft/sec (330 m/sec)
Cyclic rate: 1250 rds/min

This model was also made in limited numbers in .45 ACP calibre.

Specifications: the same, except
Magazine: 16-round box
Muzzle velocity: 787 ft/sec (240 m/sec)

VESELEY Britain
BSA

V42

1942. Cylindrical receiver, perforated barrel jacket, large magazine housing for special magazine which held two columns one behind the other. Wooden butt which contained part of the return spring. Submitted, passed trials, but turned down since Sten production was then at its peak.

Cartridge: 9mm Parabellum
Length: 32.0in (813mm)
Weight: 9lb 3oz (4.17kg)
Barrel: 10.0in (254mm), 6 grooves, rh
Magazine: 60-round box
Muzzle velocity: 1350 ft/sec (412 m/sec)
Cyclic rate: 750 rds/min

VIGNERON Belgium
Liègeoise

M2

1953. Cylindrical receiver, adjustable sliding wire butt set at an angle to the frame, long barrel with rear section finned, muzzle compensator. Pistol grip has grip safety locking the bolt. Adopted by Belgian Army, quantity left in the Congo, hence not uncommon in central Africa.

Cartridge: 9mm Parabellum
Length, butt extended: 35.00in (890mm)
Length, butt retracted: 27.75in (704mm)
Weight: 7lb 4oz (3.29kg)
Barrel: 12.0in (305mm), 6 grooves, rh
Magazine: 32-round box
Muzzle velocity: 1200 ft/sec (365 m/sec)
Cyclic rate: 625 rds/min

VIKING
Viking & WSI

1983–87. Cylindrical receiver, protruding short barrel, plastic fore-end and grip, cocking handle upper left of receiver. Sliding wire butt similar to that of the US M3. Sound suppressor, collimating sights and other accessories were offered, but very few guns were ever made. Designed by Frank Csongor, it appears to have been originally made by W.S.I., then by Csongor's own company, Viking.

Cartridge: 9 × 19mm Parabellum
Length, butt extended: 15.75in (600mm)
Length, butt folded: 29.0in (400mm)
Weight: 7lb 12oz (3.52kg)
Barrel: 8.66in (220mm), 6 grooves, rh
Magazine: 32- or 36-round box
Muzzle velocity: 1312 ft/sec (400 m/sec)
Cyclic rate: 750 rds/min

VILLAR PEROSA Italy
OVP

M15

1915. Often called the first submachine gun, but actually designed as an infantry support machine gun and did not became a submachine gun until converted into the OVP (*qv*). Delayed blowback by helical groove in receiver and cam on bolt. Cylindrical receiver, overhead magazine. Mounted in pairs on a bipod, with spade grip and trigger.

Cartridge: 9 × 19mm Glisenti
Length: 21.00in (533mm)
Weight: 14lb 6oz (6.52kg)
Barrel: 12.50in (318mm), 6 grooves, rh
Magazine: 25-round box

Muzzle velocity: 1200 ft/sec (365 m/sec)
Cyclic rate: 1200 rds/min for each barrel

WALTHER Germany
Walther

MP-K

1963. Pressed steel receiver with cylindrical upper section within which the major portion of the bolt moves. Barrel lies below, and receiver is ventilated. Side-folding stock which also acts as a forward handgrip when folded.

Cartridge: 9mm Parabellum
Length, butt extended: 25.71in (653mm)
Length, butt retracted: 14.48in (368mm)
Weight: 6lb 3oz (2.82kg)
Barrel: 6.73in (171mm), 6 grooves, rh
Magazine: 32-round box
Muzzle velocity: 1167 ft/sec (356 m/sec)
Cyclic rate: 550 rds/min

MP-L

This is exactly the same weapon as the MP-K *above*, but with a longer barrel and hence an extended forward section to the receiver.

Cartridge: 9mm Parabellum
Length, butt extended: 29.0in (737mm)
Length, butt retracted: 17.91in (455mm)
Weight: 6lb 10oz (3.0kg)
Barrel: 10.12in (257mm), 6 grooves, rh
Magazine: 32-round box
Muzzle velocity: 1300 ft/sec (396 m/sec)
Cyclic rate: 600 rds/min

WEAVER
Weaver Arms

PKS-9 Ultralite

1985. Largely made of aluminium castings to save weight. Rectangular receiver, short wooden fore-end, pistol grip acts as magazine housing. Rear sight in large housing, fore-sight on large triangular casting, exposed muzzle. Magazine protrudes from pistol grip for over half its length. Limited production. Some models had a clumsy tubular stock which folded forward over the receiver.

Cartridge: 9 × 19mm Parabellum
Length, without stock: 16.4in (416mm)
Weight: 6.0 lb (2.72kg)
Barrel: 7.125in (181mm), 6 grooves, rh
Magazine: 25-, 32- or 40-round box
Muzzle velocity: 1250 ft/sec (380 m/sec)
Cyclic rate: 1000 rds/min

WELGUN Britain
BSA

1944. Developed as a light and handy gun for airborne troops. Open-sided receiver with cylindrical bolt, barrel jacket containing the return spring which pulled the bolt forward. Pistol grip, single-strut folding butt, vertical magazine. Not adopted.

Cartridge: 9mm Parabellum
Length, butt extended: 27.5in (700mm)

Length, butt retracted: 17.00in (432mm)
Weight: 6lb 13oz (3.09kg)
Barrel: 7.75in (196mm), 6 grooves, rh
Magazine: 32-round box
Muzzle velocity: 1250 ft/sec (381 m/sec)
Cyclic rate: 650 rds/min

YUGOSLAVIA
Kragujevac
M49

1949. Based on the Russian PPSh-41, but with several detail differences. The receiver and jacket are machined steel instead of stampings, there is a push-through safety catch in the fore-end ahead of the trigger-guard, and the jacket has small circular holes instead of slots. The Soviet 71-round drum will no longer fit, but the Soviet PPSh-41, Yugoslav and Chinese Type 50 magazines can be interchanged.

Cartridge: 7.62 × 25mm Soviet Pistol
Length: 34.25in (870mm)
Weight: 8lb 11oz (3.95kg)
Barrel: 10.75in (273mm), 4 grooves, rh
Magazine: 35-round box
Muzzle velocity: 1640 ft/sec (500 m/sec)
Cyclic rate: 700 rds/min

M56

1956. Generally resembles the Erma MP40, but with longer body and barrel, and has curved magazine in front of the fore-end. Similar folding butt, simpler bolt and return spring assembly. Fitted for bayonet.

Cartridge: 7.62 × 25mm Soviet Pistol
Length, butt extended: 34.25in (870mm)
Length, butt retracted: 25.39in (645mm)
Weight: 6lb 10oz (3.0kg)
Barrel: 9.84in (250mm), 4 grooves, rh
Magazine: 35-round box
Muzzle velocity: 1640 ft/sec (500 m/sec)
Cyclic rate: 600 rds/min

M65

1965. Designed for export sale, this was simply the M56 re-barrelled to 9mm Parabellum and with a straight magazine instead of a curved one.

Cartridge: 9mm Parabellum
Length, butt extended: 34.45in (875mm)
Length, butt retracted: 25.0in (635mm)
Weight: 6lb 10oz (3.0kg)
Barrel: 9.84in (250mm), 6 grooves, rh
Magazine: 30-round box
Muzzle velocity: 1260 ft/sec (384 m/sec)
Cyclic rate: 600 rds/min

M84

1984. This is the Skorpion in 7.65mm calibre built under licence. The dimensions are as for the Czech original.

COMPARATIVE TABLES

Weapons are arranged in ascending order of calibre. Overall lengths and barrel lengths are given in inches, weights in pounds and muzzle velocities in feet per second. Multiple magazine size options are not shown; only the most usual magazine capacity is given.

Types of action are abbreviated as follows: Blowback – BB; Delayed blowback – DBB; Recoil – Rec.

Name	Year	Calibre	Action	Length	Barrel	Weight	Magazine	Velocity	Rate
American 180	1960	.22LR	BB	35.25	16.5	5.75	177	1350	1200
Russia: A-91	1995	5.45 × 39.5	Gas	23.78	7.97	3.81	20	2230	900
Daewoo K1A	1988	5.56 × 45	Gas	33.00	10.35	6.31	30	2690	800
Heckler & Koch HK53	1970	5.56 × 45	DBB	29.70	8.30	6.75	25	2460	700
FN P-90	1990	5.7 × 28	BB	19.68	10.35	5.56	50	2345	900
Lercker	1950	6.35 Auto	BB	7.25	4.00	2.06	20	820	1000
China: Type 50	1950	7.62 × 25	BB	33.75	10.75	8.00	35	1400	900
China: Type 64 Silent	1964	7.62 × 25	BB	33.20	9.60	7.50	30	980	1000
China: Type 79	1980	7.62 × 25	Gas	29.13	n/a	4.19	20	1640	650
China: Type 85	1985	7.62 × 25	BB	24.72	n/a	4.19	30	1640	780
China: Type 85 Silent	1985	7.62 × 25	BB	34.20	9.80	5.50	30	985	800
CZ 24	1951	7.62 × 25	BB	26.60	11.20	7.25	32	1800	600
CZ26	1952	7.62 × 25	BB	27.00	11.20	7.25	32	1800	600
Iran: Model 22	1943	7.62 × 25	BB	33.19	10.55	8.25	35	1500	900
North Vietnam: K-50M	1965	7.62 × 25	BB	29.76	10.60	7.50	35	1600	700
Russia: PPS-34/38	1938	7.62 × 25	BB	30.70	10.62	8.25	71	1590	800
Russia: PPD-40	1940	7.62 × 25	BB	30.60	10.63	8.12	71	1590	800
Russia: PPS-42	1942	7.62 × 25	BB	35.04	10.83	6.56	35	1590	700
Russia: PPS-43	1943	7.62 × 25	BB	32.28	10.00	7.50	35	1590	700
Russia: PPSh-41	1941	7.62 × 25	BB	33.00	10.50	8.00	71	1590	900
Yugoslavia: M49	1949	7.62 × 25	BB	34.25	10.75	8.69	35	1640	700
Yugoslavia M56	1956	7.62 × 25	BB	34.25	9.84	6.62	35	1640	600
Brondby	1933	7.63 × 25	Gas	34.25	16.73	5.12	15	1650	800
Skorpion vz/61	1960	7.65 × 17	BB	28.95	4.53	2.88	20	968	700
MAS MAS38	1938	7.65 × 19	BB	28.90	8.82	6.31	32	1151	60
SIG M1920	1920	7.65 × 21.5	BB	33.07	8.27	11.12	50	1200	600
Suomi M26	1926	7.65 × 21.5	BB	36.02	13.58	9.69	36	1250	750
Japan: Type100/40	1940	8 × 21	BB	36.00	9.00	7.50	30	1100	450
Japan: Type 100/44	1944	8 × 21	BB	36.00	9.20	8.50	30	1100	800
CZ 1938	1938	9 × 17	BB	31.00	8.50	8.00	24	950	600
Ingram Model 11	1970	9 × 17	BB	18.10	5.08	3.50	32	961	1200
Arsenal Shipka	1996	9 × 18	BB	24.60	5.90	4.88	32	1050	700
Baksan	1995	9 × 18	Rec	25.60	n/a	3.94	20	1100	900
Bison	1990	9 × 18	BB	26.00	n/a	4.62	64	1115	700

Name	Year	Calibre	Action	Length	Barrel	Weight	Magazine	Velocity	Rate
KEDR	1973	9 × 18	BB	21.25	4.70	3.06	30	1117	850
Kiparis	1997	9 × 18	BB	23.20	n/a	3.44	30	1100	900
KLIN	1994	9 × 18	BB	21.25	4.70	3.06	30	1410	1100
Kovrov AEK 919	1997	9 × 18	BB	19.50	8.85	3.62	30	1115	n/a
Poland: PM63	1964	9 × 18	BB	22.95	6.00	3.94	25	1060	600
Poland: PM84	1983	9 × 18	BB	22.64	7.28	4.56	25	1083	600
Adasa	1953	9 × 19	BB	32.00	9.85	7.00	30	1200	600
Agram	1997	9 × 19	BB	13.80	6.00	4.19	32	1200	n/a
Akaba	1970	9 × 19	BB	29.00	5.90	n/a	36	1250	700
Alfa GP-1	1978	9 × 19	BB	24.50	9.00	7.06	30	1350	550
Andrews (Australia)	1943	9 × 19	BB	26.50	6.80	6.19	30	1180	660
Arac	1950	9 × 19	BB	34.75	11.85	7.00	32	1300	600
Ares	1984	9 × 19	BB	19.80	7.25	5.25	20	1250	650
Argentina: FMK-3	1986	9 × 19	BB	27.20	11.40	7.94	40	1312	600
Argentina: PAM-1	1952	9 × 19	BB	28.54	7.87	6.56	40	1200	450
Armaguerra O.G.44	1944	9 × 19	BB	31.00	11.50	7.00	40	1280	500
Arms Research KF-AMP	1985	9 × 19	BB	20.55	5.00	3.94	36	1181	800
Arsenal Shipka	1996	9 × 19	BB	28.00	7.80	5.31	25	1250	700
Austen Mk I	1943	9 × 19	BB	33.25	7.80	8.75	28	1200	500
Austen Mk II	1944	9 × 19	BB	33.25	7.80	8.50	28	1200	500
Australia: F-1	1962	9 × 19	BB	28.15	8.00	7.19	34	1250	600
Beretta 1918	1918	9 × 19	BB	33.50	21.50	7.19	25	1250	900
Beretta 1938A	1938	9 × 19	BB	37.25	12.40	9.25	40	1378	600
Beretta 38/42	1943	9 × 19	BB	31.50	8.40	7.20	40	1250	550
Beretta 38/44	1945	9 × 19	BB	31.50	8.40	7.20	40	1250	550
Beretta 38/49	1949	9 × 19	BB	31.50	8.40	7.20	40	1250	550
Beretta Model 1	1941	9 × 19	BB	28.00	7.80	8.00	40	1250	550
Beretta Model 3	1956	9 × 19	BB	28.00	7.80	7.62	40	1250	550
Beretta Model 5	1957	9 × 19	BB	31.50	8.40	7.20	40	1250	550
Beretta Model 12	1959	9 × 19	BB	26.00	7.90	6.56	40	1250	550
Beretta Model 12S	1983	9 × 19	BB	26.00	7.80	7.06	40	1250	550
Bergmann MP18	1916	9 × 19	BB	32.10	7.80	9.19	32	1250	400
Bergmann MP28	1928	9 × 19	BB	32.00	7.80	8.94	32	1250	650
Bergmann MP34	1934	9 × 19	BB	33.00	7.80	8.94	32	1250	650
Bernardelli VB	1947	9 × 19	BB	32.70	11.80	7.44	40	1350	600
BSA	1945	9 × 19	BB	27.50	8.00	5.62	32	1300	530
Burma: BA52	1949	9 × 19	BB	32.00	10.00	6.75	40	1377	500
Bushman	1990	9 × 19	BB	10.86	3.24	6.44	32	1155	450
BXP	1984	9 × 19	BB	23.90	8.18	5.75	32	1250	800
Canada: C1	1958	9 × 19	BB	27.00	7.79	6.50	30	1200	550
Carl Gustav m/45B	1945	9 × 19	BB	31.80	8.38	7.88	36	1345	600
CETME C-2	1977	9 × 19	BB	28.35	8.35	6.31	32	1066	600
CEV M9-M1	1982	9 × 19	BB	n/a	9.00	6.62	30	1312	600
Colt Model 635	1992	9 × 19	BB	28.75	10.50	5.75	32	1300	900
Cook	1950	9 × 19	BB	23.28	9.50	7.00	32	1200	550
CZ 47	1947	9 × 19	BB	30.85	7.80	6.37	40	1250	560
CZ23	1948	9 × 19	BB	27.00	11.20	6.81	40	1250	600
CZ ZK 383	1933	9 × 19	BB	35.43	12.79	9.56	30	1250	500/700
Daugs M44	1944	9 × 19	BB	32.70	9.84	6.19	71	1300	650

Name	Year	Calibre	Action	Length	Barrel	Weight	Magazine	Velocity	Rate
Dux 53	1953	9×19	BB	32.50	9.84	7.69	50	1300	500
Dux 59	1959	9×19	BB	31.20	9.84	6.62	40	1300	550
El Salvador: HB-1	1958	9×19	BB	34.00	10.00	8.25	30	1300	740
Erma MPE	1931	9×19	BB	35.04	9.84	9.19	30	1250	500
Erma MP38	1936	9×19	BB	32.75	9.72	9.00	32	1250	500
Erma MP40	1940	9×19	BB	32.80	9.84	8.88	32	1250	500
Erma EMP44	1944	9×19	BB	28.34	9.84	8.00	32	1300	500
Erma EMP58	1958	9×19	BB	27.56	6.49	6.62	32	1250	700
Erma EMP59	1959	9×19	BB	28.75	8.27	7.06	30	1250	620
Erma EMP60	1960	9×19	BB	31.10	9.45	7.31	36	1300	500
FN	1953	9×19	BB	34.45	9.80	8.19	40	1310	600
FNAB	1943	9×19	DBB	31.30	7.80	7.06	40	1250	400
Franchi LF-57	1957	9×19	BB	26.70	8.10	7.12	40	1260	500
Furrer MP41/44	1943	9×19	Rec	30.50	9.80	11.37	40	1312	900
Germany: MP-3008	1945	9×19	BB	31.50	7.72	6.50	32	1250	500
Gevarm D3, D4	1956	9×19	BB	31.20	12.60	8.06	32	1310	600
Haenel MP41	1941	9×19	BB	34.05	9.84	8.12	32	1250	500
Hafdasa C-4	1949	9×19	BB	31.20	7.75	7.00	30	1200	600
Halcon ML-57	1957	9×19	BB	30.70	8.86	6.94	40	1200	520
Halcon ML-63	1963	9×19	BB	23.62	6.69	8.06	42	1148	600
Heckler & Koch MP5A2	1964	9×19	DBB	26.70	8.86	5.62	30	1312	800
H&K MP5A3	1964	9×19	DBB	26.00	8.86	5.62	30	1312	800
H&K MP5SD1	1970	9×19	DBB	21.65	5.75	6.19	30	935	800
H&K MP5SD2	1975	9×19	DBB	30.70	5.75	6.81	30	935	800
H&K MP5SD3	1975	9×19	DBB	30.70	5.75	7.50	30	935	800
H&K MP5K	1976	9×19	DBB	12.80	4.52	4.37	15	1230	900
H&K MP5PDW	1992	9×19	DBB	31.50	5.50	6.15	30	1230	900
H&K MP200	1988	9×19	BB	22.24	n/a	6.12	30	1245	880
Hispano-Suiza MP43/44	1943	9×19	BB	34.00	12.50	10.50	50	1300	800
Hotchkiss Universal	1949	9×19	BB	30.60	10.80	7.50	32	1312	650
Hovea m/49	1949	9×19	BB	31.80	8.46	7.37	36	1250	600
Hungary: KGP-9	1990	9×19	BB	24.20	7.48	6.06	25	1280	900
IMBEL MD-2	1980	9×19	BB	30.31	8.70	7.94	30	1312	700
Imperia MI-53	1954	9×19	BB	31.50	8.00	6.94	32	1200	600
INDEP LUSA A1	1986	9×19	BB	23.60	6.30	5.50	30	1280	900
INDEP LUSA A2	1994	9×19	BB	23.00	6.30	6.19	30	1280	900
Indonesia: PM Model 7	1957	9×19	BB	33.07	10.78	7.25	33	1250	600
Ingram Model 10	1964	9×19	BB	22.0	5.75	6.00	32	1200	1050
Interdynamic	1985	9×19	BB	20.55	5.00	3.94	36	1245	900
IOG MP2	1980	9×19	BB	13.25	n/a	4.00	32	1085	750
Italy: TZ-45	1945	9×19	BB	33.46	9.05	7.19	40	1198	550
Jati-Matic	1985	9×19	BB	14.76	8.00	4.31	40	1181	650
Lanchester	1941	9×19	BB	33.50	7.90	9.62	50	1200	600
Madsen m/45	1945	9×19	BB	31.50	12.40	7.00	50	1312	850
Madsen m/46	1946	9×19	BB	31.50	7.75	7.00	32	1250	500
Madsen m/50	1950	9×19	BB	30.75	7.83	7.00	32	1250	550
Madsen m/53	1953	9×19	BB	31.50	7.80	7.00	32	1250	550
MAS STA-1924	1924	9×19	BB	32.83	8.86	7.69	32	1200	600
MAT MAT-49	1949	9×19	BB	28.35	8.97	7.69	32	1283	600

Name	Year	Calibre	Action	Length	Barrel	Weight	Magazine	Velocity	Rate
Mauser Model 57	1957	9×19	BB	24.00	10.24	6.94	32	1197	800
MEMS Mod 67	1967	9×19	BB	31.50	7.08	7.31	40	1197	850
Mendoza HM-3	1975	9×19	BB	25.00	10.04	5.94	32	1300	600
Mini-ERO	1996	9×19	BB	21.46	5.90	4.88	30	1155	1100
Orita M1941	1941	9×19	BB	35.20	11.69	7.62	25	1250	600
OVP	1920	9×19	BB	35.50	11.00	8.06	25	1250	900
Owen Mk 1	1941	9×19	BB	32.00	9.75	9.31	33	1378	700
Owen Mk 2	1943	9×19	BB	32.00	9.75	7.62	33	1378	700
Patchett Mk 1	1944	9×19	BB	28.00	8.25	6.19	32	1200	600
Pelo	1956	9×19	BB	20.07	8.86	4.62	30	1200	600
Poland: PM84P	1985	9×19	BB	22.64	7.28	4.75	25	1181	640
Poland: PM98	1998	9×19	BB	23.82	7.28	5.06	25	1181	640
Port Said	1960	9×19	BB	31.81	8.38	8.06	36	1312	600
Portugal: FBP M/948	1948	9×19	BB	32.00	9.80	8.19	32	1260	500
Portugal: FBP M/976	1978	9×19	BB	31.50	9.80	6.88	36	1260	650
RAN	1953	9×19	BB	31.25	11.81	6.50	32	1395	630
Ratmil	1995	9×19	BB	25.60	n/a	5.94	30	1214	650
Rexim Favor	1952	9×19	BB	34.35	13.35	10.31	32	1400	600
Rhodesia: R-76	1976	9×19	BB	30.00	10.00	6.69	30	1300	500
Rhogun	1978	9×19	BB	26.00	10.00	8.81	25	1250	660
Ruger MP-9	1994	9×19	BB	21.89	6.81	6.62	32	1148	600
Russia: PP-90	1995	9×19	BB	19.29	5.12	4.06	30	1050	650
Saco Model 683	1985	9×19	BB	27.52	8.00	7.31	25	1300	650
SAF	1990	9×19	BB	25.28	7.87	5.94	30	1280	1200
SAF Mini-SAF	1990	9×19	BB	12.20	4.53	5.06	30	1214	1200
Sedgley	1940	9×19	BB	35.00	11.00	7.50	20	1312	450
SIG MKPO	1935	9×19	DBB	32.38	11.81	8.37	30	1312	900
SIG MP41	1940	9×19	BB	31.50	12.05	9.60	40	1312	850
SIG MP44	1943	9×19	BB	32.38	11.81	8.69	40	1378	800
SIG MP48	1948	9×19	BB	28.15	7.87	8.12	40	1200	700
SIG MP310	1958	9×19	BB	28.94	7.87	7.56	40	1200	900
Sima-Cifar MGP-79A	1979	9×19	BB	31.85	9.33	6.81	32	1345	700
Sima-Cifar MGP-84	1982	9×19	BB	19.29	6.00	5.06	32	1122	650
Sima-Cifar MGP-87	1987	9×19	BB	30.16	7.64	6.37	32	1187	700
Smith & Wesson Light Rifle	1939	9×19	BB	30.50	9.75	8.62	20	1240	No
Smith & Wesson Type 76	1967	9×19	BB	28.95	8.00	7.25	36	1250	720
Socimi Type 821	1985	9×19	BB	23.62	7.87	5.37	32	1247	600
Sola Super	1954	9×19	BB	35.00	12.00	6.37	32	1400	550
Sola Light	1957	9×19	BB	31.00	7.87	6.00	32	1250	550
Spectre M-4	1985	9×19	BB	22.83	5.12	6.37	50	1312	850
Star Z-62	1962	9×19	BB	27.60	7.91	6.31	40	1200	550
Star Z-70/B	1971	9×19	BB	27.60	7.91	6.31	40	1247	550
Star Z-84	1984	9×19	BB	24.21	8.46	6.62	30	1312	600
Sten Mk 1	1940	9×19	BB	35.25	7.75	7.19	32	1250	550
Sten Mk 1*	1941	9×19	BB	31.25	7.80	7.00	32	1250	550
Sten Mk 2	1942	9×19	BB	30.00	7.75	6.50	32	1250	550
Sten Mk 2S	1942	9×19	BB	35.75	3.50	7.75	32	1000	450
Sten Mk 3	1942	9×19	BB	30.00	7.75	7.00	32	1250	550
Sten Mk 4	1943	9×19	BB	27.50	3.75	7.50	32	1250	550

Name	Year	Calibre	Action	Length	Barrel	Weight	Magazine	Velocity	Rate
Sten Mk 5	1944	9 × 19	BB	30.00	7.75	8.56	32	1250	600
Sten Mk 6	1944	9 × 19	BB	33.75	3.75	9.50	32	1000	475
Sterling L2A1	1953	9 × 19	BB	27.17	7.80	6.00	34	1280	550
Sterling L34A1	1960	9 × 19	BB	34.02	7.80	7.94	34	1017	550
Steyr MPi 69	1969	9 × 19	BB	26.38	10.24	6.88	32	1250	550
Steyr AUG-9	1986	9 × 19	BB	26.18	16.54	7.31	32	1312	700
Steyr TMP	1990	9 × 19	Rec	11.10	5.12	2.88	30	1180	900
Steyr-Solothurn MP-34	1930	9 × 19	BB	33.50	7.75	8.50	32	1250	500
Suomi M31	1931	9 × 19	BB	36.02	13.58	9.69	50	1312	900
Suomi M37-39	1939	9 × 19	BB	30.31	8.38	8.56	50	1200	900
Suomi MP44/46	1946	9 × 19	BB	32.50	9.80	6.19	36	1310	650
Tallinn	1923	9 × 19	BB	31.89	8.27	9.50	40	1200	600
United Defense M42	1941	9 × 19	BB	32.25	11.00	9.06	20	1312	700
Uru Model 2	1977	9 × 19	BB	26.42	6.89	6.56	30	1276	750
Uzi	1954	9 × 19	BB	25.60	10.23	8.25	32	1312	600
Uzi: Mini-Uzi	1981	9 × 19	BB	23.62	7.75	5.94	32	1155	950
Uzi: Micro-Uzi	1982	9 × 19	BB	18.11	4.61	4.31	20	1082	1250
Veseley V-42	1942	9 × 19	BB	32.00	10.00	9.19	60	1350	750
Vigneron M2	1953	9 × 19	BB	35.00	12.00	7.25	32	1200	625
Viking	1983	9 × 19	BB	15.75	8.66	7.75	36	1312	750
Villar Perosa M15	1915	9 × 19	DBB	21.00	12.50	14.37	25	1200	1200
Walther MP-K	1963	9 × 19	BB	25.71	6.73	6.19	32	1167	550
Walther MP-L	1963	9 × 19	BB	29.00	10.12	6.62	32	1300	600
Weaver PKS-9	1985	9 × 19	BB	16.40	7.12	6.00	32	1250	1000
Welgun (UK)	1944	9 × 19	BB	27.50	7.75	6.81	32	1250	650
Yugoslavia: M65	1965	9 × 19	BB	34.45	9.84	6.62	30	1260	600
Labora	1938	9 × 23	BB	31.75	10.25	9.37	36	1312	750
Parinco CI-3R	1958	9 × 23	BB	31.50	10.00	6.00	32	1200	600
Star SI-35	1935	9 × 23	DBB	35.45	10.60	8.25	40	1350	300/700
Star Z-45	1944	9 × 23	BB	33.00	7.80	8.50	30	1250	450
BSA-Kiraly	1939	9 × 25	DBB	38.75	16.13	8.50	40	1480	730
Danuvia 39M	1939	9 × 25	DBB	41.25	19.65	8.19	40	1525	750
Danuvia 43M	1943	9 × 25	DBB	37.50	16.70	8.00	40	1450	750
SIG MKMO	1933	9 × 25	DBB	40.35	19.68	9.25	40	1600	900
Heckler & Koch MP5/10	1992	10 Auto	DBB	26.80	8.86	5.88	30	1450	800
Heckler & Koch MP5/40	1992	.40 S&W	DBB	26.80	8.86	5.88	30	1150	800
Demro TAC-1	1974	.45	BB	19.37	10.50	7.75	30	935	700
Halcon M/943	1943	.45	BB	33.40	11.50	10.44	30	950	700
Halcon M/946	1946	.45	BB	31.10	6.00	8.88	30	920	700
Hyde Model 35	1935	.45	BB	35.00	11.25	9.50	20	920	725
Hyde-Inland (US M2)	1942	.45	BB	32.10	12.10	9.25	20	960	500
INA M/950	1950	.45	BB	31.25	8.38	7.50	30	920	650
Ingram Model 6	1949	.45	BB	30.00	9.00	7.25	30	920	600
Ingram Model 10	1964	.45	BB	22.00	5.75	6.00	30	920	1145
La France M16K	1996	.45	BB	26.61	7.24	8.50	30	853	625
P.O.C. Model 6	1951	.45	BB	30.25	9.00	7.00	30	950	650
Reising Model 50	1941	.45	DBB	35.75	11.00	6.75	20	920	550
Reising Model 55	1943	.45	DBB	31.25	10.50	6.25	20	920	550
Thompson M1928A1	1928	.45	DBB	33.75	10.50	10.75	50	920	700

Name	Year	Calibre	Action	Length	Barrel	Weight	Magazine	Velocity	Rate
Thompson M1	1942	.45	BB	32.00	10.50	10.44	30	920	700
USA: M3	1942	.45	BB	30.00	8.00	8.94	30	920	450
USA: M3A1	1944	.45	BB	29.75	8.00	8.19	30	920	450
Uzi: Micro-Uzi	1983	.45	BB	18.11	4.61	4.31	16	787	1000

RIFLES

Where no magazine capacity is given weapons are single shot. Armour penetration figures are given for anti-tank rifles as follows 21/300/0, meaning that the bullet will penetrate 21mm of armour at 300m range, striking at an angle of 0° – that is at right angles to the target plate.

ACCURACY INTERNATIONAL Britain
Accuracy International

PM Sniper Rifle

1985. Bolt action repeating rifle built on an aluminium frame, around which a synthetic fibre stock is assembled. Thumb-hole stock, bipod attached to fore-end. Iron sights to 700 metres, but usually fitted with telescope. Developed commercially, adopted by British Army as **L96A1** sniper rifle. Also available in other calibres.

Cartridge: 7.62 × 51mm NATO
Length: 47.0in (1194mm)
Weight: 14lb 5oz (6.50kg)
Barrel: 25.78in (655mm), 4 grooves, rh
Magazine: 10-round box
Muzzle velocity: 2788 ft/sec (850 m/sec)

AW Sniper Rifle

Developed *ca* 1993 as an improvement on the PM and specifically to meet a Swedish Army specification. Adopted as **Psg 90** sniping rifle by Sweden in 1996. Bolt action repeating rifle, heavy barrel, muzzle brake, adjustable thumb-hole stock, bipod attached to fore-end. Particular attention paid to reliability in sub-zero climate.

Cartridge: 7.62 × 51mm NATO
Length: 47.25in (1200mm)
Weight: 14lb 5oz (6.50kg)
Barrel: 25.60in (650mm), 4 grooves, rh
Magazine: 9-round box
Muzzle velocity: 2788 ft/sec (850 m/sec)

ADVANCED COMBAT RIFLE USA

1984–90. A programme to develop an infantry rifle showing a substantial improvement in first-round hit probability over the standard M16A2 rifle. Four designs were tested in 1989–90; all worked satisfactorily but none showed the required degree of improvement and the programme was closed down. The four rifles tested are listed below since significant numbers were made and because there is every possibility that they may form the basis of some future designs. Unfortunately, not all details of these rifles have been released, nor can the details of their ammunition be given in the cartridge section.

AAI ACR Prototype
AAI

Gas-operated; locking system never revealed but probably an arcuate swinging block. Single shots and three-round bursts. Conventional butt, trigger-guard and receiver; short fore-end, long slotted handguard, large tubular muzzle compensator. Fired a flechette cartridge based on the 5.56 x 45mm case.

Cartridge: 5.56 × 45mm Flechette
Length: 40.59in (1016mm)
Weight: 7lb 12oz (3.53kg)
Barrel: not known
Magazine: 30-round box
Muzzle velocity: 4600 ft/sec (1402 m/sec)
Cyclic rate: not known

Colt ACR Prototype
Colt

Gas-operated, rotating bolt, selective fire. Straight-line layout with telescoping tubular butt, M16-pattern receiver, heavy barrel with muzzle brake/compensator, fore-end with perforated rib above to provide a quick sight line for snap-shooting. Fired a Duplex (two bullet) round based on the existing 5.56 x 45mm case.

Cartridge: 5.56 × 45mm Duplex
Length, butt extended: 40.59in (1031mm)
Length, butt retracted: 36.73in (933mm)
Weight: 7lb 5oz (3.306kg)
Barrel: not known
Magazine: 30-round box
Muzzle velocity: 2900 ft/sec (884 m/sec)
Cyclic rate: not known

Heckler & Koch ACR Prototype
Heckler & Koch

This was little more than the existing German G11 rifle (*see* H&K, G11K3) with some slight modifications to suit American tastes. Gas operated, rotating chamber breech, caseless cartridge. Note that the calibre is noted as being different to the German weapon; it wasn't, but in an attempt to disguise its origins the US authorities decreed that the calibre would be measured from the bottom of the rifling grooves.

Cartridge: 4.92 × 34mm caseless
Length: 29.53in (750mm)
Weight: 8lb 10oz (3.90kg)
Barrel: not known
Magazine: 50-round box
Muzzle velocity: 3000 ft/sec (914 m/sec)
Cyclic rate: 600 rds/min automatic
Three-round burst rate: 2200 rds/min

Steyr ACR Prototype
Steyr

Bullpup, smoothly streamlined plastic body with carrying-handle/sight base extending to the muzzle, Translucent magazine in butt, short exposed flash eliminator, hand-sized trigger-guard. Gas operated using an annular piston arrangement driving a rising-block breech. Fired a special plastic-cased, annular-primed, rimless and grooveless flechette cartridge. Single shots and three-round bursts.

Cartridge: 5.56mm synthetic-cased flechette
Length: 30.08in (764mm)
Weight: 7lb 2oz (3.23kg)
Barrel: not known
Magazine: 24-round box
Muzzle velocity: 4855 ft/sec (1480 m/sec)
Cyclic rate: not known

ALBINI-BRAENDLIN Belgium
Dresse-Laloux

Breech-loading conversions to a design by Albini, perfected and engineered by Braendlin.

M1867 Infantry Rifle

Conversions from earlier smooth-bore (SB) muskets or muzzle-loading rifles to the Albini 'trap-door' breech system. SB muskets had new rifled barrels. Full-stocked, external side-hammers driving a bolt which locked the breech-block and then struck the firing pin.

Cartridge: 11 × 50R Albini
Length: 53.07in (1348mm)
Weight: 10lb 1oz (4.57kg)
Barrel: 34.76in (883mm), 4 grooves, rh
Muzzle velocity: 1360 ft/sec (415 m/sec)

M1873 Infantry Rifle

Lifting 'trap-door' breech; full stocked, external hammer with locking bolt, firing pin inside breech-block, tangent sight to 1100m. Bayonet fittings and cleaning rod.

Cartridge: 11 × 50R Albini
Length: 53.03in (1347mm)
Weight: 9lb 14oz (4.49kg)
Barrel: 34.72in (882mm), 4 grooves, rh

Muzzle velocity: 1380 ft/sec (420 m/sec)

M1873 Short Rifle

Similar breech design to the Infantry Rifle but shorter, for Gendarmerie and cavalry. Cheek pad on butt, bayonet fittings, sling loop on butt. Sighted to 500m.

Cartridge: 11 × 42R
Length: 45.08in (1145mm)
Weight: 8lb (3.64kg)
Barrel: 26.77in (680mm), 4 grooves, rh
Muzzle velocity: 1165 ft/sec (355 m/sec)

M1880 Infantry Rifle

As for the M1873 but new sights, graduated to 1400m with additional sight notch for ranges to 2100m.

AL-KADISA Iraq
State factories

Al-Kadisa Sniping Rifle

This is the standard Russian Dragunov SVD sniping rifle manufactured under licence in Iraq. It differs in having four long slots in the handguard instead of six short, and the magazine has a stylised palm tree design impressed into it. Slight dimensional differences from the SVD.

Cartridge: 7.62 × 54R
Length: 48.43in (1230mm)
Weight: 9lb 7oz (4.30kg)
Barrel: 24.41in (620mm), 4 grooves, rh
Magazine: 10-round box
Muzzle velocity: 2723ft/sec (830 m/sec)

ALLIN-SPRINGFIELD USA
Springfield

Or **Allin Conversions**. Conversions of muzzle-loading rifles and muskets to breech-loading, using a lifting 'trap-door' breech-block patented by Allin in 1865. New weapons were then manufactured using the same breech system.

M1866 Infantry Rifle

Conversions of M1863 percussion rifles by boring out and inserting barrel liners and the Allin breech mechanism.

Cartridge: .50-70 US Government
Length: 56.00in (1422mm)
Weight: 9lb 14oz (4.48kg)
Barrel: 36.60in (929mm), 3 grooves, rh
Muzzle velocity: 1260 ft/sec (384 m/sec)

M1873 Infantry Rifle

New manufacture 1873–78. Full-stocked, external hammer, lifting block breech, leaf sight to 2000 yards, fitted for socket bayonet.

Cartridge: .45-70 Government
Length: 51.92in (1319mm)
Weight: 9lb 3oz (4.17kg)
Barrel: 32.38in (822mm), 3 grooves, rh
Muzzle velocity: 1320 ft/sec (402 m/sec)

M1879 Infantry Rifle

New manufacture 1879–81. Improved sights and various other details, otherwise essentially the same as the M1873.

Cartridge: .45-70 Government
Length: 51.75in (1308mm)
Weight: 9lb 2.4oz (4.15kg)
Barrel: 32.38in (822mm), 3 grooves, rh
Muzzle velocity: 1320 ft/sec (402 m/sec)

M1879 Carbine

As for M1879 Rifle but shorter and with butt-trap for cleaning kit.

Cartridge: .45-70 Government
Length: 41.30in (1049mm)
Weight: 9lb 3oz (4.17kg)
Barrel: 21.88in (556mm), 3 grooves, rh
Muzzle velocity: ca 1200 ft/sec (365 m/sec)

M1884 Infantry Rifle

New manufacture 1884–89. Improved sight with windage adjustment; minor manufacturing improvements.

Specifications: as for M1873

M1874 Carbine

New manufacture 1884–89, changes as for rifle.

Specifications: as for M1879 Carbine

M1889 Infantry Rifle

New manufacture 1889–92. Similar to the M1874 Rifle but fitted for a new rod bayonet.

Specifications: as for M1879

ARISAKA Japan

Meiji 29th Year Rifle
Koishikawa

1896. Turnbolt, locked by two lugs on bolt head and the handle acting as a third lug. Safety hook on cocking piece. Leaf sight to 2000m. Full-stocked, cleaning rod. Small numbers made for troop trials.

Cartridge: 6.5 × 51SR
Length: 50.04in (1271mm)
Weight: 9lb (4.08kg)
Barrel: 30.98in (787mm), 6 grooves, rh
Magazine: 5-round integral
Muzzle velocity: 2493 ft/sec (760 m/sec)

Meiji 30th Year Rifle
Koishikawa

1897. Generally similar to 29th Year model but with manufacturing improvements. Half-length hand-guard. This rifle was employed in British service, 1915–21, as **Rifle, Magazine, 0.256in, Pattern 1900**.

Cartridge: 6.5 × 51SR
Length: 50.16in (1274mm)
Weight: 8lb 13oz (4.01kg)
Barrel: 31.06in (789mm), 6 grooves, rh
Magazine: 5-round integral
Muzzle velocity: 2542 ft/sec (775 m/sec)

Meiji 30th Year Cavalry Carbine
Koishikawa

1900. Shorter version of the 30th Year Rifle, no handguard, sighted to 1500m.

Cartridge: 6.5 × 51SR
Length: 37.87in (962mm)
Weight: 7lb 7.5oz (3.39kg)
Barrel: 18.90in (480mm), 6 grooves, rh
Magazine: 5-round integral
Muzzle velocity: ca 2360 ft/sec (720 m/sec)

Meiji 35th Year Infantry Rifle
Koishikawa

1902. Improved version of the 30th Year Rifle: improved bolt, new tangent sight, longer handguard, sliding bolt cover. Intended for troop trials but Russo-Japanese War intervened and the rifles were issued to the Navy.

Cartridge: 6.5 × 51SR
Length: 50.19in (1275mm)
Weight: 8lb 15oz (4.07kg)
Barrel: 31.10in (790mm), 6 grooves, rh
Magazine: 5-round integral
Muzzle velocity: 2542 ft/sec (775 m/sec)

Meiji 38th Year Infantry Rifle
Koishikawa, Kokura, Mukden, Nagoya, Nanking & Tientsin

1905. Improved 30th Year Rifle with simplified bolt, improved extractor, sliding bolt cover, large knurled safety knob on rear of bolt. Leaf sight to 2400m. This rifle was employed in British service, 1915-21, as **Rifle, Magazine, 0.256in, Pattern 1907**.

Cartridge: 6.5 × 51SR
Length: 50.19in (1275mm)
Weight: 9lb 2oz (4.12kg)
Barrel: 31.45in (799mm), 4 or 6 grooves, rh
Magazine: 5-round integral
Muzzle velocity: 2400 ft/sec (730 m/sec)

Meiji 38th Year Cavalry Carbine
Koishikawa, Mukden & Nagoya

1905. Short version of the 38th Year Rifle, short handguard, sighted to 2000m. This carbine was employed in British service, 1915–21, as **Carbine, Magazine, 0.256in, Pattern 1907**.

Cartridge: 6.5 × 51SR
Length: 37.91in (963mm)
Weight: 7lb 6oz (3.35kg)
Barrel: 19.17in (487mm), 4 or 6 grooves, rh
Magazine: 5-round integral
Muzzle velocity: 2250 ft/sec (685 m/sec)

Meiji 44th Year Cavalry Carbine
Koishikawa, Mukden & Nagoya

1911. As for the 38th Year Carbine, but with a permanently-attached bayonet hinged below the muzzle.

Cartridge: 6.5 × 51SR
Length: 38.50in (978mm)
Weight: 8lb 13oz (4.01kg)
Barrel: 18.50in (469mm), 6 grooves, rh
Magazine: 5-round integral
Muzzle velocity: 2250 ft/sec (685 m/sec)

Type 99 Infantry Rifle
Dai-Nippon, Kayaba, Kokura, Jinsen, Nagoya & Toyo Juki
1939. Re-design of the 38th Year Rifle as a short rifle to suit a new 7.7mm cartridge. Leaf sight to 1500m, plus anti-aircraft sight and wire bipod.

Cartridge: 7.7 × 58mm Arisaka
Length: 45.00in (1143mm)
Weight: 9lb 2oz (4.19kg)
Barrel: 25.75in (654mm), 4 grooves, rh
Magazine: 5-round integral
Muzzle velocity: 2400 ft/sec (730 m/sec)

Type 0 Parachutists' Rifle
Nagoya
1940. A variant of the Type 99 Infantry Rifle with an interrupted screw joint between barrel and receiver to permit dismantling. 500 produced for trials.

Type 1 Parachutists' Rifle
Nagoya
1941. Variant of the Type 38 Cavalry Carbine with a side-hinged butt, developed as an interim design for parachute troops.

Type 2 Parachutists' Rifle
Nagoya
1942. A second variant of the Type 0 Parachutists' Rifle using a sliding wedge joint instead of the interrupted screw joint. 25,000 produced 1943–44.

Cartridge: 7.7 × 58mm Arisaka
Length: 45.27in (1150mm)
Weight: 8lb 15oz (4.05kg)
Barrel: 25.39in (645mm), 4 grooves, rh
Magazine: 5-round integral
Muzzle velocity: 2368 ft/sec (722 m/sec)

ARMALITE USA
ArmaLite

AR-10
1957. Gas-operated, selective-fire. Plastic butt and pistol grip, large magazine housing ahead of trigger. Perforated handguard with prominent gas tube on left front. Raised sight line; rear sight in carrying handle, with hooked cocking handle beneath. Produced in limited numbers, adopted by Burma, Portugal, Nicaragua and Sudan.

Cartridge: 7.62 × 51mm NATO
Length: 40.51in (1029mm)
Weight: 9lb 1oz (4.1kg)
Barrel: 20.00in (508mm), 4 grooves, rh
Magazine: 20-round box
Muzzle velocity: 2772 ft/sec (845 m/sec)
Cyclic rate: 700 rds/min

AR-10B
ArmaLite Inc
1996. Entirely new weapon developed from the original AR-10 by Eagle Arms, who purchased the ArmaLite trademark in 1995. In broad terms it is a 7.62mm version of the Colt M16 and uses several common parts. It is unlikely to appear in military inventories, being aimed at the collector market, and is noted here merely to prevent confusion.

AR-15
1957. Plastic butt, plastic fore-end/handguard, pistol grip with magazine housing ahead of trigger. Raised sight line, rear sight in carrying handle. Cocking handle at rear end of receiver. Exposed barrel with flash hider. Gas operated, selective fire, rotating bolt. Eventually became the US military's M16 (*see* Colt M16).

Cartridge: 5.56 × 45mm M193
Length: 39.0in (990mm)
Weight: 6lb 5oz (2.9kg)
Barrel: 20.00in (508mm), 4 grooves, rh
Magazine: 30-round box
Muzzle velocity: 3240 ft/sec (988 m/sec)
Cyclic rate: 800 rds/min

AR-18
1964. Plastic butt, side-hinged; plastic fore-end/handguard; pistol grip with magazine housing in front of trigger. Exposed barrel with flash-hider. Aperture rear sight at rear of receiver, post foresight front of handguard. Gas-operated, selective fire, rotating bolt. Intended to be a cheaper equivalent to the AR-15. Produced in limited numbers.

Cartridge: 5.56 × 45mm M193
Length, butt extended: 37.0in (940mm)
Length, butt folded: 28.98in (736mm)
Weight: 6lb 15oz (3.17kg)
Barrel: 18.26in (464mm), 6 grooves, rh
Magazine: 20-, 30- or 40-round box
Muzzle velocity: 3280 ft/sec (1000 m/sec)
Cyclic rate: 800 rds/min

AR-18S
1970. Short version of the AR-18; used the same mechanism but with short barrel and handguard and forward pistol grip. Limited quantity.

Cartridge: 5.56 × 45mm M193
Length, butt extended: 30.11in (765mm)
Length, butt folded: 22.0in (560mm)
Weight: 6lb 13oz (3.1kg)
Barrel: 10.1in (257mm), 6 grooves, rh
Magazine: 20- or 30-round box
Muzzle velocity: 2560 ft/sec (780 m/sec)
Cyclic rate: 800 rds/min

ARMENIA
State factory

K3 Rifle
1996. Bullpup design using the Kalashnikov gas-operated turning bolt system. Magazine behind pistol grip, rear of receiver shaped into shoulder rest, short fore-end, exposed barrel, flash hider. Nylon-based plastic furniture and magazine.

Cartridge: 5.45 × 39.5mm
Length: 27.56in (700mm)
Weight (loaded): 8lb 13oz (4.00kg)
Barrel: 16.34in (415mm), 4 grooves, rh
Magazine: 30-round box
Muzzle velocity: 2952ft/sec (900 m/sec)
Cyclic rate: 600 rds/min

K11 Sniping Rifle

1996. Bolt-action repeating rifle, wooden furniture, skeleton stock with pistol grip, bipod, iron sights plus optical sight, muzzle threaded for silencer.

Cartridge: 5.45 x 39.5mm
Length: 36.22in (920mm)
Weight: 7lb 11oz (3.5kg)
Barrel: 16.34in (415mm), 4 grooves, rh
Magazine: 30-round box
Muzzle velocity: 2952ft/sec (900 m/sec)

BALLESTER RIGAUD Argentina
Hafdasa

Semi-automatic carbine used by military & police *ca* 1946–55. Tubular receiver, fluted barrel, wood furniture, may have a folding bayonet on left side of barrel.

Cartridge: 9mm Parabellum
Length: 33.5in (850mm)
Weight: n/a
Barrel: 12.6in (320mm), 6 grooves, rh
Magazine: 54-round box
Muzzle velocity: *ca* 1250 ft/sec (380 m/sec)

BANG Denmark

Soren H. Bang developed a number of rifles using a muzzle cap to trap emerging gas and drive an operating rod to open the breech. These were extensively tested between *ca* 1910 and 1930 by various countries but none was ever accepted for service. No data are given since virtually every one was different, Bang tailoring his design to his potential market. They were all full-stocked rifles and recognisable by the perforated full-length handguard, muzzle cap, and curiously unbalanced breech mechanism which lies well forward of the trigger.

BARRETT USA
Barrett

M82A1 'Light Fifty'

1983. Semi-automatic, recoil-operated, rotating bolt. Fluted barrel with muzzle brake; bipod, adjustable butt; telescope sight.

Cartridge: .50 Browning (12.7 x 99mm)
Length: 61.0in (1549mm)
Weight: 44lb (13.40kg)
Barrel: 29.0in (737mm), 8 grooves, rh
Magazine: 11-round box
Muzzle velocity: 2798 ft/sec (853 m/sec)

M82A2

1992. Simplified and smaller version of the M82A1 mechanism set in a bullpup form. Shoulder rest and magazine housing below receiver, pistol grip midway, forward hand grip, fluted barrel, two-port muzzle brake.

Cartridge: .50 Browning (12.7 x 99mm)
Length: 55.47in (1409mm)
Weight: 29lb (12.24kg)
Barrel: 29.0in (736mm), 8 grooves, rh
Magazine: 5-round box
Muzzle velocity: 2798 ft/sec (853 m/sec)

M90

1990. Bolt action repeating rifle in bullpup form; bolt and magazine at rear of receiver, pistol grip in front of magazine, bipod, heavy smooth barrel with large muzzle brake.

Cartridge: .50 Browning (12.7 x 99mm)
Length: 45.0in (1143mm)
Weight: 22.0lb (9.98kg)
Barrel: 29.0in (736mm), 8 grooves, rh
Magazine: 5-round box
Muzzle velocity: 2798 ft/sec (853 m/sec)

BEAUMONT Netherlands
Beaumont

M1871 Infantry Rifle

Bolt action single shot rifle, full-stocked but no handguards and barrel entirely exposed. Prominent rear sight in front of chamber. Concave rear face to trigger guard. Sighted to 1100m.

Cartridge: 11 x 51R Beaumont
Length: 52.00in (1320mm)
Weight: 9lb 10oz (4.38kg)
Barrel: 32.67in (830mm), 4 grooves, rh
Muzzle velocity: 1328 ft/sec (405 m/sec)

M1871/88 Infantry Rifle

The Model 1871 modified to take a Vetterli magazine, sighted to 1300m for an improved cartridge.

Specifications: as for M1871, except
Weight: 10 lb (4.53kg)
Magazine: 4-round box
Muzzle velocity: 1476 ft/sec (450 m/sec)

BERDAN USA

Although Colonel Hiram Berdan was an American, his rifles were adopted only by Spain, Bulgaria and Russia.

SPAIN
Euskalduna, Ibarzabal & Orbea

M1867 Infantry Rifle

Breech-loading conversion of rifle muskets by fitting a 'trap-door' breech-block hinging up and forward. External hammer.

Cartridge: 14.5 x 41R
Length: 54.70in (1389mm)
Weight: 9lb 7oz (4.28kg)
Barrel: 36.22in (920mm), 4 grooves, rh
Muzzle velocity: 1197 ft/sec (365 m/sec)

M1867 Light Infantry Rifle

Similar conversion to the Infantry Rifle, but performed on the lighter M1857 percussion rifle.

Cartridge: 14.5 x 41R
Length: 48.42in (1230mm)
Weight: 8lb 7oz (3.83kg)
Barrel: 30.31in (770mm), 4 grooves, rh
Muzzle velocity: 1100 ft/sec (335 m/sec)

M1867 Carbine

Similar conversion to the Infantry Rifle, but performed on the M1857 Engineer Carbine.

Cartridge: 14.5 x 41R
Length: 48.42in (1230mm)
Weight: 8lb 5oz (3.77kg)
Barrel: 30.31in (770mm), 4 grooves, rh
Muzzle velocity: 1197 ft/sec (365 m/sec)

RUSSIA

M1868 Infantry Rifle
Colt

Also called the 'Berdan I' Rifle, a lifting block type similar to the Albini in that it uses the hammer to drive a locking bolt into the breech-block and then strike the firing pin.

Cartridge: 10.6 x 57.5R
Length: 53.0in (1346mm)
Weight: 9lb 6oz (4.25kg)
Barrel: 32.48in (825mm), 6 grooves, rh
Muzzle velocity: 1450 ft/sec (442 m/sec)

M1870 Infantry Rifle
Tula

Also called the 'Berdan II' Rifle. Bolt action, single shot, full-stocked, no handguards, cleaning rod. Leaf sight to 1500 paces (about 1250 yards/1140m). Also adopted by Bulgaria as the **M1880**.

Cartridge: 10.6 x 57.5R
Length: 53.35in (1355mm)
Weight: 9lb 9oz (4.35kg)
Barrel: 32.80in (833mm), 6 grooves, rh
Muzzle velocity: 1433 ft/sec (437 m/sec)

M1870 Carbine
Tula

Short version of the Infantry Rifle, stocked almost to the muzzle. Also adopted by Bulgaria as the **M1880**.

Cartridge: 10.6 x 57.5R
Length: 38.0in (965mm)
Weight: 6lb 3oz (2.80kg)
Barrel: 18.70in (475mm), 6 grooves, rh
Muzzle velocity: 1187 ft/sec (362 m/sec)

M1870 Dragoon Rifle
Izhevsk & Tula

Variant of the M1870 Infantry Rifle recognisable by the use of sling slots instead of metal swivels.

Cartridge: 10.6 x 57.5R
Length: 48.70in (1237mm)
Weight: 7lb 14oz (3.58kg)
Barrel: 28.35in (720mm), 6 grooves, rh
Muzzle velocity: 1263 ft/sec (385 m/sec)

M1870 Cossack Rifle
Tula

Generally as for the Dragoon Rifle, except as below.

Length: 48.0in (1219mm)
Weight: 7lb 8oz (3.38kg)

M1895 Three-Line Berdan
Nagant, Pieper & possibly Francotte

Conversion of the M1870 Infantry Rifle and Cavalry Carbine to fire the 7.62 x 54R cartridge adopted with the Mosin-Nagant M1891 rifle. Conversion involved re-barrelling, cutting a second locking recess in the receiver floor, providing a new bolt with two locking lugs instead of the original one, and fitting the M1891 rifle sight graduated to 2700 paces. Surviving weapons were eventually sent to the Republicans in the Spanish Civil War. The following data are for the rifle version.

Cartridge: 7.62 x 54R
Length: 52.05in (1322mm)
Weight: 9lb 5oz (4.23kg)
Barrel: 31.57in (802mm), 4 grooves, rh
Muzzle velocity: 1985 ft/sec (605 m/sec)

BERETTA Italy
Beretta

P30 Carbine

1957. Generally resembles the American Winchester M1 carbine but with a different cocking handle and using a tilting breech block to lock the breech. Selective fire by double trigger, grooved wooden fore-end, exposed muzzle with bayonet lug. Numbers sold to Morocco.

Cartridge: .30 US Carbine
Length: 37.25in (946mm)
Weight: 7lb 3oz (3.26kg)
Barrel: 17.91in (455mm), 4 grooves, rh
Magazine: 30-round box
Muzzle velocity: 1968 ft/sec (600 m/sec)
Cyclic rate: *ca* 500 rds/min

BM59 Infantry Rifle

1960. Basically a Garand M1 with a 7.62mm barrel, automatic fire and a removable 20-round magazine. The magazine can be loaded from chargers while on the gun, and there are also modifications to almost all the operating parts. The barrel has a prominent flash eliminator which may be externally shaped for use as a grenade launcher.

Cartridge: 7.62 x 51mm NATO
Length: 43.00in (1095mm)
Weight: 9lb 9oz (4.4kg)
Barrel: 19.30in (491mm), 4 grooves, rh
Magazine: 20-round box
Muzzle velocity: 2700 ft/sec (823 m/sec)
Cyclic rate: 800 rds/min

BM59 Alpini Rifle

1960. Modified version for use by Alpine troops. Folding tubular metal butt, pistol grip, short fore-end, bipod attached to gas cylinder.

Cartridge: 7.62 x 51mm NATO
Length: 43.20in (1097mm)
Weight: 10lb 1oz (4.56kg)
Barrel: 19.30in (491mm), 4 grooves, rh
Magazine: 20-round box
Muzzle velocity: 2700 ft/sec (823 m/sec)
Cyclic rate: 800 rds/min

BM59 Parachutist Rifle

1960. Similar to the Alpini, but with shorter barrel and detachable flash eliminator.

Cartridge: 7.62 x 51mm NATO
Length: 43.70in (1110mm)
Weight: 9lb 10oz (4.46kg)
Barrel: 18.40in (468mm), 4 grooves, rh
Magazine: 20-round box
Muzzle velocity: 2625 ft/sec (800 m/sec)
Cyclic rate: 810 rds/min

BM59 Mark 4 Squad Automatic

1964. Heavy-barrel version with pistol grip, wooden butt with hinged butt-plate, heavy bipod, short fore-end and handguard.

Cartridge: 7.62 x 51mm NATO
Length: 48.9in (1242mm)
Weight: 12lb (5.44kg)
Barrel: 21.0in (533mm), 4 grooves, rh
Magazine: 20-round box
Muzzle velocity: 2730 ft/sec (832 m/sec)
Cyclic rate: 750 rds/min

AR70 Assault Rifle

1970. Gas-operated, rotating bolt, lightweight rifle made of steel stampings and plastic furniture. Solid butt, tapering ribbed handguard, gas cylinder above barrel, pistol grip, curved magazine.

Cartridge: 5.56 x 45mm M193
Length: 37.60in (955mm)
Weight: 7lb 10oz (3.50kg)
Barrel: 17.8in (450mm), 4 grooves, rh
Magazine: 30-round box
Muzzle velocity: 3116 ft/sec (950 m/sec)
Cyclic rate: 650 rds/min

SC70 Assault Carbine

1970. Variant version of the assault rifle with folding metal tubular butt.

Cartridge: 5.56 x 45mm M193
Length, butt extended: 37.80in (960mm)
Length, butt folded: 28.90in (734mm)
Weight: 7lb 12oz (3.55kg)
Barrel: 17.8in (450mm), 4 grooves, rh
Magazine: 30-round box
Muzzle velocity: 3116 ft/sec (950 m/sec)
Cyclic rate: 650 rds/min

SCS70 Short Carbine

1975. Short version of the SC-70.

Cartridge: 5.56 x 45mm M193
Length, butt extended: 32.28in (820mm)
Length, butt folded: 23.46in (596mm)
Weight: 8lb 2.5oz (3.70kg)
Barrel: 12.60in (320mm), 4 grooves, rh
Magazine: 30-round box
Muzzle velocity: 2903 ft/sec (885 m/sec)
Cyclic rate: 600 rds/min

AR70/90

1990. Greatly improved version of the AR70. Receiver strengthened, butt re-shaped to give straight-line layout, detachable carrying handle. Selective fire with three-round bursts. Gas operated with rotating bolt. Takes any M16-type magazine.

Cartridge: 5.56 x 45mm NATO
Length: 39.29in (998mm)
Weight: 8lb 13oz (3.99kg)
Barrel: 17.71in (450mm), 6 grooves, rh
Magazine: 30-round box
Muzzle velocity: 3050 ft/sec (930 m/sec)
Cyclic rate: 625 rds/min

SC70/90

1990. Folding butt version of the AR70/90. The same mechanism and features.

Cartridge: 5.56 x 45mm NATO
Length, butt extended: 38.81in (986mm)
Length, butt folded: 29.80in (757mm)
Weight: 8lb 12oz (3.99kg)
Barrel: 17.8in (450mm), 6 grooves, rh
Magazine: 30-round box
Muzzle velocity: 3150 ft/sec (960 m/sec)
Cyclic rate: 700 rds/min

SCS 70/90

1990. Short barrel version of the SC70/90, folding butt, no gas regulator and no ability to fire grenades.

Cartridge: 5.56 x 45mm
Length, butt extended: 34.48in (876mm)
Length, butt folded: 25.47in (647mm)
Weight: 8lb 5oz (3.79kg)
Barrel: 13.86in (352mm), 6 grooves, rh
Magazine: 30-round box
Muzzle velocity: 2952 ft/sec (900 m/sec)
Cyclic rate: 700 rds/min

SCP70/90

1995. Similar to the SCS70/90 but with gas regulator and attachable grenade launcher.

Specifications: as for SCS70/90

Sniper Rifle

1985. Bolt action repeating rifle using Mauser-type bolt, based on Beretta 500 sporting rifle. Heavy free-floating barrel, thumb-hole stock, bipod, harmonic balancer in fore-end. NATO standard sight mount for optical sights, target quality iron sights standard. Adjustable recoil pad, butt cheek-piece, hand stop under fore-end.

Cartridge: 7.62 x 51mm NATO
Length: 45.86in (1165mm)
Weight: 12lb 7oz (5.55kg)
Barrel: 23.07in (586mm), 4 grooves, rh
Magazine: 5-round box
Muzzle velocity: *ca* 2854 ft/sec (870 m/sec)

BERNARDELLI Italy
Bernardelli

B2 Infantry Rifle
1985. RIfle put forward for Italian Army trials; few details were released but it is known that it was based on the Galil (*qv*) and was gas-operated with selective fire and grenade-launching capability. Carrying handle. Rifle was beaten in trials by Beretta and development ceased in 1990.

Cartridge: 5.56 × 45mm M193
Length, butt extended: 38.54in (979mm)
Length, butt folded: 29.21in (742mm)
Weight: 8lb 9.5oz (3.9kg)
Barrel: 18.10in (460mm), 6 grooves, rh
Magazine: 30- or 50-round box
Muzzle velocity: 3002 ft/sec (915 m/sec)
Cyclic rate: 600 rds/min

B2S Assault Carbine
1985. Short-barrel version of the B2 rifle, similar features.

Cartridge: 5.56 × 45mm
Length, butt extended: 33.50in (851mm)
Length, butt folded: 24.17in (614mm)
Weight: 8lb (3.65kg)
Barrel: 13.07in (332mm), 6 grooves, rh
Magazine: 30- or 50-round box
Muzzle velocity: 2756 ft/sec (840 m/sec)
Cyclic rate: 720 rds/min

BERTHIER France
Rifles designed by Adolph Berthier for French service were essentially Lebel (*qv*) actions remodelled to improve locking and speed of action and replaced the Lebel tube magazine with a Mannlicher-type clip magazine concealed in the stock.

1890 Cavalry Carbine
St Étienne
Typical carbine of the period; combless stock, turned-down bolt handle, sling ring attached to the left side of the stock. Cleaning rod, no handguard. Leaf sight to 1800m; in 1901 had new sight to 2000m due to adoption of Balle D cartridge.

Cartridge: 8 × 50R Lebel
Length: 37.20in (945mm)
Weight: 6lb 11oz (3.02kg)
Barrel: 17.85in (453mm), 4 grooves, lh
Magazine: 3-round box
Muzzle velocity: *ca* 2000 ft/sec (609 m/sec)

1890 Cuirassiers' Carbine
St Étienne
Similar to the Cavalry Carbine, but with a leather butt-pad.

Specifications: as for Cavalry Carbine, except
Weight: 6lb 10oz (2.98kg)

1890 Gendarmerie Carbine
St Étienne
As for Cavalry Carbine, but with a nose-cap adapted to fitting a bayonet.

Specifications: similar, except
Weight: 6lb 13oz (3.10kg)

1892 Artillery Musketoon
St Étienne
'Musketoon' is French for a carbine fitted with a bayonet. This weapon is essentially the 1890 Cavalry Carbine with a changed nosecap to accept a bayonet.

1902 Colonial Rifle
St Étienne
The action of the 1890 carbines mounted in a light rifle for use by locally-raised troops in French Indo-China.

Cartridge: 8 × 50R Lebel
Length: 44.33in (1126mm)
Weight: 7lb 3oz (3.26kg)
Barrel: 24.92in (633mm), 4 grooves, lh
Magazine: 3-round box
Muzzle velocity (Balle D): 2274 ft/sec (693 m/sec)

1907 Colonial Rifle
St Étienne
Similar to the M1902 but larger to suit taller Senegalese troops. Bolt handle turned down, no cleaning rod.

Cartridge: 8 × 50R Lebel
Length: 51.42in (1306mm)
Weight: 8lb 7oz (3.82kg)
Barrel: 31.61in (803mm), 4 grooves, lh
Magazine: 3-round box
Muzzle velocity: 2300 ft/sec (701 m/sec)

1907/15 Infantry Rifle
MAC Chatellerault, MAS & MAT
1915. To replace the Lebel M1886 as the standard French infantry rifle. It is simply the 1907 Colonial Rifle with a straight bolt handle and a cleaning rod

Cartridge: 8 × 50R Lebel
Length: 51.24in (1303mm)
Weight: 8lb 6oz (3.79kg)
Barrel: 31.40in (798mm), 4 grooves, lh
Magazine: 3-round box
Muzzle velocity: 2350 ft/sec (716 m/sec)

1916 Infantry Rifle
MAC Chatellerault, MAS, MAT & Remington
The 07/15 with an enlarged and visible magazine to accept a 5-round clip.

Cartridge: 8 × 50R Lebel
Length: 51.24in (1303mm)
Weight: 8lb 6oz (3.79kg)
Barrel: 31.40in (798mm), 4 grooves, lh
Magazine: 5-round box
Muzzle velocity: 2350 ft/sec (716 m/sec)

1892/16 Artillery Musketoon
MAC Chatellerault, MAS & MAT
The Model 1892 Musketoon re-designed to take the 5-round clip, sling ring, sling slot in butt, cleaning rod inlet into left side of stock

Cartridge: 8 × 50R Lebel
Length: 37.20in (945mm)
Weight: 7lb 3oz (3.25kg)
Barrel: 17.83in (453mm), 4 grooves, lh
Magazine: 3-round box
Muzzle velocity: 2090 ft/sec (637 m/sec)

1907-15-34 Rifle
MAS

Interim design of short rifle for all arms, basically the Model 07/15 rebarrelled and modified so as to accept the 7.5mm M1929 cartridge. Magazine modified to Mauser integral pattern, charger-loaded. Those for cavalry units had a sling bar on the butt and a turned-down bolt handle.

Cartridge: 7.5 × 54mm French M1929
Length: 42.52in (1080mm)
Weight: 8lb 2oz (3.68kg)
Barrel: 22.83in (580mm), 4 grooves, lh
Magazine: 5-round integral box
Muzzle velocity: 2674 ft/sec (815 m/sec)

1902-37 Short Rifle
MAS

Modification of the 1902 Colonial Rifle to 7.5mm calibre and charger-loading.

Cartridge: 7.5 × 54mm French M1929
Length: 42.32in (1075mm)
Weight: 8lb 1oz (3.65kg)
Barrel: 22.44in (570mm), 4 grooves, lh
Magazine: 5-round box
Muzzle velocity: 2674 ft/sec (815 m/sec)

BERYL Poland
Lucznik

Model 96

1996. Usual Kalashnikov mechanism but outwardly different. Black plastic furniture, more barrel and gas cylinder exposed, folding bipod in front of gas regulator, side-folding skeleton metal stock, receiver top dove-tailed for telescope sight. Muzzle compensator/grenade launcher. Selective fire with three-round burst. Tangent sight adjustable to 1000m range

Cartridge: 5.56 × 45mm, all types
Length, butt extended: 37.13in (943mm)
Length, butt retracted: 29.21in (742mm)
Weight: 7lb 6oz (3.35kg)
Barrel: 18.0in (457mm), 6 grooves, rh
Magazine: 30-round box
Muzzle velocity: 3018 ft/sec (920 m/sec) (NATO 5.56)
Cyclic rate: 700 rds/min

Mini-Beryl Model 96

1996. Short-barrelled version of the Beryl. Receiver differs in having a rear sight with additional telescope mounting grooves and with three set positions to 400m range.

Cartridge: 5.56 × 45mm, all types
Length, butt extended: 28.74in (730mm)
Length, butt retracted: 20.66in (525mm)
Weight: 6lb 10oz (3.00kg)
Barrel: 9.25in (235mm), 6 grooves, rh
Magazine: 20- or 30-round box
Muzzle velocity: 2526ft/sec (770m/sec) (NATO 5.56)
Cyclic rate: 700 rds/min

BLAKE USA
Blake

Repeating Rifle

Bolt action, detachable rotary magazine, full-stocked, short handguard, exposed muzzle, cleaning rod, pistol-grip butt-stock. Submitted for military tests 1893, refused; tested by NY Militia 1896, recommended for adoption, but political obstacles caused it to be refused again. Thereafter offered commercially in various sporting calibres.

Cartridge: .30-40 Krag
Length: 49.50in (1257mm)
Weight: 9lb 10oz (4.37kg)
Barrel: 30.0in (762mm), 4 grooves, rh
Magazine: 7-round rotary
Muzzle velocity: 2000 ft/sec (610 m/sec)

BOFORS Sweden
Bofors

Rifle manufacture in Sweden was originally by the Carl Gustav and Husqvarna companies; they amalgamated in the 1970s to become FFV, and were taken over in 1993 by Bofors.

CGA 5 (Ak5)

1986. A specially-modified version of the Fabrique Nationale FNC (*qv*). New folding butt, bolt, extractor, hand-guard, sights, cocking handle, magazine, selector switch and special winter trigger-guard. Three-round burst removed.

Cartridge: 5.56 × 45mm NATO
Length, butt extended: 39.57in (1005mm)
Length, butt folded: 29.53in (750mm)
Weight: 8lb 9oz (3.90kg)
Barrel: 17.71in (450mm), 6 grooves, rh
Magazine: 30-round box
Muzzle velocity: 3051 ft/sec (930 m/sec)
Cyclic rate: 700 rds/min

CGA5B (Ak5B)

1993. Variant model of the CGA 5 with the British Sight Unit, Small Arms, Trilux (SUSAT) optical sight, no iron sights, cheek-piece on butt.

Specifications: the same

CGA5D

1995. Variant model of the CGA 5 with iron sights, a Picatinny Rail sight mount, cheek-piece on butt.

Specifications: the same

CGA5-C2

1995. Short version of the CGA 5 for use by vehicle crewmen and others requiring a carbine.

Cartridge: 5.56 × 45mm NATO
Length, butt extended: 32.09in (815mm)
Length, butt folded: 21.85in (555mm)
Weight: 7lb 5oz (3.30kg)
Barrel: 9.84in (250mm), 6 grooves, rh
Magazine: 30-round box
Muzzle velocity: 2887 ft/sec (880 m/sec)
Cyclic rate: 750 rds/min

BOYS Britain
Enfield

Mark I Anti-tank Rifle

1937. Bolt action repeating rifle, action recoiling in cradle. Bipod attached to cradle, forward-leaning pistol grip, similar handgrip on padded butt, top-mounted box magazine, muzzle brake. Note that the word is not Boy's, Boys' or Boyes; the weapon was actually named for Captain Boys, one of the design team.

Cartridge: .55in Boys
Length: 63.50in (1614mm)
Weight: 36lb 0oz (16.56kg)
Barrel: 36.0in (914mm), 7 grooves, rh
Magazine: 5-round box
Muzzle velocity: 3250 ft/sec (990 m/sec)
Armour penetration: 21/300/0

BREDA Italy
Breda

Model PG

1935. Gas-operated by annular piston surrounding barrel, hence abnormally thick barrel and stock. Curved magazine with open sides allowing ammunition to be seen. Nose cap with bayonet lug and sling swivel. Selective fire, single shot or four-round bursts. Small number supplied to Costa Rica.

Cartridge: 7 × 57mm Mauser
Length: 43.90in (1115mm)
Weight: 11lb 9oz (5.25kg)
Barrel: 17.90in (455mm), 4 grooves, lh
Magazine: 20-round box
Muzzle velocity: *ca* 1885 ft/sec (575m/sec)

BROWNING AUTOMATIC RIFLE BAR USA

M1918
Colt, Marlin & Winchester

Original model. Selective fire, tubular flash hider, no bipod, butt plate not hinged, rear sight similar to Enfield M1917 rifle

Cartridge: .30-06
Length: 47.0in (1194mm)
Weight: 16lb 0oz (7.26kg)
Barrel: 24.0in (610mm), 4 grooves, rh
Magazine: 20-round box
Muzzle velocity: 2805 ft/sec (855 m/sec)
Cyclic rate: 550 rds/min

M1918A1

1927. Improved model. Butt plate has hinged shoulder support; bipod with spike feet attached to gas cylinder, selective fire.

Cartridge: .30-06
Length: 47.0in (1194mm)
Weight: 18lb 8oz (8.39kg)
Barrel: 24.0in (610mm), 4 grooves, rh
Magazine: 20-round box
Muzzle velocity: 2805 ft/sec (855 m/sec)
Cyclic rate: 550 rds/min

M1918A2

1939. Bipod with skid feet attached to flash hider; monopod beneath butt; fore-end reduced in height to expose barrel for cooling; magazine guards fitted to trigger guard; rear sight from the Browning M1919A4 machine gun, adjustable for windage. Rate of fire regulator. Wartime and postwar versions had sundry improvements and simplifications.

Cartridge: .30-06
Length: 47.8in (1214mm)
Weight: 19lb 6oz (8.80kg)
Barrel: 24.0in (610mm), 4 grooves, rh
Magazine: 20-round box
Muzzle velocity: 2805 ft/sec (855 m/sec)
Cyclic rate: 450 or 650 rds/min

M1922

Generally similar to the M1918, but with a heavy finned barrel, butt grooves for the monopod clamp, bipod attached to the barrel, rear sight as for M1919 machine gun and adjustable for windage. Designed as a light machine gun for US Cavalry, issued in limited numbers, obsolete 1940.

Cartridge: .30-06
Length: 41.0in (1042mm)
Weight: 19lb 3oz (8.71kg)
Barrel: 18.0in (457mm), 4 grooves, rh
Magazine: 20-round box
Muzzle velocity: 2700 ft/sec (823m/sec)
Cyclic rate: 550 rds/min

BELGIUM
FN

M30

Similar to US M1918, but with pistol grip, ribbed barrel, magazine and ejection port covers, ribbed barrel, domed gas regulator. Made in 7.65mm calibre for Belgium, 7.92mm for China, 7mm for Chile

Cartridge: 7.65 × 53mm
Length: 45.27in (1150mm)
Weight: 20lb 8oz (9.3kg)
Barrel: 22.0in (560mm), 4 grooves, rh
Magazine: 20-round box
Muzzle velocity: 1890 ft/sec (620 m/sec)
Cyclic rate: 500 rds/min

Type D

Based on US M1918, but with pistol grip, ribbed quick-change barrel, carrying handle, bipod, hinged butt to permit rapid field stripping, escapement rate controller, recoil spring in butt. May have monopod beneath butt. Supplied to Belgium in .30-06 calibre, to Egypt in 7.92 x 57mm calibre.

Cartridge: 7.92 × 57mm Mauser
Length: 45.10in (1145mm)
Weight: 20lb 5oz (9.21kg)
Barrel: 19.7in (500mm), 4 grooves, rh
Magazine: 20-round box
Muzzle velocity: *ca* 2500 ft/sec (762m/sec)
Cyclic rate: 480 rds/min

POLAND
M28
Radom
Generally as for the US M1918, but with short, low-set fore-end exposing all barrel, high bipod attached to gas cylinder, pistol grip, upswept butt.

Cartridge: 7.92 × 57mm Mauser
Length: 47.83in (1215mm)
Weight: 20lb 15oz (9.5kg)
Barrel: 24.0in (610mm), 4 grooves, rh
Magazine: 20-round box
Muzzle velocity: 2788 ft/sec (850 m/sec)
Cyclic rate: 600 rds/min

SWEDEN
M21
Carl Gustav
As for the US M1918, but with a pistol grip and covers for the magazine housing and ejection port.

Cartridge: 6.5 × 55mm Mauser
Length: 44.0in (1117mm)
Weight: 19lb 3oz (8.71kg)
Barrel: 26.4in (670mm), 4 grooves, rh
Magazine: 20-round box
Muzzle velocity: 2460 ft/sec (740 m/sec)
Cyclic rate: 500 rds/min

M37
Generally as for the US M1918, but with recoil spring in butt, hooded foresight and flash hider.

Cartridge: 6.5 × 55mm Mauser
Length: 46.10in (1171mm)
Weight: 20lb 14oz (9.48kg)
Barrel: 24.0in (610mm), 4 grooves, rh
Magazine: 20-round box
Muzzle velocity: 2460 ft/sec (740 m/sec)
Cyclic rate: 480 rds/min

BSA Britain
BSA

P-28
Experimental, submitted to British Army *ca* 1950. Chambered for .280 round, was rejected when the .280in cartridge was abandoned. Gas-operated, breech locking by lateral shift of the block. Half-stocked, prominent rear sight, flash hider formed externally for grenade launching, bayonet lug.

Cartridge: .280 British
Length: 42.20in (1072mm)
Weight: 9lb 9oz (4.35kg)
Barrel: 22.24in (565mm), 6 grooves, rh
Magazine: 20-round box
Muzzle velocity: 2525 ft/sec (770 m/sec)

BURTON USA

Lee-Burton
Enfield
Experimental, submitted to British Army 1882–87. Combined a modified Lee bolt action with a large hopper-type magazine on the right side. Full stocked, no handguard.

Cartridge: .402 Enfield-Martini
Length: 50.18in (1274mm)
Weight: 10lb 4oz (4.65kg)
Barrel: 30.20in (767mm), 7 grooves, lh
Magazine: 5-round hopper
Muzzle velocity: 1570 ft/sec (478 m/sec)

Ward-Burton
Springfield
Experimental, submitted to US Army 1870–72. Used Burton's bolt action single shot mechanism. Rejected in favour of the Allin-Springfield conversion (*qv*).

Cartridge: .50-70 US Government
Length: 51.88in (1318mm)
Weight: 9lb 1oz (4.11kg)
Barrel: 32.63in (829mm), 3 grooves, rh
Muzzle velocity: 1250 ft/sec (381 m/sec)

CEI-RIGOTTI Italy
Glisenti
1900. Full-stocked, exposed muzzle, magazine housing in front of trigger guard. Gas-operated selective fire; mechanism similar to that of the US Winchester M1 carbine. One of the earliest selective-fire rifles which worked.

Cartridge: 6.5 × 52mm Mannlicher-Carcano
Length: 39.37in (1000mm)
Weight: 9lb 9oz (4.30kg)
Barrel: 19.0in (483mm), 4 grooves, rh
Magazine: 10-, 20- or 50-round box
Muzzle velocity: 2400 ft/sec (730 m/sec)
Cyclic rate: n/a

CETME Spain
Model 58
Santa Barbara
1958. Similar in appearance to the Heckler & Koch G3, but fired a special 7.62 × 51mm NATO cartridge with a reduced propellant charge. Delayed blowback by rollers, selective fire.

Cartridge: 7.62 × 51mm CETME
Length: 39.37in (1000mm)
Weight: 11lb 5oz (5.13kg)
Barrel: 17.0in (432mm), 4 grooves, rh
Magazine: 20-round box
Muzzle velocity: 2493 ft/sec (760m/sec)
Cyclic rate: 600 rds/min

Model C
1965. Improved version of the Model 58 for the full-charge NATO cartridge. Wooden furniture, some models have bipod. Flash hider.

Cartridge: 7.62 × 51mm NATO
Length: 39.96in (1015mm)
Weight: 9lb 4oz (4.20kg)
Barrel: 17.72in (450mm), 4 grooves, rh
Magazine: 5- or 20-round box
Muzzle velocity: 2560 ft/sec (780 m/sec)
Cyclic rate: 600 rds/min

Model L

1984. Similar to the previous models, but built for the 5.56mm cartridge and used more synthetic material.

Cartridge: 5.56 × 45mm NATO
Length: 36.42in (925mm)
Weight: 7lb 8oz (3.40kg)
Barrel: 15.75in (400mm), 6 grooves, rh
Magazine: 12- or 30-round box
Muzzle velocity: 2870 ft/sec (875m/sec)
Cyclic rate: 700 rds/min

Model Ll

1985. This was an export version of the Model L, having a magazine housing which would accept the US Colt M16 and similar magazines. It is doubtful if many were made.

Model LC

1984. A carbine version of the Model L, same mechanism but shorter and lighter and with a telescoping stock.

Cartridge: 5.56 × 45mm NATO
Length, butt extended: 33.86in (860mm)
Length, butt folded: 26.18in (665mm)
Weight: 7lb 0oz (3.20kg)
Barrel: 12.60in (320mm), 6 grooves, rh
Magazine: 12- or 30-round box
Muzzle velocity: 2730ft/sec (832 m/sec)
Cyclic rate: 750 rds/min

Model R

Firing port weapon for use from armoured vehicles fitted with a special mounting. Based on the Model E rifle (an experimental model) the mechanism is the same as that of the Model C, except that a new cocking device, employing the cocking handle of the German MG3 machine gun, is used. The weapon has no butt, and a large cylindrical collar surrounds the rear half of the barrel and acts as a mounting device. Automatic fire only.

Cartridge: 7.62 × 51mm NATO
Length: 26.18in (665mm)
Weight: 14lb 2oz (6.4kg)
Barrel: 12.0in (305mm), 4 grooves, rh
Magazine: 20-round box
Muzzle velocity: 2263 ft/sec (690 m/sec)
Cyclic rate: 600 rds/min

CHAFFEE-REECE USA
Springfield

1882. Experimental bolt-action rifle with tubular magazine in the butt, cartridges delivered by a ratchet system driven by the bolt movement. About 750 made, unsuccessful in troop trials, disposed of commercially.

Cartridge: .45-70 Government
Length: 49.0in (1244mm)
Weight: 9lb 3oz (4.16kg)
Barrel: 27.9in (708mm), 3 grooves, rh
Magazine: 5-round tube
Muzzle velocity: 1300 ft/sec (396 m/sec)

CHARTERED INDUSTRIES Singapore
CIS
SAR-80

1980. Gas-operated, selective fire. Tapered plastic fore-end similar to that of the M16. Slotted flash hider, pressed steel slab-sided receiver, optional bipod.

Cartridge: 5.56 × 45mm M193
Length: 38.18in (970mm)
Weight: 8lb 3oz (3.70Kg)
Barrel: 18.07in (459mm), 4 grooves, rh
Magazine: 5- or 20-round box
Muzzle velocity: 3182 ft/sec (970 m/sec)
Cyclic rate: 600 rds/min

SR-88

1988. Improved model. Forged aluminium receiver, glass-reinforced nylon furniture, chromed gas piston assembly, modular bolt group, fixed or folding butt. Four-position gas regulator.

Cartridge: 5.56 × 45mm NATO
Length, butt fixed or extended: 38.19in (970mm)
Length, butt folded: 29.37in (746mm)
Weight: 8lb 1oz (3.66kg)
Barrel: 18.07in (459mm), 6 grooves, rh
Magazine: 20- or 30-round box
Muzzle velocity: 3182 ft/sec (970 m/sec)
Cyclic rate: 750 rds/min

SR-88-A Rifle

1990. Further improvement. Lower receiver aluminium forging, upper receiver pressed steel; hammer-forged barrel with chromed chamber; barrel attached to receiver by locknut and detent system. Three-position gas regulator.

Cartridge: 5.56 × 45mm NATO
Length, butt fixed or extended: 37.80in (960mm)
Length, butt folded: 31.89in (810mm)
Weight: 8lb 2oz (3.68kg)
Barrel: 18.11in (460mm), 6 grooves, rh
Magazine: 30-round box
Muzzle velocity: 3084 ft/sec (940 m/sec)
Cyclic rate: 800 rds/min

SR-88-A Carbine

1990. Short version of the SR-88-A rifle, similar characteristics. Folding butt version only.

Cartridge: 5.56 × 45mm NATO
Length, butt extended: 31.89in (810mm)
Length, butt folded: 25.98in (660mm)
Weight: 8lb 6oz (3.81kg)
Barrel: 11.50in (292mm), 6 grooves, rh
Magazine: 30-round box
Muzzle velocity: 2730ft/sec (832 m/sec)
Cyclic rate: 800 rds/min

CHINA
State factories
See also Kalashnikov & Mauser

'Hanyang' Rifle

Manufactured some time between 1912 and 1925, and more or less based on the German Commission Rifle M1888. Turnbolt action, Mannlicher-type clip-loading magazine, full-stocked with a handguard and bayonet fittings.

Cartridge: 7.92 × 57mm Mauser
Length: 49.25in (1251mm)
Weight: 8lb 8oz (3.87kg)
Barrel: 29.25in (743mm), 4 grooves, lh
Magazine: 5-round box
Muzzle velocity: *ca* 2067 ft/sec (630 m/sec)

'Generalissimo' or 'Chiang-Kai-Shek' Rifle
Manufactured 1936–49, and based on the Mauser M1898. Full-stocked, exposed muzzle, bayonet bar, finger groove in fore-end, one barrel band.

Cartridge: 7.92 × 57mm Mauser
Length: 43.75in (1111mm)
Weight: 9lb 0oz (4.08kg)
Barrel: 23.62in (600mm), 4 grooves, rh
Magazine: 5-round integral box
Muzzle velocity: *ca* 2690 ft/sec (825 m/sec)

Type 56 Assault Rifle
See Kalashnikov Clones

Type 56 Carbine.
This is an exact copy of the Russian Simonov SKS.

Type 68 Rifle
This looks like the Simonov SKS but actually uses the Kalashnikov bolt system, permits automatic fire and has a different gas regulator.

Cartridge: 7.62 × 39mm Soviet M1943
Length: 40.50in (1030mm)
Weight: 7lb 11oz (3.49kg)
Barrel: 20.50in (521mm), 4 grooves, rh
Magazine: 15- round box
Muzzle velocity: 2395 ft/sec (730 m/sec)
Cyclic rate: 750 rds/min

Type 79 Sniping Rifle
Exact copy of the Russian Dragunov SVD sniping rifle.

Type 81 Assault Rifle
A highly modified and improved version of the Type 68. Uses the same gas-operated bolt system but the receiver and butt are modelled on the AK47. Short fore-end/handguard leaving much of the gas cylinder and barrel exposed. Muzzle shaped for grenade firing.

Cartridge: 7.62 × 39mm Soviet M1943
Length: 37.60in (955mm)
Weight: 7lb 8oz (3.40kg)
Barrel: 15.75in (400mm), 4 grooves, rh
Magazine: 30-round box
Muzzle velocity: 2395 ft/sec (730 m/sec)
Cyclic rate: 750 rds/min

Type CQ Assault Rifle
This is a copy of the M16A1, though the method of dismantling differs. The pistol grip's curved shape distinguishes it from the genuine article.

Cartridge: 5.56 × 45mm M193
Length: 38.86in (987mm)
Weight: 7lb 1oz (3.20kg)
Barrel: 19.88in (505mm), 6 grooves, rh

Magazine: 20- round box
Muzzle velocity: 3248 ft/sec (990 m/sec)
Cyclic rate: 750 rds/min

COLT USA
Colt
M16
This was the military designation of the ArmaLite AR-15 rifle (*qv*) upon acceptance into US military service.

M16A1 Rifle
1967. M16 with a forward bolt closing plunger added, improved bolt buffer and various minor manufacturing modifications.

Cartridge: 5.56 × 45mm M193
Length: 39.00in (990mm)
Weight: 6lb 5oz (2.90kg)
Barrel: 20.00in (508mm), 6 grooves, rh
Magazine: 20- or 30-round box
Muzzle velocity: 3250 ft/sec (988 m/sec)
Cyclic rate: 800 rds/min

M16A2 Rifle
1982. Rifling changed to suit NATO standard 5.56mm bullet, optional three-round burst device, revised rear sight with windage adjustment, aluminium heat shield inside circular handguard/fore-end assembly, heavier barrel, improved muzzle compensator.

Cartridge: 5.56 × 45mm NATO
Length: 39.37in (1000mm)
Weight: 7lb 8oz (3.40kg)
Barrel: 20.00in (508mm), 6 grooves, rh
Magazine: 20- or 30-round box
Muzzle velocity: 3110 ft/sec (948 m/sec)
Cyclic rate: 800 rds/min

M16A3 Rifle
As for M16A2 but with removable carrying handle and 'Picatinny Rail' optical sight mount on receiver.

Specifications: as for M16A2

M16A4 Carbine
Short version of the M16A2 with telescoping butt-stock.

Cartridge: 5.56 × 45mm NATO
Length, butt extended: 33.00in (838mm)
Length, butt retracted: 29.80in (757mm)
Weight: 5lb 13oz (2.64kg)
Barrel: 14.57in (370mm), 6 grooves, rh
Magazine: 20- or 30-round box
Muzzle velocity: 3022 ft/sec (921 m/sec)
Cyclic rate: 700 rds/min

M231 Firing Port Weapon
Specialised form of the M16 rifle for use from armoured vehicles through special firing ports. The receiver and mechanism are the same but the cylindrical fore-end incorporates a bayonet-joint for fitting into the firing port and the barrel has no front sight. There is a sliding wire butt; in emergency the weapon can be taken from the port and used separately.

Cartridge: 5.56 × 45mm NATO
Length, butt extended: 32.28in (820mm)

Length, butt folded: 27.95in (710mm)
Weight: 8lb 9oz (3.90kg)
Barrel: 14.5in (368mm), 6 grooves, rh
Magazine: 30-round box
Muzzle velocity: 3000 ft/sec (914 m/sec)
Cyclic rate: 1100 rds/min

COMBLAIN Belgium
Petit Syndicat

M1870 Civil Guard Carbine
Half-stocked carbine with falling-block breech operated by an underlever. Metal-tipped fore-end with sling swivel. Lead and ramp sight to 1000m. The same carbine was adopted by the Brazilian Army in 1874 but using a slightly different cartridge, the 11 x 53R Brazilian Comblain.

Cartridge: 11 x 50R Albini
Length: 47.24in (1200mm)
Weight: 9lb 13oz (4.46kg)
Barrel: 31.81in (808mm), 4 grooves, rh
Muzzle velocity: 1410 ft/sec (430 m/sec)

M1871 Short Rifle
Similar to the M1870 carbine but shorter. Sighted to 500 metres. Late models had bayonet fittings.

Cartridge: 11 x 42R Albini-Comblain
Length: 31.49in (800mm)
Weight: 6lb 10oz (3.03kg)
Barrel: 17.91in (455mm), 4 grooves, rh
Muzzle velocity: 968 ft/sec (295 m/sec)

COMMISSION RIFLE Germany
This, an amalgam of Mannlicher and other ideas assembled by a Military Commission, is sometimes listed as a Mauser, sometimes as a Mannlicher. It being entirely neither, I prefer to list it separately.

M1888 Infantry Rifle
Amberg, Danzig, Erfurt, Loewe, Spandau & Steyr
Bolt action, clip-loading repeater, using the Mannlicher clip and magazine. Full-stocked, jacketed barrel, box magazine ahead of trigger-guard.

Cartridge: 7.92 x 57mm Mauser
Length: 48.80in (1240mm)
Weight: 8lb 6oz (3.81kg)
Barrel: 29.13in (740mm), 4 grooves, rh
Magazine: 5-round box
Muzzle velocity: 2100 ft/sec (640 m/sec)

M1888 Cavalry Carbine
Erfurt, Haenel & Schilling
1890. As for the rifle, but shorter. Stocked to the nose-cap, one barrel band, flattened bolt handle turned down.

Cartridge: 7.92 x 57mm Mauser
Length: 37.40in (950mm)
Weight: 6lb 13oz (3.10kg)
Barrel: 17.12in (435mm), 4 grooves, rh
Magazine: 5-round box
Muzzle velocity: 1886 ft/sec (575 m/sec)

M1888/05 and M1888/14 Infantry Rifles
Spandau
These were a number of M1888 rifles converted to charger loading in 1907 as an economy measure, and more in 1915 as an emergency wartime expedient, so as to conform with the standard issue ammunition. Their dimensions were the same as the original rifle and the external indication of the change is a thumb-notch cut into the receiver wall and the provision of charger guides.

M1891 Artillery Carbine
Erfurt, Haenel & Schilling
As for the M1888 Cavalry Carbine, but with a piling hook and a steel plate under the fore-end behind the nose cap.

Specifications: as for M1888, except
Weight: 7lb 2oz (3.23kg)

M1907 Rifle
Haenel
Generally as for the M1888 Rifle but changes to the bolt, addition of charger guides and a turned-down bolt handle. Magazine replaced by an internal 5-round box. Made for sale to China but the Chinese preferred a Mauser. Those weapons which had been made were impressed into German Army service in 1914.

Cartridge: 7.92 x 57mm Mauser
Length: 47.95in (1218mm)
Weight: 8lb 9oz (3.87kg)
Barrel: 27.95in (710mm), 4 grooves, rh
Magazine: 5-round box
Muzzle velocity: 2805 ft/sec (855 m/sec)

CRISTÓBAL Dominican Republic
Armeria San Cristóbal

Carbine M2
1953. Generally resembles the Beretta Model 1938 submachine gun, half-stocked, tubular receiver, two triggers, but thin exposed barrel and slender box magazine canted forward. Delayed blowback using Kiraly's two-part bolt. Used by Dominican Republic and also sold to Cuba.

Cartridge: .30 US Carbine
Length: 37.20in (945mm)
Weight: 7lb 12oz (3.52kg)
Barrel: 16.22in (412mm), 4 grooves, rh
Magazine: 25- or 30-round box
Muzzle velocity: 1876 ft/sec (572 m/sec)
Cyclic rate: 580 rds/min

Rifle M62
1962. Gas-operated semi-automatic rifle, locked by lowering the breech-block into a recess in the receiver floor. Half-stocked, prominent gas cylinder.

Cartridge: 7.62 x 51mm NATO
Length: 42.5in (1080mm)
Weight: 10lb 6oz (4.72kg)
Barrel: 21.3in (540mm), 4 grooves, rh
Magazine: 20-round box
Muzzle velocity: 2705t/sec (825 m/sec)

CROATIA
RH-ALAN

APS95 Assault Rifle

1995. Based on the Israeli Galil, uses similar gas piston and rotating bolt. Pressed steel receiver, slotted synthetic fore-end, folding metal skeleton butt, prominent carrying handle with optical sight, Muzzle compensator/grenade launcher.

Cartridge: 5.56 × 45mm NATO
Length, butt extended: 38.58in (980mm)
Length, butt folded: 28.74in (730mm)
Weight: 8lb 2.5oz (3.70kg)
Barrel: 17.71in (450mm), 6 grooves, rh
Magazine: 35-round box
Muzzle velocity: 3002 ft/sec (915 m/sec)
Cyclic rate: 650 rds/min

EM 992 Sniping Rifle

1995. Bolt-action repeating rifle; deep stock conceals the magazine, wood furniture, bipod, high comb butt with pronounced 'pistol-grip'. Iron sights and telescope mount.

Cartridge: 7.62 × 51mm NATO
Length: 47.83in (1215mm)
Weight: 14lb 5oz (6.50kg)
Barrel: 22.24in (565mm), 4 grooves, rh
Magazine: 5-round box
Muzzle velocity: 2854 ft/sec (870 m/sec)

EMM 992 Sniping Rifle

1995. The same rifle as the EM 992 but chambered and rifled for the .300 Winchester Magnum cartridge, leading to some small dimensional differences.

Cartridge: .300 Winchester Magnum
Length: 49.02in (1245mm)
Weight: 14lb 9oz (6.60kg)
Barrel: 22.83in (580mm), 4 grooves, rh
Muzzle velocity: 3395 ft/sec (1035 m/sec)
Magazine: 4-round box

MACS Sniping Rifle

Single shot, bolt action. Half-stocked, heavy barrel with muzzle brake. Skeleton butt attached to pistol grip. No iron sights, telescope mount on receiver.

Cartridge: .50 Browning
Length: 57.87in (1470mm)
Weight: 25lb 6oz (11.50kg)
Barrel: 30.70in (780mm), 8 grooves, rh
Muzzle velocity: 2805 ft/sec (855 m/sec)

CZECHOSLOVAKIA

ZH 29 Rifle
CZ Brno

1929. Designed by Emmanuel Holek of Ceskoslovenska Zbrojovka, Brno, extensively tested in the 1930s. Semi-automatic, using gas piston and tilting bolt. Three-quarter-stocked, with aluminium handguard, box magazine some distance from the trigger, exposed muzzle, bayonet lug.

Cartridge: 7.92 × 57mm Mauser
Length: 45.50in (1155mm)
Weight: 10lb 0oz (4.54kg)

Barrel: 21.50in (545mm), 4 grooves, rh
Magazine: 10- or 25-round box
Muzzle velocity: 2700 ft/sec (823 m/sec)

ZK 420
CZ Brno

1946. Designed by Josef and Frantisek Koucky of CZ, Brno. Last of a series of ZK models dating from 1941. Gas piston with bolt carrier and rotating bolt very similar to Kalashnikov's later AK pattern. Half-stocked, gas cylinder and barrel exposed, box magazine, handguard. Extensively tested but abandoned in favour of the vz 52.

Cartridge: 7.92 × 57mm Mauser
Length: 41.25in (1047mm)
Weight: 10lb 0oz (4.54kg)
Barrel: 21.0in (533mm), 4 grooves, rh
Magazine: 10-round box
Muzzle velocity: 2700 ft/sec (823 m/sec)

vz 52
CZ Brno

1953. Semi-automatic, gas operated with tilting bolt. Full-stocked, with handguard, exposed muzzle, bayonet hinged to the front cap and folding alongside the fore-end.

Cartridge: 7.62 × 45mm
Length: 40.0in (1015mm)
Weight: 9lb 0oz (4.08kg)
Barrel: 20.50in (520mm), 4 grooves, rh
Magazine: 10-round box
Muzzle velocity: 2440 ft/sec (743 m/sec)

vz 52/56
CZ Brno

The vz 52 rifle re-barrelled to fire the Warsaw Pact standardised 7.62 × 39mm cartridge. No change in basic dimensions but muzzle velocity reduced to *ca* 2705 ft/sec (825 m/sec).

vz 58
CZ Brno & Povaske Strojarne

Assault rifle which has some resemblance to the AK series on the outside but uses a similar gas-operated tilting bolt mechanism to the vz 52. Early production with wood furniture, later with plastic-impregnated wood fibre composition or plastic material. Two versions: **vz58P** with fixed butt, **vz 58V** with single-strut side-swinging folding butt.

Cartridge: 7.62 × 39mm M1943
Length, fixed or extended butt: 33.20in (843mm)
Length, folded butt: 25.16in (640mm)
Weight: 6lb 14oz (3.11kg)
Barrel: 15.80in (400mm), 4 grooves, rh
Magazine: 30-round box
Muzzle velocity: 2330 ft/sec (710 m/sec)
Cyclic rate: 800 rds/min.

CZ 2000 Assault Rifle
CZ Brno

1995. Newly-developed rifle designed for the 5.56mm NATO cartridge, on the assumption that the Czech Republic will join NATO at some future date. Currently on hold while the politicians argue. Gas operated, using a rotating bolt system loosely based on the Kalashnikov, selective fire with three-round burst. Pressed steel receiver, plastic fore-end/handguard, gas cylinder above the barrel, prominent fore-sight with optional bipod attached underneath. Tubular skeleton stock, pistol grip, and a translucent plastic magazine.

Cartridge: 5.56 × 45mm NATO
Length: 33.46in (850mm)
Weight: 6lb 9oz (3.0kg)
Barrel: 15.04in (382mm), 6 grooves, rh
Magazine: 30-round box
Muzzle velocity: 2985 ft/sec (910 m/sec)
Cyclic rate: 800 rds/min

CZ 2000 Short Assault Rifle
CZ Brno
1995. A short-barrelled version of the assault rifle. Same butt, pistol grip and receiver but shorter barrel, gas cylinder and fore-end, and a conical flash hider instead of a pronged flash eliminator.

Cartridge: 5.56 × 45mm NATO
Length: 26.57in (675mm)
Weight: 5lb 12oz (2.60kg)
Barrel: 7.28in (185mm), 6 grooves, rh
Magazine: 30-round box
Muzzle velocity: 2887 ft/sec (880 m/sec)
Cyclic rate: 800 rds/min

M96 Falcon Anti-materiel Rifle
Vsetín
1995. Bolt action magazine rifle. Straight-line layout of cylindrical receiver and long barrel, pistol grip and mechanism is small frame beneath chamber area, with bipod on front end. Iron sights and with telescope mount. Muzzle brake.

Cartridge: 12.7 × 108mm DShK
Length: 54.33in (1380mm)
Weight, loaded, with 5 rounds: 32lb 14oz (14.92kg)
Barrel: 36.50in (927mm), 8 grooves, rh
Magazine: 2- or 5-round box
Muzzle velocity: 2789 ft/sec (850 m/sec)

DAEWOO South Korea
Daewoo

K1 Carbine
1982. Based on the US Colt M16 design and used the same gas impingement system of operation. Relatively few appear to have been made.

Cartridge: 5.56 × 45mm NATO
Length, butt extended: 30.90in (785mm)
Length, butt folded: 23.03in (585mm)
Weight: 6lb 5oz (2.85kg)
Barrel: 10.35in (263mm), 6 grooves, rh
Magazine: 30-round box
Muzzle velocity: 2730 ft/sec (832 m/sec)
Cyclic rate: 750 rds/min

K2 Rifle
1987. Gas-operated by long-stroke piston; plastic folding butt, short ribbed plastic fore-end/handguard, receiver of milled aluminium forgings. Selective fire with added three-round burst. Muzzle brake/compensator.

Cartridge: 5.56 × 45mm NATO
Length, butt extended: 38.58in (980mm)
Length, butt folded: 28.74in (730mm)
Weight: 7lb 3oz (3.26kg)
Barrel: 18.30in (465mm), 6 grooves, rh
Magazine: 30-round box
Muzzle velocity: 3018 ft/sec (920 m/sec)
Cyclic rate: 800 rds/min

K1A1 Carbine
1987. Resembles a shortened K2 rifle but uses direct gas impingement on the bolt carrier instead of a gas piston. Telescoping butt. Large muzzle brake/compensator. Selective fire with three-round burst.

Cartridge: 5.56 × 45mm NATO
Length, butt extended: 32.68in (830mm)
Length, butt folded: 25.40in (645mm)
Weight: 6lb 6oz (2.88kg)
Barrel: 10.35in (263mm), 2grooves, rh
Magazine: 30-round box
Muzzle velocity: 2690 ft/sec (820 m/sec)
Cyclic rate: 800 rds/min

DAUDETEAU France
St Chamond

M1896 Rifle
Full-stocked, half-length handguard, bolt action repeater with fixed box magazine in front of trigger guard. Issued to French Navy in 1896, withdrawn *ca* 1905, replaced by Lebel rifles.

Cartridge: 6.5 × 53.5SR Daudeteau No 12
Length: 50.67in (1287mm)
Weight: 8lb 11oz (3.95kg)
Barrel: 32.48in (825mm), 4 grooves, lh
Magazine: 5-round integral box
Muzzle velocity: 2526 ft/sec (770 m/sec)

DEGTYAREV Russia
State factories

PTRD Anti-tank Rifle
1941. Bolt action, single shot, automatically opened by the recoil of the barrel and receiver, manually closed. Very long barrel, crude muzzle brake, bipod, cylindrical fore-end/handguard, pistol grip and single-strut metal butt with cheek-piece.

Cartridge: 14.5 × 114mm Soviet
Length: 78.74in (2000mm)
Weight: 38lb 2oz (17.29kg)
Barrel: 48.30in (1227mm), 8 grooves, rh
Muzzle velocity: 3320 ft/sec (1010 m/sec)
Armour penetration: 25/500/0

DE LISLE Britain
Sterling
One of the few really silent weapons ever produced in quantity, this is a Lee-Enfield bolt action attached to a .45in barrel enclosed in a large and highly efficient silencer. Normally fitted with a wooden stock, but a few with metal folding stocks similar to that of the Sterling submachine

gun (*qv*) were specially produced for issue to airborne troops.

Cartridge: .45 ACP
Length: 35.50in (901mm)
Weight: 7lb 8oz (3.42kg)
Barrel: 8.27in (210mm), 4 grooves, rh
Magazine: 8-round box (Colt M1911A1)
Muzzle velocity: 853 ft/sec (260 m/sec)

DIEMACO Canada
Diemaco

C7 Rifle
1984. Canadian-made version of the M16A2. Minor differences include removal of the three-round burst facility, flip-type rear sight, spent case deflector, and cold-hammered barrel with rifling to suit both M193 and NATO ammunition. Used by Canada, Denmark and the Netherlands.

Cartridge: 5.56 × 45mm NATO
Length: 40.15in (1020mm)
Weight: 7lb 4oz (3.30kg)
Barrel: 20.0in (510mm), 6 grooves, rh
Magazine: 30-round box
Muzzle velocity: 3035 ft/sec (925 m/sec)
Cyclic rate: 800 rds/min

C7A1 Rifle
1990. Improved version of the C7 using a low-mounted optical sight. The receiver top is formed into a sight rail.

Specifications: the same

C8 Assault Carbine
1984. Compact version of the C7 rifle, using a telescoping butt and shorter barrel.

Cartridge: 5.56 × 45mm NATO
Length, butt extended: 33.07in (840mm)
Length, butt folded: 29.92in (760mm)
Weight: 5 lb 15oz (2.7kg)
Barrel: 14.57in (370mm), 6 grooves, rh
Magazine: 30-round box
Muzzle velocity: 2952 ft/sec (900 m/sec)
Cyclic rate: 800 rds/min

C8A1 Assault Carbine.
1990. Variant of the C8 which mounts a telescope sight. Used by Netherlands special forces. No significant change in dimensions.

DRAGUNOV Russia
State factories

SVD Sniping Rifle
1963. Long, slender barrel; skeleton stock with cheek-rest and pistol grip; optical sight; slotted fore-end/handguard. Basically Kalashnikov mechanism but using a short-stroke piston to avoid the shift of balance encountered with long-stroke systems. Semi-automatic only. Made under licence in China, Iran and Romania.

Cartridge: 7.62 × 54R Russian
Length: 48.23in (1225mm)
Weight: 9lb 7oz (4.30kg)

Barrel: 24.48in (622mm), 4 grooves, rh
Magazine: 10-round box
Muzzle velocity: 2723 ft/sec (830 m/sec)

ENFIELD Britain
Enfield

Rifle, Magazine, .276in, Pattern 1913
1913. Mauser bolt action, integral magazine, full-stocked, exposed muzzle with winged foresight, aperture backsight at the rear of the action, charger loading.

Cartridge: .276 Enfield
Length: 46.18in (1173mm)
Weight: 8lb 9oz (3.88kg)
Barrel: 26.0in (660mm), 5 grooves, lh
Magazine: 5-round integral
Muzzle velocity: 2785 ft/sec (849 m/sec)

Rifle, Magazine, .303in, Pattern 1914, Mark 1e
Remington
1916. This is the Pattern 1913 rifle mass-produced in .303 chambering to meet wartime demands. Due to lack of full standardisation of parts, American production was divided into three sub-marks; the Mark 1e was made by Remington Arms-UMC at their Eddystone, Pennsylvania, factory.

Cartridge: .303 British
Length: 46.16in (1172mm)
Weight: 9lb 2oz (4.14kg)
Barrel: 26.0in (660mm), 5 grooves, lh
Magazine: 5-round integral
Muzzle velocity: 2525 ft/sec (770 m/sec)

Rifle, Magazine, .303in, Pattern 1914, Mark 1r
Remington
1916. Manufactured by Remington Arms-UMC at the Remington factory Ilion, New York.

Rifle, Magazine, .303in, Pattern 1914, Mark 1w
Winchester
1916. Manufactured by the Winchester Repeating Arms Co at New Haven, Connecticut.

Rifle, Magazine, .303in, Pattern 1914, Mark 1e*
Rifle, Magazine, .303in, Pattern 1914, Mark 1r*
Rifle, Magazine, .303in, Pattern 1914, Mark 1w*
1917. These were improved designs, in which the left locking lug on the bolt was lengthened and corresponding changes made to its seat on the rifle's receiver. These rifles are identified by a five-pointed star stamped on the bolt handle and chamber.

Rifle, Magazine, .303in, Pattern 1914, Mark 1e* (F)
Rifle, Magazine, .303in, Pattern 1914, Mark 1r* (F)
Rifle, Magazine, .303in, Pattern 1914, Mark 1w* (F)
1917. Mark 1★ rifles which were fitted with finely-adjustable rear sights were given the added notation '(F)'.

Rifle, Magazine, .303in, Pattern 1914, Mark 1w* (T)
1918. Selected Mark 1w★ rifles fitted with Aldis P1918 sighting telescopes in a high mount above the bolt.

All Pattern 1914 rifles were placed in reserve storage in 1926 and re-introduced into service as the **Rifle No 3 Mark 1** on 1 December 1941.

Rifle No 3 Mark I

1926. Pattern 1914 Mark 1 rifles of any manufacture were given this title upon the re-numbering of British rifles in 1926.

Rifle No 3 Mark I*

1926. Pattern 1914 Mark 1★ rifles of any manufacture were given this title upon the re-numbering of British rifles in 1926.

Rifle No 3 Mark I (F)

1926. Pattern 1914 Mark 1 or 1★ rifles fitted with fine-adjustment sights were given this title upon the re-numbering of British rifles in 1926.

Rifle No 3 Mark I (T)

1926. Pattern 1914 Mark 1w★ (T) rifles were given this title upon the re-numbering of British rifles in 1926.

Rifle No 3 Mark I (T) A

1941. Nomenclature allotted to a small (less than 100) number of No 3 Mark 1 or 1★ rifles fitted with low-set Aldis sighting telescopes.

US Rifle, Cal. 30, M1917

1917. This is the Enfield Pattern 1914 rifle re-designed to accept US .30-06 cartridges and adopted as Substitute Standard to alleviate the shortage of Springfield M1903 rifles in 1917. The factories which had produced the .303 P'14 continued with the .30 P'17, and 2,192,450 were manufactured. Apart from the chambering and calibre and some minor manufacturing differences, these rifles were identical to the Enfield P'14. Rifles issued to the British Home Guard in 1940–41 were marked with a red stripe around the fore-end to distinguish them from the P'14, also issued.

Cartridge: .30-06 Springfield
Length: 46.30in (1174mm)
Weight: 9lb 0oz (4.08kg)
Barrel: 26.0in (660mm), 5 grooves, rh
Magazine: 5-round integral
Muzzle velocity: 2750 ft/sec (838 m/sec)

Rifle, .280in, EM1

1947. Bullpup, with magazine behind the curved pistol grip; straight-line layout, optical sight in carrying handle, exposed muzzle, bulbous fore-end. Gas operated, roller locked.

Cartridge: .280 Enfield
Length: 35.98in (914mm)
Weight: 10lb 2oz (4.66kg)
Barrel: 24.48in (622mm), 5 grooves, rh
Magazine: 20-round box
Muzzle velocity: 2530 ft/sec (771 m/sec)
Cyclic rate: 600 rds/min

Rifle, 7mm, No 9 Mark I

1949. Originally known as the **EM2**. Bullpup, with magazine behind the straight pistol grip; straight-line layout with raised optical sight in carrying handle. Bulbous ribbed fore-

end, exposed barrel. Gas operated, locking by hinged lugs. Introduction rescinded in 1951.

Cartridge: .280 Enfield
Length: 35.0in (889mm)
Weight: 7lb 13oz (4.14kg)
Barrel: 24.48in (622mm), 5 grooves, lh
Magazine: 20-round box
Muzzle velocity: 2530 ft/sec (771 m/sec)
Cyclic rate: 650 rds/min

L85A1 SA80

1986. Gas-operated, rotating bolt, selective fire bullpup design. Wedge-shaped rectangular receiver with butt-plate, magazine behind pistol grip, ventilated fore-end and hand-guard, exposed barrel shaped for grenade launching and with compensator. Infantry version has SUSAT optical sight as standard; other arms version has carrying handle with iron sights and prominent foresight.

Cartridge: 5.56 × 45mm NATO
Length: 30.90in (785mm)
Weight: 8lb 6oz (3.81kg)
Barrel: 20.40in (518mm), 6 grooves, rh
Magazine: 30-round box
Muzzle velocity: 3084 ft/sec (940 m/sec)
Cyclic rate: 650–800 rds/min

L86A1 Cadet Rifle

A modification of the L85A1 by removing the gas system and substituting a manual bolt handle. Carrying handle and flip aperture sight. Army Cadet Force training use. May be fitted with a .22RF adapter for indoor range shooting.

Cartridge: 5.56 × 45mm NATO
Length: 29.75in (755mm)
Weight: 8lb 14oz (4.02kg)
Barrel: 19.5in (495mm), 6 grooves, rh
Magazine: 10-round box
Muzzle velocity: 3084 ft/sec (940 m/sec)

EVANS USA

Evans

Old Model Rifle

1872. Lever action, rolling block breech, screw-type helical magazine inside the butt operated by under-lever. Submitted to US Army, turned down, sold commercially.

Cartridge: .44 Evans Short
Length: 47.25in (1200mm)
Weight: 10lb 2oz (4.58kg)
Barrel: 30.0in (762mm), 4 grooves, rh
Magazine: 24-round helical
Muzzle velocity: 850 ft/sec (260 m/sec)

New Model Rifle

1877. Slight modifications to Old Model, including locking catch on the under-lever, ejection port cover and external hammer. 1000 purchased by Russian Navy in 1878.

Cartridge: .44 Evans Long
Length: 43.25in (1098mm)
Weight: 9lb 10oz (4.37kg)
Barrel: 26.0in (660mm), 4 grooves, rh
Magazine: 26-round helical
Muzzle velocity: 1443 ft/sec (440 m/sec)

Top: Hinged frame, self-extracting. (Austrian 11mm Montenegrin Gasser)

Above: Folding trigger, solid frame, gate-loading. (Italian 10.4mm Bodeo M1889)

Left: Tip-up revolver, finger spur on trigger-guard.
(Belgian non-military HDH)

Right: Tip-down barrel automatic pistol.
(French 9mm Le Français)

Above: Open frame, trigger-guard lever operates extracting mechanism. (French 9mm Galand M1878, non-military)

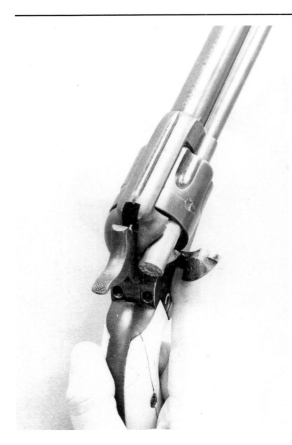

Left: Gate-loading a solid frame Colt M1873 Army revolver.

Below: Modern construction; the Belgian FN 5.7mm Five-SeveN; note the rails under the front of the barrel for attachment of a laser aiming device.

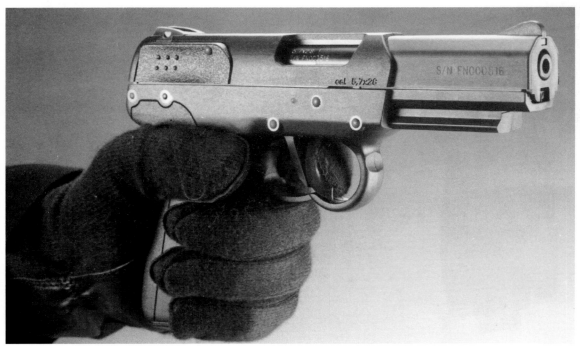

Left: Wooden holster stock attached to the butt. (Belgian 9mm Browning FN High-Power)

Right: Open-topped slide. (Beretta 9mm Model 92SB)

Below: One-handed cocking on an automatic pistol: the Chinese Type 77.

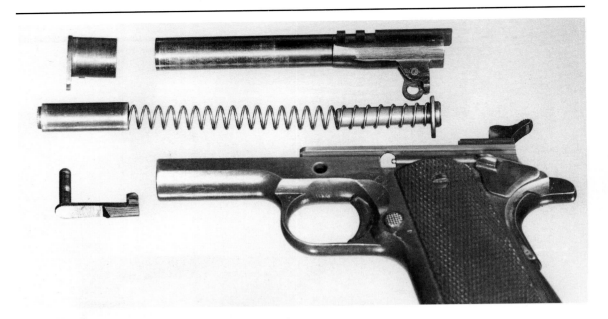

Browning locking systems.

Top: the Browning link.
(Colt M1911A1)
Centre: the Browning cam.
(Browning BDA 9);
Bottom: the Browning-Petter
cam. (SIG P210)

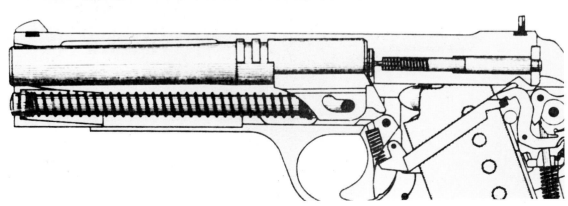

Above: Wood-stocked, perforated barrel jacket, side-feeding magazine. (German 9mm Bergmann MP28/II)

Top: The shape of things to come? (Belgian 5.7mm FN P-90)

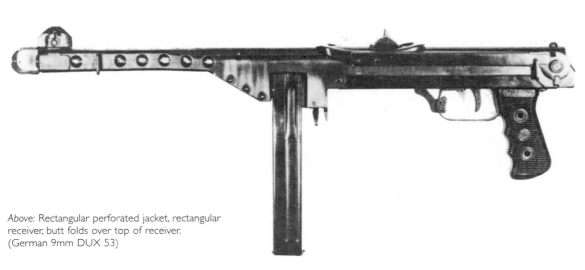

Above: Rectangular perforated jacket, rectangular receiver, butt folds over top of receiver. (German 9mm DUX 53)

Right: Slotted barrel jacket, synthetic receiver cover, butt folding underneath, box magazine. (Spanish 9mm Star Z-45)

Centre, far right: Retracting wire butt, pistol grip/magazine housing, sling cocking. (Austrian 9mm Steyr MPi 69)

Bottom far right: Single-strut butts; a comparison between the British 9mm Sten Mark 2 (*above*) and the German 9mm Potsdam Gerät (*below*).

Below: Rifle-stocked, folding bayonet; without the magazine this could easily be mistaken for a rifle-calibre carbine by a casual observer. (Italian 9mm Beretta M1918)

Bottom: Rectangular receiver, short barrel retained by knurled nut, pivoting folding stock, pistol grip/magazine housing. (Italian 9mm Socimi)

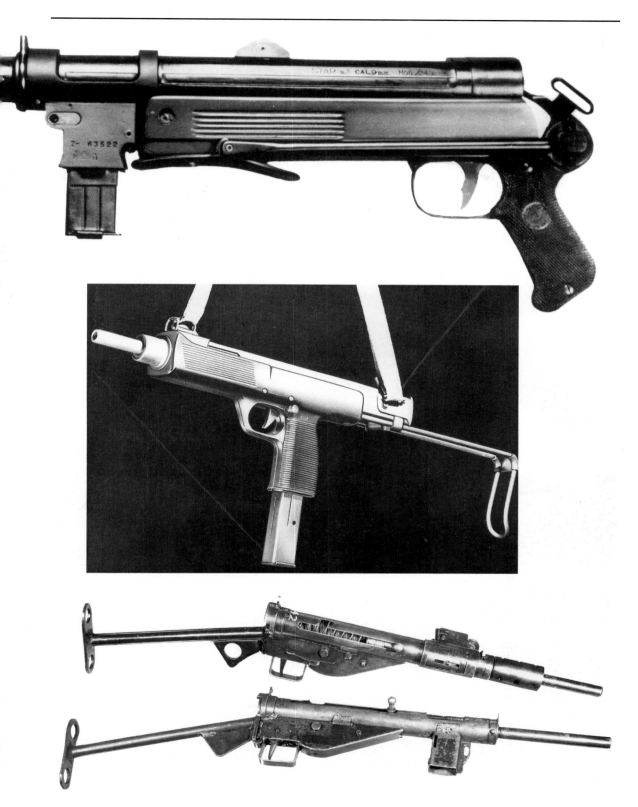

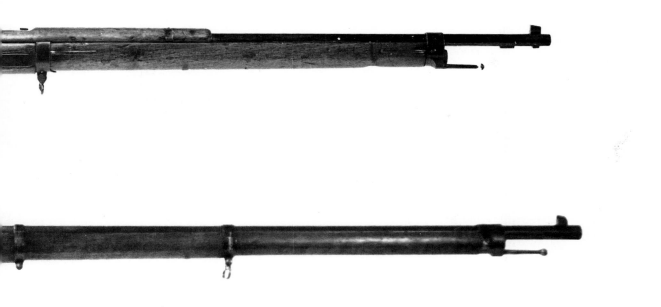

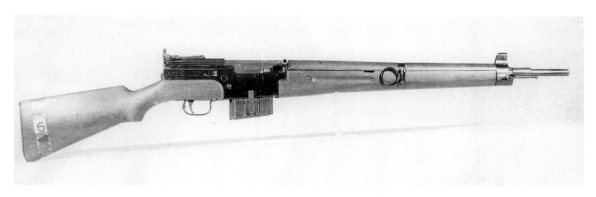

Top: Full-stocked, exposed muzzle, piling hook, straight-wrist butt-stock. (French 8mm MAS M1917)

Above, centre: Full-stocked, no handguard, exposed muzzle, piling hook, pistol-grip butt-stock, box magazine. (Austrian 11mm Mannlicher M1886)

Left: Bullpup design. Notice how the action is underneath the firer's face and the magazine is behind the pistol grip. (French 5.56mm FA-MAS F-1)

Above: Full-stocked, full-length handguard, exposed muzzle, slab-sided receiver, box magazine, pistol-grip butt-stock. (French 7.5mm MAS 49)

Above: Butt pad with hand grip, cradle with bipod, long unsupported barrel with muzzle brake, bolt action, overhead magazine. A typical anti-tank rifle. (British Boys Mk 1)

Top: Full-stocked, half-length handguard, toggle action. (Pedersen T2)

Right: Clip-loaded, through the action. (US Garand M1)

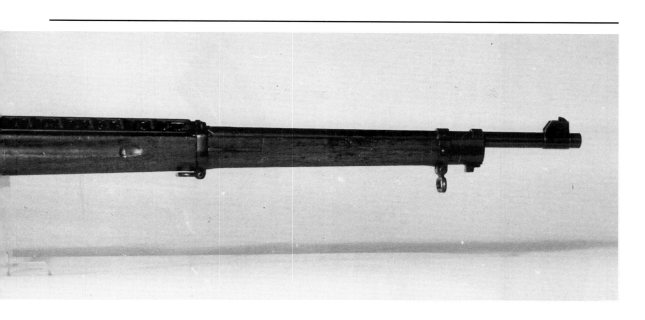

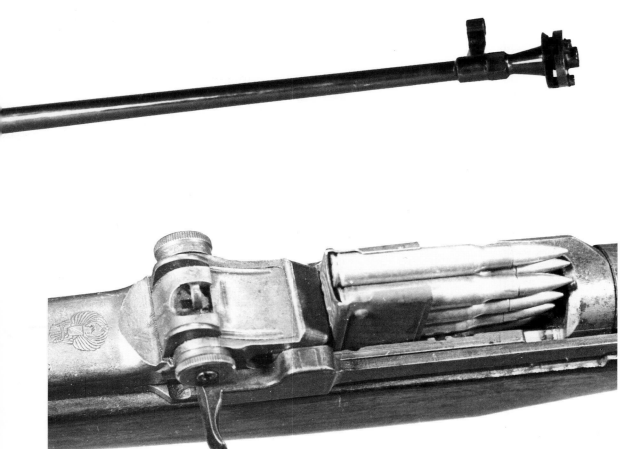

Left: Finned barrel, overhead magazine, non-adjustable bipod, short fore-end grip and monopod. (British .303in Vickers-Berthier)

Below left: Slotted barrel jacket, bipod, wood butt and pistol grip, side-feeding magazine. (Swiss 7.5mm M25)

Bottom left: Drum magazine, exposed barrel with flash eliminator, forward hand-grip, bipod, cut-away butt. (Singapore 5.56mm Ultimax 100)

Below: Corrugated water jacket, muzzle booster, spade grips and trigger. (British .303in Vickers Mark 1)

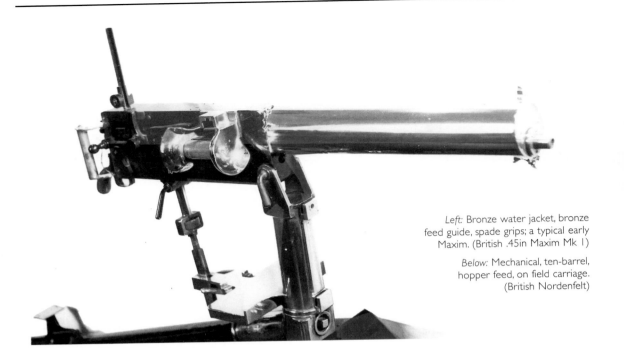

Left: Bronze water jacket, bronze feed guide, spade grips; a typical early Maxim. (British .45in Maxim Mk 1)

Below: Mechanical, ten-barrel, hopper feed, on field carriage. (British Nordenfelt)

FABRIQUE NATIONALE Belgium
FN

This company was originally set up to manufacture the Mauser Rifle for the Belgian Army (*see* Mauser). It subsequently made Mausers under licence for a number of countries, and in the 1920s developed its own Mauser model. Work on automatic weapons began with making the Browning Automatic Rifle (*see* Rifles, Browning) under licence, and moved on to develop the company's own designs. The 1939–45 war interrupted this process, but in the postwar years the company has produced several notably successful weapons.

Model 1949 or SAFN

Design began in the mid-1930s, was shelved during WWII and completed in the late 1940s. Gas-operated, semi-automatic, using a tilting bolt. Full-stocked, full-length handguard, exposed muzzle, box magazine, pistol-grip butt. Sold in various calibres to South America, the Middle and Far East.

Cartridge: 7.92 x 57mm Mauser
Length: 44.0in (1116mm)
Weight: 9lb 8oz (4.31kg)
Barrel: 22.25in (590mm), 6 grooves, rh
Magazine: 10-round box
Muzzle velocity: 2400 ft/sec (730 m/sec)

FAL Model 50-00

1953. Improved version of the M1949 mechanism in a completely new shape. Pressed-steel receiver, pistol grip, ventilated fore-end/handguard, exposed barrel with flash eliminator. Aperture rear sight, foresight on nosecap. May be selective fire or semi-automatic only.

Cartridge: 7.62 x 51mm NATO
Length: 42.91in (1090mm)
Weight: 9lb 6oz (4.25kg)
Barrel: 20.98in (533mm), 4 grooves, rh
Magazine: 20-round box
Muzzle velocity: 2756 ft/sec (840 m/sec)
Cyclic rate: 650–700 rds/min

FAL Model 50-64

This is the same weapon as the basic FAL 50-00, but with a side-folding tubular steel stock.

Cartridge: 7.62 x 51mm NATO
Length, butt extended: 43.11in (1095mm)
Length, butt folded: 33.27in (845mm)
Weight: 8lb 9oz (3.90kg)
Barrel: 20.98in (533mm), 4 grooves, rh
Magazine: 20-round box
Muzzle velocity: 2756 ft/sec (840 m/sec)
Cyclic rate: 650–700 rds/min

FAL Model 50-63

The 'Paratrooper' model with short barrel and side-folding stock.

Cartridge: 7.62 x 51mm NATO
Length, butt extended: 40.15in (1020mm)
Length, butt folded: 30.31in (770mm)
Weight: 8lb 4oz (3.75kg)
Barrel: 17.17in (436mm), 4 grooves, rh
Magazine: 20-round box

Muzzle velocity: 2657 ft/sec (810 m/sec)
Cyclic rate: 650–700 rds/min

FAL Model 50-41

1958. The 'Heavy Barrel' model. Similar layout to the standard rifle, but heavier barrel, short fore-end to permit barrel cooling, carrying handle and bipod.

Cartridge: 7.62 x 51mm NATO
Length: 45.28in (1150mm)
Weight: 13lb 3oz (6.0kg)
Barrel: 20.98in (533mm), 4 grooves, rh
Magazine: 20-round box
Muzzle velocity: 2756 ft/sec (840 m/sec)
Cyclic rate: 650–700 rds/min

CAL

1966. This was more or less a scaled-down version of the FAL, using the same gas system and tipping bolt. It was expensive and ahead of its time, the 5.56mm revolution not having taken off, and it found few takers.

Cartridge: 5.56 x 45mm M193
Length: 38.50in (978mm)
Weight: 6lb 8oz (2.94kg)
Barrel: 18.46in (469mm), 6 grooves, rh
Magazine: 20-round box
Muzzle velocity: 3200 ft/sec (975 m/sec)
Cyclic rate: 850 rds/min

FNC Rifle

1976. Replacement for the CAL, easier to make and maintain. Operation changed to gas piston, bolt carrier and rotating bolt. Slab-sided receiver, round ribbed fore-end with flutes, folding tubular light alloy butt. Selective fire with three-round burst control.

Cartridge: 5.56 x 45mm NATO
Length, butt extended: 39.25in (997mm)
Length, butt folded: 30.16in (766mm)
Weight: 8lb 6oz (3.80kg)
Barrel: 17.68in (449mm), 6 grooves, rh
Magazine: 30-round box
Muzzle velocity: 3166 ft/sec (965 m/sec)
Cyclic rate: 650–700 rds/min

FNC Carbine

1976. Similar to the FNC rifle but shorter barrel.

Cartridge: 5.56 x 45mm NATO
Length, butt extended: 35.87in (911mm)
Length, butt folded: 26.77in (680mm)
Weight: 7lb 12oz (3.50kg)
Barrel: 14.29in (363mm), 4 grooves, rh
Magazine: 20-round box
Muzzle velocity: 3117 ft/sec (950m/sec)
Cyclic rate: 650–700 rds/min

Model 30-11 Sniping Rifle

Ca 1970–90. Probably the last Mauser bolt-action rifle to be built by FN, this was a half-stocked heavy barrel weapon with flash eliminator and a fully adjustable wooden butt with high comb. Mounts were available for various types of optical and optronic sights, and the FN-MAG machine gun bipod could be fitted to the fore-end.

Cartridge: 7.62 × 51mm NATO
Length: 43.98in (1117mm)
Weight: 10lb 11oz (4.85kg)
Barrel: 19.76in (502mm), 6 grooves, rh
Magazine: 5-round integral box
Muzzle velocity: 2790 ft/sec (850 m/sec)

FARA Argentina
FMAP

FARA 83 Assault Rifle

Gas-operated, rotating bolt, selective fire. Slab-sided receiver, pistol grip, short fore-end, exposed barrel with gas cylinder above. Side-folding plastic butt.

Cartridge: 5.56 × 45mm NATO
Length, butt extended: 39.37in (1000mm)
Length, butt folded: 29.33in (745mm)
Weight: 8lb 11oz (3.95kg)
Barrel: 17.80in (452mm), 6 grooves, rh
Magazine: 30-round box
Muzzle velocity: 3166 ft/sec (965 m/sec)
Cyclic rate: 750 rds/min

FEDEROV Russia
Sestroretsk

AVF Automat

1913. Short-recoil selective fire, full-stocked, integral magazine.

Cartridge: 6.5 × 51SR Arisaka
Length: 49.41in (1255mm)
Weight: 10lb 2oz (4.60kg)
Barrel: 31.50in (800mm), 6 grooves, rh
Magazine: 5-round box
Muzzle velocity: 2400 ft/sec (730 m/sec)
Cyclic rate: not known

AVF Automat
Sestroretsk 1916, Kovrov 1920

1916. Improved and reduced in size; short wood stock, forward hand-grip, curved detachable magazine. About 3500 made 1920–25.

Cartridge: 6.5 × 51SR Arisaka
Length: 38.38in (975mm)
Weight: 9lb 13oz (4.45kg)
Barrel: 20.47in (520mm), 6 grooves, rh
Magazine: 25-round box
Muzzle velocity: 2313 ft/sec (705 m/sec)
Cyclic rate: not known

FFV Sweden
FFV

FFV-890C

1983. Based upon the Galil and developed by FFV for the Swedish Army. The principal change was to the rifling, to permit firing the FN SS109/NATO 5.56mm bullet. Pressed steel receiver, perforated fore-end, side-folding butt, pistol grip, hooded foresight, flash hider/grenade launcher. Rifle was not selected for service.

Cartridge: 5.56 × 45mm NATO
Length, butt extended: 33.86in (860mm)
Length, butt folded: 24.60in (625mm)
Weight: 7lb 11oz (3.50kg)
Barrel: 13.39in (340mm), 6 grooves, rh
Magazine: 35-round box
Muzzle velocity: 2730 ft/sec (860 m/sec)
Cyclic rate: 650 rds/min

FRÜWIRTH Austria
Steyr

Gendarmerie Carbine M1872

Bolt action, tubular magazine beneath barrel, full-stocked. Long turned-down bolt handle, prominent spur cocking piece on bolt.

Cartridge: 11 × 42R Werndl
Length: 40.86in (1038mm)
Weight: 8lb 2oz (3.69kg)
Barrel: 22.44in (570mm), 6 grooves, rh
Magazine: 6-round tube
Muzzle velocity: 978 ft/sec (298 m/sec) .

GALIL Israel
IMI

7.62mm ARM Assault Rifle/Light Machine Gun

Broadly based on the Kalashnikov gas and rotating bolt system, with a firing mechanism taken from the Garand. Slab-sided receiver, plastic pistol grip and short fore-end, no handguard, gas cylinder above the barrel, prong-type flash eliminator. Tubular metal butt folds to the right side. Vertical cocking handle on right. Bipod and carrying handle.

Cartridge: 7.62 × 51mm NATO
Length, butt extended: 41.34in (1050mm)
Length, butt folded: 31.89in (810mm)
Weight: 9lb 11oz (4.40kg)
Barrel: 21.06in (535mm), 4 grooves, rh
Magazine: 25-round box
Muzzle velocity: 2788 ft/sec (850 m/sec)
Cyclic rate: 650 rds/min

7.62mm AR Assault Rifle

This is the same as the ARM but without the bipod and carrying handle.

Specifications: the same, except
Weight: 8lb 11oz (3.95kg)

7.62mm SAR Short Assault Rifle

A shorter version of the AR rifle.

Cartridge: 7.62 × 51mm NATO
Length, butt extended: 36.02in (915mm)
Length, butt folded: 26.57in (675mm)
Weight: 8lb 5oz (3.75kg)
Barrel: 15.75in (400mm), 4 grooves, rh
Magazine: 25-round box
Muzzle velocity: 2625 ft/sec (800 m/sec)
Cyclic rate: 750 rds/min

5.56mm ARM Assault Rifle/Machine Gun

A scaled-down model of the 7.62mm ARM, with bipod and carrying handle. The only visible difference, when size cannot be determined, is the magazine which is curved instead of straight.

Cartridge: 5.56 × 45mm NATO
Length, butt extended: 38.54in (979mm)
Length, butt folded: 29.21in (742mm)
Weight: 9lb 9oz (4.35kg)
Barrel: 18.11in (460mm), 6 grooves, rh
Magazine: 35- or 50-round box
Muzzle velocity: 3116 ft/sec (950 m/sec)
Cyclic rate: 650–700 rds/min

5.56mm AR Assault Rifle

The same weapon as the ARM but without the bipod and carrying handle.

Specifications: the same, except
Weight: 8lb 11oz (3.95kg)

5.56mm SAR Short Assault Rifle

Short version of the AR rifle.

Cartridge: 5.56 × 45mm NATO
Length, butt extended: 33.07in (840mm)
Length, butt folded: 24.17in (614mm)
Weight: 8lb 5oz (3.75kg)
Barrel: 13.07in (332mm), 6 grooves, rh
Magazine: 35- or 50-round box
Muzzle velocity: 2953 ft/sec (900 m/sec)
Cyclic rate: 650–700 rds/min

MAR Micro Assault Rifle

Much-shortened AR rifle intended for special forces. Standard Galil receiver, short barrel, special short fore-end with pronounced front lip to prevent the firer's hand reaching the muzzle. Folding tubular stock.

Cartridge: 5.56 × 45mm NATO
Length, butt extended: 27.16in (690mm)
Length, butt folded: 17.52in (445mm)
Weight: 6lb 8oz (2.95kg)
Barrel: 7.68in (195mm), 6 grooves, rh
Magazine: 35-round box
Muzzle velocity: 2330 ft/sec (710 m/sec)
Cyclic rate: 650 rds/min

Galil Sniper

Based upon the standard Galil rifle, but with special modifications: bipod attached to the receiver front end, heavy barrel, muzzle brake, telescope sight mount on left side of receiver, two-stage trigger. Semi-automatic fire only. Folding wooden butt with adjustable cheek-piece and rubber recoil pad.

Cartridge: 7.62 × 51mm NATO
Length, butt extended: 43.90in (1115mm)
Length, butt folded: 33.07in (840mm)
Weight, with bipod and sling: 14lb 2oz (6.4kg)
Barrel: 20.0in (508mm), 4 grooves, rh
Magazine: 30-round box
Muzzle velocity: 2674 ft/sec (815 m/sec)

GALLAGER USA
Richardson

Single-shot Carbine

Made during the Civil War, the majority of Gallager weapons were percussion breech-loaders, but some 5000 of the final production model were chambered for the .56-52 Spencer rimfire cartridge. Half-stocked, external hammer, trigger-guard lever which slides the barrel forward to load.

Cartridge: .56-52 Spencer
Length: 41.0in (1040mm)
Weight: 8lb 3oz (3.71kg)
Barrel: 22.25in (565mm), 4 grooves, rh
Muzzle velocity: 900 ft/sec (274 m/sec)

GARAND USA
Harrington, International Harvester, Springfield & Winchester

US Rifle M1

1932. Semi-automatic, gas-operated, rotating bolt, clip-loaded integral magazine. Full-stocked, exposed barrel and gas cylinder. Bayonet fittings.

Cartridge: .30-06 Springfield
Length: 43.50in (1103mm)
Weight: 9lb 8oz (4.37kg)
Barrel: 24.0in (610mm), 4 grooves, rh
Magazine: 8-round integral
Muzzle velocity: 2740 ft/sec (835 m/sec)

US Rifle M1E1

M1 with changes to the cam angle opening the bolt and to the general fit of the operating mechanism. Few made; no dimensional changes.

US Rifle M1E2

M1 rifle adapted for an optical sight; experimental, few made.

US Rifle M1E3

M1 with roller bearing cam lug on the bolt and other changes to the operating system to make for smoother operation. Few made.

US Rifle M1E4

Another attempt to make a smoother action, this time by inserting an expansion chamber into the gas system. Few made.

US Rifle M1E5

Shortened version with 18.00in (457mm) barrel and folding stock. Delivered excessive muzzle blast, abandoned.

US Rifle M1E6

M1 with offset telescope sight so as to permit retention of iron sights for emergency use. Few made.

US Sniper's Rifle M1C M1E7

M1 with telescope Sight M73 (Lyman 'Alaskan') or M73B1 (Weaver 330). The butt was fitted with a cheek pad and the muzzle with a flash hider.

US Sniper's Rifle M1D M1E8

M1 with Sight M81, M82 or M84 in block mount.

US Rifle M1E9
Variant of the M1E4 using a tappet system of gas operation.

US Rifle T26
Short version of the M1 demanded by the Pacific Warfare Board in June 1945. Some prototypes were manufactured in Manila but the project was abandoned when the war ended, no production having taken place.

US Rifle M14
Harrington, Springfield, Winchester & TRW
1957. The logical improvement of the Garand, doing away with the clip system and adopting a charger-loaded 20-round box, converting the calibre to 7.62mm NATO and turning it into a selective fire weapon. This latter feature proved to be superfluous and most service rifles had the selective option locked out, being returned to single shot only.

Cartridge: 7.62 x 51mm NATO
Length: 44.14in (1121mm)
Weight: 8lb 9oz (3.88kg)
Barrel: 22.0in (559mm), 4 grooves, rh
Magazine: 20-round box
Muzzle velocity: 2800 ft/sec (853 m/sec)
Cyclic rate: 750 rds/min

US Rifle M14A1
The squad automatic (LMG) version of the M14 rifle, with selective fire, bipod, straight-line stock with pistol grip, folding forward hand-grip, rubber butt pad, shoulder rest and muzzle compensator.

Cartridge: 7.62 x 51mm NATO
Length: 44.30in (1125mm)
Weight: 12lb 12oz 5.78kg)
Barrel: 22.0in (559mm), 4 grooves, rh
Magazine: 20-round box
Muzzle velocity: 2800 ft/sec (853 m/sec)
Cyclic rate: 750 rds/min

US Rifle M21
Sniper version of the M14, fitted with Leatherwood telescope sight.

Specifications: as for the M14

GEPARD Hungary
Technika

Gepard M1 Anti-materiel Rifle
Single shot heavy rifle using interrupted-lug breech block attached to the pistol grip. Cylindrical cradle with recoil buffer, long unsupported barrel with muzzle brake, bipod attached to cradle. Butt formed at rear end of receiver. No iron sights, telescope mount.

Cartridge: 12.7 x 108mm DShK
Length: 61.81in (1570mm)
Weight: 41lb 14oz (19.0kg)
Barrel: 43.40in (1100mm), 8 grooves, rh
Muzzle velocity: 2756 ft/sec (840 m/sec)

Gepard M1A1 Anti-materiel Rifle
The Gepard M1 rifle but mounted on a back-packing frame which also doubles as a firing support.

Specifications: as for M1, except
Weight: 48lb 8oz (22kg)

Gepard M2 Anti-materiel Rifle
Semi-automatic using long recoil system. Cylindrical receiver, cylindrical cradle extending from it and supporting most of the barrel. Bipod, short butt with cheek-piece, box magazine alongside pistol grip, preventing its use by left-hand firers.

Cartridge: 12.7 x 108mm DShK
Length: 60.24in (1530mm)
Weight: 26lb 7oz (12.0kg)
Barrel: 43.40in (1100mm), 8 grooves, rh
Magazine: 5- or 10-round box
Muzzle velocity: 2756 ft/sec (840 m/sec)
Armour penetration: 15/600/0

Gepard M2A1 Anti-materiel Rifle
Shorter version of the M2 intended for airborne and other high-mobility troops.

Cartridge: 12.7 x 108mm DShK
Length: 49.61in (1260mm)
Weight: 22lb 1oz (10.0kg)
Barrel: 32.68in (830mm), 8 grooves, rh
Magazine: 5- or 10-round box
Muzzle velocity: 2592 ft/sec (790 m/sec)

Gepard M3 Anti-materiel Rifle
This is a scaled up version of the M2 rifle, chambered for the Soviet 14.5mm cartridge. Cradle contains an hydraulic recoil buffer, otherwise of the same operation and general appearance as the M2.

Cartridge: 14.5 x 114mm Soviet
Length: 74.0in (1880mm)
Weight: 44lb 1oz (20.0kg)
Barrel: 58.27in (1480mm), 8 grooves, rh
Magazine: 5- or 10-round box
Muzzle velocity: 3280 ft/sec (1000 m/sec)

GRAS France
M1874 Rifle
MAC Chatellerault, MAS, MAT & Steyr
Full-stocked, single shot, bolt action with straight handle, ramp leaf sight to 1800m, cleaning rod, bayonet lug.

Cartridge: 11 x 59R Gras
Length: 51.38in (1305mm)
Weight: 9lb 4oz (4.19kg)
Barrel: 32.32in (821mm), 4 grooves, lh
Muzzle velocity: 1443 ft/sec (440 m/sec)

M1874 Cavalry Carbine
MAC Chatellerault, MAS & MAT
Similar to the rifle but shorter, full-stocked, turned-down bolt handle.

Cartridge: 11 x 59R Gras
Length: 46.26in (1175mm)
Weight: 7lb 13.5oz (3.56kg)
Barrel: 27.64in (702mm), 4 grooves, lh
Muzzle velocity: 1404 ft/sec (428m/sec)

M1874 Mounted Gendarmerie Carbine
MAC Chatellerault, MAS & MAT
Similar to the cavalry carbine but fitted for M1874 bayonet.

Specifications: the same

M1874 Dismounted Gendarmerie Carbine
MAC Chatellerault, MAS & MAT
Similar to the cavalry carbine but fitted for M1866 bayonet.

Specifications: the same

M1874 Artillery Musketoon
MAC Chatellerault, MAS & MAT
Generally a shortened infantry rifle, but with the bolt handle turned down and fitted for the M1866 bayonet.

Cartridge: 11 × 59R Gras
Length: 38.98in (990mm)
Weight: 7lb 3oz (3.26kg)
Barrel: 20.08in (510mm), 4 grooves, lh
Muzzle velocity: 1332 ft/sec (406m/sec)

M1874/80/14 Rifle
MAC Chatellerault, MAS, MAT & civil contract
1914. Conversion of old Gras rifles to 8mm calibre to fire the Lebel cartridge. A short handguard was fitted and there was a small modification to the bolt face, but otherwise the action was unchanged. Sight graduated to 2000m.

Cartridge: 8 × 50R Lebel
Length: 51.38in (1305mm)
Weight: 9lb (4.08kg)
Barrel: 32.28in (820mm), 4 grooves, lh
Muzzle velocity: 2296 ft/sec (700 m/sec)

GRÜNEL Switzerland
Grünig

Sniping Rifle
1988. Based upon existing match rifle. Used ball-bearings to provide smooth bolt operation, and an electronic trigger mechanism to give constant pressure. Walnut ventilated stock, adjustable butt, exposed heavy barrel, muzzle brake, no iron sights.

Cartridge: 7.62 × 51mm NATO
Length: 45.27in (1150mm)
Weight: 11lb 11oz (5.30kg)
Barrel: 25.60in (650mm), 4 grooves, rh
Magazine: 10-round box
Muzzle velocity: 2690 ft/sec (820 m/sec)

GUEDES Portugal
Steyr

M1885 Rifle
Block breech operated by trigger guard. Full stocked, single shot. Adopted by Portuguese Army but made in Austria.

Cartridge: 8 × 60R Guedes
Length: 47.91in (1217mm)
Weight: 9lb 0oz (4.10kg)
Barrel: 33.27in (845mm), 4 grooves, rh
Muzzle velocity: 1706 ft/sec (520 m/sec)

GUSTLOFF Germany
Gustloff

Volksgewehr VG1-5
1945. Semi-automatic, delayed blowback using gas leaked into the receiver to delay opening of the receiver and bolt. Sheet-metal crude construction, wood stock, MP43 magazine. Intended for the Volkssturm 'Home Guard' but few were ever made.

Cartridge: 7.92 × 33mm Kurz
Length: 34.85in (885mm)
Weight: 10lb 2oz (4.62kg)
Barrel: 14.9in (378mm), 4 grooves, rh
Magazine: 30-round box
Muzzle velocity: 2150 ft/sec (655 m/sec)

HAENEL Germany
MKb 42 (H)
Haenel
1942. Prototype selective fire assault rifle to fire the new 7.92mm Kurz cartridge developed by Polte. Gas-operated, tipping bolt, straight-line layout, pressed steel construction, gas cylinder above barrel. About 8000 made.

Cartridge: 7.92 × 33mm Kurz
Length: 37.0in (940mm)
Weight: 10lb 13oz (4.90kg)
Barrel: 14.37in (364mm), 4 grooves, rh
Magazine: 30-round box
Muzzle velocity: 2100 ft/sec (640 m/sec)
Cyclic rate: 500 rds/min

MP43 (StG 44)
Erfurt, Erma, Haenel & Mauser
1943. Improved model of the MKb 42(H). Similar appearance but shorter gas cylinder and longer barrel. Several manufacturers.

Cartridge: 7.92 × 33mm Kurz
Length: 37.0in (940mm)
Weight: 11lb 4oz (5.12kg)
Barrel: 16.50in (418mm), 4 grooves, rh
Magazine: 30-round box
Muzzle velocity: 2125 ft/sec (647 m/sec)
Cyclic rate: 500 rds/min

HARRIS USA
Harris & McMillan
Name now attached to the rifles previously known as McMillan.

M87R Sniper Rifle
Bolt-action, magazine, anti-materiel rifle. Half-stocked, synthetic, with a thumb hole and pistol grip butt. Box magazine, heavy barrel, no handguard, pepper-pot muzzle brake, bipod attached to the fore-end.

Cartridge: .50 Browning
Length: 53.0in (1346mm)
Weight: 21lb 0oz (9.52kg)
Barrel: 29.0in (736mm), 8 grooves, rh
Magazine: 5-round box
Muzzle velocity: 2798 ft/sec (853 m/sec)

M92 Sniper Rifle

A modified version of the M87R in bullpup form. The same barrel, bolt action and muzzle brake are mounted in a large and deep plastic stock formed into a shoulder-rest and pistol grip. Bipod attached midway along the fore-end.

Cartridge: .50 Browning
Length: *ca* 35.0in (890mm)
Weight: *ca* 21lb 0oz (9.52kg)
Barrel: 29.0in (736mm), 8 grooves, rh
Magazine: 5-round box
Muzzle velocity: 2798 ft/sec (853 m/sec)

M93 Sniper Rifle

An improved version of the M87R which is generally the same but has the butt-stock hinged behind the receiver so as to fold to the left side for transport. It also has a monopod in the pistol grip portion of the butt.

Specifications: as for the M87R

HECKLER & KOCH Germany
Heckler & Koch

Until 1995 H&K's 'trade-mark' was the roller-delayed blowback system inherited from CETME when they undertook to develop the original CETME design for the German Army in the early 1950s. This became the G3, and with the exception of the G11 every rifle developed by H&K until the G36 was a variation of that basic design.

G3 Rifle

1961. Adopted by German Army. Extensive use of steel pressings and stampings, wood butt. Selective fire, pistol grip, fixed butt, hooded foresight, flip rear sight.

Cartridge: 7.62 × 51mm NATO
Length: 40.20in (1021mm)
Weight: : 9lb 11oz (4.40kg)
Barrel: 17.72in (450mm), 4 grooves, rh
Magazine: 20-round box
Muzzle velocity: 2625 ft/sec (800 m/sec)
Cyclic rate: 550 rds/min

G3A1 Rifle.

1963. The G3 with a retractable butt.

Specifications: similar, except
Length, butt retracted: 31.5in (800mm)
Weight: 10lb 6oz (4.70kg)

G3A2 Rifle.

1962. Improved G3 with free-floating barrel. Most G3s were rebuilt to this standard.

Specifications: as for G3

G3A3 Rifle

1964. New flash suppressor/muzzle brake dimensioned to NATO standard for grenade launching; new drum rear sight; plastic fixed butt; plastic fore-end may be solid or perforated.

Cartridge: 7.62 × 51mm NATO
Length: 40.35in (1025mm)
Weight: 9lb 11oz (4.40kg)
Barrel: 17.72in (450mm), 4 grooves, rh
Magazine: 20-round box

Muzzle velocity: 2625 ft/sec (800 m/sec)
Cyclic rate: 550 rds/min

G3A3ZF Sniping Rifle

1964. Specially-selected G3A3 rifles fitted with a telescope sight.

Specifications: as for G3A3

G3A4 Rifle

1964. This was the retracting-butt version of the G3A3.

Specifications: similar, except
Length, butt retracted: 33.07in (840mm)
Weight: 10lb 6oz (4.7kg)

G3A6
Maker not known

Company designation for Iran-manufactured version of the G3A3.

G3A7
MKEK

Company designation for Turkish-manufactured version of the G3A3. Slight dimensional differences due to manufacturing techniques.

Cartridge: 7.62 × 51mm NATO
Length: 40.16in (1020mm)
Weight: 9lb 6oz (4.25kg)
Barrel: 17.71in (450mm), 4 grooves, rh
Magazine: 20-round box
Muzzle velocity: 2690 ft/sec (820 m/sec)
Cyclic rate: 600 rds/min

G3A7A1
MKEK

Turkish-manufactured version of the G3A4. Slight dimensional differences.

Cartridge: 7.62 × 51mm NATO
Length, butt extended: 40.16in (1020mm)
Length, butt folded: 33.07in (840mm)
Weight: 10lb 0oz (4.52kg)
Barrel: 17.71in (450mm), 6 grooves, rh
Magazine: 20-round box
Muzzle velocity: 2690ft/sec (820 m/sec)
Cyclic rate: 600 rds/min

G3SG/1 Sniping Rifle

1973. Specially selected G3A3 rifles fitted with a set trigger and telescope sight, folding bipod and cheek-rest on the butt.

Specifications: as for G3A3, except
Weight, with sight: 12lb 3oz (5.54kg)

PSG1 Marksman's Rifle

1985. Specially built, used the standard action but with self-loading action only, a heavy free-floating barrel, adjustable butt, hand rest on the pistol grip and telescope sight.

Cartridge: 7.62 × 51mm NATO
Length: 47.56in (1208mm)
Weight: 17lb 13oz (8.10kg)
Barrel: 25.60in (650mm), 4 grooves, rh, polygonal
Magazine: 5- or 20-round box
Muzzle velocity: 2723 ft/sec (830m/sec)

MSG90 Sniping Rifle

1987. A less expensive alternative to the PSG1, this uses the standard action with self-loading only, heavy free-floating hammered barrel, no iron sights, telescope sight standard, adjustable butt. There is a T-rail in the fore-end for attachment of bipod, sling or hand-stop, and a NATO STANAG 2324 sight mount built into the top of the receiver.

Cartridge: 7.62 x 51mm NATO
Length: 45.87in (1165mm)
Weight: 14lb 2oz (6.4kg)
Barrel: 23.62in (600mm), 4 grooves, rh
Magazine: 5- or 20-round box
Muzzle velocity: 2690 ft/sec (820 m/sec)

MSG90A1 Sniping Rifle

1997. MSG90 with added iron sights, windage adjustment, empty case deflector. Developed for US Department of Defense.

Specifications: as for MSG90, except
Weight: 14lb 11oz (6.67kg)

MSG3

1987. Generally similar to the MSG90 and with similar dimensions, but is fitted with standard iron sights as well as the telescope mount. Developed solely for the German Army.

HK32A2 Rifle

1965. A variant of the G3A2 chambered for the 7.62 x 39mm Soviet M1943 cartridge. Prototypes and demonstration weapons were produced, but since nobody appeared to want them, they were never manufactured in quantity.

Cartridge: 7.62 x 39mm M1943
Length: 40.20in (1021mm)
Weight: 7lb 11oz (3.50kg)
Barrel: 15.35in (390mm), 4 grooves, rh
Magazine: 20-, 30- or 40-round box
Muzzle velocity: 2360 ft/sec (720 m/sec)
Cyclic rate: 600 rds/min

HK32A3

1965. Retracting-butt version of the HK32A2.

Specifications: similar, except
Length, butt extended: 37.00in (940mm)
Length, butt retracted: 28.70in (729mm)
Weight: 8lb 8oz (3.49kg)

HK32KA1

1965. Short-barrelled, retracting butt carbine version.

Cartridge: 7.62 x 39mm M1943
Length, butt extended: 34.0in (864mm)
Length, butt retracted: 26.40in (670mm)
Weight: 8lb 6oz (3.80kg)
Barrel: 12.67in (322mm), 4 grooves, rh
Magazine: 20-, 30- or 40-round box
Muzzle velocity: 2295 ft/sec (700 m/sec)
Cyclic rate: 600 rds/min

HK33A2 Rifle

1965. Virtually a G3 down-sized to accept the 5.56mm cartridge.

Cartridge: 5.56 x 45mm M193
Length: 36.22in (920mm)
Weight: 8lb 1oz (3.65kg)
Barrel: 15.35in (390mm), 6 grooves, rh
Magazine: 20- or 40-round box
Muzzle velocity: 3018 ft/sec (920 m/sec)
Cyclic rate: 750 rds/min

HK33A3 Rifle

1965. As for the HK33A2, but with retractable butt.

Specifications: similar, except
Length, butt extended: 37.0in (940mm)
Length, butt retracted: 28.93in (735mm)
Weight: 8lb 12oz (3.98kg)

HK33KA1

1965. Short-barrelled, retracting butt carbine version.

Cartridge: 5.56 x 45mm M193
Length, butt extended: 33.97in (863mm)
Length, butt retracted: 26.77in (680mm)
Weight: 8lb 12oz (3.98kg)
Barrel: 12.67in (322mm), 6 grooves, rh
Magazine: 20- or 40-round box
Muzzle velocity: 3008 ft/sec (917 m/sec)
Cyclic rate: 650 rds/min

HK33EA2

1985. Improved version of the fixed butt HK33A2 with added provision of ambidextrous selector/safety. Rifling to suit either type of 5.56mm cartridge. Normally with black furniture, it could be supplied in camouflage pattern or in sand colour, when the designation became **HK33ECA2** or **ECS2**.

Cartridge: 5.56 x 45mm M193 or NATO
Length: 36.22in (920mm)
Weight: 8lb 1oz (3.65kg)
Barrel: 15.35in (390mm), 6 grooves, rh
Magazine: 25-round box
Muzzle velocity: 3018 ft/sec (920 m/sec)
Cyclic rate: 750 rds/min

HK33EK

1985. Retracting butt, short barrel carbine version.

Cartridge: 5.56 x 45mm M193 or NATO
Length, butt extended: 34.05in (865mm)
Length, butt retracted: 26.57in (675mm)
Weight: 8lb 12oz (3.89kg)
Barrel: 12.67in (322mm), 6 grooves, rh
Magazine: 25-round box
Muzzle velocity: 2887 ft/sec (880 m/sec)
Cyclic rate: 650 rds/min

HK33 SG/1

1985. Sniping version of the HK33 family. Fixed butt, bipod, cheek pad, telescope sight.

Cartridge: 5.56 x 45mm M193 or NATO
Length: 36.22in (940mm)
Weight: 8lb 1oz (4.08kg)
Barrel: 15.35in (390mm), 6 grooves, rh
Magazine: 5- or 25-round box
Muzzle velocity: 3018 ft/sec (920 m/sec)
Cyclic rate: 750 rds/min

HK36 Rifle

1971. Experimental rifle developed round a 4.6 x 36mm cartridge. Upswept side-folding butt, short fore-end, long exposed barrel with flash suppressor, carrying handle with collimating sight, pistol grip. Fixed magazine loaded from pre-packed box into the rear of the magazine. Selective fire capability with burst-fire facility giving 2, 3, 4 or 5 rounds as required. Standard H&K roller-locked delayed blowback operation. Development abandoned in 1976 in favour of the G11.

Cartridge: 4.6 x 36mm Löffelspitz
Length, butt extended: 35.04in (890mm)
Length, butt folded: 31.38in (797mm)
Weight: 6lb 4oz (2.85kg)
Barrel: 15.0in (381mm), 6 grooves, rh
Magazine: 30-round box
Muzzle velocity: 2811 ft/sec (857 m/sec)
Cyclic rate: 1100 rds/min

HK53 Short Assault Rifle

Ca 1973. Originally called a submachine gun, this is an extremely compact carbine and can be considered as the baby of the HK33 family. It is similar in appearance to the HK33K but with a shorter barrel and fore-end and a special magazine.

Cartridge: 5.56 x 45mm M193 or NATO
Length, butt extended: 29.72in (755mm)
Length, butt retracted: 22.16in (563mm)
Weight: 6lb 11oz (3.05kg)
Barrel: 8.85in (225mm), 6 grooves, rh
Magazine: 40-round box
Muzzle velocity: 2460 ft/sec (750 m/sec)
Cyclic rate: 700 rds/min

G8 Rifle

1985. This weapon originally appeared as the HK11 machine gun, but after modifications to meet a German Border Police requirement was re-designated as a rifle. It can be configured, by add-on kits, as a rifle or as a magazine-fed or belt-fed machine gun. The receiver is similar to all other H&K rifles but the quick-change heavy barrel is encased almost to the muzzle. Bipod; may have forward hand grip and/or telescope sight.

Cartridge: 7.62 x 51mm NATO
Length: 40.55in (1030mm)
Weight: 17lb 15oz (8.15kg)
Barrel: 17.71in (450mm), 4 grooves, rh
Magazine: 20- round box or 50-round drum, or belt
Muzzle velocity: 2625 ft/sec (800 m/sec)
Cyclic rate: 800 rds/min

G8A1 Rifle

1985. A variant of the G8 rifle which will not accept the belt-feed modification and is restricted to using magazines only.

Specifications: the same

G11K3 Rifle

1990 (in service). Unconventional caseless cartridge rifle. Unique 'boxy' plastic casing contains the mechanism; magazine inserts above barrel, rotary cocking handle on left side, optical sight in carrying handle. Selective fire with three-round burst. Gas operated, rotating chamber breech mechanism.

Cartridge: 4.73 x 33 DM11
Length: 29.53in (750mm)
Weight: 8lb 1oz (3.65kg)
Barrel: 21.26in (540mm), 4 grooves, rh, increasing
Magazine: 45-round box
Muzzle velocity: 3051 ft/sec (930 m/sec)
Cyclic rate: 600 rds/min
Three-round burst rate: 2100 rds/min

G36 Rifle

1995. Designed for the German Army to take the place of the G11, financial approval for which had been withheld after an initial issue to Special Forces. Gas-operated, rotating bolt locking. Folding skeleton butt, carrying handle with built-in 3x optical sight, optional bipod, perforated hand-guard, muzzle compensator/flash hider.

Cartridge: 5.56 x 45mm NATO
Length, butt extended: 39.29in (998mm)
Length, butt retracted: 29.84in (758mm)
Weight: 7lb 9oz (3.43kg)
Barrel: 18.90in (480mm), 6 grooves, rh
Magazine: 30-round box
Muzzle velocity: 3018 ft/sec (920 m/sec)
Cyclic rate: 750 rds/min

G36K Short Rifle

1995. Issued to German Special Forces. Short version of the G36.

Cartridge: 5.56 x 45mm NATO
Length, butt extended: 33.78in (858mm)
Length, butt retracted: 24.13in (613mm)
Weight: 6lb 14oz (3.13kg)
Barrel: 13.0in (320mm), 6 grooves, rh
Magazine: 30-round box
Muzzle velocity: 2789 ft/sec (850 m/sec)
Cyclic rate: 750 rds/min

G36E & G36KE Assault Rifles

Export version of the G36 and G36K; differ only in that the optical sight is of 1.5x power.

Specifications: the same

G41 Rifle

1985. An improved HK33, designed around the SS109 NATO-standard cartridge. Incorporated a low-noise bolt closing device, hold-open device, dust-proof cover on the ejection port, STANAG 4179 magazine housing to accept any M16-type magazine, STANAG 2324 sight mount for all NATO optical or electro-optical sights, carrying handle and a minimum service life of 20,000 rounds.

Cartridge: 5.56 x 45mm NATO
Length: 39.25in (997mm)
Weight: 9lb 1oz (4.10kg)
Barrel: 17.71in (450mm), 6 grooves, rh
Magazine: 30-round box
Muzzle velocity: 3150 ft/sec (960 m/sec)
Cyclic rate: 850 rds/min

G41A2

1985. G41 rifle with retractable butt.

Cartridge: 5.56 × 45mm NATO
Length, butt extended: 39.24in (996mm)
Length, butt retracted: 31.73in (806mm)
Weight: 9lb 9oz (4.35kg)
Barrel: 17.71in (450mm), 6 grooves, rh
Magazine: 30-round box
Muzzle velocity: 3150 ft/sec (960 m/sec)
Cyclic rate: 850 rds/min

G41K

1985. Retracting butt, short-barrelled carbine member of the family.

Cartridge: 5.56 × 45mm NATO
Length, butt extended: 36.61in (930mm)
Length, butt retracted: 29.13in (740mm)
Weight: 9lb 6oz (4.25kg)
Barrel: 14.96in (380mm), 6 grooves, rh
Magazine: 30-round box
Muzzle velocity: 3000 ft/sec (915 m/sec)
Cyclic rate: 900 rds/min

HELENIUS Finland

APH-RK-97 Anti-materiel Rifle

1996. Single shot heavy rifle using vertical sliding breech-block operated by pump action of the sliding forward handgrip. Slab-sided receiver, pistol grip, L-shaped stock, muzzle brake, bipod.

Cartridge: .50 Browning
Length: 52.36in (1330mm)
Weight: 30lb 14oz (14.0kg)
Barrel: 37.0in (940mm), 8 grooves, rh
Muzzle velocity: 2723 ft/sec (830 m/sec)

HOTCHKISS USA

Winchester

Designed by B.B. Hotchkiss, manufactured by Winchester, who bought the manufacturing rights.

Winchester-Hotchkiss M1879

Bolt-action, tube magazine in butt, loaded through trap, full stocked, combined safety catch and magazine cut-off. Purchased by US Army and Navy.

Cartridge: .45-70 Government
Length: 48.60in (1234mm)
Weight: 9lb 2oz (4.14kg)
Barrel: 28.65in (728mm), 3 grooves, rh
Magazine: 5-round tube
Muzzle velocity: ca 1300 ft/sec (396 m/sec);

Winchester-Hotchkiss M1883

Improved model; magazine loaded through open action. Tested by US Army, rejected, but a small quantity sold commercially.

Cartridge: .45-70 Government
Length: 51.75in (1314mm)
Weight: 8lb 15oz (4.06kg)
Barrel: 32.0in (813mm), 3 grooves, rh
Magazine: 6-round tube
Muzzle velocity: ca 1300 ft/sec (396 m/sec)

HOWA Japan
Howa

Type 64 Rifle

1964. Gas-operated, selective fire, tilting breech-block. Perforated fore-end/handguard, bipod, exposed barrel with four-port muzzle brake. Straight-line layout, pistol grip. Notably shorter than usual, to suit Japanese stature, and regulated for a reduced-load cartridge. About 250,000 made.

Cartridge: 7.62 × 51mm
Length: 38.97in (990mm)
Weight: 9lb 11oz (4.40kg)
Barrel: 17.71in (450mm), 4 grooves, rh
Magazine: 20-round box
Muzzle velocity: 2296 ft/sec (700 m/sec)
Cyclic rate: 500 rds/min

Type 89 Rifle

1989. Gas-operated, selective fire, rotating bolt. Perforated handguard, bipod, hooded front sight, exposed barrel, muzzle brake. Plastic butt, pistol grip. Replaced Type 64 in Japanese forces. Fixed or side-folding butt versions.

Cartridge: 5.56 × 45mm NATO
Length, fixed or extended butt: 36.06in (916mm)
Length, folded butt: 26.50in (673mm)
Weight: 7lb 11oz (3.5kg)
Barrel: 16.54in (420mm), 6 grooves, rh
Magazine: 20- or 30-round box
Muzzle velocity: 3018 ft/sec (920 m/sec)
Cyclic rate: 750 rds/min

IMBEL Brazil
IMBEL

MD2

1985. A 5.56mm rifle based upon the FN-FAL, which Imbel made under licence. It has a similar outline, layout and operating system to the FN-FAL, with a side-folding tubular butt and a removable bipod.

Cartridge: 5.56 × 45mm M193 or NATO
Length, butt extended: 40.55in (1030mm)
Length, butt folded: 30.08in (764mm)
Weight: 9lb 11oz (4.40kg)
Barrel: 17.83in (453mm), 6 grooves, rh
Magazine: 20- or 30-round box
Muzzle velocity: 3150 ft/sec (960 m/sec)
Cyclic rate: 700 rds/min

MD3

1985. Similar to the MD2, but with a fixed plastic butt.

Specifications: the same, except
Weight: 10lb 1oz (4.56kg)

INSAS India
Ishapore

INSAS Assault Rifle

Indian Small Arms System. 1993. Gas-operated, selective fire, rotating bolt, largely based on Kalashnikov. Barrel, gas cylinder and front sight resemble the FN-FAL and the fore-end leans towards the ArmaLite AR-15. The fixed butt model uses the old Lee-Enfield butt-plate, and the folding butt model seems to have taken the FN-CAL as its guide. The cartridge is based on the Belgian SS109 but is to not NATO standard.

Cartridge: 5.56 × 45mm
Length, fixed butt: 37.20in (945mm)
Length, extended butt: 37.80in (960mm)
Length, folded butt: 29.53in (750mm)
Weight: 7lb 1oz (3.20kg)
Barrel: 18.26in (464mm), 6 grooves, rh
Magazine: 20- or 30-round box
Muzzle velocity: 3000 ft/sec (915 m/sec)
Cyclic rate: 650 rds/min

JAPAN
See also Arisaka, Howa & Murata
Type 97 Anti-tank Rifle
Kokura
Gas-operated, full-automatic fire, recoiling in bipod-supported cradle. Top-mounted magazine, monopod beneath butt. Pistol grip with whole-hand trigger-guard.

Cartridge: 20 × 124
Length: 80.0in (2035mm)
Weight: 152lb 0oz (68.93kg)
Barrel: 47.0in (1195mm), 8 grooves, rh
Magazine: 7-round vertical box
Muzzle velocity: 2000 ft/sec (609 m/sec)
Cyclic rate: 350 rds/min
Armour penetration: 12/200/0

JARMANN Norway
Kongsberg
M1884 Rifle
Bolt-action, tube magazine beneath barrel, full-stocked, auxiliary long range sight on left side of stock.

Cartridge: 10.15 × 61R Jarmann
Length: 56.95in (1345mm)
Weight: 9lb 15oz (4.43kg)
Barrel: 32.60in (828mm), 4 grooves, lh
Magazine: 8-round tube
Muzzle velocity: 1362 ft/sec (415m/sec)

M1884/87 Rifle
As for the M1884 but with recalibrated sights consequent upon adopting smokeless powder and a jacketed bullet.

Specifications: the same, except
Muzzle velocity: 1625 ft/sec (495 m/sec)

JOHNSON USA
M1941
Cranston & Johnson
Recoil-operated, semi-automatic, rotating bolt, rotary magazine. Half-stocked, with perforated handguard and long exposed barrel. Used by US Marines, Dutch East Indies Army and US special forces in 1941–45.

Cartridge: .30-06 Springfield
Length: 45.50in (1156mm)
Weight: 9lb 8oz (4.31kg)

Barrel: 22.0in (558mm), 4 grooves, rh
Magazine: 10-round rotary integral
Muzzle velocity: 2650 ft/sec (807 m/sec)

JOSLYN USA
Joslyn
Model 1862 Carbine
Single shot, side-pivoting breech-block. Half-stocked, round barrel, one barrel band, side-hammer. Hook latch holds breech-block closed. Exposed firing pin.

Cartridge: .56-50 Spencer
Length: 39.50in (1003mm)
Weight: 8lb 7oz (2.92kg)
Barrel: 22.0in (558mm), 4 grooves, rh
Muzzle velocity: *ca* 900 ft/sec (274 m/sec)

Model 1864 Carbine
Similar to the M1862 model, but with hooded firing pin and pull-out latch with knob for holding breech-block closed.

Specifications: as for M1862

KALASHNIKOV Russia
State factories, unless noted otherwise
All Kalashnikov rifles in military service operate using the same basic gas-piston and rotating-bolt system and have the same type of external safety-catch/selector lever on the right side of the receiver. Other recognisable features are the short fore-end and handguard, the gas cylinder above the barrel and the curved magazine.

AK-47
1949. Machined steel receiver, polished bolt and carrier, wood butt and fore-end, wood or plastic grips.

Cartridge: 7.62 × 39mm M1943
Length: 34.21in (869mm)
Weight: 9lb 7oz (4.30kg)
Barrel: 16.30in (414mm), 4 grooves, rh
Magazine: 30-round box
Muzzle velocity: 2329 ft/sec (710 m/sec)
Cyclic rate: 775 rds/min

AK-S
1950. As for the AK-47 but with a double-strut steel butt which folded down and forward to lie beneath the receiver.

Specifications: similar, plus
Length, butt folded: 27.52in (699mm)

AKM
1959. Modified AK-47 with pressed-steel receiver body and cover and other manufacturing short-cuts. Laminated wood furniture, plastic grips. Early production had the muzzle cut square, but after 1961 it was cut obliquely to provide a compensating thrust to the muzzle.

Cartridge: 7.62 × 39mm M1943
Length: 34.49in (876mm)
Weight: 8lb 7oz (3.82kg)
Barrel: 16.30in (414mm), 4 grooves, rh
Magazine: 30-round box
Muzzle velocity: 2329 ft/sec (710 m/sec)
Cyclic rate: 775 rds/min

AKM-S

1960. As for the AKM, but with the same two-strut steel folding stock as the AK-S.

Specifications: as for AKM, except
Length, butt folded: 25.87in (657mm)
Length, butt extended: 35.24in (895mm)
Weight: 7lb 13oz (3.55kg)

AKM-SU

1975. Short version of the AKM-S for use by armoured infantry. Folding butt, short fore-end, finned expansion chamber, muzzle brake.

Cartridge: 7.62 × 39mm M1943
Length: 28.42in (722mm)
Weight: 7lb 6oz (3.35kg)
Barrel: 8.86in (225mm), 4 grooves, rh
Magazine: 30-round box
Muzzle velocity: 2116 ft/sec (645 m/sec)
Cyclic rate: 800 rds/min

AK-74

1974. Reduced-calibre version of the AKM. Grooved wooden butt, plastic magazine, prominent muzzle-brake/compensator.

Cartridge: 5.45 × 39.5mm
Length: 36.53in (928mm)
Weight: 8lb 8oz (3.86kg)
Barrel: 15.75in (400mm), 4 grooves, rh
Magazine: 30-round box
Muzzle velocity: 2953 ft/sec (900 m/sec)
Cyclic rate: 650 rds/min

AKS-74

1974. Folding-stock version of the AK-74.

Specifications: the same, except
Length, butt folded: 27.16in (690mm)

AK-74-SU

1980. Reduced calibre version of the AKM-SU with a similar folding butt, expansion chamber and flash hider. Receiver cover is hinged at the front to open instead of lift off.

Cartridge: 5.45 × 39.5mm
Length, butt extended: 26.57in (675mm)
Length, butt folded: 16.61in (422mm)
Weight: 5lb 15oz (2.70kg)
Barrel: 8.11in (206mm), 4 grooves, rh
Magazine: 30-round box
Muzzle velocity: 2411 ft/sec (735 m/sec)
Cyclic rate: 700 rds/min

Hundred Series

At the time of writing (mid-1998), a new family of Kalashnikov rifles, known as the Hundred Series is being touted as the future Russian service rifle. Apart from being made available for export in NATO calibres, and claiming to be manufactured with more modern technology, there appears to be little difference from the older design, and under the current economic difficulties, it is unlikely that it will be adopted in the near future.

AK101

1996. Similar to the basic AK-74, black synthetic furniture.

Cartridge: 5.56 × 45mm NATO
Length: 37.12in (943mm)
Weight: 7lb 8oz (3.40kg)
Barrel: 16.34in (415mm), 4 grooves, rh
Magazine: 30-round box
Muzzle velocity: 2985 ft/sec (910 m/sec)
Cyclic rate: 600 rds/min

KALASHNIKOV CLONES

By which we mean copies of, or minor modifications to, standard Kalashnikov designs, manufactured elsewhere. It does not include weapons based upon the Kalashnikov system of operation but with characteristics of their own, *eg* the Galil, and Vektor rifles. The listing is arranged by countries. Where no dimensions are given it can be taken that they do not differ significantly from the parent Russian model.

BULGARIA

AK47

Identical copy of Russian AK-47, though it may have black plastic furniture.

AKS47

Identical copy of Russian AK-S.

AKN-47

An AK47 fitted with a night vision sight

AK47-M1

An AK47 fitted with a 40mm grenade launcher.

AK74, AK-S 74

Identical copies of Russian models. Also offered for export in 5.56 × 45mm chambering.

AKN74

AK-74 fitted with night sight.

CHINA

Type 56

Similar to the Russian AK-47 but with a folding bayonet hinged below the muzzle

Type 56-1

Similar to the Russian AK-S but has prominent rivets on the metal butt arms. No bayonet.

Type 56-2

Generally as for the 56-1 but the butt-stock is a skeleton tubular type which folds to the right side of the receiver. No bayonet.

Type 56-C

Appears to have been influenced by the AK-74 design; uses plastic furniture. The side-folding butt has a cheek-piece, new muzzle compensator, cleaning kit stored in pistol grip, new sights.

Cartridge: 7.62 × 39mm M1943
Length, butt extended: 30.11in (765mm)
Length, butt folded: 22.17in (563mm)

Weight: 7lb 11oz (3.50kg)
Barrel: 13.58in (345mm), 4 grooves, rh
Magazine: 30-round box
Muzzle velocity: 2296 ft/sec (700m/sec)
Cyclic rate: 700 rds/min

EGYPT

Misr

Copy of the AKM, very minor dimensional differences. May also be found with a single-strut side-folding metal buttstock.

ARM

A Misr converted to semi-automatic fire only and with a wooden thumb-hole stock. Promoted as a sporting weapon, equally serviceable for police and security force use. May be found with small 10-round box magazine.

GERMANY (EAST)

MPiK

Copy of the AK-47, differs in having no cleaning rod under the barrel.

MPiKS

Copy of the AK-S, no cleaning rod.

MPiKM

Copy of the AKM. Cleaning rod. Early manufacture used wooden furniture with a forward handgrip, later used plastic furniture, the butt having a prominently 'dimpled' surface. No muzzle compensator.

MPiKMS

Identical copy of the AKM-S but without the shaped muzzle.

MPiKMS-72

As for the MPiKM, but has a single-strut side-folding metal butt-stock and the muzzle shaped as a compensator.

KKMPi69

An MPiKM except that the barrel comes out of the upper part of the fore-end and there is no gas cylinder. Actually a training rifle chambered for the .22 Long Rifle rimfire cartridge.

HUNGARY

AKM-63

As for the AKM, but with polypropylene plastic furniture, including a forward pistol grip beneath the fore-end. Weighs about 8oz (250g) less than the Russian AKM.

AMD-65

This is the AKM-63 with a short barrel, two-port Solothurn pattern muzzle brake and side-folding single-strut metal butt.

Cartridge: 7.62 × 39mm M1943
Length, butt extended: 33.50in (851mm)
Length, butt folded: 25.50in (648mm)
Weight: 7lb 3oz (3.27kg)
Barrel: 12.52in (318mm), 4 grooves, rh
Magazine: 30-round box
Muzzle velocity: 2296 ft/sec (700 m/sec)
Cyclic rate: 600 rds/min

NGM Assault Rifle

Hungarian version of the AK-74 but chambered for the 5.56mm cartridge for export. Cold hammered barrel with chrome lining and rifled one turn in 200mm as a compromise to suit both M193 and NATO ammunition.

Cartridge: 5.56 × 45mm M193 or NATO
Length: 36.81in (935mm)
Weight: 7lb 0oz (3.18kg)
Barrel: 16.23in (412mm), 4 grooves, rh
Magazine: 30-round box
Muzzle velocity: 2953 ft/sec (900 m/sec)
Cyclic rate: 600 rds/min

IRAQ

Tabuk

Copy of the AKM; slight differences in the contour of the butt and fore-end. It is also offered for export in 5.56mm calibre.

NORTH KOREA

Type 58

Copy of the AKM, differing only in having no finger grooves in the fore-end.

Type 68

Copy of the AKM-S and differs only in having holes drilled in the side-arms of the folding butt.

POLAND

PMK

Copy of the AK-47. The same title is applied to a copy of the AK-S.

PMKM

Copies of both the AKM and AKM-S are covered by this designation.

Both the PMK and PMKM may be found with extended grenade launchers attached to the muzzle.

Tantal 88

This is the Polish version of the AKS-74, with a side-folding single-strut butt apparently copied from the East German MPiKMS72. Black plastic furniture, light bipod, muzzle compensator also modified to act as a bayonet mounting.

Cartridge: 5.45 × 39mm
Length, butt extended: 37.13in (943mm)
Length, butt folded: 29.21in (742mm)
Weight: 7lb 8oz (3.40kg)
Barrel: 16.65in (423mm), 4 grooves, rh
Magazine: 30-round box
Muzzle velocity: 2887 ft/sec (880 m/sec)
Cyclic rate: 650 rds/min

Tantal 89

As for Tantal 88 but chambered for 5.56 x 45mm cartridge.

Muzzle velocity: 2953 ft/sec (900 m/sec)

ROMANIA
AKM
Copies of Russian AKM and AKM-S both found under this designation. The only significant difference is the presence of a curved front hand grip formed from the same piece of wood as the fore-end.

AKM-R
Compact version of the AKM. Short barrel ending at the front sight, smaller magazine, single-strut side-folding metal butt.

Cartridge: 7.62 × 39mm M1943
Length, butt extended: 29.53in (750mm)
Length, butt folded: 21.65in (550mm)
Weight: 6lb 13oz (3.10kg)
Barrel: 8.11in (305mm), 4 grooves, rh
Magazine: 20-round box
Muzzle velocity: 2854 ft/sec (870 m/sec)
Cyclic rate: 600 rds/min

AK-74
Generally very similar to the Russian AK-74, but the front handguard extends all the way to the end of the gas cylinder, and it may have a wooden or tubular steel skeleton fixed stock. The fore-end has the usual Romanian handgrip.

Cartridge: 5.45 × 39mm
Length: 37.0in (940mm)
Weight: 7lb 8oz (3.40kg)
Barrel: 16.34in (415mm), 4 grooves, rh
Magazine: 30-round box
Muzzle velocity: 2887 ft/sec (880 m/sec)
Cyclic rate: 700 rds/min

YUGOSLAVIA
M70B1
Copy of the AKM. Differs in having a grenade sight on the gas port which, when raised, cuts off the gas flow for grenade launching.

M70AB2
Copy of the AKM-S.

M76 Sniping Rifle
This is basically an AKM with long barrel and wooden fixed butt, chambered for the 7.92mm Mauser cartridge. The usual iron sights are retained and there is also a mount for optical or electro-optical sights. Semi-automatic only, small straight magazine.

Cartridge: 7.92 × 57mm Mauser
Length: 44.68in (1135mm)
Weight: 9lb 4oz (4.20kg)
Barrel: 21.65in (550mm), 4 grooves, rh
Magazine: 30-round box
Muzzle velocity: 2887 ft/sec (880 m/sec)

M77B1
Another long-barrelled AKM with a fixed wooden butt and straight magazine, this time chambered for the NATO standard 7.62 × 51mm cartridge and intended for use as an infantry rifle.

Cartridge: 7.62 × 51mm NATO
Length: 38.97in (990mm)
Weight: 7lb 8oz (3.40kg)
Barrel: 16.34in (415mm), 4 grooves, rh
Magazine: 20-round box
Muzzle velocity: 2887 ft/sec (880 m/sec)
Cyclic rate: 700 rds/min

M80
Chambered for the 5.56mm cartridge, this generally resembles the AK-74 but fitted with a plain slotted flashhider.

Cartridge: 5.56 × 45mm
Length: 38.97in (990mm)
Weight: 7lb 11oz (3.50kg)
Barrel: 18.11in (460mm), 6 grooves, rh
Magazine: 10-round box
Muzzle velocity: 3182 ft/sec (970 m/sec)
Cyclic rate: 750 rds/min

M80A
Folding-butt version of the M80.

M85
1986. This appears to be a copy of the Russian AKS-74U, though somewhat longer and better-finished and chambered for the 5.56 × 45mm cartridge. The stock is a two-strut type which folds down and under the receiver.

Cartridge: 5.56 × 45mm
Length, butt extended: 31.10in (790mm)
Length, butt folded: 22.44in (570mm)
Weight: 7lb 1oz (3.20kg)
Barrel: 12.40in (315mm), 6 grooves, rh
Magazine: 20- or 30-round box
Muzzle velocity: 2592 ft/sec (790 m/sec)
Cyclic rate: 700 rds/min

KEENE or Remington-Keene USA
Remington
M1880
Bolt action with tubular magazine beneath barrel. Halfstocked. Manual cocking after bolt closure by hook on the rear end of the striker. Tested by the US Army and Navy but rejected. A small number issued to Indian Agency police.

Cartridge: .45-70 Government
Length: 48.50in (1232mm)
Weight: 9lb 0oz (4.08kg)
Barrel: 30.0in (762mm), 5 grooves, lh
Magazine: 8-round tube
Muzzle velocity: 1275 ft/sec (388 m/sec)

KOKA MAUSER
See Mauser, Serbia, M1878/80 Rifle

KRAG-JÖRGENSEN Norway

Developed in Norway, subsequently in military service with Denmark, Norway and the USA The common characteristic is the right-side side-loading magazine, feeding under the bolt and up to the feedway on the left side.

DENMARK

M1889 Rifle
København & Tøjhus

Bolt action, full stocked. Magazine loading trap opens forward. Hooked cocking piece spur, no safety other than half-cock, jacketed barrel.

Cartridge: 8 × 58R Danish Krag
Length: 52.28in (1328mm)
Weight: 10lb 1oz (4.58kg)
Barrel: 37.40in (950mm), 6 grooves, rh, increasing
Magazine: 5-round integral
Muzzle velocity: 1968 ft/sec (600 m/sec)

M1889-08 Rifle
København & Tøjhus

1908. As for the M1889, but sighted for a new cartridge with pointed bullet.

Muzzle velocity: 2460 ft/sec (750 m/sec)

M1889-10 Rifle
København & Tøjhus

1910. As for the M1889, but with 4-groove constant pitch rifling.

M1889 Cavalry Carbine
Tøjhus

1912. Modified M1889 rifle; shorter, unjacketed barrel, full stocked with full length handguard. Large grooved stud in left side of stock for sling.

Cartridge: 8 × 58R Danish Krag
Length: 43.30in (1100mm)
Weight: 8lb 14oz (4.04kg)
Barrel: 23.62in (600mm), 6 grooves, rh, increasing
Magazine: 5-round integral
Muzzle velocity: 2035 ft/sec (620 m/sec)

M1889 Engineer Carbine
Haerens T

1917. As cavalry carbine but fitted to take a bayonet.

Specifications: the same

M1889-23 Cavalry Carbine
Haerens R

1923. As for the M1889 Cavalry Carbine but fitted for a bayonet.

M1889-24 Infantry Carbine
Haerens V

1924. Originally built from converted M1889 rifles, later manufactured new but to the same specification. Barrel jacket retained. Originally with increasing twist rifling, changed to constant twist after 1925.

Cartridge: 8 × 58R Danish Krag
Length: 43.50in (1105mm)
Weight: 8lb 12oz (3.97kg)

Barrel: 24.00in (610mm), 6 grooves, rh, increasing; or 4 grooves, rh
Magazine: 5-round integral
Muzzle velocity: 2035 ft/sec (620 m/sec)

M1889-24 Artillery Carbine
Haerens R

1924. Generally as for the 1889 Cavalry Carbine, but with the bolt handle turned down, and a triangular sling swivel attached to the barrel band.

M1928 Sniping Rifle
Haerens R

1928. Based on the M1894 Infantry Rifle, but half-stocked, with a free-floating heavy barrel, micrometer rear sight, short handguard, hooded fore-sight, and turned-down bolt handle.

Cartridge: 8 × 58R Danish Krag
Length: 46.06in (1170mm)
Weight: 11lb 13oz (5.36kg)
Barrel: 23.03in (585mm), 6 grooves, rh, increasing; or 4 grooves, rh
Magazine: 5-round integral
Muzzle velocity: 2460 ft/sec (750 m/sec)

NORWAY

M1894 Rifle
FN Herstal, Kongsberg & Steyr

Bolt action, full-stocked, half-length handguard, cleaning rod. Loading trap opens downward, Mauser-type 'flag' safety on bolt.

Cartridge: 6.5 × 55mm Swedish Mauser
Length: 49.61in (1260mm)
Weight: 8lb 14oz (4.05kg)
Barrel: 29.92in (760mm), 4 grooves, lh
Magazine: 5-round integral
Muzzle velocity: 2395 ft/sec (730 m/sec)

M1895 Cavalry Carbine
Kongsberg

Half-stocked, short handguard, action as for the rifle.

Cartridge: 6.5 × 55mm Swedish Mauser
Length: 39.96in (1015mm)
Weight: 7lb 8oz (3.40kg)
Barrel: 20.47in (520mm), 4 grooves, lh
Magazine: 5-round integral
Muzzle velocity: 2100 ft/sec (640 m/sec)

M1897 Artillery and Engineer Carbine
Kongsberg

As for the cavalry carbine except for the position of the rear sling swivel, close to the toe of the butt.

M1904 Engineer Carbine
Kongsberg

Full-stocked with full-length handguard, cleaning rod. Bayonet fittings. Sling swivels underneath fore-end and left side of stock.

Cartridge: 6.5 × 55mm Swedish Mauser
Length: 39.96in (1015mm)
Weight: 8lb 6oz (3.81kg)
Barrel: 20.47in (520mm), 4 grooves, lh

Magazine: 5-round integral
Muzzle velocity: 2100 ft/sec (640 m/sec)

M1907 Artillery Carbine
Kongsberg

As for the 1904 Engineer Carbine except for the sling swivels, left side of fore-end and underneath the butt.

M1912 Short Rifle
Kongsberg

Full-stocked with nose-cap having bayonet lug and cleaning rod hole.

Cartridge: 6.5 × 55mm Swedish Mauser
Length: 43.54in (1106mm)
Weight: 8lb 14oz (4.02kg)
Barrel: 24.00in (610mm), 4 grooves, lh
Magazine: 5-round integral
Muzzle velocity: 2330 ft/sec (710 m/sec)

M1923 Sniping Rifle
Kongsberg

Full-stock and handguard, nose cap, chequered pistol-grip stock, free-floating heavy barrel. Few were made and it was soon replaced.

Cartridge: 6.5 × 55mm Swedish Mauser
Length: 44.0in (1117mm)
Weight: 9lb 1oz (4.11kg)
Barrel: 24.00in (610mm), 4 grooves, lh
Magazine: 5-round integral
Muzzle velocity: 2330 ft/sec (710 m/sec)

M1925 Sniping Rifle
Kongsberg

Generally as for the M1894 Rifle, but with heavy barrel and a front sight with protectors.

Cartridge: 6.5 × 55mm Swedish Mauser
Length: 49.70in (1262mm)
Weight: 9lb 14oz (4.48kg)
Barrel: 30.00in (762mm), 4 grooves, lh
Magazine: 5-round integral
Muzzle velocity: 2625 ft/sec (800 m/sec)

M1930 Sniping Rifle
Kongsberg

Half-stocked, free-floating heavy barrel, micrometer rear sight, hooded foresight. May be of new manufacture or converted from M1923 rifles.

Cartridge: 6.5 × 55mm Swedish Mauser
Length: 48.0in (1219mm)
Weight: 11lb 7oz (5.20kg)
Barrel: 29.50in (749mm), 4 grooves, lh
Magazine: 5-round integral
Muzzle velocity: 2625 ft/sec (800 m/sec)

USA

M1892 Rifle
Springfield

Bolt action, full stocked with short handguard. Loading trap opens downward. Cleaning rod, piling swivel, bayonet fittings.

Cartridge: .30-40 Krag
Length: 49.14in (1248mm)

Weight: 9lb 6oz (4.25kg)
Barrel: 30.0in (762mm), 4 grooves, rh
Magazine: 5-round integral
Muzzle velocity: 2000 ft/sec (610 m/sec)

M1896 Rifle
Springfield

As for the M1892 but with a three-piece cleaning rod carried in butt trap, new sights. Magazine cut-off turns down instead of up. Many M1892 rifles were modified to this standard.

Cartridge: .30-40 Krag
Length: 49.10in (1245mm)
Weight: 8lb 15oz (4.25kg)
Barrel: 30.0in (762mm), 4 grooves, rh
Magazine: 5-round integral
Muzzle velocity: 2000 ft/sec (610 m/sec)

M1896 Cavalry Carbine
Springfield

Same action as the rifle, with the addition of a saddle ring and rail on stock. Two-piece cleaning rod and oil-can in butt-trap.

Cartridge: .30-40 Krag
Length: 41.15in (1045mm)
Weight: 7lb 12oz (3.51kg)
Barrel: 22.0in (559mm), 4 grooves, rh
Magazine: 5-round integral
Muzzle velocity: 1750 ft/sec (533 m/sec)

M1898 Rifle
Springfield

Same action and general appearance as M1892, but with sights graduated to 2000 yards for new higher velocity ammunition. This was a failure and sights were then changed to a fresh type graduated to 2300 yards.

Cartridge: .30-40 Krag
Length: 49.13in (1248mm)
Weight: 9lb 0oz (4.08kg)
Barrel: 30.0in (762mm), 4 grooves, rh
Magazine: 5-round integral
Muzzle velocity: 2200 ft/sec (670 m/sec)

M1898 Cavalry Carbine
Springfield

Generally as for the M1896, but with high-velocity sights, which were changed as those of the rifle.

Cartridge: .30-40 Krag
Length: 41.15in (1045mm)
Weight: 7lb 12oz (3.52kg)
Barrel: 22.0in (762mm), 4 grooves, rh
Magazine: 5-round integral
Muzzle velocity: 1970 ft/sec (600 m/sec)

M1899 Cavalry Carbine
Springfield

A modified M1898 carbine, with the fore-end made somewhat longer; it was later provided with a new handguard to give better protection to the rear sight.

Specifications: no significant difference, except
Weight: 7lb 14oz (3.57kg)

Philippine Constabulary Short Rifle
Rock Island & Springfield
Converted from various models of rifle to provide a suitably short rifle for the Philippine police.

Cartridge: .30-40 Krag
Length: 41.15in (1045mm)
Weight: 8lb 1oz (3.64kg)
Barrel: 22.0in (559mm), 4 grooves, rh
Magazine: 5-round integral
Muzzle velocity: 1750 ft/sec (533 m/sec)

KRAG-PETERSON Norway/Sweden
Although designed by Krag this has no resemblance to the Krag-Jörgensen family of weapons.

M1877 Marine Carbine Denmark
København
Short rifle with full length stock but no handguard, muzzle cap. Dropping block breech with operating lever above the breech. This opened the breech and fed a round from the tube magazine under the barrel. The receiver body resembles a Martini type at first glance.

Cartridge: 11.7 x 42R rimfire
Length: 37.48in (952mm)
Weight: 8lb 15oz (4.05kg)
Barrel: 20.07in (510mm), 5 grooves, rh
Magazine: 7-round tube
Muzzle velocity: 1148 ft/sec (350 m/sec)

KROPATSCHEK Austria-Hungary
AUSTRIA-HUNGARY
Steyr
M1881 Gendarmerie Carbine
Full-stocked, bolt action, tubular magazine underneath the barrel.

Cartridge: 11.15 x 58R Werndl
Length: 40.95in (1040mm)
Weight: 8lb 6oz (3.80kg)
Barrel: 22.44in (570mm), 6 grooves, rh
Magazine: 5-round tube
Muzzle velocity: 1007 ft/sec (307 m/sec)

FRANCE
M1878 Marine Rifle
Steyr
Bolt action, full-stocked, no handguard, tubular magazine underneath the barrel.

Cartridge: 11 x 59R Gras
Length: 48.98in (1244mm)
Weight: 9lb 15oz (4.50kg)
Barrel: 29.25in (743mm), 4 grooves, rh
Magazine: 7-round tube
Muzzle velocity: 1493 ft/sec (455 m/sec)

M1884 Infantry Rifle
MAC Chatellerault & MAS
A French re-work of the original Kropatschek M1878 design which increased the magazine capacity.

Specifications: the same, except
Magazine: 8 rounds
Weight: 9lb 6oz (4.26kg)

M1885 Infantry Rifle
MAS
Full stocked but in two pieces separated by the full-depth receiver. Single barrel band.

Cartridge: 11 x 59R Gras
Length: 48.98in (1244mm)
Weight: 9lb 4oz (4.20kg)
Barrel: 29.57in (751mm), 4 grooves, rh
Magazine: 8-round tube
Muzzle velocity: 1493 ft/sec (455 m/sec)

PORTUGAL
M1886 Infantry Rifle
Steyr
Bolt action, full-stocked, tubular magazine. Generally the same as the French M1878 rifle but with a new bolt and elevator mechanism.

Cartridge: 8 x 60R Guedes (M73)
Length: 51.97in (1320mm)
Weight: 10lb 1oz (4.57kg)
Barrel: 31.57in (802mm), 4 grooves, rh
Magazine: 8-round tube
Muzzle velocity: 1755 ft/sec (535 m/sec)

M1886/89 Infantry Rifle
Steyr
M1886 rifles fitted with handguard, for colonial troops.

M1886 Fiscal Guard Carbine
Steyr
A short version of the M1886 rifle. Full-stocked and with bayonet fittings.

Cartridge: 8 x 60R Guedes
Length: 45.87in (1165mm)
Weight: 9lb 6oz (4.25kg)
Barrel: 25.86in (657mm), 4 grooves, rh
Magazine: 6-round tube
Muzzle velocity: 1558 ft/sec (475 m/sec)

M1886 Cavalry Carbine
Steyr
Full-stocked to the muzzle and fitted for a bayonet, but otherwise simply a short version of the infantry rifle

Cartridge: 8 x 60R Guedes
Length: 40.4in (1025mm)
Weight: 8lb 13oz (4.0kg)
Barrel: 20.50in (521mm), 4 grooves, rh
Magazine: 5-round tube
Muzzle velocity: 1394 ft/sec (425 m/sec)

LEBEL France
MAC Chatellerault, MAP, MAS & MAT
Generally acclaimed as the first 'modern' military rifle, being the first to appear using smokeless powder and a small-calibre bullet.

M1886 Infantry Rifle

Bolt-action, full-stocked but in two parts, divided by the receiver; tubular magazine in the fore-end, exposed muzzle. Ramp sight to 2000m.

Cartridge: 8 × 50R Lebel
Length: 51.45in (1307mm)
Weight: 9lb 3oz (4.18kg)
Barrel: 32.08in (815mm), 4 grooves, lh
Magazine: 8-round tube
Muzzle velocity: 2067 ft/sec (630 m/sec)

M1886/93 Infantry Rifle

Improved version of the M1886; lighter striker and other small changes. Recognisable by a piling hook under the muzzle. No significant change in dimensions.

M1886 R35

1935. M1886/93 rifles shortened to provide arms for motorised infantry as an interim measure while production of the MAS 1936 (*qv*) got under way.

Cartridge: 8 × 50R Lebel
Length: 37.72in (958mm)
Weight: 8lb 5oz (3.77kg)
Barrel: 17.71in (450mm), 4 grooves, lh
Magazine: 3-round tube
Muzzle velocity: 1985 ft/sec (605 m/sec)

Development of the Lebel is covered under Berthier, *above*

LEE USA

James Paris Lee developed both turnbolt and straight-pull bolt actions, together with a box magazine. The straight-pull action was adopted by the US Navy and also sold commercially by Winchester. The turn-bolt action was adopted by Britain and the USA for military use and sold commercially by Remington.

Lee M1895 Navy Rifle
Lee Arms

Straight-pull bolt, locked by a wedge. Full-stocked, short handguard, short exposed muzzle. Small fixed magazine ahead of trigger guard.

Cartridge: .236 Lee US Navy
Length: 47.00in (1194mm)
Weight: 8lb 0oz (3.63kg)
Barrel: 27.25in (692mm), 5 grooves, lh
Magazine: 5-round integral box
Muzzle velocity: 2400 ft/sec (732 m/sec)

Remington-Lee M1879 Rifle
Remington

Turn-bolt, full-stocked, removable magazine ahead of trigger guard, no handguard, exposed muzzle. Adopted by US Navy.

Cartridge: .45-70 Government
Length: 48.50in (1232mm)
Weight: 8lb 8oz (3.85kg)
Barrel: 29.50in (749mm), 3 grooves, rh
Magazine: 5-round box
Muzzle velocity: 1320 ft/sec (402 m/sec)

Remington-Lee M1882 Rifle
Remington

Turn-bolt, fully stocked, removable box magazine. Tested by US Army but refused. Dimensions the same as the M1879, it being an improved version of that weapon.

Remington-Lee M1885 Rifle
Remington

Further improvement on the M1879, principally a magazine which could be removed and still retain its cartridges, a separate bolt-head with improved extractor, and an enlarged cocking-piece. Tested by Denmark, adopted by US Navy.

Cartridge: .45-70 Government
Length: 52.0in (1321mm)
Weight: 8lb 8oz (3.85kg)
Barrel: 33.50in (851mm), 3 grooves, rh
Magazine: 5-round box
Muzzle velocity: 1350 ft/sec (411 m/sec)

Remington-Lee M1889 Rifle
Remington

Generally similar to the M1885 but sold by Remington to various military forces in Central and South America in the 1890s.

Cartridge: various, to customer requirements
Length: 47.60in (1209mm)
Weight: 8lb 8oz (3.85kg)
Barrel: 29.0in (749mm), 4 grooves, rh
Magazine: 10-round box
Muzzle velocity: *ca* 2000 ft/sec (610 m/sec), depending on calibre

LEE-ENFIELD Britain
BSA, Enfield, LSA, NRF1 & SSA

The adoption of cordite as a propellant meant that the earlier Metford system of rifling (*see* the next set of entries on Lee-Metford), designed for black powder, was no longer effective, being eroded very quickly by the hotter Cordite. Enfield rifling, using deeper and more clearly defined grooves, was better suited to the new propellant and led to the Lee-Enfield rifle family.

Rifle, Magazine, Lee-Enfield, Mark I

1895. This was much the same as the Lee-Metford Mark 2★, differing only in the rifling. Full-stocked, cleaning rod, barleycorn foresight, square notch rear sight, long range sight, magazine cut-off.

Cartridge: .303 British
Length: 49.50in (1257mm)
Weight: 9lb 4oz (4.19kg)
Barrel: 30.2in (769mm), 5 grooves, lh
Magazine: 10-round box
Muzzle velocity: *ca* 2200 ft/sec (670 m/sec)

Rifle, Magazine, Lee-Enfield, Mark 1★

1899. Differed from Mark 1 in omitting the cleaning rod and fittings.

Rifle, Charger Loading, Magazine, Lee-Enfield, Mark 1*

1907. Conversion of Lee-Enfield Rifles Marks 1 and 1* or Lee-Metford Mark 2* by the addition of a bridge charger guide, new magazine and new backsight.

Specifications: as for the Magazine Lee-Enfield Mark 1*, except
Weight: 9lb 5oz (4.22kg)

Rifle, Short, Magazine, Lee-Enfield, Mark 1

SMLE. 1903. A complete re-design in order to replace the existing division between rifles and carbines and produce one rifle which could be used by all troops. Lee bolt action, fully stocked with snub nose-cap having protecting wings for the foresight and fittings for the sword bayonet. Charger loading, using guides formed on the bolt head. Magazine cut-off. Long range sight. Barleycorn foresight, V-notch rear sight.

Cartridge: .303 British
Length: 44.56in (1132mm)
Weight: 8lb 2.5oz (3.70kg)
Barrel: 25.187in (640mm), 5 grooves, lh
Magazine: 10-round box
Muzzle velocity: *ca* 2000 ft/sec (610 m/sec)

Rifle, Short, Magazine, Lee-Enfield, Mark 1*

1906. Differs from Mark 1 in having butt-plate of gun-metal, with trap; Number 2 magazine (deeper at the front end); a keeper screw for the striker which had a slot allowing it to be unscrewed using a coin.

Specifications: as for Mark 1

Rifle, Short, Magazine, Lee-Enfield, Converted, Mark 1

1903. Conversions made from Lee-Metford Mark 1* by fitting new sights, shorter and lighter barrel, and adapting them for charger loading. Only the Sealed Pattern arm was ever made, and the weapon was declared obsolete in 1906.

Rifle, Short, Magazine, Lee-Enfield, Converted, Mark 2

1903. A conversion of the Lee-Enfield Marks 1 and 1* and Lee-Metford Marks 2 and 2* achieved by fitting new sights, shorter and lighter barrels and modifications to permit charger loading.

Specifications: as for Mark 1

Rifle, Short, Magazine, Lee-Enfield, Converted, Mark 2*

1906. Similar to the Converted Mark 2, from which it differed in having the butt recessed for the sling swivel, provision for a butt trap, and a Number 2 magazine.

Specifications: as for Mark 1, except
Weight: 8lb 7oz (3.82kg).

Rifle, Short, Magazine, Lee-Enfield, Mark 3

1907. As for the SMLE Mark 1 but the foresight was a blade instead of a barleycorn and was supplied in five heights. The rear sight bed was wider, and the sight leaf graduated to 2000 yards and with a fine adjustment worm wheel. A 'U' notch replaced the former 'V' notch. The body was fitted with a bridge charger-guide and the charger guide on

the bolt head was removed. From 1916, wartime concessions permitted the omission of the long range sights, replacement of the rear sight wind gauge by a fixed cap, alteration of the contours of the striker, and omission of the piling swivel lugs.

Weight: 8lb 10.5oz (3.94kg)

Rifle, Short, Magazine, Lee-Enfield, Converted, Mark 4

1907. This differed from the Converted Mark 2* insofar as it embodied the special features of the SMLE Mark 3.

Weight: 8lb 14.5oz (4.13kg)

Rifle, Short, Magazine, Lee-Enfield, Mark 1**

1909. This weapon was issued only to the Royal Navy, and was a conversion from SMLE Mark 1 rifles consisting of fitting a SMLE Mark 3 foresight, and a rear sight wind-gauge with a 'U' notch to suit.

Rifle, Short, Magazine, Lee-Enfield, Converted, Mark 2**

1909. Another naval conversion, the same as the Mark 1** but performed on the SMLE Mark 2 rifle.

Rifle, Short, Magazine, Lee-Enfield, Converted, Mark 2***

1909. The third naval conversion, as before, but applied to the SMLE Converted Mark 2*.

Rifle, Short, Magazine, Lee-Enfield, Mark 1***

1914. A conversion from the SMLE Mark 1* by fitting a wind-gauge with 'U' notch to the rear sight and a new blade foresight to suit Mark 7 ball ammunition.

Rifle, Short, Magazine, Lee-Enfield, Mark 3*

1916. This was a wartime model differing from the Mark 3 in having the magazine cut-off omitted during manufacture. It could also incorporate any of the wartime concessions noted under the Mark 3.

Rifle, Number 4, Mark 1

BSA, ROF (F), ROF (M), Long Branch & Savage
1941. The Number 4 was similar to the Short Magazine Lee-Enfield but with an aperture rear sight hinged at the rear of the body, the nosecap abolished and the muzzle exposed for about three inches and fitted with lugs for the spike bayonet. All screw threads were to national standards instead of being to the Enfield standard.

Cartridge: .303 British
Length: 44.43in (1128mm)
Weight: 9lb 1oz (4.10kg)
Barrel: 25.19in (522mm), 5 grooves, lh
Magazine: 10-round box
Muzzle velocity: *ca* 2440 ft/sec (743 m/sec)

Rifle, Number 4, Mark 1 (T)

1942. The Rifle, No 4, Mk 1 fitted with a tangent rear sight and prepared for a telescopic sight; the butt was fitted with a check rest.

Rifle, Number 4, Mark 1*

1941. Similar to the Mark 1 pattern, but a simplified method of removing the bolt. Most of these Mark 1 rifles were made in the USA or Canada and will be marked 'US PROPERTY' or 'LONG BRANCH'.

Rifle, Number 4, Mark 2

1949. Similar to the Mark 1 but with a new design of trigger mechanism in which the trigger was hinged about a pin located in a bracket forged integrally with the body, instead of being hinged to the trigger guard as hitherto.

Rifle, Number 4, Mark 1/2

1949. A Number 4 Mark 1 modified to approximate to Mark 2 by having the trigger rebuilt.

Rifle, Number 4, Mark 1/2 (T)

A Number 4 Mk 1 (T) with the new trigger mechanism.

Rifle, Number 4, Mark 1/3

1949. A Number 4 Mark 1* with trigger modified to approximate to Mark 2.

Rifle, Number 4, T/W3 Mark 2

1956. Specially selected Number 4 Mark 2 rifles fitted with a Number 32 Mark 3 sighting telescope.

Rifle, Number 5, Mark 1
BSA & ROF (F)

1945. The 'Jungle Carbine'. A short rifle using the bolt and magazine of the Number 4 rifle but with a short barrel, short fore-end stock, muzzle flash eliminator and rubber butt pad.

Cartridge: .303 British
Length: 39.5in (1003mm)
Weight: 7lb 2.5oz (3.25kg)
Barrel: 18.75in (475mm), 5 grooves, lh
Magazine: 10-round box
Muzzle velocity: *ca* 2400 ft/sec (731 m/sec)

Rifle, 7.62mm, L39A1
Enfield

A modified Rifle Number 4, fitted with a shortened fore-end, heavy barrel and with the action modified to fire the 7.62mm NATO cartridge. Used as a military competition rifle.

Cartridge: 7.62 × 51mm NATO
Length: 46.50in (1180mm)
Weight: 9lb 11oz (4.42kg)
Barrel: 27.55in (700mm), 4 grooves, rh
Magazine: 10-round box
Muzzle velocity: *ca* 2758 ft/sec (841 m/sec)

Rifle, 7.62mm, L42A1
Enfield

A conversion of the Rifle Number 4 Mark 1 or Mark 1* (T) sniping rifle to fire the 7.62mm NATO cartridge. It has a shortened fore-end and is fitted with the Telescope, Sighting, Straight, L1A1. The same rifle, fitted with a commercial zoom sight, was marketed to police forces as the 'Enfield Enforcer'.

Cartridge: 7.62 × 51mm NATO
Length: 46.49in (1181mm)
Weight: 9lb 11oz (4.42kg)
Barrel: 27.55in (700mm), 4 grooves, rh
Magazine: 10-round box
Muzzle velocity: *ca* 2750 ft/sec (838 m/sec)

Carbine, Magazine, Lee-Enfield, Mark 1

1902. When Carbines, Magazine, Lee-Metford, Mark 1 are fitted with Lee-Enfield barrels and have the wings of the nose caps drawn out to the same height as that on the Lee-Enfield Carbines, they will be described as above. The barrels will be marked by the manufacturer on the Knox-form with the letter 'E'.

Carbine, Magazine, Lee-Enfield, Cavalry, Mark 1

1907. Basically the Lee-Metford Carbine Mark 1 with Enfield rifling, improved sights, the sling fittings omitted, and an attached leather cover for the rear sight. The weight and dimensions remained the same as for the earlier gun.

Cartridge: .303 British
Length: 39.94in (1014mm)
Weight: 7lb 7oz (3.37kg)
Barrel: 20.75in (527mm), 5 grooves, lh
Magazine: 6-round single-column box
Muzzle velocity: *ca* 2000 ft/sec (610 m/sec)

Carbine, Magazine, Lee-Enfield, Cavalry, Mark 1*

1899. Similar to the Mark 1 Cavalry Carbine but without the clearing rod and fittings.

Note that the foresight wings were removed from all carbines in April 1903. All Magazine Lee-Enfield carbines were sentenced 'Drill Purposes Only' in August 1925, rendered incapable of firing ammunition, and issued to Officer Training Corps units.

LEE-METFORD Britain
BSA, Enfield & LSA

The Lee-Metford rifle was introduced into British service in 1888, under the official designation of Rifle, Magazine, Mark 1, This utilised the turnbolt action and magazine of James Lee, together with a rifled barrel designed by William Metford, specifically to combat the fouling inherent in the gunpowder propelling charges of the time.

Rifle, Magazine, Mark 1

A fully-stocked bolt-action rifle with dust-cover, removable box magazine ahead of the trigger and attached by a chain link, and a cleaning rod inserted into the fore-end beneath the muzzle. The foresight was a square block with a vertical slot in it, and the rear sight was a square notch, fixed in its lowest place at 300 yards and graduated to 1900 yards. On the side of the stock were a set of 'Extreme Range Sights' graduated from 1800 yards to 3500 yards. Safety catch on left side of body, magazine cut-off on right side. In August 1891, the designation of this rifle was officially changed to **Rifle, Magazine, Lee-Metford Mark 1**.

Cartridge: .303 British
Length: 49.50in (1257mm)
Weight: 9lb 8oz (4.37kg)
Barrel: 30.2in (769mm), 7 grooves, lh
Magazine: 8-round single-column box
Muzzle velocity: *ca* 2200 ft/sec (670 m/sec)

Rifle, Magazine, Lee-Metford, Mark I*
1892. This was an improved Mark 1, with several modifications found desirable after the rifle had been put into service use. The safety catch was removed, the only safety being a half-cock position. The sights were modified to cater for the ballistics of smokeless propellant (Cordite) and the foresight became a barleycorn (vertically tapered) blade pinned into the original sight block, and the rear sight became a square notch, adjustable to 1800 yards. The Extreme Range sight was graduated from 1600–2900 yards. The magazine spring had four coils instead of three, and the striker spring was 3.25in long instead of 5in. The hole in the butt, which in the Mark 1 held an oil-bottle and jag, was deepened to accept a pull-through. A brass disc was inlet into the side of the butt for the regimental number.

Specifications: as for the Mark 1, except
Muzzle velocity: 2000 ft/sec (610 m/sec)

Rifle, Magazine, Lee-Metford, Mark 2
1892. The principal difference between this and the previous models was that the magazine was changed to a pattern holding ten rounds in two columns, and as a result, the body was somewhat modified in contour. The magazine spring was of C shape instead of a coil, the barrel was lighter, and there were minor variations in the construction of the bolt and magazine cut-off.

Specifications: as for Mark 1, except
Weight: 9lb 4oz (4.25kg)
Magazine: 10-round box

Rifle, Magazine, Lee-Metford, Mark 2*
1895. This differed from the Mark 2 in that the bolt was lengthened by 1.00in (25.4mm) and fitted with two grooves for a safety catch, and the cocking piece was also lengthened and carried the safety catch.

Rifle, Charger-Loading, Magazine, Lee-Metford, Mark 2
1907. This was a conversion from the Mark 2, achieved by fitting a bridge charger guide across the bolt way, and a new magazine; the rifle also had an adjustable blade foresight with a fixed protector, and a new rear sight graduated from 600–1800 yards The butt-plate was of bronze instead of steel.

Cartridge: .303 British
Length: 49.50in (1257mm)
Weight: 9lb 8oz (4.37kg)
Barrel: 30.18in (766mm), 7 grooves, lh
Magazine: 10-round double-column box
Muzzle velocity: ca 2060 ft/sec (628m/sec)

Carbine, Magazine, Lee-Metford, Mark I
1894. This was a short rifle issued only to cavalry; it was based on the Mark 2 rifle but differed in dimensions and magazine capacity, as well as various minor details. The bolt-knob was flattened on top.

Cartridge: .303 British
Length: 39.94in (1014mm)
Weight: 7lb 7oz (3.37kg)
Barrel: 20.75in (527mm), 7 grooves, lh
Magazine: 6-round single-column box
Muzzle velocity: ca 2000 ft/sec (610 m/sec)

Note that the foresight wings were removed from all carbines in April 1903. All Magazine Lee-Metford carbines were sentenced 'Drill Purposes Only' in August 1925, rendered incapable of firing ammunition, and issued to Officer Training Corps units.

LJUNGMANN Sweden
Ag42 Rifle
Husqvarna
1942. Gas-operated semi-automatic locking by tilting the bolt down into a recess in the receiver floor. Bolt carrier driven by direct gas impingement. Full-stocked, exposed muzzle with brake perforations, detachable box magazine.

Cartridge: 6.5 x 55mm Swedish Mauser
Length: 47.9in (1216mm)
Weight: 9lb 11oz (4.40kg)
Barrel: 25.10in (637mm), 6 grooves, rh
Magazine: 10-round box
Muzzle velocity: 2460 ft/sec (750 m/sec)

Ag42B Rifle
Husqvarna
Improved version. Stainless steel gas tube, changes to bolt and firing mechanism, magazine modified.

Cartridge: 6.5 x 55mm Swedish Mauser
Length: 47.8in (1215mm)
Weight: 10lb 6oz (4.74kg)
Barrel: 24.50in (623mm), 6 grooves, rh
Magazine: 10-round box
Muzzle velocity: 2450 ft/sec (745 m/sec)

DENMARK
Madsen-Ljungmann
Madsen
This is effectively the Ag42 built by Madsen under licence to tempt the Danish Army. Dimensionally similar, it differed in having the gas tube wrapped around the barrel. It was not adopted.

EGYPT
Hakim
Maadi
1955. Manufactured in Egypt on machinery purchased from Sweden, this was the Ag42B, but with an adjustable gas port and generally somewhat more substantial in order to take a more powerful cartridge.

Cartridge: 7.92 x 57mm Mauser
Length: 47.60in (1209mm)
Weight: 10lb 10oz (4.82kg)
Barrel: 23.23in (590mm), 4 grooves, rh
Magazine: 10-round box
Muzzle velocity: 2854 ft/sec (870 m/sec)

Rashid
Maadi
1960. A completely Egyptian derivative of the Ljungmann, this used the same gas system but was chambered for the Soviet 7.62 x 39mm cartridge. Half-stocked, with a perforated handguard and folding bayonet hinged below the muzzle. It also added a cocking handle, rather than the Ljungmann system of using the breech cover to cock.

Cartridge: 7.62 × 39mm M1943
Length: 42.40in (1077mm)
Weight: 8lb 6oz (3.80kg)
Barrel: 22.44in (570mm), 4 grooves, rh
Magazine: 10-round box
Muzzle velocity: 2395 ft/sec (730 m/sec)

McMILLAN USA

This company was taken over in 1995 by the Harris Company and the rifles are now known (and listed *above*) by that name.

MADSEN Denmark
Madsen

M62 Light Automatic Rifle LAR

Gas-operated, selective-fire, rotating bolt in carrier. Light alloy receiver with gas tube above free-floating barrel and a support rail beneath the barrel, the two connected by a vertical bar through which the barrel passed. Perforated metal handguard, small wooden fore-end, sliding steel butt, box magazine. Aperture rear sight, hooded foresight. Muzzle brake shaped for grenade launching.

Cartridge: 7.62 × 51mm NATO
Length: 42.30in (1074mm)
Weight: 10lb 9oz (4.79kg)
Barrel: 21.10in (536mm), 4 grooves, rh
Magazine: 20-round box
Muzzle velocity: 2651 ft/sec (808 m/sec)
Cyclic rate: 600 rds/min

MANNLICHER Austria
Steyr

AUSTRIA-HUNGARY
M1885 Rifle

Straight-pull bolt action and wedge-locked. Clip-loaded magazine with clip-ejecting lever on right side. Magazine distinctly separate from trigger-guard. Full-stocked, exposed muzzle, cleaning rod.

Cartridge: 11.15 × 58R Werndl
Length: 52.28in (1328mm)
Weight: 10lb 8oz (4.75kg)
Barrel: 31.81in (808mm), 6 grooves, rh
Magazine: 5-round box
Muzzle velocity: 1444 ft/sec (440 m/sec)

M1886 Rifle

Generally as the M1885, but clip ejecting catch moved to rear of magazine, cleaning rod removed, piling hook beneath muzzle, new sights.

Cartridge: 11.15 × 58R Werndl
Length: 52.20in (1326mm)
Weight: 9lb 15oz (4.52kg)
Barrel: 31.73in (806mm), 6 grooves, rh
Magazine: 5-round box
Muzzle velocity: 1444 ft/sec (440 m/sec)

M1886/90 Rifle

M1886 rifles converted to 8 x 50R Mannlicher. Chambering and sights for semi-smokeless powder loading.

Muzzle velocity: 2035 ft/sec (620 m/sec)

M1888 Rifle

A small-calibre replacement for the M1886, this was simply the M1886 with a new barrel and action and a new sight for the black-powder cartridge. The magazine is the principal visible difference, being smaller.

Cartridge: 8 × 50R Austrian Mannlicher
Length: 50.43in (1281mm)
Weight: 9lb 11oz (4.41kg)
Barrel: 30.12in (765mm), 4 grooves, rh
Magazine: 5-round box
Muzzle velocity: *ca* 1755ft/sec (535m/sec)

M1888/90 Rifle

The Model 1888 re-sighted for the semi-smokeless M88/90 cartridge.

Muzzle velocity: 2028 ft/sec (618 m/sec)

M1890 Cavalry Carbine

Straight-pull bolt locking by cam action on the rotating head. Shorter action, magazine and trigger-guard in one piece. Full-stocked, exposed muzzle, sling swivels on the left side of the stock.

Cartridge: 8 × 50R Austrian Mannlicher
Length: 39.57in (1005mm)
Weight: 7lb 5oz (3.30kg)
Barrel: 19.61in (498mm), 4 grooves, rh
Magazine: 5-round box
Muzzle velocity: 1886 ft/sec (575 m/sec)

M1890 Gendarmerie Carbine

1892. As for the cavalry carbine, but with bayonet fittings and a piling hook.

Specifications: the same

M1895 Rifle
Fegyvergyar & Steyr

Straight-pull bolt locking by cam action. Full-stocked with full-length handguard, sighted for the smokeless M88/93 cartridge.

Cartridge: 8 × 50R Austrian Mannlicher
Length: 50.40in (1280mm)
Weight: 8lb 5oz (3.78kg)
Barrel: 30.19in (765mm), 4 grooves, rh
Magazine: 5-round box
Muzzle velocity: 2030 ft/sec (620 m/sec)

M1895 Short Rifle
Fegyvergyar & Steyr

Straight-pull bolt locking by cam action. Full-stocked with full-length handguard, sighted for the smokeless M88/93 cartridge. Swivels beneath stock, piling hook at side and bayonet fittings.

Cartridge: 8 × 50R Austrian Mannlicher
Length: 39.49in (1003mm)
Weight: 6lb 13oz (3.09kg)
Barrel: 19.68in (500mm), 4 grooves, rh
Magazine: 5-round box
Muzzle velocity: 1902ft/sec (580 m/sec)

M1895 Cavalry Carbine
Fegyvergyar & Steyr
Similar to the short rifle, but swivels on the side of stock, no piling hook, no bayonet fittings.

Specifications: the same

CHINA
M1904 Rifle
Steyr
Turnbolt action, clip-loader. Full-stocked with half-length handguard, bayonet lug on side of nose-cap. Not adopted by Austria, but sold to China.

Cartridge: 7.92 × 57mm Mauser
Length: 48.23in (1225mm)
Weight: 8lb 13oz (4.0kg)
Barrel: 28.54in (725mm), 4 grooves, rh
Magazine: 5-round box
Muzzle velocity: 2247 ft/sec (685 m/sec)

HUNGARY
M1935 Short Rifle
Fegyvergyar
Short rifle based on the Romanian M1893, but using the Hungarian 8 x 56R M31 cartridge. Turnbolt, clip-loaded, two-piece stock bolted to the receiver, full-stocked, full-length handguard, exposed muzzle, box magazine.

Cartridge: 8 × 56R Hungarian Mannlicher
Length: 48.75in (1110mm)
Weight: 8lb 14oz (4.04kg)
Barrel: 23.60in (600mm), 4 grooves, rh
Magazine: 5-round box
Muzzle velocity: 2400 ft/sec (730 m/sec)

M1943 Short Rifle
Fegyvergyar
Fresh design based on the German M98/40 (*see* Mauser) and which therefore used a Mauser-type charger-loading magazine. The bolt was still Mannlicher, but very little else was. The result has a very Mauser look about it except for the split-bridge receiver and bolt.

Cartridge: 8 × 56R Hungarian Mannlicher
Length: 43.00in (1092mm)
Weight: 8lb 10oz (3.92kg)
Barrel: 23.60in (600mm), 4 grooves, rh
Magazine: 5-round integral box
Muzzle velocity: 2400 ft/sec (730 m/sec)

NETHERLANDS
M1895 Infantry Rifle
Hembrug & Steyr
Turning bolt action, clip-loaded magazine, full-stocked with half-length handguard, box magazine, nose cap with bayonet bar.

Cartridge: 6.5 × 54R Dutch Mannlicher
Length: 50.98in (1295mm)
Weight: 9lb 8oz (4.30kg)
Barrel: 31.10in (790mm), 4 grooves, rh
Magazine: 5-round box
Muzzle velocity: 2428 ft/sec (740 m/sec)

M1895 No 1 Cavalry Carbine
Hembrug & Steyr
Action as for the M1895 rifle, half-stocked, no handguard, sling bars on the left side.

Cartridge: 6.5 × 54R Dutch Mannlicher
Length: 37.48in (952mm)
Weight: 6lb 13oz (3.10kg)
Barrel: 17.71in (450mm), 4 grooves, rh
Magazine: 5-round box
Muzzle velocity: 2050 ft/sec (625 m/sec)

M1895 No 2 Gendarmerie Carbine
Hembrug & Steyr
Similar to the cavalry carbine but full-stocked and with bayonet fittings.

Specifications: the same, except
Weight: 7lb 1oz (3.22kg).

M1895 No 3 Engineer and Artillery Carbine
Hembrug & Steyr
Similar to the No 2 Carbine, but with a long handguard which ended just behind the fore-sight.

Specifications: the same, except
Weight: 6lb 15oz (3.14kg)

M1895 No 4 Bicycle Troops' Carbine
Hembrug & Steyr
Similar to the No 3 Carbine, but with the handguard the same length as the stock.

Specifications: the same

M1895A5 Carbine
Hembrug
1930. Issued to the Dutch Air Force, this was a cut-down M1895 rifle.

Cartridge: 6.5 × 54R Dutch Mannlicher
Length: 37.80in (960mm)
Weight: 7lb 13oz (3.56kg)
Barrel: 17.91in (455mm), 4 grooves, rh
Magazine: 5-round box
Muzzle velocity: 2050 ft/sec (625 m/sec)

ROMANIA
M1892 Rifle
Steyr
Turnbolt, clip-loading box magazine, straight butt, full-stocked with half-length handguard, exposed muzzle, cleaning rod, bayonet fittings.

Cartridge: 6.5 × 54R Romanian Mannlicher
Length: 48.31in (1227mm)
Weight: 8lb 15oz (4.05kg)
Barrel: 28.54in (725mm), 4 grooves, rh
Magazine: 5-round box
Muzzle velocity: 2395 ft/sec (730 m/sec)

M1893 Rifle
Steyr
Improved M1892; piling hook added, reinforcing rib added to the magazine sides, and changes to the bolt to prevent it being used if wrongly assembled.

Specifications: as for M1892

M1893-03 Carbine
Steyr
Short version of the rifle, with a turned-down bolt handle, no handguard, short exposed muzzle, no bayonet fittings.

Cartridge: 6.5 × 54R Romanian Mannlicher
Length: 37.50in (952mm)
Weight: 7lb 4oz (3.29kg)
Barrel: 17.71in (450mm), 4 grooves, rh
Magazine: 5-round box
Muzzle velocity: 2312 ft/sec (705 m/sec)

SWITZERLAND

M1893 Cavalry Carbine
SIG & W+F Bern
Straight pull bolt action, locking by cam action on the rotating head. Full-stocked with full-length handguard. Clip-loaded box magazine.

Cartridge: 7.5 × 53mm M1890 Schmidt-Rubin
Length: 40.0in (1016mm)
Weight: 6lb 13oz (3.08kg)
Barrel: 21.65in (550mm), 4 grooves, rh
Magazine: 6-round box
Muzzle velocity: 1837 ft/sec (560 m/sec)

MANNLICHER-CARCANO Italy
A combination of the Mannlicher clip-loading magazine and a simplified one-piece bolt developed by Sr. Carcano of the Turin arsenal. Adopted only by Italy.

M1891 Rifle
Brescia & Terni
Turnbolt, clip-loading, full-stocked with half-length handguard, exposed muzzle, piling hook on right side of nose-cap.

Cartridge: 6.5 × 52mm Mannlicher-Carcano
Length: 50.80in (1290mm)
Weight: 8lb 6oz (3.80kg)
Barrel: 30.71in (780mm), 4 grooves, rh
Magazine: 6-round box
Muzzle velocity: 2400 ft/sec (730 m/sec)

M1891 Cavalry Carbine
Brescia & Terni
Short version of the rifle; half-stocked, with a folding bayonet attached under the muzzle.

Cartridge: 6.5 × 52mm Mannlicher-Carcano
Length: 37.52in (953mm)
Weight: 6lb 15oz (3.16kg)
Barrel: 17.75in (451mm), 4 grooves, rh
Magazine: 6-round box
Muzzle velocity: 2083 ft/sec (635 m/sec)

M1891TS Special Troops' Carbine
Brescia & Terni
Short version of the rifle, full-stocked with nose-cap and exposed muzzle. Bayonet fittings on nosecap.

Cartridge: 6.5 × 52mm Mannlicher-Carcano
Length: 37.52in (953mm)
Weight: 7lb 2oz (3.22kg)

Barrel: 17.75in (451mm), 4 grooves, rh
Magazine: 6-round box
Muzzle velocity: 2083 ft/sec (635 m/sec)

M1891/24 Carbine
Terni
As for the M1891 special carbine but with the rifle sight and different bayonet fittings.

Specifications: as for the 1891 Cavalry Carbine

M1891/38 Short Rifle
Terni
An M1891 Rifle cut down and re-modelled to correspond to the 7.35mm M1938 rifle in appearance but retaining the 6.5mm cartridge.

M1938 Short Rifle
Terni
A redesign of the 1891 rifle to adapt it to a new 7.35mm cartridge. Full-stocked, exposed barrel, bayonet lug, Mannlicher magazine, simplified rear sight.

Cartridge: 7.35 × 51mm Carcano
Length: 40.16in (1020mm)
Weight: 8lb 2oz (3.68kg)
Barrel: 22.13in (562mm), 4 grooves, rh
Magazine: 6-round box
Muzzle velocity: 2477ft/sec (755 m/sec)

M1938 Carbine
Terni
A re-barrelled M1891 Cavalry or TS Carbine for use with 7.35mm ammunition.

Specifications: as for the original weapon, except
Muzzle velocity: 2378 ft/sec (725 m/sec)

MANNLICHER-SCHOENAUER Austria
A combination of Mannlicher's turnbolt action and a rotary magazine developed by Otto Schoenauer. The design saw most application in the sporting and commercial field, but the Greeks adopted it as a military weapon. For the modern application, *see* Steyr-Mannlicher.

GREECE
M1903 Rifle
Steyr
Turnbolt, rotary magazine, full-stocked, half-length handguard, exposed muzzle, cleaning rod. The principal visual difference between this and any other Mannlicher is the absence of an external magazine, the rotary being completely concealed within the stock, though there was access to it through a floor plate.

Cartridge: 6.5 × 54mm Mannlicher-Schoenauer
Length: 48.23in (1225mm)
Weight: 8lb 5oz (3.77kg)
Barrel: 28.54in (725mm), 4 grooves, rh
Magazine: 5-round charger-loaded spool
Muzzle velocity: 2231ft/sec (680 m/sec)

M1905 Cavalry Carbine
Steyr
A shortened version of the M1903 rifle.

Cartridge: 6.5 × 54mm Mannlicher-Schoenauer
Length: 40.35in (1025mm)
Weight: 7lb 12oz (3.53kg)
Barrel: 20.67in (525mm), 4 grooves, rh
Magazine: 5-round charger-loaded spool
Muzzle velocity: 2057 ft/sec (627 m/sec)

M1903/14 Rifle
Breda & Steyr
Minor improvement to the M1903; full-length handguard, piling hook added, and may be found with either straight or turned-down bolt handles.

Specifications: the same, except
Weight: 8lb 7oz (3.83kg)

M1905/14 Cavalry Carbine
Breda & Steyr
Similar modifications as the rifle.

Weight: 7lb 14oz (3.58kg)

MAROSCZEK Poland

wz/35 Anti-tank Rifle
Radom
Bolt-action repeating rifle of conventional half-stocked form, abnormally-long unsupported barrel, muzzle brake.

Cartridge: 7.92 × 107mm Marosczek
Length: 70.0in (1780mm)
Weight: 19lb 8oz (8.85kg)
Barrel: 47.25in (1200mm), 4 grooves, rh
Magazine: 10-round box
Muzzle velocity: 4198 ft/sec (1280 m/sec)
Armour penetration: 20/300/0

MARTINI Switzerland
A modification of the American Peabody dropping block system by Martini of Switzerland, in which the Peabody hammer was replaced by a firing pin, spring and cocking mechanism contained inside the breech block. The Martini was never used by Switzerland; its principal military application was by the British in the Martini-Henry and derivatives, listed below, but three independent military patterns existed. It was, of course, also widely used commercially.

ROMANIA

M1879 Peabody-Martini Rifle
Witten
Lever-action dropping block, single shot rifle, based upon the Turkish M1874 which itself was virtually the same as the British Martini-Henry. Full-stocked, two barrel bands.

Cartridge: 11.43 × 60R Peabody-Martini
Length: 49.0in (1245mm)
Weight: 9lb 10oz (4.36kg)
Barrel: 33.26in (845mm), 5 grooves, rh
Muzzle velocity: ca 1492ft/sec (450 m/sec)

SOUTH AFRICAN REPUBLIC

Martini-Richards Rifle
Westley Richards
1895. Made by Westley Richards using British Martini-Henry Mark 4 rifle actions slightly modified by his own views on a cocking indicator and a dismantling screw.

Cartridge: .577/450 Martini-Henry
Length: 49.53in (1260mm)
Weight: 9lb 0oz (4.08kg)
Barrel: 33.25in (843mm), 7 grooves, rh
Muzzle velocity: ca 1350ft/sec (411 m/sec)

TURKEY

M1874 Peabody Martini Rifle
Providence
Made by the Providence Tool Co in the USA, these were almost identical with the British Martini-Henry Mark 1 rifle.

Cartridge: .450 Turkish Martini
Length: 49.0in (1245mm)
Weight: 8lb 12oz (4.33kg)
Barrel: 33.22in (843mm), 5 grooves, rh
Muzzle velocity: ca 1263ft/sec (385 m/sec)

MARTINI-ENFIELD Britain
Beardmore or Enfield, unless noted otherwise
Rifle, Martini-Enfield, Mark 1
1895. Conversion of Martini-Henry Mark 3 rifles by fitting them with a new, shorter, barrel rifled to the Enfield system. Fitted to accept the converted triangular Martini-Enfield bayonet, About 200 were made fitted for sword bayonets and sighted for use with black powder cartridges, for use in Western Australia.

Cartridge: .303 British
Length: 46.5in (1181mm)
Weight: 8lb 5oz (3.77kg)
Barrel: 30.187in (767mm), 5 grooves, lh
Muzzle velocity: ca 2000 ft/sec (610 m/sec)

Rifle, Martini-Enfield, Mark 1*
The Mark 1 but fitted with an adjustable barleycorn foresight in three sizes, differing by 0.015in. Doubtful if many were made.

Specifications: as for Mark 1

Rifle, Martini-Enfield, Mark 2
1896. Conversion of the Martini-Henry Rifle Mark 2 in a similar manner to the Mark 1.

Specifications: as for Mark 1

Rifle, Martini-Enfield, Mark 2*
1903. The Mark 2 fitted with the adjustable foresight as for the Mark 1*.

Carbine, Martini-Enfield, Mark 1
General title covering any Martini-Metford Carbine which was re-barrelled to Enfield standard in 1903.

Carbine, Martini-Enfield, Artillery, Mark 1
Beardmore, Enfield & Henry
1895. A conversion of the Martini-Henry Rifle Mark 3 by fitting a shorter barrel rifled on the Enfield system. With fittings for the Sword Bayonet Pattern 1888 Mark 1. Sights: fore barleycorn with protecting wings; rear V-notch.

Cartridge: .303 British
Length: 37.31in (948mm)
Weight: 7lb 4.5oz (3.30kg)
Barrel: 21.0in (533mm), 5 grooves, lh
Muzzle velocity: *ca* 1800 ft/sec (610 m/sec)

Carbine, Martini-Enfield, Artillery, Mark 1*
Beardmore, Enfield & Henry
1899. Differs from Artillery Mark 1 by the omission of clearing rod and fittings.

Carbine, Martini-Enfield, Artillery, Mark 2
Beardmore, Enfield & Henry
1897. Conversion from the Martini-Henry Carbine Marks 1 and 3 by fitting new barrels.

Carbine, Martini-Enfield, Artillery, Mark 2*
Enfield
1899. Differs from Artillery Mark 2 by the omission of clearing rod and fittings.

Carbine, Martini-Enfield, Artillery, Mark 3.
Beardmore, Enfield & Henry
1899. Conversion from the Martini-Henry Rifle Mark 2 by fitting a new .303in barrel.

Specifications: as for Mark 1

Carbine, Martini-Enfield, Cavalry, Mark 1
Enfield
1896. Conversion from Martini-Henry Rifle Mark 2 by fitting .303 inch barrel etc., but differing from the Artillery models by the absence of bayonet fittings.

Specifications: as for Artillery Mark 1, except
Weight: 7lb 3oz (3.26kg)

Carbine, Martini-Enfield, Cavalry, Mark 1*
Enfield
1899. Differs from Cavalry Mark 1 by the omission of clearing rod and fittings.

Note that the foresight wings were removed from all carbines in April 1903. All Martini-Enfield rifles and carbines were sentenced 'Drill Purposes Only' in August 1925, rendered incapable of firing ammunition, and issued to Officer Training Corps units.

MARTINI-HENRY Britain
A combination of the Martini block action and a barrel rifled on the system of Alexander Henry, which involved the gradual deepening of the rifling grooves for about 11 inches from the breech face before they attained full depth.

The cartridge tables list four varieties of Martini-Henry ammunition, two for rifles and two for carbines, which were less powerful and had a lighter bullet. The earlier Rolled Case varieties were fragile and prone to jamming in dusty or sandy conditions and from 1885 they were replaced by the improved Solid Case versions, though the stocks of Rolled Case ammunition continued to be used for training for some time.

So that soldiers should have rifles and carbines suited to their stature, from the time of the Martini-Henry until the last days of the Lee-Enfield, a proportion of British Army rifles was made with butts half an inch (13mm) longer or half an inch shorter than standard. These were stamped 'L' or 'S' and known as Long Butt or Short Butt models. They are not shown separately here, since they differ only in overall length, but their existence should be borne in mind.

Rifle, Martini-Henry, Mark 1
Enfield
1874. Lever-operated dropping block, steel barrel, full-stocked, no handguard, muzzle fitted for bayonet.

Cartridge: .577/450 Martini-Henry
Length: 49.0in (1245mm)
Weight: 8lb 12oz (3.97kg)
Barrel: 33.22in (843mm), 7 grooves, lh
Muzzle velocity: *ca* 1315ft/sec (400 m/sec)

Rifle, Martini-Henry, Mark 2
BSA, Enfield & LSA
1877. Similar to Mark 1 but the action modified to obtain a better trigger pull.

Specifications: as for Mark 1

Rifle, Martini-Henry, Mark 3
Enfield
1879. Improved Mark 2; backsight set 'so that when the sight is raised it is inclined 1° 6' to the left' to compensate for bullet drift; barrel has a double lump at the breech end; breech-block wider at the front; and other small details. Also note that 'the average weight is about 9lb depending upon the quality of wood in the stock.'

Specifications: as for Mark 1, except as described above

Rifle, Martini-Henry, Mark 4
Enfield
1887. Constructed from components made for a .402 calibre rifle which had been cancelled due to the impending approval of the .303 calibre. There were three patterns differing slightly according to how much modification had to be done to the components. All patterns had similar features differing from the Mark 3 rifle: a longer lever to give more powerful extraction; the breech-block reduced in thickness and fitted with modified extractor; the body reduced so as to give a better grip; and the buttstock narrowed and cut so that the butt plate was at a more comfortable angle. All were fitted to take the P1887 sword bayonet.

Cartridge: .577/450 Martini-Henry
Length: 49.38in (1254mm)
Weight: 9lb 2oz (4.14kg)
Barrel: 33.06in (840mm), 7 grooves, lh
Muzzle velocity: *ca* 1350ft/sec (411 m/sec)

Carbine, Martini-Henry, Cavalry, Mark 1
Enfield
1877. A short version of the rifle; full-stocked, no handguard, foresight with protecting wings. Although a

reduced-charge carbine cartridge was provided, the rifle cartridge could be fired.

Cartridge: .577/450 Martini-Henry Carbine
Length: 37.68in (957mm)
Weight: 7lb 8oz (3.40kg)
Barrel: 21.38in (543mm), 7 grooves, lh
Muzzle velocity: *ca* 1100 ft/sec (335 m/sec)

Carbine, Martini-Henry, Artillery, Mark 1
Enfield

1879. Generally similar to the cavalry carbine but fitted for a bayonet.

Specifications: the same, except
Weight: 7lb 10oz (3.46kg)

MARTINI-METFORD Britain

Rifle, Martini-Metford, Mark 1
Enfield

1889. Originally sealed as the Rifle, Martini-Henry, Mark 5 this was the normal lever-action M-H design but with a .303in Metford-rifled barrel. The name was changed to Martini-Metford to avoid confusion. The Sealed Pattern weapon was made, but the design was never produced in quantity or issued for service.

Cartridge: .303 British
Length: 49.69in (1262mm)
Weight: 9lb 6.5oz (4.27kg)
Barrel: 33.19in (843mm), 7 grooves, lh
Muzzle velocity: *ca* 2200 ft/sec (670 m/sec)

Rifle, Martini-Metford, Mark 2
BSA

1900. Generally similar to the Mark 1. About 10,000 made but distributed only to British colonial forces.

Cartridge: .303 British
Length: 49.5in (1257mm)
Weight: 9lb 14oz (4.48kg)
Barrel: 33.19in (843mm), 7 grooves, lh
Muzzle velocity: *ca* 2200 ft/sec (670 m/sec)

Carbine, Martini-Metford, Artillery, Mark 1
BSA, Enfield & LSA

1892. Conversion of the Martini-Henry Artillery Carbine Mark 1 by fitting a new .303in barrel, chambered and rifled as for the Lee-Metford rifle. Sights: fore barleycorn, rear V-notch graduated 200–1400 yards.

Cartridge: .303 British
Length: 37.625in (956mm)
Weight: 7lb 12.25oz (3.15kg)
Barrel: 20.56in (522mm), 7 grooves, lh
Muzzle velocity: *ca* 2000 ft/sec (610 m/sec)

Carbine, Martini-Metford, Artillery, Mark 2
BSA, Enfield & LSA

1893. Conversions from Martini-Henry Rifle Mark 2 Long Butt, fitted with .303in barrel.

Specifications: as for Mark 1, except
Weight: 7lb 1oz (3.20kg)

A small number were converted from Short Butt rifles, and thus differed in specification.

Length: 36.84in (936mm)
Weight: 6lb 15oz (3.146kg)

Carbine, Martini-Metford, Artillery, Mark 3
BSA, Enfield & LSA

1894. Conversions from Martini-Henry Rifle Mark 3, Long Butt, fitted with .303in barrel. Some of these weapons were re-barrelled with Enfield-rifled barrels in 1903, becoming **Carbines, Martini-Enfield, Mark 1**.

Cartridge: .303 British
Length: 37.625in (956mm)
Weight: 7lb 3oz (3.26kg)
Barrel: 21.0in (533mm), 7 grooves, lh
Muzzle velocity: *ca* 2000 ft/sec (610 m/sec)

Carbine, Martini-Metford, Cavalry, Mark 1
Enfield & Henry

1892. Conversion of the Martini-Henry Mark 1 Cavalry Carbine by fitting it with a .303in barrel, chambered and rifled on the Lee-Metford system. Sights: fore barleycorn, rear V-notch graduated 200–1400 yards. No foresight protecting wings.

Cartridge: .303 British
Length: 37.625in (956mm)
Weight: 8lb 1.5oz (3.67kg)
Barrel: 20.56in (527mm), 7 grooves, lh
Muzzle velocity: *ca* 2000 ft/sec (610 m/sec)

Carbine, Martini-Metford, Cavalry, Mark 1*
Enfield

1893. Differs from Mark 1 in being fitted with foresight protecting wings.

Carbine, Martini-Metford, Cavalry, Mark 2
Enfield & Henry

1892. As for Mark 1, but converted from the Martini-Henry Artillery Carbine and thus differed in the fore-end, nose cap and upper barrel, being fitted for the sword bayonet.

Specifications: as for Mark 1, except
Weight: 8 lb 4oz (3.74kg)

Carbine, Martini-Metford, Cavalry, Mark 2*
Enfield

1893. Differs from Mark 2 in having foresight protecting wings.

Carbine, Martini-Metford, Cavalry, Mark 3
Enfield & Henry

1893. Conversion from Martini-Henry Rifle Mark 2, being fitted with short .303in barrel and with foresight protecting wings.

Cartridge: .303 British
Length: 37.625in (956mm)
Weight: 6lb 12oz (3.06kg)
Barrel: 21.0in (533mm), 7 grooves, lh
Muzzle velocity: *ca* 2000 ft/sec (610 m/sec)

Note that the foresight wings were removed from all carbines in April 1903. All Martini-Metford rifles and carbines were sentenced 'Drill Purposes Only' in August 1925, rendered incapable of firing ammunition, and issued to Officer Training Corps units.

MAS France
MAS

Mle 1917

Gas-operated semi-automatic, using a piston to rotate an interrupted-thread bolt. Full-stocked, exposed barrel, cleaning rod, unique half-oval charger-loaded box magazine. Cylindrical receiver with large cocking handle on right.

Cartridge: 8 × 50R Lebel
Length: 52.40in (1331mm)
Weight: 11lb 9oz (5.25kg)
Barrel: 31.40in (798mm), 4 grooves, rh
Magazine: 5-round box
Muzzle velocity: 2350 ft/sec (716 m/sec)

Mle 1918

Improved Mle 1917; shorter, lighter, used the standard-issue cartridge charger rather than a special one, added a hold-open device and other small improvements.

Cartridge: 8 × 50R Lebel
Length: 43.10in (1095mm)
Weight: 10lb 8oz (4.79kg)
Barrel: 23.10in (586mm), 4 grooves, rh
Magazine: 5-round box
Muzzle velocity: 2200 ft/sec (670 m/sec)

Mle 1936 Infantry Rifle

Bolt action repeater, bolt locking into the receiver behind the magazine. Bolt handle slopes forward. Slab-sided receiver, two-piece stock, sling ring, foresight on nose-cap.

Cartridge: 7.5 × 54mm French M1929
Length: 40.15in (1020mm)
Weight: 8lb 5oz (3.78kg)
Barrel: 22.60in (573mm), 4 grooves, lh
Magazine: 5-round box
Muzzle velocity: 2700 ft/sec (823 m/sec)

Mle 1936/CR39 Short Rifle

1939. A short-barrelled version of the Mle 1936 with a hinged aluminium butt which folded down and forward. For parachute and mountain troops.

Cartridge: 7.5 × 54mm French M1929
Length, butt extended: 34.90in (886mm)
Length, butt folded: 34.30in (617mm)
Weight: 8lb 8oz (3.85kg)
Barrel: 17.71in (450mm), 4 grooves, lh
Magazine: 5-round box
Muzzle velocity: 2560 ft/sec (780 m/sec)

Mle 1949

1950. Work on an automatic rifle began in 1924 and was close to completion when war interrupted. It was resumed in 1944 and the resultant weapon was issued to troops in 1949. Two-piece stock similar to the MAS 1936 rifle, slab-sided receiver, exposed muzzle with foresight on the nose cap, box magazine beneath action. Gas operated, semi-automatic fire only, breech locked by tilting the bolt into a recess in the receiver.

Cartridge: 7.5 × 54mm French M1929
Length: 42.36in (1076mm)
Weight: 9lb 0oz (4.07kg)

Barrel: 22.83in (580mm), 4 grooves, lh
Magazine: 10-round box
Muzzle velocity: 2788 ft/sec (850m/sec)

Mle 1949/56

1956. A slightly improved and modified version of the Mle 1949, the principal change being the forming of the muzzle into a NATO-standard grenade-launching configuration, with 22mm diameter gas sealing rings. The fore end was shortened to permit the grenade tail to fit fully over the muzzle of the rifle and the foresight was mounted on a ramp, just behind the grenade stop ring. A special grenade sight was also fitted.

Cartridge: 7.5 × 54mm French M1929
Length: 40.24in (1022mm)
Weight: 8lb 6oz (3.88kg)
Barrel: 22.83in (580mm), 4 grooves, lh
Magazine: 10-round box
Muzzle velocity: 2750 ft/sec (838m/sec)

Mle 1962

This was intended to replace the Mle 1949 and 49/56 and chamber the 7.62 × 51mm NATO cartridge. It was more or less an improved Mle 49/56 with plastic furniture and a pistol grip, new sights and sundry other detail refinements. It was approved for service as the Mle 1962, but on second thoughts the French decided to look more closely at smaller calibres. The Mle 62 went into suspended animation and was eventually replaced by the FAMAS 5.56mm weapon (*see below*).

Cartridge: 7.62 × 51mm NATO
Length: 40.75in (1035mm)
Weight: 9lb 5oz (4.22kg)
Barrel: 22.83in (580mm), 4 grooves, lh
Magazine: 20-round box
Muzzle velocity: 2758 ft/sec (840m/sec)

Mle FR-F1 Sniping Rifle

1964. Bolt action sniping rifle based upon the action of the Mle 1936 and retaining the two-piece stock layout. Pistol grip, box magazine. Bipod legs attach to the sides of the fore-end and fold forward but are adjustable for length and height. Iron sights fitted but normally used with telescope. Originally in 7.5mm calibre, numbers were later made in 7.62mm chambering.

Cartridge: 7.5 × 54mm French M1929
Length: 44.80in (1138mm)
Weight: 11lb 7oz (5.20kg)
Barrel: 21.73in (552mm), 4 grooves, rh
Magazine: 10-round box
Muzzle velocity: 2795 ft/sec (852m/sec)

Mle FR-F2 Sniping Rifle

1984. Improved version of the FR-F1. Similar general layout but fore-end now of plastic-covered metal, bipod attached to a yoke around the barrel, barrel covered with thermal sleeve to reduce heat haze in sight line.

Specifications: the same as the FR-F1

Mle FR-G1, FR-G2

1995. Variant models of the FR-F2. The **FR-G1** has no thermal sleeve, a wooden fore-end and a fixed-angle bipod. The **FR-G2** is the G1 with an articulated bipod.

Specifications: the same

FAMAS F-1 Assault Rifle

1980. Unmistakable bullpup design. Selective fire, delayed blowback, large carrying handle with cocking handle beneath, pistol grip, magazine under the butt, muzzle shaped for grenade launching and with flash hider.

Cartridge: 5.56 × 45mm French
Length: 29.80in (757mm)
Weight: 8lb 3oz (3.70kg)
Barrel: 19.20in (488mm), 4 grooves, rh
Magazine: 25-round box
Muzzle velocity: 3150 ft/sec (960 m/sec)
Cyclic rate: 950 rds/min

FAMAS G-2 Assault Rifle

1994. Updated version of the F-1 for export. Trigger guard for fully gloved hand, breech-block buffer stronger, magazine housing to NATO STANAG 4179 to accept any M16 type. Selector/safety now inside trigger guard.

Cartridge: 5.56 × 45mm M193 or NATO
Length: 29.92in (760mm)
Weight: 8lb 6oz (3.80kg)
Barrel: 19.20in (488mm), 3 grooves, rh
Magazine: 20- or 30-round box
Muzzle velocity: 3035 ft/sec (925 m/sec)
Cyclic rate: 1100 rds/min

MAUSER Germany
Mauser, unless noted otherwise

In pre-Kalashnikov days, probably the most widely-distributed rifle of all. There was a relatively small number of basic types, but each had minor variations to suit the wants of specific customers. Rather than attempt a chronological listing, which would be confusing, the models are listed by user countries and include Mauser rifles made under licence or by other countries after the expiry of Mauser's patents. It does not include Mauser derivatives such as the Arisaka, Springfield or Enfield (which have their own entries). Unless otherwise noted, manufacture was by Mauser.

GERMANY

M1871 Infantry Rifle
Mauser, NA&ACo, Spandau, Steyr & Suhl

Bolt action, single shot, full-stocked, no handguard, exposed muzzle with bayonet fittings, cleaning rod. Bolt handle straight, and the bolt has a prominent slotted screw holding the guide block. Flag-type safety catch on rear of bolt. Locking by a rear lug turned down in front of the split receiver bridge. Leaf sight, to 1600m.

Cartridge: 11.15 × 60R Mauser
Length: 52.95in (1345mm)
Weight: 10lb 1oz (4.58kg)
Barrel: 33.66in (855mm), 4 grooves, rh
Muzzle velocity: 1411 ft/sec (430 m/sec)

M1871 Light Infantry Rifle
Danzig, Mauser & Steyr

1876. Action as for the M1871 rifle, but with a shorter barrel. Full-stocked, no handguard, spur on trigger-guard, leaf sight to 1600m.

Cartridge: 11.15 × 60R Mauser
Length: 48.82in (1240mm)
Weight: 9lb 14oz (4.48kg)
Barrel: 29.53in (750mm), 4 grooves, rh
Muzzle velocity: (418 m/sec)

M1871 Carbine
Haenel, Mauser, Schilling & Steyr

1876. Action as for M1871 rifle, stocked to the muzzle, nose-cap with foresight, no handguard. Bolt handle turned down, leaf sight to 1200m

Cartridge: 11.15 × 60R Mauser
Length: 39.17in (995mm)
Weight: 7lb 9oz (3.42kg)
Barrel: 19.88in (505mm), 4 grooves, rh
Muzzle velocity: 1280 ft/sec (390 m/sec)

M1879 Border Guards' Rifle
Haenel, Mauser, Schilling & Steyr

This was the same weapon as the M1871 Carbine, differing in having a two-position flip rear sight and in being fitted for a bayonet.

Specifications: the same

M1871/84 Infantry Rifle
Amberg, Danzig, Erfurt, Mauser & Spandau

1885. A modification of the 1871 rifle to turn it into a repeater; addition of a tube magazine under the barrel and a lifting mechanism below the bolt. The only readily visible difference lies in the shorter barrel and a subtle change in the shape of the trigger guard.

Cartridge: 11.15 × 60R Mauser
Length: 51.06in (1297mm)
Weight: 10lb 3oz (4.61kg)
Barrel: 31.50in (800mm), 4 grooves, rh
Magazine: 8-round tube
Muzzle velocity: 1411 ft/sec (430 m/sec)

M1888/97 Infantry Rifle

1895. Trials rifle, based on the Commission Rifle M1888, but with various Mauser ideas incorporated, among them the three-lug bolt and charger-loading. The army would have adopted it, but Mauser then came up with the Gewehr 98, which was a far better design.

Cartridge: 7.92 × 57mm Mauser
Length: 48.82in (1240mm)
Weight: 8lb 11oz (3.98kg)
Barrel: 29.13in (740mm), 4 grooves, rh
Magazine: 5-round box
Muzzle velocity: 2067 ft/sec (630 m/sec)

M1898 Infantry Rifle (Gewehr 98)
Amberg, Danzig, DWM, Erfurt, Haenel, Mauser, Oberspree, Schilling & Spandau

The perfected Mauser military design; three-lug bolt, charger-loaded integral box magazine, large receiver ring, recessed bolt face, and a short-travel firing pin to give fast lock time. Full-stocked, exposed muzzle, half-length handguard. Prominent curved-ramp tangent sight to 2000m.

Cartridge: 7.92 × 57mm Mauser
Length: 49.21in (1250mm)
Weight: 9lb 0oz (4.09kg)
Barrel: 33.66in (740mm), 4 grooves, rh
Magazine: 5-round integral box
Muzzle velocity: 2854 ft/sec (870 m/sec)

M1898 Carbine (Karabiner 98)
Erfurt

1899 Pattern, adopted 1900. Gew. 98 action, stocked to the muzzle, no handguard, nosecap, no bayonet fittings. Withdrawn from service 1902.

Cartridge: 7.92 × 57mm Mauser
Length: 37.20in (945mm)
Weight: 7lb 5oz (3.33kg)
Barrel: 17.13in (435mm), 4 grooves, rh
Magazine: 5-round integral box
Muzzle velocity: 1854 ft/sec (565 m/sec)

M1898 Carbine (Kar. 98A)
Erfurt

1902 Pattern. Gew. 98 action, short barrel stocked to a nosecap and leaving an exposed muzzle with a short wooden stock piece beneath. Bayonet bar, cleaning rod. Withdrawn 1905.

Cartridge: 7.92 × 57mm Mauser
Length: 37.20in (945mm)
Weight: 7lb 9oz (3.42kg)
Barrel: 17.12in (435mm), 4 grooves, rh
Magazine: 5-round integral box
Muzzle velocity: 2608 ft/sec (795 m/sec)

M1898AZ Carbine (Kar. 98AZ or Kar. 98a)
Amberg, Danzig & Erfurt

1908. Final attempt to provide an all-arms carbine without excessive muzzle blast. Full-stocked, full-length handguard, short exposed muzzle, piling hook, Rear sight simplified, front sight has wing protectors. Flattened bolt handle, turned down.

Cartridge: 7.92 × 57mm Mauser
Length: 42.91in (1090mm)
Weight: 8lb 3oz (3.71kg)
Barrel: 23.23in (590mm), 4 grooves, rh
Magazine: 5-round integral box
Muzzle velocity: 2756 ft/sec (840 m/sec)

M1898b Short Rifle (Kar. 98b)

1920. Refurbished Gew. 98 rifles issued to the Reichswehr in 1920–21. Simplified leaf backsight, turned-down bolt handle.

Specifications: as for Gew. 98

M1898k Short Rifle (Kar. 98k)
Brünn, FN, Feinmechanik, Gustloff, Lübeck, Mauser, Sauer & Sohn & Steyr

1935. Standard issue to the Wehrmacht, some 11 million being made. Generally as for the Kar. 98b but shorter. Gew. 98 action, tangent leaf sight to 2000m, full-stocked, handguard to the barrel band, bayonet bar, exposed muzzle, turned down bolt.

Cartridge: 7.92 × 57mm Mauser
Length: 43.70in (1110mm)
Weight: 8lb 10oz (3.92kg)
Barrel: 23.62in (600mm), 4 grooves, rh
Magazine: 5-round integral box
Muzzle velocity: 2477 ft/sec (755 m/sec)

Gewehr 98/40
Fegyvergyar

Listed here because of its nomenclature, this rifle has as much Mannlicher in its design as Mauser. It was based upon the Hungarian M1935 short rifle (*see* Mannlicher, Hungary) and was selected by the German Army simply because they needed rifles and the Budapest factory had nothing much to do at the time. The rifle was converted to 7.92 × 57mm calibre, and to the Mauser charger-loaded magazine system, but the bolt and the rest of the rifle retained their Mannlicher parentage. Recognisable by the two-piece stock, the bolt hand turning down in front of a split bridge, and the hook-like cocking piece on the bolt.

Cartridge: 7.92 × 57mm
Length: 43.11in (1095mm)
Weight: 9lb 0oz (4.08kg)
Barrel: 23.62in (600mm), 4 grooves, rh
Magazine: 5-round integral box
Muzzle velocity: 2477 ft/sec (755 m/sec)

M1915 Aviator's Rifle

1915. Recoil-operated semi-automatic using flaps to lock the bolt. Final one of a series of development models worked on since 1908. Adopted in small numbers to arm early aircraft observers.

Cartridge: 7.92 × 57mm Mauser
Length: 49.13in (1248mm)
Weight: 10lb 8oz (4.74kg)
Barrel: 26.57in (675mm), 4 grooves, rh
Magazine: 10- or 20-round curved box
Muzzle velocity: 2510 ft/sec (765m/sec)

M1918 Tank-Gewehr

First anti-tank rifle; a large but otherwise conventional Mauser bolt action in a half-stocked heavy single-shot rifle with bipod attached to the fore-end. Pistol grip, iron sights.

Cartridge: 13 × 92SR T-Patrone
Length: 61.81in (1680mm)
Weight: 39lb 0oz (17.6kg)
Barrel: 38.69in (983mm), 4 grooves, rh
Muzzle velocity: 3000 ft/sec (913 m/sec)
Armour penetration: 25/200/0

M29/40 Short Rifle
Steyr

1940. A version of the Kar. 98k made by Steyr-Daimler-Puch from parts held for manufacture of Mauser rifles under licence for export. Broadly based on the Polish Model 1929, the result was identical to the Kar. 98k except for a different muzzle cap and slight differences in stock contour.

M33/40
Brünn
1940. Made by the Czech factory in Brno, under German management during WWII, this was the Czech M1933 gendarmerie carbine with slight variations to suit German mountain troops. The rifle generally resembled the Kar. 98k but was full-stocked and with a full-length handguard.

Cartridge: 7.92 × 57mm Mauser
Length: 38.98in (990mm)
Weight: 8lb 6oz (3.78kg)
Barrel: 19.29in (490mm), 4 grooves, rh
Magazine: 5-round integral box
Muzzle velocity: 2247 ft/sec (685 m/sec)

Gew 41 (M) Infantry Rifle
1941. Gas-operated, rotating bolt. Gas was trapped at the muzzle, and therefore the rifle has a conspicuously bulky and sharply tapered muzzle. Full-stocked, with a rectangular box magazine well in front of the trigger. Bolt-handled cocking handle at the rear of the receiver. Tested, but turned down due to excessive fouling and weight.

Cartridge: 7.92 × 57mm Mauser
Length: 46.14in (1172mm)
Weight: 11lb 1oz (5.02kg)
Barrel: 21.65in (550mm), 4 grooves, rh
Magazine: 10-round box
Muzzle velocity: 2428 ft/sec (740 m/sec)

StG 45 Assault Rifle
1945. Design produced in prototypes only, to satisfy a demand for a lighter assault rifle than the StG 44. Cylindrical receiver, continued into a cylindrical fluted fore-end/handguard, with a long exposed muzzle with high-set hooded sight. Slight bend in stock, pistol grip, box magazine ahead of trigger guard. Introduced the original roller-locked delayed blowback mechanism which was later perfected and is currently used on almost all CETME and Heckler & Koch rifles.

Cartridge: 7.92 × 33mm Kurz
Length: 35.15in (893mm)
Weight: 8lb 3oz (3.71kg)
Barrel: 15.75in (400mm), 4 grooves, rh
Magazine: 30-round box
Muzzle velocity: 2100 ft/sec (640 m/sec)
Cyclic rate: 400 rds/min

Model SP66 Sniping Rifle
1976. Short-action bolt system in which the handle is toward the front end of the bolt. Heavy barrelled repeating rifle. Half-stocked, free-floating barrel with muzzle brake, adjustable thumb-hole butt. No iron sights, telescope mount on receiver.

Cartridge: 7.62 × 51mm NATO
Length: 44.09in (1120mm)
Weight: 13lb 12oz (6.25kg) with telescope
Barrel: 25.60in (650mm) without brake, 4 grooves, rh
Magazine: 3-round integral box
Muzzle velocity: 2362 ft/sec (720 m/sec)

Model 86 Sniping Rifle
1986. Short-action bolt system, ventilated synthetic stock, free-floating heavy barrel with muzzle brake. Adjustable thumb hole butt. No iron sights, telescope mount on receiver. Fore-end rail for bipod or hand stop.

Cartridge: 7.62 × 51mm NATO
Length: 47.64in (1210mm)
Weight: 10lb 13oz (4.90kg)
Barrel: 30.70in (780mm) with brake, 4 grooves, rh
Magazine: 9-round box
Muzzle velocity: 2362 ft/sec (720 m/sec)

Model SR93 Sniping Rifle
1993. Short-throw bolt action repeating rifle, capable of being adjusted for right or left hand use without tools. Heavy barrel supported by full-length stock, skeleton butt with cheek-piece, bipod, no iron sights, telescope mount.

Cartridge: .300 Winchester Magnum, or .338 Lapua Magnum
Length: 48.43in (1230mm)
Weight: 13lb 0oz (5.90kg)
Barrel: 25.59in (650mm), 4 grooves, rh
Magazine: 6-round box (.300), or 5-round box (.338)
Muzzle velocity, .300: 3238 ft/sec (987 m/sec)
Muzzle velocity, .338: 2998 ft/sec (914 m/sec)

ARGENTINA
M1891 Rifle
DWM & Loewe
This was an improved version of the Turkish M1890 rifle. Full-stocked with a half-length handguard, a slightly modified bolt and a strengthened extractor.

Cartridge: 7.65 × 53mm Mauser
Length: 48.62in (1235mm)
Weight: 8lb 13oz (3.99kg)
Barrel: 29.13in (740mm), 4 grooves, rh
Magazine: 5-round box
Muzzle velocity: 2133 ft/sec (650 m/sec)

M1891 Cavalry Carbine
DWM & Loewe
Same action as the rifle; stocked to the muzzle, short handguard, nose cap, bolt handle turned down. Sling bar and saddle ring.

Cartridge: 7.65 × 53mm Mauser
Length: 37.0in (940mm)
Weight: 7lb 4oz (3.28kg)
Barrel: 17.64in (448mm), 4 grooves, rh
Magazine: 5-round box
Muzzle velocity: 1893 ft/sec (577 m/sec)

M1909 Rifle
FMAP & Loewe
This used the 1898 bolt action, but with a hinged magazine floorplate. Full-stocked with half-length handguard and of much the same general appearance as the German Gew. 98. Originally supplied from Germany but made in Argentina after 1942.

Cartridge: 7.65 × 53mm Mauser
Length: 49.17in (1249mm)
Weight: 8lb 15oz (4.07kg)
Barrel: 29.13in (740mm), 4 grooves, rh
Magazine: 5-round integral box
Muzzle velocity: 2706 ft/sec (825 m/sec)

AUSTRIA
M1914 Rifle

This was to have been the next Austro-Hungarian service rifle from 1914 but the war intervened and only trial quantities were ever delivered. As for the German Gew. 98 but with a slightly different stock form.

Cartridge: 8 x 50R Austrian Mannlicher
Length: 50.19in (1275mm)
Weight: 8lb 13oz (4.00kg)
Barrel: 30.70in (780mm), 4 grooves, rh
Magazine: 5-round integral box
Muzzle velocity: 2034 ft/sec (620 m/sec)

BELGIUM
M1889 Infantry Rifle
FN, Hopkins, Liège & Pieper

1892. The first of a new small-calibre design with two locking lugs on a one-piece bolt, the handle turning down behind the receiver bridge. A charger-loaded integral box magazine was adopted, with a bridge charger guide. The barrel was jacketed throughout its length. Full-stocked, no handguard, straight stock.

Cartridge: 7.65 x 53mm Mauser
Length: 48.62in (1235mm)
Weight: 8lb 13oz (3.99kg)
Barrel: 29.13in (740mm), 4 grooves, rh
Magazine: 5-round box
Muzzle velocity: 2133 ft/sec (650 m/sec)

M1889 Civil Guard Rifle
FN

This was simply the infantry rifle but with the bolt handle turned down and using a different bayonet.

Specifications: the same

M1889 Cavalry Carbine
Liège

As for the infantry rifle but shorter. Half-stocked, bolt handle turned down, long cleaning rod under equally long exposed barrel.

Cartridge: 7.65 x 53mm Mauser
Length: 34.84in (885mm)
Weight: 6lb 10oz (3.02kg)
Barrel: 15.75in (400mm), 4 grooves, rh
Magazine: 5-round box
Muzzle velocity: 1837 ft/sec (560 m/sec)

M1889 Dismounted Troops' Carbine
Liège

Full-stocked, no handguard, bolt handle turned down, more a short rifle than a carbine.

Cartridge: 7.65 x 53mm Mauser
Length: 41.14in (1045mm)
Weight: 7lb 12oz (3.53kg)
Barrel: 21.65in (550mm), 4 grooves, rh
Magazine: 5-round box
Muzzle velocity: 1919 ft/sec (585 m/sec)

M1889 Mounted Gendarmerie Carbine
Liège

Similar to the cavalry carbine but stocked to the nose-cap and fitted for sword bayonet.

Cartridge: 7.65 x 53mm Mauser
Length: 34.84in (885mm)
Weight: 6lb 12oz (3.05kg)
Barrel: 15.75in (400mm), 4 grooves, rh
Magazine: 5-round box
Muzzle velocity: 1837 ft/sec (560 m/sec)

M1935 Short Rifle
FN

This rifle used a bolt mechanism based on that of the Gew. 98, with three-lug locking, did away with the jacket around the barrel, and placed the magazine inside the stock.

Cartridge: 7.65 x 53mm Mauser
Length: 43.38in (1107mm)
Weight: 9lb 0oz (4.08kg)
Barrel: 23.42in (595mm), 4 grooves, rh
Magazine: 5-round integral box
Muzzle velocity: 2346 ft/sec (715 m/sec)

M1889/36 Rifle
Pieper

Conversion of M1889 rifles to approximate to the M1935 specification. In effect, the M1889 bolt mechanism with a new jacket-less barrel.

Cartridge: 7.65 x 53mm Mauser
Length: 43.07in (1094mm)
Weight: 8lb 5oz (3.77kg)
Barrel: 23.62in (600mm), 4 grooves, rh
Magazine: 5-round box
Muzzle velocity: 2346 ft/sec (715 m/sec)

M1922 Rifle
FN

Commercially made by FN Herstal for sale to Brazil and other countries. A full-stocked infantry rifle using the 1898 bolt mechanism and internal magazine.

Cartridge: 7 x 57mm Mauser
Length: 48.70in (1237mm)
Weight: 8lb 13oz (4.00kg)
Barrel: 29.13in (740mm), 4 grooves, rh
Magazine: 5-round integral box
Muzzle velocity: 2575 ft/sec (785 m/sec)

M1924 Rifle
FN

Commercially made by FN Herstal, a short rifle to replace the M1922 as their export line. Full-stocked, half-length handguard, 1898 bolt and magazine, exposed muzzle, cleaning rod. Made in various calibres.

Cartridge: 7 x 57mm Mauser
Length: 42.91in (1090mm)
Weight: 8lb 6oz (3.81kg)
Barrel: 23.27in (591mm), 4 grooves, rh
Magazine: 5-round integral box
Muzzle velocity: 2379 ft/sec (725 m/sec)

M1935/46
FN
Post-1945 conversions of M1935 rifles to the US .30-06 cartridge.

Cartridge: .30-06 Springfield
Length: 43.50in (1105mm)
Weight: 8lb 15oz (4.06kg)
Barrel: 23.23in (590mm), 4 grooves, rh
Magazine: 5-round integral box
Muzzle velocity: 2740 ft/sec (835 m/sec)

BOLIVIA
M1895 Rifle
This was exactly the same weapon as the Argentine M1891 rifle.

M1907 Rifle
This was the Gewehr 98 in export form, firing the 7.65 x 53mm cartridge.

M1950 Rifle
This was the Czech Model 1924 export rifle in 7.65mm calibre and with some minor changes in the furniture and fittings.

BRAZIL
M1894 Rifle
DWM, FN & Loewe
Similar to the Spanish M1893 except for a minor change in the bolt and the omission of the hold-open feature on the magazine platform.

Cartridge: 7 x 57mm Mauser
Length: 48.62in (1235mm)
Weight: 8lb 14oz (4.03kg)
Barrel: 29.05in (738mm), 4 grooves, rh
Magazine: 5-round integral box
Muzzle velocity: 2300 ft/sec (700 m/sec)

M1904 Rifle
DWM
Much the same as the German Gewehr 98 but for the calibre; full stocked, pistol-grip butt, and fitted with the nose-cap of the M1894 rifle so that the same bayonet could be used.

Cartridge: 7 x 57mm Mauser
Length: 49.17in (1249mm)
Weight: 8lb 13oz (4.0kg)
Barrel: 29.05in (738mm), 4 grooves, rh
Magazine: 5-round integral box
Muzzle velocity: 2300 ft/sec (700 m/sec)

M1908 Rifle
DWM 1908–14; Radom 1935–37
Similar to the M1904 rifle, and of similar dimensions, the only change appears to have been a new pattern of nose-cap for a new bayonet.

CHILE
M1895 Rifle
DWM & Loewe
Similar to the Brazilian M1894 in having no hold-open stop on the magazine follower and a flush bolt face. Full-stocked, half-length handguard, exposed muzzle, cleaning rod, bayonet bar.

Cartridge: 7 x 57mm Mauser
Length: 48.50in (1232mm)
Weight: 8lb 14oz (4.03kg)
Barrel: 29.06in (738mm), 4 grooves, rh
Magazine: 5-round integral box
Muzzle velocity: 2700 ft/sec (823m/sec)

M1895 Short Rifle
A shorter version of the rifle, with the bolt handle turned down.

M1895 Carbine
Same bolt and magazine as the rifle, but shorter than the short rifle. Full-stocked, short handguard, cleaning rod, bayonet bar, bolt handle turned down.

Cartridge: 7 x 57mm Mauser
Length: 37.0in (940mm)
Weight: 7lb 8oz (3.40kg)
Barrel: 18.25in (464mm), 4 grooves, rh
Magazine: 5-round integral box
Muzzle velocity: 2600 ft/sec (790 m/sec)

M1904 Rifle
DWM
This was the same rifle as the Brazilian M1904.

CHINA
M1895 Rifle
DWM & Loewe
The same rifle as the Chilean M1895.

Model 21 Short Rifle
Kwantung Arsenal
Chinese-manufactured copy of the Belgian M1924 in 7.92mm Mauser calibre.

COLOMBIA
M1891 Rifle
DWM & Loewe
The same rifle as the Argentine M1891.

M1904 Rifle
DWM
The same rifle as the Brazilian M1904.

COSTA RICA
M1895 Rifle
DWM & Loewe
The same rifle as the Chilean M1895.

M1910 Rifle
Based on the Gew. 98 but with a half-length handguard and with the bolt face recessed.

Cartridge: 7 x 57mm Mauser
Length: 48.82in (1240mm)
Weight: 8lb 12oz (3.97kg)
Barrel: 29.13in (740mm), 4 grooves, rh
Magazine: 5-round integral box
Muzzle velocity: 2494 ft/sec (760 m/sec)

CZECHOSLOVAKIA

M1898/22 Rifle
CZ Brno

1922. Based on the Mexican M1912 rifle; M1898 bolt action, full-stocked, half-length handguard, pistol-grip butt, hooded foresight.

Cartridge: 7.92 × 57mm Mauser
Length: 48.82in (1240mm)
Weight: 9lb 5oz (4.22kg)
Barrel: 29.13in (740mm), 4 grooves, rh
Magazine: 5-round integral box
Muzzle velocity: 2854 ft/sec (870 m/sec)

M1898/29 Rifle
CZ Brno

Manufactured in Czechoslovakia for export sale and was simply a very slightly modified version of the M1898/22 service rifle.

M1898/29 Short Rifle
CZ Brno

The export version of the service M1924 short rifle.

M1924 Short Rifle
CZ Brno

Shorter version of the M1898/22 with several minor improvements in butt shape, finish, barrel bands, and may have a straight or turned-down bolt.

Cartridge: 7.92 × 57mm Mauser
Length: 43.23in (1098mm)
Weight: 9lb 2oz (4.14kg)
Barrel: 23.23in (590mm), 4 grooves, rh
Magazine: 5-round integral box
Muzzle velocity: 2756 ft/sec (840 m/sec)

M1933 Gendarmerie Carbine
CZ Brno

Shorter version of the M1924 rifle. Hollow bolt knob, sling bar.

Cartridge: 7.92 × 57mm Mauser
Length: 39.21in (996mm)
Weight: 7lb 11oz (3.48kg)
Barrel: 17.91in (455mm), 4 grooves, rh
Magazine: 5-round integral box
Muzzle velocity: 2510 ft/sec (765 m/sec)

IRAN

See Persia

MEXICO

M1895 Infantry Rifle
DWM & Loewe

Generally the same rifle as the Spanish M1893, but without the recessed bolt face. Straight butt.

Cartridge: 7 × 57mm Mauser
Length: 48.58in (1234mm)
Weight: 8lb 12oz (3.97kg)
Barrel: 29.05in (738mm), 4 grooves, rh
Magazine: 5-round integral box
Muzzle velocity: 2395 ft/sec (730 m/sec)

M1895 Carbine
DWM & Loewe

Shortened version of the M1895 rifle. Bolt handle turned down, sling swivels on the side.

Cartridge: 7 × 57mm Mauser
Length: 37.52in (953mm)
Weight: 7lb 8oz (3.40kg)
Barrel: 18.31in (465mm), 4 grooves, rh
Magazine: 5-round integral box
Muzzle velocity: 2300 ft/sec (700 m/sec)

M1902 Infantry Rifle
DWM & Steyr

As for the M1895 rifle, but with an 1898 three-lug bolt.

Cartridge: 7 × 57mm Mauser
Length: 48.58in (1234mm)
Weight: 8lb 13oz (4.01kg)
Barrel: 29.05in (738mm), 4 grooves, rh
Magazine: 5-round integral box
Muzzle velocity: 2395 ft/sec (730 m/sec)

M1907 Infantry Rifle
Steyr

Made in Austria by Steyr, this is much the same as the M1902 but with a pistol-grip butt and a different nose-cap.

Cartridge: 7 × 57mm Mauser
Length: 48.78in (1239mm)
Weight: 8lb 15oz (4.05kg)
Barrel: 29.05in (738mm), 4 grooves, rh
Magazine: 5-round integral box
Muzzle velocity: 2300 ft/sec (700 m/sec)

M1910 Infantry Rifle
FNA

This was the M1902 rifle manufactured in Mexico from about 1913 onward.

Specifications: as for the M1902

M1912 Infantry Rifle
Steyr

Production difficulties with the M1910 led to a further order for rifles from Steyr of Austria. These were very similar to the M1907 design, but the outbreak of war in 1914 led to most of the production going to the Austro-Hungarian Army. They were also sold to Yugoslavia, in 7.92mm calibre, in 1920.

M1924 Short Rifle
FN

These were the Belgian M1924 rifle in 7mm calibre.

M1936 Short Rifle
FNA

Of Mexican manufacture, this combined the Mauser 1898 bolt with the Springfield cocking-piece, barrel bands and nose-cap, but with a pistol-grip butt.

Cartridge: 7 × 57mm Mauser
Length: 42.91in (1090mm)
Weight: 8lb 5oz (3.78kg)
Barrel: 23.23in (590mm), 4 grooves, rh
Magazine: 5-round integral box
Muzzle velocity: 2300 ft/sec (715 m/sec)

M1954 Short Rifle
FNA
The M1936 altered to fire the .30-06 cartridge, adopted as standard. Laminated wood stocks, trigger-guard and magazine floor-plate one piece, aperture rear sight.

Cartridge: .30-06 Springfield
Length: 44.09in (1120mm)
Weight: 9lb 10oz (4.37kg)
Barrel: 24.0in (610mm), 4 grooves, rh
Magazine: 5-round integral box
Muzzle velocity: 2772 ft/sec (845 m/sec)

ORANGE FREE STATE

M1896
DWM
This rifle was the Chilean M1895 in 7mm calibre.

PERSIA

Model 1310, 1317
CZ Brno
1931. These were Czech M98/29 rifles and short rifles.

Model 1328
Persia
Made from 1949 onward, this was more or less the Czech M1898/29 short rifle with changes to the sling attachments.

Cartridge: 7.92 × 57mm Mauser
Length: 38.19in (970mm)
Weight: 8lb 9oz (3.90kg)
Barrel: 18.11in (460mm), 4 grooves, rh
Magazine: 5-round integral box
Muzzle velocity: 2379 ft/sec (725 m/sec)

POLAND

M1898 Infantry Rifle
Warsaw
1920. Polish-made copy of the German Gew. 98 Infantry rifle. The only discernible difference is in the markings.

M1898 Short Rifle
Warsaw
1920. Polish-made copy of the German Kar. 98AZ. It can be distinguished by the presence of a sling bar on the left side and a piling hook on the nose-cap.

M1929 Short Rifle
Radom
1930. Based on the design of the Czech M1924 rifle. Full-stocked with full-length handguard, exposed muzzle, cleaning rod. Sling bar on left side of butt.

Cartridge: 7.92 × 57mm Mauser
Length: 43.39in (1102mm)
Weight: 9lb 0oz (4.09kg)
Barrel: 23.62in (600mm), 4 grooves, rh
Magazine: 5-round integral box
Muzzle velocity: 2477 ft/sec (755 m/sec)

PORTUGAL
See also Mauser-Vergueiro

M937, 937A Short Rifle
1937. This was an off-the-shelf Mauser more or less the same as the contemporary Kar. 98k being made for the German Army. The first few were issued with the usual German type of sling slot in the butt, but from early 1938 they had sling swivels on the butt and became the **M937A**.

Cartridge: 7.92 × 57mm Mauser
Length: 43.43in (1103mm)
Weight: 8lb 12oz (3.96kg)
Barrel: 19.69in (500mm), 4 grooves, rh
Magazine: 5-round integral box
Muzzle velocity: 2428 ft/sec (740 m/sec)

SERBIA

M1878/80 Rifle Mauser-Milovanovicz
1880. Basically the German Mauser M1871 single-shot rifle with rifling due to Major Koka Milovanovicz of Kragujevac arsenal. (It is also called the 'Koka Mauser' in contemporary reports.) This rifling system was distinguished by the width of the groove diminishing as it went up the barrel. It doubtless seemed a good idea at the time but any gains in gas sealing and accuracy were countered by the trouble and expense of manufacture. It was never repeated on any other arm.

Cartridge: 10.15 × 63R Serbian Mauser
Length: 50.71in (1288mm)
Weight: 9lb 14oz (4.47kg)
Barrel: 30.71in (780mm), 4 grooves, rh
Muzzle velocity: 1673 ft/sec (510 m/sec)

M1880/06 and /07 Rifles
Kragujevac
1906. The original M1878/80 rifles converted to 7mm calibre and given a box magazine. The /06 model was a straightforward conversion with the bolt locking into the receiver, but the cartridge proved too powerful and the /07 versions have a safety latch to hold the bolt closed.

Cartridge: 7 × 57mm Mauser
Length: 50.71in (1288mm)
Weight: 9lb 14oz (4.52kg)
Barrel: 30.71in (780mm), 4 grooves, rh
Magazine: 5-round integral box
Muzzle velocity: 2330ft/sec (710 m/sec)

M1885 Cavalry Carbine
The bolt action and tube magazine of the German M1871/84 rifle in a full-stocked carbine. Notable for a receiver extension above the butt wrist which supports the bolt in opening; the butt wrist is extended to allow a good grip.

Cartridge: 10.15 × 63R Serbian Mauser
Length: 37.60in (955mm)
Weight: 8lb 5oz (3.75kg)
Barrel: 18.31in (465mm), 4 grooves, rh
Magazine: 5-round tube in fore-end
Muzzle velocity: 1525 ft/sec (465 m/sec)

M1899 Rifle
DWM & Steyr
Two-lug bolt, full-stocked, half-length handguard, nose-cap with bayonet fittings and cleaning rod. Generally similar to the Chilean M1895 rifle.

Cartridge: 7 × 57mm Mauser
Length: 48.43in (1230mm)

Weight: 8lb 14oz (4.03kg)
Barrel: 29.13in (740mm), 4 grooves, rh
Magazine: 5-round integral box
Muzzle velocity: 2329 ft/sec (710 m/sec)

M1910 Rifle

As for the Gew. 1898 but with a half-length handguard and a simplified nose-cap with bayonet fittings.

Cartridge: 7 × 57mm Mauser
Length: 48.74in (1238mm)
Weight: 9lb 1oz (4.11kg)
Barrel: 29.13in (740mm), 4 grooves, rh
Magazine: 5-round integral box
Muzzle velocity: 2329 ft/sec (710 m/sec)

SIAM

M1902 Rifle
Koishikawa

Generally as for the Gew. 98, but adapted for a rimmed cartridge. Full-stocked, half-length handguard, exposed muzzle, cleaning rod. Sliding bolt cover.

Cartridge: 8 × 50R Siamese Mannlicher
Length: 49.09in (1247mm)
Weight: 8lb 9oz (3.88kg)
Barrel: 29.13in (740mm), 4 grooves, rh
Magazine: 5-round integral box
Muzzle velocity: 2050 ft/sec (625 m/sec)

M1923 Short Rifle
Koishikawa

The 1902 rifle rebuilt (in Japan) for a new cartridge and shortened. Sling mounts on left side, new nose-cap with bayonet bar.

Cartridge: 8 × 52R Siamese Mauser
Length: 41.93in (1065mm)
Weight: 8lb 0oz (3.65kg)
Barrel: 22.05in (560mm), 4 grooves, rh
Magazine: 5-round integral box
Muzzle velocity: 2100 ft/sec (640 m/sec)

SPAIN

M1891 Infantry Rifle

Based on the Turkish M1890, a two-lug bolt action and exposed magazine. Full-stocked, no handguard, exposed muzzle, cleaning rod. Troop trial quantity only.

Cartridge: 7.65 × 53 Belgian Mauser
Length: 48.74in (1238mm)
Weight: 9lb 1oz (4.11kg)
Barrel: 29.13in (740mm), 4 grooves, rh
Magazine: 5-round box
Muzzle velocity: 2067 ft/sec (630 m/sec)

M1892 Infantry Rifle

Similar to the M1891 but with improvements suggested by the troop trials. Internal charger-loaded magazine, new extractor, removable magazine floor-plate, improvements to the bolt. Half-length handguard. Chambered for a new cartridge.

Cartridge: 7 × 57mm Spanish Mauser
Length: 48.62in (1235mm)
Weight: 9lb 1oz (4.11kg)

Barrel: 29.05in (738mm), 4 grooves, rh
Magazine: 5-round integral box
Muzzle velocity: 2198 ft/sec (670 m/sec)

M1892 Cavalry Carbine
Loewe

Same action as the M1891 rifle, stocked to the muzzle, nose-cap, turned-down bolt handle, sling bar and saddle ring.

Cartridge: 7 × 57mm Spanish Mauser
Length: 37.12in (943mm)
Weight: 7lb 4oz (3.30kg)
Barrel: 17.52in (445mm), 4 grooves, rh
Magazine: 5-round integral box
Muzzle velocity: 1837 ft/sec (560 m/sec)

M1893 Infantry Rifle
Loewe & Oviedo

The definitive 'Spanish Mauser'; the first Mauser with a charger-loading magazine concealed within the stock. The one which opened American military eyes in Cuba during the Spanish-American War and led to the Springfield rifle. Two-lug bolt action as for the M1891 rifle, charger guide in the receiver bridge, magazine follower holds bolt open. Straight buttstock, half-length handguard.

Cartridge: 7 × 57mm Spanish Mauser
Length: 48.62in (1235mm)
Weight: 8lb 11oz (3.95kg)
Barrel: 29.05in (738mm), 4 grooves, rh
Magazine: 5-round integral box
Muzzle velocity: 2231 ft/sec (680 m/sec)

M1895 Cavalry Carbine
Loewe & Oviedo

Short version of the M1893 rifle, stocked to the nose-cap, half-length handguard, turned-down bolt handle.

Cartridge: 7 × 57mm Spanish Mauser
Length: 37.12in (943mm)
Weight: 7lb 1oz (3.20kg)
Barrel: 17.56in (446mm), 4 grooves, rh
Magazine: 5-round integral box
Muzzle velocity: 2165 ft/sec (660 m/sec)

M1913 Short Rifle
Oviedo

Similar to the 1895 carbine but fitted for bayonet. Troop trial quantity only.

Specifications: as for the M1895 Carbine

M1916 Artillery Rifle
Oviedo & Tarrasa

To replace earlier carbines consequent upon adopting a new and more powerful cartridge. Used the M1891 two-lug bolt, with the left side of the action cut away to facilitate charger loading. Bolt handle turned down. Sling swivel and stock bar on left side.

Cartridge: 7 × 57mm Spanish Mauser
Length: 41.34in (1050mm)
Weight: 8lb 4oz (3.75kg)
Barrel: 21.69in (551mm), 4 grooves, rh
Magazine: 5-round integral box
Muzzle velocity: 2707 ft/sec (825 m/sec)

M1943 Short Rifle
La Coruña & Oviedo
Generally as for the German Kar. 98k, as by this time the Spanish had adopted the 7.92mm Mauser cartridge. Straight bolt handle, half-length handguard.

Cartridge: 7.92 × 57mm Mauser
Length: 43.50in (1105mm)
Weight: 8lb 10oz (3.91kg)
Barrel: 23.62in (600mm), 4 grooves, rh
Magazine: 5-round integral box
Muzzle velocity: 2460 ft/sec (750 m/sec)

SWEDEN

M1894 Carbine
Carl Gustav & Mauser
Used the two-lug bolt and integral magazine of the Spanish M1893 rifle, stocked to the nose-cap in the European carbine style, half-length handguard, turned-down bolt handle, grooved fore-end.

Cartridge: 6.5 × 55mm Swedish Mauser
Length: 37.40in (950mm)
Weight: 7lb 5oz (3.31kg)
Barrel: 17.32in (440mm), 4 grooves, rh
Magazine: 5-round integral box
Muzzle velocity: 2132 ft/sec (650 m/sec)

M1894/17 Carbine
Carl Gustav
As for the M1894, but with a new nose-cap to allow a bayonet to be fitted.

Specifications: the same

M1896 Rifle
Carl Gustav, Husqvarna & Mauser
Used the same action and magazine as the M1894 carbine but in a full-length rifle. Full-stocked, straight butt, half-length handguard, cleaning rod, bayonet lug.

Cartridge: 6.5 × 55mm Swedish Mauser
Length: 49.45in (1256mm)
Weight: 8lb 15oz (4.07kg)
Barrel: 29.09in (739mm), 4 grooves, rh
Magazine: 5-round integral box
Muzzle velocity: 2378 ft/sec (725 m/sec)

M1939 Rifle
Carl Gustav
Basically a modified German Kar. 98k with an 8mm calibre barrel so as to fire the same 8 × 63mm Browning cartridge as used in Sweden's machine guns. It was not a success, the cartridge being far too powerful.

M1940 Rifle
Carl Gustav
The M1939 design fitted with a muzzle brake to make it slightly more controllable. It was still a lemon and was not kept in service for very long.

THAILAND
See Siam

TURKEY
M1887 Rifle
Mauser's perfected black-powder design. Essentially the German M71/84 tube magazine rifle chambered for a 9.5mm cartridge, though an additional lug was provided on the bolt to secure it against the extra power.

Cartridge: 9.5 × 60R Turkish Mauser
Length: 49.25in (1251mm)
Weight: 9lb 4oz (4.19kg)
Barrel: 29.92in (760mm), 4 grooves, rh
Magazine: 8-round tube
Muzzle velocity: 1755 ft/sec (535 m/sec)

M1890 Rifle
Similar to the Belgian M1889 but without the barrel jacket. Two-lug bolt, exposed box magazine, full-stocked, half-length handguard.

Cartridge: 7.65 × 53mm Mauser
Length: 48.70in (1237mm)
Weight: 8lb 13oz (4.00kg)
Barrel: 29.13in (740mm), 4 grooves, rh
Magazine: 5-round box
Muzzle velocity: 2132 ft/sec (650 m/sec)

M1890 Cavalry Carbine
This used the same action as the rifle, with a short barrel stocked to the nosecap and a turned-down bolt handle.

Cartridge: 7.65 × 53mm Mauser
Length: 39.17in (995mm)
Weight: 7lb 11oz (3.50kg)
Barrel: 19.68in (500mm), 4 grooves, rh
Magazine: 5-round box
Muzzle velocity: 1886 ft/sec (575 m/sec)

M1893 Rifle
This was similar to the Spanish M1893, using the two-lug bolt and charger-loaded integral magazine. The Turks had a magazine cut-off fitted, uncommon on a Mauser.

Cartridge: 7.65 × 53mm Mauser
Length: 48.62in (1235mm)
Weight: 8lb 15oz (4.06kg)
Barrel: 29.05in (738mm), 4 grooves, rh
Magazine: 5-round integral box
Muzzle velocity: 2132 ft/sec (650 m/sec)

M1905 Carbine
Used the action of the M1903 rifle with a short barrel stocked to the nosecap. Turned-down bolt handle, sling swivels on the left side, wing protectors on front sight.

Cartridge: 7.65 × 53mm Mauser
Length: 41.14in (1045mm)
Weight: 8lb 4oz (3.75kg)
Barrel: 21.65in (550mm), 4 grooves, rh
Magazine: 5-round integral box
Muzzle velocity: 2083 ft/sec (635 m/sec)

YUGOSLAVIA

Model 1948
Kragujevac
More or less a copy of the German Kar. 98k, using a three-lug bolt with turned-down handle, integral magazine, full-

stocked, full-length handguard, exposed muzzle, bayonet bar, cleaning rod.

Cartridge: 7.92 × 57mm Mauser
Length: 42.90in (1089mm)
Weight: 8lb 10oz (3.91kg)
Barrel: 23.30in (592mm), 4 grooves, rh
Magazine: 5-round integral box
Muzzle velocity: 2600 ft/sec (792 m/sec)

MAUSER-MILOVANOVICZ
See Mauser, Serbia, M1878/80 Rifle

MAUSER-VERGUEIRO Portugal
M1904 Rifle
DWM
Virtually a Mauser action but with a split receiver bridge to allow the bolt handle to pass through and turn down in front as an additional safety feature. The bolt itself is closer to Mannlicher practice than to Mauser, in an attempt to keep production costs down. Full stocked, full-length handguard, exposed muzzle, cleaning rod. The same rifle, in 7mm Spanish calibre, was adopted by the Brazilian police.

Cartridge: 6.5 × 58mm Mauser-Vergueiro
Length: 48.70in (1223mm)
Weight: 8lb 6oz (3.80kg)
Barrel: 29.10in (738mm), 4 grooves, rh
Magazine: 5-round integral box
Muzzle velocity: 2345 ft/sec (715 m/sec)

MEUNIER France
MAT

Rifle A-6
Semi-automatic, recoil-operated, rotating bolt. Integral charger-loaded magazine. Full-stocked, half-length handguard, ventilation slots in fore-end, bayonet lug. Straight bolt-type cocking handle. Saw limited use 1916–17.

Cartridge: 7 × 59mm Meunier
Length: 50.90in (1293mm)
Weight: 8lb 14oz (4.04kg)
Barrel: 28.35in (720mm), 4 grooves, rh
Magazine: 6-round box
Muzzle velocity: 2608 ft/sec (795 m/sec)

MILBANK-AMSLER Switzerland
SIG
Adaptation of the American Milbank side-opening 'trap-door' breech block, with hammer and with firing pin in the block, modified by Amsler of Switzerland, and used to convert earlier percussion muzzle-loading weapons to breech-loading.

M1851/67 Rifle
Conversion as above. Double set trigger, full-stocked, tubular bayonet socket.

Cartridge: 10.4 × 38R Swiss Peabody rimfire
Length: 49.60in (1260mm)
Weight: 9lb 15oz (4.50kg)

Barrel: 29.53in (750mm), 4 grooves, rh
Muzzle velocity: 1362 ft/sec (415 m/sec)

M1856/67 Rifle
Conversion as above, from Jäger rifle.

Cartridge: 10.4 × 38R Swiss Peabody rimfire
Length: 51.93in (1319mm)
Weight: 9lb 5oz (4.23kg)
Barrel: 34.05in (865mm), 4 grooves, rh
Muzzle velocity: 1443 ft/sec (440 m/sec)

M1863/67 Infantry Rifle
Conversion as above. Sling swivel on trigger guard.

Cartridge: 10.4 × 38R Swiss Peabody rimfire
Length: 54.33in (1380mm)
Weight: 10lb 4oz (4.65kg)
Barrel: 36.45in (926mm), 4 grooves, rh
Muzzle velocity: 1476 ft/sec (450 m/sec)

M1864/67 Short Rifle
Conversion as above. Similar to the M1851/67, but has an octagonal barrel with cylindrical muzzle and fitted with a bayonet lug.

Cartridge: 10.4 × 38R Swiss Peabody rimfire
Length: 49.49in (1257mm)
Weight: 10lb 1oz (4.55kg)
Barrel: 29.60in (752mm), 4 grooves, rh
Muzzle velocity: 1362 ft/sec (415 m/sec)

MONDRAGON Mexico
Model 1908 'Porfirio Diaz' Rifle
SIG
Gas-operated semi-automatic using a rotating bolt. Designed in Mexico, made in Switzerland by SIG. Full-stocked, box magazine, exposed muzzle, full-length handguard, bayonet fitting, Gas cylinder exposed at front of fore-end. Cocking handle has lock to permit manual operation. About 400 rifles had been delivered when the 1911 revolution took place and the balance of the order was cancelled.

Cartridge: 7 × 57mm Mauser
Length: 42.04in (1068mm)
Weight: 9lb 6oz (4.25kg)
Barrel: 24.41in (620mm), 4 grooves, rh
Magazine: 8-round box
Muzzle velocity: 2050 ft/sec (625m/sec)

Model 1915 (Germany)
SIG having been left with about 3,000 Mexican rifles, they were able to sell them to Germany in 1915, where they were used by marines and aircraft observers until suitable machine guns could be made. Special 30-round drum magazines were manufactured and supplied. Apart from the magazine, the rifle was exactly the same as the Mexican M1908.

MOSIN-NAGANT Russia
Izhevsk, Sestroretsk & Tula

M1891 Infantry Rifle
Bolt action, charger-loaded box magazine, full-stocked and with a full-length handguard. The bolt locks by two lugs on the bolt head and the handle passes through the split receiver bridge and locks in front. Octagonal receiver, and an unusual cartridge control system in the feedway.

Cartridge: 7.62 × 54R
Length: 51.89in (1318mm)
Weight: 8lb 15oz (4.06kg)
Barrel: 32.28in (820mm), 4 grooves, rh
Magazine: 5-round box
Muzzle velocity: 1985 ft/sec (605m/sec)

M1891 Dragoon Rifle
A shortened version of the infantry rifle. Short handguard, sling slots in fore-end and butt. The 'Cossack rifle' was the same weapon but with a slightly different cleaning rod.

Cartridge: 7.62 × 54R
Length: 48.62in (1235mm)
Weight: 8lb 11oz (3.93kg)
Barrel: 29.92in (760mm), 4 grooves, rh
Magazine: 5-round box
Muzzle velocity: 1968 ft/sec (600m/sec)

M1907 Carbine
The same action as the 1891 rifle, but in a short weapon full-stocked and with a very short exposed muzzle. Not fitted for bayonet.

Cartridge: 7.62 × 54R
Length: 40.16in (1020mm)
Weight: 7lb 8oz (3.40kg)
Barrel: 20.08in (510mm), 4 grooves, rh
Magazine: 5-round box
Muzzle velocity: 1805 ft/sec (550m/sec)

M1891/30 Rifle
Sovietized version of the M1891 rifle; cylindrical receiver, hooded foresight.

Cartridge: 7.62 × 54R
Length: 48.43in (1230mm)
Weight: 8lb 11oz (3.95kg)
Barrel: 28.74in (730mm), 4 grooves, rh
Magazine: 5-round box
Muzzle velocity: 2641 ft/sec (805m/sec)

M1938 Carbine
A shortened version of the M1891/30 rifle, capable of accepting a bayonet.

Cartridge: 7.62 × 54R
Length: 40.16in (1020mm)
Weight: 7lb 10oz (3.45kg)
Barrel: 20.08in (510mm), 4 grooves, rh
Magazine: 5-round box
Muzzle velocity: 2575 ft/sec (785m/sec)

M1944 Carbine
As for the M1938, but with a cruciform-blade bayonet attached by a hinge on the barrel, folding back on the right-hand side of the fore-end. This was the last bolt-action carbine to be officially adopted by any army. This carbine

was later copied by China as the Type 53 (*see* China).

Cartridge: 7.62 × 54R
Length: 40.35in (1025mm)
Weight: 8lb 14oz (4.03kg)
Barrel: 20.47in (520mm), 4 grooves, rh
Magazine: 5-round box
Muzzle velocity: 1985 ft/sec (605m/sec)

CZECHOSLOVAKIA

M1954 Sniping Rifle
CZ Brno
A sniping rifle assembled from selected M1891/30 actions and barrelled to extract the best performance from the Type D heavy ball bullet cartridge. Half-stocked, pistol grip butt, handguard, usually with an optical sight.

Cartridge: 7.62 × 54R
Length: 48.42in (1230mm)
Weight: 11lb 7oz (5.20kg)
Barrel: 28.74in (730mm), 4 grooves, rh
Magazine: 5-round box
Muzzle velocity: 2640 ft/sec (805 m/sec)

FINLAND

M1924 Infantry Rifle
Valmet
New barrels (made in Switzerland) fitted to refurbished actions salvaged from worn-out M1891 ex-Russian rifles. Various small changes to the furniture resulted since the exterior contour of the Swiss barrels differed somewhat from the Russian.

Cartridge: 7.62 × 54R
Length: 51.18in (1300mm)
Weight: 9lb 4oz (4.20kg)
Barrel: 32.20in (818mm), 4 grooves, rh
Magazine: 5-round box
Muzzle velocity: 2830 ft/sec (863 m/sec)

M1927 Short Rifle
Valmet
Shortened version of the M1924, full-stocked, bayonet lug, aperture backsight.

Cartridge: 7.62 × 54R
Length: 46.65in (1185mm)
Weight: 9lb 1oz (4.11kg)
Barrel: 26.97in (685mm), 4 grooves, rh
Magazine: 5-round box
Muzzle velocity: 2428 ft/sec (740 m/sec)

M1928 Short Rifle
Sako
Another short version of the M1924 with a different stock and a new system of rifling.

Specifications: as for the M1927, except
Weight: 9lb 3oz (4.18kg)

M1928/30 Short Rifle
Sako
The M1928 short rifle with an improved magazine and a new backsight,

Specifications: as for the M1927, except
Weight: 9lb 10oz (4.36kg)

M1939 Short Rifle
Sako

A new design, though basically the same as the M1927. It had new rifling and a larger bore diameter to accommodate a new heavy ball bullet, a two-piece stock and an improved backsight.

Cartridge: 7.62 × 54R
Length: 46.65in (1185mm)
Weight: 10lb 0oz (4.55kg)
Barrel: 26.97in (685mm), 4 grooves, rh
Magazine: 5-round box
Muzzle velocity: 2297 ft/sec (700 m/sec)

MURATA Japan

Meiji 18th Year Rifle
Koishikawa

1885. Final version of a design based on elements of the Gras and Mauser rifles which had been purchased by Japan, perfected by Major Murata. Bolt action, single shot. Full-stocked with straight butt, bayonet bar on left.

Cartridge: 11 × 60R Murata
Length: 50.23in (1276mm)
Weight: 9lb 0oz (4.09kg)
Barrel: 32.00in (813mm), 4 grooves, rh
Muzzle velocity: 1427 ft/sec (435m/sec)

Meiji 22nd Year Rifle
Koishikawa

1889. Improvement of the 18th Year Rifle into a small-calibre magazine weapon. Similarly fully-stocked, with the front end of the magazine tube protruding to form part of the bayonet mounting system. Short handguard. Magazine cut-off lever behind bolt handle.

Cartridge: 8 × 53R Murata
Length: 47.52in (1207mm)
Weight: 8lb 11oz (3.94kg)
Barrel: 29.52in (750mm), 4 grooves, rh
Magazine: 8-round tube
Muzzle velocity: 1853 ft/sec (565m/sec)

Meiji 27th Year Carbine
Koishikawa

1894. Used the same bolt and magazine action as the 22nd Year Rifle but the magazine tube was not exposed. Sling swivels underneath for artillery and engineers, on the side for cavalry.

Cartridge: 8 × 53R Murata
Length: 37.48in (952mm)
Weight: 6lb 14oz (3.11kg)
Barrel: 19.29in (490mm), 4 grooves, rh
Magazine: 6-round tube
Muzzle velocity: 1706 ft/sec (520m/sec)

NEUHAUSEN Switzerland
SIG

M1889 Rifle

Conversion from Vetterli turnbolt to SIG-Neuhausen straight-pull bolt for Swiss Army trials. Full-stocked, box magazine, ring or hook safety on cocking-piece.

Cartridge: 7.5 × 53mm Schmidt-Rubin
Length: 51.18in (1300mm)
Weight: 8lb 14oz (4.02kg)
Barrel: 30.31in (770mm), 3 grooves, rh
Magazine: 12-round tube
Muzzle velocity: 2000 ft/sec (610 m/sec)

NTW South Africa
Mechem

NTW 20 Anti-materiel Rifle

Bolt action repeating rifle, can be broken into two units for carriage. Bipod attached to receiver, monopod under butt, pistol grip. Heavy barrel with muzzle brake. Side-feeding box magazine.

Cartridge: 20 × 83mm MG151
Length: 70.67in (1795mm)
Weight: 57lb 5oz (26.0kg)
Barrel: 39.37in (1000mm), 8 grooves, rh
Magazine: 3-round box
Muzzle velocity: 2362 ft/sec (720 m/sec)

NTW 14.5 Anti-materiel Rifle.

Re-chambered version of the NTW 20 rifle (*above*) with some minor manufacturing changes.

Cartridge: 14.5 × 114mm Soviet
Length: 79.33in (2015mm)
Weight: 63lb 15oz (29.0kg)
Barrel: 48.03in (1220mm), 8 grooves, rh
Magazine: 3-round box
Muzzle velocity: 3543 ft/sec (1080 m/sec)

ONYX Poland
Lucznik

Type 89

1989. More or less the Polish version of the AK-74 SU. Short Kalashnikov type weapon with muzzle expansion chamber and brake of different design, folding wire single-strut butt. Principal distinguishing mark is the prominent rear sight combined with telescope mount fitted above the ejection port.

Cartridge: 5.45 × 39.5mm
Length, butt extended: 28.35in (720mm)
Length, butt retracted: 20.43in (519mm)
Weight: 6lb 6oz (2.90kg)
Barrel: 8.15in (207mm), 6 grooves, rh
Magazine: 30-round box
Muzzle velocity: 2296 ft/sec (700m/sec)
Cyclic rate: 700 rds/min

Type 91

1991. As for the Type 89 but chambered for the 5.56 × 45mm cartridge.

Specifications: the same, except
Muzzle velocity: 2330 ft/sec (710 m/sec)

PALMER USA
Lamson

Bolt action Carbine
First US military bolt action, some 1000 purchased in 1865. Short bolt handle at rear of bolt, side-hammer. Half-stocked, single barrel band, round barrel.

Cartridge: .56-52 Spencer
Length: 38.50in (978mm)
Weight: 8lb 8oz (3.86kg)
Barrel: 20.0in (508mm), 4 grooves, rh
Muzzle velocity: *ca* 900 ft/sec (274 m/sec)

PARKER-HALE Britain
Gibbs & Parker-Hale

Primarily a maker of sporting rifles and sights, Parker-Hale produced three sniping rifles which were adopted by various military forces. The company disposed of its rifle business in 1990, after which the Model 85 *described below* was manufactured in the USA by the Gibbs Rifle Company.

M82 Sniping Rifle
Bolt-action repeater using Mauser 98 type action. Half-stocked, no handguard, butt adjustable by spacers. Heavy barrel, fore-end rail for bipod or hand stop.

Cartridge: 7.62 × 51mm NATO
Length: 45.75in (1162mm)
Weight: 10lb 9oz (4.80kg)
Barrel: 25.98in (660mm), 4 grooves, rh
Magazine: 4-round integral box
Muzzle velocity: 2821 ft/sec (860 m/sec)

M83 Sniping Rifle
Bolt action, single shot, using Mauser 98 type action. Improved Model 83 with input from 1200TX target rifle. Half-stocked, heavy barrel, hooded foresight, micrometer rear sight.

Cartridge: 7.62 × 51mm NATO
Length: 46.73in (1187mm)
Weight: 10lb 15oz (4.98kg)
Barrel: 25.98in (660mm), 4 grooves, rh
Magazine: 4-round integral box
Muzzle velocity: 2821 ft/sec (860 m/sec)

M85 Sniping Rifle
Further improvement on the M82/83 pattern. Mauser 98-type bolt action, removable box magazine, half-stocked, heavy barrel, iron sights, dovetail telescope mount on receiver. Bipod attached to bracket on fire-end, fore-end rail for hand stop or sling, adjustable butt-plate.

Cartridge: 7.62 × 51mm NATO
Length: 45.27in (1150mm)
Weight, with telescope: 12lb 7oz (5.64kg)
Barrel: 27.56in (700mm), 4 grooves, rh
Magazine: 10-round integral box
Muzzle velocity: 2855 ft/sec (870 m/sec)

PEABODY USA
Providence
SPAIN

M1868 Rifle
Lever-operated dropping breech-block, single shot. Full-stocked, exposed muzzle.

Cartridge: .56-50 Spencer
Length: 54.05in (1373mm)
Weight: 9lb 15oz (4.52kg)
Barrel: 35.90in (912mm), 3 grooves, rh
Muzzle velocity: 1230 ft/sec (375 m/sec)

M1868 Carbine
Same action as the rifle, half-stocked, sling ring on side.

Cartridge: .56-50 Spencer
Length: 38.19in (970mm)
Weight: 8lb 8oz (3.86kg)
Barrel: 19.96in (507mm), 3 grooves, rh
Muzzle velocity: 984 ft/sec (300 m/sec)

SWITZERLAND

M1867 Engineer Rifle
Lever-operated dropping breech-block, single shot. Full-stocked, exposed muzzle.

Cartridge: 10.4 × 38R Swiss Peabody
Length: 51.57in (1310mm)
Weight: 9lb 11oz (4.40kg)
Barrel: 32.80in (833mm), 3 grooves, rh
Muzzle velocity: 1427 ft/sec (435 m/sec)

PEDERSEN USA
Springfield

T2E1 Rifle
1932. Delayed blowback, toggle system, semi-automatic. Full-stocked, half-length handguard, exposed muzzle, distinctive magazine shape. Also built under licence as the **Vickers Automatic Rifle** in Britain 1930–32.

Cartridge: .276 Pedersen T2
Length: 45.0in (1143mm)
Weight: 9lb 0oz (4.10kg)
Barrel: 24.0in (610mm), 6 grooves, rh
Magazine: 10-round box
Muzzle velocity: 2500 ft/sec (762 m/sec)

PELO Finland
Maker not known

Ca 1950. Self-loading, recoil-operated. Full-stocked, fixed box magazine, exposed muzzle, bayonet bar. Prototypes in 6.5mm Swedish and 7.92mm Mauser tested in various countries, but never adopted.

Cartridge: 7.92 × 57mm Mauser
Length: 43.30in (1100mm)
Weight: 9lb 4oz (4.19kg)
Barrel: not known
Magazine: 6- or 10-round fixed box
Muzzle velocity: 2460 ft/sec (750 m/sec)

PGM France
PGM

Model UR Intervention Sniping Rifle

Bolt action repeating rifle; components mounted on an alloy frame. Adjustable butt, pistol grip, heavy ribbed free-floating barrel, bipod mounted on fore-end.

Cartridge: 7.62 × 51mm NATO
Length: 40.55in (1030mm)
Weight: 12lb 2oz (5.50kg)
Barrel: 18.50in (470mm), 4 grooves, rh
Magazine: 5-round box
Muzzle velocity: 2625 ft/sec (800 m/sec)

Model UR Commando Sniping Rifle

Based on the UR Intervention model (*above*) but with a lighter, part-fluted barrel and a folding butt.

Cartridge: 7.62 × 51mm NATO
Length, butt extended: 40.55in (1030mm)
Length, butt folded: 29.13in (740mm)
Weight: 11 lb 3oz (5.0kg)
Barrel: 18.50in (470mm), 4 grooves, rh
Magazine: 5-round box
Muzzle velocity: 2625 ft/sec (800 m/sec)

Model Hecate II Anti-materiel Rifle

Bolt action repeater, heavy barrel with muzzle brake, adjustable butt, pistol grip, bipod attached to fore-end, monopod attached to butt.

Cartridge: .50 Browning
Length: 54.33in (1380mm)
Weight: 30lb 7oz (13.80kg)
Barrel: 27.56in (700mm), 8 grooves, rh
Magazine: 7-round box
Muzzle velocity: 2788 ft/sec (850 m/sec)

REMINGTON USA
Remington

The only Remington rifle to see extensive military service was the Remington-Rider 'rolling block' model, which was very popular in the late 19th century. The system involves a rearward-pivoting breech-block which is backed-up by a conventional hammer. The block cannot be opened unless the hammer is cocked, and when the hammer falls it interlocks with the block to prevent opening. All weapons were made by Remington, except where shown.

USA

M1870 Navy Rifle

Standard rolling block breech with hammer and smaller spur for opening the block. Full-stocked, two bands, no handguard, exposed muzzle, cleaning rod. Blued barrel, case-hardened frame

Cartridge: .50-70 US Government
Length: 48.62in (1235mm)
Weight: 9lb 1oz (4.11kg)
Barrel: 32.62in (828mm), 3 grooves, rh
Muzzle velocity: 1275 ft/sec (388 m/sec)

M1870 Carbine

Same action as rifle, but half-stocked and shorter barrel. Long sling bar on fore-end secured by through-bolt, shorter bar on butt. Trials quantity only, not accepted for service.

Cartridge: .50-70 US Government
Length: 38.50in (1235mm)
Weight: 7lb 13oz (3.54kg)
Barrel: 23.25in (590mm), 3 grooves, rh
Muzzle velocity: 1100 ft/sec (335m/sec)

M1871 Army Rifle

Similar to the Navy model but the breech mechanism is fitted with the 'Locking Action' in which the hammer drops to half-cock when the block is closed and has to be full-cocked before firing.

Cartridge: .50-70 US Government
Length: 51.75in (1314mm)
Weight: 9lb 5oz (4.22kg)
Barrel: 36.0in (914mm), 3 grooves, rh
Muzzle velocity: 1315 ft/sec (400 m/sec)

M40A1 Sniping Rifle

Ca 1965. Bolt-action repeating rifle. A Remington 700 sporting rifle 'militarised' for the US Marine Corps. Wood half-stock, heavy barrel, no iron sights, telescope mount.

Cartridge: 7.62 × 51mm NATO
Length: 43.98in (1117mm)
Weight: 14lb 8oz (6.57kg)
Barrel: 24.0in (610mm), 4 grooves, rh
Magazine: 5-round integral box
Muzzle velocity: 2550 ft/sec (777 m/sec)

DENMARK

M1867 Rifle
København & Remington

Standard rolling block action, full-stocked, exposed muzzle, cleaning rod. Bayonet bar and lug on right side.

Cartridge: 11.7 × 42R Danish Remington RF
Length: 50.39in (1280mm)
Weight: 9lb 4oz (4.20kg)
Barrel: 35.71in (907mm), 5 grooves, rh
Muzzle velocity: 1230 ft/sec (375 m/sec)

M1867 Carbine
København & Remington

As for the rifle but with half-length stock; Artillery models fitted for bayonet, Engineer and Cavalry not so fitted.

Cartridge: 11.7 × 27R Danish Remington Carbine RF
Length: 36.02in (915mm)
Weight: 6lb 15oz (3.15kg)
Barrel: 21.06in (535mm), 5 grooves, rh
Muzzle velocity: 870 ft/sec (265 m/sec)

M1867/93 Marine Rifle
København

The M1867 rifle rebuilt to fire 8mm centre-fire cartridges. New fore-end, full-length handguard, nose-cap with bayonet fittings.

Cartridge: 8 × 58R Danish Krag
Length: 36.02in (1022mm)
Weight: 6lb 15oz (3.81kg)
Barrel: 21.06in (740mm), 6 grooves, rh
Muzzle velocity: 1980 ft/sec (605 m/sec)

M1867/96 Cavalry Carbine
København
The M1867 carbine re-chambered for the 11.7mm centre-fire cartridge.

Specifications: the same, except
Cartridge: 11.7 × 51R Danish Remington
Muzzle velocity: 1345 ft/sec (410 m/sec)

EGYPT
M1868 Rifle
Standard rolling block mechanism, full-stocked, three bands, bayonet lug on right side of muzzle.

Cartridge: 11.43 × 50R Egyptian Remington
Length: 50.31in (1278mm)
Weight: 9lb 2oz (4.15kg)
Barrel: 35.0in (889mm), 5 grooves, rh
Muzzle velocity: 860 ft/sec (390 m/sec)

MEXICO
M1897 Rifle
Standard rolling block mechanism, full-stocked, exposed muzzle, cleaning rod.

Cartridge: 7 × 57mm Spanish Mauser
Length: 45.51in (1156mm)
Weight: 8lb 8oz (3.86kg)
Barrel: 30.0in (762mm), 5 grooves, rh
Muzzle velocity: 2100 ft/sec (640 m/sec)

NORWAY
M1867 Rifle
Christiana, Husqvarna & Kongsberg
Manufactured in Norway, to the standard design. Iron fittings, brass butt-plate, birch-wood full-length stock.

Cartridge: 12.17 × 44R Norwegian Remington RF
Length: 53.46in (1358mm)
Weight: 9lb 15oz (4.50kg)
Barrel: 37.32in (948mm), 5 grooves, rh
Muzzle velocity: 1247 ft/sec (380 m/sec)

M1888 Carbine
Kongsberg
M1867 rifles fitted with new short barrels for the 8mm Krag cartridge and issued to cavalry and pioneers.

Cartridge: 8 × 58R Danish Krag
Length: 40.35in (1025mm)
Weight: 8lb 6oz (3.80kg)
Barrel: 24.21in (615mm), 4 grooves, rh
Muzzle velocity: 1788 ft/sec (545 m/sec)

SPAIN
M1870 Rifle
Standard Remington product; full-stocked, exposed muzzle, cleaning rod.

Cartridge: 11.15 × 57R Spanish Remington
Length: 50.31in (1278mm)
Weight: 9lb 5oz (4.20kg)
Barrel: 35.12in (892mm), 5 grooves, rh
Muzzle velocity: 1365 ft/sec (416 m/sec)

M1870 Carbine
Oviedo
As for the rifle but shorter and with two barrel bands instead of three.

Cartridge: 11.15 × 57R Spanish Remington
Length: 42.13in (1070mm)
Weight: 8lb 10oz (3.90kg)
Barrel: 27.16in (690mm), 5 grooves, rh
Muzzle velocity: 1148 ft/sec (350 m/sec)

M1870 Short Rifle
Orbea
Locally manufactured, following the M1870 pattern but with minor variations.

Cartridge: 11.15 × 57R Spanish Remington
Length: 46.85in (1190mm)
Weight: 8lb 13oz (4.0kg)
Barrel: 32.28in (820mm), 6 grooves, rh
Muzzle velocity: 1296 ft/sec (395 m/sec)

Model 1871 Infantry Rifle
Oviedo & Placencia
Standard pattern breech, full-stocked, three barrel bands, extended muzzle, cleaning rod, bayonet fittings.

Cartridge: 11.15 × 57R Spanish Remington
Length: 51.77in (1315mm)
Weight: 9lb 0oz (4.08kg)
Barrel: 37.0in (940mm), 6 grooves, rh
Muzzle velocity: 1312 ft/sec (400 m/sec)

Model 1871 Short Rifle
Placencia
Short version of the M1871 rifle, similar in appearance but with only two barrel bands.

Cartridge: 11.15 × 57R Spanish Remington
Length: 42.52in (1080mm)
Weight: 8lb 12oz (4.00kg)
Barrel: 27.95in (710mm), 6 grooves, rh
Muzzle velocity: 1214 ft/sec (370 m/sec)

M1871 Cavalry Carbine
Same action as the M1871 rifle but half-stocked with one barrel band, sling swivels and a sling bar on the left side.

Cartridge: 11.15 × 57R Spanish Remington
Length: 37.91in (963mm)
Weight: 7lb 4oz (3.28kg)
Barrel: 23.15in (588mm), 6 grooves, rh
Muzzle velocity: 1171 ft/sec (357 m/sec)

M1871 Artillery Carbine
Oviedo
Shortened version of the M1871 rifle, full-stocked but with two barrel bands; fitted for bayonet.

Cartridge: 11.15 × 57R Spanish Remington
Length: 37.91in (963mm)
Weight: 7lb 8oz (3.47kg)
Barrel: 23.15in (588mm), 6 grooves, rh
Muzzle velocity: 1171 ft/sec (357 m/sec)

Model 1889 Dragoon Carbine
Oviedo

Even though the rolling block was virtually obsolete by 1889 the Spanish introduced this for general issue. Shortened version of the 1871 rifle, full-stocked, two bands, no bayonet.

Cartridge: 11.15 × 57R Spanish Remington
Length: 46.26in (1175mm)
Weight: 8lb 11oz (3.95kg)
Barrel: 31.57in (802mm), 6 grooves, rh
Muzzle velocity: 1453 ft/sec (443 m/sec)

RHEINMETALL Germany
Rheinmetall

FG 42 Parachutists' Rifle
Gas-operated, selective fire. Fires from a closed breech in semi-auto mode, open breech in full-auto. Straight-line configuration, left-side-mounted magazine, light bipod, integral bayonet, muzzle brake, high-set sight line.

Cartridge: 7.92 × 57mm Mauser
Length: 37.00in (940mm)
Weight: 9lb 15oz (4.53kg)
Barrel: 20.0in (508mm), 4 grooves, rh
Magazine: 20-round box
Muzzle velocity: 2500 ft/sec (761 m/sec)
Cyclic rate: 750 rds/min

Panzerbuchse 38 Anti-tank Rifle
Single-shot rifle using a semi-automatic vertical sliding breech-block which opened on recoil and closed when a fresh round was inserted. Tubular butt with curved pad, fore-end surrounds barrel and controls recoil, bipod, muzzle brake.

Cartridge: 7.92 × 94mm PzB
Length: 51.0in (1295mm)
Weight: 35lb 0oz (15.88kg)
Barrel: 43.0in (1092mm), 4 grooves, rh
Muzzle velocity: 3795 ft/sec (1210 m/sec)
Armour penetration: 30/100/60

Panzerbuchse 39 Anti-tank Rifle
Simplified and cheaper version of the PzB 38; no recoil movement of barrel, breech opened by manual operation of the pistol grip. Muzzle brake, hooded foresight.

Cartridge: 7.92 × 94mm PzB
Length: 62.25in (1581mm)
Weight: 27lb 4oz (12.43kg)
Barrel: 42.75in (1086mm), 4 grooves, rh
Muzzle velocity: 4150 ft/sec (1265 m/sec)
Armour penetration: 30/100/60

Panzerbuchse 41 Anti-tank Rifle
Designed by Solothurn AG of Switzerland, made by Rheinmetall. Recoil operated, the action sliding in a cradle supported by bipod. Left-side magazine feed.

Cartridge: 20 × 138B Long Solothurn
Length: 83.0in (2108mm)
Weight: 97lb 0oz (44.0kg)
Barrel: 35.43in (900mm), 8 grooves, rh
Magazine: 5- or 10-round box

Muzzle velocity: 2400 ft/sec (731 m/sec)
Armour penetration: 30/250/0

ROBAR USA
Robar

RC-50
Ca 1980. Conventional half-stocked bolt action rifle in .50 calibre. Bipod at tip of fore-end, small box magazine, muzzle brake, telescope sights only. Used by US forces.

Cartridge: .50 Browning
Length: 55.0in (1397mm)
Weight: 25lb 0oz (11.34kg)
Barrel: 29.0in (736mm), 8 grooves, rh
Magazine: 5-round box
Muzzle velocity: *ca* 2723 ft/sec (830 m/sec)

ROSS Canada
Ross

There were, at bottom, two basic types of Ross rifle, the 1905 and the 1910. Both used straight-pull bolts; the 1905 locked by two lugs on the bolt head, the 1910 by an interrupted multiple thread. The 1905 used a Harris Controlled Platform Magazine, which had a lever allowing the platform and spring to be depressed for easier loading, while the 1910 used a standard British-pattern .303in charger. Ross was more interested in high velocity and flat trajectory than in military serviceability and some of his commercial rifles were moderately successful. His military designs were less so. Nevertheless, a 'Military Target Rifle' in non-military .280 calibre won the US and UK rifle trophies in 1913, and the US NRA promptly re-wrote the rules to prevent it happening again.

Rifle, Ross, Mark 1
1905. As described, with Harris magazine and two-lug bolt and integral magazine concealed in the stock. Magazine cut-off. Full-stocked, short handguard, pistol-grip butt, exposed muzzle with bayonet lug on nose-cap.

Cartridge: .303 British
Length: 48.63in (1235mm)
Weight: 8lb 1oz (3.64kg)
Barrel: 28.00in (711mm), 4 grooves, rh
Magazine: 5 round integral box
Muzzle velocity: 2000 ft/sec (610 m/sec)

Rifle, Ross, Mark 2
1909. As Mark 1 but with improved sight, modified bolt cocking on opening, and chamber dimensions to British service standard.

Specifications: as for Mark 1

Rifles, Ross, Marks 2*, 2**, 2***, 2**** and 2*****
These were all variations of the Mark 2 featuring different types of sight and other small modifications. The 2** also had a 30.5in (775mm) barrel.

Rifle, Ross, Short, Mark 1.
In order to conceal the inordinate quantity of modifications which had been made, the Mark 2 was re-christened the 'Short, Mark 1' in 1912.

Rifle, Ross, Short, Mark 2
This was the Mark 2★★★ or 2★★★★★ re-named, the 'star' system of sub-mark distinction becoming somewhat cumbersome by this time.

Rifle, Ross, Short, Mark 2*
Another exercise in concealment, this was the 30.5in barrel Mark 2★★ with a new name.

Rifle, Ross, Mark 3
The first of the improved 1910 pattern with conventional box magazine in front of the trigger guard, charger-loaded, and with the interrupted multiple thread breech lock. Full-stocked, shallow pistol-grip in the butt, prominent aperture sight mounted on the receiver bridge.

Rifle, Ross, Mark 3*
As for Mark 3, but with some small changes to the bolt to improve the locking, and a new foresight.

Rifle, Ross, Mark 3B
The only Ross rifle to be formally accepted into British service (the others were confined to the Canadian Army). It was the Mark 3 or 3★ with the addition of a Lee-Enfield-style magazine cut-off.

Cartridge: .303 British
Length: 50.56in (1285mm)
Weight: 9lb 14oz (4.48kg)
Barrel: 30.15in (775mm), 4 grooves, rh
Magazine: 5 round box
Muzzle velocity: 2600 ft/sec (790 m/sec)

RUGER USA
Ruger

Mini 14/20GB Infantry Rifle
1982. Military version of the commercial Mini-14 carbine. Gas-operated, rotating bolt, semi-automatic, based on the Garand rifle system. This modification added a heat-proof fibreglass handguard, flash hider, and a front sight and bayonet lug.

Cartridge: 5.56 × 45mm M193
Length: 37.40in (950mm)
Weight: 6lb 6oz (2.90kg)
Barrel: 18.50in (470mm), 6 grooves, rh
Magazine: 5- 20- or 30-round box
Muzzle velocity: 3297 ft/sec (1005 m/sec)

AC-556 Selective Fire Weapon
1984. As for the Mini 14/20GB but with ventilated hand-guard, which extends on the right side to cover the operating rod, and a three-position selector giving single shots, three-round bursts or automatic fire.

Cartridge: 5.56 × 45mm M193
Length: 37.74in (984mm)
Weight: 6lb 6oz (2.89kg)
Barrel: 18.50in (470mm), 6 grooves, rh
Magazine: 5- 20- or 30-round box
Muzzle velocity: 3470 ft/sec (1058 m/sec)
Cyclic rate: 750 rds/min

AC-556F Selective Fire Weapon
1984. A shortened version of the AC-556 with folding steel stock, shortened fore-end with nose-cap carrying foresight and bayonet lug, flash suppressor. Rifling changed from one turn in 308mm to one turn in 254mm.

Cartridge: 5.56 × 45mm M193
Length, butt extended: 32.08in (815mm)
Length, butt folded: 23.74in (603mm)
Weight: 6lb 15oz (3.15kg)
Barrel: 13.0in (330mm), 6 grooves, rh
Magazine: 5- 20- or 30-round box
Muzzle velocity: 3470 ft/sec (1058 m/sec)
Cyclic rate: 750 rds/min

KAC-556, KAC-556F
1986. Variants of the AC-556 and AC-556F in stainless steel instead of blued steel finish.

Specifications: the same

RUSSIA
See also Berdan, Degtyarev, Federov, Kalashnikov, Mosin-Nagant, Simonov & Tokarev
This section lists various Russian rifles not associated with any specific designer. Their date of origination is not known; all were revealed in the period 1990–95. Data is that supplied by the vendors.

AS Silent Assault Rifle
Precise Engineering
Based on a shortened version of the Kalashnikov gas piston and rotating bolt system, fitted into a short receiver and allied with an integral barrel/silencer. Tubular metal butt folding to the left, pistol grip, iron sights, curved magazine. Selective fire.

Cartridge: 9 × 39mm SP-6
Length, butt extended: 34.40in (875mm)
Length, butt folded: 24.21in (615mm)
Weight: 5lb 8oz (2.50kg)
Barrel: n/a
Magazine: 20-round box
Muzzle velocity: 968 ft/sec (295 m/sec)
Cyclic rate: n/a.

VSS Silent Sniper Rifle
Precise Engineering
Generally the same as the AS rifle, but with a fixed skeleton butt with cheek-piece and mounts for various type of optical and optronic sights.

Cartridge: 9 × 39mm SP-5
Length: 39.29in (894mm)
Weight: 9lb 1oz (2.60kg)
Barrel: n/a
Magazine: 10- or 20-round box
Muzzle velocity: 968 ft/sec (295 m/sec)
Cyclic rate: n/a

APS Underwater Rifle
Precise Engineering
Appears to be broadly based on the Kalashnikov mechanism, with gas cylinder above the barrel. Unique deep curved magazine, pistol grip, folding butt, selective fire.

Cartridge: 5.66mm MPS
Length, butt extended: 33.07in (840mm)
Length, butt folded: 24.17in (614mm)
Weight: 5lb 5oz (2.40kg)
Barrel: n/a
Magazine: 26-round box
Muzzle velocity: 1198 ft/sec (365 m/sec) in air
Cyclic rate: n/a

AS-94 Assault Rifle
Izhmash

Gas-operated. Receiver similar to the Kalashnikov series, but the gas cylinder is under the barrel. L-shaped butt, pistol grip, curved magazine. Selective fire with two-round burst.

Cartridge: 5.45 × 39.5mm
Length: 37.12in (943mm)
Weight: 8lb 8oz (3.85kg)
Barrel: n/a
Magazine: 30-round box
Muzzle velocity: *ca* 2952 ft/sec (900 m/sec)
Cyclic rate: 600 rds/min

V-94 Anti-materiel Rifle
KBP

Reminiscent of the Simonov PTRS anti-tank rifle: long barrel, muzzle brake, bipod, pistol grip, wooden butt. No iron sights, fitted for telescope. Gas operated, semi-automatic. Large locking lever on the receiver allows the receiver and butt to be disconnected from the barrel and folded around for compact carrying.

Cartridge: 12.7 × 108mm DShK
Length, in firing position: 66.93in (1700mm)
Length, folded for carrying: 43.30in (1100mm)
Weight: 25lb 13oz (11.70kg)
Barrel: 40.16in (1020mm), 8 grooves, rh
Magazine: 5-round box
Muzzle velocity: 2790 ft/sec (850 m/sec)

SAKO Finland
Sako

Sako originated as a government factory in the 1920s and made the M1928 and later Mosin-Nagant rifles for the Finnish Army. After 1944 the company concentrated on commercial sporting weapons until it was amalgamated with Valmet (*qv*) in 1987.

TRG-21

Bolt-action repeater, Half-stocked, no handguard, deeply curved pistol-grip butt with cheek-piece. Cold-hammered barrel with muzzle brake. Bipod. Telescope sight mount, emergency iron sights.

Cartridge: 7.62 × 51mm NATO
Length: 45.28in (1150mm)
Weight: 10lb 6oz (4.70kg)
Barrel: 26.00in (660mm), 4 grooves, rh
Magazine: 10-round box
Muzzle velocity: 2821 ft/sec (860 m/sec)

TRG-41

This is the same rifle as the TRG-21 but chambered for the .338 Lapua Magnum cartridge, resulting in some changed dimensions.

Cartridge: .338 Lapua Magnum
Length: 47.24in (1200mm)
Weight: 11lb 4oz (5.10kg)
Barrel: 27.16in (690mm), 4 grooves, rh
Magazine: 5-round box
Muzzle velocity: 2998 ft/sec (914 m/sec)

M90

Sako's improved Kalashnikov, to follow the earlier Valmet designs into Finnish service. Kalashnikov gas-operated rotating bolt action but refined and lightened. Kalashnikov-type receiver and safety latch; curved, ribbed, magazine. Prominent flash eliminator/grenade launcher muzzle. Side-folding tubular steel butt.

Cartridge: 7.62 × 39mm Soviet M1943
Length, butt extended: 36.61in (930mm)
Length, butt folded: 26.57in (675mm)
Weight: 8lb 8oz (3.85kg)
Barrel: 16.38in (416mm), 4 grooves, rh
Magazine: 30-round box
Muzzle velocity: 2625 ft/sec (800 m/sec)
Cyclic rate: 700 rds/min

SCHMIDT-RUBIN Switzerland
Bern

M1889 Infantry Rifle

Straight-pull bolt action with two lugs on the bolt sleeve locking in front of receiver lugs. Prominent box magazine and rear sight ramp. Full-stocked, exposed muzzle with foresight ahead of the nose-cap. Ring cocking-piece.

Cartridge: 7.5 × 53mm Swiss M1890
Length: 51.26in (1302mm)
Weight: 10lb 11oz (4.85kg)
Barrel: 30.71in (780mm), 3 grooves, rh
Magazine: 12-round box
Muzzle velocity: 1968 ft/sec (600 m/sec)

M1889/96 Infantry Rifle

Improvement on the M1889 by moving the bolt lugs to the front of the bolt sleeve to strengthen the action.

Cartridge: 7.5 × 53mm Swiss M1890
Length: 51.18in (1300mm)
Weight: 9lb 15oz (4.51kg)
Barrel: 30.71in (780mm), 3 grooves, rh
Magazine: 12-round box
Muzzle velocity: 1968 ft/sec (600 m/sec)

M1897 Cadet Rifle

Shorter and lighter variant of the M1889/96, using the improved bolt mechanism. Single-shot only, no magazine.

Cartridge: 7.5 × 53mm Swiss M1890
Length: 43.50in (1105mm)
Weight: 7lb 13oz (3.53kg)
Barrel: 23.30in (592mm), 3 grooves, rh
Muzzle velocity: 1853 ft/sec (565 m/sec)

M1900 Short Rifle
Shorter and lighter version of the M1889/96 with reduced-capacity magazine. Or, looked at another way, a cadet rifle with a magazine.

Cartridge: 7.5 x 53mm Swiss M1890
Length: 43.50in (1105mm)
Weight: 8lb 6oz (3.79kg)
Barrel: 23.30in (592mm), 3 grooves, rh
Magazine: 6-round box
Muzzle velocity: 1853 ft/sec (565 m/sec)

M1905 Cavalry Carbine
M1896 action, stocked to the muzzle, sling slot in the butt, no bayonet fittings.

Cartridge: 7.5 x 53mm Swiss M1890
Length: 42.12in (1070mm)
Weight: 8lb 0oz (3.63kg)
Barrel: 21.65in (550mm), 3 grooves, rh
Magazine: 6-round box
Muzzle velocity: 1805 ft/sec (550 m/sec)

M1911 Infantry Rifle
Improved and stronger bolt system, smaller magazine. Full-stocked, flatter sight. New rifling.

Cartridge: 7.5 x 55mm Swiss M1911
Length: 51.65in (1312mm)
Weight: 10lb 2oz (4.62kg)
Barrel: 30.71in (780mm), 4 grooves, rh
Magazine: 6-round box
Muzzle velocity: 2600 ft/sec (790 m/sec)

M1911 Carbine
Shorter version of the rifle, using the same action. Full-stocked.

Cartridge: 7.5 x 55mm Swiss M1911
Length: 43.40in (1100mm)
Weight: 8lb 10oz (3.93kg)
Barrel: 23.30in (590mm), 4 grooves, rh
Magazine: 6-round box
Muzzle velocity: 2500 ft/sec (760 m/sec)

M1931 Short Rifle
Straight-pull bolt, similar principle but much shorter action, bringing the magazine back to the trigger guard. Full-stocked, exposed muzzle.

Cartridge: 7.5 x 55mm Swiss M1911
Length: 43.50in (1105mm)
Weight: 8lb 13oz (4.01kg)
Barrel: 25.70in (655mm), 4 grooves, rh
Magazine: 6-round box
Muzzle velocity: 2550 ft/sec (775 m/sec)

SCHUTZ & LARSEN Denmark
Schutz & Larsen

M1942 Police Carbine
Turnbolt action repeating rifle, four-lug bolt, full-stocked to the muzzle, short handguard. Cylindrical receiver, oval ejection slot, integral magazine with removable floor-plate.

Cartridge: 8 x 58R Danish Krag
Length: 43.62in (1108mm)
Weight: 8lb 11oz (3.93kg)

Barrel: 22.64in (575mm), 4 grooves, rh
Magazine: 4-round integral box
Muzzle velocity: 2133 ft/sec (650 m/sec)

SIG Switzerland
SIG
Schweizer Industrie Gesellschaft, Neuhausen-am-Rheinfalls. SIG has manufactured rifles and machine guns since the mid-19th century, but its own designs of military weapons did not begin to prosper until the 1930s and came into their full inheritance in the post WWII period.

SK46 Rifle
Gas-operated semi-automatic, locking by tilting the breech-block. Full-stocked, exposed muzzle, piling hook, box magazine well in front of trigger-guard; appears to be modelled upon the Schmidt-Rubin rifle. Offered for export sale but few takers.

Cartridge: 7.92 x 57mm Mauser, and others
Length: 44.25in (1125mm)
Weight: 10lb 0oz (4.54kg)
Barrel: 23.63in (600mm), 4 grooves, rh
Magazine: 5- or 10-round box
Muzzle velocity: 2700 ft/sec (823 m/sec)

AK53 Rifle
A most unusual selective-fire rifle using the blow-forward system, with a fixed breech-block and a moving barrel. Straight wrist wooden butt and half-stock, barrel with jacket, muzzle brake, large curved magazine with slot showing contents.

Cartridge: 7.5 x 55mm Swiss M1911
Length: 39.37in (1000mm)
Weight: 10lb 12oz (4.90kg)
Barrel: 23.63in (600mm), 4 grooves, lh
Magazine: 30-round box
Muzzle velocity: 2450 ft/sec (750 m/sec)
Cyclic rate: 300 rds/min

Stgw 57 Assault Rifle
Delayed blowback, selective fire; uses the roller-delayed breech system which originated with the Mauser StG 45 and was developed by CETME, assisted by gas delivery via flutes in the chamber. Pressed steel receiver, short ventilated metal fore-end, folding bipod, rubber-covered wood butt, perforated barrel jacket, carrying handle, muzzle formed into grenade launcher and compensator.

Cartridge: 7.5 x 55mm Swiss M1911
Length: 43.40in (1102mm)
Weight: 12lb 5oz (5.59kg)
Barrel: 20.47in (520mm), 4 grooves, lh
Magazine: 24-round box
Muzzle velocity: 2493 ft/sec (760 m/sec)
Cyclic rate: 475 rds/min

SG510 Assault Rifle
This is the same weapon as the Stgw 57 above but in a variety of forms for export. The **SG510-1** was chambered for the 7.62 x 51mm NATO (M38) cartridge. The **SG510-2** fired the same cartridge but was lighter in construction. The **SG510-3** fired the Soviet 7.62 x 39mm cartridge and was smaller in all dimensions. None of these was ever

made in quantity. The **SG510-4** (specifications below) replaced the 510-1 as the 7.62 x 51mm member of the group. It differed from the Stgw 57 in having a wooden butt and fore-end, a bipod which folded on to the top of the barrel, and in dimensions.

Cartridge: 7.62 x 51mm NATO
Length: 40.0in (1016mm)
Weight: 9lb 6oz (4.25kg)
Barrel: 19.88in (505mm), 4 grooves, rh
Magazine: 20-round box
Muzzle velocity: 2592 ft/sec (790 m/sec)
Cyclic rate: 500 rds/min

SG530 Assault Rifle.

Virtually a scaled-down Stgw 57 chambered for the 5.56mm cartridge, but since the cartridge did not lend itself to the SIG delayed blowback system, operation changed to gas piston which withdrew the locking rollers. Pressed steel receiver, synthetic furniture, M16-type fore-end/hand-guard, gas cylinder exposed at front of handguard, long slender barrel with compensator and grenade rings. Although an excellent weapon it was too expensive to produce and was replaced by the SG540.

Cartridge: 5.56 x 45mm M193
Length: 37.0in (940mm)
Weight: 7lb 8oz (3.45kg)
Barrel: 15.50in (394mm), 4 grooves, rh
Magazine: 30-round box
Muzzle velocity: 3000 ft/sec (912 m/sec)
Cyclic rate: 600 rds/min

SG540 Assault Rifle
FAMAE, INDEP & Manurhin

Designed by SIG, manufactured under licence by Manurhin of France, of Portugal and FAMAE of Chile. Adopted by numerous armies. Gas-operated, selective fire, locking by rotating bolt. Pressed-steel receiver, pistol grip, synthetic furniture, solid or folding tubular steel butt, muzzle-compensator/grenade launcher.

Cartridge: 5.56 x 45mm NATO
Length, fixed or extended butt: 37.40in (950mm)
Length, butt folded: 28.35in (720mm)
Weight, fixed butt: 7lb 3oz (3.26kg)
Weight, folding butt: 7lb 1oz (3.21kg)
Barrel: 18.11in (460mm), 6 grooves, rh
Magazine: 20- or 30-round box
Muzzle velocity: 3215 ft/sec (980 m/sec)
Cyclic rate: 700 rds/min

SG542 Assault Rifle

Similar design to the SG540 but chambered for the 7.62mm NATO cartridge.

Cartridge: 7.62 x 51mm NATO
Length, fixed or extended butt: 39.37in (1000mm)
Length, butt folded: 29.68in (754mm)
Weight, fixed or folding butt: 7lb 13oz (3.55kg)
Barrel: 18.31in (465mm), 4 grooves, rh
Magazine: 20- or 30-round box
Muzzle velocity: 2690 ft/sec (820 m/sec)
Cyclic rate: 650 rds/min

SG543 Assault Carbine

Short-barrelled carbine version of the SG540, with fixed or folding butt.

Cartridge: 5.56 x 45mm NATO
Length, fixed or extended butt: 31.69in (805mm)
Length, butt folded: 22.40in (569mm)
Weight, fixed butt: 6lb 8oz (2.95kg)
Weight, folding butt: 6lb 10oz (3.0kg)
Barrel: 11.81in (300mm), 6 grooves, rh
Magazine: 20- or 30-round box
Muzzle velocity: 2870 ft/sec (875 m/sec)
Cyclic rate: 750 rds/min

Stgw 90 Assault Rifle SG550

1986. Designed to replace the Stgw 57 with a 5.56mm weapon. Generally follows the design of the SG540 and is an improved version, using the same gas system. Selective fire with three-round bursts, more use of synthetic materials, translucent magazine with attachment slots and studs so that two or three can be clipped side-by-side for quick changing. Made in folding-butt style only, with light bipod.

Cartridge: 5.56 x 45mm NATO
Length, butt extended: 39.29in (998mm)
Length, butt folded: 30.39in (772mm)
Weight: 9lb 1oz (4.1kg)
Barrel: 20.79in (528mm), 6 grooves, rh
Magazine: 20- or 30-round box
Muzzle velocity: 3215 ft/sec (980 m/sec)
Cyclic rate: 700 rds/min

Stgw 90 Assault Carbine SG551

Short-barrelled version of the Stgw 90 rifle. No bipod.

Cartridge: 5.56 x 45mm NATO
Length, butt extended: 32.55in (827mm)
Length, butt folded: 23.68in (601mm)
Weight: 7lb 8oz (3.40kg)
Barrel: 14.64in (372mm), 6 grooves, rh
Magazine: 20- or 30-round box
Muzzle velocity: 3018 ft/sec (920 m/sec)
Cyclic rate: 700 rds/min

SG550 Sniper

Semi-automatic version of the Stgw 90 assault rifle, with heavy extended barrel, no muzzle attachments, no iron sights, folding adjustable-length butt with cheek-rest, adjustable bipod, hand stop on pistol grip. Double-pull trigger.

Cartridge: 5.56 x 45mm NATO
Length, butt extended: 44.48in (1130mm)
Length, butt folded: 35.62in (905mm)
Weight: 15lb 8oz (7.02kg)
Barrel: 25.59in (650mm), 6 grooves, rh
Magazine: 20- or 30-round box
Muzzle velocity: 3215 ft/sec (980 m/sec)

SG551-1P/SIG 551 SWAT

1993. Described as a 'Law Enforcement Rifle' this is a modified SG551 selective fire carbine with telescope sight, folding butt with cheek-piece, ventilated fore-end and new lightweight transparent magazines. Originally called the 551-1P, it was re-launched as the 551 SWAT in 1996.

Cartridge: 5.56 x 45mm NATO
Length, butt extended: 32.79in (833mm)
Length, butt folded: 23.90in (607mm)
Weight: 7lb 8oz (3.40kg)
Barrel: 14.29in (363mm), 6 grooves, rh
Magazine: 5-, 20- or 30-round box
Muzzle velocity: 3018 ft/sec (920 m/sec)
Cyclic rate: 700 rds/min

SG550/551SP

These are commercial versions of the SG550 and 551, intended as sporting weapons or for police and security use. They are restricted to semi-automatic firing and cannot be converted to automatic operation.

Specifications: as for the military weapons

SIG552 Commando

An ultra-short semi-automatic version of the SG551 SWAT with the cheek-piece and other controls arranged for use by left- or right-handed firers.

Cartridge: 5.56 x 45mm NATO
Length, butt extended: 28.74in (730mm)
Length, butt folded: 19.84in (504mm)
Weight: 7lb 1oz (3.2kg)
Barrel: 8.90in (226mm), 6 grooves, rh
Magazine: 5-, 20- or 30-round box
Muzzle velocity: 2379 ft/sec (725 m/sec)

SIG-Sauer SSG 2000 Sniping Rifle

1990. Based on the short-throw bolt action of the Sauer 80/90 sporting and target rifle. The non-rotating bolt uses hinged lugs which are driven out by cams to lock into the receiver as the bolt handle is turned down. Half-length stock, fully-adjustable pistol-grip butt, heavy barrel with muzzle compensator, no iron sights, fore-end rail for bipod, sling or hand-rest. Produced in various calibres.

Cartridge: 7.62 x 51mm NATO
Length: 47.63in (1210mm)
Weight: 14lb 8oz (6.60kg)
Barrel: 24.0in (610mm), 4 grooves, rh
Magazine: 4-round box
Muzzle velocity: 2690 ft/sec (820 m/sec)

SIG-Sauer SSG 3000 Sniping Rifle

1992. Based on the Sauer 200STR target rifle, with cam-locked bolt as described above. Modular; barrel and receiver joined by screw clamps, trigger unit and magazine in one forged assembly which slots into the receiver. Bolt locks directly into barrel. Half-stocked, ventilated fore-end, heavy barrel with muzzle compensator, no iron sights, adjustable butt, adjustable bipod.

Cartridge: 7.62 x 51mm NATO
Length: 46.45in (1180mm)
Weight: 11lb 14oz (5.40kg)
Barrel: 24.0in (610mm), 4 grooves, rh
Magazine: 5-round box
Muzzle velocity: 2690 ft/sec (820 m/sec)

SIMONOV Russia
State factories
AVS-36

1936. Gas-operated semi-automatic, bolt locked by rising wedge. Full-stocked, three-quarter length handguard leaving front end of gas cylinder exposed. Muzzle brake, hooded foresight, bayonet lugs. Cylindrical receiver, box magazine.

Cartridge: 7.62 x 54R Russian
Length: 48.10in (1220mm)
Weight: 9lb 8oz (4.37kg)
Barrel: 24.4in (620mm), 4 grooves, rh
Magazine: 15-round box
Muzzle velocity: 2550 ft/sec (776 m/sec)

SKS

1946. Gas-operated, semi-automatic, locking by tipping bolt. Half-stocked, half-length handguard, half of barrel and gas cylinder exposed. Hooded foresight, folding bayonet, wedge-shaped box magazine.

Cartridge: 7.62 x 39mm Soviet M1943
Length: 40.20in (1022mm)
Weight: 8lb 8oz (3.86kg)
Barrel: 20.50in (520mm), 4 grooves, rh
Magazine: 10-round box
Muzzle velocity: 2410 ft/sec (735 m/sec)

PTRS41 Anti-tank Rifle

Semi-automatic, gas operated via piston, carrier and rotating bolt. Clip-loaded magazine, muzzle brake, bipod.

Cartridge: 14.5 x 114mm Soviet
Length: 84.0in (2006mm)
Weight: 46lb 0oz (20.96kg)
Barrel: 48.0in (1216mm), 8 grooves, rh
Magazine: 5-round box
Muzzle velocity: 3320 ft/sec (1010 m/sec)
Armour penetration: 23/500/0

YUGOSLAVIA
Zastava Arms
M59 Rifle

1959. The M59 was simply an identical copy of the Simonov SKS made under licence in Yugoslavia. Its appearance and dimensions were exactly the same as the Soviet weapon, only the markings differing.

M59/66 Rifle

1967. This was a locally-developed improvement on the earlier Model 59 and differed in having the muzzle extended and formed into a grenade launcher. It also had an associated ladder-type grenade-launching sight which folded down flat behind the foresight and was retained by the gas regulator cut-off valve catch. Thus, to erect the sight it was necessary to press in the catch, which reminded the firer to turn off the gas flow to the cylinder and piston when launching a grenade.

Cartridge: 7.62 x 39mm Soviet M1943
Length: 44.09in (1120mm)
Weight: 9lb 0oz (4.10kg)
Barrel: 24.33in (618mm), 4 grooves, rh

Magazine: 10-round box
Muzzle velocity: 2410 ft/sec (735 m/sec)

SNIDER USA

Although Jacob Snider was an American, this system was never used in the USA.

BRITAIN

Pattern I Rifled Musket
BSA, Enfield & LSA
1866. Snider conversion of the Enfield Rifled Musket Pattern 1853. The conversion was the insertion of a side-hinged breech-block with firing pin, thus converting muzzle-loading rifled muskets into breech-loaders. The face of the block was counter-sunk for the base of the cartridge.

Cartridge: .577 Snider
Length (with bayonet): 72.5in (1841mm)
Weight: 10lb 0oz (4.53kg)
Barrel: 39.0in (990mm), 3 grooves, rh
Muzzle velocity: 1240 ft/sec (378 m/sec)

Pattern I*
BSA, Enfield & LSA
1867. As for Pattern 1, but with the countersink having a squared edge rather than a rounded one. Pattern 1 arms were converted to P1★.

Pattern 2*
BSA, Enfield & LSA
1867. 'Arms made originally with the squared countersink but without other minor improvements'. Note that no Pattern 2 was ever made.

Pattern 2**
BSA, Enfield & LSA
1867. Arms made with the squared countersink and with a new extractor, the underside of the block truly circular so as to support the entire base of the cartridge, and improvements to the hammer.

Cartridge: .577 Snider
Length: 54.25in (1378mm)
Weight: 9lb 2oz (4.14kg)
Barrel: 36.50in (927mm), 3 grooves, rh
Muzzle velocity: 1240 ft/sec (378 m/sec)

Short Enfield Rifle P60
BSA, Enfield, LSA, NA&ACo & Sparkbrook
1867. Snider conversion to the Pattern 2★★ standard.

Cartridge: .577 Snider
Length: 48.70in (1237mm)
Weight: 8lb 12oz (3.97kg)
Barrel: 30.50in (775mm), 5 grooves, rh
Muzzle velocity: 1200 ft/sec (365 m/sec)

Artillery Carbine P61
Bonehill, BSA, Enfield, LSA & Sparkbrook
1867. Snider conversion to the Pattern 2★★ standard.

Cartridge: .577 Snider
Length: 40.25in (1022mm)
Weight: 7lb 8oz (3.40kg)
Barrel: 21.50in (546mm), 5 grooves, rh
Muzzle velocity: 1005 ft/sec (306 m/sec)

Cavalry Carbine P61
Bonehill, BSA, Enfield, LSA & Sparkbrook
1867. Snider conversion to the Pattern 2★★ standard.

Cartridge: .577 Snider
Length: 37.38in (950mm)
Weight: 6lb 10oz (3.0kg)
Barrel: 19.25in (489mm), 5 grooves, rh
Muzzle velocity: 995 ft/sec (303 m/sec)

Naval Rifle P58
BSA, Enfield, LSA & Sparkbrook
1867. Snider conversion to the Pattern 2★★ standard.

Constabulary Carbine
Enfield & Sparkbrook
1867. Conversion from Rifle, Short, P56. For Royal Irish Constabulary.

Cartridge: .577 Snider
Length: 41.10in (1044mm)
Weight: 7lb 5oz (3.32kg)
Barrel: 22.50in (571mm), 3 grooves, rh
Muzzle velocity: 1020 ft/sec (310 m/sec)

Rifle, Pattern 1853, Snider, Improved Action 1868, Interchangeable, Mark 3
Bonehill
1869. Similar to the Enfield Rifle Pattern 2★★ but steel barrel instead of iron; a locking bolt is fitted to the breech-block; hammer face squared instead of recessed; other minor changes consequent upon these arms being of new manufacture rather than conversions.

Carbine, B.L., Rifled, Snider, Yeomanry, Mark I
Sparkbrook
1880. Converted from the Snider 1853 Rifle, used the Mark 3 action, differed from the ordinary Snider cavalry carbine by being one inch longer in the stock.

Cartridge: .577 Snider
Length: 37.88in (962mm)
Weight: 7lb 0oz (3.17kg)
Barrel: 21.63in (549mm), 3 grooves, rh
Muzzle velocity: 995 ft/sec (303 m/sec)

SOLOTHURN Switzerland
Steyr

S18/100 Anti-tank Rifle
Recoil-operated semi-automatic. Barrel recoils inside receiver, checked by prominent hydro-pneumatic shock absorber above barrel. Butt formed at end of receiver. Bipod on cradle, monopod under butt. Left side mounted magazine.

Cartridge: 20 x 105B Short Solothurn
Length: 69.25in (1760mm)
Weight: 99lb 3oz (45.0kg)
Barrel: 35.40in (900mm), 4 grooves, rh
Magazine: 5- or 10-round box
Muzzle velocity: 2500 ft/sec (762 m/sec)
Armour penetration: 27/300/0

SPENCER USA

Note that the nomenclature of Spencer cartridges does not refer to the calibre of the weapon but to the dimensions of case mouth and base; the .56-56 was actually .52 calibre, and the .56-50 was .50 calibre

M1861 Rifle
Spencer

Full-stocked, no handguard, exposed muzzle. Straight wrist buttstock slab-sided brass or iron receiver with outside hammer and operating lever forming part of trigger guard. Pivoting breech-block with tubular cartridge magazine inserted into the stock via the butt-plate. 12,741 purchased by US Army and Navy. Navy models had shorter fore-end and a bayonet lug.

Cartridge: .56-56 Spencer
Length: 47.0in (1194mm)
Weight: 10lb 0oz (4.54kg)
Barrel: 30.0in (762mm), 6 grooves, rh
Magazine: 7-round tube
Muzzle velocity: 950 ft/sec (290 m/sec)

M1861 Carbine
Spencer

Similar action to the M1861 Rifle, but shorter barrel with short fore-end and longer unsupported portion of barrel.

Cartridge: .56-56 Spencer
Length: 39.0in (991mm)
Weight: 8lb 4oz (3.74kg)
Barrel: 22.0in (559mm), 6 grooves, rh
Magazine: 7-round tube
Muzzle velocity: 930 ft/sec (283 m/sec)

M1861/67 Carbine conversion
Springfield

A conversion of the M1861 carbine by Springfield Armory, re-sleeving the barrel to .50 calibre and fitting a cut-off to the magazine, the control for which is just in front of the trigger.

Specifications: similar, except
Cartridge: .56-50 Spencer
Rifling: 3 grooves
Muzzle velocity: *ca* 1075 ft/sec (327 m/sec)

M1865 Rifle
Spencer

Similar to the M1861 model rifle but in .56-50 chambering.

Specifications: as above, except
Muzzle velocity: *ca* 1125 ft/sec (343 m/sec)

M1865 Carbine
Spencer

Generally as for the M1861 but chambered for the .56-50 cartridge. About 23,000 made, about half fitted with cut-off

M1865 contract Carbine
Burnside

Identical to the M1865 Spencer-made carbine but with 3-groove rifling; about half fitted with cut-off.

M1867 Rifle
Spencer

Identical to the M1865 rifle but marked M1867; about 7000 made, unknown proportion fitted with Spencer's patent magazine cut-off which was attached to the top of the breech-block.

M1867 Carbine
Spencer

As for the M1865 but usually with Spencer magazine cut-off on breech-block.

New Model Rifle
Spencer

1868. Identical to the M1867 rifle but marked 'N.M.' May have bayonet lug beneath barrel for sword bayonet or simply use the front sight as the lug for the standard army socket bayonet.

New Model Carbine
Spencer

1868. As for the M1867 carbine but marked 'N.M.'

M1871 Rifle conversion
Springfield

A conversion of 1108 M1865 carbines to infantry rifles by replacing the barrel, Standard butt and action, new barrel, full-stocked, no handguard, two barrel bands, exposed muzzle and cleaning rod in fore-end. Original form of cut-off fitted.

Cartridge: .56-50 Spencer
Length: 49.50in (1257mm)
Weight: 10lb 10oz (4.82kg)
Barrel: 32.50in (825mm), 3 grooves, rh
Magazine: 7-round tube
Muzzle velocity: 1120 ft/sec (341 m/sec)

SPRINGFIELD USA
Springfield

The early Springfield conversions from muzzle-loading rifles are dealt with under Allin, *above*. All weapons except the M1903A4 were made by Springfield Armory, plus the additional makers shown.

M1901 Rifle

Turnbolt, licensed Mauser two-lug design, integral charger-loaded magazine. Full-stocked, full-length handguard, exposed muzzle. Typical flared knob on cocking piece. Rod bayonet carried in fore-end. Only built in trials numbers.

Cartridge: .30 M1901
Length: 49.25in (1251mm)
Weight: 9lb 8oz (4.31kg)
Barrel: 30.0in (762mm), 4 grooves, lh
Magazine: 5-round integral box
Muzzle velocity: 2300 ft/sec (701 m/sec)

M1903 Rifle

Similar to the M1901 but a short rifle so as to do away with the rifle/carbine distinction. Rod bayonet; changed in 1905 to sword bayonet and nose-cap modified.

Cartridge: .30-03 Springfield
Length: 43.41in (1103mm)
Weight: 8lb 8oz (3.85kg)
Barrel: 24.21in (615mm), 4 grooves, lh

Magazine: 5-round integral box
Muzzle velocity: 2300 ft/sec (701 m/sec)

In 1906 an improved cartridge, the .30-06, was adopted; this raised the muzzle velocity to 2805 ft/sec (855 m/sec).

M1903 Mark I The Pedersen Device

Conversion of M1903 rifles by removing the bolt and inserting a blowback pistol mechanism, feeding from an obliquely mounted box magazine. It fired a specially-designed pistol-type cartridge and was intended to deliver constant firepower during an infantry assault. It was never used in action and most were scrapped in the 1920s. The rifles converted for this device can be recognised by the ejection port cut through the left receiver wall.

Dimensions: the same

M1903A1

1929. The standard M1903 rifle fitted with a pistol-grip buttstock.

Cartridge: .30-06 Springfield
Length: 43.50in (1105mm)
Weight: 8lb 0oz (3.85kg)
Barrel: 24.21in (615mm), 4 grooves, lh
Magazine: 5-round integral box
Muzzle velocity: 2805 ft/sec (855 m/sec)

M1903A2

This is not a personal weapon but a rifle barrel mounted in blocks to fit inside an artillery piece for sub-calibre practice.

M1903A3
Remington & Smith-Corona

1942. Re-design of the M1903A1 to facilitate mass production. Aperture sight adopted.

Cartridge: .30-06 Springfield
Length: 43.25in (1098mm)
Weight: 8lb 13oz (4.00kg)
Barrel: 24.00in (610mm), 2 or 4 grooves, lh
Magazine: 5-round integral box
Muzzle velocity: 2805 ft/sec (855 m/sec)

M1903A4
Remington

Sniping rifle version, recognisable by the absence of iron sights. Various types of telescope fitted.

Cartridge: .30-06 Springfield
Length: 43.21in (1097mm)
Weight: 9lb 2oz (4.14kg)
Barrel: 24.00in (610mm), 4 grooves, lh
Magazine: 5-round integral box
Muzzle velocity: 2805 ft/sec (855 m/sec)

STEYR-MANNLICHER Austria
Steyr

Mannlicher, Mauser and similar arms made by Steyr are dealt with in the appropriate sections.

AUG Rifle

Armee Universal Gewehr. 1977. Developed to meet Austrian Army specification for assault rifle. Adopted by them as the StuG 77. Bullpup design, synthetic casing with barrel, receiver and firing mechanism modules inserted.

Modules may be exchanged to produce different sizes of weapon. Casing may be olive drab, sand or black self-coloured. Gas-operated by rotating bolt, selective fire capability. Optical 1.4x sight in carrying handle. Translucent plastic magazine. Folding forward hand grip. Later adopted by the armed forces of Oman, Morocco, Ireland, Australia, and New Zealand.

Cartridge: 5.56 × 45mm M193 or NATO
Length: 31.10in (790mm)
Weight: 7lb 15oz (3.60kg)
Barrel: 20.0in (508mm), 6 grooves, rh
Magazine: 30-round box
Muzzle velocity: 3182 ft/sec (970m/sec)
Cyclic rate: 650 rds/min

AUG Carbine

Basic units as for the rifle, but with shorter barrel.

Cartridge: 5.56 × 45mm M193 or NATO
Length: 27.16in (690mm)
Weight: 7lb 5oz (3.30kg)
Barrel: 16.02in (407mm), 6 grooves, rh
Magazine: 30-round box
Muzzle velocity: 3133 ft/sec (950 m/sec)
Cyclic rate: 700 rds/min

AUG Submachine Gun

An even shorter variant, rarely encountered.

Cartridge: 5.56 × 45mm M193 or NATO
Length: 24.65in (626mm)
Weight: 6lb 11oz (3.05kg)
Barrel: 13.78in (350mm), 6 grooves, rh
Magazine: 30-round box
Muzzle velocity: 3050 ft/sec (930 m/sec)
Cyclic rate: 700 rds/min

AUG/HB

Heavy-barrelled version with bipod and larger magazine, for use as a light machine gun.

Cartridge: 5.56 × 45mm M193 or NATO
Length: 35.43in (900mm)
Weight: 10lb 13oz (4.90kg)
Barrel: 24.45in (621mm), 6 grooves, rh
Magazine: 30- or 42-round box
Muzzle velocity: 3280 ft/sec (1000 m/sec)
Cyclic rate: 680 rds/min

SSG69 Sniping Rifle

1969. Turnbolt action repeater; six-lug bolt, bolt handle swept back, half-stocked in synthetic material, pistol-grip butt. Rotary (Schoenauer pattern) magazine with spool removable via floor-plate. There are several variants of the SSG69, with heavy barrels, short barrels, silencers etc.

Cartridge: 7.62 × 51mm NATO or .243 Winchester
Length: 44.88in (1140mm)
Weight: 8lb 9oz (3.90kg)
Barrel: 25.60in (650mm), 4 grooves, rh
Magazine: 5-round rotary
Muzzle velocity: 2822 ft/sec (860 m/sec)

IWS 2000/AMR 5075 Anti-materiel Rifle

1990. Originally called the AMR, later renamed Individual Weapon System 2000. Heavy weapon, squared-off receiver, cylindrical cradle containing recoil system wrapped around the barrel, large multi-baffle muzzle brake, bipod, telescope sight. Smoothbore, long recoil, semi-automatic firing fin-stabilised projectiles.

Cartridge: 15.2mm AMR
Length: 70.87in (1800mm)
Weight: 39lb 11oz (18.0kg)
Barrel: 47.24in (1200mm), smoothbore
Magazine: 5-round box
Muzzle velocity: 4757 ft/sec (1450 m/sec)

STONER USA
M63A1 Rifle
Cadillac Gage

Although never taken into military service, this modular rifle was something of a milestone in development and is frequently referred to. Designed by Eugene Stoner and made by Cadillac Gage, the system had 15 modules which could be assembled into rifle, carbine and light machine gun formats. The basic operation system was direct gas impingement, using a gas tube above the barrel and a bolt carrier and rotating bolt.

Cartridge: 5.56 × 45mm M193
Length: 40.25in (1023mm)
Weight: 7lb 12oz (3.56kg)
Barrel: 20.0in (508mm), 6 grooves, rh
Magazine: 30-round box
Muzzle velocity: 3250 ft/sec (988 m/sec)
Cyclic rate: 700 rds/min

SR50 Anti-materiel Rifle
Knight

1996. Semi-automatic, gas-operated by direct gas impingement, rotating bolt. Straight-line layout of butt pad, cylindrical receiver, short smooth jacket and long barrel with muzzle brake. Side-feeding magazine, bipod attached to jacket.

Cartridge: .50 Browning
Length: 58.38in (1483mm)
Weight: 31lb 7oz (14.28kg)
Barrel: 35.50in (902mm), 8 grooves, rh
Magazine: 10-round box
Muzzle velocity: *ca* 2887 ft/sec (880 m/sec)

SWINBURN Britain
Model 1875 Rifle
Westley Richards

Lever-action dropping block similar to the Martini in action and appearance though with a longer operating lever. Full-stocked, exposed muzzle, cleaning rod, no handguard.

Cartridge: .577/450 Martini-Henry
Length: 49.50in (1257mm)
Weight: 9lb 5oz (4.22kg)
Barrel: 33.0in (838mm), 7 grooves, rh
Muzzle velocity: 1350 ft/sec (411m/sec)

TAIWAN
Maker not known

Type 65 Assault Rifle

Resembling the M16, this actually uses the piston-type rotating bolt system from the ArmaLite AR18 rifle. Plastic handguard, block backsight, foresight on nose-cap, no carrying handle.

Cartridge: 5.56 × 45mm M193
Length: 38.97in (990mm)
Weight: 6lb 15oz (3.17kg)
Barrel: 20.0in (508mm), 4 grooves, rh
Magazine: 20- or 30-round box
Muzzle velocity: 3248 ft/sec (990 m/sec)
Cyclic rate: 750 rds/min

TOKAREV Russia
State factories

SVT38 Rifle

1938. Gas-operated semi-automatic, selective fire, locked by dropping breech-block. Full-stocked, three-quarter length slotted handguard leaving gas cylinder partly exposed, exposed muzzle, muzzle brake, short curved box magazine.

Cartridge: 7.62 × 54R Russian
Length: 48.10in (1222mm)
Weight: 8lb 10oz (3.95kg)
Barrel: 25.0in (635mm), 4 grooves, rh
Magazine: 10-round box
Muzzle velocity: 2725 ft/sec (830 m/sec)

SVT40 Rifle

1940. Improved model, same action. Half-stocked, half-length slotted handguard. Muzzle brake. A variant model with full-automatic capability, the **AVT40**, was built in prototype form but not adopted.

Cartridge: 7.62 × 54R Russian
Length: 48.10in (1222mm)
Weight: 8lb 9oz (3.90kg)
Barrel: 24.60in (625mm), 4 grooves, rh
Magazine: 10-round box
Muzzle velocity: 2725 ft/sec (830 m/sec)

SKT40 Carbine

1940. A shortened version of the rifle. Similar appearance, but only one slot in the handguard.

Cartridge: 7.62 × 54R Russian
Length: 41.93in (1065mm)
Weight: 8lb 1oz (3.65kg)
Barrel: 18.50in (470mm), 4 grooves, rh
Magazine: 20-round box
Muzzle velocity: 2445 ft/sec (745 m/sec)

TRIPLETT & SCOTT USA
Meriden

Repeating Carbine, Long

Half-stocked, round barrel, single barrel band. Barrel and breech pivot on the face of the butt action so as to revolve the barrel to align with the tube magazine in the butt. Central hammer. Estimated 3000 made 1864–65.

Cartridge: .56-52 Spencer
Length: 48.0in (1220mm)
Weight: 9lb 0oz (4.08kg)
Barrel: 30.0in (762mm), 4 grooves, rh
Magazine: 7-round tube
Muzzle velocity: *ca* 1025 ft/sec (312 m/sec)

Repeating Carbine, Short

Similar to the Long weapon but with a shorter barrel. Approximately 2000 made 1864–65.

Cartridge: .56-52 Spencer
Length: 40.0in (1016mm)
Weight: 8lb 6oz (3.79kg)
Barrel: 22.0in (558mm), 4 grooves, rh
Magazine: 7-round tube
Muzzle velocity: *ca* 1025 ft/sec (312 m/sec)

VALMET Finland
Valmet

M1962 Assault Rifle

Based on the Kalashnikov AK mechanism but with considerable external differences, although the shape remains much the same. Perforated plastic fore-end/handguard, thick single-tube butt, prominent backsight.

Cartridge: 7.62 × 39mm Soviet M1943
Length: 36.0in (914mm)
Weight: 9lb 0oz (4.09kg)
Barrel: 16.50in (419mm), 4 grooves, rh
Magazine: 30-round box
Muzzle velocity: 2400 ft/sec (730 m/sec)
Cyclic rate: 650 rds/min

M1971 Assault Rifle

A revised version of the M1962 which moved back towards the Kalashnikov, with a solid plastic butt, parallel-sided plastic fore-end, backsight in front of the chamber.

Cartridge: 7.62 × 39mm Soviet M1943
Length: 36.53in (928mm)
Weight: 7lb 15oz (3.59kg)
Barrel: 16.53in (420mm), 4 grooves, rh
Magazine: 30-round box
Muzzle velocity: 2400 ft/sec (730 m/sec)
Cyclic rate: 650 rds/min

M1976 Assault Rifle

Improved model of the M1971, principally changes in manufacture, using more stamped and formed metal. Backsight moved to the rear of the receiver.

Cartridge: 7.62 × 39mm Soviet M1943
Length: 35.94in (913mm)
Weight: 8lb 1oz (3.67kg)
Barrel: 16.54in (420mm), 4 grooves, rh
Magazine: 15-, 20- or 30-round box
Muzzle velocity: 2400 ft/sec (730 m/sec)
Cyclic rate: 650 rds/min

M1978 Long Rifle

Heavy-barrelled version of the M1976; slotted fore-end/handguard, bipod attached to barrel, carrying handle.

Cartridge: 7.62 × 39mm Soviet M1943
Length: 41.73in (1060mm)

Weight: 10lb 6oz (4.70kg)
Barrel: 22.36in (568mm), 4 grooves, rh
Magazine: 15- or 30-round box
Muzzle velocity: 2460 ft/sec (750 m/sec)
Cyclic rate: 650 rds/min

VÅPENSMIA Norway
NM 149S Sniping Rifle

Mauser M98 bolt action repeater. Half-stocked, no handguard, no iron sights, telescope mount.

Cartridge: 7.62 × 51mm NATO
Length: 44.10in (1120mm)
Weight: 12lb 5oz (5.60kg) with telescope
Barrel: 23.62in (600mm), 4 grooves, rh
Magazine: 5-round box
Muzzle velocity: 2690 ft/sec (820 m/sec)

VEKTOR South Africa
Vektor

R4 Rifle

1982. Essentially this is a modified copy of the Israel Galil rifle, the modifications principally relating to a larger and stronger butt and handguard more suited to the larger stature of South African troops. There have also been modifications to the dimensions to strengthen the weapon. Gas-operated, turning bolt, selective fire. Folding tubular butt, plastic fore-end, pistol grip, vertical cocking handle.

Cartridge: 5.56 × 45mm M193
Length, butt extended: 39.57in (1005mm)
Length, butt folded: 29.13in (740mm)
Weight: 9lb 7oz (4.30kg)
Barrel: 18.11in (460 mm), 6 grooves, rh
Magazine: 35-round box
Muzzle velocity: 3215 ft/sec (980 m/sec)
Cyclic rate: 700 rds/min

R5 Short Rifle

Short version of the R4, adopted by the South African Air Force and Marines.

Cartridge: 5.56 × 45mm M193
Length, butt extended: 34.57in (877mm)
Length, butt folded: 24.21in (615mm)
Weight: 8lb 3oz (3.70kg)
Barrel: 13.07in (332mm), 6 grooves, rh
Magazine: 35-round box
Muzzle velocity: 3018 ft/sec (920 m/sec)
Cyclic rate: 700 rds/min

R6 Compact Assault Rifle

An even shorter version of the R4/R5 for use by vehicle crews, paratroops and others requiring the smallest dimensions.

Cartridge: 5.56 × 45mm M193
Length, butt extended: 31.69in (805mm)
Length, butt folded: 22.24in (565mm)
Weight: 8lb 1oz (3.67kg)
Barrel: 11.02in (280mm), 6 grooves, rh
Magazine: 35-round box
Muzzle velocity: 2706 ft/sec (825 m/sec)
Cyclic rate: 585 rds/min

CR21 Assault Rifle

1998. Gas operated, rotating bolt, selective fire. Bullpup, in black synthetic material. Full-hand trigger guard, magazine behind pistol grip, ambidextrous fire selector on butt. Built-in reflex optical sight.

Cartridge: 5.56 × 45mm NATO
Length: 29.92in (760mm)
Weight, loaded: 8lb 6oz (3.80kg)
Barrel: 18.11in (460mm), 6 grooves, rh
Magazine: 20-or 35-round box
Muzzle velocity: 3215 ft/sec (980 m/sec)
Cyclic rate: 700 rds/min

VETTERLI Switzerland

M1869 Infantry Rifle
Bern, Cordier, Ost-Schweiz, Rychner, Sauerbrey, SIG, Steiger & Zürich

Bolt action repeater, tube magazine. Turnbolt action with two lugs locking into the receiver body. Full-stocked, no handguard, exposed muzzle, cleaning rod. Prominent loading gate on right side of receiver.

Cartridge: 10.4 × 38R Swiss Peabody RF
Length: 51.97in (1320mm)
Weight: 10lb 4oz (4.66kg)
Barrel: 33.11in (841mm), 4 grooves, rh
Magazine: 12-round tube
Muzzle velocity: 1427 ft/sec (435 m/sec)

M1870 Cadet Rifle
SIG

Bolt action as M1869 but single shot only. Full-stocked, exposed muzzle.

Cartridge: 10.4 × 38R Swiss Peabody RF
Length: 45.27in (1150mm)
Weight: 7lb 3oz (3.25kg)
Barrel: 26.77in (680mm), 4 grooves, rh
Muzzle velocity: 1312 ft/sec (400m/sec)

M1871 Carbine
Bern & Pfenninger

In general terms, a shorter version of the M1869 Rifle.

Cartridge: 10.4 × 38R Swiss Peabody RF
Length: 36.69in (932mm)
Weight: 7lb 3oz (3.25kg)
Barrel: 18.50in (470mm), 4 grooves, rh
Magazine: 6-round tube
Muzzle velocity: 1230 ft/sec (375 m/sec)

M1871 Short Rifle
Bern & SIG

Similar to the M1869 Rifle, but shorter, with a single barrel band, double set trigger and a thicker butt-plate. For light infantry.

Cartridge: 10.4 × 38R Swiss Peabody RF
Length: 49.61in (1260mm)
Weight: 10lb 3oz (4.63kg)
Barrel: 30.90in (785mm), 4 grooves, rh
Magazine: 10-round tube
Muzzle velocity: 1410 ft/sec (430 m/sec)

M1878 Infantry Rifle
Bern

Improved model but using the same action as the M1869. Full-stocked, single barrel band, no handguard, exposed muzzle, prominent rear sight.

Cartridge: 10.4 × 38R Swiss Peabody RF
Length: 52.20in (1326mm)
Weight: 10lb 2oz (4.58kg)
Barrel: 33.11in (841mm), 4 grooves, rh
Magazine: 12-round tube
Muzzle velocity: 1427 ft/sec (435 m/sec)

M1878 Short Rifle.
Bern

Variant of the infantry rifle fitted with a double set trigger.

Cartridge: 10.4 × 38R Swiss Peabody RF
Length: 52.20in (1326mm)
Weight: 10lb 3oz (4.62kg)
Barrel: 33.11in (841mm), 4 grooves, rh
Magazine: 12-round tube
Muzzle velocity: 1427 ft/sec (435 m/sec)

M1878 Carbine
Bern

Shortened rifle; full-stocked, stepped fore-end, no bayonet fittings.

Cartridge: 10.4 × 38R Swiss Peabody RF
Length: 36.54in (928mm)
Weight: 7lb 4oz (3.30kg)
Barrel: 18.50in (470mm), 4 grooves, rh
Magazine: 6-round tube
Muzzle velocity: 1230 ft/sec (375 m/sec)

M1878 Border Guard Carbine
Bern

Generally as for the carbine above, but with an extra barrel band and bayonet fittings.

Cartridge: 10.4 × 38R Swiss Peabody RF
Length: 37.20in (945mm)
Weight: 7lb 6oz (3.34kg)
Barrel: 19.09in (485mm), 4 grooves, rh
Magazine: 6-round tube
Muzzle velocity: 1230 ft/sec (375 m/sec)

M1881 Short Rifle
Bern

Action as for M1869, improved sights, improved trigger mechanism.

Cartridge: 10.4 × 38R Swiss Peabody RF
Length: 52.0in (1321mm)
Weight: 10lb 3oz (4.62kg)
Barrel: 33.07in (840mm), 4 grooves, rh
Magazine: 12-round tube
Muzzle velocity: 1427 ft/sec (435 m/sec)

M1881 Infantry Rifle
Bern

Little more than the M1878 with an improved sight and trigger.

Cartridge: 10.4 × 38R Swiss Peabody RF
Length: 52.20in (1326mm)

Weight: 10lb 1oz (4.58kg)
Barrel: 33.11in (841mm), 4 grooves, rh
Magazine: 12-round tube
Muzzle velocity: 1427 ft/sec (435 m/sec)

ITALY

M1870 Infantry Rifle
Beretta, Rome, Torino & Torre
Turnbolt action as for the Swiss but single shot weapon. Three-quarter length stock, spur trigger guard, bayonet fittings.

Cartridge: 10.4 × 47R Vetterli-Vitali
Length: 52.95in (1345mm)
Weight: 9lb 13oz (4.12kg)
Barrel: 33.86in (860mm), 4 grooves, rh
Muzzle velocity: 1410 ft/sec (430 m/sec)

M1870 Short Rifle
Beretta, Rome, Torino & Torre
Shortened version of the M1870 Infantry rifle. Full-stocked, single barrel band, bayonet fittings.

Cartridge: 10.4 × 47R Vetterli-Vitali
Length: 43.11in (1095mm)
Weight: 8lb 13oz (4.02kg)
Barrel: 24.0in (610mm), 4 grooves, rh
Muzzle velocity: 1345 ft/sec (410 m/sec)

M1870 Cavalry Carbine
Beretta, Rome, Torino & Torre
M1870 rifle action, short barrel, half-stocked. Fitted for bayonet.

Cartridge: 10.4 × 47R Vetterli-Vitali
Length: 36.57in (929mm)
Weight: 7lb 13oz (3.53kg)
Barrel: 17.71in (450mm), 4 grooves, rh
Muzzle velocity: 1230 ft/sec (375 m/sec)

M1882 Naval Rifle
Terni
This used the M1870 rifle action and allied it to a tube magazine in the fore-end, making it more bulky than the earlier models. No loading port, loaded through the open action. Full-stocked, with the cleaning rod in a slot on the left side of the stock.

Cartridge: 10.4 × 47R Vetterli-Vitali
Length: 47.64in (1210mm)
Weight: 8lb 15oz (4.05kg)
Barrel: 28.74in (730mm), 4 grooves, rh
Magazine: 8-round tube
Muzzle velocity: 1312 ft/sec (400 m/sec)

VETTERLI-VITALI Italy
Adaptation of original single-shot Vetterli rifles (*described above*) to a box magazine system designed by Vitali.

M1870/87 Infantry Rifle
Terni
The Vetterli Italian M1870 rifle converted by the insertion of the Vitali box magazine, the odd shape of which makes the rifle instantly recognisable.

Cartridge: 10.4 × 47R Vetterli-Vitali
Length: 52.95in (1345mm)
Weight: 9lb 13oz (4.12kg)
Barrel: 33.86in (860mm), 4 grooves, rh
Magazine: 4-round box
Muzzle velocity: 1410 ft/sec (430m/sec)

M1870/87 Short Rifle
Conversion of the Vetterli short rifle to Vitali magazine.

Specifications: as for the original model

M1870/87 Cavalry Carbine
Conversion to Vitali magazine.

Specifications: as for the original model

M1870/87/15
Terni
1915. Conversion of the conversion. This was the M1870/87 Infantry rifle re-converted to a Mannlicher-type clip-loaded magazine and re-barrelled for the standard 6.5mm cartridge. A marginally safe wartime expedient.

Cartridge: 6.5 × 52mm Mannlicher-Carcano
Length: 52.95in (1345mm)
Weight: 10lb 3oz (4.62kg)
Barrel: 33.86in (860mm), 4 grooves, rh
Magazine: 6-round box
Muzzle velocity: 2395 ft/sec (730 m/sec)

WALTHER Germany
Walther

Gewehr 41 (W) Assault Rifle
Gas-operated via a muzzle gas trap and annular piston, bolt locked by hinged flaps. Semi-automatic only. Full-stocked, obvious conical muzzle gas trap, prominent rectangular box magazine.

Cartridge: 7.92 × 57mm Mauser
Length: 44.50in (1130mm)
Weight: 11 lb 0oz (4.98kg)
Barrel: 21.45in (545mm), 4 grooves, rh
Magazine: 30-round box
Muzzle velocity: 2365 ft/sec (776 m/sec)

MKb 42 (W) Assault Rifle
Designed to use the then-new 7.92mm Kurz cartridge, this was a gas-operated rifle using a tipping bolt, driven by an annular piston around the barrel. Straight-line layout, wood butt, pressed steel receiver, pistol grip, circular fore-end/handguard with unusual raised rear sight bed. Raised hooded foresight, bayonet lug, curved box magazine.

Cartridge: 7.92 × 33mm Kurz
Length: 36.65in (931mm)
Weight: 9lb 11oz (4.39kg)
Barrel: 16.0in (406mm), 4 grooves, rh
Magazine: 30-round box
Muzzle velocity: 2120 ft/sec (646 m/sec)
Cyclic rate: 600 rds/min.

Gewehr 43 Assault Rifle
This was an improved version of the Gew. 41 (W) which retained the same flap locking but changed the gas system to a conventional piston and cylinder. Full-stocked, full-

length handguard, exposed muzzle. Wood or plastic furniture. Receiver has a dovetail for fitting telescope sights.

Cartridge: 7.92 × 57mm Mauser
Length: 44.0in (1117mm)
Weight: 9lb 9oz (24.33kg)
Barrel: 22.0in (559mm), 4 grooves, rh
Magazine: 10-round box
Muzzle velocity: 2448 ft/sec (746 m/sec)

WA2000 Sniper Rifle

1985–90. A very advanced sniping rifle based upon competition rifle practice. Barrel set in rigid frame which also forms the receiver. Massive adjustable thumb-hole stock, wood fore-end, bipod. Semi-automatic, gas-operated, rotating bolt.

Cartridge: .300 Winchester Magnum
Length: 35.63in (905mm)
Weight: 15lb 5oz (6.95kg)
Barrel: 25.59in (650mm), 4 grooves, rh
Magazine: 6-round box
Muzzle velocity: 3238 ft/sec (987 m/sec)

WÄNZL Austria-Hungary
Maker not known

M1866 Infantry Rifle

A lifting-block breech-loading conversion system applied to earlier muzzle-loading rifles. Block lifts up and forward, similar to the Allin conversion, but contains the chamber for the rimfire cartridge, which is struck by a side-hammer. Straight-wrist butt, full-stocked with two bands and a nose-cap, exposed muzzle, cleaning rod.

Cartridge: 14 × 33R Wänzl
Length: 52.32in (1329mm)
Weight: 9lb 6oz (4.27kg)
Barrel: 34.84in (885mm), 4 grooves, rh
Muzzle velocity: 1280 ft/sec (390 m/sec)

M1866 Short Rifle

Conversion of light infantry percussion rifles on the Wänzl system. Hexagonal barrel, muzzles cylindrical to accept a bayonet. Finger rest on the trigger guard.

Cartridge: 14 × 33R Wänzl
Length: 43.50in (1105mm)
Weight: 10lb 6oz (4.70kg)
Barrel: 26.02in (661mm), 4 grooves, rh
Muzzle velocity: 1240 ft/sec (378 m/sec)

M1866 Carbine

Similar to the M1866 rifle, but shorter.

Cartridge: 14 × 33R Wänzl
Length: 41.61in (1057mm)
Weight: 9lb 2oz (4.13kg)
Barrel: 24.06in (611mm), 4 grooves, rh
Muzzle velocity: 1224 ft/sec (373 m/sec)

WARNER USA

Carbine
Warner

Single shot, lifting breech-block, hand-operated extractor by tang beneath the fore-end. Half-stocked, round barrel, single barrel band. Hammer fired. Thumb lever alongside hammer releases breech block

Cartridge: .56-52 Spencer
Length: 38.0in (965mm)
Weight: 8lb 2oz (3.63kg)
Barrel: 20.0in (508mm), 4 grooves, rh
Muzzle velocity: *ca* 900 ft/sec (274 m/sec)

Carbine
Greene

As for the Warner model but some minor manufacturing changes; no lock for breech-block, sling bar on butt, larger extractor.

Specifications: the same

WERDER Bavaria

M1869 Infantry Rifle
Amberg

The Bavarian Lightning rifle. Dropping block similar to the Martini but opened by a lever inside the trigger guard and closed by an external lever on the pivoting shaft. Designed to permit firing in the prone position, something difficult to do with an underlever-action Martini.

Cartridge: 11 × 50R Werder
Length: 51.18in (1300mm)
Weight: 9lb 10oz (4.39kg)
Barrel: 35.04in (890mm), 4 grooves, rh
Muzzle velocity: 1463 ft/sec (446 m/sec)

M1869 Carbine
Francotte & Landes

Similar action to the rifle, though a shorter cartridge. Stocked to the nose-cap in typical European carbine style.

Cartridge: 11 × 41R Werder
Length: 37.80in (960mm)
Weight: 7lb 11oz (3.50kg)
Barrel: 21.65in (550mm), 4 grooves, rh
Muzzle velocity: 1148 ft/sec (350 m/sec)

M1869 n.M. Infantry Rifle
Amberg

The M1869 rifle action with a Mauser-pattern 11mm barrel and chamber so as to standardise throughout Germany.

Cartridge: 11.15 × 60R Mauser
Length: 51.85in (1317mm)
Weight: 9lb 3oz (4.18kg);
Barrel: 34.84in (885mm), 4 grooves, rh
Muzzle velocity: 1378 ft/sec (420 m/sec)

WERNDL Austria
Steyr

M1867 Infantry Rifle
Single shot, rotary block breech, external side-hammer. Full-stocked, exposed muzzle, bayonet fitting.

Cartridge: 11.15 × 58R Werndl
Length: 50.31in (1278mm)
Weight: 9lb 12oz (4.43kg)
Barrel: 33.66in (855mm), 6 grooves, rh
Muzzle velocity: 1430 ft/sec (436 m/sec)

M1867 Carbine
Similar action to the rifle, shorter barrel, stocked to the nose-cap.

Cartridge: 11 × 42R Werndl Carbine
Length: 39.02in (991mm)
Weight: 7lb 0oz (3.18kg)
Barrel: 22.44in (570mm), 6 grooves, rh
Muzzle velocity: 978 ft/sec (298 m/sec)

M1873 Infantry Rifle
Improved mechanism, central hammer, plus other detail improvements.

Cartridge: 11 × 58R Werndl
Length: 49.80in (1265mm)
Weight: 9lb 5oz (4.20kg)
Barrel: 33.07in (840mm), 6 grooves, rh
Muzzle velocity: 1430 ft/sec (436 m/sec)

M1873 Carbine
Improved mechanism, central hammer, detail changes.

Cartridge: 11 × 42R Werndl Carbine
Length: 39.53in (1004mm)
Weight: 7lb 3oz (3.25kg)
Barrel: 22.83in (580mm), 6 grooves, rh
Muzzle velocity: 984 ft/sec (300m/sec)

M1877 Infantry Rifle
As for the M1873 but for an improved cartridge. New sights.

Specifications: unchanged, except
Muzzle velocity: 1476 ft/sec (450 m/sec)

M1867/77 Rifles and Carbines
M1867 rifles and carbines re-modelled to take the new cartridges.

Specifications: unchanged, except
Muzzle velocity, rifle: 1476 ft/sec (450 m/sec)
Muzzle velocity, carbine: 1007 ft/sec (307m/sec)

M1877 Carbine
New model carbine to suit the new cartridge and replace the 67/77 conversions.

Specifications: as for the 1873 Carbine, except
Muzzle velocity: 1007 ft/sec (307 m/sec)

WHITNEY USA
Whitney

M1873 Rifle (Mexico)
Rolling block single shot mechanism similar to the Remington but not depending upon the hammer for locking the block. Full-stocked, exposed muzzle, three barrel bands.

Cartridge: 11.15 × 57R Spanish Remington
Length: 50.48in (1282mm)
Weight: 9lb 8oz (4.30kg)
Barrel: 35.0in (889mm), 4 grooves, rh
Muzzle velocity: 1450 ft/sec (442 m/sec)

M1873 Carbine
Rolling block single shot, same action as the rifle but shorter, half-stocked, and with cavalry sling bar and ring on stock.

Cartridge: 11.15 × 58R Spanish Remington
Length: 36.0in (1282mm)
Weight: 7lb 3oz (3.26kg)
Barrel: 20.5in (521mm), 4 grooves, rh
Muzzle velocity: 1312 ft/sec (400 m/sec)

WINCHESTER USA

M1873 Musket
Winchester
The familiar 1873 lever-action carbine was also produced in sporting rifle and military 'musket' forms, the latter being purchased by Spain, Turkey and various other countries for army use. The musket has the same butt and breech mechanism, central hammer and trigger-guard lever as any other Winchester lever-action, but differs in having a longer barrel and being fully-stocked, the fore-end concealing all but the tip of the magazine tube and leaving the muzzle exposed.

Cartridge: .44-40 Winchester
Length: 48.30in (1227mm)
Weight: 9lb 8oz (4.31kg)
Barrel: 30.0in (762mm), 4 grooves, rh
Magazine: 17-round tube
Muzzle velocity: 1300 ft/sec (396 m/sec)

M1895 Musket
Winchester
A similar variant to the M1895 Browning-designed lever action carbine, this series is distinguished by having a box magazine ahead of the trigger guard. The largest customer for this weapon appears to have been Russia, which purchased over 200,000 in 1915–17, many of which eventually found their way to Spain in 1936–37.

Cartridge: 7.62 × 54mm Russian
Length: 43.20in (1097mm)
Weight: 7lb 9oz (3.43kg)
Barrel: 24.0in (610mm), 6 grooves, rh
Magazine: 5-round box
Muzzle velocity: 2810 ft/sec (856 m/sec)

US Carbine M1
IBM, Inland, Irwin, National Postal, Quality, Rochester, Rock-Ola, Saginaw, Standard, Underwood & Winchester

1941. Semi-automatic, gas operated, short-stroke tappet system and rotating bolt. Half-stocked, hand-guard, single barrel band, bayonet bar on barrel, box magazine, flip aperture backsight.

Cartridge: .30 US Carbine
Length: 35.58in (904mm)
Weight: 5lb 3oz (2.35kg)
Barrel: 18.0in (457mm), 4 grooves, rh
Magazine: 15- or 30-round box
Muzzle velocity: 1970 ft/sec (600 m/sec)

US Carbine M1A1
Inland

Carbine as for the M1 but with a pistol grip and metal folding stock.

Cartridge: .30 US Carbine
Length, butt extended: 35.63in (905mm)
Weight: 5lb 9oz (2.53kg)
Barrel: 18.0in (457mm), 4 grooves, rh
Magazine: 15- or 30-round box
Muzzle velocity: 1970 ft/sec (600 m/sec)

US Carbine M2
Inland & Winchester

M1 modified to provide selective fire capability by change lever on left of action. Ramp-mounted aperture sight.

Cartridge: .30 US Carbine
Length: 35.58in (904mm)
Weight: 5lb 3oz (2.36kg)
Barrel: 18.0in (457mm), 4 grooves, rh
Magazine: 15- or 30-round box
Muzzle velocity: 1970 ft/sec (600 m/sec)
Cyclic rate: 750 rds/min

US Carbine M3
Inland & Winchester

An M2 without iron sights and specially adapted to mount an Infra-Red 'Sniperscope' lamp and sight.

COMPARATIVE TABLES

The tables list manually operated rifles and automatic rifles separately in ascending order of calibre. Overall lengths and barrel lengths are given in inches, weights in pounds and muzzle velocity in feet per second. Multiple magazine size options are not shown; only the most usual magazine is given.

The following abbreviations are used:

Manually-operated rifles:

Action: R/Bolt – rotating bolt; T/Bolt – turnbolt; SP/Bolt – straight pull bolt; Block – any kind of block breech – rolling, swinging, sliding; Trap – any kind of 'trap-door' breech, *eg* Snider, Springfield; Lever – any type of lever-action breech; Screw – breech-block using an interrupted thread or lugs to lock, not being part of a conventional bolt.

Magazine: B – box; Int – integral; T – tubular; H – hopper; Hel – Helical.

In each case the number that follows indicates the capacity. SS indicates a single shot weapon.

Automatic rifles:

Magazine as for manually-operated rifles, plus D – drum.

Action: Blowback – BB; Delayed blowback – DBB; Blow-forward – BF; Recoil – Rec.

MANUALLY OPERATED RIFLES

Name	Year	Calibre	Action	Length	Barrel	Weight	Magazine	Velocity
Armenia: K11 Sniper	1996	5.45 × 39.5	R/Bolt	36.22	16.34	7.69	B/30	2952
Enfield L86A1 Cadet	1988	5.56 × 45	R/Bolt	29.75	19.50	8.88	B/10	3084
Lee US Navy Rifle	1895	.236	SP/Bolt	47.00	27.25	8.00	Int/5	2400
Arisaka Meiji 29th Year Rifle	1896	6.5 × 50	T/Bolt	50.04	30.98	9.00	Int/5	2493
Arisaka Meiji 30th Year Rifle	1897	6.5 × 50	T/Bolt	50.16	31.06	8.81	Int/5	2542
Arisaka Meiji 30th Year Carbine	1897	6.5 × 50	T/Bolt	37.87	18.90	7.48	Int/5	2360
Arisaka Meiji 35th Year Rifle	1902	6.5 × 50	T/Bolt	50.19	31.10	8.94	Int/5	2542
Arisaka Meiji 38th Year Rifle	1905	6.5 × 50	T/Bolt	50.19	31.45	9.12	Int/5	2400
Arisaka Meiji 38th Year Carbine	1905	6.5 × 50	T/Bolt	37.91	19.17	7.37	Int/5	2250
Arisaka Meiji 44th Year Carbine	1911	6.5 × 50	T/Bolt	38.50	18.50	8.81	Int/5	2250
Mannlicher-Carcano Rifle	1891	6.5 × 52	T/Bolt	50.80	30.71	8.37	B/6	2400
Mannlicher-Carcano Cavalry Carbine	1891	6.5 × 52	T/Bolt	37.52	17.75	6.94	B/6	2083
Mannlicher-Carcano Carbine T.S.	1891	6.5 × 52	T/Bolt	37.52	17.75	7.12	B/6	2083
Vetterli-Vitali: Italy Rifle conversion	1915	6.5 × 52	T/Bolt	52.95	33.86	10.19	B/6	2395
Daudeteau Rifle	1896	6.5 × 53.5	T/Bolt	50.67	32.48	8.69	Int/5	2526
Mannlicher: Dutch Infantry Rifle	1895	6.5 × 54	T/Bolt	50.98	31.10	9.50	B/5	2428
Mannlicher: Dutch Carbine	1895	6.5 × 54	T/Bolt	37.48	17.71	6.81	B/5	2050
Mannlicher: Dutch Air Force Carbine	1930	6.5 × 54	T/Bolt	37.80	17.91	7.81	B/5	2050
Mannlicher: Romanian Rifle	1892	6.5 × 54	T/Bolt	48.31	28.54	8.94	B/5	2395
Mannlicher: Romanian Carbine	1903	6.5 × 54	T/Bolt	37.50	17.71	7.25	B/5	2312
Mannlicher-Schoenauer: Greek Rifle	1903	6.5 × 54	T/Bolt	48.23	28.54	8.31	Int/5	2231
Mannlicher-Schoenauer: Greek Carbine	1905	6.5 × 54	T/Bolt	40.35	20.67	7.75	Int/5	2057
Mannlicher-Schoenauer: Greek Rifle	1914	6.5 × 54	T/Bolt	48.23	28.54	8.44	Int/5	2231
Mannlicher-Schoenauer: Greek Carbine	1914	6.5 × 54	T/Bolt	40.35	20.67	7.88	Int/5	2057

Name	Year	Calibre	Action	Length	Barrel	Weight	Magazine	Velocity
Krag: Norway Rifle	1894	6.5×55	T/Bolt	49.61	29.92	8.88	Int/5	2395
Krag: Norway Cavalry Carbine	1895	6.5×55	T/Bolt	39.96	20.47	7.50	Int/5	2100
Krag: Norway Engineer Carbine	1904	6.5×55	T/Bolt	39.96	20.47	8.37	Int/5	2100
Krag: Norway Short Rifle	1912	6.5×55	T/Bolt	43.54	24.00	8.86	Int/5	2330
Krag: Norway Sniper	1923	6.5×55	T/Bolt	44.00	24.00	9.06	Int/5	2330
Krag: Norway Sniper	1925	6.5×55	T/Bolt	49.70	30.00	9.88	Int/5	2625
Krag: Norway Sniper	1930	6.5×55	T/Bolt	48.00	29.50	11.44	Int/5	2625
Mauser: Sweden Carbine	1894	6.5×55	T/bolt	37.40	17.32	7.31	Int/5	2132
Mauser: Sweden Infantry Rifle	1896	6.5×55	T/Bolt	49.45	29.09	8.94	Int/5	2378
Mauser-Vergueiro: Portugal Rifle	1904	6.5×58	T/Bolt	48.70	29.10	8.37	Int/5	2345
Mauser: Belgium FN M1922 Rifle	1922	7×57	T/Bolt	48.70	29.13	8.81	Int/5	2575
Mauser: Belgium FN M1924 Rifle	1924	7×57	T/Bolt	42.91	23.27	8.37	Int/5	2379
Mauser: Brazil Rifle	1894	7×57	T/Bolt	48.62	29.05	8.88	Int/5	2300
Mauser: Brazil Rifle	1904	7×57	T/Bolt	49.17	29.05	8.81	Int/5	2300
Mauser: Chile Rifle	1895	7×57	T/Bolt	48.50	29.06	8.88	Int/5	2700
Mauser: Chile Carbine	1895	7×57	T/Bolt	37.00	18.25	7.50	Int/5	2600
Mauser: Costa Rica Rifle	1910	7×57	T/Bolt	48.82	29.13	8.75	Int/5	2494
Mauser: Mexico Infantry Rifle	1895	7×57	T/Bolt	48.58	29.05	8.75	Int/5	2395
Mauser: Mexico Carbine	1895	7×57	T/Bolt	37.52	18.31	7.50	Int/5	2300
Mauser: Mexico Infantry Rifle	1902	7×57	T/Bolt	48.58	29.05	8.81	Int/5	2395
Mauser: Mexico Infantry Rifle	1907	7×57	T/Bolt	48.78	29.05	8.94	Int/5	2300
Mauser: Mexico Short Rifle	1936	7×57	T/Bolt	42.91	23.23	8.31	Int/5	2300
Mauser: Serbia '80/06	1906	7×57	T/bolt	50.71	30.71	9.88	Int/5	2330
Mauser: Serbia Rifle	1899	7×57	T/Bolt	48.43	29.13	8.88	Int/5	2329
Mauser: Serbia Rifle	1910	7×57	T/Bolt	48.74	29.13	9.06	Int/5	2329
Mauser: Spain Infantry Rifle	1892	7×57	T/Bolt	48.62	29.05	9.06	Int/5	2198
Mauser: Spain Cavalry Carbine	1892	7×57	T/Bolt	37.12	17.52	7.25	Int/5	1837
Mauser: Spain Infantry Rifle	1893	7×57	T/Bolt	48.62	29.05	8.69	Int/5	2231
Mauser: Spain Cavalry Carbine	1895	7×57	T/Bolt	37.12	17.56	7.06	Int/5	2165
Mauser: Spain Artillery Rifle	1916	7×57	T/Bolt	41.34	21.69	8.25	Int/5	2707
Remington: Mexico Rifle	1897	7×57	Block	45.51	30.00	8.50	SS	2100
Enfield, Pattern '13	1913	.276	T/Bolt	46.18	26.00	8.56	Int/5	2785
Mannlicher-Carcano Short Rifle	1938	7.35×51	T/Bolt	40.16	22.13	8.12	B/6	2477
Mannlicher-Carcano Carbine	1938	7.35×51	T/Bolt	37.52	17.75	6.94	B/6	2378
Mannlicher: Swiss Cavalry Carbine	1893	7.5×53	SP/Bolt	40.00	21.65	6.81	B/6	1837
Neuhausen: SIG M'89 Rifle	1889	7.5×53	SP/Bolt	51.18	30.31	8.88	T/12	2000
Schmidt-Rubin Infantry Rifle	1889	7.5×53	SP/Bolt	51.26	30.71	10.69	B/12	1968
Schmidt-Rubin Infantry Rifle	1896	7.5×53	SP/Bolt	51.18	30.71	9.94	B/12	1968
Schmidt-Rubin Cadet Rifle	1897	7.5×53	SP/Bolt	43.50	23.30	7.81	SS	1853
Schmidt-Rubin Short Rifle	1900	7.5×53	SP/Bolt	43.50	23.30	8.37	B/6	1853
Schmidt-Rubin Cavalry Carbine	1905	7.5×53	SP/Bolt	42.12	21.65	8.00	B/6	1805
Schmidt-Rubin Infantry Rifle	1911	7.5×53	SP/Bolt	51.65	30.71	10.12	B/6	2600
Schmidt-Rubin Carbine	1911	7.5×53	SP/Bolt	43.40	23.30	8.62	B/6	2500
Schmidt-Rubin Short Rifle	1931	7.5×53	SP/Bolt	43.50	25.70	8.81	B/6	2550
Berthier Short Rifle 07-15-34	1934	7.5×54	T/Bolt	42.52	22.83	8.12	Int/5	2674
Berthier Short Rifle 02-37	1937	7.5×54	T/Bolt	42.32	22.44	8.06	B/5	2674
MAS Mle 36 Rifle	1936	7.5×54	T/Bolt	40.15	22.60	8.31	B/5	2700
MAS 35/CR39 Rifle	1939	7.5×54	T/Bolt	34.90	17.71	8.50	B/5	2560

Name	Year	Calibre	Action	Length	Barrel	Weight	Magazine	Velocity
FA-MAS FR-F1/F2 Sniper	1964	7.5×54	T/Bolt	44.80	21.73	11.44	B/10	2795
Springfield Rifle M1901	1901	.30-01	T/Bolt	49.25	30.00	9.50	Int/5	2300
Springfield Rifle M1903	1903	.30-03	T/Bolt	43.41	24.21	8.50	Int/5	2300
Enfield M1917	1917	.30-06	T/Bolt	46.30	26.00	9.00	Int/5	2750
Mauser: Belgium FN 35/46 Rifle	1946	.30-06	T/Bolt	43.50	23.23	8/94	Int/5	2740
Mauser: Mexico Short Rifle	1954	.30-06	T/Bolt	44.09	24.00	9.62	Int/5	2772
Springfield Rifle M1903	1903	.30-06	T/Bolt	43.41	24.21	8.50	Int/5	2805
Springfield Rifle M1903A1	1929	.30-06	T/Bolt	43.50	24.21	8.00	Int/5	2805
Springfield Rifle M1903A3	1942	.30-06	T/Bolt	43.25	24.00	8.81	Int/5	2805
Springfield Rifle M1903A4	1942	.30-06	T/Bolt	43.21	24.00	9.12	Int/5	2805
Blake Repeater	1893	.30-40	T/Bolt	49.50	30.00	9.62	B/7	2000
Krag: USA Rifle	1892	.30-40	T/Bolt	49.14	30.00	9.37	Int/5	2000
Krag: USA Rifle	1896	.30-40	T/Bolt	49.10	30.00	8.94	Int/5	2000
Krag: USA Carbine	1896	.30-40	T/Bolt	41.15	22.00	7.75	Int/5	1750
Krag: USA Rifle	1898	.30-40	T/Bolt	49.13	30.00	9.00	Int/5	2200
Krag: USA Carbine	1896	.30-40	T/Bolt	41.15	22.00	7.75	Int/5	1970
Krag: USA Philippine Short Rifle	1898	.30-40	T/Bolt	41.15	22.00	8.06	Int/5	1750
Croatia: EMM992 Sniper	1995	.300	T/Bolt	49.02	22.83	14.56	B/4	3395
Mauser: Germany SR93 Sniper	1993	.300	T/Bolt	48.43	25.59	13.00	B/6	3238
Accuracy International PM Sniper	1985	7.62×51	T/Bolt	47.00	25.78	14.31	B/10	2788
Accuracy International AW Sniper	1993	7.62×51	T/Bolt	47.25	25.60	14.31	B/9	2788
Beretta Sniper	1985	7.62×51	T/Bolt	45.86	23.07	12.44	B/5	2854
Croatia: EM992 Sniper	1995	7.62×51	T/Bolt	47.83	22.24	14.31	B/5	2854
FN 30-11 Sniper	1970	7.62×51	T/Bolt	43.98	19.76	10.69	Int/5	2790
Grünel Sniper	1988	7.62×51	T/Bolt	45.27	25.60	11.69	B/10	2690
Lee-Enfield Rifle L39A1	1958	7.62×51	T/Bolt	46.50	27.55	9.69	B/10	2758
Lee-Enfield Rifle L42A1	1965	7.62×51	T/Bolt	46.49	27.55	9.69	B/10	2750
Mauser: Germany SP66 Sniper	1976	7.62×51	T/Bolt	44.09	25.60	13.75	Int/3	2362
Mauser: Germany Mod 86 Sniper	1986	7.62×51	T/Bolt	47.64	30.70	10.81	B/9	2362
Parker-Hale Model 82	1982	7.62×51	T/Bolt	45.75	25.98	10.56	Int/4	2821
Parker-Hale Model 83	1983	7.62×51	T/Bolt	46.73	25.90	10.94	Int/4	2821
Parker-Hale Model 85	1985	7.62×51	T/Bolt	45.27	27.56	12.44	Int/10	2855
PGM UR Intervention Sniper	1990	7.62×51	T/Bolt	40.55	18.50	12.12	B/5	2625
PGM UR Commando Sniper	1991	7.62×51	T/Bolt	40.55	18.50	11.19	B/5	2625
Remington US M40A1 Sniper	1965	7.62×51	T/Bolt	43.98	24.00	14.50	Int/5	2550
Sako TRG-21 Sniper	1990	7.62×51	T/Bolt	45.28	26.00	10.37	B/10	2821
SIG-Sauer SSG 2000 Sniper	1990	7.62×51	T/Bolt	47.63	24.00	14.50	B/4	2690
SIG-Sauer SSG 3000 Sniper	1992	7.62×51	T/Bolt	46.45	24.00	11.88	B/5	2690
Steyr-Mannlicher SSG69 Sniper	1969	7.62×51	T/Bolt	44.88	25.60	8.56	B/5	2822
Våpensmia NM 149S Sniper	1985	7.62×51	T/Bolt	44.10	23.62	12.31	B/5	2690
Berdan: Russia Three-Line Rifle	1895	7.62×54	T/Bolt	52.05	31.57	9.31	SS	1985
Mosin-Nagant Infantry Rifle	1891	7.62×54	T/Bolt	51.89	32.28	8.94	B/5	1985
Mosin-Nagant Dragoon/Cossack Rifle	1891	7.62×54	T/Bolt	48.62	29.92	8.69	B/5	1968
Mosin-Nagant Carbine	1907	7.62×54	T/Bolt	40.16	20.08	7.50	B/5	1805
Mosin-Nagant M91/30 Rifle	1930	7.62×54	T/Bolt	48.43	28.74	8.69	B/5	2641
Mosin-Nagant Carbine	1938	7.62×54	T/Bolt	40.16	20.08	7.62	B/5	2575
Mosin-Nagant Carbine	1944	7.62×54	T/Bolt	40.35	20.47	8.88	B/5	1985
Mosin-Nagant: Czech Sniper	1954	7.62×54	T/Bolt	48.42	28.74	11.44	B/5	2640

Name	Year	Calibre	Action	Length	Barrel	Weight	Magazine	Velocity
Mosin-Nagant: Finland Short Rifle	1928	7.62×54	T/Bolt	46.65	26.97	9.19	B/5	2428
Mosin-Nagant: Finland Short Rifle	1930	7.62×54	T/Bolt	46.65	26.97	9.62	B/5	2428
Mosin-Nagant: Finland Sako 39	1939	7.62×54	T/Bolt	46.65	26.97	10.00	B/5	2297
Winchester Musket M1895	1915	7.62×54	Lever	43.20	24.00	7.56	B/5	2810
Enfield, Pattern '14	1916	.303	T/Bolt	46.16	26.00	9.12	Int/5	2525
Lee-Enfield, Rifle Mk 1	1895	.303	T/Bolt	49.50	30.20	9.25	B/10	2200
Lee-Enfield, Short Rifle Mk 1	1903	.303	T/Bolt	44.56	25.19	8.15	B/10	2000
Lee-Enfield, Short Rifle, Mk 3	1907	.303	T/Bolt	44.56	25.19	8.65	B/10	2000
Lee-Enfield, Rifle No 4 Mk 1	1941	.303	T/Bolt	44.43	25.19	9.06	B/10	2440
Lee-Enfield, Rifle No 5 Mk 1	1945	.303	T/Bolt	39.50	18.75	7.15	B/10	2400
Lee-Enfield, Carbine, Cavalry Mk 1	1907	.303	T/Bolt	39.94	20.75	7.44	B/6	2000
Lee-Metford Mk 1	1888	.303	T/Bolt	49.50	30.20	9.50	B/8	2200
Lee-Metford Mk 2	1892	.303	T/Bolt	49.50	30.20	9.25	B/10	2000
Lee-Metford Charger Loading Mk 2	1907	.303	T/Bolt	49.50	30.18	9.50	B/10	2060
Lee-Metford Carbine Mk 1	1894	.303	T/Bolt	39.94	20.75	7.44	B/6	2000
Martini-Enfield: Britain Rifle	1895	.303	Block	46.50	30.19	8.31	SS	2000
Martini-Enfield: Britain Carbine	1895	.303	Block	37.31	21.00	7.27	SS	1800
Martini-Metford Rifle Mk 1	1889	.303	Block	49.69	33.19	9.40	SS	2200
Martini-Metford Rifle Mk 2	1900	.303	Block	49.50	33.19	9.88	SS	2200
Martini-Metford Carbine, RA, Mk 1	1892	.303	Block	37.63	20.56	7.76	SS	2000
Martini-Metford Carbine, RA, Mk 2	1893	.303	Block	37.63	20.56	7.06	SS	2000
Martini-Metford Carbine, RA, Mk 3	1894	.303	Block	37.63	21.00	7.19	SS	2000
Martini-Metford Carbine, Cav. Mk1	1892	.303	Block	37.63	20.56	8.09	SS	2000
Martini-Metford Carbine, Cav. Mk 2	1892	.303	Block	37.63	20.56	8.25	SS	2000
Martini-Metford Carbine, Cav. Mk 3	1893	.303	Block	37.63	21.00	6.75	SS	2000
Ross Rifle Mark 1	1905	.303	SP/Bolt	48.63	28.00	8.06	Int/5	2000
Ross Rifle, Mark 3B	1915	.303	SP/Bolt	50.56	30.15	9.88	B/5	2600
Mauser: Argentina Rifle	1891	7.65×53	T/bolt	48.62	29.13	8.81	B/5	2133
Mauser: Argentina Cavalry Carbine	1891	7.65×53	T/Bolt	37.00	17.64	7.25	B/5	1893
Mauser: Argentina Rifle	1909	7.65×53	T/Bolt	49.17	29.13	8.94	Int/5	2706
Mauser: Belgium Infantry Rifle	1889	7.65×53	T/Bolt	48.62	29.13	8.81	B/5	2133
Mauser: Belgium Cavalry Carbine	1889	7.65×53	T/Bolt	34.84	15.75	6.62	B/5	1837
Mauser: Belgium Foot Troops Carbine	1889	7.65×53	T/Bolt	41.14	21.65	7.75	B/5	1919
Mauser: Belgium Gendarmerie	1889	7.65×53	T/Bolt	34.84	15.75	6.75	B/5	1837
Mauser: Belgium FN Short Rifle	1935	7.65×53	T/Bolt	43.38	23.42	9.00	Int/5	2346
Mauser: Belgium '89/36 Rifle	1936	7.65×53	T/Bolt	43.07	23.62	8.31	B/5	2346
Mauser: Spain Infantry Rifle	1891	7.65×53	T/Bolt	48.74	29.13	9.06	B/5	2067
Mauser: Turkey Infantry Rifle	1890	7.65×53	T/Bolt	48.70	29.13	8.81	B/5	2132
Mauser: Turkey Cavalry Carbine	1890	7.65×53	T/Bolt	39.17	19.68	7.69	B/5	1886
Mauser: Turkey Infantry Rifle	1893	7.65×53	T/Bolt	48.62	29.05	8.94	Int/5	2132
Mauser: Turkey Carbine	1905	7.65×53	T/bolt	41.14	21.65	8.25	Int/5	2083
Arisaka Type 99 Rifle	1939	7.7×58	T/Bolt	45.00	25.75	9.12	Int/5	2400
Arisaka Type 2 Parachutist Rifle	1942	7.7×58	T/Bolt	45.27	25.39	8.93	Int/5	2368
China: Hanyang	1914	7.92×57	T/Bolt	49.25	29.25	8.50	B/5	2067
China: Generalissimo	1936	7.92×57	T/Bolt	43.75	23.62	9.00	Int/5	2690
Commission Rifle,	1888	7.92×57	T/Bolt	48.80	29.13	8.37	B/5	2100
Commission Carbine	1888	7.92×57	T/Bolt	37.40	17.12	6.81	B/5	1886
Commission Carbine	1891	7.92×57	T/Bolt	37.40	17.12	7.12	B/5	1886

Name	Year	Calibre	Action	Length	Barrel	Weight	Magazine	Velocity
Commission Rifle	1907	7.92×57	T/Bolt	47.95	27.95	8.56	B/5	2805
Mannlicher: China Rifle	1904	7.92×57	T/Bolt	48.23	28.54	8.81	B/5	2247
Mauser: Czech M1924 Short Rifle	1924	7.92×57	T/Bolt	43.23	23.23	9.12	Int/5	2756
Mauser: Czech M33 Carbine	1933	7.92×57	T/Bolt	39.21	17.91	7.69	Int/5	2510
Mauser: Czech/Germany M33/40	1940	7.92×57	T/Bolt	38.98	19.29	8.37	Int/5	2247
Mauser: Czech M98/22	1922	7.92×57	T/Bolt	48.82	29.13	9.31	Int/5	2854
Mauser: Germany Infantry Rifle 88/97	1895	7.92×57	T/Bolt	48.82	29.13	8.69	B/5	2067
Mauser: Germany Gewehr 98	1898	7.92×57	T/Bolt	49.21	33.66	9.00	Int/5	2854
Mauser: Germany Gewehr 98/40	1940	7.92×57	T/Bolt	43.11	23.62	9.00	Int/5	2477
Mauser: Germany Kar. 98	1899	7.92×57	T/Bolt	37.20	17.13	7.31	Int/5	1854
Mauser: Germany Kar. 98A	1902	7.92×57	T/Bolt	37.20	17.12	7.56	Int/5	2608
Mauser: Germany Kar. 98a	1908	7.92×57	T/Bolt	42.91	23.23	8.19	Int/5	2756
Mauser: Germany Kar. 98k	1935	7.92×57	T/Bolt	43.70	23.62	8.62	Int/5	2477
Mauser: Persia Mod 1328 Rifle	1949	7.92×57	T/Bolt	38.19	18.11	8.56	Int/5	2379
Mauser: Poland M29 Short	1930	7.92×57	T/Bolt	43.39	23.62	9.00	Int/5	2477
Mauser: Portugal 937A Short Rifle	1937	7.92×57	T/Bolt	43.43	19.69	8.75	Int/5	2428
Mauser: Spain M1943 Short Rifle	1943	7.92×57	T/Bolt	43.50	23.62	8.62	Int/5	2460
Mauser: Yugoslavia Rifle	1948	7.92×57	T/Bolt	42.90	23.30	8.62	Int/5	2600
Rheinmetall Panzerbuchse 39	1939	7.92×94	Block	62.25	42.75	27.25	SS	4150
Marosczeck Anti-tank	1935	7.92×107	T/Bolt	70.00	47.25	19.50	B/10	4198
Berthier Cavalry Carbine	1890	8×50	T/Bolt	37.20	17.85	6.69	B/3	2000
Berthier Cuirassier Carbine	1890	8×50	T/Bolt	37.20	17.85	6.62	B/3	2090
Berthier Gendarmerie Carbine	1890	8×50	T/Bolt	37.20	17.85	6.81	B/3	2090
Berthier Artillery Musketoon	1892	8×50	T/Bolt	37.20	17.85	6.70	B/3	2090
Berthier Colonial Rifle	1902	8×50	T/Bolt	44.33	24.92	7.19	B/3	2274
Berthier Colonial Rifle	1907	8×50	T/Bolt	51.42	31.61	8.44	B/3	2300
Berthier Infantry Rifle 07/15	1915	8×50	T/Bolt	51.24	31.40	8.37	B/3	2350
Berthier Infantry Rifle 16	1916	8×50	T/Bolt	51.24	31.40	8.37	B/5	2090
Berthier Artillery Musketoon 92/16	1916	8×50	T/Bolt	37.20	17.83	7.19	B/3	2090
Gras '74-80-14 Rifle	1914	8×50	T/Bolt	51.38	32.28	9.00	SS	2296
Lebel Infantry Rifle	1886	8×50	T/Bolt	51.45	32.08	9.19	T/8	2067
Lebel Rifle '86R35	1935	8×50	T/Bolt	37.72	17.71	8.31	T/3	1985
Mannlicher: Austro-Hungarian Rifle	1888	8×50	SP/Bolt	50.43	30.12	9.69	B/5	1755
Mannlicher: Austro-Hungarian Carbine	1890	8×50	SP/Bolt	39.57	19.61	7.31	B/5	1886
Mannlicher: Austro-Hungarian Rifle	1895	8×50	SP/Bolt	50.40	30.19	8.35	B/5	2030
Mannlicher: Austro-Hungarian Short Rifle	1895	8×50	SP/Bolt	39.49	19.68	6.81	B/5	1902
Mauser: Austro-Hungarian Rifle	1914	8×50	T/Bolt	50.19	29.13	8.94	Int/5	2034
Mauser: Siam Rifle	1902	8×50	T/Bolt	49.09	29.13	8.56	Int/5	2050
Mauser: Siam Short Rifle	1923	8×52	T/Bolt	41.93	22.05	8.00	Int/5	2100
Murata Meiji 22nd Year Rifle	1889	8×53	T/Bolt	47.52	29.52	8.69	T/8	1853
Murata Meiji 27th Year Carbine	1894	8×53	T/Bolt	37.48	19.29	6.88	T/6	1706
Mannlicher: Hungary Short Rifle	1935	8×56	T/Bolt	48.75	23.60	8.88	B/5	2400
Mannlicher: Hungary Short Rifle	1943	8×56	T/Bolt	43.00	23.60	8.62	B/5	2400
Krag: Denmark Rifle	1889	8×58	T/Bolt	52.28	31.40	10.06	Int/5	1968
Krag: Denmark Carbines	1889	8×58	T/Bolt	43.30	23.62	8.88	Int/5	2035
Krag: Denmark Infantry Carbine '89-24	1924	8×58	T/Bolt	43.50	24.00	8.75	Int/5	2035
Krag: Denmark Sniper	1928	8×58	T/Bolt	46.06	23.03	11.81	Int/5	2460
Remington: Denmark Marine Rifle	1893	8×58	Block	36.02	21.06	6.94	SS	1980

Name	Year	Calibre	Action	Length	Barrel	Weight	Magazine	Velocity
Remington: Norway Carbine	1888	8×58	Block	40.35	24.21	8.37	SS	1788
Schutz & Larsen: Denmark Carbine	1942	8×58	T/Bolt	43.62	22.64	8.69	Int/4	2133
Guedes Rifle	1885	8×60	Block	47.91	33.27	9.00	SS	1706
Kropatschek: Portugal Infantry Rifle	1886	8×60	T/Bolt	51.97	31.57	10.06	T/8	1755
Kropatschek: Portugal Carbine	1886	8×60	T/Bolt	45.87	25.86	9.37	T/6	1558
Kropatschek: Portugal Cavalry Carbine	1886	8×60	T/Bolt	40.40	20.50	8.81	T/5	1394
Sako TRG-41 Sniper Rifle	1991	.338	T/Bolt	47.24	27.16	11.25	B/5	2998
Mauser: Turkey Infantry Rifle	1887	9.5×60	T/Bolt	49.25	29.92	9.25	T/8	1755
Jarmann Rifle	1884	10.15×61	T/Bolt	56.95	32.60	9.94	T/8	1362
Mauser-Milovanovitch Rifle	1880	10.15×63	T/Bolt	50.71	30.71	9.88	SS	1673
Mauser: Serbia Carbine	1885	10.15×63	T/Bolt	37.60	18.31	8.31	T/5	1525
Burton, Lee-Burton	1882	.402	T/Bolt	50.18	30.20	10.25	H/5	1570
Milbank-Amsler 1851/67 Rifle	1867	10.4×38	Trap	49.60	29.53	9.94	SS	1362
Milbank-Amsler 1856/67 Rifle	1867	10.4×38	Trap	51.93	34.05	9.31	SS	1443
Milbank-Amsler 1863/67 Rifle	1867	10.4×38	Trap	54.33	36.45	10.25	SS	1476
Milbank-Amsler 1864/67 Short Rifle	1867	10.4×38	Trap	49.49	29.60	10.06	SS	1362
Peabody: Swiss Engineer Rifle	1867	10.4×38	Block	51.57	32.80	9.69	SS	1427
Vetterli: Swiss Infantry Rifle	1869	10.4×38	T/Bolt	51.97	33.11	10.25	T/12	1427
Vetterli: Swiss Cadet Rifle	1870	10.4×38	T/Bolt	45.27	26.71	7.19	SS	1312
Vetterli: Swiss Carbine	1871	10.4×38	T/Bolt	36.69	18.50	7.19	T/6	1230
Vetterli: Swiss Short Rifle	1871	10.4×38	T/Bolt	49.61	30.90	10.19	T/10	1410
Vetterli: Swiss Infantry Rifle	1878	10.4×38	T/Bolt	52.20	33.11	10.12	T/12	1427
Vetterli: Swiss Short Rifle	1878	10.4×38	T/Bolt	52.20	33.11	10.19	T/12	1427
Vetterli: Swiss Carbine	1878	10.4×38	T/Bolt	36.54	18.50	7.25	T/6	1230
Vetterli: Swiss Border Guard Carbine	1878	10.4×38	T/Bolt	37.20	19.09	7.37	T/6	1230
Vetterli: Swiss Short Rifle	1881	10.4×38	T/Bolt	52.00	33.07	10.19	T/12	1427
Vetterli: Swiss Infantry Rifle	1881	10.4×38	T/Bolt	52.20	33.11	10.06	T/12	1427
Vetterli: Italy Infantry Rifle	1870	10.4×47	T/Bolt	52.95	33.86	9.81	SS	1410
Vetterli: Italy Short Rifle	1870	10.4×47	T/Bolt	43.11	24.00	8.81	SS	1345
Vetterli: Italy Cavalry Carbine	1870	10.4×47	T/Bolt	36.57	17.71	7.81	SS	1230
Vetterli: Italy Naval Rifle	1882	10.4×47	T/Bolt	47.64	28.74	8.94	T/8	1312
Vetterli-Vitali: Italy Rifle	1887	10.4×47	T/Bolt	52.95	33.86	9.81	B/4	1410
Berdan: Russia Infantry Rifle	1868	10.6×57	Trap	53.00	32.48	9.37	SS	1450
Berdan: Russia Infantry Rifle	1870	10.6×57	T/Bolt	53.35	32.80	9.56	SS	1433
Berdan: Russia Carbine	1870	10.6×57	T/Bolt	38.00	18.70	6.19	SS	1187
Berdan: Russia Dragoon Rifle	1870	10.6×57	T/Bolt	48.70	28.35	7.80	SS	1263
Berdan: Russia Cossack Rifle	1870	10.6×57	T/Bolt	48.00	28.35	7.50	SS	1263
Werder: Bavaria Carbine	1869	11×41	Block	37.80	21.65	7.69	SS	1148
Albini-Braendlin Short	1873	11×42	Trap	45.08	26.77	8.00	SS	1165
Comblain Short Rifle	1871	11×42	Block	31.49	17.91	6.62	SS	968
Früwirth Gendarmerie Carbine	1872	11×42	T/Bolt	40.86	22.44	8.12	T/6	978
Werndl Carbine	1867	11×42	Block	39.02	22.44	7.00	SS	978
Werndl Carbine	1873	11×42	Block	39.53	22.83	7.19	SS	984
Albini-Braendlin	1867	11×50	Trap	53.07	34.76	10.07	SS	1360
Albini-Braendlin, Infantry	1873	11×50	Trap	53.03	34.72	9.88	SS	1380
Werder: Bavaria Infantry Rifle	1869	11×50	Block	51.18	35.04	9.62	SS	1463
Beaumont Infantry Rifle	1871	11×51	T/Bolt	52.00	32.67	9.62	SS	1328
Beaumont Infantry Rifle	1888	11×51	T/Bolt	52.00	32.67	10.00	B/4	1476

Name	Year	Calibre	Action	Length	Barrel	Weight	Magazine	Velocity
Comblain Civil Guard Carbine	1870	11×53	Block	47.24	31.81	9.81	SS	1410
Werndl Infantry Rifle	1873	11×58	Block	49.80	33.07	9.33	SS	1430
Gras Rifle	1874	11×59	T/Bolt	51.38	32.32	9.25	SS	1443
Gras Cavalry etc. Carbines	1874	11×59	T/Bolt	46.26	27.64	7.85	SS	1404
Gras Artillery Musketoon	1874	11×59	T/Bolt	38.98	20.08	7.19	SS	1332
Kropatschek: France Marine Rifle	1878	11×59	T/Bolt	48.98	29.25	9.94	T/7	1493
Kropatschek: France Infantry Rifle	1884	11×59	T/Bolt	48.98	29.25	9.37	T/8	1493
Kropatschek: France Infantry Rifle	1885	11×59	T/Bolt	48.98	23.57	9.25	T/8	1493
Murata Meiji 18th Year Rifle	1885	11×60	T/Bolt	50.23	32.00	9.00	SS	1427
Remington: Spain Rolling block Rifle	1870	11.15×57	Block	50.31	35.12	9.31	SS	1365
Remington: Spain Carbine	1870	11.15×57	Block	42.13	27.16	8.62	SS	1148
Remington: Spain Short Rifle	1870	11.15×57	Block	46.85	32.28	8.81	SS	1296
Remington: Spain Infantry Rifle	1871	11.15×57	Block	51.77	37.00	9.00	SS	1312
Remington: Spain Short Rifle	1871	11.15×57	Block	42.52	27.95	8.75	SS	1214
Remington: Spain Cavalry Carbine	1871	11.15×57	Block	37.91	23.15	7.25	SS	1171
Remington: Spain Artillery Carbine	1871	11.15×57	Block	37.91	23.15	7.50	SS	1171
Remington: Spain Dragoon Carbine	1889	11.15×57	Block	46.26	31.57	8.69	SS	1453
Whitney: Mexico Rifle	1873	11.15×57	Block	50.48	35.00	9.50	SS	1450
Whitney: Mexico Carbine	1873	11.15×57	Block	36.00	20.50	7.19	SS	1312
Kropatschek: Austria Carbine	1881	11.15×58	T/Bolt	40.95	22.44	8.37	T/5	1007
Mannlicher: Austro-Hungarian Rifle	1885	11.15×58	SP/Bolt	52.28	31.81	10.50	B/5	1444
Mannlicher: Austro-Hungarian Rifle	1886	11.15×58	SP/Bolt	52.20	31.73	9.94	B/5	1444
Werndl: Austro-Hungarian Rifle	1867	11.15×58	Block	50.31	33.66	9.75	SS	1430
Mauser: Germany Infantry Rifle	1871	11.15×60	T/Bolt	52.95	33.66	10.06	SS	1411
Mauser; Germany Light Infantry Rifle	1871	11.15×60	T/Bolt	48.82	29.53	9.88	SS	1371
Mauser: Germany Carbine	1871	11.15×60	T/Bolt	39.17	19.88	7.56	SS	1280
Mauser: Germany Infantry Rifle 71/84	1885	11.15×60	T/Bolt	51.06	31.50	10.19	T/8	1411
Werder: Bavaria M69 nM Rifle	1875	11.15×60	Block	51.85	34.84	9.19	SS	1378
Evans Old Model	1872	.44	Block	47.25	30.00	10.12	Hel/24	850
Evans New Model	1877	.44	Block	43.25	26.00	9.62	Hel/26	1443
Winchester Musket M1873	1873	.44-40	Lever	48.30	30.00	9.50	T/17	1300
De Lisle Silenced	1941	.45	T/Bolt	35.50	8.27	7.50	B/8	853
Allin-Springfield Infantry	1873	.45-70	Trap	51.92	32.38	9.19	SS	1320
Allin-Springfield Infantry	1879	.45-70	Trap	51.75	32.38	9.15	SS	1320
Allin-Springfield Carbine	1879	.45-70	Trap	41.30	21.88	9.19	SS	1200
Chaffee-Reece	1882	.45-70	T/Bolt	49.00	27.90	9.19	T/5	1300
Remington-Keene	1880	.45-70	T/Bolt	48.50	30.00	9.00	T/8	1275
Remington-Lee US Navy Rifle	1879	.45-70	T/Bolt	48.50	29.50	8.50	B/5	1320
Remington-Lee US Navy Rifle	1885	.45-70	T/Bolt	52.00	33.50	8.50	B/5	1350
Remington-Lee Rifle	1889	.45-70	T/Bolt	47.60	29.00	8.50	B/10	1350
Winchester-Hotchkiss	1879	.45-70	T/Bolt	48.60	28.65	9.12	T/5	1300
Winchester-Hotchkiss	1883	.45-70	T/Bolt	51.75	32.00	8.94	T/6	1300
Peabody-Martini: Turkey Rifle	1874	.450	Block	49.00	33.22	8.75	SS	1263
Remington: Egypt Rifle	1868	11.43×50	Block	50.31	35.00	9.12	SS	860
Peabody-Martini: Romania Rifle	1879	11.43×60	Block	49.00	33.26	9.62	SS	1492
Remington: Denmark Carbine	1867	11.7×27	Block	36.02	21.06	6.94	SS	870
Krag-Peterson: Denmark Carbine	1877	11.7×42	Block	37.48	20.07	8.94	T/7	1148
Remington: Denmark Rifle	1867	11.7×42	Block	50.39	35.71	9.25	SS	1230

Name	Year	Calibre	Action	Length	Barrel	Weight	Magazine	Velocity
Remington: Denmark Cavalry Carbine	1896	11.7×51	Block	36.02	21.06	6.94	SS	1345
Remington: Norway Rifle	1867	12.17×44	Block	53.46	37.92	9.94	SS	1247
Barrett M90	1990	.50 Brg	T/Bolt	45.00	29.00	22.00	B/5	2798
Croatia: MACS Sniper	1995	.50 Brg	T/Bolt	57.87	30.70	25.37	SS	2805
Harris M87R Sniper	1987	.50 Brg	T/Bolt	53.00	29.00	21.00	B/5	2798
Harris M92 Sniper	1992	.50 Brg	T/Bolt	35.00	29.00	21.00	B/5	2798
Helenius APH-RK-97	1995	.50 Brg	Block	52.36	37.00	30.88	SS	2723
PGM Hecate II Anti-materiel Rifle	1993	.50 Brg	T/Bolt	54.33	27.56	30.44	B/7	2788
Robar RC-50	1980	.50 Brg	T/Bolt	55.00	29.00	25.00	B/5	2723
Allin-Springfield Infantry	1866	.50-70	Trap	56.00	36.60	9.88	SS	1260
Burton, Ward-Burton	1870	.50-70	T/Bolt	51.88	32.63	9.06	SS	1250
Remington: USA Navy Rifle	1870	.50-70	Block	48.62	32.62	9.06	SS	1275
Remington; USA Carbine	1870	.50-70	Block	38.50	23.25	7.81	SS	1100
Remington: USA Army Rifle	1871	.50-70	Block	51.75	36.00	9.31	SS	1315
Czech: Falcon Anti-materiel	1995	12.7×108	T/Bolt	54.33	36.50	32.88	B/5	2789
Gepard M1	1987	12.7×108	Screw	61.81	43.40	41.88	SS	2756
Mauser: Germany Tank-Gewehr	1918	13×92	T/Bolt	61.81	38.69	39.00	SS	3000
Boys Anti-tank	1937	.55	T/Bolt	63.50	36.00	36.00	B/5	3250
Wänzl Infantry Rifle	1866	14×33	Trap	52.32	34.84	9.37	SS	1280
Wänzl Short Rifle	1866	14×33	Trap	43.50	26.02	10.37	SS	1240
Wänzl Carbine	1866	14×33	Trap	41.61	24.06	9.12	SS	1224
Joslyn Carbine	1862	.56-50	Block	39.50	22.00	8.44	SS	900
Peabody: Spain Rifle	1868	.56-50	Block	54.05	35.90	9.94	SS	1230
Peabody: Spain Carbine	1868	.56-50	Block	38.19	19.96	8.50	SS	984
Spencer Rifle conversion	1871	.56-50	Block	49.50	32.50	10.62	T/7	1120
Gallager Carbine	1864	.56-52	Lever	41.00	22.25	8.19	SS	900
Palmer Carbine	1865	.56-52	T/Bolt	38.50	20.00	8.50	SS	900
Triplett & Scott Long Carbine	1864	.56-52	Block	48.00	30.00	9.00	T/7	1025
Triplett & Scott Short Carbine	1864	.56-52	Block	40.00	22.00	8.37	T/7	1025
Warner Carbine	1864	.56-52	Block	38.00	20.00	8.12	SS	900
Spencer Rifle	1861	.56-56	Block	47.00	30.00	10.00	T/7	950
Spencer Carbine	1861	.56-56	Block	39.00	22.00	8.25	T/7	930
Berdan: Spain Infantry Rifle	1867	14.5×41	Trap	54.70	36.22	9.44	SS	1197
Berdan: Spain Light Rifle	1867	14.5×41	Trap	48.42	30.31	8.44	SS	1100
Berdan: Spain Carbine	1867	14.5×41	Trap	48.42	30.31	8.31	SS	1197
Degtyarev PTRD Anti-tank	1941	14.5×114	T/Bolt	78.74	48.30	38.12	SS	3320
NTW 14.5 Anti-materiel Rifle	1995	14.5×114	T/Bolt	79.33	48.03	63.94	B/3	3543
Martini-Henry Rifle Mk I	1874	.577/450	Block	49.00	33.22	8.75	SS	1315
Martini-Henry Rifle Mk 4	1887	.577/450	Block	49.38	33.06	9.12	SS	1350
Martini-Henry Carbine, Cavalry	1877	.577/450	Block	37.68	21.38	7.50	SS	1100
Martini-Henry Carbine, RA	1879	.577/450	Block	37.68	21.38	7.62	SS	1100
Martini-Richards Rifle	1895	.577/450	Block	49.53	33.25	9.00	SS	1350
Swinburn Rifle	1875	.577/450	Block	49.50	33.00	9.31	SS	1350
Snider Rifled Musket Pattern 1	1866	.577	Trap	72.50†	39.00	10.00	SS	1240
Snider Rifled Musket Pattern 2**	1867	.577	Trap	54.25	36.50	9.12	SS	1240
Snider Enfield Short Rifle P60	1867	.577	Trap	48.70	30.50	8.75	SS	1200
Snider Artillery Carbine P61	1867	.577	Trap	40.25	21.50	7.50	SS	1005
Snider Cavalry Carbine P61	1867	.577	Trap	37.38	19.25	6.62	SS	995

† including bayonet

Name	Year	Calibre	Action	Length	Barrel	Weight	Magazine	Velocity
Snider Constabulary Carbine	1867	.577	Trap	41.10	22.50	7.31	SS	1020
Snider Yeomanry Carbine	1880	.577	Trap	37.88	21.63	7.00	SS	995
NTW 20 Anti-materiel Rifle	1995	20×83	T/Bolt	70.67	39.37	57.31	B/3	2362

AUTOMATIC RIFLES

Name	Year	Calibre	Action	Length	Barrel	Weight	Feed	Velocity	Rate
H&K HK36	1971	4.6×36	DBB	35.04	15.00	6.25	B/30	2811	1100
H&K G11K3 Caseless	1990	4.73×33	Gas	29.53	21.26	8.06	B/45	3051	600
Armenia: K3 Rifle	1996	5.45×39.5	Gas	27.56	16.34	8.81	B/30	2952	600
Kalashnikov:									
AK74	1974	5.45×39.5	Gas	36.53	15.75	8.50	B/30	2953	650
AK-74-SU	1980	5.45×39.5	Gas	26.57	8.11	5.94	B/30	2411	700
Poland: Tantal 88	1990	5.45×39.5	Gas	37.13	16.65	7.50	B/30	2887	650
Romania AK-74	1980	5.45×39.5	Gas	37.00	16.34	7.50	B/30	2887	700
Onyx Type 89	1989	5.45×39.5	Gas	28.35	8.15	6.37	B/30	2296	700
Russia: AS-94 Assault Rifle	1995	5.45×39.5	Gas	37.12	n/a	8.50	B/30	2952	600
Advanced Combat Rifle:									
AAI Prototype	1985	5.56×45	Gas	40.59	n/a	7.75	B/30	4600	n/a
Colt Prototype	1985	5.56×45	Gas	40.59	n/a	7.31	B/30	2900	n/a
Heckler & Koch Prototype	1985	4.92×34	Gas	29.53	n/a	8.62	B/50	3000	600
Steyr Prototype	1985	5.56mm	Gas	30.08	n/a	7.12	B/24	4855	n/a
ArmaLite AR-15	1957	5.56×45	Gas	39.00	20.00	6.31	B/30	3240	800
ArmaLite AR-18	1964	5.56×45	Gas	37.00	18.26	6.94	B/30	3280	800
ArmaLite AR-18S	1970	5.56×45	Gas	30.11	10.10	6.81	B/30	2560	800
Beretta AR-70 Assault Rifle	1970	5.56×45	Gas	37.60	17.80	7.61	B/30	3116	650
Beretta SC-70 Carbine	1970	5.56×45	Gas	37.80	17.80	7.75	B/30	3116	650
Beretta SCS-70 Short Carbine	1975	5.56×45	Gas	32.28	12.60	8.16	B/30	2903	600
Beretta AR70/90 Rifle	1990	5.56×45	Gas	39.29	17.71	8.81	B/30	3050	625
Beretta SC70/90 Rifle	1990	5.56×45	Gas	38.81	17.80	8.75	B/30	3150	700
Beretta SCS70/90 Rifle	1990	5.56×45	Gas	34.48	13.68	8.31	B/30	2952	700
Bernardelli B-2 Rifle	1985	5.56×45	Gas	38.54	18.10	8.60	B/30	3002	600
Bernardelli B2S Carbine	1985	5.56×45	Gas	33.50	13.07	8.00	B/30	2756	720
Beryl Model 96 Rifle	1996	5.56×45	Gas	37.13	18.00	7.37	B/30	3018	700
Beryl Mini-Beryl 96 Carbine	1996	5.56×45	Gas	28.74	9.25	6.62	B/30	2526	700
Bofors CGA-5 (Ak5) Rifle	1986	5.56×45	Gas	39.57	17.71	8.56	B/30	3051	700
Bofors CGA-5-C2 Carbine	1995	5.56×45	Gas	32.09	9.84	7.31	B/30	2887	750
CETME Model L	1984	5.56×45	DBB	36.42	15.75	7.50	B/12/30	2870	700
CETME Model LC	1984	5.56×45	DBB	33.86	12.60	7.00	B/12/30	2730	750
Chartered SAR-80	1980	5.56×45	Gas	38.18	18.07	8.19	B/20	3182	600
Chartered SR-88	1988	5.56×45	Gas	38.19	18.07	8.06	B/20/30	3182	750
Chartered SR-88A	1990	5.56×45	Gas	37.80	18.11	8.12	B/30	3084	800
Chartered SR-88A Carbine	1990	5.56×45	Gas	31.89	11.50	8.37	B/30	2730	800
China: Type CQ	1986	5.56×45	Gas	38.86	19.88	7.06	B/20	3248	750
Colt M16A1	1967	5.56×45	Gas	39.00	20.00	6.31	B/30	3250	800

Name	Year	Calibre	Action	Length	Barrel	Weight	Feed	Velocity	Rate
Colt M16A2	1982	5.56×45	Gas	39.37	20.00	7.50	B/30	3110	800
Colt M16A4 Carbine	1985	5.56×45	Gas	33.00	14.57	5.81	B/30	3022	700
Colt M231 Firing Port Weapon	1983	5.56×45	Gas	32.38	14.50	8.56	B/30	3000	1100
Croatia: APS95 Assault Rifle	1995	5.56×45	Gas	38.58	17.71	8.15	B/35	3002	650
Czech: CZ2000 Assault Rifle	1995	5.56×45	Gas	33.46	15.04	6.56	B/30	2985	800
Czech: CZ2000 Short Rifle	1995	5.56×45	Gas	26.57	7.28	5.75	B/30	2887	800
Daewoo K1 Carbine	1982	5.56×45	Gas	30.90	10.35	6.31	B/30	2730	750
Daewoo K2 Rifle	1987	5.56×45	Gas	38.58	18.30	7.19	B/30	3018	800
Daewoo K1A1 Carbine	1987	5.56×45	Gas	32.68	10.35	6.37	B/30	2690	800
Diemaco C7 Rifle	1984	5.56×45	Gas	40.15	20.00	7.25	B/30	3035	800
Diemaco C8 Carbine	1984	5.56×45	Gas	33.07	14.57	5.94	B/30	2952	800
Enfield L85A1	1986	5.56×45	Gas	30.90	20.40	8.37	B/30	3084	750
FN CAL Rifle	1966	5.56×45	Gas	38.50	18.46	6.50	B/20	3200	850
FN FNC Rifle	1976	5.56×45	Gas	39.25	17.68	8.37	B/30	3166	650
FN FNC Carbine	1976	5.56×45	Gas	35.87	14.29	7.75	B/20	3117	700
FARA 83 Assault Rifle	1984	5.56×45	Gas	39.37	17.80	8.69	B/30	3166	750
FFV 890C	1983	5.56×45	Gas	33.86	13.39	7.69	B/35	2730	650
Galil ARM Rifle/LMG	1975	5.56×45	Gas	38.54	18.11	9.56	B/35	3116	700
Galil SAR Short Assault Rifle	1975	5.56×45	Gas	33.07	13.07	8.31	B/35	2953	650
Galil MAR micro Assault Rifle	1994	5.56×45	Gas	27.16	7.68	6.50	B/35	2330	650
H&K HK33A2	1965	5.56×45	Gas	36.22	15.35	8.06	B/40	3018	750
H&K HK33A3	1965	5.56×45	DBB	37.00	15.35	8.75	B/40	3018	750
H&K HK33KA1	1965	5.56×45	DBB	33.97	12.67	8.75	B/40	3008	650
H&K HK33EA2	1985	5.56×45	DBB	36.22	15.35	8.06	B/25	3018	750
H&K HK33EK	1985	5.56×45	DBB	34.05	12.67	8.75	B/25	2887	650
H&K HK33SG/1	1985	5.56×45	DBB	35.22	15.35	8.06	B/25	3018	750
H&K HK53	1975	5.56×45	DBB	29.72	8.85	6.69	B/40	2460	700
H&K G36	1995	5.56×45	Gas	39.29	18.90	7.56	B/30	3018	750
H&K G36K	1995	5.56×45	Gas	33.78	13.00	6.88	B/30	2789	750
H&K G41	1985	5.56×45	DBB	39.25	17.71	9.06	B/30	3150	850
H&K G41A2	1985	5.56×45	DBB	39.24	17.71	9.56	B/30	3150	850
H&K G41K	1985	5.56×45	DBB	36.61	14.96	9.37	B/30	3000	900
Howa Type 89	1989	5.56×45	Gas	36.06	16.54	7.69	B/30	3018	750
IMBEL MD2	1985	5.56×45	Gas	40.55	17.83	9.69	B/30	3150	700
IMBEL MD3	1985	5.56×45	Gas	40.55	17.83	10.06	B/30	3150	700
INSAS Assault Rifle	1993	5.56×45	Gas	37.20	18.26	7.06	B/30	3000	650
Kalashnikov AK101	1996	5.56×45	Gas	37.12	16.34	7.50	B/30	2985	600
K'nikov: Hungary NGM Ass. Rifle	1995	5.56×45	Gas	36.81	16.23	7.00	B/30	2953	600
Kalashnikov: Poland Tantal 89	1992	5.56×45	Gas	37.13	16.65	7.50	B/30	2953	650
Kalashnikov: Yugoslavia M80	1985	5.56×45	Gas	38.97	18.11	7.69	B/10	3182	750
Kalashnikov: Yugoslavia M85	1985	5.56×45	Gas	31.10	12.40	7.06	B/30	2592	700
MAS FAMAS F-1	1980	5.56×45	DBB	29.80	19.20	8.19	B/25	3150	950
MAS FAMAS G-2	1994	5.56×45	DBB	29.92	19.20	8.37	B/30	3035	1100
Onyx Type 91	1991	5.56×45	Gas	28.35	8.15	6.37	B/30	2330	700
Ruger Mini14/20GB	1982	5.56×45	Gas	37.40	18.50	6.37	B/30	3297	No
Ruger AC-556	1984	5.56×45	Gas	37.74	18.50	6.37	B/30	3470	750
Ruger AC-556F	1984	5.56×45	Gas	32.08	13.00	6.94	B/30	3470	750
SIG SG-530 Assault Rifle	1968	5.56×45	Gas	37.00	15.50	7.50	B/30	3000	600

Name	Year	Calibre	Action	Length	Barrel	Weight	Feed	Velocity	Rate
SIG SG-540 Assault Rifle	1972	5.56×45	Gas	37.40	18.11	7.19	B/30	3215	700
SIG SG-543 Assault Carbine	1975	5.56×45	Gas	31.69	11.81	6.50	B/30	2870	750
SIG SG-550 (Stgw90) Rifle	1986	5.56×45	Gas	39.29	20.79	9.06	B/30	3215	700
SIG SG-551 (Stgw90) Carbine	1986	5.56×45	Gas	32.55	14.64	7.50	B/30	3018	700
SIG SG-550 Sniper	1985	5.56×45	Gas	44.48	25.59	15.50	B/30	3215	No
SIG SG-551-1P (SWAT)	1993	5.56×45	Gas	32.79	14.29	7.50	B/30	3018	700
SIG SG-552 Commando	1995	5.56×45	Gas	28.74	8.90	7.06	B/30	2379	No
Steyr-Mannlicher AUG Rifle	1977	5.56×45	Gas	31.10	20.00	7.94	B/30	3182	650
Steyr-Mannlicher AUG Carbine	1977	5.56×45	Gas	27.16	16.02	7.31	B/30	3133	700
Steyr AUG Submachine gun	1977	5.56×45	Gas	24.65	13.78	6.69	B/30	3050	700
Steyr AUG/HB	1977	5.56×45	Gas	35.43	24.45	10.81	B/42	3280	680
Stoner M63A1 Rifle	1963	5.56×45	Gas	40.20	20.00	7.75	B/30	3250	700
Taiwan Type 65	1965	5.56×45	Gas	38.97	20.00	6.94	B/20	3248	750
Vektor R4	1982	5.56×45	Gas	39.57	18.11	9.44	B/35	3215	700
Vektor R5 Short Rifle	1987	5.56×45	Gas	34.57	13.07	8.19	B/35	3018	700
Vektor R6 compact	1994	5.56×45	Gas	31.69	11.02	8.06	B/35	2706	585
Vektor CR21	1998	5.56×45	Gas	29.92	18.11	8.37	B/35	3215	700
Yugoslavia: M85	1985	5.56×45	Gas	31.30	12.40	7.06	B/30	2592	700
Russia: APS Underwater Rifle	1985	5.66mm	Gas	33.07	n/a	5.31	B/26	1198	n/a
Federov Automat (Prototype)	1913	6.5×51	Rec	49.41	31.50	10.12	B/5	2400	n/a
Federov Automat (Production)	1916	6.5×51	Rec	38.38	20.47	9.81	B/25	2313	n/a
Cei-Rigotti	1900	6.5×52	Gas	39.37	19.00	9.56	B/10/20	2400	n/a
Browning BAR: Sweden M21	1922	6.5×55	Gas	44.00	26.40	19.19	B/20	2460	500
Browning BAR; Sweden M37	1937	6.5×55	Gas	46.10	24.00	20.88	B/20	2460	480
Ljungmann Ag42 Rifle	1942	6.5×55	Gas	47.90	25.10	9.69	B/10	2460	No
Ljungmann Ag42B Rifle	1953	6.5×55	Gas	47.80	24.50	10.37	B/10	2450	No
Pederson T2E1	1932	.276	DBB	45.00	24.00	9.00	B/10	2500	No
BSA P-28	1950	.280	Gas	42.20	22.24	9.56	B/20	2525	No
Enfield EM1	1947	.280	Gas	35.98	24.48	10.12	B/20	2530	600
Enfield No 9 Mk 1 (EM2)	1949	.280	Gas	35.00	24.48	7.81	B/20	2530	650
Breda: Costa Rica Rifle PG	1935	7×57	Gas	43.90	17.90	11.56	B/20	1885	No
Mondragon Mexico M1908	1908	7×57	Gas	42.04	24.40	9.37	B/8	2050	No
Meunier A-6 Rifle	1916	7×59	Rec	50.90	28.35	8.88	B/6	2608	No
MAS Mle 1949	1950	7.5×54	Gas	42.30	22.83	9.00	B/10	2750	No
MAS Mle 1949/56	1956	7.5×54	Gas	40.75	22.83	8.37	B/10	2750	No
SIG AK53	1953	7.5×55	BF	39.37	23.63	10.75	B/30	2450	300
SIG Stgw57 Assault Rifle	1957	7.5×55	DBB	43.40	20.47	12.31	B/24	2493	475
Beretta P-30 Carbine	1957	.30 Car	Gas	37.25	17.91	7.19	B/30	1968	500
Cristóbal M2 Carbine	1953	.30 Car	DBB	37.20	16.22	7.75	B/30	1876	580
Winchester US M1 Carbine	1941	.30 Car	Gas	35.58	18.00	5.19	B/15	1970	No
Winchester US M1A1 Carbine	1943	.30 Car	Gas	35.63	18.00	5.56	B/15	1970	No
Winchester US M2 Carbine	1944	.30 Car	Gas	35.58	18.00	5.19	B/30	1970	750
Browning Auto. Rifle (BAR):									
US M1918	1918	.30-06	Gas	47.00	24.00	16.00	B/20	2805	550
US M1918A1	1927	.30-06	Gas	47.00	24.00	18.50	B/20	2805	550
US M1918A2	1939	.30-06	Gas	47.80	24.00	19.37	B/20	2805	450/650
US M1922	1922	.30-06	Gas	41.00	18.00	19.19	B/20	2700	550
Garand M1	1932	.30-06	Gas	43.50	24.00	9.50	Int/8	2740	No

Name	Year	Calibre	Action	Length	Barrel	Weight	Feed	Velocity	Rate
Johnson M1941	1941	.30-06	Rec	45.50	22.00	9.50	Int/10	2650	No
Walther WA2000 Sniper	1985	.300	Gas	35.63	25.59	15.31	B/6	3238	No
China: Type 68 Rifle	1968	7.62×39	Gas	40.50	20.50	7.69	B/15	2395	750
China: Type 81 Rifle	1990	7.62×39	Gas	37.60	15.75	7.50	B/30	2395	750
Czech: vz 52/56 Rifle	1953	7.62×39	Gas	40.00	20.50	9.00	B/10	2705	No
Czech: vz 58 Rifle	1958	7.62×39	Gas	33.20	15.80	6.88	B/30	2330	800
H&K HK32A2 Rifle	1965	7.62×39	DBB	40.20	15.35	7.69	B/30	2360	600
H&K HK32A3	1965	7.62×39	DBB	37.00	15.35	8.50	B/30	2360	600
H&K HK32KA1	1965	7.62×39	DBB	34.00	12.67	8.37	B/30	2295	600
Kalashnikov:									
AK-47	1949	7.62×39	Gas	34.21	16.30	9.44	B/30	2329	775
AKM	1959	7.62×39	Gas	34.49	16.30	8.44	B/30	2329	775
AKM-S	1960	7.62×39	Gas	35.24	16.30	7.81	B/30	2329	750
AKMS-U	1975	7.62×39	Gas	28.42	8.86	7.37	B/30	2116	800
China: Type 56-C		7.62×39	Gas	30.11	13.58	7.69	B/30	2296	700
Hungary: AMD-65	1965	7.62×39	Gas	33.50	12.52	7.19	B/30	2296	600
Romania: AKM-R		7.62×39	Gas	29.53	8.11	6.81	B/20	2854	600
Ljungmann/Rashid (Egypt)	1960	7.62×39	Gas	42.40	22.44	8.37	B/10	2395	No
Sako M90	1990	7.62×39	Gas	36.61	16.38	8.50	B/30	2625	700
Simonov SKS	1946	7.62×39	Gas	40.20	20.50	8.50	B/10	2410	No
Simonov: Yugoslavia M59/66	1966	7.62×39	Gas	44.09	24.33	9.00	B/10	2410	No
Valmet M62 Assault Rifle	1962	7.62×39	Gas	36.00	16.50	9.00	B/30	2400	650
Valmet M71 Assault Rifle	1971	7.62×39	Gas	36.53	16.53	7.94	B/30	2400	650
Valmet M76 Assault Rifle	1976	7.62×39	Gas	35.94	16.54	8.06	B/30	2400	650
Valmet M78 long Rifle	1978	7.62×39	Gas	41.73	22.36	10.37	B/30	2460	650
Czech: vz 52 Rifle	1953	7.62×45	Gas	40.00	20.50	9.00	B/10	2440	No
ArmaLite AR-10	1957	7.62×51	Gas	40.51	20.00	9.06	B/20	2772	700
Beretta BM-59 Infantry Rifle	1960	7.62×51	Gas	43.00	19.30	9.56	B/20	2700	800
Beretta BM-59 Alpini Rifle	1960	7.62×51	Gas	43.20	19.30	10.06	B/20	2700	800
Beretta BM-59 Parachutist	1960	7.62×51	Gas	43.70	18.40	9.62	B/20	2625	810
Beretta BM-59 Mark 4	1964	7.62×51	Gas	48.90	21.00	12.00	B/20	2730	750
CETME Model 58	1958	7.62×51	DBB	39.37	17.00	11.31	B/20	2493	600
CETME Model C	1965	7.62×51	DBB	39.96	17.72	9.25	B/20	2560	600
CETME Model R	1981	7.62×51	DBB	26.18	12.00	14.12	B/20	2263	600
Cristóbal M62 Rifle	1962	7.62×51	Gas	42.50	21.30	10.37	B/20	2705	No
FN FAL Model 50-00	1953	7.62×51	Gas	42.90	20.98	9.37	B/20	2756	700
FN FAL Model 50-64	1953	7.62×51	Gas	43.11	20.98	8.56	B/20	2756	700
FN FAL Model 50-63	1955	7.62×51	Gas	40.15	17.17	8.25	B/20	2657	700
FN FAL Model 50-41	1958	7.62×51	Gas	45.28	20.98	13.19	B/20	2756	700
Galil ARM Rifle/LMG	1972	7.62×51	Gas	41.34	21.06	9.69	B/25	2788	650
Galil SAR Short Assault Rifle	1972	7.62×51	Gas	36.02	15.75	8.31	B/25	2625	750
Galil Sniper	1976	7.62×51	Gas	43.90	20.00	14.12	B/30	2674	No
Garand: US M14	1957	7.62×51	Gas	44.14	22.00	8.56	B/20	2800	750
Garand: US M14A1	1958	7.62×51	Gas	44.30	22.00	12.75	B/20	2800	750
H&K G3 Rifle	1961	7.62×51	DBB	40.20	17.72	9.69	B/20	2625	550
H&K G3A1	1963	7.62×51	DBB	40.20	17.72	10.37	B/20	2625	550
H&K G3A3	1964	7.62×51	DBB	40.35	17.72	9.69	B/20	2625	550
H&K G3A4	1964	7.62×51	DBB	40.35	17.72	10.37	B/20	2625	550

Name	Year	Calibre	Action	Length	Barrel	Weight	Feed	Velocity	Rate
H&K G3A7 (Turkey)	1970	7.62×51	DBB	40.16	17.71	9.37	B/20	2690	600
H&K G3A7A1 (Turkey)	1970	7.62×51	DBB	40.16	17.71	10.00	B/20	2690	600
H&K G3SG/1	1973	7.62×51	DBB	40.35	17.72	12.19	B/20	2625	550
H&K PSG1	1985	7.65×51	DBB	47.56	25.60	17.81	B/20	2723	No
H&K MSG90	1987	7.62×51	DBB	45.87	23.62	14.12	B/20	2690	No
H&K MSG90A1	1997	7.62×51	DBB	45.87	23.62	14.69	B/20	2690	No
H&K G8 Rifle	1985	7.62×51	DBB	40.55	17.71	17.94	B/D/Belt	2625	800
Howa Type 64	1964	7.62×51	Gas	38.97	17.71	9.69	B/20	2296	500
Kalashnikov: Yugoslavia M77B1 Rifle	1983	7.62×51	Gas	38.97	16.34	7.50	B/20	2887	700
Madsen M62	1962	7.62×51	Gas	42.30	21.10	10.56	B/20	2651	600
MAS Mle 1962	1962	7.62×51	Gas	40.75	22.80	9.31	B/20	2758	No
SIG SG-510	1958	7.62×51	DBB	40.00	19.88	9.37	B/20	2592	500
SIG SG-542	1974	7.62×51	Gas	39.37	18.31	7.81	B/30	2690	650
Al-Kadisa Sniper	1990	7.62×54	Gas	48.43	24.41	9.44	B/10	2723	No
Dragunov SVD	1963	7.62×54	Gas	48.23	24.48	9.44	B10	2723	No
Simonov AVS-36	1936	7.62×54	Gas	48.10	24.40	9.50	B/15	2550	No
Tokarev SVT38	1938	7.62×54	Gas	48.10	25.00	8.62	B/10	2725	No
Tokarev SVT40	1940	7.62×54	Gas	48.10	24.60	8.56	B/10	2725	No
Tokarev SKT40 Carbine	1930	7.62×54	Gas	41.93	18.50	8.06	B/20	2445	No
Browning BAR: Belgium M30	1930	7.65×53	Gas	45.27	22.00	20.50	B/20	2788	600
Haenel MKb42(H)	1942	7.92×33	Gas	37.00	14.37	10.81	B/30	2100	500
Haenel MP43 (StG 44)	1943	7.92×33	Gas	37.00	16.50	11.25	B/30	2125	500
Mauser StG 45 Assault Rifle	1945	7.92×33	DBB	35.15	15.75	8.19	B/30	2100	400
Gustloff Volksgewehr VG1-5	1945	7.92×33	DBB	34.85	14.90	10.12	B/30	2150	No
Walther MKb 42 (W)	1942	7.92×33	Gas	36.65	16.00	9.69	B/30	2120	600
Czech: ZH 29 Rifle	1929	7.92×57	Gas	45.50	21.50	10.00	B/25	2700	No
Czech: ZK 420 Rifle	1946	7.92×57	Gas	41.25	21.00	10.00	B/10	2700	No
FN SAFN Rifle	1949	7.92×57	Gas	44.00	22.25	9.50	B/10	2400	No
Kalashnikov: Yugoslavia M76 Sniper	1980	7.92×57	Gas	44.68	21.65	9.25	B/30	2887	No
Ljungmann/Hakim (Egypt)	1955	7.92×57	Gas	47.00	23.23	10.62	B/10	2854	No
Mauser Aviator's Rifle	1915	7.92×57	Gas	49.13	26.57	10.50	B/20	2510	No
Mauser Gewehr 41 (M)	1941	7.92×57	Gas	46.14	21.65	11.06	B/10	2428	No
Pelo	1950	7.92×57	Rec	43.40	n/a	9.25	B/10	2460	No
Rheinmetall FG 42 Rifle	1942	7.92×57	Gas	37.00	20.00	9.94	B/20	2500	750
SIG SK46	1946	7.92×57	Gas	44.25	23.63	10.00	B/10	2700	No
Walther Gewehr 41 (W)	1941	7.92×57	Gas	44.50	21.45	11.00	B/30	2365	No
Walther Gewehr 43	1943	7.92×57	Gas	44.00	22.00	9.56	B/10	2448	No
Panzerbuchse 38	1938	7.92×94	Rec	51.00	43.00	35.00	SS	3795	No
MAS Mle 1917	1917	8×50	Gas	52.40	31.40	11.56	B/5	2350	No
MAS Mle 1918	1918	8×50	Gas	43.10	23.10	10.50	B/5	2200	No
Ballester-Rigaud	1946	9×19	BB	33.50	12.60	n/a	54	1250	No
Russia: AS Silent Rifle	1988	9×39	Gas	34.40	n/a	5.50	B/20	968	n/a
Russia: VSS Silent Sniper	1988	9×39	Gas	39.29	n/a	9.06	B/20	968	n/a
Barrett M82A1 Light Fifty	1983	.50 Brg	Rec	61.00	29.00	44.00	B/11	2798	No
Barrett M62A2	1992	.50 Brg	Rec	55.47	29.00	29.00	B/5	2798	No
Stoner SR50 Anti-materiel	1996	.50 Brg	Gas	58.38	35.50	31.44	B/10	2887	No
Gepard M2 Anti-materiel	1990	12.7×108	Rec	60.24	43.40	26.44	B/10	2756	No
Gepard M2A1 Anti-materiel	1990	12.7×108	Rec	49.61	32.68	22.06	B/10	2592	No

Name	Year	Calibre	Action	Length	Barrel	Weight	Feed	Velocity	Rate
Russia: V-94 Anti-materiel	1995	12.7 × 108	Gas	66.93	40.16	25.88	B/5	2790	No
Gepard M3 Anti-materiel	1991	14.5 × 114	Rec	74.00	58.21	44.06	B/10	3280	No
Simonov PTRS Anti-tank	1941	14.5 × 114	Gas	84.00	48.00	46.00	B/5	3320	No
Steyr IWS 2000 Anti-material	1990	15.2mm	Rec	70.87	47.24	39.68	B/5	4757	No
Solothurn A18/100 Anti-tank	1936	20 × 105	Rec	69.25	35.40	99.19	B/10	2500	No
Japan: Type 97 Anti-tank Rifle	1940	20 × 124	Gas	80.00	47.00	152.0	B/7	2000	350
Panzerbuchse 41	1941	20 × 138	Rec	83.00	35.43	97.00	B/10	2400	No

MACHINE GUNS

NOTE: The words 'light', 'medium', 'heavy' and 'general purpose' in this section are indicative of the intended tactical role, not descriptive comments.

ADAMS-WILMOT Britain
BSA
1934. Aircraft flexible gun. Air-cooled, gas-piston operated, tilting block. Rectangular receiver, barrel with flash hider, gas cylinder underneath, large pistol grip, prominent tubular buffer behind receiver. Drum magazine.

Cartridge: .303 British
Length: not known
Weight: 20lb 0oz (9.07kg)
Barrel: not known
Feed: 99-round drum
Muzzle velocity: 2440 ft/sec (744 m/sec)
Cyclic rate: 900 rds/min

ALFA Spain
Oviedo
Model 44
1944. Medium. Air-cooled, tripod mounted, gas piston operated, lifting block to unlock the bolt. Belt fed from attached box on left side. Spade grips with trigger and safety lever. Rear portion of the barrel fluted.

Cartridge: 7.92 x 57mm Mauser
Length: 57.08in (1450mm)
Weight, gun: 28lb 10oz (13.0kg)
Weight, tripod: 59lb 8oz (27.0kg)
Barrel: 29.53in (750mm), 6 grooves, rh
Feed: 100-round metal link belt
Muzzle velocity: 2493 ft/sec (760 m/sec)
Cyclic rate: 780 rds/min

Model 55
1955. This is the Model 44 but in 7.62mm calibre.

Cartridge: 7.62 x 51mm NATO
Length: 43.30in (1100mm)
Weight, gun: 28lb 9oz (12.97kg)
Weight, tripod: 59lb 8oz (27.0kg)
Barrel: 24.00in (610mm), 6 grooves, rh
Feed: 100-round metal link belt
Muzzle velocity: 2821 ft/sec (860 m/sec)
Cyclic rate: 780 rds/min

Model 44 (Egypt)
This is the same weapon as the Spanish model, firing the 7.92mm Mauser cartridge and supplied in the 1950s. It differs only in having aluminium cooling fins for the full length of the barrel and also larger slots in the gas cylinder.

Specifications: the same as the Spanish model

AMELI Spain
Santa Barbara
Ameli
1980. Light. Air-cooled, delayed-blowback using a roller-delayed two-part bolt as in the CETME rifle. Plastic stock, pistol grip, belt fed, slotted rectangular barrel jacket with carrying handle, quick-change barrel, flash hider, bipod. Resembles a smaller MG 42.

Cartridge: 5.56 x 45mm NATO
Length: 38.19in (970mm)
Weight: 11lb 7oz (5.20kg)
Barrel: 15.75in (400mm), 6 grooves, rh
Feed: 100- or 200-round metal link belt
Muzzle velocity: 2870 ft/sec (875 m/sec)
Cyclic rate: 900 rds/min

ARES USA
Ares
Light
Light. Gas operated using a rotating bolt, rectangular receiver, folding butt, grooved fore-end, bipod, flash eliminator, pistol grip. Feeds from an ammunition box hung on the left side.

Cartridge: 5.56 x 45mm NATO
Length, butt extended: 42.24in (1073mm)
Length, butt folded: 38.23in (971mm)
Weight: 10lb 13oz (4.91kg)
Barrel: 21.65in (550mm), 6 grooves, rh
Feed: 100-round metal link belt, or can be adapted to M16 magazines
Muzzle velocity: 3100 ft/sec (945 m/sec)
Cyclic rate: 600 rds/min

Externally Powered

For tank use. Operated by an electric motor which drives a rotating cam to propel the bolt. Quick-change barrel, and feed can be altered from left to right as required. Cylindrical motor casing with gun receiver mounted on top, slender air-cooled barrel, with perforated flash hider.

Cartridge: 7.62 × 51mm NATO
Length: 31.81in (808mm)
Weight: 27lb 10oz (12.52kg)
Barrel: 23.50in (597mm), 6 grooves, rh
Feed: 100-round metal link belt
Muzzle velocity: 2755 ft/sec (840 m/sec)
Cyclic rate: variable up to 650 rds/min

BEARDMORE-FARQUHAR Britain
Beardmore & COW

Ca 1917–24. Light or aircraft. Air-cooled, gas-operated through a spring buffer. Very slender receiver with open space between it and the supporting frame of the gun. Drum feed, wooden butt, bipod in ground role.

Cartridge: .303 British
Length: 49.50in (1258mm)
Weight: 19lb 0oz (8.62kg)
Barrel: 26.50in (673mm), 4 grooves, rh
Feed: 81-round drum
Muzzle velocity: 2440 ft/sec (744 m/sec)
Cyclic rate: 500 rds/min

BENET-MERCIE USA
Hotchkiss & Springfield

Machine Rifle M1909

Developed by Hotchkiss of France. Light. Air-cooled, gas piston operated, locking bolt to barrel by a fermeture nut. Pistol grip stock with deep butt end containing a monopod. Finned barrel, bipod. Metal strip feed.

Cartridge: .30-06 Springfield
Length: 46.75in (1187mm)
Weight: 27lb 0oz (12.25kg)
Barrel: 23.50in (596mm), 4 grooves, rh
Feed: 30-round metal strip
Muzzle velocity: 2788 ft/sec (850 m/sec)
Cyclic rate: 600 rds/min

BERESIN Russia
State factories

UBT

1941. Aircraft, flexible. Air cooled, gas piston operated, bolt locked by laterally-moving yoke in receiver. Belt feed from right side. Fires from open bolt.

Cartridge: 12.7 × 108mm DShK
Length: 55.0in (1397mm)
Weight: 56lb 0oz (25.40kg)
Barrel: 35.00in (890mm), 8 grooves, rh
Feed: disintegrating link belt
Muzzle velocity: 2800 ft/sec (853 m/sec)
Cyclic rate: 1000 rds/min

UBS; UBK

These are variant models of the UBT; the **UBS** was for mounting in aircraft and synchronising for firing through the propeller arc; the **UBK** was for wing mounting outside the propeller arc. They differed in having a barrel some 2 inches (54mm) shorter than the UBT and in being fitted with a pneumatic remote cocking device.

BERETTA Italy
Beretta

AR70/78

1978. Light. Air-cooled, gas piston operated, rotating bolt. A heavy-barrel version of the AR70/.223 rifle with a quick-change barrel, bipod and larger magazine. Short plastic fore-end, no handguard, perforated bipod legs which fold in the middle, traditional butt, pistol grip.

Cartridge: 5.56 × 45mm M193
Length: 37.60in (955mm)
Weight: 11lb 11oz (5.30kg)
Barrel: 17.71in (450mm), 4 grooves, rh
Feed: 40-round box
Muzzle velocity: 3182 ft/sec (970 m/sec)
Cyclic rate: 670 rds/min

AR70/84

1984. Light. Air-cooled, gas piston operated, rotating bolt. This is an improved version of the AR70-78, using the same mechanism but without the quick-change barrel. Skeleton butt with shoulder strap, long slotted fore-end/handguard, tripod hinged in the middle for height adjustment, muzzle formed into grenade launcher. Fixed barrel, selective fire from an open bolt.

Cartridge: 5.56 × 45mm NATO
Length: 37.60in (955mm)
Weight: 11lb 11oz (5.30kg)
Barrel: 17.71in (450mm), 4 grooves, rh
Feed: 30-round box
Muzzle velocity: 3182 ft/sec (970 m/sec)
Cyclic rate: 670 rds/min

AS70/90

1990. Light. Air-cooled, gas piston operated, rotating bolt. Heavy-barrel version of the AR70/90 assault rifle, using the same mechanism but firing from an open bolt. Butt with handgrip and shoulder strap, long slotted fore-end/handguard, bipod, muzzle shaped for grenade launching. Distinguishable from the 70/84 by having a carrying handle over the receiver.

Cartridge: 5.56 × 45mm NATO
Length: 39.37in (1000mm)
Weight: 11lb 12oz (5.34kg)
Barrel: 18.30in (465mm), 6 grooves, rh
Feed: 30-round box
Muzzle velocity: 3215 ft/sec (980 m/sec)
Cyclic rate: 800 rds/min

MG 42/59

1959. This is the German MG3 manufactured under licence by Beretta and Breda. The appearance and operation is precisely the same but there are some dimensional differences due to manufacturing methods.

Cartridge: 7.62 × 51mm NATO
Length: 48.03in (1220mm)
Weight: 26lb 7oz (12,0kg)
Barrel: 20.98in (533mm), 4 grooves, rh
Feed: metal link belt
Muzzle velocity: 2690 ft/sec (820 m/sec)
Cyclic rate: 800 rds/min

BERGMANN Germany
Bergmann

MG 10
1910. Medium. Water-cooled, belt fed, recoil operated, breech-block locked by a vertical locking block. Quick-change barrel. Spade grips and trigger.

Cartridge: 7.92 × 57mm Mauser
Length: not known
Weight: 36lb 0oz (16.33kg)
Barrel: not known
Feed: metal link belt
Muzzle velocity: 2950 ft/sec (900 m/sec)
Cyclic rate: 550 rds/min

MG 15
1915. So far as can be ascertained this appears to be the M1910 gun altered to feed from the standard Maxim cloth belt instead of Bergmann's original aluminium-link belt.

MG15nA
1916. (*nA = neuer Art* = new pattern) This was the M1912 gun with the water jacket removed and with a slotted barrel jacket, pistol grip, butt-pad on the rear end of the receiver, and a round-topped belt drum box on the right side of the receiver. Carrying handle on the barrel jacket, high-set foresight. Sometimes with small tripod, sometimes bipod.

Cartridge: 7.92 × 57mm Mauser
Length: 44.13in (1121mm)
Weight: 28lb 8oz (12.92kg)
Barrel: 28.50in (726mm), 4 grooves, rh
Feed: 200-round cloth belt
Muzzle velocity: 2925 ft/sec (892 m/sec)
Cyclic rate: 550 rds/min

BERTHIER France
USA

M1917
USMG
1916. Light. Water-cooled, very slender water-jacket supplied by flexible tube, pump and reservoir by assistant gunner. Single-strut butt, pistol grip, bipod, curved top-mounted magazine, offset sights.

Cartridge: .30-06 Springfield
Length: 48.0in (1220mm)
Weight: 15lb 12oz (7.14kg)
Barrel: not known
Feed: 20-round box
Muzzle velocity: 2625 ft/sec (800 m/sec)
Cyclic rate: 500 rds/min

For the development of Berthier's design, see Vickers-Berthier

BESA Britain
BSA

7.92mm Mark I
1939. Originally the Czech ZB vz/53, design bought by Britain and made by BSA Ltd. Tank co-axial gun. Air cooled, gas piston operated, tilting breech-block. Barrel recoils and firing takes place during the forward counter-recoil movement to reduce trunnion pull. Exceptionally accurate.

Cartridge: 7.92 × 57mm Mauser
Length: 43.50in (1105mm)
Weight: 47lb 0oz (21.46kg)
Barrel: 29.0in (736mm), 4 grooves, rh
Feed: 225-round belt
Muzzle velocity: 2700 ft/sec (823 m/sec)
Cyclic rates: 500 or 800 rds/min

7.92mm Mark 2
1940. As for Mark 1 but with some minor engineering changes to facilitate production.

Specifications: the same, except
Weight: 48lb 0oz (21.84kg)

7.92mm Mark 2*
1941. More engineering changes and simplified components to speed up wartime manufacture. No change in dimensions. All component parts interchangeable with Mark 2 guns

7.92mm Mark 3
1941. Further simplification, but components no longer interchangeable with Mark 2 guns. Rate regulator omitted and thus only one rate of fire: 800 rds/min.

7.92mm Mark 3*
1941. Similar to Mark 3, but with the rate of fire fixed at 500 rds/min.

7.92mm Mark 3/2
1952. As for Mark 3, but with a new receiver cover and mounting bracket.

7.92mm Mark 3/3
1952. As for Mark 3, but with new gas cylinder and barrel. Guns were converted from Mark 3/2 but no new manufacture to this mark took place.

15mm Mark I
1940. Originally the Czech ZB vz/60; design bought by Britain and produced by BSA Ltd. Armoured car armament. Air cooled, selective fire, gas piston operated, tilting breech-block, belt fed. In most respects, a scaled up version of the 7.92mm BESA gun.

Cartridge: 15 × 104mm BESA
Length: 80.70in (2050mm)
Weight: 125lb 8oz (56.93kg)
Barrel: 57.60in (1462mm), 8 grooves, rh
Feed: 25-round belt
Muzzle velocity: 2700 ft/sec (823 m/sec)
Cyclic rate: 450 rds/min

BESAL Britain
BSA
Mark 1

1941. Later called the Faulkner, after its designer. An emergency replacement for the Bren, designed by BSA, in case Bren production was reduced by German bombing. Light. Air-cooled, gas piston operated, tilting block. Square-section piston and cylinder for simple manufacture. Pistol grip, wood butt, standard Bren magazine.

Cartridge: .303 British
Length: 48.0in (1220mm)
Weight: 15lb 12oz (7.14kg)
Barrel: 22.0in (558mm), 4 grooves, rh
Feed: 20-round box
Muzzle velocity: 2450 ft/sec (745 m/sec)
Cyclic rate: 500 rds/min

Mark 2

1941. Perfected version of Mark 1, approved for service, production shelved until necessary, which never occurred. Gas cylinder covered by fish-belly shroud, pistol grip moved forward and acted as cocking handle, cooling fins at front end of gas cylinder, long flash hider.

Cartridge: .303 British
Length: 46.63in (1185mm)
Weight: 21lb 8oz (9.74kg)
Barrel: 22.0in (558mm), 4 grooves, rh
Feed: 30-round box
Muzzle velocity: 2450 ft/sec (745 m/sec)
Cyclic rate: 600 rds/min

BREDA Italy
Breda
Model 1924.

Light. Air-cooled, delayed blowback recoil-operated using a fermeture nut system Unusual combination of wooden butt and spade grip with trigger. Slender cylindrical receiver, part-finned barrel held in slotted cradle. Large feed block with attached magazine which hinges forward to be charger-loaded. Light tripod.

Specifications: not known

Model 1928

Improved version of the Model 1924 which did away with the wooden butt. Only 2000 made.

Specifications: not known

Model 1930

Final version of the Model 1924, became standard light gun. Air-cooled, recoil-operated delayed blowback, forward-swinging charger-loaded magazine. Bipod fitted to the end of the barrel cradle. Pistol grip, wooden butt with shoulder strap. Selective fire.

Cartridge: 6.5 x 52mm Carcano
Length: 48.50in (1232mm)
Weight: 22lb 12oz (10.34kg)
Barrel: 20.50in (521mm), 4 grooves, rh
Feed: 20-round box
Muzzle velocity: 2065 ft/sec (630 m/sec)
Cyclic rate: 500 rds/min

Model 1931

Heavy. Air-cooled, gas piston operated, vertical sliding breech lock. For anti-aircraft and tank use.

Cartridge: 13.2 x 99mm Breda
Length: 65in (1652mm)
Weight: 104lb 11oz (47.5kg)
Barrel: 39.37in (1000mm), 4 grooves, rh
Feed: 30-round box
Muzzle velocity: 2592 ft/sec (790m/sec)
Cyclic rate: 500 rds/min

Model 1937

Medium. Air-cooled, gas piston operated, using a vertical sliding lock to lock the breech. No primary extraction, so cases are lubricated by an oil pump during loading. Fed with a 20-round metal strip, the mechanism replacing the empty cases in the strip after extraction. This gun was also used by Portugal, who called it the **M938**.

Cartridge: 8 x 59mm Breda
Length: 50.0in (1270mm)
Weight, gun: 42lb 8oz (19.27kg)
Weight, tripod: 41lb 8oz (18.82kg)
Barrel: 25.0in (635mm), 4 grooves, rh
Feed: 20-round metal strip
Muzzle velocity: 2600 ft/sec (792 m/sec)
Cyclic rate: 450 rds/min

8mm Model 1938

A modification of the M1937 gun for use in tanks. Had a top-feeding curved magazine, a shorter barrel, and a pistol grip and trigger instead of spade grips

7.35mm Model 1938

A modification of the M1930 light gun from 6.5mm to 7.35mm calibre. Apart from re-barrelling, little change was required and the dimensions remained the same.

BREN Britain
Enfield & Inglis
Mark 1

1938. Designed in Czechoslovakia as the ZB vz/26 in 7.92mm calibre, re-designed into .303 calibre and manufactured in Britain and Canada. The Mark 1 was to the original Czech design, with offset drum rear sight, hand-grip and top strap on butt, characteristic curved top-mounted magazine, conical flash hider. Telescoping adjustable bipod, folding cocking handle.

Cartridge: .303 British
Length: 46.25in (1150mm)
Weight: 22lb 5oz (10.15kg)
Barrel: 25.0in (635mm), 6 grooves, rh
Feed: 30-round box
Muzzle velocity: 2400 ft/sec (731 m/sec)
Cyclic rate: 500 rds/min

Mark 2

1941. Simplified for faster production. Leaf type rear sight, non-adjustable bipod, fixed cocking handle, no grip or strap on butt. No significant change in dimensions.

Mark 2/1

1948. As for Mark 2 but with a new cocking handle and slide assembly.

Mark 3

1944. Similar to the Mark 1, but lighter and with a shorter barrel.

Cartridge: .303 British
Length: 42.60in (1082mm)
Weight: 19lb 5oz (8.75kg)
Barrel: 22.25in (565mm), 4 grooves, rh
Feed: 30-round box
Muzzle velocity: 2400 ft/sec (731 m/sec)
Cyclic rate: 480 rds/min

Mark 4

1944. Similar to the Mark 2, but lighter and with a shorter barrel.

Specifications: as for Mark 3, except
Weight: 19lb 2oz (8.68kg)

L4A1

1958. Conversion of Mark 3 guns to 7.62mm NATO calibre. New barrel, flash hider, ejector assembly and a Canadian 7.92mm Bren extractor. Also a modified Canadian 7.92mm Bren breechblock, and modifications to the gun body and magazine opening cover.

Specifications: as for Mark 3

L4A2

1958. As for the L4A1, but incorporating some design improvements.

L4A3

1960. Conversion of Mark 2 guns to 7.62mm NATO calibre by modifying the existing body and fitting new patterns of barrel assembly, butt, slide and gas deflector. For Navy and RAF use only.

L4A4

1960. Similar to L4A2 except that the barrel is chromium-lined and thus a spare barrel is no longer provided with each gun.

L4A6

1961. Conversion of existing L4A1 guns by fitting a new chromium-lined barrel.

7.92mm Mark 2

1941. This gun was manufactured in Canada for supply to the Chinese Nationalist Army. It was the standard British Mark 2 gun but with a special breech-block and extractor and a straight magazine (since the gun now fired a rimless cartridge). Except for the calibre and straight magazine there are no significant differences between the British .303 Mark 2 and this gun.

Cartridge: 7.92 × 57mm Mauser

BRITAIN

See also **Adams-Wilmot, Beardmore-Farquhar, Besa, Besal, Bren, Gardener, Gatling, Hefah, Hotchkiss, Lewis, Maxim, Nordenfelt, Vickers & Vickers-Berthier**

L7A1

Enfield

1961. The FN-MAG general purpose gun with minor modifications as required by the British Army, such as a heavier chrome-lined barrel and modified piston and bolt. Wood butt, rectangular receiver with pistol grip, tapered barrel with gas cylinder beneath, slotted flash eliminator, bipod.

Cartridge: 7.62 × 51mm NATO
Length: 48.50in (1232mm)
Weight: 24lb 8oz (10.90kg)
Barrel: 26.75in (679mm), 4 grooves, rh
Feed: metal link belt
Muzzle velocity: 2750 ft/sec (838 m/sec)
Cyclic rate: 800 rds/min

L7A2

1963. Modifications to the trigger and feed mechanisms, fitting of a belt box to the left side, stronger carrying handle, stronger bipod legs. No significant change in dimensions.

L8A1

Variant of the L7A2 for use as a coaxial weapon in the Chieftain tank. The trigger mechanism was replaced by a solenoid firing gear and a bore evacuator fitted to prevent firing gases entering the tank.

L8A2

A slightly improved L8A1 for coaxial mounting in the Challenger 1 tank.

L19A1

Any L7 model fitted with a heavy barrel for prolonged sustained fire duties.

L20A1

An L7A1 modified for use in helicopter mountings. Adjustable for left or right side feed, and with electric solenoid firing gear.

L20A2

An L7A2 similarly modified for helicopter fitting.

L37A1

A variant for fitting into armoured vehicles. Special barrel to permit a greater proportion of tracer ammunition to be fired; can have the spade grips removed and a butt and bipod fitted for emergency ground use. Used as a turret weapon on tanks and armoured personnel carriers.

L37A2

An improved L37A1 adapted for turret mounting in the Challenger 1 tank.

L41A1, L45A1, L46A1

Non-firing versions of the L8A1, L37A1 and L7A2 used for training and drill purposes.

L43A1

Generally similar to the L8A1, this was used briefly as a ranging machine gun for the 76mm main armament of the Scorpion light tank.

L86A1 LSW

1986. Heavy-barrelled version of the Enfield L85A1 rifle. Bullpup design with additional handgrip behind the magazine, long perforated barrel support with bipod beneath the muzzle, slotted fore-end/handguard, optical sight.

Cartridge: 5.56 × 45mm NATO
Length: 35.43in (900mm)
Weight: 13lb 7oz (6.1kg) with sight
Barrel: 25.43in (646mm), 6 grooves, rh
Feed: 30-round box
Muzzle velocity: 3182 ft/sec (970 m/sec)
Cyclic rate: 700 rds/min

L94A1

This is the British-manufactured version of the Hughes EX34 Chain Gun. It differs in having a long Stellite-lined barrel and a special mounting plate on the barrel jacket for fitting into the Warrior AFV and Challenger 2 tank.

Cartridge: 7.62 × 51mm NATO
Length: 49.21in (1250mm)
Weight: 39lb 6oz (17.86kg)
Barrel: 27.67in (703mm), 4 grooves, rh
Feed: metal link belt
Muzzle velocity: 2870 ft/sec (875 m/sec)
Cyclic rate: 520 rds/min

BRIXIA Italy
Brixia

M1920

Medium. Water-cooled, tripod-mounted. Short recoil operated, bolt locked by a pivoting block which also functions as an accelerator. Rate of fire could be varied by a gradual regulator. Also offered as an air-cooled aircraft gun, with finned barrel. Neither was ever put into quantity production.

Cartridge: 6.5 × 52mm Carcano
Length: not known
Weight, gun: 34lb 8oz (15.65kg)
Barrel: not known
Feed: 50-round box
Muzzle velocity: 2080 ft/sec (634 m/sec)
Cyclic rate: 600 rds/min

BROWNING USA
Colt, Remington & Westinghouse

.30 M1917

First designed in 1910, then slightly improved and accepted in 1917. Medium. Water-cooled, recoil-operated, bolt locked by a moving lug. Belt fed from left side. Tripod mounted. Pistol grip and trigger behind receiver.

Cartridge: .30-06 Springfield
Length: 37.50in (952mm)
Weight, gun: 32lb 10oz (14.97kg)
Weight, tripod: 45lb 8oz (20.64kg)
Barrel: 24.0in (610mm), 4 grooves, rh
Feed: 250-round cloth belt
Muzzle velocity: 2800 ft/sec (853 m/sec)
Cyclic rate: 600 rds/min

.30 M1917A1

Ca 1930. Improvements include various manufacturing changes, new steam tube cooling system, stronger feed mechanism from the M1919A4 gun, bronze parts replaced by steel, and provision for firing at higher elevation against aerial targets.

Cartridge: .30-06 Springfield
Length: 38.64in (981mm)
Weight, gun: 32lb 9oz (14.78kg)
Weight, tripod: 53lb 3oz (24.13kg)
Barrel: 23.90in (607mm), 4 grooves, rh
Feed: 250-round cloth belt
Muzzle velocity: 2800 ft/sec (853 m/sec)
Cyclic rate: 600 rds/min

.30 Aircraft M1918

Modification of the M1917 water-cooled gun to air-cooling for aircraft use. The water jacket was removed and replaced by a light, slotted barrel jacket, and various components were lightened. The .30 M1918M1 was the M1918 rebuilt with various improvements including a new trigger mechanism and spade grips.

.30 Aircraft M1919 Fixed

The Aircraft M1918 gun made as new, instead of being a conversion.

.30 Aircraft M1919 Flexible

The M1918M1 made as new, with spade grips for firing by the aircraft observer or air gunner.

.30 Tank M1919

This used the same receiver and mechanism as the M1917 gun but had an 18-inch air-cooled barrel enclosed in a slotted jacket. It was also provided with a special ball mounting and optical sight, though iron sights and a simple tripod were issued for emergency use.

.30 M1919A1

1931. The air-cooled M1919 tank gun adapted for ground use. Removable single-strut butt, hand-grip beneath the receiver, slotted barrel jacket, small simple tripod. Front sight on the front of the receiver.

Cartridge: .30-06 Springfield
Length: 35.10in (892mm) without butt
Weight, gun with tripod: 40lb 0oz (18.14kg)
Barrel: 18.0in (457mm), 4 grooves, rh
Feed: 250-round cloth belt
Muzzle velocity: 2690 ft/sec (820 m/sec)
Cyclic rate: 600 rds/min

.30 M1919A2

1931. Improved M1919A1 for cavalry use. Front sight mounted on the barrel jacket, no butt, otherwise the same weapon. The Tripod M2 was first issued with this gun and weighed 14lb (6.35kg).

.30 M1919A3

A trials and evaluation weapon of which only 72 were made. Basically the M1919A2 with the front sight moved back to the receiver.

.30 M1919A4

1934. Medium. Air-cooled with slotted barrel jacket, on M2 tripod. New sights, 24-inch barrel. Same mechanism as all previous Browning guns, though with an improved belt feed system, and replaced all previous M1919 models. Still in wide use in many armies.

Cartridge: .30-06 Springfield
Length: 41.11in (1044mm)
Weight, gun: 31lb 0oz (14.06kg)
Weight, tripod: 14lb 0oz (6.35kg)
Barrel: 24.0in (610mm), 4 grooves, rh
Feed: 250-round cloth belt
Muzzle velocity: 2800 ft/sec (853 m/sec)
Cyclic rate: 500 rds/min

M1919A5

Special version of the M1919A4 for mounting into the Light Tank M3; this demanded a special bolt-retracting slide and other changes, and the resultant weapon became the A5.

Specifications: as for A4, except
Weight: 30lb 8oz ((13.83kg)
Length: 40.80 in (1036mm)

M1919A6

1943. The M1919A4 modified for infantry use as a light machine gun. A shoulder stock was added behind the pistol grip, a carrying handle placed on the barrel jacket, a flash hider and a bipod mount fitted to the jacket just behind the muzzle.

Cartridge: .30-06 Springfield
Length: 53.0in (1346mm)
Weight, gun: 32lb 8oz (14.74kg)
Barrel: 24.0in (610mm), 4 grooves, rh
Feed: 250-round cloth belt
Muzzle velocity: 2800 ft/sec (853 m/sec)
Cyclic rate: 450 rds/min

.30 Aircraft M2

1931. A freshly designed air-cooled gun solely for aircraft use and with components not interchangeable with ground guns. In two versions: 'fixed' for mounting into aircraft wings or fuselages, and could be synchronised, and 'flexible' for use by aerial gunners. The basic difference is that the fixed gun had a solenoid firing mechanism, while the flexible gun had spade grips and a trigger. The gun is lighter than the ground weapon and has a much higher rate of fire. A retracting slide is used to cock the gun instead of the usual crank handle.

Cartridge: .30-06 Springfield
Length: 39.80in (1011mm)
Weight, fixed gun: 21lb 8oz (9.75kg)
Weight, flexible gun: 23lb 0oz (10.43kg)
Barrel: 23.90in (610mm), 4 grooves, rh
Feed: 250-round cloth belt
Muzzle velocity: 2800 ft/sec (853 m/sec)
Cyclic rate: 1200 rds/min

.30 Tank M37

A variant of the M1919A4 in which the feed mechanism was changed to permit feeding from either side as dictated by the position of the gun inside the tank. As this gun was designed to feed from a disintegrating link belt, an ejection chute was provided to discharge the links into a collector.

7.62mm NATO Mark 21 Mod 0

A US Navy variant of the M1919A4, re-barrelled to fire the 7.62 x 51mm NATO cartridge.

.50 M1921

1925. Heavy. Water-cooled, recoil operated. In effect, the .30 M1917A1 scaled up to handle the larger cartridge.

Cartridge: .50 Browning
Length: 56.0in (1422mm)
Weight, gun: 66lb 0oz (29.93kg)
Weight, tripod: 75lb 0oz (34.02kg)
Barrel: 36.0in (914mm), 8 grooves, rh
Feed: cloth belt
Muzzle velocity: 2300 ft/sec (701 m/sec)
Cyclic rate: 450 rds/min

.50 M1921A1

1930. Improved model; the principal change was the addition of a compound leverage cocking handle. No significant change in dimensions.

.50 M2

1933. Heavy. Water-cooled, recoil operated. It was simply the M1921A1 with an improved water jacket which extended past the muzzle. Flexible gun with spade grips and adjustable for right or left feeding. Originally with 36-inch barrel, in 1938 redesigned with 45-inch barrel. Principally used for anti-aircraft firing, for which a special mount was provided.

Cartridge: .50 Browning
Length: 66.0in (1676mm)
Weight, gun: 100lb 0oz (45.36kg)
Weight, M2A1 tripod: 375lb 0oz (170.10kg)
Barrel: 45.0in (1143mm), 8 grooves, rh
Feed: 110-round metal link belt
Muzzle velocity: 2930 ft/sec (893 m/sec)
Cyclic rate: 650 rds/min

.50 Aircraft M2

Ca 1928. As for the water-cooled M2, but air-cooled and with a slotted barrel jacket. In fixed or flexible variants, the flexible being provided with spade grips and trigger.

Cartridge: .50 Browning
Length: 57.0in (1448mm)
Weight, fixed: 64lb 0oz (29.03kg)
Weight, flexible: 65lb 2oz (29.53kg)
Barrel: 36.0in (914mm), 8 grooves, rh
Feed: 110-round metal link belt
Muzzle velocity: 2840 ft/sec (866 m/sec)
Cyclic rate: 850 rds/min

.50 M2HB (Heavy Barrel)
Colt, FN, Ramo, Saco & Winchester

1933. As for the M2 water-cooled, but without water jacket and with a heavy barrel so as to absorb heat during sustained fire. Originally with 36-inch barrel but after 1938 with 45-inch barrel. Invariably seen in flexible form, with spade grips, but a fixed version without the spade grips was produced in small numbers in 1941 for mounting in the M6 heavy tank. It was identical to the flexible M2 except that it weighed 2 pounds less. A third version, the 'Turret Type' was fitted with anti-aircraft sights and fittings for assembly to tank turrets; this weighed 3 pounds less than the flexible.

Cartridge: .50 Browning
Length: 65.0in (2559mm)
Weight, gun: 84lb 0oz (38.10kg)
Weight, tripod M3: 44lb 0oz (19.96kg)
Barrel: 45.0in (1143mm), 8 grooves, rh
Feed: 110-round metal link belt
Muzzle velocity: 2930 ft/sec (893 m/sec)
Cyclic rate: 450–575 rds/min

.50 M2HB-QCB
FN, Manroy, Ramo & Saco
Quick Change Barrel. 1986. Developed by FN Herstal of Belgium, this is the standard M2HB but with a quick-change barrel, the principal advantage of which was that head-space adjustment was no longer required.

Specifications: the same as the standard M2HB

Saco Fifty/.50
Saco
1987–91. A 'product-improved' version of the M2HB with a quick-change barrel, welded receiver instead of riveted, adjustable rate of fire between 500 and 750 rds/min, and a new cocking mechanism. The normal Browning operating mechanism was retained.

Cartridge: .50 Browning
Length: 61.41in (1560mm)
Weight, gun: 58lb 14oz (26.72kg)
Barrel: 36.0in (914mm), 8 grooves, rh
Feed: 110-round metal link belt
Muzzle velocity: 2841 ft/sec (866 m/sec)
Cyclic rate: 500–750 rds/min, adjustable

Ramo M2 Lightweight
Ramo
1991. This appears to be the Saco Fifty/.50 under new management and with a few manufacturing differences. A notable recognition feature is the conical flash hider.

Cartridge: .50 Browning
Length: 60.0in (1524mm)
Weight, gun: 58lb 14oz (26.72kg)
Barrel: 36.0in (914mm), 8 grooves, rh
Feed: 110-round metal link belt
Muzzle velocity: 2841 ft/sec (866 m/sec)
Cyclic rate: 550–750 rds/min, adjustable.

BSA Britain
BSA

M1924
Aircraft observers' gun. Heavy. Recoil-operated using rotating bolt sleeve. Air-cooled, though a water-cooled model was built. Often called the '0.5 Lewis' but bears no relationship other than the drum magazine.

Cartridge: .5 Vickers
Length: not known
Weight: 46lb 0oz (20.86kg)
Barrel: not known
Feed: 37-round drum
Muzzle velocity: 2600 ft/sec (792 m/sec)
Cyclic rate: 400 rds/min

CHATELLERAULT France
MAC Chatellerault

M1924/29
1929. Improved model of an earlier failure. Light. Air-cooled, gas piston operated, tilting bolt, overhead magazine. Wood butt, wood short fire-end, bipod, flash hider. Selective fire, two triggers.

Cartridge: 7.5 × 54mm French M1929
Length: 42.60in (1082mm)
Weight: 20lb 4oz (9.18kg)
Barrel: 19.70in (500mm), 4 grooves, rh
Feed: 26-round box
Muzzle velocity: 2700 ft/sec (823 m/sec)
Cyclic rate: 500 rds/min

M1931
1931. Variant of the M1924/29 for use in fixed fortress and tank mountings. It differs in having a drum magazine mounted vertically on the left or right side of the gun and having a short, down-curved butt instead of a traditionally-shaped one.

Cartridge: 7.5 × 54mm French M1929
Length: 40.50in (1029mm)
Weight: 27lb 4oz (12.36kg)
Barrel: 19.70in (500mm), 4 grooves, rh
Feed: 150-round drum
Muzzle velocity: 2700 ft/sec (823 m/sec)
Cyclic rate: 500 rds/min

34/39 Aircraft
Variant model of the M1924/29 belt fed for use by aerial gunners.

CHAUCHAT France
Puteaux

CSRG Mle 1915
Light. Air-cooled, long recoil operation, rotating bolt. Long tubular receiver, barrel jacket, flash hider. Pistol grip with fore-grip just in front. Semi-circular magazine beneath receiver. Short wood butt, long spindly bipod.

Cartridge: 8 × 50R Lebel
Length: 45.00in (1143mm)
Weight: 20lb 0oz (9.07kg)
Barrel: 18.50in (469mm), 4 grooves, rh
Feed: 20-round box
Muzzle velocity: 2300 ft/sec (700 m/sec)
Cyclic rate: 250 rds/min

USA

US M1918
This was the CSRG Mle 1915 re-designed to fire the US .30-06 cartridge. The visible difference lies in the magazine,

now a rectangular 16-round box inserted below the receiver, and the forward handgrip being moved in front of the magazine.

Specifications: the same, except
Muzzle velocity: ca 2700 ft/sec (822 m/sec)
Cyclic rate: ca 300 rds/min

CHINA
Type 24
This was the Russian Maxim M1910 purchased in the 1920s.

Type 26
This was the Czech ZB wz/26, purchased in the early 1930s.

Type 53
State factories
Licenced copy of the Russian 7.62mm DPM.
See Degtyarev

12.7mm Type 54
State factories
Licenced copy of the Russian 12.7mm DShK 38/46.
See Degtyarev

7.62mm Type 56
State factories
Licenced copy of the Russian 7.62mm RPD.
See Degtyarev

14.5mm Type 56
State factories
Licenced copy of the Russian 14.5mm KPV. The Chinese version differs slightly in some details of the feed mechanism and in having cooling fins on the barrel.
See Russia

Type 57
State factories
The Russian 7.62mm SG43.
See Goryunov

Type 58
State factories
Licenced copy of the Russian 7.62mm RP-46.
See Russia

Type 63
State factories
The Russian 7.62mm SGM.
See Degtyarev

Type 67
State factories
Chinese design using ideas from several of the guns listed above. Light. Air-cooled, gas piston operated using a tilting block. Wood butt, pistol grip, bipod attached to gas cylinder. Flash hider. Belt fed from the right.

Cartridge: 7.62 × 54R Russian
Length: 45.0in (1143mm)
Weight: 32lb 8oz (9.90kg)
Barrel: 23.50in (597mm), 4 grooves, rh

Feed: 100-round metal link belt
Muzzle velocity: 2740 ft/sec (835 m/sec)
Cyclic rate: 650 rds/min

Type 74
State factories
Light. Air-cooled, gas piston operated using a laterally-shifting bolt. Long barrel, short gas cylinder above it, wood butt, bipod, pistol grip. Normally used a drum magazine but can accept Type 56 rifle box magazines.

Cartridge: 7.62 × 39mm M1943
Length: 43.62in (1108mm)
Weight: 14lb 2oz (6.40kg)
Barrel: 20.80in (528mm) 4 grooves, rh
Feed: 101-round drum
Muzzle velocity: 2411 ft/sec (735 m/sec)
Cyclic rate: 750 rds/min

Type 77
State factories
Heavy. Air cooled, gas operated by direct gas impingement on the bolt carrier. Bolt locked by two hinged flaps. Multi-baffle muzzle brake.

Cartridge: 12.7 × 108mm DShK
Length: 85.98in (2184mm)
Weight: 89lb 8oz (40.60kg)
Barrel: 40.0in (1016mm), 8 grooves, rh
Feed: 60-round metal link belt
Muzzle velocity: 2625 ft/sec (800 m/sec)
Cyclic rate: 800 rds/min

Type 80
State factories
A slightly modified copy of the Kalashnikov PK. General purpose. Air-cooled, gas piston operated, rotating bolt. Fitted with bipod, provided with tripod.

Cartridge: 7.62 × 54R Russian
Length: 46.93in (1192mm)
Weight, gun: 17lb 6oz (7.90kg)
Weight, tripod: 10lb 6oz (4.70kg)
Barrel: 26.57in (675mm), 4 grooves, rh
Feed: 50-round drum, or 100- or 200-round metal link belt
Muzzle velocity: 2706 ft/sec (825 m/sec)
Cyclic rate: 650 rds/min

Type 81
State factories
Light. Air-cooled, gas piston operated, rotating bolt. Heavy-barrel version of the Type 81 rifle (*qv*) with which most of its parts are interchangeable. Bipod; cleaning rod beneath barrel; drum magazine but will accept Type 81 rifle magazines.

Cartridge: 7.62 × 39mm M1943
Length: 40.31in (1024mm)
Weight: 11lb 6oz (5.15kg)
Barrel: 20.80in (528mm) 4 grooves, rh
Feed: 75-round drum or 30-round box
Muzzle velocity: 2411 ft/sec (735 m/sec)
Cyclic rate: 700 rds/min

Type W-85
State factories
Heavy. Anti-aircraft, air-cooled, gas operated, probably direct gas as in the Type 77. Remarkably light for its size.

Cartridge: 12.7 × 108mm DShK
Length: 78.05in (1995mm)
Weight: 40lb 12oz (18.50kg)
Barrel: 40.00in (1016mm), 8 grooves, rh
Feed: 60-round metal link belt
Muzzle velocity: 2525ft/sec (800 m/sec)
Cyclic rate: 750 rds/min

COLT USA
Colt

M1895
Browning design, using a gas-propelled swinging arm to drive the bolt; hence the nickname 'Potato Digger'. Produced in 6mm Lee for the US Navy, in .30-40 Krag for the US Army and in other calibres commercially. Tripod mounted, air cooled, belt fed. Smooth barrel.

Cartridge: .30-40 Krag
Length: 40.80in (1036mm)
Weight: 40lb 0oz (30.0kg)
Barrel: 28.0in (711mm), 6 grooves, rh
Feed: 250-round cloth belt
Muzzle velocity: 2000 ft/sec (610 m/sec)
Cyclic rate: 430 rds/min

M1914
The M1895 gun modified to fire the .30-06 cartridge.

Specifications: the same, except
Muzzle velocity: 2800 ft/sec (853 m/sec)

M1915
Marlin
A slightly modified M1895 gun (cooling fins added to the barrel) in .30-06 made by the Marlin-Rockwell Corporation. No significant change in dimensions.

Model 715
Developed *ca* 1990 by Colt and Diemaco of Canada. Basically an M16A2 rifle with heavy barrel, selective fire, forward handgrip, rectangular fore-end/handguard, bipod. Used by Canadian Army as the C7 light support weapon, and by the Netherlands Marines.

Cartridge: 5.56 × 45mm NATO
Length: 40.15in (1020mm)
Weight: 12lb 12oz (5.80kg)
Barrel: 20.07in (510mm), 6 grooves, rh
Feed: 30-round box
Muzzle velocity: 3035 ft/sec (925 m/sec)
Cyclic rate: 625 rds/min

CZECHOSLOVAKIA
CZ Brno

ZB vz/26
Developed by Zbrojovka Brno. Light. Air-cooled, gas piston operated, tilting bolt. Barrel finned, long gas cylinder almost to the muzzle, bipod, carrying handle, overhead straight box magazine, wood butt, pistol grip. Offset sights, with drum-set rear sight. Quick-change barrel. Selective fire. Sold widely throughout the world.

Cartridge: 7.92 × 57mm Mauser
Length: 45.78in (1163mm)
Weight: 21lb 5oz (9.66kg)
Barrel: 23.70in (602mm), 4 grooves, rh
Feed: 20-round box
Muzzle velocity: 2598 ft/sec (792 m/sec)
Cyclic rate: 500 rds/min

ZB vz/27, 28
Zbrojovka Brno adopted a policy of improving their design as and when an idea occurred to them, and they also marked their guns with the year of production. As a result those guns known as the ZB27 and 28 were all minor variants of the ZB26, differing in the method of connecting the bolt to the piston and similar matters. Dimensionally they are exactly the same.

ZB vz/30
The final improved version of the vz/26, with new cam surfaces for the bolt and some manufacturing changes to make production easier. It was adopted in large numbers in China, made in Spain as the **FAO** (from Fábrica de Armas de Oviedo), and made in Iran. Manufacture continued throughout the 1939–45 war, the gun being adopted by the German Army.

Cartridge: 7.92 × 57mm Mauser
Length: 45.75in (1161mm)
Weight: 21lb 5oz (9.60kg)
Barrel: 26.50in (672mm), 4 grooves, rh
Feed: 30-round box
Muzzle velocity: 2500 ft/sec (762 m/sec)
Cyclic rate: 600 rds/min

ZGB vz/30
This was the ZB30 modified to fire British .303 ammunition and supplied to Britain for trials in 1931/32. The most obvious difference was the need for a curved 20-round magazine to accommodate the rimmed cartridge. Otherwise as for the vz/26.

ZGB32, 33, 34
The ZGB vz/30 further modified as a result of trials. The gas cylinder was shortened, the recoil buffer modified, the magazine capacity increased to 30 rounds. After testing more changes were made including reducing the rate of fire. This became the ZGB33. The ZGB34 was the title given to the last two trials guns purchased in April 1934; there appears to be no difference between these and the ZGB33. This then became the Bren gun (*qv*).

Cartridge: .303 British
Length: 45.50in (1156mm)
Weight: 22lb 2oz (10.03kg)
Barrel: 25.0in (635mm), 6 grooves, rh
Feed: 30-round box
Muzzle velocity: 2450 ft/sec (745 m/sec)
Cyclic rate: 500 rds/min

ZB vz/37
1937. Medium. Air-cooled, gas piston operated, tilting breech-block. Two rates of automatic fire. Belt fed. Finned barrel, unusual perforated barrel support forward of the

receiver. Bicycle-type handlebars under the receiver with trigger. Tripod mounted.

Cartridge: 7.92 × 57mm Mauser
Length: 43.50in (1104mm)
Weight: 41lb 0oz (18.60kg)
Barrel: 26.70in (678mm), 4 grooves, rh
Feed: 100-round metal link belt
Muzzle velocity: 2600 ft/sec (792 m/sec)
Cyclic rate: 500 or 700 rds/min

vz/52

1952. Resembles the earlier vz/26 pattern but slight differences in operation. Fires from belt or magazine, quick-change barrel, selective fire from dual trigger. Air cooled, gas piston, tilting block.

Cartridge: 7.62 × 45mm Czech
Length: 41.0in (1041mm)
Weight: 17lb 9oz (8.0kg)
Barrel: 27.0in (686mm), 4 grooves, rh
Feed: 25-round box or 100-round belt
Muzzle velocity: 2450 ft/sec (746m/sec)
Cyclic rate: 900 rds/min (magazine) or 1150 rds/min (belt)

vz/52/57

This was the vz/52 converted to fire the 7.62 x 39mm Soviet round for the sake of Warsaw Pact standardisation.

Specifications: the same, except
Muzzle velocity: 2477 ft/sec (755 m/sec)

vz/59

Generally a development of the vz/52, discarding the magazine feed and relying entirely upon belt. General purpose. Found with light barrel and bipod or heavy barrel and tripod. Bipod mounting is below the foresight.

Cartridge: 7.62 × 54R Russian
Length, light barrel: 43.93in (1116mm)
Length, heavy barrel: 47.83in (1215mm)
Weight, light barrel and bipod: 29lb 2oz (8.67kg)
Weight, heavy barrel and tripod: 42lb 6oz (19.24kg)
Barrel, light: 23.35in (593mm), 4 grooves, rh
Barrel, heavy: 27.28in (693mm), 4 grooves, rh
Feed: 30-round box
Muzzle velocity, light barrel: 2657 ft/sec (810 m/sec)
Muzzle velocity, heavy barrel: 2723 ft/sec (830 m/sec)
Cyclic rate: 750 rds/min

CZ 2000

1992. Originally called the 'Lada'. Based on the CZ 2000 assault rifle but with a heavy barrel. Gas operated with rotating bolt lock. Rectangular receiver, exposed barrel with gas cylinder above in Kalashnikov style. Short plastic fore-end, folding tubular butt. Bipod attached just below fore-sight. Magazine fed from either box or drum.

Cartridge: 5.45 × 39.5mm Soviet
Length, butt extended: 41.34in (1050mm)
Length, butt folded: 31.89in (810mm)
Weight: 9lb 1oz (4.10kg)
Barrel: 22.71in (577mm), 6 grooves, rh
Feed: 30-round box or 75-round drum
Muzzle velocity: 3150 ft/sec (960 m/sec)
Cyclic rate: 800 rds/min

DAEWOO South Korea
Daewoo

K3

Based on, if not copied from, the FN Minimi. Light. Air-cooled, gas piston operated, rotating bolt, magazine or belt feed. Bipod on gas cylinder, can also be tripod-mounted.

Cartridge: 5.56 × 45mm NATO
Length: 40.55in (1030mm)
Weight: 15lb 2oz (6.85kg)
Barrel: 21.0in (533mm), 6 grooves, rh
Feed: 30-round box or 200-round metal link belt
Muzzle velocity: 3000 ft/sec (915 m/sec)
Cyclic rate: 850 rds/min

DARNE France
Darne

Model 1918

Aircraft gun. Air cooled, gas piston operated, lifting the bolt up into a recess in the receiver to lock. Crude finish, cheap but reliable. Tall rectangular receiver, gas cylinder beneath barrel, pistol grip and various types of shoulder stock for observers' guns. Belt fed. Used by France and countries in the Balkans and South America, 1918–39. Various calibres.

Cartridge: 8 × 50R Lebel
Length: 36.89in (937mm)
Weight: 15lb 7oz (7.0kg)
Barrel: 25.98in (660mm), 4 grooves, rh
Feed: cloth belt
Muzzle velocity: 2300 ft/sec (700 m/sec)
Cyclic rate: 1100 rds/min

DEGTYAREV Russia
State factories

DP

1928. Light. Air-cooled, gas piston operated, locking by flaps. Rifle-type stock, bipod, gas cylinder beneath barrel, thin flat drum magazine. Finned barrel. Grip safety behind the trigger-guard.

Cartridge: 7.62 × 54R Russian
Length: 50.80in (1290mm)
Weight: 20lb 8oz (9.12kg)
Barrel: 23.80in (605mm), 4 grooves, rh
Feed: 47-round drum
Muzzle velocity: 2760 ft/sec (840 m/sec)
Cyclic rate: 550 rds/min

DT

1929. Tank-mounted version of the DP. Similar mechanism, but no supporting jacket around the barrel, and a prominent circular mounting block at the front of the receiver. Single-strut butt is adjustable for length. Pistol grip.

Cartridge: 7.62 × 54R Russian
Length: 47.0in (1193mm)
Weight: 28lb 0oz (12.70kg)
Barrel: 23.80in (605mm), 4 grooves, rh
Feed: 60-round drum
Muzzle velocity: 2760 ft/sec (840 m/sec)
Cyclic rate: 650 rds/min

DPM

1944. Modification of the DP by removing the return spring from underneath the barrel and placing it in a tube at the rear of the receiver, which sticks out over the butt and is an instant identification. It also prevented the firer from grasping the butt , and therefore a pistol grip was added. Bipod strengthened and attached to the barrel casing. Grip safety removed and replaced by conventional safety lever.

Cartridge: 7.62 × 54R Russian
Length: 49.80in (1265mm)
Weight: 26lb 13oz (12.20kg)
Barrel: 23.80in (605mm), 4 grooves, rh
Feed: 47-round drum
Muzzle velocity: 2760 ft/sec (840 m/sec)
Cyclic rate: 550 rds/min

DTM

1944. Modification of the DT gun in a similar manner to the DPM.

Cartridge: 7.62 × 54R Russian
Length: 46.5in (1181mm)
Weight: 28lb 6oz (12.87kg)
Barrel: 23.80in (605mm), 4 grooves, rh
Feed: 60-round drum
Muzzle velocity: 2756 ft/sec (840 m/sec)
Cyclic rate: 600 rds/min

DShK38

1938. Heavy. Air-cooled, gas piston operated, flap locking. Feed system uses a 'squirrel-cage' rotary mechanism concealed under a circular cover over the receiver, a quick recognition point for this gun. Long finned barrel, gas cylinder underneath, muzzle brake.

Cartridge: 12.7 × 108mm DShK
Length: 62.30in (1582mm)
Weight: 73lb 8oz (33.33kg)
Barrel: 39.37in (1000mm), 8 grooves, rh
Feed: 50-round metal link belt
Muzzle velocity: 2805 ft/sec (855 m/sec)
Cyclic rate: 575 rds/min

DShK 38-46

1946. Modification of the DShK38 by removing the rotary feed mechanism and replacing it with a more conventional lever system. The receiver is now flat-topped. Other modifications were made to improve operation.

Cartridge: 12.7 × 108mm DShK
Length: 62.50in (1587mm)
Weight: 78lb 8oz (35.60kg)
Barrel: 42.00in (1066mm), 8 grooves, rh
Feed: 50-round metal link belt
Muzzle velocity: 2825 ft/sec (860 m/sec)
Cyclic rate: 550 rds/min

DS39

1939. Medium. Air-cooled, gas piston operated, flap locking. Finned barrel, general appearance like that of the DShK but smaller. Made in limited numbers. Two rates of fire.

Cartridge: 7.62 × 54R Russian
Length: 46.0in (1168mm)
Weight: 26lb 6oz (11.97kg)
Barrel: 28.40in (721mm), 4 grooves, rh
Feed: 250-round cloth belt
Muzzle velocity: 2650 ft/sec (807 m/sec)
Cyclic rate: 550 or 1100 rds/min

RPD

1953. The final evolution of the DP series was the change to the short 7.62 cartridge. Feed system changed to a belt carried in a drum-type box beneath the receiver. Wood butt, pistol grip, short fore-end grip, bipod.

Cartridge: 7.62 × 39mm M1943
Length: 41.0in (1041mm)
Weight: 15lb 7oz (7.0kg)
Barrel: 20.50in (520mm), 4 grooves, rh
Feed: 100-round metal link belt
Muzzle velocity: 2410 ft/sec (734 m/sec)
Cyclic rate: 700 rds/min

FABRIQUE NATIONALE Belgium
See also **Rifles, Browning Automatic Rifle**

FN-MAG

Mitrailleuse d'Appui Générale = General Purpose Machine Gun. *Ca* 1955. General purpose. Air-cooled, gas piston operated, tilting breech-block. In basic form uses a wooden butt, smooth barrel, bipod attached to gas cylinder, pistol grip, slotted flash eliminator. But variants, due to national preferences, abound – finned barrels, spade grips and so forth. Used by Britain as the **L7**, by Sweden as the **m/58**, and by many other countries.

Cartridge: 7.62 × 51mm NATO
Length: 49.20in (1250mm)
Weight: 22lb 4oz (10.15kg)
Barrel: 21.50in (546mm), 4 grooves, rh
Feed: metal link belt
Muzzle velocity: 2800 ft/sec (853 m/sec)
Cyclic rate: 850 rds/min

FN Minimi

1974. Light. Air-cooled, gas piston operated, rotating bolt, Feeds from magazine or belt without adjustment. Quick-change barrel.

Cartridge: 5.56 × 45mm NATO
Length: 40.94in (1040mm)
Weight: 15lb 2oz (6.85kg)
Barrel: 18.35in (466mm), 6 grooves, rh
Feed: 30-round box or 200-round metal link belt
Muzzle velocity: 3000 ft/sec (915 m/sec)
Cyclic rate: 850 rds/min

FN-Minimi Para

Compact version of the Minimi with short barrel and a sliding butt.

Cartridge: 5.56 × 45mm NATO
Length: 35.15in (893mm)
Weight: 15lb 10oz (7.10kg)
Barrel: 13.66in (347mm), 6 grooves, rh
Feed: 30-round box or 200-round metal link belt
Muzzle velocity: 2952 ft/sec (900 m/sec)
Cyclic rate: 850 rds/min

15mm FN-BRG

1985. Heavy gun intended to fill the gap between .50 and 20mm. Gas piston operated, rotating bolt, dual feed. Quick-change smooth barrel, muzzle brake. Trials quantity only.

Cartridge: 15 × 115mm FN-BRG
Length: 78.74in (2000mm)
Weight: 121lb 4oz (55.0kg)
Barrel: 53.15in (1350mm);, 8 grooves, rh
Feed: two metal link belts
Muzzle velocity: 2952 ft/sec (3445 m/sec)
Cyclic rate: 700 rds/min

15.5mm FN-BRG

1988. Barrel wear problems led to a redesign of the ammunition to a projectile with a driving band and a consequent increase in calibre. Other improvements were made. Gas short-stroke piston and tappet driving rotating bolt in carrier; fluted quick-change barrel with conical flash hider. Dual belt feed. Trials quantity only, project suspended in 1991.

Cartridge: 15.5 × 106mm FN-BRG
Length: 84.65in (2150mm)
Weight: 132lb 4oz (60.0kg)
Barrel: length not known, 8 grooves, rh
Feed: dual metal link belts
Muzzle velocity: 3460 ft/sec (1055 m/sec)
Cyclic rate: 600 rds/min

FIAT-REVELLI Italy
FIAT

Model 1914

Medium. Water-cooled, belt-fed, delayed-blowback. Oiler for lubricating cartridges on loading. Stepped receiver with operating rod which reciprocates across the top. Tripod mounted. Unusual feed system. May be found with smooth or corrugated water jacket.

Cartridge: 6.5 × 52mm Carcano
Length: 46.50in (1180mm)
Weight: 37lb 8oz (17.0kg)
Barrel: 25.75in (643mm), 4 grooves, rh
Feed: 50-round strip-feed box
Muzzle velocity: 2100 ft/sec (645 m/sec)
Cyclic rate: 400 rds/min

Model 1935

The Model 1914 re-worked; water-cooling changed to air-cooling, with a slotted barrel cradle; feed changed to belt, fluted chamber adopted instead of lubrication of the cartridges, and new calibre. Many had the oiler re-installed when the fluted chamber failed to prevent separated cases.

Cartridge: 8 × 59mm Breda
Length: 50.0in (1270mm)
Weight: 40lb 0oz (18.1kg)
Barrel: 25.75in (653mm), 4 grooves, rh
Feed: 50-round metal link belt
Muzzle velocity: 2600 ft/sec (792 m/sec)
Cyclic rate: 500 rds/min

FRANCE
***See also* Berthier, Chatellerault, Chauchat, Darne, Hotchkiss, Puteaux, St Étienne & Vickers-Berthier**

AA-52 Light Barrel
MAS

Arme Automatique Transformable, 1952. General purpose. Light barrel version. Air cooled, delayed blowback using two-piece bolt, fluted chamber. Bipod, single-strut folding butt with monopod. Hump-backed receiver, quick-change barrel with carrying handle. Belt fed from the left.

Cartridge: 7.5 × 54mm French M1929
Length, butt extended: 45.08in (1145mm)
Length, butt folded: 38.58in (980mm)
Weight: 22lb 0oz (9.97kg)
Barrel: 19.68in (500mm), 4 grooves, rh
Feed: disintegrating link belt
Muzzle velocity: 2700 ft/sec (823 m/sec)
Cyclic rate: 700 rds/min

AA-52 Heavy Barrel

General purpose. Heavy barrel version. Air cooled, delayed blowback using two-piece bolt, fluted chamber. Tripod (US M2) mounted. Same gun as the light except for the heavier barrel.

Cartridge: 7.5 × 54mm French M1929
Length, butt extended: 49.0in (1245mm)
Length, butt folded: 42.52in (1080mm)
Weight, gun: 25lb 1oz (11.37kg)
Weight, tripod: 23lb 6oz (10.60kg)
Barrel: 23.62in (600mm), 4 grooves, rh
Feed: disintegrating link belt
Muzzle velocity: 2756 ft/sec (840 m/sec)
Cyclic rate: 700 rds/min

AA 7.62 F-1

The same gun but modified to fire the 7.62mm NATO cartridge.

Specifications: the same, except
Muzzle velocity, light barrel: 2723 ft/sec (830 m/sec)
Muzzle velocity, heavy barrel: 2772 ft/sec (845 m/sec)

GALIL Israel
IMI

Model ARM

Ca 1974. Heavy-barrel version of the Galil AR rifle (*qv*), with bipod, carrying handle and a selection of magazines.

Cartridge: 7.62 × 51mm NATO
Length, butt extended: 40.94in (1050mm)
Length, butt folded: 31.89in (810mm)
Weight: 15lb 2oz (4.0kg)
Barrel: 18.35in (535mm), 4 grooves, rh
Feed: 25-, 35- or 50-round box
Muzzle velocity: 2788ft/sec (850 m/sec)
Cyclic rate: 650 rds/min

GARDNER USA

M1880
Pratt & Whitney
Mechanical, crank driven, two-barrel. Mounted on two-wheeled artillery carriage.

Cartridge: .45-70 Government
Weight of gun and carriage: 500 lb (226kg)
Rate of fire: 250 rds/min

BRITAIN
Enfield
Gun, Machine, Gardner, 0.45in, 5 Barrel, Mark I
1882. Mechanical, crank driven. Five barrels side-by-side in cradle, mounted on artillery-type carriage.

Cartridge: .450 Gardner & Gatling
Length: 53.50in (1359mm)
Weight: 290lb (131.5kg)
Barrels: 33.0in (838mm), 7 grooves, rh
Feed: 30-round vertical feeder
Muzzle velocity: not known
Rate of fire: up to 800 rds/min

Gun, Gardner, 2-Barrel, 0.45in Mark I
1884 Mechanical, crank driven, two barrels side-by-side in a cylindrical gunmetal casing. For deck mounting on warships; pedestal mounting with shield.

Cartridge: .450 Gardner & Gatling
Length: 47.0in (1193mm)
Weight: 218lb (98.88kg)
Barrels: 30.0in (762mm), 7 grooves, rh
Feed: 30-round vertical feeder
Muzzle velocity: not known
Rate of fire: up to 250 rds/min

Gun, Gardner, 0.4in, 2-Barrel, Mark I
1888. Similar to the .45in Mark 1 but has shorter barrels supported only at the breech, with no barrel casing; the cartridge feeder is slightly shorter, and the sights differ. Guns used with fortress parapet mountings have the muzzle reduced in diameter to one inch (25.4mm) for a short distance.

Cartridge: .402 Enfield-Martini
Length: 45.5in (1155mm)
Weight: 88lb (39.9kg)
Barrels: 28.50in (724mm), 7 grooves, rh
Feed: 20-round vertical cartridge container
Muzzle velocity: not known
Rate of fire: up to 200 rds/min

Gun, Gardner, 0.4in, 2-Barrel, Mark I Converted
1889. Due to the abandonment of the proposed .402 cartridge, those Gardner guns which had been made were converted to the .45in Martini-Henry cartridge. The barrels were re-bored and re-chambered, the extractors and cartridge feeders altered to suit the larger cartridge. Basic dimensions remained the same.

Gun, Gardner, 2-Barrel, .303in, Converted, Mark I
1898. Conversion of the 2-barrel .45in Mark 1 guns to fire the .303 cartridge. New barrels and modifications to the mechanism as required.

Cartridge: .303 British
Length: 45.25in (1149mm)
Weight: 92lb (41.73kg)
Barrel: 28.25in (718mm), 5 grooves, rh
Feed: 20-round vertical feeder
Muzzle velocity: not known
Cyclic rate: 400 rds/min.

GAST Germany
Vorwerk
1918
Twin-barrelled, recoil-operated, the recoil of one barrel actuating the breech mechanism of the other barrel, so firing alternately. Hollow shoulder stock, pistol grip with finger rest on trigger-guard, large side-mounted drum magazines.

Cartridge: 7.92 × 57mm Mauser
Length: 54.72in (1390mm)
Weight: 40lb 13oz (18.50kg)
Barrels: 28.35in (720mm), 4 grooves, rh
Feed: two 192-round drums
Muzzle velocity: ca 2700 ft/sec (823 m/sec)
Rate of fire: 1300 rds/min (both barrels)

GATLING USA

BRITAIN
Gun, Gatling, 0.45in
Armstrong
1874. Mechanical, revolving, 10-barrel, on light artillery-type carriage.

Cartridge: .450 Gardner & Gatling
Length: 59.41in (1359mm)
Weight, with carriage: 444lb (201.39kg)
Barrels: 31.95in (812mm), 7 grooves, rh
Feed: 240-round drum
Muzzle velocity: not known
Rate of fire: up to 800 rds/min

Gun, Gatling, 0.65in
Armstrong
1875. For Naval service. 10 barrels. Similar construction to the 0.45in gun above.

Cartridge: .65 Gatling
Length: 66.60in (1692mm)
Weight: 817lb (370.60kg)
Barrel: 33.0in (838mm), 7 grooves, rh
Feed: 50-round drum
Muzzle velocity: not known
Cyclic rate: 400 rds/min

GEBAUER Hungary
Gebauer-Weich Motor Gun
Sollux
1918. Two barrel mechanically-driven from aeroplane engine so as to synchronise with the propeller at any speed. To some degree it can be considered as a mechanised Gardner (qv) gun, with a rate of fire of up to 800 rds/min per barrel. (The work of Ferencz Gebauer, a Hungarian

engineer. Not to be confused with Jan Gebauer, a Czech ballistician.) The war ended before the gun could be manufactured in quantity, and it was thereafter abandoned.

GENERAL ELECTRIC USA
GEC & Lockheed

M134 Minigun
Ca 1963. Mechanical, six barrels, Gatling type, electrically driven. For mounting in helicopters and vehicles.

Cartridge: 7.62 × 51mm NATO
Length: 31.56in (802mm)
Weight: 36lb 0oz (16.33kg)
Barrel: 22.0in (559mm), 4 grooves, rh
Feed: metal link belt
Muzzle velocity: 2850 ft/sec (869 m/sec)
Cyclic rate: selectable to 6000 rds/min

XM 214 (Six-Pak)
Ca 1968. Lightweight version of the M134 Minigun in 5.56mm calibre. Six barrels, mechanical, Gatling type. New clutched feed drive which stops feed when trigger is released; bolts removable without tools.

Cartridge: 5.56 × 45mm M193
Length: 28.80in (732mm)
Weight: 22lb 8oz (10.21kg)
Barrel: 20.14in (511mm), 6 grooves, rh
Feed: metal link belt
Muzzle velocity: 3250 ft/sec (991 m/sec)
Cyclic rate: 400–6000 rds/min, selectable

GECAL 50
Lockheed
1986. Six-barrel mechanical, Gatling type, electrically driven. 10-shot burst fire mechanism, linked belt or linkless feed, barrel length to customer's requirements.
And see USA, GAU/19A for the in-service version

Cartridge: .50 Browning
Length: 46.50in (1181mm)
Weight: 96lb 2oz (43.60kg)
Barrels: 36.0in (914mm), 8 grooves, rh
Feed: link belt or linkless
Muzzle velocity: 2900 ft/sec (884 m/sec)
Cyclic rate: 8000 rds/min

GERMANY
See also **Bergmann, Gast, Heckler & Koch, Knorr-Bremse, Maxim, Schwarzlose & TuF**

MG3A1
Beretta, Franchi, MKEK, POF, Rheinmetall, Santa Barbara & Whitehead
This is the current version of the wartime MG 42 (*see below*) and is simply the MG 42 with various improvements and in 7.62mm NATO calibre. It arrived at MG3A1 via MG1, 2 and 3 which were all gradual changes from the MG 42 design as various improvements were added.

Cartridge: 7.62 × 51mm NATO
Length: 48.22in (1225mm)
Weight: 24lb 6oz (11.05kg)
Barrel: 20.90in (531mm), 4 grooves, rh

Feed: metal link belt
Muzzle velocity: 2690 ft/sec (820 m/sec)
Cyclic rate: 1100 rds/min

MG 08
See Maxim, Germany

MG 13
Simson
Ca 1933. A rebuild of water-cooled Dreyse M1910 and 1915 medium machine guns into a lighter air-cooled model as an interim measure pending issue of the MG 34. Recoil-operated, using a vertically-swinging breech-block. Tall, thin receiver, single-strut metal butt, pistol grip, perforated barrel jacket, bipod close to muzzle, Small box magazine or larger saddle drum.

Cartridge: 7.92 × 57mm Mauser
Length: 57.75in (1466mm)
Weight: 23lb 15oz (10.89kg)
Barrel: 28.25in (717mm), 4 grooves, rh
Feed: 25-round box or 75-round saddle drum
Muzzle velocity: 2700 ft/sec (823 m/sec)
Cyclic rate: 650 rds/min

MG 15
Rheinmetall
1932. Aircraft, flexible, air cooled, short recoil operation, rotating breech-block. In 1944–45 numbers were adapted for ground use by adding a simple single-strut butt and attaching a bipod to the barrel jacket. Fired from an open bolt.

Cartridge: 7.92 × 57mm Mauser
Length: 52.50in (1334mm)
Weight: 28lb 0oz (12.70kg)
Barrel: 23.50in (595mm), 4 grooves, rh
Feed: 75-round saddle drum
Muzzle velocity: 2700 ft/sec (823 m/sec)
Cyclic rate: 850 rds/min

MG 17
Rheinmetall
1932. This was the same weapon as the MG 15 but firing from a closed bolt so that it could be synchronised to fire through an aircraft propeller.

Specifications: the same

MG 30
Rheinmetall
1930. Built by Solothurn in Switzerland, sold to Austria and Hungary. Light. Air-cooled, recoil-operated, rotating bolt. Straight line layout, quick barrel change by removing butt and receiver end cap and withdrawing bolt and barrel. Left side-mounted box magazine, perforated barrel jacket with bipod, high sight line.

Cartridge: 7.92 × 57mm Mauser
Length: 46.25in (1174mm)
Weight: 17lb 0oz (7.70kg)
Barrel: 23.50in (595mm), 4 grooves, rh
Feed: 25-round box
Muzzle velocity: 2500 ft/sec (761 m/sec)
Cyclic rate: 800 rds/min

MG 34
Mauser
1934. General purpose. Air-cooled, recoil operated, rotating bolt. Straight-line layout, synthetic butt, pistol grip, perforated barrel jacket. Quick-change barrel by swinging the receiver to one side and withdrawing barrel from jacket. Belt or magazine feed. Bipod or tripod mounting. Selective fire.

Cartridge: 7.92 × 57mm Mauser
Length: 48.0in (1219mm)
Weight: 26lb 11oz (12.10kg)
Barrel: 24.75in (627mm), 4 grooves, rh
Feed: 50-round belt or 75-round saddle drum
Muzzle velocity: 2700 ft/sec (823 m/sec)
Cyclic rate: 650 rds/min

MG 34S, MG 34/41
1940. Attempts to simplify the MG34 and increase the rate of fire by shortening the barrel and doing away with the selective fire option. Not adopted.

MG 42
Mauser
1942. Replacement for the MG 34 which was easier to make and had higher rate of fire. General purpose. Air-cooled, recoil-operated, roller-locked bolt, quick change barrel via a slot in the jacket. Short synthetic butt, pistol grip, perforated barrel jacket, muzzle recoil booster and flash hider, bipod.

Cartridge: 7.92 × 57mm Mauser
Length: 48.0in (1219mm)
Weight: 25lb 8oz (11.50kg)
Barrel: 21.0in (533mm), 4 grooves, rh
Feed: 50-round belt
Muzzle velocity: 2480 ft/sec (755 m/sec)
Cyclic rate: 1200 rds/min

MG 42/59
1959. Licenced copy of the MG3 (*above*) manufactured by Beretta and Breda in Italy, used by the Italian and Austrian armies.
See Beretta for details

MG 45
Mauser
1945. Development weapon as replacement for the MG 42. Air-cooled, delayed blowback using a form of roller lock later adopted in the CETME and G3 rifles. Development was not completed, but the SIG MG 710 (*qv*) uses much the same system.

MG 81
Mauser
1938. Originally a flexible aircraft gun, many were provided with a single-strut butt with cheek-pad and a bipod and used as ground weapons. In the aircraft role usually mounted in pairs, as the **MG 81K**. Air-cooled, recoil-operated, roller-locked bolt. Hump-backed receiver, slotted barrel jacket, large pistol grip. Ground guns had a half-sleeve around the barrel jacket to hold the bipod. Belt fed, adjustable for right or left side feed. Exceptionally high rate of fire.

Cartridge: 7.92 × 57mm Mauser
Length: 36.02in (915mm)
Weight: 14lb 5oz (6.50kg)
Barrel: 18.70in (475mm), 6 grooves, rh
Feed: metal link belt
Muzzle velocity: 2592 ft/sec (790 m/sec)
Cyclic rate: 1600 rds/min

MG 131
Rheinmetall
1936 Aircraft fixed gun. Air-cooled, recoil-operated with gas assist, rotating bolt sleeve. Belt fed, electric cocking and firing.

Cartridge: 13 × 64mm MG131
Length: 46.25in (1174mm)
Weight: 40lb 0oz (18.14kg)
Barrel: 21.75in (552mm), 6 grooves, rh
Feed: 100-round metal link belt
Muzzle velocity: 2560 ft/sec (780 m/sec)
Cyclic rate: 960 rds/min

MG 151
Mauser
1935 Standard German aircraft fixed armament in 1939. Air-cooled, recoil-operated, roller-locked bolt. No barrel jacket. Electric cocking and firing.

Cartridge: 15 × 95mm MG151
Length: 75.43in (1916mm)
Weight: 78lb 15oz (35.80kg)
Barrel: 49.37in (1254mm), 8 grooves, rh
Feed: 50-round metal link belt
Muzzle velocity: 3150 ft/sec (960 m/sec)
Cyclic rate: 700 rds/min

MG 151/20
Mauser
1938 Upgrading of the 15mm MG151 to a heavier calibre. No change in basic mechanism.

Cartridge: 20 × 83.5mm MG151
Length: 69.52in (1766mm)
Weight: 93lb 8oz (42.41kg)
Barrel: 43.46in (1104mm), 8 grooves, rh
Feed: 50-round metal link belt
Muzzle velocity: 2313 ft/sec (705 m/sec)
Cyclic rate: 700 rds/min

GORYUNOV Russia
State factories

SG43
1943. Designed to replace the Degtyarev DS. Medium. Air-cooled, gas piston operated, bolt moves sideways to lock. Smooth barrel, flash hider, spade grips and trigger with cocking handle beneath, belt fed from the right side.

Cartridge: 7.62 × 54R Russian
Length: 44.09in (1120mm)
Weight: 30lb 7oz (13.80kg)
Barrel: 28.35in (720mm), 4 grooves, rh
Feed: 250-round belt
Muzzle velocity: 2832 ft/sec (863 m/sec)
Cyclic rate: 650 rds/min

SGM

Modified version of the SG43. Fluted barrel, cocking handle moved to the right side of the receiver, improved barrel lock, dust covers on feed and ejection ports.

Cartridge: 7.62 x 54R Russian
Length: 44.09in (1120mm)
Weight: 29lb 14oz (13.60kg)
Barrel: 28.35in (720mm), 4 grooves, rh
Feed: 250-round belt
Muzzle velocity: 2870 ft/sec (875 m/sec)
Cyclic rate: 650 rds/min

SGMT

Tank co-axial version of the SGM; solenoid trigger mounted on back plate.

SGMB

Vehicle-mounted version of the SGM; as for the SGM but with a special cradle mounting.

HECKLER & KOCH Germany
Heckler & Koch

HK11

Light. Air-cooled, delayed blowback using roller-delayed bolt. Quick-change barrel. Fixed synthetic butt, pistol grip, bipod. A magazine-fed version of the HK21 (*below*).

Cartridge: 7.62 x 51mm NATO
Length: 40.15in (1020mm)
Weight: 15lb 0oz (6.80kg)
Barrel: 17.71in (450mm), 4 grooves, rh
Feed: 20-round box or 80-round dual drum
Muzzle velocity: 2560 ft/sec (780 m/sec)
Cyclic rate: 850 rds/min

HK11A1

Light. Air-cooled, delayed blowback using roller-delayed bolt. Quick-change barrel. Improved version of the HK11. Drum magazine abandoned.

Cartridge: 7.62 x 51mm NATO
Length: 40.55in (1030mm)
Weight: 16lb 15oz (7.70kg)
Barrel: 17.71in (450mm), 4 grooves, rh
Feed: 20- or 30-round box
Muzzle velocity: 2625 ft/sec (800 m/sec)
Cyclic rate: 650 rds/min

HK11E

Improved version of HK11A1. New sight, forward hand grip, three-round burst added, winter trigger attachment, improved quick-change barrel grip, quiet-closing bolt device.

Cartridge: 7.62 x 51mm NATO
Length: 40.55in (1030mm)
Weight: 17lb 15oz (8.15kg)
Barrel: 17.71in (450mm), 4 grooves, rh
Feed: 20-round box or 50-round drum
Muzzle velocity: 2625 ft/sec (800 m/sec)
Cyclic rate: 800 rds/min

HK13

Light. Air-cooled, delayed blowback using roller-delayed bolt. Quick-change barrel, fixed butt, bipod.

Cartridge: 5.56 x 45mm M193
Length: 38.58in (980mm)
Weight: 13lb 3oz (6.00kg)
Barrel: 17.71in (450mm), 6 grooves, rh
Feed: 20-, 30- or 40-round box
Muzzle velocity: 3117 ft/sec (950 m/sec)
Cyclic rate: 750 rds/min

HK13E

1983. Improved version of HK13. Lengthened receiver, new sight, forward hand grip, three-round burst added, winter trigger attachment, improved quick-change barrel grip, quiet-closing bolt device.

Cartridge: 5.56 x 45mm M193
Length: 40.55in (1030mm)
Weight: 17lb 10oz (8.0kg)
Barrel: 17.71in (450mm), 6 grooves, rh
Feed: 20- or 30-round box
Muzzle velocity: 3117 ft/sec (950 m/sec)
Cyclic rate: 750 rds/min

HK21

General purpose. Air-cooled, delayed blowback using roller-delayed bolt. Belt fed, selective fire, quick-change barrel. By changing the barrel, feed plate and bolt can be converted to 7.62 x 51mm, 5.56 x 45mm or 7.62 x 39mm calibres. An adapter can be inserted into the belt feed to accept rifle magazines

Cartridge: 7.62 x 51mm NATO
Length: 40.19in (1021mm)
Weight: 16lb 2oz (7.32kg)
Barrel: 17.71in (450mm), 4 grooves, rh
Feed: metal link belt
Muzzle velocity: 2625 ft/sec (800 m/sec)
Cyclic rate: 900 rds/min

HK21A1

General purpose. Improved version of the HK21. Improved belt feed mechanism, box magazine option removed, 7.62 x 39mm conversion removed.

Cartridge: 7.62 x 51mm NATO
Length: 40.15in (1020mm)
Weight: 17lb 10oz (8.0kg)
Barrel: 17.71in (450mm), 4 grooves, rh
Feed: metal link belt
Muzzle velocity: 2625 ft/sec (800 m/sec)
Cyclic rate: 900 rds/min

HK21E

1983. Improved version of HK21A1. Lengthened receiver, longer barrel, new sight, forward hand grip, three-round burst added, winter trigger attachment, improved quick-change barrel grip, quiet-closing bolt device.

Cartridge: 7.62 x 51mm NATO
Length: 44.88in (1140mm)
Weight: 20lb 8oz (9.30kg)
Barrel: 22.05in (560mm), 4 grooves, rh
Feed: metal link belt
Muzzle velocity: 2756 ft/sec (840 m/sec)
Cyclic rate: 800 rds/min

HK23E

Variant of the HK21 series firing the 5.56mm cartridge. Similar in all other respects to the HK21E.

Cartridge: 5.56 × 45mm M193 or SS109
Length: 40.55in (1030mm)
Weight: 19lb 5oz (8.75kg)
Barrel: 17.71in (450mm), 6 grooves, rh
Feed: 20- or 30-round box
Muzzle velocity: 3117 ft/sec (950 m/sec)
Cyclic rate: 750 rds/min

HK73

1984. A variant of the HK23E, differing in using a linkless belt feed system. The rounds were in a container which clipped to the gun and fed directly into the feedway. Dimensions as for the HK23E. It was withdrawn after a short time.

HKGR6

1984. A further variant of the HK23E, this was the HK73 with a built-in optical sight. Dimensions as for the HK23E. It was withdrawn after a short time.

G36 LSW

1995. Light Support Weapon. Partner to the H&K G36 assault rifle (*qv*). Gas operated, using a rotating bolt, air-cooled. Folding metal skeleton butt, rectangular receiver, magazine fed, long slotted fore-end/handguard, bipod. Flash hider on muzzle, shaped for grenade launching. Prominent carrying handle with sight incorporated.

Cartridge: 5.56 × 45mm NATO
Length, butt extended: 38.98in (990mm)
Length, butt folded: 29.92in (760mm)
Weight: 7lb 11oz (3.50kg)
Barrel: 18.90in (480mm), 6 grooves, rh
Feed: 30-round box
Muzzle velocity: 3018 ft/sec (920 m/sec)
Cyclic rate: 750 rds/min

HEFAH Britain
Ductile Steel & Hefah

V Mark I

1942. Light. Air-cooled, gas piston operated, rotating bolt. Basically the Lewis mechanism but using a return spring in a tube behind the receiver. Modified Bren drum magazine beneath the receiver. Adopted for anti-aircraft use by Royal Navy, limited numbers.

Cartridge: .303 British
Length: 48.0in (1220mm)
Weight: 15lb 2oz (6.85kg)
Barrel: 24.50in (622mm), 4 grooves, rh
Feed: 60-round drum
Muzzle velocity: 2500 ft/sec (762 m/sec)
Cyclic rate: 600 rds/min

HOTCHKISS France
Hotchkiss

Mle 1897

Medium. Air-cooled, gas piston operated using a lug forced up from the bolt to lock into the barrel. Five large brass cooling fins. Fed by a metal strip holding the cartridges.

Cartridge: 8 × 50R Lebel
Length: not known
Weight: 55lb 0oz (25.40kg)
Barrel: not known
Feed: 30-round metal strip
Muzzle velocity: 2400 ft/sec (731 m/sec)
Cyclic rate: 600 rds/min

Mle 1909

Light. Air-cooled, gas piston operated, fermeture nut locking system. Upswept butt springing from the pistol grip, part-finned barrel with gas cylinder below. Small tripod or bipod attached at front of receiver. Selective fire.

Cartridge: 8 × 50R Lebel
Length: 46.75in (1187mm)
Weight: 27lb 0oz (12.25kg)
Barrel: 23.50in (596mm), 4 grooves, rh
Feed: 30-round metal strip
Muzzle velocity: 2180 ft/sec (665 m/sec)
Cyclic rate: 500 rds/min

1914

Slight improvement on the M1897 model; the most obvious change is that the barrel fins are steel instead of brass and there is no form of safety device whatever.

Cartridge: 8 × 50R Lebel
Length: 51.60in (1310mm)
Weight: 55lb 11oz (25.26kg)
Barrel: 31.0in (787mm), 6 grooves, rh
Feed: 24- or 30-round metal strip, or 250-round articulated strip belt
Muzzle velocity: 2325 ft/sec (708 m/sec)
Cyclic rate: 500 rds/min

BRITAIN

Gun, Hotchkiss, .303in, Mark I
Enfield

1916. This was the French Mle 1909 gun as manufactured in England. The dimensions are exactly the same as those of the Mle 1909, but the change of ammunition increased the muzzle velocity to 2450 ft/sec.

Gun, Hotchkiss, .303in, Mark I*

1917. The Mark 1 gun converted to belt feed for use in tanks.

Specifications: the same as the Mark 1 gun.

HUGHES USA

EX34 Chain Gun
Hughes & McDonnell

Ca 1975. Mechanical, externally electrically powered. Motor drives a loop of chain in the floor of the receiver which propels the bolt carrier and drives the belt feed. Short, square receiver, feeding at top edge, short perforated barrel jacket, slender barrel, prong-type flash eliminator.

Cartridge: 7.62 x 51mm NATO
Length: 25.98in (660mm)
Weight: 30lb 3oz (13.70kg)
Barrel: 22.83in (580mm), 4 grooves, rh
Feed: metal link belt
Muzzle velocity: 2828 ft/sec (862 m/sec)
Cyclic rate: 520 rds/min

INSAS India
Ishapore
INSAS

1997. Heavy barrel version of the INSAS assault rifle (*qv*). Light. Air-cooled, gas piston operated, rotating bolt. Conventional butt, fore-end, bipod. Sighted to 1000 metres.

Cartridge: 5.56 x 45mm
Length: 41.34in (1050mm)
Weight: 13lb 8oz (6.11kg)
Barrel: 21.06in (535mm), 4 grooves, rh
Feed: 30-round box
Muzzle velocity: 3130 ft/sec (954 m/sec)
Cyclic rate: 650 rds/min

INSAS Para

1997. The same weapon as the Insas gun above, but with a folding butt and slightly shorter barrel for use by airborne troops.

Cartridge: 5.56 x 45mm
Length, butt extended: 40.35in (1025mm)
Length, butt folded: 30.51in (775mm)
Weight: 13lb 7oz (6.10kg)
Barrel: 20.07in (510mm), 4 grooves, rh
Feed: 30-round box
Muzzle velocity: 3117 ft/sec (950 m/sec)
Cyclic rate: 650 rds/min

JAPAN
State factories
Type 1

1941. Further improvement on the Type 92 (*below*); lighter, and chambered for a rimless cartridge. Appearance similar to the Type 92 but the barrel fins are the same diameter throughout except for a short section in front of the receiver, and the muzzle has a conical flash hider.

Cartridge: 7.7 x 58mm Arisaka
Length: 42.40in (1077mm)
Weight: 77lb 0oz (34.92kg), with tripod
Barrel: 23.23in (590mm), 4 grooves, rh
Feed: 30-round metal strip
Muzzle velocity: 2400 ft/sec (731 m/sec)
Cyclic rate: 550 rds/min

Type 1 Aircraft

1941 Copy of the US Browning .50 M2 aircraft gun in 13.2 x 99mm calibre.

Type 2 Aircraft

1942. Copy of the German 13mm MG 131 (*see* Germany, MG 131).

Type 3

1914. Heavy. Air-cooled, gas piston operated, locking flap. A copy of the Hotchkiss Mle 1897, slightly modified to suit Japanese manufacturing methods. Cooling fins on barrel, large behind gas port, small in front. Spade grips and trigger, tripod mount with sockets for carrying poles.

Cartridge: 6.5 x 51SR Arisaka
Length: 45.50in (1156mm)
Weight: 62lb 0oz (28.12kg)
Barrel: 29.52in (750mm), 4 grooves, lh
Feed: 30-round metal strip
Muzzle velocity: 2400 ft/sec (731 m/sec)
Cyclic rate: 400 rds/min

Type 11

1922. Light. Air-cooled, gas piston operated. Unusual hopper feed system using rifle chargers. Finned barrel, upswept butt springing from the pistol grip. Bipod.

Cartridge: 6.5 x 51SR Arisaka
Length: 43.50in (1104mm)
Weight: 22lb 8oz (10.19kg)
Barrel: 19.0in (482mm), 4 grooves, rh
Feed: 30-round hopper
Muzzle velocity: 2300 ft/sec (701 m/sec)
Cyclic rate: 500 rds/min

Type 89 Aircraft

1929. Copy of the British Vickers aircraft gun in 7.7 x 58R calibre

Type 91

1931. This was the tank version of the Type 11 and differed only in having a larger feed hopper. In later years many were removed from tanks and fitted with a bipod and telescope sight for use by infantry.

Cartridge: 6.5 x 51SR Arisaka
Length: 42.0in (1066mm)
Weight: 24lb 7oz (11.0kg)
Barrel: 19.20in (488mm), 4 grooves, rh
Feed: 50-round hopper
Muzzle velocity: 2300 ft/sec (701 m/sec)
Cyclic rate: 500 rds/min

Type 92

1932. This was an improved Type 3 for the new 7.7mm semi-rimmed ammunition. Principal distinguishing features are the dropped 'handlebar' grips behind and below the receiver instead of spade grips.

Cartridge: 7.7 x 58SR Arisaka
Length: 45.50in (1156mm)
Weight: 61lb 0oz (27.67kg)
Barrel: 27.56in (700mm), 4 grooves, rh
Feed: 30-round metal strip
Muzzle velocity: 2400 ft/sec (731 m/sec)
Cyclic rate: 450 rds/min

Type 92 Aircraft

1932. Copy of the Lewis gun (*qv*) in 7.7 x 58R calibre.

Type 93

1933. Heavy. Air-cooled, gas piston operated. Usually twin-mounted for air defence role. Top mounted box magazine.

Cartridge: 13.2 x 99mm Hotchkiss & Breda
Length: 95in (2413mm)
Weight: 87lb 0oz (39.46kg)
Barrel: 65.0in (450mm), 6 grooves, rh
Feed: 30-round box
Muzzle velocity: 2210 ft/sec (674 m/sec)
Cyclic rate: 450 rds/min

Type 96

1936. Light. Air-cooled, gas piston operated. tilting block. An improved version of the Type 11 using a conventional top-mounted box magazine. Finned quick-change barrel with carrying handle, pistol grip, wood butt, bipod.

Cartridge: 6.5 x 51SR Arisaka
Length: 41.50in (1054mm)
Weight: 20lb 0oz (9.07kg)
Barrel: 21.70in (552mm), 4 grooves, rh
Feed: 30-round box
Muzzle velocity: 2400 ft/sec (731 m/sec)
Cyclic rate: 550 rds/min

Type 97

1937. Tank gun to replace the Type 92. Air-cooled, long finned barrel with long gas cylinder, overhead magazine, pistol grip, short butt-pad. Mechanically based on the Czech vz/26 using a gas piston and tilting bolt. First Japanese machine gun which did not demand lubricated ammunition.

Cartridge: 7.7 x 58SR Arisaka
Length: 46.50in (1181mm)
Weight: 24lb 0oz (10.88kg)
Barrel: 28.0in (711mm), 4 grooves, rh
Feed: 30-round box
Muzzle velocity: 2400 ft/sec (731 m/sec)
Cyclic rate: 500 rds/min

Type 98

1938. Copy of the German MG 15 (*qv*).

Type 99

1939. New design consequent upon the introduction of the 7.7mm rimless cartridge. More or less the Type 96 built to closer tolerances and with cartridge headspace adjustment, Finned barrel, bipod, monopod under the toe of the butt. Carrying handle on the quick-change barrel, overhead magazine.

Cartridge: 7.7 x 58mm Arisaka
Length: 46.50in (1181mm)
Weight: 23lb 0oz (10.43kg)
Barrel: 23.60in (600mm), 4 grooves, rh
Feed: 30-round box
Muzzle velocity: 2350 ft/sec (715 m/sec)
Cyclic rate: 850 rds/min

Model 62
Sumitomo

1962. General purpose. Air-cooled, gas piston operated, tilting block. Finned barrel, bipod or tripod mounted, butt with shoulder strap, pistol grip, belt fed from left. Quick change barrel.

Cartridge: 7.62 x 51mm
Length: 45.50in (1200mm)
Weight: 23lb 9oz (10.70kg)
Barrel: 20.63in (524mm), 4 grooves, rh
Feed: metal link belt
Muzzle velocity: 2400 ft/sec (732 m/sec)
Cyclic rate: 600 rds/min

Model 74
Sumitomo

1974. Co-axial tank gun, heavy variant of the Model 62. Spade grip and manual trigger or solenoid trigger, adjustable rate of fire. Plain barrel.

Cartridge: 7.62 x 51mm
Length: 42.72in (1085mm)
Weight: 44lb 15oz (20.40kg)
Barrel: 24.60in (625mm), 4 grooves, rh
Feed: metal link belt
Muzzle velocity: 2805 ft/sec (855 m/sec)
Cyclic rate: 700–1000 rds/min, adjustable.

JOHNSON USA
Cranston & Johnson

M1941

Light. Air-cooled, recoil-operated. Straight-line layout, buffer in the wooden butt, bipod in front of fore-end, Box magazine feeds from the left side and can be topped up from the right. Perforated handguard. Selective fire, firing from open bolt at automatic, closed bolt for single shots.

Cartridge: .30-06 Springfield
Length: 42.30in (1074mm)
Weight: 12lb 8oz (5.67kg)
Barrel: 22.0in (558mm), 4 grooves, rh
Feed: 20-round box
Muzzle velocity: 2800 ft/sec (853 m/sec)
Cyclic rate: 600 rds/min

M1944
Johnson

Light. Air-cooled, recoil-operated. Generally as for the M1941, but used a butt made of two tubes and a butt-pad, and had a monopod and shoe instead of a bipod.

Cartridge: .30-06 Springfield
Length: 42.0in (1067mm)
Weight: 14lb 5oz (6.49kg)
Barrel: 22.0in (558mm), 4 grooves, rh
Feed: 30-round box
Muzzle velocity: 2800 ft/sec (853 m/sec)
Cyclic rate: 300–900 rds/min, adjustable by buffer tension

KALASHNIKOV Russia
State factories

PK

1963. General purpose. Combination of the Kalashnikov gas piston and rotating bolt, the RPD trigger and a feed system apparently inspired by the Czech vz/52. Air-cooled, bipod, belt box carried beneath the receiver Quick-change fluted barrel with carrying handle, hollowed-out butt.

Cartridge: 7.62 × 54R Russian
Length: 45.67in (1160mm)
Weight: 19lb 13oz (9.0kg)
Barrel: 25.90in (658mm), 4 grooves, rh
Feed: 30-round box
Muzzle velocity: 2706 ft/sec (825 m/sec)
Cyclic rate: 700 rds/min

PKS

The PK gun (*above*) mounted on a tripod in the sustained fire role.

PKT

The PK gun modified for co-axial mounting in tanks. Sights, butt, pistol grip and trigger, and bipod are removed and a solenoid firing gear fitted to the rear of the receiver.

PKM

'Product-improved' version of the PK. Smooth barrel, lighter components.

Weight: 18lb 8oz (8.40kg)

PKMS

PKM mounted on a tripod.

PKB

The PKM with butt, bipod, pistol grip and trigger removed and a spade grip with trigger fitted to the receiver backplate.

RPK

Ca 1960. More or less a heavy-barrel version of the AK rifle, using the same gas and rotating bolt system and the same magazines, although it is provided with its own 75-round drum. Long barrel with cleaning rod beneath, gas cylinder on top, wood fore-end and butt, bipod attached behind muzzle.

Cartridge: 7.62 × 39mm M1943
Length: 41.00in (1041mm)
Weight: 10lb 8oz (4.76kg)
Barrel: 23.23in (590mm), 4 grooves, rh
Feed: 30- or 40-round box, or 75-round drum
Muzzle velocity: 2400 ft/sec (734 m/sec)
Cyclic rate: 600 rds/min

RPK-74

1974. Heavy-barrel version of the AK-74 rifle, or the 5.45mm version of the RPK. Similar in appearance, with the usual drop-curved machine-gun butt which gives a grip for the non-firing hand, and a long curved magazine which necessitates a high-set bipod.

Cartridge: 5.45 × 39.5mm
Length: 41.73in (1060mm)
Weight: 10lb 2oz (4.60kg)
Barrel: 24.25in (616mm), 4 grooves, rh
Feed: 30-, 40- or 45-round box

Muzzle velocity: 3150 ft/sec (960 m/sec)
Cyclic rate: 650 rds/min

KNORR-BREMSE Germany
Knorr

M/35.

Designed in Sweden as the **LH33**, patents sold to the German Knorr-Bremse company. Light. Air-cooled, gas operated, side-feeding box magazine. Cheap, poorly made, and has some unpleasant surprises – if the safety is wrongly applied the gun will fire when the safety is released. Used by the Waffen SS as a training weapon and some sold to Finland and Sweden.

Cartridge: 7.92 × 57mm Mauser
Length: 51.48in (1308mm)
Weight: 22lb 1oz (10.0kg)
Barrel: 27.25in (691mm), 4 grooves, rh
Feed: 20-round box
Muzzle velocity: 2600 ft/sec (792 m/sec)
Cyclic rate: 500 rds/min

LEWIS USA

BRITAIN
BSA & Savage

Gun, Machine, Lewis, .303in, Mark 1

1914. Light. Air-cooled by finned aluminium radiator around the barrel concealed in a light metal jacket. Gas piston operated, rotating bolt. Helical return spring in casing beneath receiver is recognition feature. Flat drum magazine on top of receiver, wooden butt, pistol grip, bipod.

Cartridge: .303 British
Length: 50.63in (1285mm)
Weight: 26lb 0oz (11.79kg)
Barrel: 26.25in (667mm), 4 grooves, lh
Feed: 47- or 97-round drum
Muzzle velocity: 2450 ft/sec (745 m/sec)
Cyclic rate: 550 rds/min

Gun, Machine, Lewis, Mark 1*

1946. Mark 1 guns modified to approximate to the Mark 4 standard. Doubtful if any were made: they were declared obsolete on the same day as they were introduced.

Gun, Machine, Lewis, .303in, Mark 2

1915. The Mark 1 gun with the radiator and jacket removed, leaving the barrel and gas cylinder exposed. Butt removed and a spade grip fitted. For aircraft use. A 97-round drum magazine was introduced for this gun in 1916.

Gun, Machine, Lewis, Mark 2*

Existing Mark 2 guns modified by enlarging the gas port and modifying other parts to increase the rate of fire to about 800 rds/min. Air service.

Gun, Machine, Lewis, Mark 3

Similar to Mark 2* but of new manufacture.

Gun, Machine, Lewis, Mark 4

1946. A redesign of the Mark 3 gun to simplify manufacture. Doubtful if any were made as, like the Mark 1*, it was made obsolete by the same approval which introduced it.

Gun Machine, Lewis, SS

1942. SS = Shoulder Shooting. Issued to naval auxiliary vessels for air defence. The radiator was removed and barrel exposed, a muzzle brake and a short butt fitted, a fore-grip welded to a guard fitted round the gas cylinder. Any gun could be converted to this form, and a star added to the existing mark number, but in the event they appear to have been called the 'Mark 11S' in Royal Navy records.

Gun, Machine, Savage-Lewis, .30in

Nomenclature applied to American Lewis guns made by the Savage Arms Co and bought by the Royal Navy in 1940. They were later allotted to the Home Guard and fitted with a skeleton butt attached to the original spade grip, and a simple bipod. They were marked with a two-inch red stripe around the receiver in front of the magazine post, and magazine centres were also painted red to distinguish them from .303 guns.

Cartridge: .30-06 Springfield

USA

Machine Gun, Lewis, Cal .30 M1917
Savage

The British Mark 1 re-barrelled for the US .30 cartridge.

Cartridge: .30-06 Springfield
Length: 51.75in (1314mm)
Weight: 25lb 4oz (11.45kg)
Barrel: 26.25in (667mm), 4 grooves, lh
Feed: 47-round drum
Muzzle velocity: 2830 ft/sec (863 m/sec)
Cyclic rate: 500 rds/min

Machine Gun, Lewis, Cal .30 M1918

This was the same gun as the M1917 but with some small but vital modifications to the gas piston system to slow down the breech opening, due to the greater power of the US .30-06 cartridge compared to the British .303.

Machine Gun, Aircraft, Lewis, Cal .303 M1917

The British .303 Mark 2 gun supplied to the US Army Air Service in France.

Machine Gun, Aircraft, Lewis, Cal .30 M1918

This was the M1918 ground gun stripped of its radiator and provided with a spade grip and 97-round drum magazine in a similar manner to the British Mark 2.

MADSEN Denmark
Madsen

1904–56

The year notation merely points out that the Madsen remained fundamentally unchanged throughout its life, most of the apparent changes being more or less cosmetic. In effect, a recoil-operated version of the Peabody-Martini breech-block, it was adopted by over 30 countries. Light. Air-cooled, short bulky receiver, curved overhead magazine, bipod, barrel jacket, curved rifle-type butt and trigger. Found in various calibres.

Cartridge: 7.92 x 57mm Mauser
Length: 45.0in (1143mm)
Weight: 20lb 0oz (9.07kg)
Barrel: 23.0in (584mm), 4 grooves, rh
Feed: 20, 30 or 40-round box
Muzzle velocity: ca 2460 ft/sec (750 m/sec)
Cyclic rate: 450 rds/min

MADSEN-SAETTER Denmark
Madsen

Mark 3

1959. General purpose. Air-cooled; gas piston operated, bolt locked by lugs. Long receiver, butt, pistol grip, barrel finned over rear section, flash hider, gas cylinder beneath barrel, bipod. The design never went into production.

Cartridge: 7.62 x 51mm NATO
Length: 45.90in (1165mm)
Weight: 23lb 8oz (10.65kg)
Barrel: 22.20in (565mm), 4 grooves, rh
Feed: 49-round metal link belt
Muzzle velocity: 2800 ft/sec (853 m/sec)
Cyclic rate: 650–1000 rds/min, adjustable

Tank

1959. Tank or tripod-mounted version of the Mark 3. Similar to the Mark 3 but somewhat heavier barrel, no butt.

Cartridge: 7.62 x 51mm NATO
Length: 38.20in (970mm)
Weight: 22lb 5oz (10.12kg)
Barrel: 22.20in (565mm), 4 grooves, rh
Feed: 49-round metal link belt
Muzzle velocity: 2800 ft/sec (853 m/sec)
Cyclic rate: 750 rds/min

Heavy

1959. Tank or anti-aircraft. Air-cooled, gas piston operated, bolt locked by lugs. Spade grips and trigger, long receiver, mid-length perforated barrel jacket, gas cylinder beneath barrel, flash hider.

Cartridge: .50 Browning
Length: 64.0in (1626mm)
Weight: 61lb 11oz (27.98kg)
Barrel: 39.37in (1000mm), 8 grooves, rh
Feed: 50-round metal link belt
Muzzle velocity: 2850 ft/sec (868 m/sec)
Cyclic rate: 1000 rds/min

MARLIN USA
Marlin

M1917

This is actually the Colt M1895 'Potato Digger' but re-modelled into a more conventional type with gas piston operating in a cylinder beneath the barrel. In aircraft and tank versions; the former with a long, finned, aluminium radiator surrounding the barrel, the latter with a heavy armoured jacket.

Cartridge: .30-06 Springfield
Length: 40.00in (1016mm)
Weight: 22lb 8oz (10.10kg)
Barrel: 28.0in (711mm), 4 grooves, rh
Feed: 250-round cloth belt
Muzzle velocity: 2800 ft/sec (853 m/sec)
Cyclic rate: 600 rds/min

MAXIM

BELGIUM
Liège

Mitrailleur Modèle 1900

Standard Maxim pattern: smooth phosphor-bronze water jacket, fusee spring casing on left of receiver upturned, spade grips and trigger. Recoil-operated using a toggle which broke downwards, belt fed.

Cartridge: 7.65 × 53mm Belgian Mauser
Length: 46.46in (1180mm)
Weight: 39lb 11oz (18.0kg)
Barrel: 28.22in (717mm), 4 grooves, rh
Feed: 250-round cloth belt
Muzzle velocity: 2132 ft/sec (650 m/sec)
Cyclic rate: *ca* 450 rds/min

Mitr. Model 1910

Generally as for the German MG 08, with steel water jacket.

Cartridge: 7.65 × 52mm Mauser

Mitr. Maxim légère

1920. Modification of the German MG 08/15 to 7.65mm calibre.

Cartridge: 7.65 × 53mm Belgian Mauser
Length: 49.50in (1400mm)
Weight: 33lb 1oz (15.0kg)
Barrel: 28.34in (720mm), 4 grooves, rh
Feed: 100- or 250-round cloth belt
Muzzle velocity: 2025 ft/sec (617 m/sec)
Cyclic rate: 450 rds/min

BRITAIN
Vickers

Gun, Maxim, 0.45in Mark 1

1889. Standard pattern. Brass, smooth, water jacket, brass feed plates.

Cartridge: .577/450 Martini-Henry
Length: 43.50in (1105mm)
Weight: 60lb (27.20kg)
Barrel: length not known, 7 grooves, rh
Feed: 250-round cloth belt
Muzzle velocity: *ca* 1350 ft/sec (411 m/sec)
Cyclic rate: 400 rds/min

Gun, Maxim, 0.45in Mark 1, Gardner-Gatling Chamber

1892. Naval service. As for the 0.45in Mark 1 *above* but for the .45 Gardner & Gatling cartridge.

Cartridge: .450 Gardner & Gatling
Length: 43.75in (1111mm)
Weight: 60lb (27.20kg)
Barrel: length not known, 7 grooves, rh
Feed: 140- or 334-round cloth belt
Muzzle velocity: *ca* 1200 ft/sec (365 m/sec)
Cyclic rate: 400 rds/min

Gun, Maxim, .303in Mark 1.

1889. Land service. As for the 0.45in gun but adapted to the .303 cartridge. In 1912 the manufacturing cost of this gun was £64.75.

Cartridge: .303 British
Length: 42.38in (1076mm)
Weight: 60lb (27.20kg)
Barrel: 28.0in (1102mm), 5 grooves, rh
Feed: 250-round cloth belt
Muzzle velocity: *ca* 1800 ft/sec (548 m/sec)
Cyclic rate: 400 rds/min

Gun, Maxim, .303in Converted, Mark 1

1897. Conversion from 0.45in guns by changing the barrel and other parts of the mechanism as necessary.

Cartridge: .303 British
Length: 45.0in (1143mm)
Weight: 64lb (29.03kg)
Barrel: 28.0in (1102mm) 5 grooves, rh
Feed: 250-round cloth belt
Muzzle velocity: *ca* 1800 ft/sec (548 m/sec)
Cyclic rate: 400 rds/min

Gun, Maxim, .303in Converted, Mark 2

1901. This conversion differed from the Mark 1 by adapting the mechanism to suit the currently-produced service barrel with muzzle attachment, and by the introduction of new parts.

Cartridge: .303 British
Length: 46.50in (1180mm)
Weight: 40lb 0oz (18.14kg)
Barrel: 28.25in (717mm), 4 grooves, rh
Feed: 250-round cloth belt
Muzzle velocity: 2750 ft/sec (838 m/sec)
Cyclic rate: 600 rds/min

Gun, Maxim, 'G', .303in.

1915. A number of captured German Maxim M1908 guns were converted from 7.92mm calibre to .303 calibre and placed in service under this nomenclature.

BULGARIA
DWM

MG 08

As for the German MG 08.

Cartridge: 8 × 50R Bulgarian Mannlicher

CHINA
Maker not known

Type 24

Standard water-cooled model, prominent blast shield behind flash hider. Complex tripod with seat, elevation and traverse controls.

Cartridge: 7.92 × 57mm Mauser
Length: 48.0in (1219mm)
Weight, gun: 52lb 8oz (23.81kg)
Weight, tripod: 67lb (30.40kg)
Barrel: 28.54in (725mm), 4 grooves, rh
Feed: 250-round cloth belt
Muzzle velocity: *ca* 2920 ft/sec (890 m/sec)
Cyclic rate: 350 rds/min

GERMANY
DWM & Spandau
MG01
Standard Maxim pattern, as for Belgian M1900.

Cartridge: 7.92 × 57mm Mauser

MG 08
1908. Standard Maxim pattern, but plain steel water-jacket and muzzle recoil booster with conical flash hider. Originally issued with a heavy 'sledge' tripod mounting.

Cartridge: 7.92 × 57mm Mauser
Length: 46.25in (1175mm)
Weight, gun: 58lb 5oz (26.50kg)
Weight, tripod: 70lb 8oz (31.97kg)
Barrel: 28.35in (720mm), 4 grooves, rh
Feed: 250-round cloth belt
Muzzle velocity: *ca* 2838ft/sec (865 m/sec)
Cyclic rate: 450 rds/min

MG 09
This was simply the MG 08 commercially manufactured for export by DWM, existing stocks of which were hurriedly adopted by the German Army in 1914 to augment MG 08 supplies.

MG 08/15
An attempt to provide a light machine gun for the infantry squad. Simply the standard 08 without tripod, but with a wooden butt and pistol grip added and a lighter water jacket and receiver casing, belt carried in a rounded box on the right side of the gun, and a bipod attached to the front of the receiver.

Cartridge: 7.92 × 57mm Mauser
Length: 56.90in (1445mm)
Weight: 31lb 0oz (14.06kg)
Barrel: 28.35in (720mm), 4 grooves, rh
Feed: 250-round cloth belt
Muzzle velocity: *ca* 2838 ft/sec (865 m/sec)
Cyclic rate: 450 rds/min

lMG 08/15
1916. The 'l' means *luftgekühlt* (air-cooled) and this weapon was the 08/15 with the water jacket replaced by a slotted jacket acting solely as a barrel support and allowing air to pass through; for use on aircraft. It was fitted for synchronising gear for forward firing through the propeller arc.

MG 08/18
Similar to the 08/15, but with the water jacket discarded and a thin perforated barrel jacket in its place.

Specifications: as for the 08/15, except
Weight: 33lb 1oz (15.0kg)

RUSSIA
Tula
M1905
Standard Maxim pattern as for Belgian M1900.

Cartridge: 7.62 × 54R Russian

M1910
Russian-built modified version of the M1905, using a smooth steel water jacket and with some minor modifica-

tions to the feed mechanism. The jacket was later changed for a corrugated type, similar to the Vickers, and finally was given (*ca* 1941) a very large water filling cap which would allow the jacket to be filled with handfuls of snow in extreme conditions.

Cartridge: 7.62 × 54R
Length: 43.60in (1107mm)
Weight, gun: 52lb 8oz (23.81kg)
Weight, tripod: 70lb (31.75kg)
Barrel: 28.25in (718mm), 4 grooves, rh
Feed: 250-round cloth belt
Muzzle velocity: *ca* 2830 ft/sec (863 m/sec)
Cyclic rate: 550 rds/min

PV1
Aircraft version of the M1910 gun, with slotted jacket to permit air cooling.

MK; Maxim-Kolesnikov
Ca 1923. An attempt to turn the M1910 into a tank weapon by fitting a short, down-curved butt and rifle-type trigger to the rear of the receiver and surrounding the barrel with a thin perforated barrel jacket with a mounting collar a few inches in front of the receiver. Unsuccessful. Some were converted but not put into service; they were later fitted with bipods and passed to the Spanish Republicans in 1937.

MT; Maxim-Tokarev
Ca 1923. An attempt to make a light machine gun for infantry use, resulting in a similar weapon to the German MG 08/18. The normal receiver was fitted with a pistol-grip rifle stock and trigger at the rear end, and a thin perforated jacket round the barrel, with a bipod behind the muzzle. As with the MK gun, the experiment was not a success and, of the guns which were made, 2000 were eventually off-loaded to Spain in 1937.

SWITZERLAND
Bern
MG Model 00
Standard Maxim pattern as for Belgian M1900.

Cartridge: 7.5 × 53mm Swiss M1890

MG Model 11
1911. As for the German MG 08, with plain steel water-jacket.

Cartridge: 7.5 × 55mm Swiss M1911

TURKEY
M8/15
The German 7.92mm MG 08/15 acquired during WWI. No differences.

USA
Colt
M1904
Standard Maxim pattern as for Belgian M1900, but chambered for the .30-03, and then altered for the .30-06 cartridge.

Cartridge: .30-06 Springfield
Length: 48.0in (1219mm)
Weight, gun: 68lb 8oz (31.07kg)

Weight, tripod: 80lb (36.29kg)
Barrel: 28.54in (725mm), 4 grooves, rh
Feed: 250-round cloth belt
Muzzle velocity: *ca* 2825 ft/sec (861 m/sec)
Cyclic rate: 600 rds/min

YUGOSLAVIA

LM M8/15M

The German 7.92mm MG 08/15 acquired in the 1920s. No differences.

MENDOZA Mexico
Mendoza

C-1934

1934. Light. Gas-operated using a rotating bolt, selective fire. Partially-finned barrel with conical flash hider, wooden butt and long fore-end, bipod attached to gas cylinder beneath barrel. Magazine beneath receiver. Quick-change barrel.

Cartridge: 7 × 57mm Mauser
Length: 46.0in (1168mm)
Weight: 18lb 8oz (8.39kg)
Barrel: 25.0in (635mm), 4 grooves, rh
Feed: 20-round box
Muzzle velocity: *ca* 2700 ft/sec (823 m/sec)
Cyclic rate: 450 rds/min

RM2

1960. Gas operated, rotating bolt, selective fire. Wooden butt, short separate fore-end, exposed fixed barrel and gas cylinder, with bipod attached. Muzzle brake/compensator, overhead magazine.

Cartridge: .30-06 Springfield
Length: 43.3in (1100mm)
Weight: 14lb 2oz (6.40kg)
Barrel: 24.0in (610mm), 4 grooves, rh
Feed: 20-round box
Muzzle velocity: *ca* 2750 ft/sec (838 m/sec)
Cyclic rate: 450–650 rds/min, adjustable.

MINI-GUN

See General Electric

NEGEV Israel
IMI

Light Machine Gun

Ca 1990. Light. Air-cooled, gas piston operated, rotating bolt, selective fire. Receiver with folding skeleton butt, pistol grip. Fore-end conceals gas cylinder and carries bipod. Carrying handle, quick-change barrel. Fires from open bolt. Feeds from magazines or from belt, with adapter in place.

Cartridge: 5.56 × 45mm M193) or NATO
Length, butt extended: 40.15in (1020mm)
Length, butt folded: 30.71in (780mm)
Weight: 16lb 8oz (7.50kg)
Barrel: 18.11in (460mm), 6 grooves, rh
Feed: 30- or 35-round box, or metal link belt

Muzzle velocity: 3280 ft/sec (1000 m/sec)
Cyclic rate: 700–800 or 850–1000 rds/min, depending upon the setting of the gas regulator

Assault Machine Gun

Ca 1990. This has the same receiver, pistol grip and butt as the light gun above, but with no bipod and with a shorter barrel. It is claimed that in this guise it can be used as an assault rifle or as a machine gun.

Cartridge: 5.56 × 45mm M193 or NATO
Length, butt extended: 35.04in (890mm)
Length, butt folded: 25.59in (650mm)
Weight: 15lb 7oz (7.0kg)
Barrel: 13.0in (330mm), 6 grooves, rh
Feed: 30- or 35-round box, or metal link belt
Muzzle velocity: 3280 ft/sec (1000 m/sec)
Cyclic rate: 700–800 or 850–1000 rds/min, depending upon the setting of the gas regulator

NORDENFELT Sweden

BRITAIN
Maxim

Gun, Machine, Nordenfelt, 0.45in, 5-Barrel, Mark 1

1884. Naval service. Barrels side-by-side, supported by cross-pieces held by side girders. Rectangular flat receiver. A vertical cartridge hopper feeds ammunition via a distributor to the individual barrels. Fired by a reciprocating hand lever on the right side. On pedestal deck mounting.

Cartridge: .450 Gardner & Gatling
Length: 46.0in (1168mm)
Weight: 154lb (69.85kg)
Barrel: 28.50in (724mm), 7 grooves, rh
Feed: 50-round distributor, fed by 50-round hopper
Muzzle velocity: *ca* 1250 ft/sec (381 m/sec)
Cyclic rate: up to 300 rds/min

Gun, Machine, Nordenfelt, 0.45in, 5-Barrel, Mark 2

1886. Land and naval service. Differs from Mark 1 in detail of construction.

Cartridge: .450 Gardner & Gatling
Length: 42.25in (1073mm)
Weight: 133lb (60.32kg)
Barrel: 28.50in (724mm), 7 grooves, rh
Feed: 50-round distributor, fed by 50-round hopper
Muzzle velocity: *ca* 1250 ft/sec (381 m/sec)
Cyclic rate: up to 300 rds/min

Gun, Machine, Nordenfelt, 0.45in, 3-Barrel, Mark 1

1887. Land service. Three barrels side-by-side in an open frame. Designed to fire .45 Martini-Henry solid-cased cartridges.

Cartridge: .577/450 Martini-Henry Solid Case
Length: 41.50in (1054mm)
Weight: 93lb (42.18kg)
Barrel: 28.50in (724mm), 7 grooves, rh
Feed: 27-round feed box
Muzzle velocity: *ca* 1350 ft/sec (411 m/sec)
Cyclic rate: up to 300 rds/min

Gun, Nordenfelt, 3-Barrel, .303in Converted, Mark I
1898. Conversion of .45in calibre guns to .303 for mounting in forts.

Cartridge: .303 British
Length: 41.25in (1047mm)
Weight: 98lb (44.45kg)
Barrel: 28.50in (724mm), 5 grooves, rh
Feed: 27-round feed box
Muzzle velocity: 1800 ft/sec (548 m/sec)
Cyclic rate: up to 300 rds/min.

PERINO Italy
Maker unknown

Model 1908
Medium. Air-cooled, recoil operation assisted by a muzzle gas booster, using a lever locking the tilting breech-block. The recoil of the barrel inside its jacket pumped air to cool the chamber and barrel; an alternative version had a water jacket. Fed from a magazine box containing five trays of 12 rounds each. Reports indicate that it was a practical weapon but bureaucratic delay meant that it was not ready for production when Italy entered World War I and the design was abandoned.

Cartridge: 6.5 × 52mm Carcano
Length: 43.60in (1107mm)
Weight, gun: 50lb 8oz (22.90kg)
Barrel: 27.56in (700mm), 6 grooves, rh
Feed: 60-round tray magazine
Muzzle velocity: *ca* 2000 ft/sec (610 m/sec)
Cyclic rate: 600 rds/min

PIRAT Poland
Maker not known

KPWT
Name of a complete equipment comprising a Polish-made version of the Russian KPV (*qv*) fitted to a Polish-designed tripod with recoil-absorbing cradle, thus converting what originated as an anti-aircraft machine gun into a somewhat cumbersome ground support gun which has to be dismantled before it can be moved any distance.

Cartridge: 14.5 × 114mm Soviet
Length, gun: 77.95in (1980mm)
Weight, gun: 115lb 0oz (52.20kg)
Weight, tripod: 330lb (150kg)
Barrel: 53.0in (1346mm), 8 grooves, rh
Feed: 10-round metal link belt
Muzzle velocity: *ca* 3280 ft/sec (100 m/sec)
Cyclic rate: 600 rds/min

PUTEAUX France
Puteaux

Mle 1905
An attempt by the Puteaux Arsenal to bypass the Hotchkiss patents and 'improve' the Hotchkiss machine gun. Resembled the St Étienne (*below*) for which it acted as a prototype. Basic Hotchkiss gas piston mechanism, fitted with rate regulator, barrel encased in brass finned radiator.

Cartridge: 8 × 50R Lebel
Length: 49.21in (1250mm)
Weight, gun: 54lb 0oz (24.49kg)
Barrel: 30.70in (780mm), 6 grooves, rh
Feed: 23-round metal strip
Muzzle velocity: *ca* 2300 ft/sec (700 m/sec)
Cyclic rate: 650 rds/min

RUSSIA
***See also* Beresin, Degtyarev, Goryunov, Kalashnikov & Maxim**

KPV
1955. Heavy. Air-cooled, recoil operated, rotating bolt. Quick-change barrel in perforated jacket, muzzle booster and conical flash hider. Cylindrical receiver with rectangular feed mechanism casing on top. Carrying handle on jacket.

Cartridge: 14.5 × 114mm Soviet
Length: 78.98in (2006mm)
Weight: 108lb 4oz (49.10kg)
Barrel: 53.0in (1346mm), 8 grooves, rh
Feed: metal link belt
Muzzle velocity: *ca* 3280 ft/sec (1000 m/sec)
Cyclic rate: 600 rds/min

RP-46
1946. More or less a remake of the Degtyarev DPM to take belt feed and, by changing the receiver top cover, still fire the DPM flat drum. Light. Air-cooled, gas piston operated, flap-locked bolt. Wooden butt, tubular extension behind the receiver holds the return spring, pistol grip, half-length slotted barrel jacket with gas cylinder beneath, bipod, conical flash hider.

Cartridge: 7.62 × 54R Russian
Length: 50.51in (1283mm)
Weight: 28lb 11oz (13.0kg)
Barrel: 23.90in (607mm), 4 grooves, rh
Feed: 250-round metal link belt
Muzzle velocity: *ca* 2760 ft/sec (840 m/sec)
Cyclic rate: 600 rds/min

NSV
1971. Heavy. Air-cooled, gas piston operated, three-part bolt locked by lugs. Rectangular receiver with prominent feed mechanism cover on top; exposed barrel with gas cylinder beneath, conical flash hider. Tripod mounted, or as a flexible air defence gun on tank turrets. Pistol grip and unusual skeleton butt. Weapon also made under licence in Bulgaria, Poland and Serbia.

Cartridge: 12.7 × 108mm Russian
Length: 61.42in (1560mm)
Weight, gun: 55lb 2oz (25.0kg)
Weight, tripod: 35lb 4oz (16.0kg)
Barrel: 44.50in (1130mm), 8 grooves, rh
Feed: 50-round metal link belt
Muzzle velocity: *ca* 2772 ft/sec (845 m/sec)
Cyclic rate: 750 rds/min

NSV-N4
This is the tripod-mounted NSV fitted with a night vision sight.

NSVT

This is a variant for co-axial mounting in tanks. Pistol grip and butt removed, electrical solenoid firing trigger fitted.

ShKAS

1933. Aircraft gun. Light. Air-cooled, could be fixed or flexible. Gas piston operated, with cylinder above barrel and concealed in a ribbed shroud. Exposed barrel with raised sight. Prominent cylindrical section of receiver concealed squirrel-cage feed mechanism. Spade grip handle at rear of receiver acts as cocking handle. Pistol grip. Fixed guns have no pistol grip or spade grip, uses Bowden wire control for cocking and electric firing.

Cartridge: 7.62 × 54R Russian
Length: 27.56in (700mm)
Weight: 23lb 8oz (10.66kg)
Barrel: 17.52in (445mm), 4 grooves, rh
Feed: 250-round metal link belt
Muzzle velocity: *ca* 2760 ft/sec (840 m/sec)
Cyclic rate: 600 rds/min

ST ÉTIENNE France
MAS

Mle. 1907

A second attempt to improve on the Hotchkiss, this time by the St Étienne arsenal. Gas action reversed, pulling the piston forward and operating the bolt through a rack and pinion. Bolt locking by over-centre toggle. Rate of fire is regulated by changing the gas cylinder volume. Large receiver with sloped front, half-length barrel jacket, exposed gas cylinder and return spring beneath barrel, spade grips and trigger.

Cartridge: 8 × 50R Lebel
Length: 46.50in (1180mm)
Weight: 56lb 12oz (25.40kg)
Barrel: 28.0in (710mm), 6 grooves, rh
Feed: 24- or 30-round metal strip
Muzzle velocity: 2300 ft/sec (700 m/sec)
Cyclic rate: 400-500 rds/min

SCHWARZLOSE Germany
Schwarzlose

AUSTRIA-HUNGARY

M1907

Medium. Water-cooled, delayed blowback operation relying on a heavy breech-block with a toggle and powerful return spring. It also needed a short barrel, restricting the range and rate of fire. Rectangular receiver with unusual curved back, handle-bar grips, smooth water jacket, long conical flash hider. Heavy tubular tripod with large election arcs. Also used by Dutch (in 6.5mm), Greek (6.5mm) and German (7.92mm calibre) Armies before 1918. Many taken by Italy as WWI reparations were used until 1945.

Cartridge: 8 × 50R Austrian Mannlicher
Length: 41.93in (1065mm)
Weight, gun: 43lb 14oz (19.90kg)
Weight, tripod: 40lb 13oz (18.50kg)
Barrel: 20.66in (525mm), 4 grooves, rh
Feed: 250-round cloth belt

Muzzle velocity: 2050 ft/sec (625 m/sec)
Cyclic rate: 400 rds/min

M07/12

Improved M1912; rate of fire increased to 500 rds/min, larger oil reservoir now carries enough oil for 4500 rounds instead of 2000. No change in principal dimensions.

M07/16

Aircraft gun. First applications of the M1907 to aircraft were water-cooled; then the water jacket was slotted to provide air cooling. Finally the jacket was removed, leaving the barrel exposed to the air and this design became the M07/16. Some had the original handle-bar grips, later conversions used a form of pistol grip on an extension bar behind the receiver. The **M07/16A** was an 07/16 with a more powerful return spring which boosted the rate of fire to 600 rds/min.

SIA Italy
SIA

Ca 1913–25. Light. Air-cooled, gas piston operated, using the firing pin to rotate and lock the bolt. The first gun to use a fluted chamber, patented by Agnelli.

Cartridge: 6.5 × 52mm Carcano
Length: not known
Weight: 23lb 8oz (10.66kg)
Barrel: not known
Feed: 25-round metal strip
Muzzle velocity: *ca* 2100 ft/sec (645 m/sec)
Cyclic rate: 700 rds/min

SIG Switzerland
SIG

KE7

1936. Kiraly-Ende. Light. Air-cooled, recoil-operated, two-part bolt locked by a lug. Rifle-type butt, slender receiver with pistol grip, magazine beneath. Barrel enclosed in slotted jacket, long wooden fore-end, bipod. Sold to China and some South American countries.

Cartridge: 7.92 × 57mm Mauser
Length: 46.87in (1190mm)
Weight: 17lb 4oz (7.80kg)
Barrel: 23.63in (600mm), 4 grooves, rh
Feed: 20-round box
Muzzle velocity: *ca* 2625 ft/sec (800m/sec)
Cyclic rate: 550 rds/min

MG 51

Based on the German MG 42 but manufactured from milled steel instead of metal pressings. Wooden butt at rear of receiver, pistol grip, cylindrical half-jacket holding bipod, exposed barrel with carrying handle and flash hider. Quick-change barrel.

Cartridge: 7.5 × 55mm Swiss M1911
Length: 50.0in (1270mm)
Weight: 35lb 6oz (16.0kg)
Barrel: 22.20in (564mm), 4 grooves, rh
Feed: 250-round metal link belt
Muzzle velocity: *ca* 2600 ft/sec (792 m/sec)
Cyclic rate: 1000 rds/min

MG 710-1

Ca 1960. Medium. Air-cooled, delayed blowback, roller-delayed bolt. Based on the German MG 42 improved model, under development as the war ended. Similar general form to the MG 42 with similar quick-change barrel. Fluted chamber. Barrel jacket is open down the right side to permit barrel changing to the right and rear.

Cartridge: 7.5 × 55mm Swiss M1911
Length: 46.85in (1190mm)
Weight: 24lb 14oz (11.30kg)
Barrel: 19.68in (500mm), 4 grooves, rh
Feed: 200-round metal link belt
Muzzle velocity: *ca* 2600 ft/sec (792 m/sec)
Cyclic rate: 800 rds/min

MG710-2

Ca 1960. Similar to the MG 710-1 but differs in barrel change; has a half-length perforated jacket, in front of which is the barrel carrying handle. The barrel is unlocked and withdrawn forward.

Cartridge: 7.5 × 55mm Swiss M1911
Length: 46.85in (1190mm)
Weight: 24lb 0oz (10.90kg)
Barrel: 21.65in (550mm), 4 grooves, rh
Feed: 200-round metal link belt
Muzzle velocity: *ca* 2600 ft/sec (792 m/sec)
Cyclic rate: 800 rds/min

MG 710-3

Ca 1965. Improved and final version of the 710. Pressed steel perforated half-length barrel jacket, barrel with T-shaped removal handle, withdraws to right and rear. More use of metal stampings in manufacture.

Cartridge: 7.5 × 55mm Swiss M1911
Length: 45.0in (1146mm)
Weight: 21lb 4oz (9.65kg)
Barrel: 22.0in (560mm), 4 grooves, rh
Feed: 200-round metal link belt
Muzzle velocity: *ca* 2600 ft/sec (792 m/sec)
Cyclic rate: 900 rds/min

SINGAPORE
CIS

CIS .50

1988. Heavy. Air-cooled, gas piston operated, rotating bolt. Fires from an open bolt. Dual feed – *ie* feeds a belt in at each side and the gunner selects which to use.

Cartridge: .50 Browning
Length: 70.0in (1778mm)
Weight, gun: 66lb 2oz (30.0kg)
Weight, tripod: 50lb 11oz (23.0kg)
Barrel: 45.0in (1143mm), 8 grooves, rh
Feed: dual disintegrating link belts
Muzzle velocity: 2920 ft/sec (890 m/sec)
Cyclic rate: 500 rds/min

Ultimax 100

Ca 1982. Light. Air-cooled, gas piston operated, rotating bolt. Synthetic cutaway butt, pistol grip, drum magazine beneath receiver, forward pistol-type grip, bipod. Gas cylinder above quick-change barrel.

Cartridge: 5.56 × 45mm M193 or NATO
Length: 40.31in (1024mm)
Weight: 10lb 13oz (4.90kg)
Barrel: 20.0in (508mm), 6 grooves, rh
Feed: 100-round drum, or 20- or 30-round box
Muzzle velocity: 3182 ft/sec (970 m/sec)
Cyclic rate: 500 rds/min

SKODA Austria-Hungary
Skoda

M1893

Medium. Air-cooled. Developed by Skodawerke to a design by Archduke Salvator and Count von Dormus. An eccentric weapon, even by 1893 standards. Delayed blowback, delay due to interlocking wedges and a powerful spring in a tube behind the receiver. Rate of fire variable between 180 and 250 rds/min by means of an adjustable-length pendulum suspended beneath the receiver (necessitating a high-set mounting). Overhead gravity-feed magazine. Used in naval and land fortress applications only.

Cartridge: 8 × 50R Austrian Mannlicher
Dimensions: none available

M1902

Improved design, adding a water-jacket but retaining the pendulum rate-of-fire regulator, thus requiring an odd high-set tripod for field use.

M1909

Further improvement to compete with Schwarzlose. Gravity feed abandoned in favour of a cloth belt feed which entered at the bottom left side of the receiver and left at the top left side. Pendulum rate regulator scrapped. Rate of fire increased to 425 rds/min, but this meant adding an oil pump to lubricate the cartridges.

M1913

The M1909 with some modifications to improve the feed system and with an improved tripod with armoured shield. Skoda's last throw, it armed some Austrian reserve regiments for a short period in 1914–15 until replaced by the Schwarzlose.

STEYR Austria
Steyr

AUG LSW

Heavy-barrelled version of the Steyr AUG rifle (*qv*), with bipod and larger magazine, for use as a light machine gun.

Cartridge: 5.56 × 45mm M193 or NATO
Length: 35.43in (900mm)
Weight: 10lb 13oz (4.90kg)
Barrel: 24.45in (621mm), 6 grooves, rh
Feed: 30- or 42-round box
Muzzle velocity: 3280 ft/sec (1000 m/sec)
Cyclic rate: 680 rds/min

STONER USA

Stoner 63
Cadillac Gage

Ca 1965. Light. Air-cooled, gas piston operated, rotating bolt. Belt feed, or overhead magazine by changing receiver top cover. Synthetic butt, pistol grip and ribbed fore-end, barrel with gas cylinder beneath, slotted flash eliminator, bipod.

Cartridge: 5.56 × 45mm M193
Length: 40.24in (1029mm)
Weight: 12lb 8oz (5.65kg)
Barrel: 21.69in (551mm), 4 grooves, rh
Feed: 30-round box or metal link belt
Muzzle velocity: 3250 ft/sec (990 m/sec)
Cyclic rate: 700 rds/min

SWITZERLAND
See also SIG

M25
Bern

1926. Light. Air-cooled, recoil-operated using a toggle action which opens sideways. Wood butt, pistol grip, right side mounted magazine, slotted barrel jacket with bipod, short conical flash hider.

Cartridge: 7.5 × 55mm Swiss M1911
Length: 45.67in (1160mm)
Weight, with bipod: 23lb 12oz (10.80kg)
Barrel: 22.24in (565mm), 4 grooves, rh
Feed: 30-round box
Muzzle velocity: *ca* 2460 ft/sec (750 m/sec)
Cyclic rate: 450 rds/min

Model 87
Bern

For tanks and other armoured vehicles. Recoil operated, bolt locking by flaps, based on the mechanism of the Model 51 (*see* SIG). Receiver similar to the Model 51 (or MG 42) with very short shoulder pad, electric firing, heavy armoured barrel and jacket with mantlet mounting. Can be adapted to 7.62mm NATO ammunition by changing barrel and bolt.

Cartridge: 7.5 × 55mm Swiss M1911
Length: 46.25in (1175mm)
Weight, with mounting and jacket: 66lb 2oz (30.0kg)
Barrel: 18.70in (475mm), 4 grooves, rh
Feed: metal link belt
Muzzle velocity: *ca* 2625 ft/sec (800 m/sec)
Cyclic rate: 1000 rds/min

TuF: Tank und Flieger Germany
MAN

1918 Basically an enlarged Maxim gun, using the same recoil-operated breech mechanism, and water-cooled. Designed as a heavy gun for use in tanks or aircraft but development was not completed before the war ended.

Cartridge: 13 × 92SR
Length: n/a
Weight, gun: 85lb 0oz (38.55kg)
Barrel: n/a
Feed: 100-round cloth belt

Muzzle velocity: *ca* 2600 ft/sec (792m/sec)
Cyclic rate: 400 rds/min

USA
See also **Ares, Benet-Mercie, Berthier, Browning, Chauchat, Colt, Gardner, Gatling, General Electric, Hughes, Johnson, Lewis, Marlin, Maxim & Stoner**

M60
Bridge & Inland

General purpose. Air-cooled, belt fed, gas piston operated, using a rotating bolt. Straight-line layout; rubber-bonded butt with shoulder strap, pistol grip, ribbed plastic fore-end, bipod attached to barrel.

Cartridge: 7.62 × 51mm NATO
Length: 43.50in (1105mm)
Weight: 23lb 3oz (10.51kg)
Barrel: 22.04in (560mm), 4 grooves, rh
Feed: metal link belt
Muzzle velocity: 2838 ft/sec (865 m/sec)
Cyclic rate: 550 rds/min

M60E2

Highly modified version of the M60 for co-axial tank mounting. The butt and fore-end are removed and an extension tube fitted to the barrel and another to the gas cylinder, the latter acting to vent the operating gases outside the tank. Length of extension tubes, and hence of the gun, depend entirely upon the installation and armour thickness of the carrying vehicle.

M60E3
Saco

Lightweight version of the M60 developed by Saco Defense. Lightweight bipod mounted on receiver; carrying handle on barrel to assist changing; forward hand grip, simplified gas system and feed system.

Cartridge: 7.62 × 51mm NATO
Length: 42.0in (1067mm)
Weight: 18lb 15oz (8.61kg)
Barrel: 22.0in (559mm), 4 grooves, rh
Feed: metal link belt
Muzzle velocity: 2822 ft/sec (860 m/sec)
Cyclic rate: 550 rds/min

M60E4
Saco

Further improvement on the M60, designed by Saco Defense. Bipod strengthened; feed system improved to give better belt lift; optical sight mount integrated into the receiver cover; three optional barrel lengths; improved gas system; improved flash eliminator. Adopted by US Navy. Data for standard LMG version.

Cartridge: 7.62 × 51mm NATO
Length: 37.71in (958mm)
Weight: 22lb 8oz (10.20kg)
Barrel: 22.0in (559mm), 4 grooves, rh
Feed: metal link belt
Muzzle velocity: 2800 ft/sec (854 m/sec)
Cyclic rate: 600 rds/min

M73
Springfield
Tank co-axial machine gun. Receiver can be swung to one side to permit withdrawal of barrel from the perforated jacket for changing. To keep the receiver short, the breech is a vertical sliding block, necessitating separate extraction and ramming mechanisms. Can be adjusted to feed from left or right side. Not an outstanding success.

Cartridge: 7.62 × 51mm NATO
Length: 35.0in (889mm)
Weight: 30lb 14oz (14.0kg)
Barrel: 22.0in (559mm), 4 grooves, rh
Feed: metal link belt
Muzzle velocity: 2800 ft/sec (854 m/sec)
Cyclic rate: 600 rds/min

M85
AAI & GEC
Ca 1963. Intended to replace the .50 Browning as a tank co-axial or flexible machine gun. Air-cooled, recoil-operated, bolt locks to receiver by lugs. Dual rate of fire. Generally similar to the .50 Browning M2 but with a prong-type flash eliminator, and a hump-backed feed cover on the receiver.

Cartridge: .50 Browning
Length: 50.55in (1384mm)
Weight: 61lb 8oz (27.90kg)
Barrel: 36.0in (914mm), 8 grooves, rh
Feed: metal link belt
Muzzle velocity: 2842 ft/sec (866 m/sec)
Cyclic rate: 400 or 1050 rds/min

M219
This is a considerably improved version of the M73, the improvements being so great that a separate identity was necessary. The entire feed system and the timing cams inside the gun have been redesigned. Other than being slightly lighter, there are no dimensional changes.

M240
FNMI
1976. A licence-produced version of the Belgian FN-MAG (*qv*), adopted as a tank co-axial machine gun. Air-cooled, gas piston operated, tilting breech-block. Fitted with spade grips it is also used as a flexible turret-mounted gun.

M240G
FNMI
1995. In view of the reliability of the M240 via-à-vis the M60, it was decided to fit a bipod and provide tripods for use as a ground gun, thus bringing it back to its originally-designed form. In this guise it becomes the M240G. There are some minor differences between it and the FN-MAG due to the convoluted development history.

Cartridge: 7.62 × 51mm NATO
Length: 48.03in (1220mm)
Weight: 25lb 13oz (11.70kg)
Barrel: 24.68in (627mm), 4 grooves, rh
Feed: metal link belt
Muzzle velocity: 2800 ft/sec (854 m/sec)
Cyclic rate: 750 rds/min

M249
FNMI
1990. The Belgian FN Minimi with some variations to meet US military specifications and suit US manufacturing techniques. The main external differences are in the shape of the butt and fore-end/handguard.

Cartridge: 5.56 × 45mm NATO
Length: 40.94in (1040mm)
Weight: 15lb 2oz (6.85kg)
Barrel: 20.59in (523mm), 6 grooves, rh
Feed: 200-round metal link belt or 30-round box
Muzzle velocity: 3000 ft/sec (915 m/sec)
Cyclic rate: 750 rds/min

GAU-19/A
GEC & Lockheed
The nomenclature adopted for the GECAL 50 (see General Electric) when it was standardised for US Army service. Various developmental improvements have changed some of the dimensions. Six-barrel, mechanical, Gatling type, electrically driven.

Cartridge: .50 Browning
Length: 46.50in (1181mm)
Weight: 74lb 0oz (33.60kg)
Barrels: 36.0in (914mm), 4 grooves, rh
Feed: metal link belt or linkless
Muzzle velocity: 2900 ft/sec (884 m/sec)
Cyclic rate: 1000 or 2000 rds/min, selectable.

VALMET Finland
Valmet

M62
1966. Light. Air-cooled, gas piston operated, tilting breech block based on the Czech ZB26. Wood butt, pistol grip, short wood fore-end, heavy barrel with bipod just behind foresight.

Cartridge: 7.62 × 39mm M1943
Length: 42.72in (1085mm)
Weight: 18lb 5oz (8.30kg)
Barrel: 18.50in (470mm), 4 grooves, rh
Feed: 100-round metal link belt
Muzzle velocity: 2395 ft/sec (730 m/sec)
Cyclic rate: 1050 rds/min

VEKTOR South Africa
LIW

SS-77
1986. General purpose. Air-cooled, gas piston operated, laterally-shifting block locking. Skeleton synthetic folding butt, pistol grip, belt feed, part-fluted barrel with carrying/quick-change handle, perforated flash hider. Short fore-end, bipod attached to gas cylinder.

Cartridge: 7.62 × 51mm NATO
Length, butt extended: 45.47in (1155mm)
Length, butt folded: 37.0in (940mm)
Weight: 21lb 3oz (9.60kg)
Barrel: 21.65in (550mm), 4 grooves, rh
Feed: metal link belt
Muzzle velocity: 2756 ft/sec (840 m/sec)
Cyclic rate: 750 rds/min

Mini-SS

1994. Conversion (by means of a kit) of the SS-77 to fire 5.56mm ammunition. Kit includes barrel, feed cover, bolt, and gas piston. A folding bipod is added and a fixed butt is normal, though a folding butt is an option.

Cartridge: 5.56 × 45mm NATO
Length: 39.37in (1000mm)
Weight: 17lb 9oz (7.96kg)
Barrel: 20.19in (513mm), 6 grooves, rh
Feed: metal link belt
Muzzle velocity: 3215 ft/sec (980 m/sec)
Cyclic rate: 800 rds/min

MG4

Medium. Air-cooled, recoil operated. Based on the Browning M1919A4 (*qv*) but with considerable modification to the feed and trigger system, permitting firing from an open bolt. May be tripod or vehicle mounted.

Cartridge: 7.62 × 51mm NATO
Length: 37.0in (940mm)
Weight: 33lb 1oz (15.0kg)
Barrel: 23.42in (595mm), 4 grooves, rh
Feed: metal link belt
Muzzle velocity: 2756 ft/sec (840 m/sec)
Cyclic rate: 700 rds/min

VICKERS Britain
Vickers

Gun, Vickers, .303 inch, Mark 1

1912. An improved Maxim; toggle action is inverted, so that it breaks upwards, and the whole gun lightened by use of high grade steel instead of phosphor bronze. The water jacket is corrugated longitudinally, a simple distinguishing mark which actually added strength to the structure.

Cartridge: .303 British
Length: 45.50in (1155mm)
Weight: 40lb 0oz (18.10kg)
Barrel: 28.50in (723mm), 4 grooves, rh
Feed: 250-round cloth belt
Muzzle velocity: 2450 ft/sec (745 m/sec)
Cyclic rate: 450 rds/min

Gun, Vickers, .303 inch, Mark 1*

1916. Aircraft gun. The jacket is pierced on the front face and louvered at the rear to allow the flow of air around the barrel and there were minor modifications to the front cover and crank handle to accommodate the trigger motor of the synchronising apparatus. Basic dimensions remained the same but the weight fell to 27lb 8oz (12.47kg). Some guns of this type were fitted with muzzle boosters and new buffer springs to increase the rate of fire to about 850 rds/min; such guns were marked 'SU' (Speeded Up).

Gun, Vickers, .303 inch, Mark 2

1917. Aircraft gun. Similar to Mark 1* but with a smaller-diameter jacket perforated with 0.5 inch holes and some other minor manufacturing changes. Weight reduced to 22lb (9.97kg). Some guns converted to 'SU' specification.

Gun, Machine, Vickers, .303in, Mark 2*

1917. Aircraft gun. In two forms, the **Mark 2*A** with right-hand feed, **Mark 2*B** with left-hand feed to suit

their mounting alongside the aircraft engine. Minor alterations to the crank handle and provision for attaching a loading handle. Otherwise as for Mark 2.

Gun, Machine, Vickers, .303in, Mark 4A

1933. Tank gun. Converted from Mark 1 guns and differing principally in the cooling arrangements, using flexible hose to connect the water jacket with a water supply inside the vehicle.

Gun, Machine, Vickers, .303in, Mark 4B

1933. Tank gun. As for Mark 4A but with some differences in the cooling arrangements

Gun, Machine, Vickers, .303in, Mark 5

1932. Aircraft gun. Generally as for the Mark 2 but with some changes in the receiver to facilitate opening the cover in restricted spaces.

Gun, Machine, Vickers, .303in, Mark 6

1934. Tank gun. Similar to the Mark 4B, with left or right-hand feed. The fusee spring box on the left side is of aluminium alloy. Plain water jacket.

Gun, Machine, Vickers, .303in, Mark 6*

1936. Tank gun. Similar to the Mark 6 but with inlet and outlet pipes for connection to a water supply in the vehicle.

Length: 41.75in (1060mm)
Weight: 42lb 12oz (19.39kg)
Cyclic rate: 500 rds/min

Gun, Machine, Vickers, .303in, Mark 7

1938. Similar to Mark 6 but with corrugated water jacket, stronger front cover, new fusee spring box.

Gun, Vickers, .303 inch, GO

GO = Gas Operated. Also known as the **Type K.** *Ca* 1937. Aircraft gun, though during World War II it was adopted by special forces. Gas piston operated, adapted from the Vickers-Berthier (*qv*) action. Single spade grip and trigger behind receiver, exposed barrel with spoon-type flash eliminator and gas cylinder beneath. Saw little air service as it was soon replaced by belt-fed guns in turrets.

Cartridge: .303 British
Length: 40.0in (1016mm)
Weight: 21lb 0oz (9.52kg)
Barrel: 20.0in (508mm), 5 grooves, rh
Feed: 100-round flat drum
Muzzle velocity: 2450 ft/sec (745 m/sec)
Cyclic rate: 1050 rds/min

Gun, Machine, Vickers, .5 inch, Mark 1

1932. Ground gun. Issued in limited numbers for trials. A scaled-up version of the .303 Mark 1, of similar appearance but bigger and with a conical flash hider. Two rates of fire, governed by a delay pawl in the firing mechanism.

Cartridge: .50 Vickers
Length: 54.0in (1372mm)
Weight: 52lb 0oz (23.58kg)
Barrel: 31.10in (790mm), 7 grooves, lh
Feed: 100-round metal link belt
Muzzle velocity: 2600 ft/sec (792 m/sec)
Cyclic rate: 450 or 675 rds/min

Gun, Machine, Vickers, .5 inch, Mark 2

1932. Tank pattern. Offset pistol grip trigger, selective fire, delay pawl in firing mechanism.

Specifications: as for Mark 1, except
Cyclic rate: 450 rds/min

Gun, Machine, Vickers, .5 inch, Mark 3

1934. For naval service as an air defence gun. As for Mark 1 but no delay pawl, so cyclic rate 675 rds/min, automatic fire only. Wire toggle cocking system, with a bronze guide block attached to the rear of the receiver to support the cocking wire. Left- or right-hand feed according to its position on the mounting.

Gun, Machine, Vickers, .5 inch, Mark 4

1935. Similar to Mark 1 but with a mounting plate which allowed it to fit in place of .303in guns in some vehicles.

Weight: 58lb (26.37kg)
Cyclic rate: 675 rds/min

VICKERS-BERTHIER France/Britain
Ishapore & Vickers
Designed by Berthier, rights acquired by Vickers in 1925.

Mark 1
1928. Light. Air-cooled, gas piston operated, tilting bolt. Wood butt with monopod, pistol grip, curved top-mounted magazine, finned barrel with gas cylinder beneath, conical flash hider. Squared-off wood fore-end. Bipod attached to gas cylinder.

Mark 2.
1929. As for Mark 1 but the fore-end is more rounded and extends in front of the receiver and around the gas cylinder.

Light Mark 2
1931, for Indian trials. Short fore-end, smooth barrel, no monopod and cutaway butt.

Mark 3
1933. As for the Light Mark 2 but somewhat heavier and more robust. Adopted by the Indian Army. **Mark 3B** was similar but had some small changes in the gas system to improve reliability.

Cartridge: .303 British
Length: 46.50in (1180mm)
Weight: 22lb 0oz (9.98kg)
Barrel: 23.50in (597mm), 5 grooves, rh
Feed: 30-round box
Muzzle velocity: 2450 ft/sec (745 m/sec)
Cyclic rate: 600 rds/min

VILLAR PEROSA
See Submachine Guns, Villar Perosa

YUGOSLAVIA
Kragujevac

M53
General purpose. Air-cooled, recoil-operated, locking by bolt lugs. Generally based on the German MG 42 (*qv*) with similar type of quick-change barrel inside a slotted jacket.

Normally fitted with bipod but also tripod mounted.

Cartridge: 7.92 × 57mm Mauser
Length: 35.0in (889mm)
Weight: 30lb 14oz (14.0kg)
Barrel: 22.0in (559mm), 4 grooves, rh
Feed: metal link belt
Muzzle velocity: 2800 ft/sec (854 m/sec)
Cyclic rate: 600 rds/min

M72B1
A heavy-barrelled version of the Kalashnikov AK47 rifle, with a few variations. The barrel is finned below the gas cylinder and longer than normal, with a cleaning rod stowed beneath it. Wood butt, pistol grip, bipod attached behind the foresight.

Cartridge: 7.62 × 39mm M1943
Length: 47.64in (1210mm)
Weight, gun: 27lb 8oz (12.5kg)
Weight, tripod: 48lb 8oz (22.0kg)
Barrel: 22.05in (560mm), 4 grooves, rh
Feed: 50-round drum or 50-round metal link belt
Muzzle velocity: 2346 ft/sec (715 m/sec)
Cyclic rate: 1000 rds/min

M77B1
Same design as M72B1 *above*, but for export and chambered for the 7.62 x 51mm NATO cartridge.

Cartridge: 7.62 × 51mm NATO
Length: 40.35in (1025mm)
Weight: 11lb 4oz (5.1kg)
Barrel: 21.06in (535mm), 4 grooves, rh
Feed: 20-round box
Muzzle velocity: 2756 ft/sec (840 m/sec)
Cyclic rate: 600 rds/min

M82
Similar to the M72B1 in general design but no fins on the barrel and a folding carrying handle above the receiver. For export, chambered for the 5.56 x 45mm M193 cartridge.

Cartridge: 5.56 × 45mm M193
Length: 40.15in (1020mm)
Weight: 8lb 13oz (4.0kg)
Barrel: 21.34in (542mm), 6 grooves, rh
Feed: 30-round box
Muzzle velocity: 3280 ft/sec (1000 m/sec)
Cyclic rate: 700 rds/min

M84
General purpose. Air-cooled; gas piston operated, rotating bolt. Appears to be based on the Kalashnikov PKM (*qv*). Wooden butt, pistol grip, carrying handle on barrel, bipod mounted on gas cylinder, slotted flash hider.

Cartridge: 7.62 × 54R Russian
Length: 46.26in (1175mm)
Weight: 33lb 1oz (15.0kg)
Barrel: 25.90in (658mm), 4 grooves, rh
Feed: 100- or 250-round metal link belt
Muzzle velocity: 2706 ft/sec (825 m/sec)
Cyclic rate: 700 rds/min

COMPARATIVE TABLES

Weapons are arranged in ascending order of calibre. Overall and barrel lengths are given in inches, weights in pounds, muzzle velocities in feet per second and rates of fire in rounds per minute. Entries include the following abbreviations and conventions:

Action: Blowback – BB; Delayed blowback – DBB; Externally powered – EP; Hand operated crank or lever – Hand.

Feed system: Box – B; Drum – D; Strip – S; Hopper – H; Vertical guide – G; Tray – T. Belt/B and similar combinations indicate that both the systems shown can be used. Multiple magazine size options are not shown; only the most usual magazine is given.

Rate: two figures divided by an oblique stroke indicate two selectable rates of fire. A single figure preceded by < indicates a variable rate to the maximum figure as shown.

Name	Year	Calibre	Action	Length	Barrel	Weight	Feed	Velocity	Rate
Czech CZ2000	1992	5.45×39.5	Gas	41.34	22.71	9.12	D/75	3150	800
Kalashnikov RPK-74	1974	5.45×39.5	Gas	41.73	24.25	10.12	B/45	3150	650
Ameli	1980	5.56×45	DBB	38.19	15.75	11.44	Belt	2870	900
Ares Light		5.56×45	Gas	42.24	21.65	10.81	Belt/B	3100	600
Beretta AR70-78	1978	5.56×45	Gas	37.60	17.71	11.69	B/40	3182	670
Beretta AR70-84	1984	5.56×45	Gas	37.60	17.71	11.69	B/30	3182	670
Beretta AS 70/90	1990	5.56×45	Gas	39.37	18.30	11.75	B/30	3215	800
Britain: L86A1 LSW	1986	5.56×45	Gas	35.43	25.43	13.44	B/30	3182	700
Colt Model 715	1990	5.56×45	Gas	40.15	20.07	12.75	B/30	3035	625
Daewoo K3	1990	5.56×45	Gas	40.55	21.00	15.12	Belt/B	3000	850
FN Minimi	1974	5.56×45	Gas	40.94	18.35	15.12	Belt/B	3000	850
FN Minimi Para	1982	5.56×45	Gas	35.15	13.66	15.65	Belt/B	2952	850
GE XM 214 Six-Pak	1958	5.56×45	EP	28.80	20.14	22.50	Belt	3250	<6000
Heckler & Koch HK13		5.56×45	DBB	38.58	17.71	13.19	B/40	3117	750
Heckler & Koch HK13E		5.56×45	DBB	40.55	17.71	17.62	B/30	3117	750
Heckler & Koch HK23E		5.56×45	DBB	40.55	17.71	19.33	B/30	3117	750
Heckler & Koch HK G36 LSW	1995	5.56×45	Gas	38.98	18.90	7.69	B/30	3018	750
INSAS	1997	5.56×45	Gas	41.34	21.06	13.50	B/30	3130	650
INSAS Para	1997	5.56×45	Gas	40.35	20.07	13.44	B/30	3117	650
Negev Light	1990	5.56×45	Gas	40.15	18.11	16.50	Belt/B	3280	750/900
Negev Assault	1990	5.56×45	Gas	35.04	13.00	15.44	Belt/B	3280	750/900
Singapore: Ultimax	1982	5.56×45	Gas	40.31	20.00	10.81	D/100	3182	500
Steyr AUG LSW	1980	5.56×45	Gas	35.43	24.45	10.81	B/42	3280	680
Stoner 63	1965	5.56×45	Gas	40.24	21.69	12.50	Belt/B	3250	700
USA M249	1990	5.56×45	Gas	40.94	20.59	15.12	Belt/B	3000	750
Vektor Mini-SS	1994	5.56×45	Gas	39.37	20.19	17.56	Belt	3215	800
Yugoslavia: M82	1982	5.56×45	Gas	40.15	21.34	8.81	B/30	3280	700
Japan: Type 3	1914	6.5×51	Gas	45.50	29.52	62.00	S/30	2400	400
Japan: Type 11	1922	6.5×51	Gas	43.50	19.0	22.50	H/30	2300	500
Japan: Type 91	1931	6.5×51	Gas	42.00	19.20	24.44	H/50	2300	500
Japan: Type 96	1936	6.5×51	Gas	41.50	21.70	20.00	B/30	2400	550
Breda M1930	1930	6.5×52	DBB	48.50	20.50	22.75	B/20	2065	500
Brixia M1920	1920	6.5×52	Recoil	n/a	n/a	34.50	B/50	2080	600

Name	Year	Calibre	Action	Length	Barrel	Weight	Feed	Velocity	Rate
FIAT-Revelli M1914	1914	6.5×52	DBB	46.50	25.75	37.50	B/50	2100	400
Perino 1908	1908	6.5×52	Recoil	43.60	27.56	50.50	T/60	2000	600
SIA	1913	6.5×52	Gas	n/a	n/a	23.50	S/25	2100	700
Mendoza C-34	1934	7×57	Gas	46.00	25.00	18.50	B/20	2700	450
Chatellerault M1924/29	1929	7.5×54	Gas	42.60	19.70	20.25	B/26	2700	500
Chatellerault M1931	1931	7.5×54	Gas	40.50	19.70	27.25	D/150	2700	500
France: AA-52 Light	1952	7.5×54	DBB	45.08	19.68	22.00	Belt	2700	700
France: AA-52 Heavy	1952	7.5×54	DBB	49.00	23.62	25.06	Belt	2756	700
SIG MG 51	1951	7.5×55	Recoil	50.00	22.20	35.37	Belt	2600	1000
SIG MG 710-1	1960	7.5×55	DBB	46.85	19.68	24.88	Belt	2600	800
SIG MG 710-2	1960	7.5×55	DBB	46.85	21.65	24.00	Belt	2600	800
SIG MG 710-3	1965	7.5×55	DBB	45.00	22.00	21.25	Belt	2600	900
Swiss: M25	1925	7.5×55	Recoil	45.67	22.24	23.75	B/30	2460	450
Swiss: M97	1987	7.5×55	Recoil	46.25	18.70	66.12	Belt	2625	1000
Benet-Mercie (USA) M1909	1909	.30-06	Gas	46.75	23.50	27.00	S/30	2788	600
Berthier (USA) M1917	1916	.30-06	Gas	48.00	n/a	15.75	B/20	2625	500
Browning M1917	1917	.30-06	Recoil	37.50	24.00	32.62	Belt	2800	600
Browning M1917A1	1930	.30-06	Recoil	38.64	23.90	32.57	Belt	2800	600
Browning M1919A1	1931	.30-06	Recoil	35.10	18.00	40.00	Belt	2690	600
Browning M1919A4	1934	.30-06	Recoil	41.11	24.00	31.00	Belt	2800	500
Browning M1919A5	1941	.30-06	Recoil	40.80	24.00	30.50	Belt	2800	500
Browning M1919A6	1943	.30-06	Recoil	53.00	24.00	32.50	Belt	2800	450
Browning Aircraft M2	1931	.30-06	Recoil	39.80	23.90	21.50	Belt	2800	1200
Chauchat (USA) M1918	1918	.30-06	Recoil	45.00	18.50	20.00	B/16	2700	300
Colt M1914	1895	.30-06	Gas	40.80	28.00	40.00	Belt	2800	430
Johnson 1941	1941	.30-06	Recoil	42.30	22.00	12.50	B/20	2800	600
Johnson 1944	1944	.30-06	Recoil	42.00	22.00	14.31	B/30	2800	600
Lewis (USA) M1917	1917	.30-06	Gas	51.75	26.25	25.25	D/47	2830	500
Marlin	1917	.30-06	Gas	40.00	28.00	22.50	Belt	2800	600
Maxim (USA) M1904	1904	.30-06	Recoil	48.00	28.54	68.50	Belt	2825	600
Mendoza RM2	1960	.30-06	Gas	43.30	24.00	14.12	B/20	2750	650
Colt M1895	1895	.30-40	Gas	40.80	28.00	40.00	Belt	2000	430
China: Type 74	1974	7.62×39	Gas	43.62	20.80	14.12	D/101	2411	750
China: Type 81	1981	7.62×39	Gas	40.31	20.80	11.37	D/75	2411	700
Czech vz52/57	1957	7.62×39	Gas	41.00	27.00	17.56	Belt/B	2477	1150
Degtyarev RPD	1953	7.62×39	Gas	41.00	20.50	15.44	Belt	2410	700
Kalashnikov RPK	1960	7.62×39	Gas	41.00	23.23	10.50	D/75	2400	600
Valmet M62	1966	7.62×39	Gas	42.72	18.50	18.31	Belt	2395	1050
Yugoslavia: M72B1	1978	7.62×39	Gas	47.64	22.05	27.50	Belt/D	2346	1000
Czech vz/52	1952	7.62×45	Gas	41.00	27.00	17.56	Belt/B	2450	900/1150
Alfa Model 55	1955	7.62×51	Gas	43.30	24.00	28.56	Belt	2821	780
Ares Ext. Powered		7.62×51	EP	31.81	23.50	27.62	Belt	2765	<650
Beretta MG 42/59	1959	7.62×51	Recoil	48.03	20.98	26.44	Belt	2690	800
Britain: L7A1 GPMG	1961	7.62×51	Gas	48.50	26.75	24.50	Belt	2750	800
Britain: L94A1 Chain Gun		7.62×51	EP	49.21	27.67	39.37	Belt	2870	520
FN-MAG	1955	7.62×51	Gas	49.20	21.50	22.25	Belt	2800	850
Galil ARM	1974	7.62×51	Gas	40.94	18.35	15.12	B/50	2788	650
GE M134 Minigun	1963	7.62×51	EP	31.56	22.00	36.00	Belt	2850	<6000
Germany: MG3A1	1958	7.62×51	Recoil	48.22	20.90	24.37	Belt	2690	1100
Heckler & Koch HK11		7.62×51	DBB	40.15	17.71	15.00	D/80	2560	850

Name	Year	Calibre	Action	Length	Barrel	Weight	Feed	Velocity	Rate
Heckler & Koch HK11A1		7.62×51	DBB	40.55	17.71	16.94	B/30	2625	650
Heckler & Koch HK11E		7.62×51	DBB	40.55	17.71	17.94	D/50	2625	800
Heckler & Koch HK21		7.62×51	DBB	40.19	17.71	16.12	Belt	2625	900
Heckler & Koch HK21A1		7.62×51	DBB	40.15	17.71	17.62	Belt	2625	900
Heckler & Koch HK21E	1983	7.62×51	DBB	44.88	22.05	20.50	Belt	2756	800
Hughes EX34 Chain Gun	1975	7.62×51	EP	25.98	22.83	30.19	Belt	2828	520
Japan: Model 62	1962	7.62×51	Gas	45.50	20.63	23.56	Belt	2400	600
Japan: Model 74	1974	7.62×51	Gas	42.72	24.60	44.94	Belt	2805	700/1000
Madsen-Saetter	1959	7.62×51	Gas	45.90	22.20	23.50	Belt	2800	650/1000
Madsen-Saetter Tank	1959	7.62×51	Gas	38.20	22.20	22.31	Belt	2800	750
USA: M60	1963	7.62×51	Gas	43.50	22.04	23.19	Belt	2838	550
USA: M60E3	1986	7.62×51	Gas	42.00	22.00	18.94	Belt	2822	550
USA: M60E4	1991	7.62×51	Gas	37.71	22.0	22.50	Belt	2800	600
USA: M73	1962	7.62×51	Recoil	35.00	22.00	30.88	Belt	2800	600
USA: M240G	1995	7.62×51	Gas	48.03	24.68	25.81	Belt	2800	750
Vektor SS-77	1977	7.62×51	Gas	45.47	21.65	21.19	Belt	2756	750
Vektor MG-4	1980	7.62×51	Recoil	37.00	23.42	33.06	Belt	2756	700
Yugoslavia: M77B1	1980	7.62×51	Gas	40.35	21.06	11.25	B/20	2750	600
China: Type 67	1967	7.62×54	Gas	45.00	23.50	32.50	Belt	2740	650
China: Type 80	1980	7.62×54	Gas	46.93	26.57	17.37	D/50	2706	650
Czech vz/59, Light	1959	7.62×54	Gas	43.93	23.35	29.12	B/30	2657	750
Czech vz/59, Heavy	1959	7.62×54	Gas	47.83	27.28	42.37	B/30	2723	750
Degtyarev DP	1928	7.62×54	Gas	50.80	23.80	20.50	D/47	2760	550
Degtyarev DT	1929	7.62×54	Gas	47.00	23.80	28.00	D/60	2760	650
Degtyarev DPM	1944	7.62×54	Gas	49.80	23.80	26.81	D/47	2760	550
Degtyarev DTM	1944	7.62×54	Gas	46.50	23.80	28.37	D/60	2760	600
Degtyarev DS39	1939	7.62×54	Gas	46.00	28.40	26.37	Belt	2650	550/1100
Degtyarev RP-46	1946	7.62×54	Gas	50.51	23.90	28.69	Belt	2760	600
Goryunov SG-43	1943	7.62×54	Gas	44.09	28.35	30.44	Belt	2832	650
Goryunov SGM		7.62×54	Gas	44.09	28.35	29.88	Belt	2870	650
Kalashnikov PK	1963	7.62×54	Gas	45.67	25.90	19.81	B/30	2706	700
Maxim (Russia) M1910	1910	7.62×54	Recoil	43.60	28.25	52.50	Belt	2830	550
Russia: ShKAS	1933	7.62×54	Gas	27.56	17.52	23.50	Belt	2760	600
Yugoslavia: M84	1984	7.62×54	Gas	46.26	25.90	33.06	Belt	2706	700
Maxim: Belgium M1900	1900	7.65×53	Recoil	46.46	28.22	39.69	Belt	2132	450
Maxim: Belgium légère	1920	7.65×53	Recoil	49.50	28.34	33.06	Belt	2025	450
Adams-Wilmot	1934	.303	Gas	n/a	n/a	20.00	D/99	2440	900
Beardmore-Farquhar	1920	.303	Gas	49.50	26.50	19.00	D/81	2440	500
Besal Mk 1	1941	.303	Gas	48.00	22.00	15.75	B/20	2450	500
Besal Mk 2	1941	.303	Gas	46.63	22.00	21.50	B/30	2450	600
Bren Mk 1, Mk 2	1938	.303	Gas	46.25	25.00	22.31	B/30	2400	500
Bren Mk 3	1944	.303	Gas	42.60	22.25	19.31	B/30	2400	480
Czech ZGB33	1933	303	Gas	45.50	25.00	22.12	B/30	2450	500
Gardner (Britain), 2-bbl; Conv'd	1898	.303	Hand	45.25	28.25	92.00	G/20	n/a	400
Hefah V Mk 1 (Britain)	1942	.303	Gas	48.00	24.50	15.12	D/60	2500	600
Hotchkiss (Britain) Mk 1	1916	.303	Gas	46.75	23.50	27.00	S/30	2450	500
Lewis (Britain) Mark 1	1914	.303	Gas	50.63	26.25	26.00	D/47	2450	550
Maxim (Britain) .303 Mk 1	1889	.303	Recoil	42.38	28.00	60.00	Belt	1800	400
Maxim (Britain) .303 Conv'd Mk 1	1897	.303	Recoil	45.00	28.00	64.00	Belt	1800	400
Maxim (Britain) .303 Conv'd Mk 2	1901	.303	Recoil	46.50	28.25	40.00	Belt	2750	600

Name	Year	Calibre	Action	Length	Barrel	Weight	Feed	Velocity	Rate
Nordenfelt (Britain) Conv'd Mk I	1898	.303	Hand	41.25	28.50	98.00	B/27	1800	<300
Vickers Mk I	1912	.303	Recoil	45.50	28.50	40.00	Belt	2450	450
Vickers GO (or Type K)	1937	.303	Gas	40.00	20.00	21.00	D/100	2450	1050
Vickers-Berthier Mk 3	1933	.303	Gas	46.50	23.50	22.00	B/30	2450	600
Japan: Type I	1941	7.7×58	Gas	42.40	23.23	77.00	S/30	2400	550
Japan: Type 92	1932	7.7×58	Gas	45.50	27.56	61.00	S/30	2400	450
Japan: Type 97	1937	7.7×58	Gas	46.50	28.00	24.00	B/30	2400	500
Japan: Type 99	1939	7.7×58	Gas	46.50	23.60	23.00	B/30	2350	850
Alfa Model 44	1944	7.92×57	Gas	57.08	29.53	28.62	Belt	2493	780
Bergmann MG 10	1910	7.92×57	Recoil	n/a	n/a	36.00	Belt	2950	550
Bergmann MG 15nA	1916	7.92×57	Recoil	44.13	28.50	28.50	Belt	2925	550
Besa Mk I	1939	7.92×57	Gas	43.50	29.00	47.00	Belt	2700	500/800
Besa Mk 2	1940	7.92×57	Gas	43.50	29.00	48.00	Belt	2700	500/800
Czech ZB vz/26	1926	7.92×57	Gas	45.78	23.70	21.31	B/20	2598	500
Czech ZB vz/30	1930	7.92×57	Gas	45.75	26.50	21.31	B/30	2500	600
Czech ZB vz/37	1937	7.92×57	Gas	43.50	26.70	41.00	Belt	2600	500/700
Gast	1918	7.92×57	Recoil	54.72	28.35	40.81	D/192	2700	1300
Germany: MG 13	1933	7.92×57	Recoil	57.75	28.25	23.94	D/75	2700	650
Germany: MG 15	1932	7.92×57	Recoil	52.50	23.50	28.00	D/75	2700	850
Germany: MG 30	1930	7.92×57	Recoil	46.25	23.50	17.00	B/25	2500	800
Germany: MG 34	1934	7.92×57	Recoil	48.00	24.75	26.69	D/75	2700	650
Germany: MG 42	1942	7.92×57	Recoil	48.0	21.00	25.50	Belt	2480	1200
Germany: MG 81	1938	7.92×57	Recoil	36.02	18.70	14.37	Belt	2592	1600
Knorr-Bremse M/35	1933	7.92×57	Gas	51.48	27.25	22.06	B/20	2600	500
Madsen	1904-	7.92×57	Recoil	45.00	23.00	20.00	B/40	2460	450
Maxim: (China) Type 24	1924	7.92×57	Recoil	48.00	28.54	52.50	Belt	2920	350
Maxim: (Germany) MG 08	1908	7.92×57	Recoil	46.25	28.35	58.31	Belt	2838	450
Maxim (Germany): MG 08/15	1915	7.92×57	Recoil	56.90	28.35	31.00	Belt	2838	450
SIG KE7	1936	7.92×57	Recoil	46.87	23.63	17.25	B/20	2625	550
Yugoslavia: M53	1953	7.92×57	Recoil	35.00	22.00	30.88	Belt	2800	600
Chauchat Mle 1915	1915	8×50	Recoil	45.00	18.50	20.00	B/20	2300	250
Darne M1918	1918	8×50	Gas	36.89	25.98	15.44	Belt	2300	1100
Hotchkiss Mle 1897	1897	8×50	Gas	n/a	n/a	55.00	S/30	2400	600
Hotchkiss Mle 1909	1909	8×50	Gas	46.75	23.50	27.00	S/30	2180	500
Hotckiss Mle 1914	1914	8×50	Gas	51.60	31.00	55.69	Belt/S	2325	500
Puteaux	1905	8×50	Gas	49.21	30.70	54.00	S/23	2300	650
St Étienne	1907	8×50	Gas	46.50	28.00	56.75	S/30	2300	450
Schwarzlose (Austria)	1907	8×50	DBB	41.93	20.66	43.88	Belt	2050	400
Breda Model 37	1937	8×59	Gas	50.00	25.00	42.50	S/20	2600	450
FIAT-Revelli M1935	1935	8×59	DBB	50.00	25.75	40.00	Belt	2600	500
Gardner (Britain) 2-bbl Mk I	1888	.402	Hand	45.50	28.50	88.00	G/20	n/a	<200
Gardner (Britain) 5-bbl Mk I	1882	.45	Hand	53.50	33.00	290.00	G/30	n/a	<800
Gardner, (Britain) 2-bbl Mk I	1884	.45	Hand	47.00	30.00	218.00	G/30	n/a	<250
Gatling (Britain)	1874	.45	Hand	59.41	31.95	444.00*	D/240	n/a	<800
Maxim (Britain) .45 Mk I	1889	.45	Recoil	43.50	n/a	60.00	Belt	1350	400
Maxim (Britain) .45 GG Mk I	1892	.45	Recoil	43.75	n/a	60.00	Belt	1200	400
Nordenfelt (Britain) 5-bbl Mk I	1884	.45	Hand	46.00	28.50	154.00	H/50	1250	<300
Nordenfelt (Britain) 5-bbl; Mk 2	1886	.45	Hand	42.25	28.50	133.00	H/50	1250	<300
Nordenfelt (Britain) 3-bbl Mk I	1887	.45	Hand	41.50	28.50	93.00	B/27	1350	<300

* complete with wheeled carriage

Name	Year	Calibre	Action	Length	Barrel	Weight	Feed	Velocity	Rate
BSA M24 Observer's	1924	.5 Vic	Recoil	n/a	n/a	46.00	D/37	2600	400
Vickers, .5in Mark I	1932	.5 Vic	Recoil	54.00	31.10	52.00	Belt	2600	450/675
Browning M1927	1927	.50 Brg	Recoil	56.00	36.00	66.00	Belt	2300	450
Browning M2	1933	.50 Brg	Recoil	66.00	45.00	100.00	Belt	2930	650
Browning Aircraft M2	1928	.50 Brg	Recoil	57.00	36.00	64.00	Belt	2840	850
Browning M2HB	1933	.50 Brg	Recoil	65.00	45.00	84.00	Belt	2930	525
Browning Saco Fifty/.50	1987	.50 Brg	Recoil	61.41	36.00	58.88	Belt	2841	500/750
Browning Ramo M2 Light	1991	.50 Brg	Recoil	60.00	36.00	58.88	Belt	2841	500/750
GECAL 50	1986	.50 Brg	EP	46.50	36.00	96.12	Belt	2900	8000
Madsen-Saetter Heavy	1959	.50 Brg	Gas	64.00	39.37	61.69	Belt	2850	1000
Singapore: CIS .50	1988	.50 Brg	Gas	70.00	45.00	66.12	Belt	2920	500
USA: M85	1963	.50 Brg	Recoil	50.55	36.00	61.50	Belt	2842	400/1050
USA: GAU-19/A		.50 Brg	EP	46.50	36.00	74.00	Belt	2900	1000/2000
Beresin UBT	1941	12.7×108	Gas	55.00	35.00	56.00	Belt	2800	1000
China: Type 77	1977	12.7×108	Gas	85.98	40.00	89.50	Belt	2625	800
China: Type W-85	1985	12.7×108	Gas	78.05	40.00	40.75	Belt	2625	750
Degtyarev DShK 38	1938	12.7×108	Gas	62.30	39.37	73.50	Belt	2805	575
Degtyarev DShK 38-46	1946	12.7×108	Gas	62.50	42.00	78.50	Belt	2825	550
Russia: NSV	1971	12.7×108	Gas	61.42	44.50	55.12	Belt	2772	750
Germany: MG 131	1936	13×64	Recoil	46.25	21.75	40.00	Belt	2560	960
Tank und Flieger	1918	13×92	Recoil	n/a	n/a	85.00	Belt	2600	400
Breda Model 1931	1931	13.2×99	Gas	65.00	39.37	104.69	B/30	2592	500
Japan: Type 93	1933	13.2×99	Gas	95.00	65.00	87.00	B/30	2210	450
Pirat KPWT	1995	14.5×114	Recoil	77.95	53.00	115.00	Belt	3280	600
Russia: KPV	1955	14.5×114	Recoil	78.98	53.00	108.25	Belt	3280	600
Germany: MG 151	1935	15×95	Recoil	75.43	49.37	78.94	Belt	3150	700
Besa Mk I	1940	15×104	Gas	80.70	57.60	125.50	Belt	2700	450
FN-BRG	1985	15×115	Gas	78.74	53.15	121.25	2 Belt	2952	700
FN-BRG15	1988	15.5×106	Gas	84.65	n/a	132.25	2 Belt	3460	600
Gatling (Britain)	1875	.65	Hand	66.60	33.00	817.00	D/50	n/a	<400
Germany: MG 151/20	1938	20×84	Recoil	69.52	43.40	93.50	Belt	2313	700

INVENTORS, DESIGNERS & MANUFACTURERS

Cross references to other articles within this chapter are indicated by **bold** type.

ABADIE

Belgian gunsmith, believed to have worked for **Nagant**. In 1874 he patented a revolver loading gate which disconnected the hammer, allowing the trigger to be used to rotate the cylinder for loading. Revolvers using this system were widely adopted, and in Portugal bore the Abadie name.

ACCURACY INTERNATIONAL

Accuracy International, Portsmouth, England. Founded by Malcom & Sarah Cooper in *ca* 1980 as importers and retailers, Cooper then designed a sniping rifle which was adopted by the British Army as the L96A1. An improved design was then adopted by the Swedish Army, and several variant models were developed for police and security forces. The company also manufactures competition sights and rifles.

ADAMS

There were several notable gunmakers called Adams in the 19th century, but the two who concern us most here are Robert (1809–70) and his brother John, both gunmakers of London. They were both patentees of various designs of, and improvements to revolvers, and John was principally responsible for the Adams revolvers adopted by the British Army. At various times, they operated independently; as partners; as Adams & Co. with another Adams, Henry, whose relationship is not known; and with the Deane brothers as Deane, Adams & Deane. They were also connected with the London Armoury Company in the late 1850s, and opened an American office, the Adams Revolving Arms Co., in order to profit from the American Civil War.

AGNELLI

Guiseppe Agnelli was an Italian engineer who designed a light machine gun and took out patents in about 1912. The patents were subsequently taken over by the Società Italiana Ansaldo and promoted as the SIA machine gun, but the company was unable to get it into a workable form before World War I ended, and eventually a small number of guns were made as training weapons in the late 1920s before the design was finally abandoned.

The weapon was of no particular merit, but earns a mention here because Agnelli elected to use a delayed blowback system and, like many inventors before and since, discovered that delayed blowback plus a necked high-pressure cartridge equals difficult extraction. But instead of adding an oil pump, which was the usual solution, Agnelli had the idea of milling grooves along the length of the chamber, so allowing a portion of the propellant gas to leak between the case and the chamber wall and thus 'float' the case on a layer of high-pressure gas. This prevented the case from expanding and sticking to the chamber walls, so that, as the breech began to open, so the case began to slide out without sticking. The idea has seen many applications since then, mostly in the second half of the century, but Agnelli deserves the credit for originating it.

ALBINI

Augusto Albini (1850–1909) was an Italian naval officer who designed a lifting-block breech mechanism for rifles. He enlisted the aid of Francis **Braendlin**, an engineer, to perfect the design and the two took out patents in 1866/67. Widely tested, the Albini-Braendlin rifle was adopted by the Belgian Army, largely because the system lent itself to cheap conversion of existing muzzle-loading rifles. Albini also designed a side-swinging cylinder for use with revolvers, essentially the same type as that used with most present-day revolvers. He patented the idea in 1869, but appears never to have pursued the matter.

ALLIN

Erskine S. Allin (1809–79), Master Armorer at Springfield Armory in the 1860s who developed a method of converting muzzle-loading muskets into breech-loading arms, the so-called 'Springfield Trap-door' system.

ARISAKA

Colonel Nariake Arisaka, Japanese Army. Superintendent of Tokyo Arsenal and President of a Commission which sat in the 1890s and developed a bolt-action rifle to replace the **Murata**.

ARMALITE

(1) The ArmaLite Division of Fairchild Aircraft & Engine Corporation was formed in 1954 to exploit the use of aluminium alloys and plastic materials for the manufacture of firearms. Eugene Stoner was retained as designer, and he developed the .308in AR-3 using a rotating bolt mechanism. This was followed by the AR-10 in 1957, and 100 AR-10 rifles were made for extensive testing. The Netherlands showed interest and ArmaLite granted a licence to Artillerie-Inrichtingen. However, military trials invariably chose the FN-FAL rifle instead of the AR-10, and Artillerie-Inrichtingen lost interest and relinquished its licence.

In 1957 the US Army issued a specification for a lightweight rifle, and two ArmaLite engineers modified an AR-10 to use the .222 Remington cartridge. The US Army then moved the goalposts by demanding longer range performance, and ArmaLite responded by chambering the design for an improved .222 cartridge which, to differentiate it, became known as the .223 Remington. Although this AR-15 rifle performed well, the Ordnance Department was not convinced that the small calibre was effective and approved the 7.62mm M14 as the future service rifle. With this, Fairchild lost interest and licensed the design to Colt.

(2) ArmaLite Incorporated was now registered as a new company, Fairchild having withdrawn from firearms and Stoner having gone to work for Cadillac Gage. The US Air Force now showed interest in the .223 AR-15 design, trials were conducted, and in January 1962 it was standardised as the M16 by the Air Force. In November Colt received the first orders for military supply. The rifle was distributed in Vietnam to airfield guards and there attracted the attention of the US Army, which eventually adopted it.

There were complaints of unreliability in the field, eventually traced to a fatal combination of a change in propellant composition (of which the manufacturers were not informed) and user instructions which suggested that the rifle need not be cleaned. The new powder fouled the mechanism and the lack of cleaning made things worse This was eventually cured, but the M16 took time to live down the poor reputation it had gained in Vietnam.

(3) The ArmaLite Corporation of Costa Mesa California replaced ArmaLite Inc and took an early, neglected, 7.62mm design by Stoner, the AR-16, scaled it down to 5.56mm calibre and put it forward as the AR-18, a simple rifle which could be easily made by any engineering company without the need for specialist machinery. Licences for this weapon were taken out by Howa Machinery of Japan in 1969 and Sterling Armaments of England in 1973, but neither company was able to make a success of the design.

ASTRA

Brand name used by Astra-Unceta y Cia SA of Guernica, Spain. The company was founded in 1907 as Pedro Unceta y Juan Esperanza in Eibar, Guipuzcoa province, the first product being an automatic pistol called the 'Victoria' which was the usual 'Eibar copy' of the Browning 1903 design in both 6.35mm and 7.65mm calibres.

In 1913 the factory was moved to Guernica and the name changed to Esperanza y Unceta, and in addition to making the Victoria the firm undertook to manufacture the Campo-Giro pistols for the Spanish Army. In 1914 the trade name 'Astra' was adopted, and during the First World War the company was very active in supplying pistols for French and Italian Army contracts.

After the war Astra redesigned the Campo-Giro pistol to produce the 'Astra Modelo 1921' for the Spanish Army, which was also sold commercially as the Astra 400. This was of a peculiar 'tubular' design based on the Campo-Giro, and was to serve the Spanish forces until the 1970s. In the 1920–36 period the company produced a number of models based upon the **Mauser** military pistol, both semi- and full-automatic, as well as a variety of commercial automatic pistols in a numbered series. They also continued to produce cheap 'Eibar' designs under the names Brunswig, Fortuna, Museum, Salso and Union.

The Spanish Civil War interrupted Astra's commercial operations, though military production continued, and after the Civil War the firm was one of the few permitted to manufacture pistols. Since 1945 its products have been a series of automatic pistols (Cub, Constable, Falcon, Firefox) and revolvers (Cadix) of good quality. Between 1957 and 1968 Astra made the '**Colt** Junior', actually their Astra Model 200 in 6.35mm calibre, for sale under the Colt name in the USA. Their most recent designs appear to owe something to the **SIG** P220 series, but this can be said of many other firms as well.

AUG

Armee Universal Gewehr (Army Universal Rifle). A 5.56mm calibre assault rifle manufactured by **Steyr-Mannlicher** of Steyr, Austria, since 1977. Design began in the late 1960s in answer to a request from the Austrian Army, who also collaborated with Steyr-Mannlicher in the design.

At the army's request the rifling was set at one turn in 9 inches, faster than the then-standard one turn in 12 inches pioneered by the AR-15 rifle, in the interests of better accuracy and less destructive wounding performance. The rifle takes its 'Universal' name from being modular; the barrel, receiver and firing mechanism can be changed for other units of different size or performance so that the weapon can be configured in several ways, from ultra-short carbine to heavy-barrelled squad automatic.

The basic weapon consists of a tough synthetic casing into which the steel barrel and receiver are fitted and retained by catches. The firing mechanism, entirely synthetic apart from pins and springs, fits into the butt, and the magazine is translucent. It is of bullpup design, and the receiver is formed into a carrying handle which contains a 1.4-power optical sight. Four barrels, of different lengths and weights, are available; two receivers, one with optical sight and the other with a sight mount for fitting electro-optical sights; three firing mechanisms, one offering single shots and automatic fire, one giving single shots and three-round bursts or single shots and auto fire by selecting an internal switch; and one, for police use, allowing single shots only. Magazines holding 30 and 42 rounds are available. The rifle has a cyclic rate of automatic fire of 650 rounds per minute.

The AUG has been adopted by the armies of Austria, Australia, New Zealand, Malaysia, Morocco, Oman and Saudi Arabia, and a number of police and security agencies including the US Customs Service. It is, or has been, made under licence in Australia and Malaysia.

AUTO-ORDNANCE

Founded in 1916 as the Auto-Ordnance Corporation of New York. The financial backer was Thomas F. Ryan, banker and entrepreneur; John T. **Thompson**, John B. **Blish** and George Harvey were the other shareholders, with Ryan holding the greater part. Chief Engineer was Theodor Eickhoff, who had worked with Thompson in the Ordnance Department, notably on the development of the M1911 pistol. Oscar Payne was appointed draughtsman in August 1916. Between them they eventually produced the Thompson submachine gun, though manufacture was performed by the Colt company. The company passed through various hands after 1945 but survives today as a subsidiary of Numrich Arms Corporation, manufacturing semi-automatic replicas of the Thompson.

BALLE D

Standard bullet for the 8mm M1886 **Lebel** rifle of the French Army from 1898 until 1932, when it was replaced by a compound bullet. However, vast numbers were then in existence and it continued to be used until the end of World War II.

When introduced it was the first pointed and streamlined (boat-tailed) bullet to be adopted as a military standard, and it was unusual in being a solid copper-zinc alloy bullet rather than the usual compound lead-core/steel-jacket type of the period. The shape reduced air drag at both nose and base, thus improving the bullet's velocity and accuracy throughout its range, and the solid construction was chosen in order to avoid the tendency of compound bullets to 'set up' or deform when subjected to the chamber pressure, thus becoming cylindrical-based instead of boat-tailed.

The letter D commemorates Captain Desaleux, the designer of the bullet.

BARTHELMES

Fritz Barthelmes (d.1973) was the chief engineer of the **Walther** company in the 1930s and largely responsible for the design of the Walther P38 pistol. He escaped from the Russian Zone in 1945 to set up his own light engineering firm in Heidenheim, making, among other things, starting and signal pistols. After his death his son Martin continued the business and developed some successful air pistols.

BEARDMORE-FARQUHAR

A machine gun made by the Beardmore Engineering Co. to the patents of Mowbray Farquhar during WWI. It was extensively tested by the RAF in 1919 and by the British Army in 1920, but although light in weight, much of its working parts were exposed and this affected its reliability and it was not adopted for service. Improved models were developed, up to .5in calibre, but without success, and work on the design ceased in the early 1930s. It was revived during WWII and submitted for service use, but

was refused by the Ordnance Board; reading between the lines of their reports one gets the impression that they had seen all they wanted to see of Farquhar and his gun by that time and were not anxious to see a revival.

The gun was gas- and spring-actuated in a manner which considerably reduced the recoil blow and thus permitted lightweight construction.

BEAUMONT

Frederick Edward Blackett Beaumont, Lieutenant, Royal Engineers (d.1899). In 1855 he patented the first double-action revolver lock, which was incorporated in subsequent **Adams** revolvers. Prior to this, Adams had met with considerable sales resistance because his revolver was self-cocking, but could not be thumb-cocked by pulling back the hammer.

BENELLI

Engineering company of Urbino, Italy, it moved into firearms in the early 1920s, making shotguns and sporting rifles. In 1975 it decided to concentrate on firearms and became Benelli Armi; a subsidiary factory was established in Vitoria, Spain, in 1975.

The company makes a range of pistols, rifles and shotguns in both factories, but has had comparatively few ventures into military weapons. One which is worth noting was their development of a 'caseless cartridge' submachine gun in the 1970s. This used a round of ammunition which was a hollow-based bullet, the hollow being loaded with propellant and closed by a combustible primer. On firing, the bullet was blown out of the gun by the propellant but left no case to be extracted. The weapon worked, and was successfully demonstrated to several armies, but none was prepared to make the leap into a totally new technology, and Benelli gave up and abandoned the design in about 1984.

BENET

Laurence V. Benet was the son of Stephen Vincent Benet, author and one-time Chief of Ordnance, US Army. He became the manager of Hotchkiss et Cie in Paris and was responsible for obtaining the **Odkolek** patent in 1898, which was the foundation of the **Hotchkiss** machine gun.

BERDAN

Colonel Hiram Berdan, USA. (d.1893). After raising and leading a sharp-shooting regiment in the Union Army, Berdan resigned his commission in 1864 in order to devote his time to designing weapons. In 1865 he developed a centre-fire cartridge with drawn brass case which carried its own cap anvil, which became the military standard of the world. He then developed a bolt-action rifle which was adopted by the Russians in 1870.

BERETTA

Pietro Beretta SpA of Gardone Val Trompia, Italy, can trace its origins back to a barrel-making smith in 1680 and is probably the oldest-established gunmaking business in existence. Its products were confined to sporting rifles and shotguns until World War I, when the factory turned to military production. In 1919 the company returned to its sporting firearms but now added pistols to its line, and kept a foot in the military door. Military production expanded once more during World War II, and since then military work has formed a high proportion of the company's output. However, its reputation for high quality sporting weapons has been maintained.

BERGMANN

With a partner called Flörscheim (other details unknown), Theodor Bergmann set up an engineering factory, the Eisenwerke Gaggenau, in 1877 to make railway track and structural ironwork. This prospered but in the early 1890s Bergmann sold out and set up his own business, Bergmann's Industriewerke, to manufacture pistols and other firearms designed by his employee Louis **Schmeisser**. This prospered, sub-contracting much of the manufacture to an outside firm.

In 1904 Bergmann sold a successful military pistol to Spain, but immediately after receiving the contract, his sub-contractor was bought up by a competitor and Bergmann was without manufacturing facilities. He sold the pistol patents and contract to Pieper of Liège, then moved to Berlin, designed a machine gun, had it accepted by the army and set up a new factory to produce it. This company remained in existence until 1945, though from the 1920s appears to have been a general engineering works producing a few pocket pistols and then weapon components for other makers.

BERNARDELLI

Vincenzo Bernardelli SpA of Gardone Val Trompia, Italy. A manufacturer of sporting weapons and pocket pistols, who competed for the Italian Army rifle contract in the 1980s. The Bernardelli B2 assault rifle was actually the Israeli 5.56mm **Galil** rifle with some slight cosmetic changes. It was rejected in favour of the **Beretta** AR70/90 design, and Bernardelli returned to the commercial field.

BERTHIER

Adolph V.P.M. Berthier was a French Army officer who, in the late 1880s, developed a bolt-action rifle for the French Army which was adopted in various forms.

In the early 1900s he worked on a machine gun design which was provisionally approved by the US Army in 1918 but, on post-war examination, proved to be insufficiently developed. Berthier then took his design to **Vickers**, who completed the development, and as the Vickers-Berthier machine gun it was adopted by the Indian Army in the 1930s.

BLISH

John Bell Blish (1860–1921). Entered the US Navy, graduating from Annapolis in 1875. He served as coastal survey officer, then as a deck officer during the Spanish-American War. He retired in 1905 as a commander, but returned to active duty during WWI.

Blish developed his 'principle of metallic adhesion' for securing a breech-block and patented it in 1913. It is generally said that he was inspired by seeing the screw breech of a heavy naval gun stay closed during the high-pressure phase of the cartridge explosion, and then open itself as the pressure dropped; which, if true, only shows that the US Navy had some desperately unsafe breech mechanisms in those days. He was contacted by **Thompson** in

1915 and allowed Thompson to use his patent in return for a share in the proposed **Auto-Ordnance** company to make an automatic rifle.

BORCHARDT

Hugo Borchardt was born in Germany *ca* 1847 and emigrated to America when he was 16 years old. He worked for the Pioneer Breech-Loading Arms Co. in 1871, then the Singer Sewing Machine Co. and Colt, ending up with **Winchester**. He was factory superintendent on the Sharps Rifle Factory in 1876, developing the Sharps-Borchardt rifle.

When the Sharps firm folded in 1880 he returned to Europe and worked with **Frommer** in Budapest. After a brief return to the USA in 1892 he returned once more to Europe and went to Berlin where, working for Ludwig **Loewe**, he developed his automatic pistol. He patented a few designs of toggle-locked rifles and pistols in the 1900s, but thereafter appears to have abandoned firearms and his actions are unrecorded. He died in Berlin on 8 May 1924.

BOXER

Colonel Edward Mounier Boxer, RA, FRS (1823–1898). Commissioned into the Royal Artillery in 1839 Boxer became interested in ammunition and gunnery, and in 1849, whilst still a captain, he developed a wooden time fuze which was accepted for service and remained in use for many years. He was appointed Superintendent of the Royal Laboratory, the ammunition branch of the Royal Arsenal at Woolwich. Here he developed metallic cartridges, fuzes and artillery projectiles, including a modern design of shrapnel shell for use with rifled guns.

Boxer's name is best remembered in the Boxer primer, used with most sporting ammunition to this day, and which contains its own anvil, so that re-capping and reloading a cartridge becomes a fairly simple task. He was eventually criticised for his connections with commercial companies exploiting his patents, and was forced to resign in 1869, but he retired with the honorary rank of major-general.

BRAENDLIN

A gunsmith of Belgian origin, Francis Augustus Braendlin worked for Mont Storm in the USA in the 1860s. Patented a breech-loading rifle in 1863 and co.-patented, with **Albini**, a breech-loading system which appeared as the Albini-Braendlin rifle. Operated in Birmingham, England, 1867–71 as Braendlin & Sommerville making Albini-Braendlin rifles and **Galand** & Sommerville revolvers. This was succeeded by the Braendlin Armoury Company, operated by George C. Braendlin, Francis' son and which went into liquidation in 1888. The name was bought and operated by Charles Greener until he, too, went under in 1915.

BREDA

The Società Anonima Ernesto Breda of Brescia was a heavy engineering company which specialised in railway rolling stock until, during World War I, it accepted a contract to manufacture the FIAT-Revelli machine gun for the Italian Army. This appears to have convinced the company that there as an untapped gold mine awaiting it in the armaments field, and after the war it set about designing a machine gun of its own.

Breda produced a light machine gun in 1924 and thereafter improved it and was able to sell numbers to the Italian Army. In 1930 the company acquired the Società Anonima Fiat Armamentos de Torino (SAFAT), a company that had been set up by **FIAT** during the war in order to manufacture arms; FIAT had decided to quit the armaments business. Henceforth the weapons produced by Breda were properly known as Breda-SAFAT, although most people simply called them Breda. More designs, variations upon their basic 1924 model, followed, and aircraft machine guns were added to the repertoire.

All this enterprise collapsed, of course, with the end of World War II, but the basic Breda engineering concern survived and re-established itself, and is still marginally concerned with military arms, though it now only produces small arms under licence from other makers.

BRNO

Ceskoslovenska Zbrojovka Brno, the Czech arms factory, was set up in March 1919. It was originally state-owned, but this placed various political obstacles in the way of trading and it was re-organised as a limited liability company in 1924. Its first task was the manufacture of rifles for the nascent Czech Army, and the company entered into an agreement with **Mauser**. This led, via a roundabout route, to their commencing production of an automatic pistol, but a policy decision was taken in 1923 to concentrate pistol production in the **Ceska Zbrojovka** concern, and after that Brno concentrated on rifles and machine guns.

Brno was the birthplace of the ZB series of light machine guns which culminated in the ZB 30 and the Bren gun and of the heavier designs such as the Besa.

In post-war years the company gradually assumed the title of Zbrojovka Brno and specialised in sporting rifles. Since the independence of the Czech Republic, the products of Brno and Ceska Zbrojovka appear to have become interchangeable and made at either factory.

BROWNING

John Moses Browning (1855–1926). Son of a gunsmith, Browning made his first rifle whilst still a boy, and patented his dropping-block design in 1879. This was subsequently taken up by **Winchester**, and Browning went on to develop virtually every kind of firearm – pistols, rifles and shotguns, slide-action, lever-action, block-action, single-shot, repeating, gas-operated automatic and recoil-operated automatic.

When refused by American makers, he took his automatic shotgun and early automatic pistols to Belgium and had them built by Fabrique Nationale (**FN**), but he remained a freelance, offering his designs to those makers whom he felt could best utilise them. His pistols, automatic shotgun and machine guns are still being manufactured and will probably continue well into the 21st century.

BSA

(1) Birmingham Small Arms Co. Ltd, Small Heath, Birmingham. Founded in June 1861 by a consortium of Birmingham gunmakers in order to tender for the supply of rifles to the British Army. The company obtained a contract to convert **Enfield** rifle muskets to the **Snider** breech-loading system, delivering about 250,000 weapons by 1869. There followed a contract for Martini-Henry rifles in 1871 but the company went into voluntary liquidation in 1875.

(2) It re-appeared within a few days as the Birmingham Small Arms & Metals Co. Ltd and completed the Martini-Henry contract. After this it went through a quiet period until receiving a contract for the Lee-Metford rifle and for the manufacture of .303 ammunition. It also produced Lee-Metford and Lee-Enfield rifles for both military and commercial sale and then, in 1897 went into voluntary liquidation once more.

(3) After a period of reconstruction, during which the factories continued working on military contracts, in 1901 it became the Birmingham Small Arms Co. Ltd once again. By this time it had added bicycles to its repertoire, and in 1909 added motor-cycles, and in 1910 bought up the Daimler car company. During World War I it operated four factories in Birmingham, producing rifles and **Lewis** machine guns. In 1919 it split into three autonomous divisions: BSA Guns, BSA Cycles and BSA Tools.

(4) BSA Guns Ltd subsisted on commercial production through the 1920s and early 1930s, after which the re-armament programme produced military contracts for rifles, machine guns (Besa and Besal), **Browning** aircraft machine guns, Bren gun components and many other military stores. By 1945 the company was operating over 60 factories and employing over 28,000 people. Military contracts ceased after 1945, and, although the company produced good designs for a submachine gun and a 7mm automatic rifle to compete for British Army adoption, these had been insufficiently developed and were not adopted.

Thereafter the company gradually ran down its firearms production, concentrating upon air guns. In 1973 the assets were sold to Manganese Bronze Holdings and the firm continued to operate under the BSA name until in 1984 it was placed in liquidation.

The assets were again sold, this time to a new firm called BSA Guns (1984) Ltd. The firearms production machinery was sold to Pakistan, and small-scale manufacture of air guns continued until the early 1990s when the remains were bought by the El Gamo company of Spain.

BURNSIDE

General Ambrose Everett Burnside, USA (1824–1881). After graduating from West Point Burnside served for some years in the US Army before resigning in 1855 to form a company to manufacture his breech-loading rifle. He got into financial difficulties and had to sell his patents, and although the Burnside carbine was later issued to Union troops in some numbers, Burnside made little or nothing out of it. On the outbreak of the Civil War he raised a regiment of volunteers and rapidly advanced in rank to major-general. At this level he left a staggering record of incompetence in several posts and eventually went into politics, which perhaps better suited his limited abilities.

CARCANO

Salvatore Carcano was the Chief Inspector of the Reale Fabricca d'Armi, Turin and collaborator with Colonel Paravicino in the design of the Italian M1891 service rifle, commonly called the **Mannlicher**-Carcano. Carcano's contribution was principally the bolt, which though generally resembling that of the **Mauser** rifle, has a different type of safety and has the handle rather further forward.

CARL GUSTAV

Carl Gustav Stads Gevärsfabrik, Eskilstuna, Sweden, a major Swedish government small arms factory. Amalgamated with Husqvarna in 1970 to become **FFV**, which in turn was taken over by Bofors in 1992 and is now Bofors Ordnance.

CEI-RIGOTTI

Captain Amerigo Cei-Rigotti, Italian Army. The designer of a gas-operated automatic rifle patented in Italy in 1895. It was tested in Britain in 1901, and in Italy until 1905, with the result that numbers were adopted by the Carabinieri. Although not perfect, it was basically sound and could have been developed into a quite serviceable weapon, given the time and will.

CESKA ZBROJOVKA

Ceska Zbrojovka of Pilsen was set up in 1919; in 1921 it moved to new premises in Strakonice and shortly thereafter was given the task of producing military pistols. Production then expanded to cover rifles, machine guns, bicycles, artillery and virtually all kinds of munitions, and a second factory appeared in Prague. In 1938 an entirely new factory was built in Uhersky Brod, principally for the manufacture of aircraft machine guns, and this gradually became the main CZ factory.

After World War II its products moved more towards commercial markets and the name changed to the Czech Motorcycle Corporation, but this phase was soon abandoned and by the middle 1970s it was CZ Arms and it then produced the CZ 75 pistol which became a notable success. It now operates as Ceska Zbrojovka Uhersky Brod and is linked with Zbrojovka Brno.

CETME

Centro de Estudios Technicos de Materiales Especiales. (Centre for Technical Studies into Military Materiel), Madrid. Spanish research and development centre set up in 1944 to conduct the development of weapons for the Spanish Army. Weapons developed by CETME are then passed to the Empresa Nacional de Santa Barbara, the national arsenal organisation, for manufacture.

COLONEY

Myron Coloney was one of the lunatic fringe of the firearms world. Little is known of his antecedents, but he appeared in about 1878, together with another of the same breed, Doctor James H. MacLean. MacLean was a qualified doctor of medicine who had made a substantial fortune from patent medicines, while Coloney had an inventive turn of mind and a certain degree of mechanical aptitude. Between them they obtained a variety of patents for improbable firearms, collectively known as 'MacLean's Peacemakers', and proceeded to sell stock in their various enterprises. Their designs included such items as a 48-shot repeating pistol, a 128-shot rifle, three-barrelled pistols, machine guns and repeating artillery, none of which ever got past the prospectus and drawing-board stage.

It is ironic that, among the real ragbag of nonsense embodied in Coloney's British Patent 5613 of 1881, there is a rimless cartridge case, many years ahead of the first production of such a design. But neither MacLean nor Coloney recognised the significance of this piece of casual sketching, and the idea lay neglected until it was rediscovered elsewhere. It was the only practical idea the pair ever had, and they missed it. They vanished into obscurity, doubtless pursued by investors and creditors, in the early 1890s.

COLT

Samuel Colt (1814–1862) was undoubtedly the man who brought the revolver into prominence, though he did little inventing. His principal ability lay in organising mass production using interchangeable parts so that, given a sound design to start with, his revolvers could be quickly assembled without hand fitting and easily repaired without the services of a skilled gunsmith.

According to legend, Colt was the cabin boy of the brig *Corvo* when he was inspired by the ship's wheel to invent a revolver and carve a working model from wood; it seems most probable that this tale was the later invention of the infant public relations industry.

After leaving the sea, he became 'Doctor Coult', a travelling medicine man and with the proceeds of this enterprise had a revolver made to his design. His first attempts, by a man called Anson Chase, appear to have been unsuccessful, largely because of Chase's poor workmanship, and Colt subsequently found John Pearson of Baltimore who, in 1834, produced what Colt had envisaged. Colt then sailed to England and took out British Patent 6909 on 22 October 1835, then returned to the USA to take out US Patent 9430X on 25 February 1836.

Colt's design was an amalgam of existing ideas plus one or two improvements of his own, and the prime substance of his patents was his method of rotating the cylinder by means of a ratchet linked to the hammer and a method of locking the cylinder in place whilst the shot was fired. The American patent succeeded in preventing any competitor developing similar mechanisms or, indeed, any method of mechanically rotating the cylinder, until its expiry in 1857, which gave Colt a strangle-hold on the revolver market. This, though, did him little good in the early days since America was at peace and there was little call for revolvers. The Mexican War of 1847, the 1849 Gold Rush and the opening up of the West were the market opportunities which, in succession, enabled Colt to establish a major factory and become a household name.

After Colt's untimely death at an early age, a succession of directors was able to keep up the company' eminent position, though some of their decisions and their subsequent weapons were not always a success. On the whole, however, the successes outweighed the failures and the company has survived to the present day and still retains its high reputation.

COMBLAIN

Hubert Joseph Comblain was a Belgian gunsmith who, with his partner Mangeot, produced a percussion revolver with an odd side-hammer. His main claim to fame, however, came with the adoption, in 1870, of his dropping-block rifle as a Belgian and Brazilian service weapon.

CUTTS COMPENSATOR

A muzzle attachment invented by Colonel Richard M. Cutts and his son Richard M., Jnr., both of the US Marine Corps, for the purpose of stabilising a weapon during automatic fire. It takes the form of a cylinder with slots in the top, so that when the weapon is fired a proportion of the gas behind the bullet is ejected upwards and thus thrusts the muzzle down, counteracting the natural rise of the muzzle due to recoil forces.

A common defect of light automatic weapons fired from the shoulder is that the recoil thrust, acting with the firer's shoulder as a pivot, causes the muzzle of the gun to rise during sustained fire so that a high proportion of the burst of fire goes over the top of the target. The Cutts Compensator claimed to prevent this, making the weapon more effective by placing more bullets in the target. It was adopted for the **Thompson** submachine gun in 1928 and became a distinctive feature of that weapon, but it was never adopted for any other weapon. However, the same principle has been used by many designers by means of various types of muzzle attachment which, though producing similar effects, evaded the Cutts patents.

Opinions as to its efficiency are mixed. After testing the Thompson with compensator in 1928 the British Small Arms Committee were of the view that it made little or no difference to the results; perhaps the best that can be said is that it does no harm and might do some good. The principal British objection appears to have been that it added $20 to the price of a Thompson submachine gun.

DANUVIA

The Danuvia Arms Company of Budapest, of which far too little is known, existed in the 1930s and employed Pal **Kiraly** as its designer and chief engineer. He, naturally enough, brought his two-part breech block with him and applied it to the design of a powerful submachine gun, the 39M. He had already offered something similar to BSA in England; it is believed that this was turned down by the British Army, and that BSA had made some suggestions for improvement, which he now incorporated into the 39M. This gun was followed by a variant model, the 43M, after which nothing much was heard from the Danuvia company for many years. In 1996, however, the name suddenly re-appeared advertising a fairly commonplace automatic pistol.

DARNE

H. Darne, a French gunmaker, established in St Étienne in 1881. He became famous for his distinctive design of double-barrelled shotguns in which the barrels are fixed and the breech-block slides back to extract and reload. During World War I the company was drawn into military contracts, and realised that there was room for a cheap but reliable machine gun, particularly for use in aircraft. In the 1920s they designed such a gun, had it built in Spain in the first instance, and sold it widely. Although cheap and apparently flimsy, the guns were deceptively strong and reliable, and were among the final contenders for the Royal Air Force standard machine gun in the 1930s.

The collapse of France in 1940 and, subsequently, the abandonment of rifle-calibre machine guns for aerial use, put an end to the Darne machine gun, and the company returned to the manufacture of sporting weapons, recording its 300,000th double-barrel gun in 1970.

DAUDETEAU

Commandant Louis Daudeteau of the French Navy developed a bolt-action magazine rifle in 1889–92 which, in 6.5mm calibre, was taken into French Navy service in 1896. Although the design appears to be somewhat more tidy than the **Lebel**, it was not favoured due to its small calibre, and in 1905 the navy discarded the rifles and reverted to the Lebel. Numbers were sold to some South American countries, and Daudeteau worked with the French Army for several years, testing and experimenting with various bolt-action rifle designs until the 1900s.

DAUGS

Willy Daugs was a German ordnance engineer. He appears to have been some sort of an entrepreneur in pre-war years, since his name has been mentioned in connection with the supply of weapons to the Spanish Republicans during the Civil War. He then appeared managing the Tikkakoski arsenal in Finland in 1942, and in 1943 he negotiated a licence to Hispano-Suiza allowing them to make the Suomi SMG in Switzerland.

Daugs fled from Finland in 1945, first to Sweden, then Holland, where he attempted to interest various people in the drawings of the M44 submachine gun, then finally to Spain where he went to Oviedo and worked with Vorgrimmler, late chief designer at Mauserwerke. There they produced the DUX 53 submachine gun, based upon the M44 design, of which 1000 were made for the (West) German Bundesgrenz-schutz (Border Guard) in the mid-1950s.

Daugs then returned to Germany and worked for some time with Anschütz, at Ulm, on the DUX 59 SMG, but due to personality clashes with the Anschütz management he cancelled the licence he had issued to Anschütz, sold it elsewhere, and left Germany. His movements thereafter are unknown.

DEGTYAREV

Vasily Alexeyevitch Degtyarev (1879–1949). Degtyarev was apprenticed at the Imperial Arms Factory at Tula, Russia. His forebears had been gunsmiths, and his natural ability soon saw him promoted to foreman. During his compulsory military service he was posted to a research establishment where he familiarised himself with machine guns.

In 1906 Degtyarev was appointed assistant to Vladimir **Federov**, who was then developing an automatic rifle, and under his instruction soon acquired an unrivalled knowledge of automatic arms. Degtyarev held his post throughout the Revolution, and in the 1920s completed the design of a light machine gun which was introduced as the DP (Degtyarev Pulyemet) in 1928. This was followed by tank and aircraft guns.

During the later 1930s Degtyarev worked with **Shpagin** and Komaritsky to develop the DShK heavy machine gun, and then, at very short notice, produced the PTRD anti-tank rifle. In post-war years he developed the RPD light machine gun and co.-operated on other designs before retiring laden with honours.

DRAGUNOV

Yevgeni Fyordorov Dragunov was born in Izhevsk in 1920, one of long line of gunsmiths. At the age of 14 he went into the Industrial-Technical school and, on completion of his studies there, went straight to work in the Izhevsk rifle factory. In 1939 he was inducted into the Soviet Army and spent the war as a foreman gunsmith in a repair shop. He returned to the rifle factory after leaving the army in 1945, and in subsequent years busied himself with various minor improvements to existing designs and then developed the SVD sniping rifle.

DREYSE

Johann Nikolas von Dreyse (1787–1867). Born to a family of gunsmiths, he spent his early years in the trade working for Pauly in Paris when Pauly was experimenting with breech-loading and self-contained cartridges, By the 1820s he had returned to Prussia and was making percussion muzzle-loading sporting guns and by 1828 he had begun making breech-loading arms, culminating in the famous 'Needle Gun'.

Upon von Dreyse's death, his business was carried on by his son Franz, who developed pistols and shotguns working on the needle-gun system. But these failed to compete with more modern designs and in 1901 the moribund company was bought out by the Rheinische Metallwaren und Maschinenfabrik of Düsseldorf. This was a heavy engineering company at that time; it then decided to go into firearms, and revived the Dreyse name as its trademark, attaching it to various pistols and machine guns. The RMM company eventually adopted the short form of **Rheinmetall**, which it retains to this day.

DWM

Deutsche Waffen und Munitionsfabrik. This firm began in Karlsruhe in 1872 as Henri Ehrmann & Co., cartridge manufacturers. It was liquidated in 1877, bought up, and re-named Wilkelm Holtz & Co., and in 1878 was sold to Wilhelm Lorenz, who re-organised it as the Deutsche Metall-Patronenfabrik Lorenz, Karlsruhe. He made a success of the business and in 1889 sold out to Ludwig **Loewe** of Berlin.

Loewe foresaw the adoption of smokeless powder and acquired near-monopoly agreements with the two principal propellant companies, so that when the Germany Army decided to adopt smokeless powder in April 1889, Loewe had the business virtually to himself. He then went on to acquire percussion cap makers, establish his own primer factory, and in 1896 amalgamated all this ammunition business with his existing engineering works to form Deutsche Waffen und Munitionsfabrik. It continued to acquire companies and also held sizeable shares in **Mauser** and **FN** of Belgium.

The organisation was dismantled by the Allied Control and Disarmament Commission in 1918–19, but the company was reformed in 1923 as the Berlin-Karlsruhe Industriewerke, and operated as a general engineering concern. In the early 1930s it came back into the armaments busniess, and in 1936 resumed its former name as DWM. In 1945–46 it was dismantled once more by the occupying ppowers, but reformed as the Industriewerke Karlsruhe in 1947, and has operated since as a general engineering company.

ENFIELD

Name broadly applied to the various designs of rifle and revolver developed and manufactured by the Royal Small Arms Factory, Enfield Lock, Middlesex, England, between 1854 and 1987. They include the Enfield percussion rifle of 1853; the Lee-Enfield military rifles; the Enfield Pattern '14 and Pattern '17 rifles of 1914–18; the Enfield revolvers Marks I and II of 1880–87; the Enfield .38 revolver of 1932–45; and the 'SA80' automatic rifle made in the late 1980s.

The Royal Small Arms Factory at Enfield Lock was actually established in 1804 but was principally concerned with repair work and the assembling of weapons from parts received from contractors. However, the Crimean War of 1854–56 revealed serious shortcomings in the system of supply by contractors, particularly when war-inspired urgency was involved, and the government decided that a state-controlled arms factory was imperative. Machine tools were procured from the USA, new buildings erected, and production began with the Enfield Rifle, Pattern of 1853.

In the mid-1980s the Royal Ordnance Factory organisation which owned and operated the RSAF was sold to British Aerospace in the 'privatisation' craze of the time, and shortly afterwards all production at Enfield ceased, the usable machinery was transferred to the Royal Ordnance Factory Nottingham, and the Enfield plant closed, sold and demolished.

British military small arms production is now carried out at Nottingham under the banner of **Heckler & Koch** (UK) plc, a subsidiary of British Aerospace Defence.

ERMA

Acronym derived from Erfurter Maschinenwerke B. Giepel GmbH, a gunmaking company of Erfurt, Germany; also called Erma-Werke. This company began as a general engineering works in 1919 and manufactured components for Vollmer, who was a gunsmith making small quantities of submachine guns. In 1931 Erma licensed the production rights for Vollmer's submachine gun; shortly afterwards Vollmer, who had run his business on the proverbial shoestring, sold up completely and went to work for Erma as their chief designer, and the Vollmer submachine gun became the ERMA MPE.

The heart of Vollmer's design was the unified breech-block and return spring in a telescoping casing, and this feature was continued into other Erma products, culminating in the immortal MP38 and MP40.

After 1945 the company was re-established in Dachau; it made a brief foray into submachine gun design in the early 1960s without success and thereafter abandoned the field and concentrated on sporting weapons.

E.Y. RIFLE

Name applied to British service rifles which were bound round the chamber and barrel by several layers of wire, secured by soldering. They were reserved for firing grenades by means of muzzle cups, the binding being in order to strengthen them against the additional pressure and also to remind soldiers not to fire them with ball ammunition, since their continued use for grenade firing ruined their barrels for accurate shooting. The greater number of EY rifles were Enfield P'14 and P'17 types which had been sentenced unrepairable due to the rifling being worn, but which were still serviceable enough in the grenade launching role, though a smaller number of Lee-Enfields were similarly converted.

The origin of the name has long defied explanation. Some people claim that it came from *E*mergency use onl*Y*, others that it comes from Edgar Yule, the inventor of the idea. No official explanation has ever been traced.

FAZAKERLEY

British Royal Ordnance Factory located on the outskirts of Liverpool and which manufactured Lee-Enfield rifles, bayonets and, particularly, Sten submachine guns during World War II. Established in 1940, it was closed down shortly after the end of the war.

FEDEROV

Vladimir Grigorevitch Federov (1874–1960). Entered the Artillery School in 1897 and then worked at the Sestroretsk Arms Factory under Colonel S.I. **Mosin**. In 1900 he was appointed to the Test Section of the Artillery Commission, where he continued studying firearms and gradually began to concentrate on automatic weapon design.

In 1905 Federov produced a gas-operated conversion of the Mosin-**Nagant** bolt-action rifle, and followed this with a recoil-operated automatic rifle. This was favourably received, and a prototype made with the help of **Degtyarev**. Chambered for the standard 7.62 x 54R cartridge, it rapidly convinced Federov that a smaller cartridge would result in a more practical weapon, and he designed his next rifle around the 6.5mm **Arisaka**, several thousands of rounds of which had been acquired during the Russo-Japanese War.

In 1916 Federov produced his 'Automat' rifle, which was approved, but production had hardly begun when the 1917 Revolutions stopped all work. After some delay work was resumed under Soviet control, and a number of Automats were made for the Red Army.

In the 1920s Federov was given an arms factory to manage and also became the patron of such new designers as Degtyarev, **Simonov** and **Shpagin**. In 1943 he was appointed Lieutenant-General of the Red Army, and received many other awards and decorations.

FEG

Fegyver es Gepgyar Reszvenytarsasag, Budapest, Hungary. This arms factory and engineering works was set up in the early 1880s and, at various times, manufactured Mannlicher rifles and a variety of pistols, most of which were designed by Rudolf **Frommer**, the managing director 1906–35.

After 1945 and the Sovietisation of Hungary it became Femaru es Szerszazamgepgyar NV until *ca* 1985 when it became the FEG Arms & Gas Appliances Factory. In the 1980s it began production of a range of pistols copied from the **FN Browning** High-Power.

FFV

Forsvarets Fabriksverk (Military Factory). The principal government armaments factory of Sweden, it was absorbed by the Bofors organisation in the early 1990s.

FIAT

Fabbrica Italiana Automibili Torino. The well-known Italian engineering and automobile company which, during World War I, entered the armaments field manufacturing the **Revelli** medium machine gun, which is consequently known as the FIAT-Revelli. The company then set up a subsidiary under the name Società Anonima Fiat Armamentos de Torino (SAFAT) to manufacture armaments, but in 1930 decided to concentrate on car manufacture and sold the SAFAT factory to **Breda**. The guns produced after that became known as Breda-SAFAT.

FN

Fabrique Nationale des Armes de Guerre was established in Herstal, Liège, Belgium in 1889 for the purpose of manufacturing rifles for the Belgian Army. The shareholders were a collection of the principal gunmakers of Liège, and the company was formed because the army requirement of 150,000 rifles was beyond the ability of any single company. But after completing the army order by building **Mauser** rifles under licence, the firm went on to buy up an ammunition company, expand it, and commence making ammunition for the army. The efficiency of the company became known abroad, and in 1892 it received a contract from Russia to renovate 400,000 **Berdan** rifles. There then followed several contracts from South American countries for rifles and ammunition.

By early 1894 come of the shareholders were apprehensive of the Frankenstein monster they had created. They had intended that it should complete the army orders and then dissolve; instead it was becoming a serious competitor. Several of the more influential shareholders resigned and sold their shares.

In late 1894 the Chilean government gave FN an order for 40,000 Mauser rifles of the 1893 pattern as supplied to Spain. FN accepted, whereupon Mauser pointed out that its licence did not cover that weapon and, if FN continued with the contract, Mauser would sue. FN gave up contract, which was taken over by Mauser and in February 1896 the entire board resigned, having sold fifty percent of the shares to Ludwig **Loewe** of Berlin.

Loewe re-organised the company and formed an affiliation with Mauser (in which he held a substantial share) so that Mauser and FN divided the future manufacture of Mauser rifles between them. This work, though, did not suffice to keep the factory occupied and solvent, and in 1896 FN began the manufacture of bicycles, followed by shotguns and sporting rifles.

In that year, too, Hart Berg, a director of FN, travelled to the USA to study the mass-production of bicycles, and whilst there was introduced to John **Browning**. Browning had developed an automatic pistol; he had sold the American rights to **Colt** but had reserved the rights for the rest of the world and, after talking to Berg, offered the pistol to FN. Berg returned to Liège in 1897 and in July an agreement was drawn up with Browning which was to stay in force until his death in 1926.

With the German occupation of Belgium in 1914 manufacture ceased; many of the machines were removed by the Germans, who later demanded that the firm re-start production of arms. The directors refused, and after two directors had been sent off to prison camps the Germans commandeered the factory and used it as a motor vehicle repair workshop.

In 1918 the first task was to regain control of the company, which had become the property of the German **DWM** firm during the war. A syndicate of bankers was formed, and in 1919 control passed back into Belgian hands. In the 1920s and 1930s it was principally occupied in making Mauser rifles and Browning pistols, shotguns and rifles, motor-cycles, motor-cars and sewing machines. It also bought up a number of small ammunition and gunmaking firms in Belgium and France, and set up rifle manufacturing plants in Yugoslavia.

In 1940 the Germans re-appeared, the company was once again taken over by DWM, German managers were brought in, and the factory continued producing weapons but entirely for the German Army. Most of the directors and design staff vanished, to reappear in Britain where they formed a design team inside the Royal Small Arms Factory and continued working on automatic rifle designs.

1945 saw the departure of the Germans and the return of the firm to Belgian ownership once more. In the years that followed the FAL rifle and MAG machine gun, fruits of the wartime work carried out in Britain, became the preferred armament of more than half the world's armies. Since then the company has had its financial ups and downs, was briefly owned by **GIAT**, the French consortium, but in 1997 went back into entirely Belgian ownership and now appears to have settled down to a moderate prosperity.

FROMMER

Rudolf Frommer (1868–1936). Studied engineering, joined **FEG** in 1896, eventually became managing director from 1906 until his retirement due to ill health in 1935. He took a particular interest in the design of automatic weapons using the long recoil system in the 1900s, patenting several pistols, and in later years he extended his interests to cover self-loading sporting and military rifles. He was intimately connected with Georg Roth and Karel **Krnka**, and the individual idiosyncrasies of this 'Bohemian Trio' are often discernible in patents taken out by any or all of them.

FURRER

Colonel Adolf Furrer was the Superintendent of the Swiss Arsenal at Thun in the 1920–40 period. Whilst doubtless an efficient officer, there is also no doubt that he had a fixation on the toggle system of breech locking, which probably came from his early association with the Thun production of Parabellum pistols. He eventually applied toggle-locking systems to a range of submachine guns, machine guns, anti-tank rifles, infantry support cannons

and air defence cannons of ever-increasing complexity.

There is no argument but that his designs worked, and worked quite well – under peacetime conditions. Whether they would have worked so well under the more strenuous conditions of war is a matter for speculation. What is certain is that they were all difficult, expensive, and slow to produce.

GALAND

Charles François Galand (fl 1870–1914)was a prominent gunmaker of Liège, Belgium, who appears to have had a branch in Paris since pistols can be found marked 'Galand Liège' or 'Galand Paris'. His first noteworthy contribution was a 'self-extracting' revolver which, together with Alfred Sommerville a Birmingham gunmaker, he patented in 1868.

This 'Galand & Sommerville' revolver was an open-frame, double-action weapon in which extraction of the spent cases was done by forcing down a lever which extended from beneath the barrel back towards the butt and forming part of the trigger guard. This forced the barrel and chamber to slide forward on the pistol frame. After a short movement the extractor plate stopped, while the remainder continued to move and thus the plate drew the cases from the cylinder. The lever was returned until the cylinder moved back and met the extractor plate, whereupon the chambers could be loaded. Then a final closing of the lever brought the cylinder and barrel back to the firing position and locked them.

In Paris Galand was an associate of M. Perrin, who had, among other things, developed the cartridge variously called the 'French Rim', 'Welt Rim' or 'Thick Rim' pattern. This was developed to suit revolvers converted from pinfire to centre-fire, and the abnormally thick rim was necessary to cover the slot in the chamber into which the pinfire cartridge pin had fitted. Galand therefore produced a large number of his self-extracting revolvers chambered for these Perrin cartridges, in 7mm, 9mm and 12mm calibres, which have inevitably come to be known as 'Galand-Perrin' revolvers. In 12mm calibre this pattern was adopted by the Romanian Army in 1874 and the Russian Navy in about 1875.

His patent of 1868 covered three variant versions of the self-extracting system. The most common is the under-lever type just described; a second type, also manufactured in Birmingham under the Galand-Sommerville name and found in conventional .38 and .45 chambering, has a shorter and neater lever which ends in front of the cylinder; while the third model, which appears only to have been manufactured in France or Belgium, has the lever shaped so as to lie along the right side of the frame above the trigger.

GALIL

Israeli service rifle developed by Major Israel Galil. It is a gas-operated automatic weapon, largely based upon the **Kalashnikov** design and using a similar bolt and bolt carrier system to lock the breech. The first models appeared in the early 1970s and were in 5.56mm calibre, but an enlarged model in 7.62 x 51mm calibre appeared shortly afterwards and was used by the Israeli Defence Force as well as being sold to other countries.

The design was later adopted by the South African

Army as the R4 rifle (made by Lyttleton Engineering), though with some minor modifications to suit African climatic conditions and the slightly different physique of South Africa's troops. A specialised sniping version in 7.62mm calibre was also developed for the Israeli Army in the 1980s.

GARAND

John C. Garand (1887–1974) was born Jean Garand, a French-Canadian, in Saint-Rémi, Quebec. His family moved to Connecticut when he was a child and after leaving school he found employment as an apprentice millwright, eventually becoming a skilled toolmaker. He became a naturalised US citizen in 1912, adopting the Anglicised form of his fore-name, and set up a small engineering company.

In 1916, moved by the news of the war, he submitted a design of machine gun to the US Army authorities. The design was favourably received and he was invited to continue working and bring it to a more perfect state. In 1919 he was offered a post in the design office of Springfield Arsenal, and he was to remain there until his retirement in 1953.

GARDNER

William Gardner (1844–1887) was a native of Ohio who went to England some time in the 1860s to study law. Of a mechanical turn of mind, he soon abandoned law for the study of firearms and in 1870 offered a magazine pistol to the British War Office, who refused it. He then developed the Gardner machine gun which was accepted and entered British service in 1882.

He was a prolific patentee of all sorts of improvements to firearms and developed a tubular-magazine rifle in about 1880, specimens of which exist, and also drew up designs for a cartridge-loaded cannon but his sudden death from illness prevented further development of these weapons.

The Gardner machine gun was a mechanical gun, operated by a crank handle which drove a reciprocating breech block to load, fire and extract. Generally in a two-barrelled form, the barrels firing alternately, but also found as a single- and a five-barrel weapon.

GASSER

Leopold Gasser (1836–1871) was descended from a long line of gunsmiths, served his apprenticeship with his family in Spittal-am-Drau (now in Austria), and then, in 1858, a qualified journeyman, moved to Vienna to complete his training. He began to specialise in revolver manufacture, and in 1869 developed a design of his own which was adopted by the Austrian Army. He then produced a 'generic' design which attained wide popularity in the Balkans as the 'Montenegrin Gasser'. By the late 1860s he was operating two factories which turned out over 100,000 revolvers a year.

After his death in 1871 the business was carried on by his son *Johann*, who was able to make various improvements on his father's designs. The adoption of automatic pistols by the Austro-Hungarian Army in 1908 and 1912 made a sharp reduction in the demand for revolvers, and the company did not survive World War I.

GAST

German machine gun for use by aircraft observers, developed during World War I. It actually consisted of two guns side-by-side, their breech-blocks connected by a mechanical linkage, so that when the first gun fired, the opening of the block closed that of the other gun and fired it, the recoil of which, in turn, closed the first gun's bolt and fired it, this alternating sequence continuing so long as the trigger was pressed. Each gun was fed by its own 192-round drum, and the effective rate of fire was 1300 rounds per minute.

The invention of Carl Gast, a German engineer, the guns were made by the Vorwerke Company of Barmen-Eberfelde. Work began in 1917, and service evaluation began early in 1918. Some minor modifications were made and production commenced, but the war ended with only 1314 guns having been made. Almost all these were destroyed by the Allied Disarmament Commission, and only a few Gast guns remain in museums.

According to interrogation reports one or more guns in 13mm calibre were made for trial, but none has ever been seen and all the service guns were in standard 7.92mm Mauser calibre.

GATLING

Dr Richard Jordan Gatling, MD, (1818–1903). Gatling was a *bona fide* doctor of medicine, though he never practised as such; it is generally said that he qualified solely to be better able to look after his family during the periodic epidemics of the time. His vocation was mechanical engineering, and at the age of 21 he patented a machine for sowing rice. In 1844 he set up as a manufacturer of agricultural implements and in a short time had expanded to have three factories in operation.

In 1862, doubtless spurred on by the Civil War, he applied for his first patent for a 'rapid-firing gun'. He continued developing this primitive design, taking out further patents, but he did not receive any major encouragement from the US Army until after the Civil War had ended. Sales to armies in various parts of the world followed, and Gatling spent many years perfecting improvements to his gun, eventually selling the patent rights to **Colt**.

Gatling then returned to his agricultural machinery business, and in 1900 developed a motor-driven plough. Whilst on a business trip in connection with the manufacture of this device, he contracted influenza and died.

GIAT

Groupement Industriel d'Armes de Terre. A French agency set up in 1950 to act as sales agents for the products of the various French state arsenals and ordnance factories. In 1990 it was 'privatised' and set about enlarging its scope by purchasing **FN**, Manurhin, and various other French munitions companies which were in financial difficulties. It also had interests in British Aerospace, **Beretta**, and other foreign firms, principally by trade and manufacturing agreements. By 1995 GIAT itself was in financial trouble, being overstretched in a shrinking defence market, and in 1997 sold the FN holding back to the Walloon government in Belgium.

GLOCK

Glock GmbH of Deutsche Wagram, Austria, was originally a small company manufacturing high quality knives, bayonets, folding shovels, entrenching tools and other edged ware for military use. Very quietly in the early 1980s the company began development of a radically new automatic pistol, using synthetic materials ('plastics') for many of the component parts. The design also incorporated an automatic trigger safety system and a self-cocking striker system which ensured that the pistol could only be discharged by deliberate intent.

In 1984 the Austrian Army announced that it would entertain tenders for the supply of 25,000 pistols; it was generally assumed that **Steyr** would supply its GB pistol and that would be that, but to everyone's surprise the Glock 17 pistol was selected. Even Glock was surprised; it had to sub-contract some of the components to other firms in order to meet the army contract. From then on, its future was assured.

GORYUNOV

Piotr Maximovitch Goryunov (1902–43). Trained as a locksmith, Goryunov fought in the Civil War of the 1920s. After the war he managed to get a foothold in the arms factory operated by **Federov** and was trained as a gunsmith. He then appears to have specialised in machine guns and his major work was the design of the SG machine gun, completed shortly before his death.

GRAS

Captain Basile Gras (1836–1904). An officer of the French Army, Gras developed his turnbolt rifle in the aftermath of the Franco-Prussian War and submitted it for approval in 1873. Essentially it was a conversion of the Chassepot to fire a metallic centre-fire cartridge instead of the semi-combustible Chassepot round. Several models were developed and adopted before the rifle was replaced by the **Lebel** in 1886. Even so, Gras rifles remained in use for many years, and there were sufficient in reserve in 1914 for them to be brought out and re-barrelled to 8mm calibre. The rifle was also adopted by Greece in 1876.

GUEDES

Lieutenant Guedes Dias of the Portuguese Army designed a drop-block lever-action rifle in the early 1880s, and a small number were made in 11mm calibre in Portugal for military tests. During the course of these tests the news of the forthcoming French adoption of a small calibre smokeless cartridge caused the Portuguese Army to ask Dias to redesign his rifle around an 8mm smokeless cartridge. This he did, and in order to speed up supply the manufacture was contracted to **Steyr** of Austria in 1885. However, in 1886 the Portuguese changed their minds and decided to adopt the **Kropatschek** rifle, cancelling their contract with Steyr. Steyr was left with several thousand rifles on its hands which were eventually disposed of to the Boers in South Africa in the late 1890s.

GUIDE LAMP

A division of General Motors, the Guide Lamp company was concerned with the manufacture of automobile lighting equipment, and had developed metal-pressing techniques for the rapid production of headlamps and similar

items. In this capacity it was approached in 1942 to manufacture the Liberator pistol and produced one million pistols in three months. Probably the only pistol on record which could be manufactured faster than it could be loaded and fired. The company later applied its metal-pressing expertise to the production of the M3 submachine gun.

HAENEL

The C. & G. Haenel Gewehr-und Waffenfabrik of Suhl, Germany, was established in 1840 but was a light general engineering company – the 'Waffen' part of the title came much later. Its first appearance in the military arms field appears to have been a contract to manufacture the Reichsrevolver of 1879, when it formed a partnership with the sporting gun manufacturer Schilling and set up a separate workshop to make the revolvers. The bicycle craze then occupied Haenel for some year, but it appears to have returned to the firearms business around the turn of the century, building sporting rifles around the bolt action of the Mauser M1888 rifle.

During World War I Haenel was busy making Gewehr 98 rifles under contract from **Mauser**. In 1921 Hugo **Schmeisser**, son of Louis, joined the company which then produced Schmeisser's patented 6.35mm pocket automatic pistol for several years. Towards the end of the 1920s Haenel moved into the air rifle field and rapidly made a reputation for high quality work.

During World War II the company was again involved in production for the military, notably making the MP38 and MP40 submachine guns.

At the end of the war Suhl was in the Russian Zone of Occupation, which later became East Germany, and the company was absorbed into the state-owned arms co.-operative. The position since the reunification of Germany is not entirely clear, but it seems probable that Haenel has regained its identity and trademarks and is returning to the manufacture of air weapons.

HECKLER & KOCH

This company set up in business in the mid-1950s in the old **Mauser** factory in Oberndorf-am-Neckar, which had been totally dismantled by the French as part of the reparations process after the war. H&K began by making a pocket pistol and then obtained a contract from the German Army to develop the **CETME**-inspired design of delayed blowback rifle which Artillerie-Inrichtingen of the Netherlands had offered to Germany. The result of this was the G3 rifle, a highly successful design which was adopted as the standard German Army rifle and was also acquired by many countries outside Germany.

Knowing a good thing when they saw one, Heckler & Koch took the roller-locked delayed blowback mechanism of the rifle and adapted it to a variety of weapons – pistols, submachine guns, rifles and machine guns. The company was among the first European gunmakers to embrace the 5.56mm cartridge and produced scaled-down versions of the G3 in the mid-1960s, although it was to be rather later than that before the idea caught on.

In the early 1970s H&K began work, under its chief designer Tilo Moller, on the G11 caseless cartridge rifle, a development which H&K brought to a brilliant completion, only to have the rug pulled from under its feet when the German government, desperate for money to rebuild former East Germany after the re-unification, slashed the defence budget and cancelled the contract for the G11 weapon.

The company's hopes, and financial future, were inextricably tied up in the G11, and when that collapsed, so did the company. It was bought by British Aerospace/ Royal Ordnance and now runs more or less autonomously, with subsidiary factories in Britain and the USA.

HENRY

Benjamin Tyler Henry (1821–1898). Born in New Hampshire, Henry was trained as a machinist in a gun-making firm and after serving his apprenticeship worked as a journeyman for several gunmakers.

In 1842 Henry went to work for the firm of Robbins, Kendall & Lawrence, where he worked on the 'Volition' repeating rifle, a primitive lever-action breech-loader using a self-contained cartridge. At the same works, Horace **Smith** and Daniel **Wesson** worked on a further improvement of this rifle which they called the 'Volcanic'. They later left to form the Volcanic Repeating Firearms Co. which eventually went into liquidation. The remains of that company were bought by Oliver **Winchester** and in 1857 he hired Tyler Henry to become his chief engineer and take on the further development of the Volcanic.

Henry decided that the first step would be to improve the ammunition, and he jettisoned the Volcanic self-propelled bullet and developed a large-calibre rimfire cartridge. He then re-designed the rifle so as to operate with this cartridge, using a tubular magazine beneath the barrel, loaded from the front end. Henry patented this new combination in 1860, and it went into production in time to see some degree of service during the Civil War. He later improved the design and this became the Winchester Model 1866 rifle.

Henry then left Winchester's employment and set up his own general engineering business in New Haven, which he ran until his death.

HOTCHKISS

Benjamin Berkeley Hotchkiss (1826–1885). Born in Connecticut, he served his apprenticeship as a millwright and then worked in his father's hardware factory. He became interested in firearms and began designing and patenting various improvements.

Hotchkiss' first major weapon success was a multiple-barrelled weapon similar to a **Gatling** gun, but of larger calibre, which was widely adopted by navies. He had designed this whilst working in France during the Franco-Prussian War, and after his return to the USA he developed a bolt-action magazine rifle which was bought by **Winchester** and produced in both military and sporting guise.

During all this time Hotchkiss had maintained an interest in artillery, and in 1882 he formed the Hotchkiss Company and began developing a number of designs for light artillery and rapid-firing guns of various sorts, which were subsequently widely adopted both by navies and armies. However, he never saw this success, since he died suddenly during a visit to Paris in 1885, and the subsequent development of his ideas was carried out by other

hands.

IBM

IBM is world-famous today for computers, but before the electronic era, and then called the International Business Machines Corporation, the company had made its name by manufacturing mechanical calculators and office machines, so that precision engineering was a familiar area. As a result, during World War II IBM became a major arms manufacturer for a short time, making 346,500 US M1 Carbines in 1943–44 at its factory in Poughkeepsie, New York. IBM then returned to hoeing its own particular row.

IMBEL

Indústrias de Materiais Bélico de Brasil; Brazilian national armaments factory. Currently manufactures **Colt** pattern pistols and **FN** pattern rifles under licence.

INA

Indústrias Nacional de Armas, São Paulo, Brazil; earlier name for what is now IMBEL (*see above*). Manufactured various arms including **Mauser** rifles, **Madsen** sub-machine guns and **Smith & Wesson** pattern revolvers in the period 1945–70

INAGAKI

Iwakichi Inagaki was a Japanese engineer who, after working in the **Koishikawa** arsenal, retired in 1924 and opened a gunsmithing business in Tokyo. In the late 1930s he concentrated on military contract work and in 1941 developed a 7.65mm blowback automatic pistol. Although turned down by the Japanese Army, several hundred were purchased by the Imperial Navy for use by pilots.

INGLIS

John Inglis & Co. of Toronto, Canada, was a general engineering company with no particular interest in firearms until 1938, when the company contracted to make 5000 Bren light machine guns, the first of which was proved in March 1940. Between then and 1943 some 120,000 guns were made for the Canadian and British Armies in .303 calibre, and from 1943 to 1945 a further 43,000 were made in 7.92mm **Mauser** calibre for supply to the Chinese Nationalist Army.

In 1942 the company received a further contract to manufacture the **Browning** Model 1935 automatic pistol for supply to the Chinese Army. Drawings were not available, and six **FN**-made pistols were received from China and 'reverse engineered' to produce working drawings. Eventually 151,816 pistols were made, some being supplied to the British and Canadian Armies. With the completion of this contract Inglis closed the production line and left the firearms business.

INGRAM

Submachine guns designed by Gordon Ingram and originally manufactured by the Police Ordnance Company of Los Angeles. This firm made the Model 6 in .45 calibre and the Model 7 in .38 Super calibre. Both were well-made, simple blowback weapons and both achieved some degree of success, being adopted by various police and military forces. Ingram left the firm in 1952, after which it closed down. Ingram then developed the Model 8, an improved Model 6, and sold the design to Thailand. Based upon this, in 1959 he developed the Model 9, which was a slightly improved 8 with a telescoping wire stock.

In 1963 he developed the Model 10, an extremely compact and simple weapon which could be fitted with a silencer. In 1964 Ingram joined the Erquiaga Arms Co. of Industry, California, and there developed the M10. This firm collapsed in 1965 and Ingram then contracted with Sionics Co., Atlanta, Ga., to manufacture the gun. This firm moved to Powder Springs, Georgia, and Ingram became its Chief Engineer in 1969. Further models, the 11 in .380 and a .45 version of the 10, were also made, production commencing in 1969.

In 1970 Sionics was bought out by the Military Armaments Company (MAC) but there were differences between management and Ingram which resulted in long legal altercations. In 1975 MAC went bankrupt, the stock of weapons and parts being sold at auction.

Rights in the design then appear to have been acquired by SWD Inc., of Atlanta, Georgia., who offered it as the Cobray for a sort time before vanishing. Other companies have since attempted to revive production with varying degrees of success, but it appears that very little manufacture took place after about 1983.

The M-10 weapon was a reasonable design, but sales were relatively poor because of poor management, constant changes of policy and ownership and futile pursuit of new designs. Little more than 10,000 weapons of all calibres were ever produced, and the Ingram has probably seen more employment in adventure movies than in real life.

INLAND

The Inland Manufacturing Division of General Motors, at Dayton, Ohio, was another of the many non-firearms-related companies which turned to manufacturing weapons for the US Government in World War II. In this case they made about 3 million US M1, M1A1 and M2 Carbines in 1942–45.

In addition, though, the company also developed the M2 submachine gun, designed by George Hyde, and brought it up to the point of acceptance for service, after which the manufacturing contract was given to another company in order to spread the manufacturing base as widely as possible.

The company was also involved in the development phase of the M3 submachine gun, another Hyde design, being largely responsible for those elements of the design which bore upon the ease of production. Again, once the development phase was over the manufacturing contract went elsewhere, since by that time Inland was fully committed to carbine production.

INSAS

Indian Small Arms System. Developed in the mid-1980s, the INSAS consists of an assault rifle in 5.56mm calibre and a light machine gun, also in 5.56mm, using similar basic components. The design shows a blend of features taken from other weapons; the receiver and pistol grip show **Kalashnikov** influence, the butt, gas regulator and flash hider are based on the **FN**-FAL, the fore-end has

echoes of the **ArmaLite** AR-15, and the forward cocking handle is based upon **Heckler & Koch** practice.

The weapons are gas operated, a piston propelling a bolt carrier carrying the usual front-lug rotating bolt. The machine gun version has a longer and heavier barrel and a bipod which appears to have been copied from the adjustable Bren bipod.

Issue of these weapons was to begin in 1994 with a first batch of 7000 rifles, but production was delayed since there was no indigenous source of manufacture for the 5.56mm ammunition which, although generally based on the SS109 type, is not to the NATO specification.

IISHAPORE

Indian government arsenal, originally founded in 1794 by the East India Company as a powder mill. Taken over by the government after the 1857 Mutiny, in 1902 the powder mill was closed down and the factory re-organised to become an 'out-station' of the Royal Small Arms Factory, **Enfield**, for the manufacture of **Lee**-Enfield rifles. Later manufactured **Vickers-Berthier** machine guns. Taken over by the Indian government after Partition, it made **FN**-FAL rifles under licence and is currently making the **INSAS** (Indian Small Arms System) 5.56mm rifle and light machine gun.

ISRAEL MILITARY INDUSTRIES

A trading company which markets the products of various Israeli government munitions manufacturers, covering small arms as well as electronic equipment, sights and similar products. In the civilian market it operates under the trade-name of 'Samson'. The Uzi sub-machine gun, **Galil** rifle, Negev light machine gun and Desert Eagle and Jericho pistols are sold by IMI and they also promoted the 9 x 21mm pistol cartridge which thus became generally known as the '9mm IMI'. In 1993 the company was re-organised and became the Ta'as Israel Industries Company, but this change was apparently ignored by the rest of the arms world, who continued to refer to it as IMI, and in 1996 they bowed to popular choice and reverted to its original name.

ITHACA GUN Co.

Originally known as the W.H. Baker Gunworks, this company was founded in 1883 in Ithaca, New York. In 1889 Baker died and the company was re-named the Ithaca Gun Company. From its inception, the company's speciality has been shotguns, but for a short period in World War II the company also made **Colt** M1911A1 .45 automatic pistols on contract for the US armed forces.

IZHEVSK RIFLE FACTORY

A Russian arms manufacturer which was founded as an ammunition factory in 1807 and later expanded to make small arms. It has been principally concerned with the manufacture of military rifles and machine guns but has also produced a small number of .22 competition pistols, both single-shot and semi-automatic.

In the early 1990s it was privatised as the Izhevsk Machinery Factory 'Izhmashzavod' and has since also seemingly become involved in a number of joint-stock companies set up in co.-operation with the leaders of the various former Soviet design bureaus. In its new guise it has developed a 5.45mm military rifle to compete against the **Kalashnikov** designs for military acceptance. This, the AS-94 assault rifle, claims to be a delayed blowback, though it obviously has a gas cylinder beneath the barrel, claims to fire a two-round burst at 1800 rounds per minute, and claims outstanding accuracy at 1000 yards.

JANUSZCZEWSKI

A Polish ordnance engineer who came to Britain in 1939 and was part of the 'Polish Design Team' at the Royal Small Arms Factory, **Enfield** Lock. He adopted the name Kenneth Jansen on naturalisation, and in the late 1940s developed the EM1 and EM2 rifles. He later emigrated to Canada and then to the USA where he continued designing firearms and became the Director of Weapons Research & Development for the **Winchester** company.

JOHNSON

Melvin M. Johnson (1909–70) was a law graduate who found firearms more interesting, Johnson became an officer in the US Marine Reserve and in the early 1930s began designing an automatic rifle, followed by a light machine gun. Both were recoil-operated weapons; the barrel recoiled a short distance with the locked bolt, after which the bolt was rotated to unlock and blowback action of the cartridge case completed the opening movement. The rifle used a five-shot rotary magazine which was loaded from the standard .30-06 five-shot charger or with single rounds whether the bolt was open or closed. It was a good design, but by the time Johnson had perfected it the US Army had committed itself to the **Garand** M1 rifle, and since the Johnson showed no advantage great enough to warrant changing, the design was turned down.

It was later purchased by the Dutch government who ordered 50,000 for their forces in the Dutch East Indies in 1940. The Japanese occupation of the East Indies prevented the delivery of most of these, and the balance was taken by the US Marine Corps, since in 1941 they were having difficulty in obtaining Garand rifles. Numbers of these were later passed across to the Brazilian Army contingent operating in Italy in 1944.

The machine gun used the same mechanism as the rifle but was fed by a box magazine inserted into the left side of the receiver. It showed no improvement over the existing **Browning** Automatic Rifle and could not be adapted to belt feed, which the army demanded on any replacement for the BAR, and was therefore not officially adopted. As with the rifle, the Dutch ordered a quantity for the East Indies and, as with the rifle, most of these were taken by the US Marine Corps.

JONES

An inventor, of Philadelphia, USA., Owen Jones designed and patented the extraction system used in the **Enfield** Mark 1 revolver in which tipping the barrel down caused the cylinder to move forward, away from a fixed extraction plate. He later designed a magazine feed for the **Martini** rifle action, 2000 of which were purchased by the Royal Navy in 1885.

JÖRGENSEN

Erik Jörgensen was the Works Manager of the gun factory forming part of the Norwegian Arsenal at Kongsberg in the 1880s. He was associated with O.H.J. **Krag** in the design of the various Krag-Jörgensen rifles and also appears to have been a partner, with Krag, in the Krag Jörgensen Rifle Company which obtained various magazine rifle patents in 1898–1900.

JOSLYN CARBINE

Also called the 'Monkey-Tail Carbine' from the curled handle of the breech mechanism, this weapon was made by A.H. Waters of Milbury, Massachusetts, to a design by B.F. Joslyn in 1855–56. About 1000 were made, and during the same period a few hundred rifles using the same breech system were also made.

Waters went out of business before 1860, and when Joslyn received an order for more weapons during the Civil War he set up his own manufactory in Stonington, Connecticut. Here he made some 16,500 Model 1862 and 1864 carbines, single shot breech-loaders with a 22-inch barrel. A few of the first 1862 models used the standard percussion cap system, but the greater part of the production was in .56-50 Spencer rimfire calibre.

KALASHNIKOV

Mikhail Timofeivitch Kalashnikov was born in 1920 in a remote area of Siberia and at the age of 17 obtained employment as a railway clerk. He was conscripted in 1939 and became a tank driver. When the Germans invaded Russia in 1941 he was a senior sergeant, and tank commander. He was awarded the Order of the Red Star for bravery in combat, and was later severely wounded in the fighting around Bryansk in early October 1941.

Whilst convalescing he amused himself by designing a submachine gun. He submitted the design for approval, and although it was refused, it was thought to be of sufficient merit to warrant sending Kalashnikov to a design office to nourish his talent. He later designed a carbine, which was turned down, and was then given one of the new 7.62 x 39mm cartridges and invited to design a rifle around it. His first attempt was not viable, but he subsequently refined his ideas until he achieved an acceptable design which became the AK-47 rifle.

The AK-47 was improved into the AKM, and when the Soviets decided to reduce their rifle calibre to 5.45mm the Kalashnikov design was simply scaled-down. The basic mechanism was applied to a variety of machine guns, and after the de-Sovietisation of Russia, Kalashnikov formed a joint stock company and produced a number of modernised designs, although they are still recognisably 'sons of AK-47'. Whether he will have any commercial success with these remains to be seen.

KIRALY

Pal Kiraly, a Hungarian, is a somewhat shadowy figure with a long association with firearms. He appears first in 1912 as patentee of a two-part breech bolt mechanism which lies at the heart of a delayed blowback operating system. He next appears working for **SIG** of Switzerland in the 1920s, where he collaborated with Ende (another mysterious figure) in the design of the KE-7 machine gun. He then developed the SIG MKMO series of submachine guns, using his two-part bolt mechanism.

Kiraly next appeared as an employee of the **Danuvia** company of Budapest, trying to interest the British Army, via the **BSA** Company, in a submachine gun of similar form to the MKMO. On being turned down by the British, he went back to Hungary and produced the Model 39M and 43M submachine guns for the Danuvia firm.

Kiraly then vanished once more and re-appeared in the Dominican Republic in the late 1950s operating their national arsenal and producing the Cristóbal 62 carbine. This venture ended in the mid-1960s and Mr. Kiraly disappeared once again.

KNIL

Koninklijke Nederlandsch Indisch Leger; Royal Dutch Indies Legion; that branch of the Dutch armed forces established in the 1880s to garrison the Dutch East Indies. Although generally issued with the same weapons as the Netherlands Army, the KNIL occasionally used variant models of pistols and carbines specifically adapted for their use in tropical climates. These, and any special ammunition required, are identified by the marking KNIL, which is sometimes found on the weapons. The force was disbanded in 1949 when Indonesia was given independence.

KNORR-BREMSE

A German engineering company of Berlin, principally concerned with the manufacture of automobile brake components. In the mid-1930s, attracted by the prospects of lucrative contracts due to the re-armament of the German Army, it purchased the patents of a Swedish machine gun, the LH33, and manufactured it under their own name. A gas-operated, magazine-fed light machine gun, it was not particularly reliable and was refused by the Army, though numbers were bought by the Waffen-SS as training weapons to cover the interim period before supplies of the MG34 became plentiful. They were later offloaded on to the various 'ethnic' SS Legions, notably the Latvian, by whom they were eventually used up.

KOISHIKAWA

Japanese arsenal in Tokyo was established 1870 to make **Murata** rifles. Subsequently it made **Arisaka** rifles, machine guns, artillery and other equipment but was damaged in the 1923 earthquake. In order to remove the principal military manufacturing facility from the earthquake zone the various manufacturing sections were removed to other arsenals in subsequent years, the small arms facility being moved to **Kokura** arsenal. Koishikawa ceased manufacturing operations in 1932.

KOKURA

Japanese arsenal which took over responsibility for small arms from **Koishikawa** in the late 1920s. Manufacture of **Arisaka** rifles began in 1932, and of 7.7mm Type 99 rifles in 1940.

KRAG

Ole Hermann Johannes Krag (1837–1912) joined the Norwegian Army artillery in 1857. He exhibited considerable proficiency in the design of small arms and spent almost all his service in the Kongsberg Arsenal, becoming its Director in 1880. By 1885 he had become a General, Master of the Ordnance, and retired in 1902.

Krag patented a number of magazine rifle designs, but his principal claim to fame was the magazine rifle he developed in conjunction with **Jörgensen** and which was adopted by the Danish, Norwegian and United States armies in the 1889–95 period. The unique feature was the Krag magazine which opened at the side of the action and was fed horizontally with loose cartridges; on closing the hinged door of the magazine, pressure was applied to the cartridges by a sprung follower to push them across the action beneath the bolt and then deliver them up the left side of the bolt to a feed way alongside the bolt.

KRNKA

Karel Krnka was a gifted and prolific designer, the son of Sylvester Krnka, a Bohemian gunsmith and inventor of some distinction in the field of military rifles and ammunition. Karel was born in 1858, served with the Austro-Hungarian Army and developed various rifle improvements before leaving military service and moving to England where he became the chief engineer for the short-lived **Gatling** Arms & Ammunition Company in Birmingham.

When this firm collapsed in 1890 Krnka returned to Prague and spent some years as a patent agent. In 1898 he became manager of the Georg Roth cartridge factory and in conjunction with Roth patented a number of automatic pistol designs. Roth died in 1909 and Krnka moved to the Hirtenberger Cartridge Company and remained there until 1922, when he moved to Czechoslovakia and became a designer with the Ceskoslovenska Zbrojovka (*see* Brno), working on automatic rifle designs until his death in 1926.

KROPATSCHEK

Alfred Kropatschek (1838–1911). He entered the Austro-Hungarian artillery as a cadet in 1854 and in 1856–59 attended the Artillery School. After a brief spell of regimental service he returned to sit the advanced course, and, as a captain, was appointed to a post on the Budapest Arsenal. In subsequent years he sat on a number of arms commissions.

He was responsible for the alterations which resulted in the **Gasser**-Kropatschek revolver, and in 1874 he submitted a design of repeating rifle with tubular magazine which was adopted by the French and Hungarian governments. In 1877 he became the Commandant of the Artillery Academy. He then developed various artillery equipments, attained the rank of general, was knighted and loaded with a variety of honours for his versatility. continuing as gunmakers until 1945.

LEBEL

Nicolas Lebel (1838–1891) was an officer in the French Army. He was appointed to command an infantry training school, where he began to take an interest in firearms design. Promoted to lieutenant-colonel, he was appointed to a commission set up to design a new rifle for the infantry. He concentrated on the development of a small-calibre jacketed cartridge with smokeless powder propellant, and also collaborated on the design of the rifle. The eventual weapon, the Mle 1886, has always, therefore, been known as the Lebel rifle.

LEE

James Paris Lee (1831–1904) was born in Hawick, Roxburghshire, Scotland. His family emigrated to Canada when he was an infant. After being apprenticed as a clock-maker under his father, he left home in about 1850 and travelled to the USA, settling in Wisconsin.

Here Lee became interested in firearms, and in 1862 he obtained patents for a breech-loading conversion to the US Army's Springfield rifle. Several other patents followed, but the design for which Lee is remembered is that of the bolt action with removable box magazine which he patented in 1879 and which subsequently became the basis of the British service Lee-**Metford** and Lee-**Enfield** rifles. He subsequently took out patents improving this basic design, and in 1893 he patented a straight-pull bolt action which was adopted by the US Navy.

LEWIS

Colonel Isaac Newton Lewis, US Army (1858–1931). Lewis graduated from West Point in 1880 and was commissioned into the Coast Artillery. He developed various fire control instruments, including the Lewis Depression Position Finder of 1891. He was the Recorder, Board of Ordnance & Fortification in 1898; Instructor and Director, Coast Artillery School Fortress Monroe 1904–11. He then retired due to ill-health in 1913.

During his last years in the army he had been approached by the Automatic Arms Co. to examine and perfect Samuel MacLean's machine gun design, and there is a strong suspicion that his 'ill-health' was a euphemism for a severe disagreement between Lewis and General Crozier, Chief of Ordnance, over the propriety of working on a commercial design whilst Lewis was still a serving officer. (This apparently ignored Crozier's successful development of the Buffington-Crozier seacoast gun carriage during his service days.)

Whatever the case, after Lewis' retirement he went to work for the Automatic Gun Co., and perfected the design. But when it was offered to the US Army, Crozier again intervened and it was refused. Lewis then obtained the rights to the design and went to Belgium where he set up a company to manufacture the gun.

LITHGOW

Australian government arms factory, Lithgow, NSW. Built 1908–12 to manufacture **Lee-Enfield** rifles, moved on to **Vickers** machine guns in 1920 and Bren guns in 1941. During 1920–39 numbers of commercial .22 rimfire and centrefire rifles were made and .410 shotguns using the Lee bolt action. The factory was expanded by subsidiaries in 1941–45, but after the war production reverted to Lithgow and the last Lee-Enfields were made *ca* 1956.

Licenced production of the **FN-FAL** in its Australian form took place in 1958–86, after which the production line was rebuilt to permit the licenced manufacture of the Austrian **Steyr AUG** rifle as the Australian F88.

LLAMA

Trade name adopted by the company originally founded in 1904 as Gabilondos y Urresti of Eibar, Spain. It began by making cheap revolvers and then in 1914 produced a cheap 7.65mm automatic pistol called the 'Ruby', which was simply a copy of the **Browning** Model of 1903. The 'Ruby' was of reasonably good quality and the French Army, desperate for pistols, gave Gabilondo an open-ended contract in 1915, calling for the delivery of 10,000 pistols a month until further notice. Gabilondo was unable to cope and sub-contracted much of the work, which eventually led to the rash of cheap pocket pistols which appeared from Eibar in the 1920s.

After 1919 the firm moved to Elgoeibar, abandoned the cheap 'Ruby' and set about making a better quality copy of the Browning 1910 model called the 'Danton'. In 1931, however, the company abandoned that design and appeared with a completely new range of pistols based upon the **Colt** M1911A1, some with locked breeches, some pure blowbacks, under the name 'Llama'. These were of good quality, and after the Civil War Gabilondo was one of the few companies permitted to resume manufacture of pistols.

Its products since then have been of the highest quality, and all have appeared under the Llama name; the company formally changed its title to 'Llama-Gabilondo' in 1936.

LOEWE

Ludwig Loewe (1837–1886). Loewe owned a small engineering factory which made machine tools in the 1860s, and when the mass-produced sewing machine appeared, he decided to concentrate on this. He went to the USA to study methods of manufacture and acquire machine tools, returned and began making sewing machines in January 1870.

The outbreak of the Franco-Prussian War later that year brought Loewe some contracts to make small arms, and he arrived at the conclusion that small arms were likely to be more profitable than sewing machines. His first major contract was for the manufacture and supply of **Smith & Wesson** revolvers to Russia. He then acquired a controlling interest in a bank which held about 40 percent of **Mauser**'s shares, so that he had an influence on Mauser's affairs and obtained contracts from them. Next he began acquiring companies making ammunition, powder and component parts, until, in 1896, his successors combined all their holdings to form the Deutsche Waffen- und Munitionsfabrik (**DWM**).

LONG BRANCH

Canadian small arms factory set up in 1940 in Long Branch, Ontario. Manufactured **Lee-Enfield** No 4 Mark 1 rifles, Sten guns, **Browning** .300 and .303 machine guns and 20mm Polsten cannon. Taken over by Canadian Arsenals Ltd in 1946, it continued making Lee-Enfield and **FN-FAL** rifles until its closure in June 1976.

LUGER

Georg Luger (1849–1923). Born at Steinach, in the Austrian Tyrol, Luger served in the Austro-Hungarian Militia in 1865–72, when he left and married. He then became a railway engineer and in this work became acquainted with **Mannlicher** and worked with him on the conversion of the Austrian **Werndl** rifle into a magazine weapon. He also spent some time studying designs for an automatic rifle.

In 1891 Luger moved to Ludwig **Loewe** & Co. in Berlin, and shortly afterwards Hugo **Borchardt** came to

Loewe with his design for an automatic pistol. The Borchardt pistol went into production in 1893 but was not a commercial success. What was more serious was that it was not a military success either, and this has been ascribed to the fact that Borchardt had no military experience and thus, having produced a pistol which worked, could not understand why the military wanted alterations to make it a more practical military weapon.

In 1895 the Borchardt was tested by the Swiss and rejected; the Loewe management then apparently asked Luger to overhaul the design and turn it into a combat-worthy weapon. This he did, in a series of steps, until he finally arrived at what we might call the definitive model, the German Army's Pistole '08. Luger continued to devise improvements to the design, though these were largely paper exercises, until his death.

MADSEN

The Madsen machine gun is named after the Danish Minister of War at the time of its introduction in the early 1900s. The actual inventor was probably a man called Rasmussen, an engineer at the Royal Danish Arsenal in Copenhagen. He designed it as an automatic rifle, and a small number were made and issued to the Danish Marines in about 1896. It was unsatisfactory, was withdrawn, and reworked into a light machine gun, the first such weapon to be made.

This appeared in 1904 and was immediately bought by Russia who put it to use in the Russo-Japanese War with good effect. From then on the Madsen sold steadily, was employed all over the world, and yet never achieved the distinction of being adopted as the official machine gun of any major army. The design remained essentially unchanged until production ceased some time in the 1950s.

The weapons were made by a syndicate, founded in 1896, called the Dansk Rekylriffel Syndikat. It occasionally ventured into other weapons, notably a 20mm anti-aircraft cannon, but for most of its existence was satisfied to produce the Madsen machine gun. In 1936 the name was changed to the Dansk Industri Syndikat and after 1945 it attempted to promote an automatic rifle and a new medium machine gun, though without success.

The syndicate ceased the manufacture of arms in the early 1960s and moved into general engineering, though it still makes machine gun mounts and tripods of various types.

MAKAROV

Nikolai Fyedorovitch Makarov was born in 1914, the son of a railway machinist. In 1929 he entered an apprentice school and specialised in metal-work and in 1931–35 he worked in a railway locomotive repair shop. He then took further technical education, which was completed in 1941, subsequently spending the war years in a factory manufacturing the PPSh submachine gun. He then began work on his design of automatic pistol which was accepted into service in 1951.

MANNLICHER

Ferdinand, Ritter von Mannlicher (1848–1904). Although renowned for his firearms, von Mannlicher was actually a railway engineer, working all his life as a designer for the Austrian State Railways. A visit to the World Exposition in Philadelphia in 1876, ostensibly to study railway equipment developments, introduced him to firearms and he then began to design a repeating rifle.

From 1880 onwards Mannlicher produced a variety of designs using tubular and box magazines, turn and straight-pull bolts. Many of these were commercially successful, being manufactured by **Steyr** and others, and one was adopted by the Austro-Hungarian Army in 1886, to be followed by adoption by many other armies. Mannlicher then turned his attention to automatic weapons, developing a self-loading rifle in 1885 and a number of self-loading pistols.

MARTINI

Friedrich Martini was a Swiss who took the falling-block breech system designed by Peabody in the USA and improved it; the original Peabody used a block with a firing pin which was struck by an external hammer. Martini did away with the hammer and arranged a self-cocking striker mechanism inside the block which was cocked as the block was opened and closed. It was widely adopted in Europe – perhaps the best-known use of the system being in the British Martini-**Henry** rifles – and is still manufactured today for target rifles, since the design gives a very short lock time.

MASON

William Mason was a **Colt** employee who devised several detail mechanisms incorporated into Colt designs. Among these were an improved ejector, a cylinder locking system, a loading gate, and the double-action trigger mechanism of the Lightning revolver, a design generally considered not to be one of Colt's better achievements. He was on a better roll when he patented the swing-out cylinder subsequently adopted by Colt for all its later revolver designs.

MAUSER

Peter Paul Mauser (1838–1914) and Wilhelm Mauser (1834–82). The two Mauser brothers were both trained as gunsmiths and worked at the Royal Württemberg Arms Factory. Peter devised his bolt action, and after an abortive and salutary experience with a would-be sharp American entrepreneur, the two brothers returned to Oberndorf and offered their rifle to the Prussian authorities.

They had no success until, in the wake of the Franco-Prussian War which revealed a few defects in the **Dreyse** rifle, their design was adopted for the new German Army as the Model 1871 rifle. In 1872 the brothers set up their factory in Oberndorf, and the rest is history. Peter Paul was the inventor and engineer, Wilhelm the salesman and administrator, and they formed an ideal working partnership until Wilhelm's untimely and early death.

MAXIM

Hiram Stevens Maxim (1840–1916). Hiram Maxim was originally a coach-builder, but he studied at technical school and eventually his inventions and designs reached into every branch of engineering. In 1881 Maxim attended an exhibition in Paris where he was reputedly advised by a friend to 'invent something that would enable these fool Europeans to kill each other quicker.'

Maxim took a small workshop in Hatton Garden, London, and began experimenting with various firearms, eventually producing the world's first automatic machine gun in 1884. He demonstrated this to some British officers and, guided by their comments, improved the weapon and in 1885 perfected his design into the basic Maxim machine gun.

MAXIM GUN Co. Ltd & successors

This was set up in 1884 by Hiram **Maxim** in order to market the Maxim machine gun and also license the patents to suitable applicants. The Chairman of the Board was Albert **Vickers**. A factory was prepared at Crayford, Kent, by 1888 but the firm was then absorbed by the newly-formed Maxim-**Nordenfelt** Gun and Ammunition Co. Ltd, the managing director being Sigmund Loewe, brother of Ludwig **Loewe**. The company then manufactured and promoted both Vickers and Nordenfelt machine guns until 1897, when it was absorbed by Vickers, which then assumed a new title of Vickers, Sons and Maxim. The whole series of transactions was very involved but it serves to show the interdependence between Vickers, Maxim, Nordenfelt and (via the Loewes) **DWM** and **Mauser**.

METFORD

William Ellis Metford (1824–1899). Like Ferdinand **Mannlicher**, William Metford was actually a railway engineer, but he had a wide range of interests which took in pyrotechnics and firearms, with the result that he invented rockets and bullets as a pastime. In 1857 he was appointed Chief Engineer to the East Indian Railway company, but ill-health led him to give up the post and return to England where he thereafter busied himself with designing rifle barrels and bullets. His rifled barrels became famous for their accuracy and were the most popular for target rifles until the end of the 19th century. His name is, of course, perpetuated in the **Lee**-Metford rifle, for which he designed the barrel and rifling in order to resist gunpowder fouling.

MONDRAGON

General Manuel Mondragon of the Mexican Army began designing an automatic rifle in the 1890s, and finally obtained a United States patent in 1907. Since there were no adequate facilities in Mexico and no US manufacturer was interested, he was forced to seek a European manufacturer, and the weapons were eventually produced by **SIG** in Switzerland.

The Mondragon used gas, tapped from the barrel, to drive an actuating piston to the rear and open the bolt, a now common-place method. Locking was achieved by lugs on the bolt, which was rotated by projections on the bolt operating handle engaging in cam tracks cut into the bolt body; there is some degree of resemblance between this and the Schmidt-**Rubin** straight-pull bolt action. As with many automatic designs of the period, it was possible to disconnect the bolt from the gas mechanism and thus turn the rifle into a manually operated straight-pull bolt-action weapon, a proviso often insisted upon by military authorities with small faith in the reliability of any automatic mechanism.

Some 400 rifles had been delivered to Mexico when

the 1911 Revolution removed President Diaz, and the new government repudiated the contract with SIG, leaving the Swiss company with the balance of the 4000-rifle order on its hands. SIG attempted to sell them to whoever was interested, but at the outbreak of war in 1914 about 3000 of the rifles were still on SIG's shelves and these were bought by Germany for issue to aviators as the Fliegerselbstladekarabine Modell 1915. Most of these were fitted with a 30-shot helical 'snail' magazine, similar in principle to that used on the **Luger** pistol and **Bergmann** submachine-gun. After being replaced on aircraft by machine guns, some of the rifles were sent for infantry use but the mud of the Western Front soon defeated them and the survivors were withdrawn. A large number were issued to the German Navy with which most survived until the war's end.

MOSIN

Colonel Sergei Ivanovitch Mosin, Imperial Russian Artillery (1849–1902). After graduating from the Artillery Academy he was appointed to Tula Arsenal as an assistant superintendent and then Superintendent. In 1882 he designed an eight-shot magazine, and then, in conjunction with Emile **Nagant** of Liège, a magazine rifle which was adopted as the Model 1891. The design was subsequently improved and remained in Russian service until the 1950s.

MURATA

Major Tsuneyoshi Murata was appointed to superintend the manufacture of Japanese small arms in the late 1870s, and his brief also covered the development of a rifle to replace the collection of European weapons which had been acquired. Murata studied the various weapons and then produced a single-shot bolt action rifle based upon the French **Gras** design in 1880. This was adopted, and some variant models followed.

In 1887, after the appearance of the French **Lebel**, Murata designed a new rifle in 8mm calibre with a tubular magazine under the barrel which became the Japanese standard in 1889. However the Sino-Japanese War of 1894 showed up some defects in the Murata design, and a fresh commission was appointed, resulting in the development of the **Arisaka** rifle and retirement of the Murata.

NAGANT

Emile and Leon Nagant were brothers who went into the firearms business in Liège, Belgium, some time in the 1870s. They set up independently as Emile Nagant and as the Fabrique d'Armes Leon Nagant, but they collaborated in design and marketing. Emile took out a patent in 1879 for various improvements in solid-framed revolvers, which were incorporated in the Belgian Officers' Model M1878 and later designs, as well as similar revolvers adopted by Argentina, Brazil, Norway and Sweden. He also collaborated with Colonel S.I. **Mosin** of the Imperial Russian Army in the design of the bolt action Mosin-Nagant rifle which, in various forms, armed the bulk of the Russian and Soviet armies until the 1950s.

The brothers appear to have been forward-looking; they were among the original share-holders, and Leon was elected as a director, of Fabrique Nationale when it was set up in July 1889. But in 1894 they sold their shares and resigned, fearful that **FN** was going beyond its original purpose (that of making **Mauser** rifles for the Belgian Army) and setting up in competition with the established gunmakers of Liège.

In 1892 Leon patented a design of gas-seal revolver in which the cylinder was moved forward during the cocking movement of the hammer so that the mouth of the aligned chamber enclosed the coned end of the barrel. This, together with a specially-designed cartridge case which entered the rear end of the barrel, ensured that none of the propelling gas from the cartridge could leak through the gap between chamber and barrel, as was the case with conventional revolvers.

The brothers marketed this design with some success, and, probably due to Emile's connection with Mosin, were able to sell the design to the Russian Army who adopted it as their M1895 revolver. It was a solid-frame, gate-loaded, seven-shot weapon in 7.62mm calibre, issued first as a single-action troopers' model and later as a double action officers' model. The calibre appears to have been chosen so as to permit the use of rifling machinery developed for the standard 7.62mm rifle.

The first supplies of this revolver were made in Liège and shipped to Russia, whilst the brothers made a similar pistol in 7.5mm calibre for commercial sale, but in 1900 the Russian government purchased the patent rights to the revolver outright and put it into production at Tula Arsenal, continuing to produce it until the late 1930s.

This Russian purchase prevented the Nagants from making or selling similar revolvers on the commercial market, and they therefore reverted to the manufacture of conventional solid-frame non-gas-seal pattern revolvers while working on a design for a gas-seal revolver using a side-swinging cylinder. This was finally achieved and marketed in 1910, but by that time the conventional revolver was being made to sufficiently close tolerances to have reduced the gas leak to a minimum and few people were prepared to pay for the extra complication and special ammunition in order to gain perhaps an additional 50 feet per second of velocity. As a result sales were poor and specimens are rare.

However, the firm had already begun to diversify, making surveying instruments, machine tools and motor car components, and in 1910 the brothers decided that the automobile was perhaps a more fruitful source of income and formed a new company, the Fabrique d'Armes et Automobiles Nagant Frères, which managed to survive until World War I closed it down permanently.

NAMBU

Lieutenant-General Kijiro Nambu, Imperial Japanese Army. As a captain he was posted to **Koishikawa** Arsenal in 1897 where he developed the 38th Year Rifle, the Nambu pistols and numerous machine guns, eventually becoming the Superintendent of the Arsenal and retiring in 1924 to form his own company to develop and manufacture firearms.

The Nambu Rifle Mfg Co. was established in 1927. Due, no doubt, to Nambu's military connections, the company appears never to have been short of contract work, making training rifles and machine guns and service weapons, refurbishing service weapons, and developing and manufacturing pistols and other weapons for

military submission. The firm was absorbed by Chuo Kogyu in 1936.

NEUHAUSEN

Name under which products of the Schweizerische Industrie Gesellschaft (**SIG**) of Neuhausen-am-Rheinfalls, Switzerland, were sold in the 1930s. The name is most generally applied to the submachine gun designed by **Kiraly** and manufactured by SIG as the MKMO in 1933–38. The name appears to have been adopted in order to distinguish SIG's commercial products from their official production for the Swiss Army.

NORDENFELT

Torsten Wilhelm Nordenfelt (1842–1920). Born in Orby, Sweden, Nordenfelt started a hardware company in the 1860s, which became highly successful, and in 1872 he was approached by Helge Palmcrantz with a design for a multi-barrel hand-operated machine gun. Nordenfelt set up a company to make the gun, giving it his own name, and it was one of the more successful mechanical designs, in calibres from .303 to one inch. Nordenfelt later built some of the first practical submarines.

In 1888 the Nordenfelt Gun and Ammunition Company merged with **Maxim**'s firm to become the Maxim-Nordenfelt Gun & Ammunition Company. This lasted until 1897 when it was absorbed by **Vickers**, and Nordenfelt resigned, went to Paris, and there set up a design bureau from which he attempted to promote a machine gun designed by a Captain Bergman, a Swedish officer who had no connection with the better-known Theodor **Bergmann**. The Bergman design was a somewhat eccentric weapon which could operated as an automatic or as a mechanical gun. It failed to prosper, and Nordenfelt closed his Paris office, returned to Sweden and shortly afterwards retired.

OBJECTIVE INDIVIDUAL COMBAT WEAPON

Basic infantry weapon currently under investigation by the US Army. It has been decided that the future infantry weapon will have to be a combination capable of firing a conventional 5.56mm bullet for point targets and an explosive air-bursting munition for area targets, and the latter is to be a specially-developed 20mm round carrying an electronic time or distance fuze. The fire control system will incorporate laser range-finding and a computer which will automatically set the 20mm fuze to the appropriate range. As of 1996 two prototypes had been designed, by the AAI Corporation and by **Heckler & Koch**. The former uses side-by-side barrels, the latter an over-and-under configuration. Mock-ups have been displayed but no firm information on performance can yet be offered.

ODKOLEK

Adolf, Freiherr von Odkolek von Augezd, was an officer of the Austro-Hungarian Army who, in 1903, patented a machine gun. He later sold the design to **Hotchkiss**, who developed it into the Hotchkiss machine gun.

OWEN

Mr Evelyn Owen was a mechanically-minded Australian civilian who designed a submachine gun and submitted it to the Army Inventions Board in July 1939. The Army

Board considered it for a rather long time and in January 1941 asked the Lysaght Company, – who were steel sheet rollers and galvanisers – to make a prototype in .38 revolver calibre. There being no .38 ammunition handy, Lysaghts made it in .32 calibre, with a side-feeding magazine, and it worked satisfactorily. They then made others in .45 ACP and .38 calibre, and in June 1941 an order for 100 guns in .38 calibre was given. This went ahead but then it was found that Australian .38 revolver ammunition gave only 590 ft/sec velocity, which was not considered sufficient for a submachine gun.

In September 1941 supplies of 9mm Parabellum ammunition became available, and the design was forthwith changed to this calibre. Three guns were completed in time for the competitive trial between the Owen, the **Thompson** and the Sten. The latter two failed dismally in the mud and sand tests, but the Owen sailed through without a fault.

After a few minor modifications the gun was put into production, but due to a shortage of machine tools it was not until August 1942 that production reached its target of 2000 guns per month. Manufacture continued at Lysaght until September 1944, when the production line was closed down and the tooling sent to the **Lithgow** rifle factory. It is not widely known that the US Army wanted to buy 60,000 Owen guns for its troops in the Pacific but the Australian Ordnance Production Directorate refused; the machine tools were needed elsewhere.

PARKER-HALE

This Birmingham company began as Alfred Gray Parker in 1890, then became A.G. Parker & Co. in 1900. Alfred Hale invested in the firm and provided a design of air pistol which was a commercial success, and the company also converted Lee-Enfield actions into sporting rifles. More importantly it became an acknowledged specialist in sights, especially for target shooting, and developed various training and practice devices including .22 conversion units for **Webley** revolvers.

In 1936 the firm became Parker-Hale Ltd and during World War II manufactured military ammunition and refurbished and repaired service rifles. In the post-war years Parker-Hale returned to the target-shooting field and then began a series of **Lee-Enfield** type sporting rifles once more, following this by a new range of rifles with Santa Barbara **Mauser** actions.

The Parker-Hale Model 82 sniping rifle was adopted by the Australian and Canadian armies. The Model 85 was entered for the British Army's sniping rifle contest in the late 1980s but, whilst being commended, was not selected for service. By that time the civil market for rifles had become extremely small, and the loss of the potentially profitable military contract led the company to cease manufacture of firearms altogether.

In 1992 the complete line of products, including the Model 85 sniping rifle, various sporting rifles and a range of reproduction percussion rifles, was sold to the American company Navy Arms, who then set up a subsidiary called the Gibbs Rifle Company to produce and sell the Parker-Hale line.

PEDERSEN

John D. Pedersen was an engineer and designer who took out a number of patents for automatic and other weapons in the early 1900s. He developed a number of guns for the **Remington** Company, but his name is particularly remembered for the military semi-automatic rifle developed in the 1920s which came very close to being accepted as the US Army's service weapon. He is also known for the 'Pedersen Device' conversion of the Springfield rifle to automatic fire.

The Pedersen rifle used a toggle as a delaying device in a blowback system of operation. The principal drawback was that in order to ensure smooth working and avoid the ever-present danger of separated cases, the ammunition had to be lubricated, and Pedersen developed a perfectly serviceable dry-wax coating for the .276 cartridge which did away with all the difficulties. It seemed highly likely that the Pedersen rifle would be approved for service, but in February 1932 the US Chief of Staff, General Douglas MacArthur, refused to countenance any reduction in calibre below .30 inch. To redesign the Pedersen to work with the standard .30 service cartridge was virtually impossible; to redesign the **Garand** far easier, and as a result work on the Pedersen ceased on 1 June 1932.

Pedersen had, some time previously, interested the **Vickers** company of England in his rifle and had visited England to advise the company during their initial production. Vickers submitted the rifle as the Vickers Automatic Rifle to the Small Arms Committee in 1929, and this was so successful that further trials took place in 1930–33. But the British Army had little enough time for lubricated ammunition, and when the US Army turned down the Pedersen, the British also lost interest in it.

It is interesting to speculate on what might have happened had Pedersen made a rifle with a fluted chamber instead of relying on wax lubrication.

PELO

Captain Carl Pelo was a Finnish officer who designed a recoil-operated semi-automatic rifle in the late 1940s. Prototypes were made in Sweden in 6.5mm and 7.92mm calibre and submitted for trial to Britain and Sweden and probably other countries, but although the rifle was of elegant appearance and relatively simple mechanism, the moving barrel was a drawback which the military were not prepared to accept, and the Pelo rifle got no further. He then turned his hand to a submachine gun design which, again, was perfectly serviceable but appeared at a time when nobody wanted submachine guns, so he had no success with that either.

REMINGTON

Eliphalet Remington was born in 1793 and according to legend, at the age of 16 he forged a gun-barrel and took it to a gunsmith to be finished and rifled. The gunsmith, impressed with the work, encouraged Eli to make more barrels, and in time he became a skilled barrelsmith. By 1828 he was making complete guns, and shortly after that he moved his workshop to a site on the newly opened Erie Canal. A small community grew up around his workshop, which in time became the town of Ilion, New York. A major order to complete a contract for rifles for the US Army led him to organise his workshop for quantity production, and he pioneered interchangeability and mass-production techniques which spread to other industries.

Eli Remington died in 1861, leaving the business to his two sons, and the Civil War brought them more orders and expanded production. Known by this time as Remington & Sons, in 1886 it became the Remington Arms Company. In 1912 it merged with the Union Metallic Cartridge Company to become Remington-UMC. It later reverted to the Remington Arms Company and passed from family ownership (today a major share is owned by **FN**) but throughout its history it has produced weapons and ammunition of the highest quality.

REVELLI

Abiel Bethel Revelli-Beaumont (1864–1930). Revelli, as he is more generally known, was an Italian Army officer who first revealed his talents by designing an automatic rifle, the Revelli-Terni, which was favourably reported upon but not adopted. He then designed the Glisenti automatic pistol which was adopted by the Italian Army in 1910, and followed this by the Fiat-Revelli medium machine gun of 1914. In later years he worked with **FIAT** as a designer and was responsible for most of the company's machine gun designs.

RHEINMETALL

Rheinische Metallwaren und Maschinenfabrik was founded in Düsseldorf in 1889 by Dr Heinrich Erhardt (1840–1928). A general engineering works, it then became noted for its artillery, producing, among other designs, the 15-pounder which was the first modern quick-firing field gun to be adopted by the British Army. It purchased the moribund **Dreyse** company and used the Dreyse name as a trademark on pistols and machine guns developed in the first two decades of this century. It was largely dismantled after World War I and what remained was more or less a general engineering firm with a rather large drawing office.

In the late 1920s it established a subsidiary in Holland called Hollandische Artillerie Industrie und Hemboltsmattschappisch – HAIHA – which for a short time in the 1930s attempted to market a 20mm anti-tank rifle, which was actually an Erhardt 20mm semi-automatic cannon which had been developed during World War I. HAIHA folded in the early 1930s.

At much the same time RMM operated a design agency in Moscow called BUTAST. It was authorised by the German government as part of the extensive undercover co.-operation with the Soviet government.

In about 1929 the company acquired the Solothurn firm to do research and development work, marketing the results through **Steyr-Solothurn** Waffen AG.

In 1936 RMM merged with Borsig, a heavy engineering company , to form Rheinmetall-Borsig. By 1939 R-B was operating five major factories and had its own proving ground at Unterluss. At the end of the war it was running 12 major plants and manufactured everything from small arms to the heaviest artillery.

R-B was broken up in 1945 by the Allies, but the core company re-formed in the 1950s and, when the West Germany Army began to assemble in the 1950s, it went back into the arms business to manufacture the MG3 machine gun. Since then, though, it has rarely concerned itself with anything smaller than a 20mm cannon and currently manufactures artillery weapons and ammunition.

ROSS

Sir Charles Henry Augustus Frederick Lockhart Ross, ninth Baron of Balnagown (1872–1942). Reputed to be one of the richest men in Britain in the 1890s, Ross was not content merely to live on the income from his estates, but became a competent engineer, businessman, administrator, agriculturalist and inventor.

Firearms were a particular field of interest, and he took out his first rifle patents in 1893 when he was an engineering student at Cambridge. More designs followed, and in 1897 he had a rifle made for him by Charles Lancaster of London.

The straight-pull bolt action fascinated Ross, and he developed a system using a sleeve around the bolt. The sleeve, moved back and forth by the bolt handle, had grooves internally which mated with lugs on the bolt to rotate it to lock into the chamber.

Following service in the Boer War as a major in Lovat's Scouts, Ross went to Canada, had a rifle made for him in the USA, and then submitted it for trial to the Canadian Army. He set up a factory in Quebec and began producing rifles for sporting use, as well as taking every opportunity to push for military adoption. In 1902 he received an order for 1000 rifles for the Royal Northwest Mounted Police, and then a further order for 12,000 rifles for the militia.

The Ross rifle went through innumerable variations in design over the next few years, but it eventually became the standard Canadian Army rifle. It was superbly accurate, but that is about as much as can be said for it. When the Canadian Army went to France in 1914 to join the British Expeditionary Force there, the conditions in the trenches in 1914/15 soon exposed the weaknesses of the straight-pull bolt design, and Canadian troops were soon throwing their Ross rifles away. Confidence was lost and the rifles were ordered to be withdrawn and replaced by **Lee-Enfield**s. The Ross Rifle Company was wound up, contracts cancelled, and the factory was taken over by the Canadian government and eventually sold to the North American Arms Company

Numbers of Ross rifles made a re-appearance in 1940 when they were sent to Britain to arm the Home Guard, but their career was short, most being replaced by P'14 or P'18 Enfields before the end of 1942.

RUBIN

Major Édouard Rubin was the Director of the Swiss Army Laboratory at Thun in the late 1870s when he decided to tackle the problem of lead fouling in rifles. Lead bullets, desirable for their mass and consequent momentum, tended to leave traces of lead in the rifling as they passed through, and the faster they moved, the more fouling they left. Paper sleeves around the bullet or coatings of lubricant were effective to some degree, but merely delayed the inevitable.

Rubin went further, and began reviewing the whole question of bullets and calibres, and he eventually developed a small-calibre bullet comprised of a lead core surrounded by a copper jacket. This gave a jacket soft enough to engrave in the rifling but which left far less of a deposit and thus extended the useful life of the rifle.

In 1883 Rubin put forward a design for a 7.5mm calibre compound bullet propelled by a compressed black powder charge in a brass cartridge case and this was tested by the Swiss Army. While they were still deliberating on this, in 1886 Vielle, a French chemist, developed smokeless powder. Rubin now re-designed his cartridge to take advantage of the new propellant, and then sat down with Colonel Rudolf Schmidt, a weapons technician of the Swiss Army, to develop the Schmidt-Rubin rifle, which in one form or another remained in Swiss service until the late 1950s.

Rubin's development of the small-calibre compound bullet affected the design of every military rifle in the 1886–95 period.

SAUER

J.P. Sauer & Sohn was established in 1751 and claimed to be the first arms factory to be built in Suhl. In the cartridge era the firm built a variety of sporting weapons and specialised in **Mauser**-action sporters from 1901 onwards. The company was wound up in 1945 when Suhl vanished into the Russian Zone of occupation. It was re-started in Eckernförde, West Germany, in 1948 and made sporting rifles once more as well as **Colt**-pattern 'Western' revolvers for the 'quick-draw' craze of the 1960s. It later became allied with **SIG** of Switzerland and since the 1970s has produced a number of SIG-Sauer pistols and rifles.

SCHMEISSER

Louis Schmeisser (1848–1917). After his apprenticeship, Schmeisser travelled widely around Europe working for various gunmakers before settling down in Jena and starting his own gunsmithing business. Here he began designing various types of weapon, but lacking the capital and engineering plant to produce them he came to an agreement with Theodor **Bergmann** who at this time was running an ironworks in Gaggenau, near Baden-Baden. Bergmann produced the weapons, usually by subcontracting them to various makers, since his factory was equipped to produce heavy iron structures and not small precision articles.

In the early 1890s Schmeisser designed and Bergmann produced a series of blowback automatic pistols, the first such weapons to be a commercial proposition; Schmeisser later designed the Bergmann machine gun and, in 1916, developed the Bergmann Machine Pistole, the first practical submachine gun.

His son, *Hugo*, also worked for Bergmann but was more of a production manager than a designer. In 1921 he left Bergmann to work for **Haenel** as their chief engineer and there produced a small pocket automatic pistol of no particular distinction which he had patented in 1920; its novelty consisted solely of its method of assembly. Under Schmeisser's urging Haenel began to develop submachine guns, but the company's principal contribution in this field was as a production base for the Erma MP40; and it may be that Schmeisser's position as manager of the factory making the MP40 led to its being commonly called the 'Schmeisser' submachine gun. He certainly had nothing to do with the design, and his attempt to improve it (the MP41) was a retrograde step. When Suhl vanished into the Russian Zone in 1945 Schmeisser vanished with it, and his subsequent career is not recorded.

SCHOENAUER

Otto Schoenauer (1844–1915) was an employee of the Österreichische Waffenfabrik **Steyr** who eventually rose to become Technical Director in 1896. Although a trained gunsmith, there seems little doubt that his forte was administration and organisation, and his only lasting contribution to weapon design was his development of the rotary rifle magazine employed in the Greek infantry rifle of 1903 and subsequently in several sporting rifles and carbines. It is still in use today in the Steyr SSG69 sniping rifle.

SCHOFIELD

Major George W. Schofield, US Army. This officer patented various improvements to revolvers in April 1874, notably a barrel catch for a hinged-frame revolver, and improvements to the collective ejecting system. These were purchased by **Smith & Wesson** for their .45 Smith & Wesson Schofield revolver which was adopted for service, together with the more famous **Colt**, in 1873. About 8000 were purchased by the US Army and a further 1000 or so sold commercially. Schofield is said to have shot himself with one in 1882.

SCHWARZLOSE

Andreas Wilhelm Schwarzlose (1867–1936). A farmer's son, his German military service introduced him to firearms, and he received training at an ordnance technical school which whetted his appetite. On leaving the army he went to Suhl and worked for various gunsmiths there to complete his training, and in 1898 designed an automatic pistol which met with moderate success.

Schwarzlose then designed a machine gun using a toggle to delay the opening of the breech, and this was adopted by the Austro-Hungarian Army in 1907 and retained in service until 1945. He is also to be remembered for his 'blow-forward' pistol, one of the few such designs to have any degree of success

SHPAGIN

Georgii Semyonovitch Shpagin (1897–1952). Shpagin came from peasant stock, and in 1916 was called up for service in the Russian Army and found himself assigned to a regimental weapons workshop. Here he familiarised himself with all the service weapons and became a competent gunsmith.

On leaving the army in 1920 Shpagin found employment at the weapon factory in which both **Federov** and **Degtyarev** were working. He gradually turned his hand to designing weapons and his most significant efforts were his collaboration with Degtyarev on the 1938 DShK heavy machine gun and his development of the PPSh sub-machine gun in 1941.

SIG

This notable business began as the Schweizerische Waggon Fabrik in 1853 at Schaffhausen making railway rolling stock. This developed into the Société pour l'Industrie Schweiz of Neuhausen. In 1860 it accepted a contract to manufacture weapons for the Swiss Army. In 1865 the weapon factory was split off as a separate enterprise, the Schweizerische Waffenfabrik, under Friedrich **Vetterli** as general manager, where he developed the

M1869 rifle. In about 1879 the company was reorganised as the Schweizerische Industrie Gesellschaft (SIG) of Neuhausen. As well as competing against the Swiss national arsenals for the manufacture of Swiss Army weapons, the firm made weapons for all and sundry until the Swiss embargoed weapon exports in 1938.

In 1971 SIG took over Hammerli, and in 1974 went into co.-operation with **Sauer**. SIG currently makes the Swiss Army Stgw 90 rifle, two sniping rifles and a range of military pistols, match rifles and hunting rifles, all of the very highest quality.

SIMONOV

Sergei Gavrilovich Simonov (1894–). Simonov was apprenticed to the village blacksmith for five years, after which he worked in a general engineering factory. He then took an advanced technical course, after which he worked in a machine gun factory and became involved with the development of the **Federov** Automat. In 1922 he became a Master Gunsmith and by the late 1920s was in charge of the experimental department of the concern.

In the early 1920s he began work on designs for a light machine gun and an automatic rifle, and in 1936 the latter design was adopted by the Soviet Army as the AVS-36. He followed this with the PTRS anti-tank rifle and, being introduced to the 7.62 x 39mm short cartridge, developed the SKS carbine which entered service in 1946.

SMITH & WESSON

Horace Smith (1808–93) and Daniel Baird Wesson (1825–1906). Smith was an expert machinist, and worked for a number of gunmakers in New England; in 1851 he took out a patent for a breech-loading arm; he also acquired the **Henry** breech-loading patent. Smith had met Daniel Wesson, both being employed by a gunmaker called Robbins, Kendall & Lawrence at the time, and the two now went into partnership to manufacture a repeating pistol. They then incorporated the Volcanic Repeating Firearms Co. and licensed their patents to it.

Smith soon left the firm and went to work with his brother-in-law (another gunsmith) whilst Wesson stayed with Volcanic until 1856 when he left the company (which was in difficulties) and began work on a design of cartridge revolver. Having perfected this he contacted Horace Smith, and in October 1857, as 'Smith & Wesson', they began producing a .22 tip-up revolver. Due to their possession of **White**'s 'master patent' for cylinders bored completely through, they were able to control the revolver market until the expiry of the patent in 1869 and their company's future was assured.

SNIDER

In the early 1860s the British Army was contemplating a breech-loading rifle, but in view of the various designs being put forward, and their lack of practical experience, it was decided to look for some simple method of converting existing muzzle-loading percussion rifles into cartridge-firing breech-loaders as cheaply as possible. This, it was felt, would suffice to introduce the army to the new system, but leave the way clear for the adoption of a more advanced design when one should make itself apparent.

The design which was accepted, out of fifty or more systems which were put forward, was the invention of Jacob Snider, of New York, USA. Snider's solution was to cut away a section of the barrel at the rear end and insert a breech block with firing pin, hinged at the side so that it could be opened and a cartridge pushed into the chamber. The block was then closed, the rifle fired by an external hammer, and the block opened and drawn back to operate an extractor which eased the empty case out of the chamber so that it could be removed.

Snider also produced a suitable cartridge, using a metal base and cardboard body, but this proved unsatisfactory and an improved design was produced by Colonel Boxer at Woolwich Arsenal.

The Snider was eventually replaced in British service by the **Martini-Henry** action.

STECHKIN

A Soviet machine pistol in 9mm **Makarov** calibre. A blowback weapon, it can be described as an enlarged **Walther** PP but with the firing mechanism modified to permit automatic fire. It was provided with a shoulder stock and the official handbook recommended the fitting of this wherever possible in order to improve control of the weapon and thus accuracy. It was formally adopted in 1951, appears to have been issued from 1955 onwards, and survived for about 20 years. Numbers were passed to other countries but they are not common. The designer was Igor Yakovlevich Stechkin (*b*.1922).

STERLING

The Sterling Armaments Company of Dagenham, Essex, entered the arms business during World War II by manufacturing the Lanchester submachine gun. It followed this by making the De Lisle silent carbine and producing components for other weapons. Sterling was then approached by George William Patchett with a design of submachine gun and began working with Patchett to develop it. About 100 pre-production models were made in early 1944, most of which were used in action in Normandy and later in the Arnhem battle by the British airborne troops, but post-war trials dragged so slowly that it was not until 1953 that it was formally approved for adoption by the British Army.

Thereafter the Sterling submachine gun (as the Patchett design came to be called) sold in large numbers throughout the world until the early 1970s when demand fell away in the face of competition from smaller and more modern designs.

Sterling tried to expand into rifles (obtaining a licence for the **ArmaLite** AR-18) and revolvers, but without success. The company went into liquidation in the late 1980s and the remains were purchased by Royal Ordnance plc, who promptly closed the Dagenham factory and removed the submachine gun production machinery to the Royal Small Arms Factory. No subsequent production has ever taken place.

STEYR-MANNLICHER

The company now called Steyr-Mannlicher was founded in Steyr, Austria, by Josef **Werndl** in 1864, and its initial operation was the conversion of about 80,000 muzzle-loaders into Wänzl breech-loading rifles. This was followed by manufacture of the Werndl rifle; other contracts were then gained, and Werndl set up a subsidiary factory in Budapest to provide rifles for the Honved, the Hungarian militia element of the Austro-Hungarian Army.

In order to acquire capital the company became the Österreichische Waffenfabrik Steyr in 1869. It acquired the Früwirth factory in Vienna, closed it down and transferred the machinery to Steyr.

From then on, orders flowed in regularly, including one in 1873 from the Prussian Army to make 100,000 **Mauser** M1871 rifles. More foreign contracts followed but in 1882 the arms business slumped and Werndl turned to electrical engineering, Steyr supposedly being the first town in the world to have electric street lighting in 1884. But in 1885 the first **Mannlicher** magazine rifle went into production and business took off again. Werndl died of a lung infection in 1889 and the factory continued under local control until Otto Schoenauer took over as the general manager in 1896

After 1919 the company became the Steyr-Werke AG and began manufacturing motor vehicles and other light engineering tasks. In the late 1920s, through some unrecorded manoeuvres, the company formed an alliance with **Rheinmetall** and set up **Steyr-Solothurn** AG to sell Rheinmetall designed weapons. In 1934 Steyr merged with the Austro-Daimler-Puch motor works to become Steyr-Daimler-Puch, and after the German annexation of Austria in 1938 the factory was absorbed into the Hermann-Göring-Werke organisation.

After 1945 Steyr was occupied by the Soviet Army and the factory was thoroughly looted, much of the machinery being dismantled and transported into Russia. The area was later handed over to the Americans, and the rest of the gunmaking machinery was removed and replaced by new machinery for the manufacture of tractors and motor-cycles.

In 1950 the company was permitted to manufacture sporting arms once more, and in the 1960s the development of military weapons began. Steyr made its mark with the introduction of the **AUG** assault rifle in the middle 1970s, setting the pattern for future designs of rifle and introducing the concept of a modular design which could be configured into various different weapons.

STEYR-SOLOTHURN

Steyr-Solothurn Waffen AG of Vienna was a 'shell' company set up in the 1930s to enable **Rheinmetall** of Germany to evade the restrictions of the Versailles Treaty. This treaty prevented Rheinmetall from producing military small arms. The company therefore bought a small engineering concern in Switzerland, the Maschinenwerke Solothurn AG of Solothurn. Next a link was formed, which even now is not entirely clear, with Steyr-Daimler-Puch in Austria which resulted in the formation of Steyr-Solothurn AG.

With all these companies in place, the routine went as follows: Rheinmetall's design office would produce a design for a weapon. The drawings would then be sent to Solothurn, where the engineering plant would produced prototypes and test them. Once they had the weapon perfected, the production drawings went to Steyr-Daimler-Puch, where the weapons were actually manufactured. Once manufactured they were sold and shipped by Steyr-

Solothurn AG. In this way the origins of the weapon were concealed and the various links in the chain were all able to earn a living.

The full extent of this linkage was not known until well after World War II and for several years it was assumed that all 'Solothurn' weapons were actually of Swiss origin.

SUDAYEV

Alexei Ivanovitch Sudayev (1912–1946) was first employed as a metal worker with a railway until his induction into the Soviet Army in 1934. He left the army in 1936 and attended an industrial technical school, then moved to the Artillery Academy for advanced technical training. In 1941 he developed a number of new manufacturing techniques to speed up the production of anti-aircraft guns, and then found himself in Leningrad when that city was besieged. There, using only those materials and machines which he found in the city, he developed a submachine gun (the PPS-42) which was of significant value in arming the besieged Leningraders. His sudden death at the age of 34 cut short what might have been a highly talented career.

THOMPSON

John Tagliaferro Thompson, USA (1860–1940). Thompson graduated from West Point in 1882 and joined the artillery. After some years of regimental service, in 1890 he transferred to the Ordnance Corps. In 1898, when the Spanish-American War broke out, he was appointed Chief Ordnance Officer to the American force sent to Cuba. The army's logistic system collapsed completely and Thompson single-handedly restored order and imposed some organisation on the supply of equipment to the expeditionary force.

On reaching Cuba Thompson was able to examine the variety of weapons in use there and reached the conclusion that American small arms needed replacement. He was then appointed to the Springfield Armory, where he supervised the development of the Springfield M1903 rifle. He was also associated with the development and introduction of the **Colt** M1911 automatic pistol, conducting, with Colonel La Grande, the famous series of 'stopping power' tests on cattle and corpses. In 1907, a major, he became Assistant Chief of Ordnance in charge of small arms design and production, finally retiring in 1914 with the rank of colonel.

In his retirement he set about designing an automatic rifle, since he considered such a weapon to be the next step for the US Army. However, he discovered that virtually every practical method of operating an automatic weapon was covered by a patent. He eventually decided upon the **Blish** system of slipping inclined faces, since it was an unworked patent which he could obtain for nothing more than sharing the profits with Blish.

Before he could get very far with his rifle, the USA was brought into World War I. Recalled to duty in 1917, he was appointed Director of Arsenals and was thus in charge of the entire US small arms programme, for which he received the DSM. He was promoted to brigadier-general in August 1918 and released from active duty in December.

By this time his associates in the **Auto-Ordnance**

Company, who had continued to work on his rifle, had reported that the Blish system was unworkable with a high-powered rifle cartridge, but worked perfectly with the .45 pistol cartridge. Thompson thereupon decided on a 'trench broom' but the war ended before this idea was perfected. He then invented the term 'submachine gun' and in 1920 produced the perfected Thompson gun design. Sales were relatively poor during the 1920s and early 1930s, in spite of considerable publicity, and Thompson died just as the demands of World War II were about to crown his efforts with the success which had hitherto eluded him.

TOKAREV

Fyedor Vassilevich Tokarev was born in 1871 to a poor Cossack family in the Don Basin. He studied metal-working at school, and during his military service attended a military weapons school. He remained in the army and eventually reached commissioned rank as a weapons specialist.

In 1907 Tokarev began working on an automatic rifle design, and he continued this during a tour of duty at the Sestroretsk rifle factory in 1908–14. On the outbreak of war he was sent out on active service, and did not return to the rifle factory until mid-1916. He survived the Revolution and made a successful translation to Communism, continuing his work on weapons design and producing the **Maxim**-Tokarev machine gun in the early 1920s. The came his automatic pistol, adopted in 1930, and his SVT automatic rifles of 1938 and 1940. He received numerous awards and the honorary degree of Doctor of Technical Sciences.

US MACHINE GUN Co.

This company was established in Meriden. Connecticut, by William Haskell to promote the **Berthier** machine gun. The design was provisionally accepted by the US Army as the M1916 but due to difficulties in obtaining machine tools and raw materials the war ended before any were made, and more leisurely post-war trials revealed defects in the design, which was abandoned. The company was closed down in 1922.

U.S. PROPERTY

Marking found on all US service arms and also on the receiver of **Lee-Enfield** No 4 Mark 1★ rifles made by the Savage Arms Co. and other US manufacturers during World War II. The marking was a legal requirement on all military arms made on contract to the US War Department and, since the wording of the regulation was somewhat ambiguous, it was extended to cover those made for the British Army on Lend-Lease contracts.

VESELEY

Josef Veseley was a Czech ordnance engineer who came to Britain in 1938 to advise the BSA Company during its tooling-up for the manufacture of the Besa machine gun. Upon the outbreak of war in 1939 he remained in Britain and became an employee of BSA.

In August 1940 he submitted a design of submachine gun to the Chief Inspector of Small Arms. Although the design was a good one, it was turned down on the grounds that manufacture of the Lanchester had already

been approved and was being prepared, and the design of the Sten gun was well advanced, and to introduce a third design at such a fraught period, with factory space at a premium and a desperate shortage of approved weapons, would merely add to the confusion.

Veseley, however, built a prototype gun in his spare time and in late 1942 submitted it for test. It was a blow-back weapon with an unusual two-column magazine in which the front column was fired off first and the second column was then released to the feedway. The weapon was tested and found to be generally sound, though it failed the mud test, as did most designs on their first appearance. Veseley made some modifications and six more prototypes which were tested in 1944–45, but by that time the Patchett (**Sterling**) design was being considered for adoption, and the Veseley submachine gun was finally refused in October 1945.

Veseley was later responsible for the design of the X16 sustained-fire machine gun which, after a competitive trial, was turned down in favour of the **FN** MAG.

VETTERLI

Friedrich Vetterli, (1822–1882) was apprenticed in Switzerland, then worked in Germany and subsequently in Paris, St Étienne and London. In 1864 he returned to Switzerland and joined the Société Suisse pour l'Industrie of Neuhausen (one of the fore-runners of **SIG**) and was appointed to head its newly-formed firearms department. There he was able to develop the Vetterli breech-loading rifle which was taken into service by the Swiss Army in 1869 and subsequently by the Italian Army.

VICKERS

This company began as steel-makers in Sheffield, then moved into shipbuilding. In 1883 Hiram **Maxim** entered into an agreement with Albert Vickers for the production of the Maxim machine gun, and the company later became Vickers, Son and Maxim. It gradually entered into every field of armaments, building battleships, tanks, aircraft and artillery, In the small arms field, however, its output has been restricted and highly specialised.

The company's name is, of course, best known for the Vickers machine gun, a re-design of the Maxim carried out at the Vickers factory at Erith in 1911–12. The principal change was that the toggle was inverted so as to break upwards, and the whole design was re-calculated so as to avoid excess weight without sacrificing strength or reliability.

During World War I the Vickers was in constant use and performed many legendary feats of sustained fire; 10,000 rounds non-stop was relatively commonplace.

In addition to use as a ground gun, it was adopted as an aircraft weapon, the water-cooled jacket being replaced by a louvred jacket which cooled the barrel by the air-flow around the aircraft. In post-war years a .50 calibre model, essentially an enlarged .303 model, was adopted for use in tanks.

In the 1920s the company began producing the Vickers-**Berthier** light machine gun, and also obtained a license for the patents of **Pedersen**, producing a slightly modified Pedersen rifle as the Vickers self-loading rifle. Though frequently tested by various military authorities, it was never adopted and did not go into production.

The company was also instrumental in supplying several thousand Parabellum (**Luger**) pistols to the Dutch Government in the early 1920s. Due to the restrictions of the Versailles Treaty, **DWM** could not manufacture pistols to fulfil an order from the Dutch government. They therefore made the component parts, which were sent to England, polished, blued and assembled in the Vickers factory, marked 'Vickers Ltd' on the toggle, and then supplied to the Netherlands East Indies.

VIGNERON

The Vigneron submachine gun was designed by Colonel Vigneron, a retired Belgian Amy officer, and produced by the SA Precision Liègeoise of Herstal. It was adopted throughout the Belgian forces in 1953 and remained in service for some years. The gun was a simple blowback weapon, well made from steel pressings, and with an unusually long barrel which carried a muzzle compensator. The butt was a folding wire affair, and the weapon was chambered for the 9mm Parabellum cartridge.

VILLAR PEROSA

The Villar-Perosa machine gun is often cited as the first submachine gun, on the grounds that it was a delayed blowback weapon of light weight, firing a pistol cartridge. This is perfectly correct, but the tactical purpose of the V-P machine gun and its actual physical appearance both argue against it being given status as a submachine gun.

The weapon was designed by A.B. Revelli and patented in 1915, the patents being assigned to the Officina Villar Perosa. It was adopted by the Italian Army as the M1915 and was also manufactured by **FIAT**, which led to it being variously known as the V-P, the FIAT or the Revelli light machine gun. It was also made in Canada by the Canadian General Electric Company for the Italian government, in 1917–1918, being known there as the FIAT-Revelli.

The Italian Army was not well-equipped with machine guns in 1915, and in particular it required a light gun for use by its Alpine mountain troops. The Villar Perosa was therefore designed as an infantry support weapon, though it was also used in aircraft and light coastal motor-boats. The weapon actually consisted of two guns mounted side-by-side, each an independent unit. Each had a tubular receiver, barrel and bolt, fed from an overhead magazine and chambered for the 9mm Glisenti pistol cartridge. Control was by a spade grip at the rear end with two triggers, one for each gun, and it could be placed on a light bipod or on a pivot mount.

The gun was a blowback type, but the bolt was made to rotate through 45° during its movement so as to allow the firing pin to pass through it; only when the bolt had fully closed was it possible for the pin to strike the cartridge. Thus the rotation was purely a safety measure, but since it also, to some slight degree, impeded the opening of the bolt, it has some claim to being a delayed blowback system. Even so, the light bolt and strong return spring meant an exceptionally high rate of fire; pressing both triggers at once delivered almost 3000 rds/min.

In order to utilise this gun during the assault, it was mounted on a platform suspended from a man's neck by straps, so that he walked into action firing the guns from the hip and looking rather like an ice-cream seller in a cin-ema. Some success was had with this tactic, but in 1918 the Army had had enough, and withdrew the guns, passing them to Beretta and the Officina Villar Perosa for conversion into single-barrel submachine guns. In this form they became the Beretta M1918 and the OVP respectively, and original V-P twin guns are now a rarity.

VITALI

General Giuseppe Vitali, Italian Army (1845–1921). As a major, in 1885, he patented an eight-shot repeating pistol which does not appear to have got beyond the prototype stage. In 1887 he adopted **Lee**'s removable box magazine and fitted it to the existing **Vetterli** single-shot rifles of the Italian Army to produce the Vetterli-Vitali repeating rifle. These are easily recognised by the unusual shape of the magazine, with the wider central vertical section housing a coil spring instead of the usual leaf spring.

WALTHER

The Waffenfabrik Walther of Zella St Blasii was founded in 1886 by Carl Walther, and for many years produced a variety of sporting rifles and shotguns. In 1908, assisted by his cousin Friedrich Pickert, a well-known revolver maker, Walther began production of a 6.35mm automatic pistol. This was followed by others and World War I saw considerable expansion of the factory. In 1915 Carl Walther died and the business was continued by his sons, and in the post-war years production of small-bore target rifles, target pistols, automatic pistols, hunting rifles and shotguns continued. The company also developed a successful mechanical calculating machine.

After World War II, the factory fell into Russian hands, and the company transferred its operations to Ulm-a-d-Donau, building itself up by its calculating machine production and by licensing the production of its pistols to the French firm of Manurhin. In the late 1950s pistol and sporting arm production was resumed, and a submachine gun was developed in the 1960s.

The early Walther pistols were all blowback types of simple construction and first class quality, but the PP Model of 1929 introduced the double-action lock to common usage, and it was followed by the PPK model, a smaller version for plain-clothes police.

In the early 1930s the German Army was looking for a new design to replace the service Parabellum and Walther put forward a 9mm Parabellum version of the PP; it was refused, since the army would not consider a blowback pistol in that calibre. The next attempt was the Model AP (for Army Pistole), a locked breech weapon using a wedge to lock slide and barrel together. It incorporated the double action lock of the PP and had the hammer concealed under the slide. While it was successful in its performance, the army was reluctant to approve it since the unseen hammer meant that it was not readily apparent whether or not the gun was cocked. Walther responded to this with the Model HP (for Heeres Pistole, which also means 'army pistol') in which the hammer was moved to an external position. This was approved, and became the Pistole 38.

In the 1950s production of the P38 pistol resumed with it renamed as the P1, with the substitution of an alloy frame, and it is in military use in many countries. The same locking mechanism is used in the P5 pistol, which was developed in response to a German police requirement for a pistol with a high standard of handling safety, but with the ability to be fired quickly without its user having to operate safety devices. To meet this the P5 has its firing pin held out of line with the hammer except when the trigger is being pressed, while a safety notch on the hammer stops the hammer falling unless the trigger is fully pressed. For those who insist on a manual safety device, the P1A1 was virtually the P5 with a cross-bolt safety catch in the slide.

In 1988 the company produced the P88 pistol. This is a double-action automatic using the **Colt-Browning** dropping barrel system, the barrel locking into the ejection opening in the slide.

WEBLEY

This famous firm can trace its roots to James Webley, born in 1808, son of a button-maker, who became a 'percussioner' and set up in business some time in the early 1830s. His brother Philip, born in 1812, was apprenticed to a gun lock filer when he was 14 years old. After seven years apprenticeship he became a journeyman gun lock filer and joined his brother James in business in 1834. In 1838 Philip married Caroline Davis, daughter of a deceased 'bullet mould and gun implement manufacturer' whose business was being continued by his widow. Shortly thereafter Mrs Davis died and Philip Webley succeeded to the Davis business and premises, via his wife. In 1838 his first son, Thomas William, was born, and in 1859, when T.W. reached his majority, the firm became P. Webley & Son. Philip had four children, but the only other who concerns us is Henry, born in 1846, who also joined his father when of age, after which the firm was sometimes known as P. Webley & Sons.

Both James and Philip had specialised in making percussion revolvers and each developed a respectable business, but in 1856 James suddenly died and his business was absorbed by Philip Webley. At much the same time Samuel **Colt** decided that there was insufficient of a market in Europe to warrant a separate factory and closed his London factory, leaving the revolver market wide open, and Webley moved promptly to fill it, expanding his business to meet the demand. He obtained several government contracts and from 1887 was the sole supplier of revolvers to the British armed forces for almost 40 years.

Philip Webley died in 1888, aged 76; his wife died three years later, and thereafter the company was in the hands of Thomas William and Henry. In 1897 they amalgamated P. Webley & Son (as the firm was still officially known) with W.C. Scott & Sons (shotgun makers) and Richard Ellis & Sons (rifles & shotguns) to form the Webley & Scott Revolver & Arms Co. Ltd. Henry retired from business (though he returned to become a director some years later), while Thomas William became managing director until his death in 1904. A further name change took place in 1906, the firm becoming Webley & Scott Ltd.

In 1958 the company was acquired by R.H. Windsor Ltd; in 1959 the Windsor group was taken over by Arusha Industries, who later became General & Engineering Industries Ltd. In 1965 this company acquired W.W. Greener, and in 1973 sold Greener and Webley & Scott to the Harris & Sheldon Group.

In 1980 firearms production ceased; the shotgun business was re-established as W. & C. Scott, and subsequently sold to Holland & Holland, and the revolver designs and tooling were sold to Pakistan in 1983. However, the Harris & Sheldon group still manufactures air rifles and pistols under the Webley name.

WERDER

Johann Ludwig Werder (1808–85). Born in Narva, Russia, Werder was trained as a locksmith and after his apprenticeship was over he spent the rest of his life in Switzerland and Germany. A remarkably versatile engineer, he designed and built bridges, wagons, steel-framed buildings, machine tools, steam boilers, engines and railway locomotives. His only association with firearms comes from his design of a breech-loading rifle for the Bavarian Army in 1868. This was the famous 'Bavarian Lightning' breech mechanism, a variation of the dropping block of Peabody and **Martini** which was operated by a thumb lever alongside the breech instead of an under-lever. This made it easier to operate in the prone position and somewhat faster that an under-lever – hence the 'Lightning' appellation.

WERNDL

Josef Werndl (1831–1889) of Steyr, Austria. Josef's father Leopold was a gunsmith with a small firm making rifle parts. Josef joined his father's business but was not impressed by the antique production methods. He entered military service in 1849 and was sent to work in a Viennese rifle factory where he first saw modern production methods. His father bought him out and he came back to the family business but still failed to see eye-to-eye, so in 1852 he went to Germany and worked for various firms before going to the USA to work for **Remington** and **Colt**. He returned to Austria in 1853 and set up his own workshop in Wehrgraben.

On his father's death from cholera in 1855 Werndl returned to Steyr to take over the family business. and drastically modernised it. He then set about developing a breech-loader and made two more trips to the USA taking with him Karl Holub, his designer. In 1866 he set up the Steyr company (*see* Steyr-Mannlicher) and ran this successful business until shortly before his death in 1889.

WHITE

Rollin White (1818–1892) was born in Vermont, USA, and learned gunsmithing in the workshop of his elder brother. He then worked for **Colt** for several years, as a sub-contractor producing barrels and other components, and occupied himself with developing improvements to revolvers.

In 1855 White took out a patent which, among other things, laid claim to the idea of boring a chamber from one end of a cylinder to the other. Colt took no interest in his patent, but Daniel Wesson saw the significance of the bored-through cylinder, since he was working on the design of a self-contained rimfire cartridge, and he obtained the exclusive rights to the patent in return for a royalty of 25 cents per revolver made. The possession of this 'master patent' until its expiry in 1869 gave **Smith & Wesson** a commanding monopoly of revolver production and earned White over $70,000. He spent a good deal of this on legal expenses, however, since the agreement with Wesson left the responsibility for proceeding against patent infringers to White.

WINCHESTER

Oliver Fisher Winchester (1810–1880) was a shirt manufacturer who became a financier and then became a gunmaker. He knew virtually nothing about firearms but he was an excellent organiser who understood business better than most of his contemporaries, He first ventured into firearms by buying shares in the Volcanic Repeating Firearms Company which had been set up by Horace Smith and Daniel Wesson to produce their improved model of the Volcanic rifle. The company went bankrupt in 1857 and Winchester purchased the remains, reorganised it as the New Haven Arms company, ensured that he had a controlling quantity of the shares, and commenced production of the Volcanic rifle.

Winchester had little better luck than had **Smith & Wesson**, but in 1857 he met Tyler **Henry** and hired him to improve the Volcanic design. Henry began by developing a suitable rimfire cartridge, then followed this by improving the Volcanic out of all recognition into the very successful Henry rifle of 1860.

After the Civil War Winchester reorganised his company once more, it now becoming the Winchester Repeating Arms Company, and started off by launching the Model of 1866 Henry rifle with the King improvement to the loading system. This was followed by the Model 1873 which introduced an iron frame and a centre-fire cartridge, With those two designs Winchester became one of the world's premier rifle makers and has retained that position ever since.

CARTRIDGE DIMENSIONS

ABBREVIATIONS

Case Type (shape of cartridge) is defined as follows:

BN	belted, necked	RN	rimmed necked	RS	rimmed straight
RLN	rimless necked	RLS	rimless straight	SRN	semi-rimmed necked
SRS	semi-rimmed straight	RBN	rebated rim necked	RBS	rebated rim straight

All dimensions are in thousandths of an inch; bullet weights in grains. A conversion table is appended to allow quick conversion into metric measure. Metric calibres are given first, in ascending order of size, then Imperial calibres.

Name and Metric Calibre	Case Type	— Length —			Diameter			Bullet Weight
		Round	Case	Rim	Head	Neck	Bullet	
4.6 x 36mm Löffelspitz	RN	1949	1417	351	348	208	185	42
4.73 x 33mm DM11 caseless	na	1291	na	——	311 square	——	186	49
5.45 x 18mm Soviet Pistol	RLN	980	700	297	297		222	40
5.45 x 39.5mm	RLN	2224	1555	394	394	244	221	53
5.56 x 45mm M193	RLN	2256	1752	375	375	253	223	55
5.56 x 45mm NATO	RLN	2260	1760	378	378	253	223	62
5.56 x 45mm French	RLN	2255	1750	375	375	253	223	54
5.66mm Russian MPS	RLN	5905	1535	445	443	442	223	35
5.7 x 28mm P90	RLN	1708	1134	311	311	249	224	23
6 x 59mm Lee USN	RLN	3110	2345	446	445	246	244	112
6.35 x 16mm Auto Pistol	SRS	910	612	301	276	276	251	50
6.5 x 51SR Arisaka	SRN	3003	1995	471	450	293	260	137
6.5 x 52mm Mannlicher-Carcano	RLN	3004	2067	448	445	295	265	161
6.5 x 53.5SR Daudeteau No 12	SRN	3043	2090	524	490	298	263	150
6.5 x 54R Dutch/Romanian Mannlicher	RN	3102	2110	527	450	294	263	156
6.5 x 54mm Mannlicher-Schoenauer	RLN	3035	2112	454	452	295	264	159
6.5 x 55mm Swedish Mauser/Norway Krag	RLN	3150	2165	480	476	281	263	156
6.5 x 58R Danish Krag	RN	3110	2268	575	502	300	264	137
6.5 x 58mm Mauser-Vergueiro	RLN	3260	2280	466	466	290	263	154
7 x 20mm Nambu	RLN	1060	780	357	351	297	278	55
7 x 57mm Spanish Mauser	RLN	3063	2240	474	470	320	284	154
7 x 59mm Meunier	RLN	3122	1496	510	510	303	292	166
7.35 x 51mm Carcano	RLN	2905	2010	449	445	323	298	128
7.5 x 22R Norwegian Nagant	RS	1315	883	405	357	325	324	103
7.5 x 23R Swiss Revolver	RS	1352	897	409	354	331	315	105
7.5 x 53mm Swiss M1890 Schmidt-Rubin	RLN	3070	2102	490	487	362	320	220

| Name and Metric Calibre | Case Type | — Length — | | Diameter | | | | Bullet Weight |
		Round	Case	Rim	Head	Neck	Bullet	
7.5 x 54mm French M1929	RLN	2992	2115	482	480	340	308	190
7.5 x 55mm Swiss M1911	RLN	3062	2180	496	494	334	304	174
7.5 x 58mm French M1924	RLN	3157	2275	486	484	336	307	139
7.62 x 25mm Soviet Pistol (Tokarev)	RLN	1365	965	390	385	328	307	85
7.62 x 38R Nagant	RN	1515	1515	405	357	303	307	105
7.62 x 39mm M1943	RLN	2193	1510	445	443	340	310	123
7.62 x 40mm CETME	RLN	2913	1645	468	466	339	312	123
7.62 x 45mm Czech	RLN	2364	1770	441	442	334	311	130
7.62 x 51mm NATO	RLN	2750	2010	470	466	338	308	150
7.62 x 54R Russian	RN	3020	2110	564	489	335	310	185
7.62 x 62.8 PZAM	RLS	3031	2472	500	500	500	307	123
7.63 x 21mm Mannlicher M1901	RLS	1115	840	345	332	331	308	85
7.63 x 25mm Mauser	RLN	1350	990	393	388	333	309	85
7.65 x 17mm rimless (China Type 64)	RLS	970	664	331	331	330	307	74
7.65 x 17SR Browning (.32ACP)	SRS	975	680	352	336	336	309	73
7.65 x 19.8mm Longue	RLS	1192	780	334	337	336	309	85
7.65 x 21.5mm Parabellum	RLN	1145	850	393	391	332	309	93
7.65 x 53mm Belgian/Turkish Mauser	RLN	3063	2105	470	470	338	311	226
7.65 x 61mm Argentine Navy	RLN	3205	2393	467	467	339	310	173
7.7 x 58mm Arisaka	RLN	3138	2275	472	472	338	311	200
7.7 x 58R Arisaka	RN	3020	2210	528	456	341	311	175
7.7 x 58SR Arisaka	SRN	3134	2283	500	470	340	313	200
7.92 x 33mm Kurz	RLN	1677	1295	468	467	354	321	125
7.92 x 40mm CETME	RLN	2850	1628	470	465	354	310	108
7.92 x 57mm Mauser	RLN	3173	2244	473	469	353	323	198
7.92 x 57R Dutch	RN	2642	2240	530	471	382	356	197
7.92 x 61RB Norwegian Browning	RBN	3295	2389	468	484	340	319	220
7.92 x 94mm PzB	RLN	4645	3720	825	825	355	324	222
7.92 x 107mm Marosczek	RLN	5204	4175	645	647	360	322	223
8 x 19mm Roth-Steyr	RLS	1130	734	348	348	346	321	112
8 x 21mm Nambu	RLN	1245	848	411	410	340	319	102
8 x 22R Serbian Nagant	RS	1281	896	401	350	332	317	120
8 x 27R Lebel revolver	RS	1430	1075	409	355	344	320	145
8 x 27R Rast & Gasser	RS	1415	1063	381	339	337	319	120
8 x 41R Mexican Pieper	RS	1615	1615	392	340	290	320	125
8 x 50R Austrian/Bulgarian Mannlicher	RN	3000	1980	553	492	351	323	240
8 x 50R Lebel	RN	2948	1980	621	535	350	323	200
8 x 50R Siamese Mannlicher	RN	2973	1980	550	488	348	321	220
8 x 52R Siamese Mauser	RN	2940	2045	560	506	348	320	180
8 x 53R Murata	RN	2945	2060	558	493	361	320	235
8 x 56R Hungarian Mannlicher	RN	3000	2196	554	491	348	329	205
8 x 56R Kropatschek	RN	3236	2197	617	543	352	322	247
8 x 58R Danish Krag	RN	3014	2280	575	503	355	322	198
8 x 59mm Breda	RLN	3161	2320	470	491	360	326	210
8 x 60R Guedes	RN	3165	2346	618	542	349	316	247
8 x 63mm Swedish Browning	RLN	3338	2477	479	485	256	321	220
9 x 15R French Thick Rim	RS	900	525	437	396	390	366	115
9 x 17mm Browning Short (.380 Auto)	RLS	980	675	374	374	372	356	94
9 x 17R Danish Revolver	RS	1075	685	430	385	375	370	124

| Name and Metric Calibre | Case Type | — Length — | | — Diameter — | | | | Bullet Weight |
		Round	Case	Rim	Head	Neck	Bullet	
9 × 18mm Makarov	RLS	976	710	396	392	384	363	94
9 × 18mm Police	RLS	990	709	374	380	380	355	94
9 × 19mm Glisenti	RLS	1140	745	390	388	380	350	125
9 × 19mm Parabellum	RLS	1153	750	390	390	380	355	115
9 × 19R Federal	RS	1163	760	435	386	382	355	115
9 × 20SR Browning Long	SRS	1100	800	402	384	376	355	112
9 × 21mm IMI	RLS	1100	830	391	390	390	354	123
9 × 21mm Gyurza	RLS	1299	819	380	380	370	354	10
9 × 22R Belgian Nagant revolver	RS	1335	875	475	423	390	365	185
9 × 22R Japanese revolver	RS	1161	860	432	386	375	353	148
9 × 23mm Bergmann-Bayard/Largo	RLS	1319	910	388	390	375	355	127
9 × 23mm Steyr	RLS	1300	913	382	382	379	355	115
9 × 23R Belgian Nagant	RS	1330	875	480	426	395	370	187
9 × 25mm Mauser Export	RLS	1378	981	391	390	377	355	127
9 × 26R Gasser-Kropatschek	RS	1330	1022	438	382	378	365	158
9 × 39mm Russian SP-5/SP-6	RLN	2185	1516	445	443	372	362	250
9.1 × 17.5R Portuguese Abadie M1878	RS	1102	688	432	378	370	360	129
9.35 × 17.5R Portuguese Abadie M1886	RS	1105	688	432	378	370	370	130
9.4 × 20R Dutch revolver	RS	1250	815	483	415	407	385	200
9.5 × 60R Turkish Mauser	RN	2965	2360	584	515	407	382	280
10mm Auto	RLS	1255	985	424	423	423	399	170
10.15 × 61R Jarmann	RN	3070	2360	613	548	430	405	337
10.15 × 63R Serbian Mauser	RN	3098	2475	585	513	432	395	340
10.4 × 20R Italian Ordnance	RS	1257	780	520	465	427	437	170
10.4 × 20R Swiss Ordnance revolver	RS	1245	785	527	440	430	425	193
10.4 × 27R Dutch East Indies revolver	RS	1300	1066	485	431	403	396	193
10.4 × 47R Vetterli-Vitali	RN	2366	1840	626	537	437	411	308
10.4 × 38R Swiss Peabody rimfire	RN	2232	1520	620	540	437	415	312
10.6 × 24.5R German Ordnance	RS	1435	970	510	455	450	450	262
10.6 × 47R Russian Berdan Carbine	RN	2560	1830	442	516	452	424	366
10.6 × 57.5R Russian Berdan Rifle	RN	2937	2268	598	515	451	430	365
11 × 17.5R French Ordnance revolver	RS	1165	690	490	467	460	449	170
11 × 41R Werder Carbine	RN	2193	1380	600	514	473	449	340
11 × 42R Albini-Comblain	RN	2236	1626	686	587	465	443	386
11 × 42R Werndl Carbine	RN	2335	1630	607	521	468	442	370
11 × 50R Albini	RN	2588	2080	678	577	482	433	386
11 × 50R Werder Rifle	RN	2508	1972	624	516	474	450	340
11 × 51R Beaumont	RN	2708	2010	665	576	484	457	375
11 × 51R Gras Cadet	RN	2232	1992	657	538	464	443	131
11 × 53R Brazilian Comblain	RN	2768	2100	673	575	460	436	380
11 × 59R Gras	RN	3020	2350	667	544	468	445	388
11 × 60R Murata	RN	2846	2360	632	542	465	432	420
11 × 70R Montigny	RN	3185	2752	598	589	466	451	
11.15 × 58R Spanish Remington	RN	2976	2240	642	520	457	439	387
11.15 × 58R Werndl Rifle 1877	RN	2913	2270	617	545	466	441	370
11.15 × 60R Mauser	RN	3094	2370	586	513	463	440	386
11.2 × 29.5 Austrian Gasser revolver	RS	1530	1154	565	490	477	442	310
11.2 × 36 Fruwirth	RS	2090	1418	572	487	464	440	370
11.2 × 57R Bulgarian Berdan	RN	2858	2248	637	522	458	437	

Name and Metric Calibre	Case Type	— Length —		Diameter				Bullet Weight
		Round	Case	Rim	Head	Neck	Bullet	
11.3 x 35R Austrian Gasser	RS	1780	1390	580	490	467	447	285
11.3 x 45R Dutch Remington	RS	2208	1768	589	512	476	459	337
11.3 x 50R Beaumont	RN	2490	1970	666	581	486	464	336
11.35 x 62 Madsen	RLN	3276	2433	627	628	492	457	306
11.4 x 50R Werndl 1873	RS	2550	1970	571	493	472	449	340
11.43 x 50R Egyptian Remington	RN	2545	1940	668	581	479	448	400
11.43 x 60R Peabody-Martini	RN	3300	2316	660	578	482	457	474
11.5 x 35R Werder	RN	1937	1374	618	515	479	464	339
11.5 x 36R Montenegrin Gasser	RN	1850	1410	561	490	455	432	262
11.5 x 57R Reformado	RN	3060	2260	631	525	486	454	395
11.7 x 27R Danish Rem. Carbine RF	RS	1606	1075	582	500	480	466	386
11.7 x 42R Danish Remington RF	RS	2083	1635	583	500	483	468	386
11.7 x 51R Danish Remington CF	RS	2708	2020	585	514	482	454	380
12 x 15R French Thick Rim	RS	1055	616	518	474	468	450	200
12.17 x 29R Lund Carbine CF	RS	1567	1138	633	552	538	494	
12.17 x 44R Norwegian/Swedish Remington	RS	2102	1728	633	550	534	504	370
12.7 x 45R Papal Remington	RS	2307	1768	618	561	528	501	478
12.7 x 81SR Breda	SRN	4220	3200	775	720	545	496	565
12.7 x 108R ShVAK	RN	5587	4244	992	854	548	511	790
12.7 x 108mm DShK	RLN	5776	4170	852	855	547	510	790
13 x 64B MG131	BN	4130	2520	672	belt 705	546	533	1150
13 x 92SR Tankpatrone (TuF)	SRN	5232	3614	910	863	574	522	965
13 x 94mm PzB	RLN	4645	3724	864	823	575	520	226
13.2 x 96mm Short Hotchkiss	RLN	5354	3790	797	792	551	530	802
13.2 x 99mm Hotchkiss & Breda	RLN	5366	3898	797	792	567	530	802
14 x 33R Wänzl	RS	2008	1288	692	606	581	571	458
14.5 x 41R Madrid Berdan	RS	2040	1600	759	658	631	587	500
14.5 x 114mm Soviet	RLN	6114	4500	1060	1061	640	570	968
15 x 83B Mauser MG 151	BN	5448	3772	992	belt 867	626	594	837
15 x 95mm Mauser MG 151	RLN	5783	3760	790	793	626	614	880
15 x 104mm BESA	RLN	5820	4085	975	975	664	587	1160
15 x 115mm FN-BRG	RLN	6283	4519	970	972	643	604	1080
15.2 x 170 Steyr AMR	RLN	8150	6693	1020	1020	669	216	540
15.24 x 41R Krnka	RS	2157	1598	787	651	651	608	570
15.5 x 35R Serbian Peabody	RS	1980	1398	703	646	622	620	
15.5 x 106mm FN-BRG	RLN	6925	4173	1055	1055	650	610	1203
17 x 28R Danish Snider	RS	1584	1083	787	706	703	668	
17.5 x 29R Dutch Snider	RS	1708	1162	814	741	739	710	610
18 x 25R Millbank Amsler	RS	1567	1000	818	735	722	706	617
18 x 35R Tabatiere	RS	1878	1350	896	798	739	712	555
20 x 72RB	RBN	5512	2834	748	882	811	783	1235
20 x 83.5mm MG151	RLN	5768	3288	986	988	790	784	1697
20 x 105B Short Solothurn	BN	6693	4134	984	belt 1035	815	783	
20 x 124 Japan Type 97	RLN	7638	4901	1122	1130	799	783	2105
20 x 138B Long Solothurn	BN	8071	5417	1055	belt 1122	819	783	2253

Name and Imperial Calibre	Case Type	| — Length — |		| ——— Diameter ——— |				Bullet Weight
		Round	Case	Rim	Head	Neck	Bullet	
.22 Long Rifle rimfire	RS	974	613	278	226	225	225	40
.236 Lee U.S.Navy	RN	3180	2350	513	445	268	238	135
.243 Winchester	RLN	2710	2045	473	470	276	243	100
.276 Enfield	RLN	3244	2350	515	525	320	282	165
.276 Pedersen T2	RLN	2843	2070	470	467	315	283	150
.280 (7mm Mk 1Z) Enfield	RLN	2540	1700	460	467	312	284	130
.30 US Carbine	RLS	1673	1290	360	356	336	304	108
.30 M1901	RLN	3335	2560	473	473	339	308	220
.30-03 Springfield	RLN	3326	2560	473	472	340	308	220
.30-06 Springfield	RLN	3320	2490	470	470	338	308	150
.30-40 Krag	RN	3078	2314	545	461	338	309	220
.300 Winchester Magnum	BN	3300	2620	532	belt 532	334	308	150
.303 British, Marks I–VI	RN	3050	2151	530	460	330	311	215
.303 British, Marks VII–VIII	RN	3050	2211	530	460	330	311	174
.338 Lapua Magnum (8.6 x 70mm)	RLN	3602	3512	587	588	365	338	250
.357 Magnum	RS	1515	1290	440	379	379	359	158
.357 SIG	RLN	1120	860	419	419		357	125
.380 Revolver British	RS	1225	770	432	384	380	353	180
.38 Special	RS	1550	1155	440	379	379	360	132
.38 Super Auto	SRS	1280	900	406	384	384	356	130
.38 Long Colt	RS	1320	1035	440	379	378	359	150
.38 Smith & Wesson	RS	1200	775	432	385	383	358	145
.40 Smith & Wesson	RLS	1130	850	424	420	420	398	178
.402 Enfield-Martini (and Gardner MG)	RN	3280	2740	677	586	432	404	384
.41 Action Express	RBS	1170	866	394	435	434	410	200
.41 Magnum	RS	1580	1280	488	433	432	410	210
.44 Brazilian Nagant revolver	RS	1310	785	508	440	436	435	240
.44 Colt	RS	1500	1100	483	456	450	443	225
.44 Evans Short	RS	1440	990	513	440	439	419	215
.44 Evans Long	RS	2000	1540	509	449	434	419	280
.44 Magnum	RS	1610	1285	515	457	456	432	240
.44 Remington	RS	1540	1055	480	450	448	444	248
.44 Special	RS	1620	1160	514	457	456	432	245
.44 S&W American	RS	1450	910	506	440	438	434	218
.44 S&W Russian	RS	1430	978	515	457	456	431	246
.44-40 Winchester	RS	1550	1310	525	471	443	427	200
.442 Revolver	RS	1100	690	503	472	470	436	219
.45 ACP	RLS	1170	900	474	472	470	450	230
.45 Colt	RS	1600	1285	512	480	480	455	255
.45 Colt US Government M1909	RS	1580	1280	540	480	476	423	250
.45 Smith & Wesson	RS	1426	1115	518	480	478	445	230
.45 Webley	RS	1155	825	510	478	470	444	230
.45-70 Government	RS	2700	2100	600	500	475	457	405
.450 Short CF	RS	990	685	510	470	465	450	230
.577/450 Martini-Henry Rolled Case	RN	3150	2320	750	660	490	450	480
.577/450 Martini-Henry Carbine, RC	RN	3150	2320	750	660	490	450	405
.577/450 Martini-Henry Solid Case	RN	3150	2355	757	666	496	450	480
.577/450 Martini-Henry Carbine, SC	RN	3150	2355	757	666	496	450	405
.450 Turkish Martini	RN	2937	2311	616	579	474	449	474

Name and Imperial Calibre	Case Type	— Length —		Diameter				Bullet Weight
		Round	Case	Rim	Head	Neck	Bullet	
.450 Adams Mk I	RS	1151	715	508	478	478	455	225
.450 Adams Mk 3	RS	1067	685	505	477	477	445	225
.450 Gardner & Gatling	RN	3305	2450	662	580	484	450	480
.450 Gatling	RN	3000	2343	661	580	483	470	480
.455 Enfield Mk 2	RS	1480	850	532	477	475	457	265
.455 Webley Mk I	RS	1435	860	533	477	475	455	265
.455 Webley Mk 2	RS	1250	750	530	477	477	454	265
.455 Webley Mk 6	RS	1235	750	530	477	477	455	265
.455 Webley & Scott Auto	RLS	1222	915	505	477	476	455	224
.46 Remington rimfire	RS	1858	1110	533	458	464	455	290
.476 Enfield Mark 3	RS	1485	870	530	478	474	460	270
.5 Vickers	RLN	4340	3160	715	723	545	514	580
.50 Browning (12.7 x 99mm)	RLN	5425	3910	800	800	557	510	662
.50 Remington Navy RF	RS	1280	860	642	562	535	510	297
.50 Remington Navy CF	RS	1270	875	650	560	540	515	308
.50 US Carbine	RS	1708	1750	660	565	535	515	409
.50-70 U.S. Government	RS	2250	1750	660	565	535	515	445
.55 Boys	BN	5310	3950	797	belt 850	606	563	735
.56-60 Spencer RF	RS	1632	1156	639	556	543	512	345
.56-56 Spencer RF	RS	1545	878	643	561	558	534	444
.56-52 Spencer RF	RS	1673	968	644	561	546	515	486
.56-50 Spencer RF	RS	1614	1173	645	560	532	500	448
.577 Snider	RS	2484	2000	750	665	603	574	518
.577 Revolver	RS	1380	815	738	660	635	605	490
.58 Remington	RS	1598	1093	747	654	616	583	525
.65 Gatling (UK Mk I)	RN	4662	3815	955	785	707	650	1422

CONVERSION TABLES

The dimensions and measurements on this book are given principally in Imperial measures: inches, pounds, ounces and grains. It is anticipated that the majority of readers will be more familiar with this system than with the metric system, and certainly the major manufacturers of weapons in the Western Hemisphere all work in the Imperial system.

For those who need to convert from one system to the other, conversion tables are as follows:

WEIGHT

437.5 grains (gr) =	1 ounce (oz)	=	28.35 grammes (g)	
1.0 g		=	0.035 oz	
16 oz		=	1 pound (lb)	=	0.454 kg
1.0 kg		=	2.2045 lb	

To convert grains to grammes divide by 15.432.
To convert grammes to grains multiply by 15.432.

Some Common Bullet Weights Converted

Grains	Grammes	Grammes	Grains
50	3.24	2.55	39.35
55	3.56	3.45	53.24
80	5.18	4.70	72.53
100	6.48	8.00	123.45
110	7.13	9.50	146.60
120	7.78	11.30	174.38
147	9.53	12.10	186.73
150	9.72		
180	11.66		
200	12.96		
220	14.26		
250	16.20		
300	19.44		

LINEAR MEASUREMENT

	1 inch	=	25.40 mm		1 mm	=	0.0394 in
12 inches	= 1 foot	=	304.80 mm	10 mm =	1 cm	=	0.3937 in
3 feet	= 1 yard	=	914.40 mm	100 cm =	1 m	=	39.370078 in
1760 yards	= 1 mile	=	1609.34 mm	1000 m =	1 km	=	3280.84 ft

MUZZLE VELOCITY

To convert metres per second into feet per second multiply by 3.28.
To convert feet per second to metres per second divide by 3.28.

CARTRIDGE DIMENSIONS

Conversion tables in thousandths of an inch/millimetres, for the conversion of cartridge dimensions, are printed overleaf.

CONVERSION CHART: METRIC TO IMPERIAL

Millimetres to thousandths of an inch

mm	.0	.1	.2	.3	.4	.5	.6	.7	.8	.9
0	000	.004	.008	.012	.016	.020	.024	.027	.031	.035
1.0	.039	.043	.047	.051	.055	.059	.063	.067	.071	.075
2.0	.079	.083	.087	.090	.094	.098	.102	.106	.111	.114
3.0	.118	.122	.126	.130	.134	.137	.142	.146	.150	.154
4.0	.157	.161	.165	.169	.173	.177	.181	.185	.189	.192
5.0	.197	.200	.205	.208	.213	.217	.220	.224	.228	.232
6.0	.236	.240	.244	.248	.252	.256	.260	.264	.268	.272
7.0	.276	.280	.283	.287	.291	.295	.299	.303	.307	.311
8.0	.315	.319	.323	.327	.331	.335	.339	.343	.346	.350
9.0	.354	.358	.362	.366	.370	.374	.378	.382	.386	.390
10.0	.3937									

Enter the chart at the left-hand column, read across to the required value.
Example: 4.6mm = 0.181in

To build up a dimension:
Example - 6.56mm to thousandths of an inch:

6.50mm	=	0.256 in
+ .06mm	=	0.002 in
6.56mm	=	0.258 in

CONVERSION CHART: IMPERIAL TO METRIC

Thousandths of an inch to millimetres

Inch	.0	.010	.020	.030	.040	.050	.060	.070	.080	.090
.000	000	.254	.508	.762	1.016	1.270	1.524	1.778	2.032	2.286
.100	2.540	2.794	3.048	3.302	3.556	3.810	4.064	4.318	4.572	4.826
.200	5.080	5.334	5.588	5.842	6.096	6.350	6.604	6.858	7.112	7.366
.300	7.620	7.874	8.128	8.382	8.636	8.890	9.144	9.398	9.652	9.906
.400	10.160	10.414	10.668	10.922	11.176	11.430	11.684	11.938	12.192	12.446
.500	12.700	12.954	13.208	13.462	13.716	13.970	14.224	14.478	14.732	14.986
.600	15.240	15.494	15.748	16.002	16.256	16.510	16.764	17.018	17.272	17.526
.700	17.780	18.034	18.288	18.542	18.796	19.050	19.304	19.558	19.812	20.066
.800	20.320	20.574	20.828	21.082	21.336	21.590	21.844	22.098	22.352	22.606
.900	22.860	23.114	23.368	23.622	23.876	24.130	24.384	24.638	24.892	25.146
1.000	25.400									

INDEX